MW00443638

"Graham Hill has gone to the ends of the earth and back—crossing theological traditions, cultures, and even oceans and continents—to bear witness to the gospel through the many perspectives of world Christianity at the beginning of the twenty-first century. Here is a missional heart that is wide open to the winds of God's Spirit coming from and going in unexpected directions. *GlobalChurch* unfolds the many tribes, languages, peoples and nations that anticipate the coming reign of God. Here is a discerning guide to what all this means today."

Amos Yong, professor of theology and mission, Fuller Theological Seminary

"It is long past time those of us from the West learned how to learn from our global colleagues. Graham Hill leads us across a large and varied terrain of glocalized Christian holistic reflection and action, helping us see not simply how to listen but to learn and grow from the insights, actions and priorities of the Majority World church. Western Christians absolutely need this book. I pray that God will use it to spark a movement toward genuine servanthood among those who have been privileged to glean from the wise counsel Hill has gathered and brought to the table. At the same time, Majority World Christians also absolutely need this book. I pray that for them it will affirm the central role they have in contributing to God's work in every nook and cranny of our globalized planet and spur them on to continue living and reflecting on God's word in their own contexts for the benefit of all of us."

Scott Moreau, associate dean, professor of intercultural studies, Wheaton College Graduate School

GLOBAL
CHURCH

RESHAPING OUR CONVERSATIONS,
RENEWING OUR MISSION,
REVITALIZING OUR CHURCHES

GRAHAM HILL
Foreword by SCOT McKNIGHT

IVP Academic
An imprint of InterVarsity Press
Downers Grove, Illinois

InterVarsity Press
P.O. Box 1400, Downers Grove, IL 60515-1426
ivpress.com
email@ivpress.com

InterVarsity Press® is the book-publishing division of InterVarsity Christian Fellowship/USA®, a movement of
students and faculty active on campus at hundreds of universities, colleges and schools of nursing in the United
States of America, and a member movement of the International Fellowship of Evangelical Students. For
information about local and regional activities, visit intervarsity.org.

All Scripture quotations, unless otherwise indicated, are taken from the Holy Bible, Today's New International
Version™ Copyright © 2001 by International Bible Society. All rights reserved.

Cover design: David Fassett
Interior design: Beth McGill
Images: orange water color square: © kentarcajuan/iStockphoto
     icons of Copenhagen, Brussels, Austria, Israel, Cuba, Portugal, Budapest, Ireland, Berlin and France:
     © artefy/iStockphoto
     blue under water: © Achim Prill/iStockphoto

ISBN 978-0-8308-4085-4 (print)
ISBN 978-0-8308-9903-6 (digital)

Printed in the United States of America ∞

Library of Congress Cataloging-in-Publication Data

Hill, Graham, Reverend.
  GlobalChurch : reshaping our conversations, renewing our mission, revitalizing our churches / Graham Hill ;
foreword by Scot McKnight.
     pages cm
  Includes index.
  ISBN 978-0-8308-4085-4 (casebound : alk. paper)
  1. Church. 2. Globalization—Religious aspects—Christianity. I. Title. II. Title: Global Church.
  BV600.3.H54 2015
  269—dc23
                                                                                          2015036015

P   23 22 21 20 19 18 17 16 15 14 13 12 11 10 9 8 7 6 5 4 3 2 1

Y   35 34 33 32 31 30 29 28 27 26 25 24 23 22 21 20 19 18 17 16

To the African, Asian, Caribbean, Eastern European,

First Nations, indigenous, Latin American,

Middle Eastern and Oceanian Christians

who opened up their lives to me while we

filmed the GlobalChurch Project video series.

Your passion for Jesus is inspirational.

The gospel is like a seed and you have to sow it. When you sow the seed of the gospel in Palestine, a plant that can be called Palestinian Christianity grows. When you sow it in Rome, a plant of Roman Christianity grows. You sow the gospel in Great Britain and you get British Christianity. The seed of the gospel is later brought to America and a plant grows of American Christianity. Now when missionaries came to our lands they brought not only the seed of the gospel, but their own plant of Christianity, flowerpot included! So, what we have to do is to break the flowerpot, take out the seed of the gospel, sow it in our own cultural soil, and let our own version of Christianity grow.

DANIEL THAMBYRAJAH NILES

CONTENTS

LIST OF FIGURES
AND TABLES

FOREWORD

Scot McKnight

When you and I think of the "face" of the church today, who do we see? Who do we think God sees? Besides the obvious—God sees each of us (that's nice and that's right and now let's move on to the answer to the question)—I'd like to suggest that God sees the face of the church in global perspective. Which means the face of the church is morphing from a European-North American face to an African-Latin American-Asian face. God sees the church for what it is while we see the church through our own lens.

For those who are willingly shifting to a more global perspective on the church, there is also a change in what mission means, and no one is more alert to the global and theological shape of missions today than Graham Hill, an Australian theologian who made his mark with an informed and distinguished book called *Salt, Light, and a City: Introducing Missional Ecclesiology*.

Strikingly, the first-century church—by divine design—was not locked into a culture the way we can be today. The apostle Paul's vision, which he called at times the "mystery," was to expand God's old people, Israel, not by abandoning Israel or by imposing on Israel but by *adding to Israel God's new people who were Gentiles*. The heartbeat of the apostle Paul, then, was a missiology of new creation in which Paul would have to learn to express the gospel in new contexts, see what God created in new contexts and keep *all these people in one fellowship*. His vision, if you know anything about the Roman Empire, was breathtakingly radical and seen as foolhardy by more than one people group, including the apostle Paul's own countrymen.

Graham Hill, if I may put my own way of framing this book, asks us to return to the New Testament era so we can learn how to be the church of divine intent. He is asking to change our conversations from monolithic and monocultural to multicultural exchanges. Gone will be the paternalism of previous generations and up will arise a whole new conversation where the

"Majority World" churches will contribute to the Euro-shaped cultures. We are only salty and full of light when we let Paul's "mystery" of including Gentiles and Jews at the one table become the fertile ground in which we plant the gospel and learn from one another.

What Graham Hill has done, however, is offered a challenge, not least in taking what has become a famous line about American elitism from the days of our founding fathers—a "city set on a hill"—and turning it into a multi-cultural, global ecclesiology and mission: the city set on a hill, he proposes, is the global church in its mission.

How can this happen? In typical missiology, missions and missional classes we ask one another to read and discuss, well, the standard Euro-centric theologians of brilliance—but Graham Hill discusses in this book theologians many of us never assign or even read. We enter into Paul's "mystery" when we become a fellowship of "differents" by listening to our brothers and sisters in their lived theology around the world. Before you turn the page to begin this wonderful book, skip to appendix three and tally up the percentage of these global theologians you recognize and read. My guess is that you will, like me, be embarrassed enough to start reading this book seriously—in a listening mode.

INTRODUCTION

BEING SALT, LIGHT AND A CITY

*By 2025 fully two-thirds of Christians will live in
Africa, Latin America, and Asia. . . . The "average
Christian" today is female, black, and lives in a
Brazilian* favela *or an African village.*

STEPHEN BEVANS

Majority World and indigenous churches are redefining twenty-first-century Christianity. Western churches must decide how they'll respond. Stephen Bevans puts it well:

> We are now living in a "world church" where the vast majority of Christians are [from the Majority World]. David Barrett's statistical studies have basically confirmed this shift, and Philip Jenkins has predicted that by 2025 fully two-thirds of Christians will live in Africa, Latin America, and Asia. . . . Scholars are fairly unanimous in acknowledging the accuracy of the facts. The "average Christian" today is female, black, and lives in a Brazilian *favela* or an African village.[1]

Some statistics illustrate this shift in twenty-first-century global Christianity. The Pew Research Center's report *Global Christianity* analyzes the size and distribution of the world's Christian population. The report maps the changes over the last century (1910 to 2010). It concludes, "A century ago, the Global North (commonly defined as North America, Europe, Australia, Japan

---

[1]Stephen B. Bevans, Roger Schroeder and L. J. Luzbetak, "Missiology After Bosch: Reverencing a Classic by Moving Beyond," *International Bulletin of Missionary Research* 29, no. 2 (2005): 69.

and New Zealand) contained more than four times as many Christians as the Global South (the rest of the world). Today, the Pew Forum study finds, more than 1.3 billion Christians live in the Global South [61% of all Christians live in Asia, Africa and Latin America], compared with about 860 million in the Global North (39%)."[2] That is an astounding shift in only one hundred years.[3]

Using the World Christian Database, Philip Jenkins offers table 1.1, "Changing distribution of Christian believers."

Table 1.1. Changing distribution of Christian believers: 1900 to 2050 (number of Christians in millions)

	1900	1970	2010	2050
Africa	10	143	493	1,031
Asia	22	96	352	601
North America	79	211	286	333
Latin America	62	270	544	655
Europe	381	492	588	530
Oceania	5	18	28	38
Total	558	1,230	2,291	3,188

Source: Philip Jenkins, *The Next Christendom: The Coming of Global Christianity*, 3rd ed. (Oxford: Oxford University Press, 2011), 3. Data is taken from World Christian Database, www.worldchristiandatabase.org/wcd.

Christianity in North America, Europe and Oceania grew from 465 million in 1900 to 902 million in 2010.[4] This number is likely to *shrink* to 901 million by 2050.

Christianity in Africa, Asia and Latin America grew from 94 million in 1900 to 1.389 billion in 2010. This number is likely to *grow* to 2.287 billion by 2050.

Let's take China, for example. Professor Fenggang Yang of Purdue University makes an important prediction. If current rates of growth continue, within one generation China will have more Christians than any other nation on earth.

In 1949, Protestant churches in China had one million members. In 2010, that number was 58 million (compare that with 40 million in Brazil and 36 million

[2]Pew Research Center, *Global Christianity: A Report on the Size and Distribution of the World's Christian Population*, December 19, 2011, www.pewforum.org/2011/12/19/global-christianity-exec/.
[3]See David B. Barrett, George T. Kurian and Todd M. Johnson, *World Christian Encyclopedia: A Comparative Survey of Churches and Religions in the Modern World*, 2nd ed., 2 vols. (New York: Oxford University Press, 2001), 12-15, and www.globalchristianity.org.
[4]Oceania includes Australia and Micronesian, Melanesian, and Polynesian countries.

in South Africa). By 2025, there are likely to be 160 million Christians in China. By 2030, this number is likely to be 247 million (outnumbering Christians in Mexico, Brazil and the United States). In an interview with the *Telegraph*, Fenggang Yang says, "Mao thought he could eliminate religion. He thought he had accomplished this. It's ironic—they didn't. They actually failed completely."[5]

Philip Jenkins concludes,

> We are currently living through one of the transforming moments in the history of religion worldwide. Over the last five centuries, the story of Christianity has been inextricably bound up with that of Europe and European-derived civilizations overseas, above all in North America. Until recently, the overwhelming majority of Christians have lived in white nations. . . . Over the last century, however, the center of gravity in the Christian world has shifted inexorably away from Europe, southward, to Africa and Latin America, and eastward, toward Asia. Today, the largest Christian communities on the planet are to be found in those regions.[6]

What does all this mean for the mission and theology and worship and communities of the church worldwide? And what does it mean particularly for the Western church?

In Matthew 5:13-16 Jesus provides three remarkable images of the church—*salt, light* and a *city*. Jesus confronts his disciples with a missional description of the church. The church in mission is the salt of the earth, the light of the world and a city set on a hill. The church's purpose is to let its "light shine before others, that they may see your good deeds and glorify your Father in heaven." The purpose of the church's missionary nature is the worship and glorification of the Father and Son and Holy Spirit.[7]

The church is *another city*, constituted by every tribe, language, people

---

[5]Tom Phillips, "China on Course to Become 'World's Most Christian Nation' Within 15 Years," *Telegraph*, April 19, 2014, www.telegraph.co.uk/news/worldnews/asia/china/10776023/China-on-course-to-become-worlds-most-Christian-nation-within-15-years.html. See Fenggang Yang and Joseph B. Tamney, eds., *Confucianism and Spiritual Traditions in Modern China and Beyond*, Religion in Chinese Societies (Boston: Brill, 2012); Fenggang Yang and Graeme Lang, eds., *Social Scientific Studies of Religion in China: Methodology, Theories, and Findings* (Leiden: Brill, 2011); Fenggang Yang, *Religion in China: Survival and Revival Under Communist Rule* (Oxford: Oxford University Press, 2012).

[6]Philip Jenkins, *The Next Christendom: The Coming of Global Christianity*, 3rd ed. (Oxford: Oxford University Press, 2011), 1.

[7]J. Driver, *Images of the Church in Mission* (Scottdale, PA: Herald, 1997), 170-81; Graham Hill, *Salt, Light, and a City: Introducing Missional Ecclesiology* (Eugene, OR: Wipf and Stock, 2012), xiii.

and nation. The church must cultivate a distinct social existence, shaping its community and mission around its commitment to plurality and diversity and unity.[8] God calls his church to be a *global* and *missional* "city on a hill." This is a church constituted and enriched and represented by Western and indigenous and Majority World peoples.

Those of us in the West need a new narrative. It's time to abandon our flawed Eurocentric and Americentric worldviews. We need a new, global and missional narrative, and for that we must turn to the churches of Majority World and indigenous cultures. They can help us explore what it means to be a global missional community. Many Christian communities in Majority World and indigenous contexts have been wrestling with these issues for generations. Marginalization and persecution and alienation have been their lot. Yet somehow, in spite of or because of that, they have flourished. In fact, they've grown exponentially.

So, whom am I talking about when I refer to Majority World and indigenous Christians? *Majority World* Christians are those in Africa, Asia, the Caribbean, Eastern Europe, Latin America, the Middle East and Oceania.[9] I use the term *Majority World* because the majority of the world's population is in those cultures today. The majority of the church is in those cultures too. I don't use the terms *non-Western* or *Third World* or *Developing World*. These terms use Western cultures as their point of reference. They imply Western

---

[8]Barry A. Harvey, *Another City: An Ecclesiological Primer for a Post-Christian World* (New York: Trinity, 1999), 23-25.

[9]I don't deal with the diasporas in this book. For example, I've made no mention of Hispanic, Portuguese, or Asian minorities in the United States, United Kingdom, Canada, Europe, Australia and so on. I'm aware that, right now, Latin American and Chinese diasporas are active in evangelism and mission in Europe in the same way in which the Filipino or the Salvadoran diasporas carry on mission in the United States. I've chosen not to include voices from the diasporas, mainly because there are so many worthy contributors in that group, and I don't have the space to treat them well in this book. In the future, I hope that I (or someone else) will write a book exploring what we can learn from the diasporas. Hispanic minorities, for example, are making significant contributions to the theological and missiological conversation in the United States that are relevant to this subject. Methodist historian Justo L. González and Pentecostal theologian Eldin Villafañe are examples. In *Mañana*, González describes the shape and form of a theology developed in the Hispanic margin of the United States. In *Out of Every Tribe and Nation*, he shows what would be implied in listening to minorities within a denominational setting. Villafañe's *The Liberating Spirit* is a milestone in the reflection about the relationship between pneumatology and social ethics. See Justo L. González, *Out of Every Tribe and Nation: Christian Theology at the Ethnic Roundtable* (Nashville: Abingdon, 1992); González, *Mañana: Christian Theology from a Hispanic Perspective* (Nashville: Abingdon, 1990); Eldin Villafañe, *The Liberating Spirit: Toward an Hispanic American Pentecostal Social Ethic* (Grand Rapids: Eerdmans, 1993).

superiority or centricity. The term *Global South* is too limiting, given the breadth of the group I am engaging. *Majority World* seems to work best.

In 2004, The Lausanne Forum for World Evangelization in Pattaya, Thailand, voted unanimously that the phrase *Majority World Church* replace other terms. People from all over the globe participated in this forum. Timothy C. Tennent agrees that this is the best phrase: "It helps to highlight the basic point that Africa, Asia, and Latin America are where the majority of the world's Christians are now located."[10] I expand the phrase *Majority World* beyond Africa, Asia and Latin America to include the Caribbean, Eastern Europe, Oceania and the Middle East.

Indigenous and *First Nations* peoples are "those ethnic groups that were indigenous to a territory prior to being incorporated into a national state, and who are politically and culturally separate from the majority ethnic identity of the state that they are a part of." This includes people groups like the Australian Aborigines and American Indians.[11]

The aim of this book is to help Western churches rediscover what it means to be salt, light and a city by engaging in global missional conversations. To do this, Western Christians need to enter into conversation with Majority World and indigenous Christians. Listening to others helps us grow in our understanding and practice of mission and church and theology. For far too long we've marginalized or ignored Majority World and indigenous voices. We must truly become a *GlobalChurch*.

This aim shapes the book's structure, as summarized below.

PART 1. SALT: RESHAPING OUR CONVERSATIONS

"You are the salt of the earth. But if the salt loses its saltiness, how can it be made salty again? It is no longer good for anything, except to be thrown out and trampled underfoot." *Globally* and *locally*, you are the salt of the earth. *Be* salt.

Salt preserves, seasons, flavors and purifies. We are salt when we glorify the Father, Son and Holy Spirit in our mission, worship, faith, hope, truth and love. We are salt when we reject a Eurocentric or Americentric vision

---

[10]Timothy C. Tennent, *Theology in the Context of World Christianity: How the Global Church Is Influencing the Way We Think About and Discuss Theology* (Grand Rapids: Zondervan, 2007), xx.

[11]Douglas Sanders, "Indigenous Peoples: Issues of Definition," *International Journal of Cultural Property* 8, no. 1 (1999): 4.

of the church, and become the global missional church Christ envisioned.

In part one, I show how Western conversations are impoverished and insufficient in isolation from indigenous and Majority World Christians. We enhance our "saltiness" through local-global (*glocal*) exchanges. To do this we must *reshape our conversations*. We need global and local exchanges that we characterize by mutuality, respect, partnership and symbiosis. Such exchanges help us learn from each other, whether we're in Western, indigenous, or Majority World settings. It helps us stay "salty." It enables us to pursue global missional theology and practice. Globally and locally, we can pursue missional vitality and truly be "the salt of the earth."

PART 2. LIGHT: RENEWING OUR MISSION

"You are the light of the world. A city on a hill cannot be hidden. Neither do people light a lamp and put it under a bowl. Instead they put it on its stand, and it gives light to everyone in the house. In the same way, let your light shine before others, that they may see your good deeds and glorify your Father in heaven" (Mt 5:14-17). *Globally* and *locally*, you are the light of the world. *Be* light.

Light illuminates, reveals and dispels darkness. The church is light when it does good deeds—healing and liberating and redemptive deeds. It's light when its being and faith and deeds bring glorify to the Father. The church is light when it participates in God's redemptive mission in the world as a global missional community.

To do this we must *renew our mission*. In part two, I explore how indigenous and Majority World Christians teach us to renew mission. We renew mission through contextualization, liberation, hospitality, Spirit empowerment, creation care, ethics and the transformation of neighborhoods.

PART 3. CITY: REVITALIZING OUR CHURCHES

You are a city set on a hill. "A city on a hill cannot be hidden." *Globally* and *locally*, you are a city set on a hill. *Be* a city set on a hill.

This means that we are an alternative and countercultural movement. We have a distinct culture and politic and social existence. We are a people gathered from every tribe, language, people and nation. We are *in* the world but not *of* the world. We are *in* the world but *distinct from* the world. We are *within* the world and *for the sake of* the world.

To be this kind of alternative city or culture, we must renew our mission, community, ethics and worship. We need to pursue the *revitalization of our churches*, so that they *are* distinct. And by distinct, I mean an alternative city (*altera civitas*).

We are a "city on a hill" that witnesses to Jesus Christ and his eternal kingdom when we are a global missional church. In part three, I demonstrate how indigenous and Majority World Christians teach us to revitalize churches. We revitalize churches by indigenizing faith, devouring Scripture, renewing education, practicing *servantship* (servant leadership), recovering community and developing spirituality and discipleship. We inspire our churches when we develop our theology and practices relating to beauty and the arts.[12]

In the final chapter, I wrap things up by addressing an important question: In light of all the material covered in this book, what would it now look like to engage in global missional theology, ecclesiology, interpretation, history, pneumatology, worship and education?

Here's how you can get the most out of this book:

Community: You can read this book alone, in a small group, with some friends at home or at a coffee shop, or as part of a ministry team. However, you get a lot more out of this book when you read it with others. Together you can think about the book's implications. What do the chapters mean for your ministry, church, agency, family or team?

GlobalChurch Project video series: I've made a video series to go along with this book. Appendix one has the details.

Study guide: You'll get a lot more out of this book if you spend time working through the study guide in appendix two. Try to do this in a group. The study guide includes reflection questions, suggested practices and Further Reading

Characters: As you read this book, you'll come across names and people you've never heard of before. For a glimpse of who they are, and what issues concern them, see appendix three.

My website: To help you get the most out of this book, I've included more resources on my website, TheGlobalChurchProject.com. These include videos, reading lists, important links, a glossary and other resources. I've

---

[12]I've put a separate chapter on the theme of beauty and the arts on my website. It's additional to this book.

also provided ways that you can contact me. See appendix four.

In my first book, *Salt, Light, and a City*, I developed a missional theology of the church. I did this in conversation with twelve theologians from the four major Christian traditions. That volume offered a window into the thought of European and American theologians. It showed how they are making sense of the nature and mission of the church in their Western cultural context.

The book that you're now reading takes a different approach. I have stepped away from European and American voices. I now ask, What can those in the Majority World and indigenous cultures teach us in the West? What can they teach us about the church's mission, worship, theology and community? The quality and quantity of material coming out of the Majority World is astonishing. Any theology that ignores the insights of indigenous and Majority World Christians is deficient and impoverished.

White, middle-class, European, North American, tertiary-educated men dominate Western theology. They dominate the Western missional conversation. I know I fit that profile! This group still monopolizes missional church conferences and seminars. They get all the book contracts. In fact, this group still controls theology and the church in many settings. But this is changing. New voices are rising. These include women, minorities, the poor, indigenous groups and Majority World leaders. Missional conversations aren't attentive to the Spirit and to God's mission if they ignore these voices. Majority World and indigenous churches often have extraordinary missional vitality. Openness to other voices needs to happen now. It is time for Western churches, theologies and mission to mature and to reflect God's global mission.

In this book I could have consulted the work of many thousands of indigenous and Majority World thinkers and writers and practitioners. But I have limited myself to a sample of those who speak directly to its themes. These African, Asian, Eastern European, Middle Eastern, Caribbean, Latin American, First Nation and indigenous thinkers challenge us. They dare us to examine our theologies and missions and churches. And they inspire us to renew the worship and community and mission of Jesus' church. They stir us to think in fresh ways about what it means to be salt, light and a city. They help us become a global missional church—a truly *GlobalChurch*.

PART ONE

SALT
Reshaping Our Conversations

GLOCALIZING CONVERSATIONS

HOW DO WE DEVELOP
GLOCAL CONVERSATIONS?

*Rather than taking one contextual version of the Gospel and imposing
it as the Gospel throughout the world via the missionary enterprise,
the shapers of Mission as Transformation have recognized the
plurality of localities that has created an intercontextual,
"pan-local," global phenomenon in theology.*

AL TIZON

The International Society for Urban Mission (ISUM) is a group of urban missionaries who are passionate about cultivating hope and love and renewal in cities. I've connected with this group for some years. ISUM held its first annual Summit on Integral Urban Mission in Bangkok, Thailand. The team from Urban Neighbours of Hope (UNOH), under the leadership of my Australian friends Ash and Anj Barker, organized much of the summit. UNOH teams covenant with God and each other to "live out our passion for loving God and neighbour. Focus on releasing neighbourhoods from urban poverty. Grow through equipping each other, neighbours, and the broader church to radically follow Jesus and join God's Kingdom coming. UNOH workers live and serve in small, responsive, neighbourhood-based teams."[1]

---

[1]See www.unoh.org.

This summit involved interactive, participatory, hands-on, immersion opportunities, keynotes, lectures and workshops. Keynote speakers came from Africa, Australia, Myanmar, New Zealand, North America, the Philippines, South America, Thailand and First Nations. A few hundred Majority World and Western thinkers and activists came together for those days. They explored the theology and practices of integral, transformational and urban mission.

These thinkers and activists pursued a range of aims.[2] This included collaboration between urban Christians from a variety of backgrounds (Majority World and Western theologians, activists, ecumenicals, Pentecostals, evangelicals, colleges, church movements and development agencies). They aimed for collective action and thought in an international and integral context. They sought to gain mutual understanding for a comprehensive picture of urban mission around the globe. They encouraged information sharing and best practices—learning from our mistakes and seeking solutions. They developed recommendations and calls to action to the broader church. Working groups wrote briefing papers after each summit based on key issues in urban mission. And they endeavored to build trust, wisdom and inspiration to better engage our new urban world.

Majority World and Western leaders participated in discussion, prayer, integral mission and working groups. The goal was to grapple with key issues and ask key questions: How do we recruit, equip and sustain urban mission today? How do we release church movements among the urban poor? How can we immerse ourselves in and transform urban neighborhoods? How do we empower urban children and young people? How does the church serve and liberate the oppressed—and others suffering from urban injustice? What needs to happen for poorer urban centers to develop economically, socially and spiritually? How do we join God in the challenges and opportunities of multifaith cities?

Workshops included urban gardening, child protection and collaborating with local churches in urban mission. Workshops also included organic church growth and mission as well as developing NGO and government partnerships. Groups considered the good, the bad and the ugly of short-term urban mission teams.

---

[2]These aims are detailed at "International Society for Urban Mission Summit," http://newurbanworld.org/summit/.

The summit was a thrilling example of how Majority World and Western leaders can cooperate. It was a time to come together in an environment of mutual learning and enrichment. It was a window into how local contexts and global themes can enrich each other. This resulted from ISUM's commitment to "solidarity, fellowship, and insight between urban Christian leaders in the Western and Majority Worlds."

The summit was a success due to ISUM's core values. What are they?[3] Christ-honoring urban mission values *bottom-up*, grassroots perspectives—rather than *top-down*, distanced perspectives. It allows local theology to reveal new insights and perspectives about God's activity. It shares insights and experiences through narratives embedded within urban poor communities and cities. It cultivates ongoing practical and personal solidarity with the world's urban poor. This Spirit-empowered urban mission honors networks, relationships and partnerships. It sees such relationships as the primary method of serving together. It listens to and amplifies the voices of the urban poor—especially those from the Majority World, and in particular the 10/40 window cities. It is attentive to signs of the kingdom of God. Urban mission that glorifies God is willing to reflect and respond with active and sacrificial commitment. It shares and extends the life of the body of Christ among the urban poor.

This summit was a milestone in urban missiology. It enriched communication between Western and Majority World thinker-activists. This resulted from the aims and values I've mentioned. Effective urban mission needs to be a conversation on many levels. It is attentive to context and immersed in local settings. It appreciates global and universal missional themes. It cultivates dialogue between these local-global (glocal) realities. It involves mutual learning between Western and Majority World thinker-activists. Moreover, solidarity between all parties is a defining feature. This solidarity is due to a compelling vision of the kingdom of God.

These collaborative, glocal features of the ISUM urban mission summit in Bangkok are critical for the aims of this book, *GlobalChurch*.

Majority World, indigenous and Western leaders, thinkers and churches can stretch and enrich each other. But they need to be open and attentive to each other. They need learning postures and open hearts and minds. They

---

[3]"About ISUM," http://newurbanworld.org/about.

require passion for learning and collaboration and Jesus and his kingdom. And their vision and values must align with those of the kingdom of God.

The global church needs a glocalized theology. This chapter considers how Kōsuke Koyama, Al Tizon, R. S. Sugirtharajah and others guide us as we form glocal theologies and learn from Majority World and indigenous ideas and expressions. They help us as we ask, How do we apply these insights in our settings while being true to our own cultures? They also help us consider how we might feed local theologies back into global conversations.

All local theologies—Western, indigenous, or Majority World—can contribute to global conversations. Local and global conversations must meet and enrich each other in constructive ways. When they do, we end up with worthwhile glocalized theologies and practices.

I believe that we must develop a missional theology of the church through glocal conversations. Glocalization can help us apply this theology in missional practices. Worthwhile glocalization is about dialogue, learning and partnership. It's about the courage to listen to others and venture into the unknown.

This conversation needs to involve Majority World, indigenous and Western thinkers. But not just thinkers and theologians: also activists, communities and ordinary believers. This chapter asks, *How do we develop glocal conversations?*

WHAT IS GLOCALIZATION?

Glocalization is a term developed by Japanese economists and popularized by Roland Robertson. It means the local (the local, contextual, homogenous) and the global (the global, universal, heterogeneous) interconnect. Our globalized world has blurred the boundaries between the local and the global. The local is a dimension of the global and the global shapes the local. The two are interdependent. They enable each other. They form each other, reciprocally. While tensions exist, the global and local are not opposing forces. They connect—deeply and inextricably. "Not only are the global and the local inseparably intertwined; they also determine each other's respective forms. From a sociological perspective, glocalization means generally the organic and symbiotic relationship between the global and the local."[4]

Al Tizon says that transformational mission is always contextual. It is

---

[4]Al Tizon, *Transformation After Lausanne: Radical Evangelical Mission in Global-Local Perspective* (Eugene, OR: Wipf and Stock, 2008), 207.

always rooted in the local and particular—as local churches embody the gospel and witness to Christ. These churches forge their own theological understandings as they do mission together. They engage in transformational practices among the people in their settings. They enjoy worship, mission and community in their local and particular context. Ideally, the result is unique, contextual theologies and missions.

Simultaneously, global conversations form. They form because of this multitude of local theologies and practices. Local conversations inform and enrich other local conversations, catalyzing global themes and voices. Tizon observes that the global "owes its existence to local contexts. . . . Shared convictions among the theologies and practices of local contextual realities give shape to its global dimensions."[5]

Majority World, indigenous and Western theologies are equally contextual. They are equally culture bound. They are equally particular to their time and location. At times they are all enlightened or myopic, liberating or constraining, humanizing or objectifying, beautiful or offensive, prophetic or tepid. The local, particular and cultural shape all these theologies. Conversely, these particular theologies feed and influence global conversations. There is no place, then, for ethnocentrism, colonialism, or elitism. There is no place for theological, missional, cultural, or institutionalized arrogance.

Multiple local contexts and voices come together—intentionally or not—to form global themes and theologies. Conversely, these global realities shape local contexts. Today, local contexts must grapple with "an emerging global culture, i.e., the interacting realities of modernity, postmodernity, and the phenomenon of globalization."[6] Hence, the interdependent and symbiotic relationship between the *local/particular* and the *global/universal*. We call this interdependent relationship between the local and the global glocalization.

The global church needs a thrilling glocal exchange. We need one that we characterize by mutuality, respect, partnership and symbiosis. Such exchange helps Majority World, indigenous and Western churches learn from each other. It enables them to pursue missional theology and practice. Together, the church becomes a "city on a hill."

---

[5]Ibid., 10.
[6]Ibid., 84.

WHAT REQUIRES GLOCALIZATION?

The glocal exchange described above needs to be broader than transformational mission. This is necessary if the church is to develop a robust, intercultural and glocal missional ecclesiology.

In my first book, *Salt, Light, and a City*, I outlined the foundational themes of missional ecclesiology.[7] Majority World and Western leaders need to engage these themes in local and contextual ways. Their insights can then enrich global conversations. These global conversations in turn shape local understandings and practices. This way a glocal appreciation of these themes emerges.

Local, regional and global theologies and practices are thereby enriched. The church becomes healthier and more missional—a truer expression of the kingdom. The church becomes a fuller witness to Christ, his passion for the nations and his ability to bring unity in diversity.

Stephen Bevans and Roger Schroeder outline the *six constants* of mission. These are our theologies about Jesus, the church, the end times, salvation, human nature and culture. Bevans and Schroeder describe the relationship between these six and their historical, cultural and theological *contexts*. This is why they call these six *constants in context*. Our understanding of these six constants develops in relation to local and global movements. Sometimes local voices influence our understandings of these six. Other times it is regional or global voices. For all of us, local, regional and global influences are at play at once. Collectively, they form our appreciation of the six constants of mission.[8]

Here are eight theological themes that the church can develop through processes of glocalization. I presented these in my book *Salt, Light, and a City*. They are vital to the church's health, mission, community and future. We could add many other themes to these eight, but these will suffice for now.[9]

Scripture. The Scriptures are the infallible, authoritative Word of God. Christ's Spirit has inspired them. They have absolute and final authority in all aspects of corporate and individual faith, ethics, conduct and witness. Christians interpret and apply Scripture in local contexts and in particular

---

[7]Graham Hill, *Salt, Light, and a City: Introducing Missional Ecclesiology* (Eugene, OR: Wipf and Stock, 2012), 149-274.
[8]Stephen B. Bevans and Roger Schroeder, *Constants in Context: A Theology of Mission for Today*, American Society of Missiology Series (Maryknoll, NY: Orbis, 2004), part one.
[9]These points first appeared in my book *Salt, Light, and a City*, xxii-xxiv.

social settings. Conversely, we learn from the interpretations and readings of other groups.

Glocal theology asks, *How does a glocal conversation shape our local-global theology of Scripture and biblical interpretation?*

Evangelicalism, Pentecostalism, missional movements and so forth. I have charismatic, missional and evangelical convictions. Glocal conversations help me understand and practice these convictions better.

I will use evangelicalism as an example. Michael Horton says that our beliefs and practices are evangelical when they are "committed to the sufficiency of Scripture, the priesthood of all believers, the total lostness of humans, the sole mediation of Christ, the gracious efficacy and finality of God's redemptive work in Christ through election, propitiation, calling and keeping. The linchpin for all of this was the doctrine of justification by grace alone, through faith alone, because of Christ alone."[10]

Such convictions are necessary if we are to be faithful to the gospel and to a biblical vision of church and mission. The gospel defines God's purposes for humanity, the church and the universe. The triune God controls the church. He is its Lord and Savior, Sanctifier and Liberator, Master and King. He is completely sovereign over its nature, affairs, mission and history. God is the church's only source of grace, election, atonement, salvation and perseverance. The church's justification and hope are by grace alone, through faith alone, by Christ alone.

Here's the challenge I face. My understanding of evangelicalism is Western. I am a product of the Western theological tradition and my Western evangelical heritage. Much of this is wonderful. But I need indigenous and Majority World evangelicals and others to help me expand and reshape these insights. The same would be true if I were a Pentecostal.

Glocal theology asks, *How does a glocal conversation shape our understanding of our theological traditions and convictions?*

Jesus Christ. We must center our theology on Jesus Christ, the Lord of the church. The church needs to reflect on the person and work of Christ and respond to him. This means gathering and going in the name and power of Christ. It means allowing Christ's Spirit to shape our community and

---

[10]Michael Horton, "Evangelical Arminians," *Modern Reformation* 1, no. 3 (1992): 17.

identity and mission. It means developing our Christology, ecclesiology and missiology concurrently. The early church developed these three areas and more in a concurrent and integrated way. There was no linear progression. The same is true in the contemporary, global church.

How can the glocal church best explore its nature, structure, mission and hope? Through the centrality and the lordship of Christ.

Majority World and indigenous Christians help us appreciate Jesus and his mission afresh. They show us how Jesus identifies with the marginalized, outcast, oppressed, rejected and broken. He prefers them. We find him among "the least of these."

Glocal theology asks, *How does a glocal conversation shape our understanding of who Jesus Christ is? How does it help us appreciate him better? What has Jesus done for and in his church and his world? What does he care about? What individual and corporate responsibilities has he given us? How do we express these at local, regional and global levels?*

The Spirit. Missional ecclesiology is inadequate without pneumatological foundations. In other words, our theology of church and Spirit go together. The Spirit creates and animates the church. He empowers it to witness to Jesus and his gospel. The Spirit enables the church to be a missional, transformational community. He shapes the church into an alternative society embodying the reign of God. The church exists for the glory and mission of Christ. The power and presence of the Spirit enables this mission, worship and glorification.

The Spirit pours out gifts on the local-global church "for the common good" and "to equip his people for works of service, so that the body of Christ may be built up." This includes, but isn't limited to, the ministry gifts, manifestation gifts and motivational gifts (1 Cor 12:7; Eph 4:11-12; Rom 12:6-8).

The Spirit forms the glocal church. He empowers it for service and witness. He fills it with Christ's empowering presence. He leads it into the *missio Dei*—the mission of the Father, Son and Holy Spirit.

Recently, Pentecostal and renewalist movements have grown dramatically in the Majority World. They have increased in status, size and influence. Many have matured theologically. The churches of the West must take notice.

Glocal theology asks, *How does a glocal conversation shape our understanding of the power and presence of the Spirit?*

The Trinity. There are clear limitations to the analogy between the church and the Trinity. The church can only *image* the Trinity. Yet the church is at its best when it reflects the relational and missional passion of the Trinity.

What is the source and inspiration of the church's local-global mission? Ultimately, it is the missional nature, passion and actions of the Father, Son and Holy Spirit. God's nature is missional. His passion is infectious. His actions are historical, redemptive and eternal. The Trinity invites the church into a sending community. The Father sends the Son. The Father and Son send the Spirit. Finally, the Trinity sends the church in mission into the world.

Glocal theology asks, *How does a glocal conversation shape our understanding of the Trinity? How does it enable our participation in the mission and community of the triune God?*

Association and dialogue. These need to happen across denominational, cultural, ethnic, gender and theological traditions and divides. Authentic dialogue is indispensable to the health and mission of the church. What do those marginal to the life of the church have to say to us? What do "others" have to teach us? Other ethnicities and cultures? Other socioeconomic groups? Other ages and genders? Other theological and confessing traditions? Other persons from times long gone?

We need to listen. Share. Be vulnerable. Be authentic. Open up to criticism, correction and change.

We need more than dialogue. We need communion and association. It is possible, in a qualified way, to say that God is present in all the various forms of the church (i.e., the various theological, ecclesiological, sociocultural, historical and other permutations of the church). We discern this presence through attention to Scripture, history, tradition, culture and the Spirit. Discernment involves critical dialogue, theological exchange, biblical study and real relationship. Only the Spirit of Jesus can enable this.

Glocal theology asks, *How does a glocal conversation shape our understanding of association and dialogue?*

Mission and the **missio Dei.** The church is missional at its core. It serves, obeys and images a missionary God. David Bosch says, "The church's mission is not secondary to its being; the church exists in being sent and in building up itself for its mission." He goes on to say, "Ecclesiology does not precede missiology; there cannot be church without an intrinsic missionary dimension."[11]

Jesus is Lord. Lord of his church and Lord of his world. His mission determines and forms the church. His mission shapes the nature, purposes, structures, ministries and activities of his church. Majority World and indigenous thinkers help us understand the implications of this mission. They help us form glocal theologies of mission. They reveal "mission in context as transformation."[12]

Glocal theology asks, *How does a glocal conversation shape our understanding of mission and the* missio Dei?

Church theology and practice. Glocal conversations can inform and enrich many aspects of the church (when practiced well). Theologies and practices benefit from robust and critical glocal conversations. These conversations enrich many areas (community, spirituality, discipleship, liturgy, worship, hospitality, eco-justice, education, social ethics, servantship, liberation, place, suffering, beauty and so on).

Glocal theology asks, *How does a glocal conversation shape our understanding of these many dimensions of church and mission?*

Glocal processes shape these eight themes and their practices. We need to facilitate and enable these conversations and processes. This is urgent. It must be a priority. No theology of mission or missional ecclesiology is adequate without glocal conversations.[13]

THE LOCAL AND GLOBAL ENRICH EACH OTHER

Glocalization takes the *local/particular* context and *global/universal* themes seriously. Contextual and global conversations enter an enriching and informing relationship. These two always have an active and symbiotic relationship. This is true whether we deliberately put them into conversation or not. The local shapes the global, and the global shapes the local. Many local

---

[11]David J. Bosch, *Believing in the Future: Toward a Missiology of Western Culture* (New York: Trinity, 1995), 32.

[12]Tizon, *Transformation After Lausanne*, 7-9.

[13]Not all of these themes are dealt with in this present volume, since either (1) I have dealt with them in my book *Salt, Light, and a City*, (2) they are not all key themes in the writings of the thirty-five Majority World thinkers considered in this volume, or (3) there is not adequate space in a book this size.

voices converge to form global conversations and theologies. Using the Philippines as a case study, Tizon illustrates this by showing the interdependence between local and global themes in mission.[14]

Dialogue between local and global conversations is critical. Kōsuke Koyama wrote an important book on contextual mission called *Water Buffalo Theology*. Koyama is a Japanese missionary who served in Chiang Mai, Thailand. He writes of the joys and challenges of doing local, particular, *water buffalo* theology. He considers the relationship between local theology, global missional themes and transforming cultures. "*Water Buffalo Theology* sees certain specific challenges. Contextualization of theology implies two critical movements. First, to articulate Jesus Christ in culturally appropriate, communicatively apt words; and second, to criticize, reform, dethrone, or oppose culture if it is found to be against what the name of Jesus Christ stands for."[15]

Kōsuke Koyama challenges us to recognize what we bring to the task of local theology. For him, it was doing theology in Thailand while being Japanese. We also need to notice the particular culture we're located in as we do the work of theology. This means we avoid speaking of an "Asian theology," "African theology" and the like. We need to cultivate local theologies that engage regional and global themes. But these theologies must be "distinctly local," and a "theology from below."[16]

Simultaneously, we need to pursue a reformation of theology and practice "in the global context." This means entering "the disturbing spaciousness of Jesus Christ." Jesus calls us to reject enmity and exceptionalism. We seem him present in our culture, language, stories and relationships. But we also choose to embrace the "other." We choose to see him present in other cultures—shaping a global people to serve and worship him, joining in his mission.[17]

Kōsuke Koyama roots the gospel in the local, contextual and particular. This is why he roots his water buffalo theology in Northern Thai culture. He is careful not to say, "Here is how you contextualize in your setting." Instead,

---

[14]Tizon, *Transformation After Lausanne*, 7-13, 149-202.

[15]Kōsuke Koyama, *Water Buffalo Theology*, 25th anniversary ed. (Maryknoll, NY: Orbis, 1999), xiii-xv.

[16]Kōsuke Koyama, "The Asian Approach to Christ," *Missiology* 12, no. 4 (1984): 435-38.

[17]Kōsuke Koyama, "Reformation in the Global Context: The Disturbing Spaciousness of Jesus Christ," *Currents in Theology and Mission* 30, no. 2 (2003): 119-28.

he tells us a story. It's the story of how he contextualized theology in northern Thailand while being open to global conversations. Koyama asks us to form our own local expressions of church, mission and theology. At the same time, we must stay attentive to what God is saying and doing beyond that context. This way, local and global and particular and universal become mutually enriching conversation partners.

GLOCALIZATION AND HISTORICALLY SILENCED VOICES

Glocal theologies and conversations pay attention to voices that powers, institutions, religions and societies have silenced. R. S. Sugirtharajah pushes back a little on Tizon's ideas. Sugirtharajah says that the church should privilege local conversations. He emphasizes the local, contextual and *postcolonial* reading of biblical texts.[18]

The church needs to listen. The church ought to be attentive to the theologies and biblical interpretations of groups that cultures and religions have ignored. Historically, powerful secular and religious forces have silenced these groups. They have marginalized, oppressed and colonized them. It is time for the church to address this injustice. We must start listening to important but silenced voices. We need to privilege the voices of the former victims of Western colonialism. We need to develop postcolonial biblical interpretations, theologies and expressions of church and mission.

How do we take such perspectives seriously as we develop glocal conversations? How do these themes help us foster vital relationships between local and global voices?

It is time for us to embrace values that enable conversations with those often ignored by the church. We need values that help us learn from these groups and individuals.

Valuing equal partnership. Colonizing powers oppressed, silenced and colonized certain groups. At times, the church was complicit. These colonized groups have become "confident, indomitable, and indispensable partners in the dialogue and collaboration with the dispossessed and disad-

---

[18]R. S. Sugirtharajah, *Asian Biblical Hermeneutics and Postcolonialism: Contesting the Interpretations,* The Bible and Liberation Series (Maryknoll, NY: Orbis, 1998), 15-16.

vantaged in the West."[19] This calls for attentiveness to these voices and responsiveness to their prophetic challenges. It also demands a critical evaluation of colonial readings of Scripture. Colonial models of theology and church and mission are no longer the benchmark. The global church must examine them afresh.

Valuing equal status. Those on the margins have now taken their rightful place on the global stage. They have claimed appropriate and equal status at the table. Subaltern readings of theology, church and mission are invaluable contributors to global theological conversations. This means that we esteem them. But we also test them.

What do we mean by *subaltern*? Subalterns are those who are downtrodden and silenced (or have been treated this way in the past). Dominant or colonizing groups treat them as invisible nonentities. They enjoy limited or no access to power. Sometimes these are women, certain tribal and ethnic groups, and those considered "untouchable." In *Voices from the Margin*, Sugirtharajah provides a platform for postcolonial, subaltern readings of Scripture and theology. These readings challenge colonial—often Western—readings of Bible and theology and cultures. They claim equal status with other ways of doing theology.[20]

Valuing equal identity. People groups need freedom to explore their new and emerging identities. These emerge in response to local and global influences. Local culture is not the only thing at work here. Global forces also shape identity, as do imported practices, ideas, readings, rituals and technologies. But each group should be free to explore and construct their particular forms of Christian identity.

Valuing equal interpretations. "Postcolonialism is concerned with the question of cultural and discursive domination." Colonialism led to oppressive and controlling forms of culture and discourse. These were usually not contextual or indigenous. Western powers, for instance, brought colonial forms of theology, church, biblical interpretation and mission.[21]

Postcolonialism calls for alternative ways of approaching these things. Those

---

[19]Ibid., 16.

[20]R. S. Sugirtharajah, *Voices from the Margin: Interpreting the Bible in the Third World* (Maryknoll, NY: Orbis, 1991).

[21]Sugirtharajah, *Asian Biblical Hermeneutics and Postcolonialism*, 17.

who were once marginalized, oppressed and silenced need to lead these fresh approaches in their own settings. These, then, influence global conversations. We need to support the new readings and insights and experiments from these groups. To be genuine, this support must be both critical and collegial.

Valuing equal empowerment. Sugirtharajah says that postcolonialism is valuable when it empowers actual communities and real people. Postcolonial thought empowers when it addresses the difficulties, hopes and experiences of ordinary people. It should never be about power plays and the clever use of language. It's pointless if it's obsessed with forming new—and "colonizing"—theories. It's a waste of time if it's a self-indulgent pursuit of new and hybrid identities. Rather, "the worth and credibility of postcolonial criticism will be judged by how it orchestrates the unique and fragile and imagined claims of one community against another." Empowerment happens in a variety of ways. One way is contributing equally to global conversations.[22]

Al Tizon examines postcolonialism in the Philippines. He says that it can teach the global church a lot about healthy local-global conversations. Filipino contextual theology resists many Western forms of mission and theology. It finds them patronizing and controlling. This indigenous theology values prophetic sociopolitical engagement in institutions and the society at large. It emphasizes ministry to whole persons and communities. It constructs a Filipino theology of beauty and mission and worship and community. And it fosters indigenous theological approaches to the spirit world and cosmology.

Tizon says that postcolonial theology has played a constructive role in the Philippines. But he is uncomfortable with the label *postcolonialism.* He prefers to describe historical events as "beyond colonialism." And he says that global conversations enrich local theologies, and vice versa.[23]

Postcolonial thought informs our understanding of the relationship between the local and global. It also shows how theology can emerge at the intersection between the local/particular and the global/universal. It reminds us that worthwhile glocalization listens to all voices. This includes heeding those that have been historically silenced.

---

[22]Ibid., 24.
[23]Tizon, *Transformation After Lausanne,* 102, 167-87.

GLOCALIZATION AND THE GLOBALCHURCH:
CONCLUDING REFLECTIONS

How do we go about developing a model for glocal conversations? Tizon has recently provided a useful model that is instructive as we seek to learn from the Majority World. It has at least two key features.

First, the local is in the global (globalization from below). Global theologies and ideas have origins in many particular, local contexts. In that sense, globalization is from below. Global ideas have local roots. Ideas about integral mission, liberation theology and missional church have local origins. They have their roots in the prayers, hopes, discoveries, mission and theologies of thousands of local communities. "The global does not, *cannot*, exist without the local—but the coming together of localities creates a global reality that becomes greater than the sum of its parts; it creates a gestalt entity to which localities make themselves accountable."[24]

Second, the global is in the local (panlocalization from above). The concerns and voices of multitudes of locales form global conversations. These global discussions can provide a "positive accountability" back to local contexts. This is true when they enrich, affirm, serve, guide and strengthen local contexts. It is also true when they avoid homogenization, control, imposition and judgment. Glocalization is best when it sees itself as interdependent: deeply connected with the local.[25]

That's a helpful starting point. But we need to go further. Besides Tizon's proposals, I'm convinced that robust glocal conversations cultivate six core practices.

1. Glocal theology practices its values. We root glocal theology in core values. These values include solidarity, understanding and mutual learning. Do we value fellowship with Christians of all cultures? Do we value learning from them?

We prove our values through our practices. What practices emerge out of these values? We need to collaborate, act collectively and share information. We must find ways to foster grassroots perspectives and local theologies. We need to share stories and learnings and cultivate networks, relationships and partnerships. We need attentiveness to local voices and global themes. We

[24]Ibid., 210-14.
[25]Ibid., 214-18.

ought to find ways to put these local and global voices into conversation.

Mutual learning, humility and solidarity are key. Worthwhile glocal conversations can never be merely theoretical or academic. It is up to us to root our values in our practices.

2. Glocal theology practices humility (and it tells a new narrative). We have noted that the local is in the global, and the global is in the local. The two are interdependent. They form each other, reciprocally. Since this is the case, we must practice humility. There is no place for ethnocentrism, colonialism, or theological and cultural arrogance. I have seen these unhealthy postures far too often in Western settings.

Recently I attended a missional leadership conference. On that occasion the keynote speaker—a leading missional author and speaker—said that North American missional conversations and innovations hold the key to the future of the Western church. This Euro American view is wrong. (I'm being kind. To be frank, it's complete nonsense.) It's arrogant and Euro American–centric. And it's completely out of step with what is happening in the glocal church. We need a new narrative.

In June 2013, The Center for the Study of Global Christianity reported the top 20 countries where Christianity has the highest percentage growth rate. Nineteen of the top twenty are in Asia and Africa. Eleven of them are in Muslim majority countries. Not a single country from Europe or North America makes the top twenty list.[26]

It's time to cultivate a new narrative. The future of the church is emerging from the Majority World. Rather than North America, the churches of Eastern Asia, Western Africa, the Arabian Peninsula and other parts of the Majority World reveal the future of the global church. We need the contributions of all contexts: Western, indigenous and Majority World. All contribute to glocal conversations. All are important as we learn from each other about mission, theology and faith. But let's stop pretending that North Americans and Europeans will reveal the future of the global church. Let's start listening to what God is saying about the future of the global church. And he's speaking to us through the churches of Asia, Africa, Latin America,

---

[26]Russ Mitchell, "The Top 20 Countries Where Christianity Is Growing the Fastest," *Disciple All Nations* (blog), August 25, 2013, https://discipleallnations.wordpress.com/2013/08/25/the-top-20-countries-where-christianity-is-growing-the-fastest.

Muslim majority settings and so on. We must cultivate a new, glocal narrative—one soaked in humility.

Glocal theology must be humble theology. Meek theology. Receptive theology. Discerning theology. Prayerful theology. Dialogical theology. Dependent theology. A theology that celebrates the interdependence between the *local/particular* and the *global/universal.*

3. *Glocal theology practices expansiveness.* Glocalization is, by nature, comprehensive. Local and global influences permeate much of our lives. These glocal forces shape our theologies and churches whether we like it or not.

But intentionality is also important. We need to commit to an expansive approach to glocal theology. How do we *deliberately cultivate glocal conversations* in our biblical interpretation? Do we foster them in our understanding of the person and work of Christ? How does glocalization shape the way the Spirit empowers and constitutes the church? How can it form our understanding of the nature and mission of the Trinity? How does it influence the way we practice fellowship and conversation across denominational, cultural, ethnic, economic, sociocultural, political, gender and theological divides? How might it shape our theologies of mission, community, beauty, spirituality, suffering, discipleship, hospitality, eco-justice, place, education, social ethics, Christian leadership and so forth?

4. *Glocal theology practices attention.* Glocal theology doesn't need to accept all the assumptions or assertions of postcolonial or Majority World thought. But it does need to engage with them and take them seriously. Postcolonial theology, for instance, gives the marginalized and colonized and forgotten and silenced both dignity and voice. Our glocal conversations must also include and esteem these groups. We need to be attentive to others: weak and powerful, female and male, dominant and downtrodden, old and young, rich and poor, privileged and marginalized, influential and subaltern, educated and illiterate. We need to practice the art of attention, being especially attentive to those who are different to us.

5. *Glocal theology practices embrace.* What do colonial, ethnocentric or Western-centric perspectives do? They silence. They control. They commodify. They institutionalize. They colonize. They domesticate. They replace. They import. They exclude. They do these things to the beliefs, experiences and practices of other cultures. A worthwhile glocal theology refuses to do these things. Instead, it adopts a responsive, humble, celebratory, open, inclusive and embracing attitude.

6. Glocal theology practices discernment. Finally, we need discernment as we engage these ideas and practices. Discernment is a huge topic that's hard to cover comprehensively in a few words. Discernment happens when the Spirit of Christ and his Word renew our minds. The Spirit grants us spiritual wisdom as we meditate on him and his Word and as we practice discipleship to Jesus Christ. Romans 12 provides guidance: we need (1) to be transformed by the renewal of our minds, (2) to serve Christ's body and (3) to put love into action. Discernment also happens in conversation, both locally and glocally.

I pray these core values and six practices come across in the following chapters of *GlobalChurch*.

Glocalization can never be just theoretical. Are we committed to moving glocalization from an abstract idea to a living communion? Are we determined to construct a missional theology of the church in the context of glocal conversations? This must involve dialogue between Majority World, indigenous and Western scholars, activists and groups.

Will glocalization be an *abstract notion*? Or will it be a formative and genuine *communion* between local, regional and global voices? Glocal dynamics are at play whether we like it or not. They're in our churches, theologies and missions. But we can choose to relinquish isolationist, colonial, parochial and arrogant approaches. Instead, we can adopt responsive, dialogical, learning, humble and embracing postures.

Through healthy approaches to glocalization, the Spirit challenges us to value local contexts. We immerse ourselves in local and particular communities and conversations. He inspires us to open ourselves to global theological conversations. He rouses us to value the symbiotic relationship between the *local/particular* and the *global/universal*.

Through glocal relationships the Spirit leads us to put local, contextual theologies into conversation with global ones. He prompts us to explore the ways in which the *local is in the glocal* and the *global is in the local*. He persuades us to pursue collaboration and dialogue and mutual learning. We engage with Christians from different backgrounds and cultures: ecumenicals, Pentecostals, evangelicals and so on from Western, indigenous and

Majority World contexts. He motivates us to express solidarity between all parties. We appreciate our unity in diversity.

Through glocal conversations the Spirit moves us to ensure that unity and solidarity emerge from a compelling vision of Jesus' kingdom and gospel and person. He challenges us to share information, theology and practices. He urges us to learn from each other—our successes and mistakes. We seek glocal solutions.

The Spirit calls us to develop glocal conversations about Christian ideas and practices. These include Scripture, Evangelicalism, ecumenism, Pentecostalism, Jesus Christ, the Holy Spirit, God the Father, the Trinity, community, spirituality, discipleship, liturgy, worship, hospitality, prayer, ecojustice, education, social ethics, Christian leadership, gospel and culture, beauty, place, suffering, liberation and so forth.

Finally, through glocal conversations the Spirit leads us to adopt a new posture. This is a responsive, humble, celebratory, open, inclusive and embracing attitude to the "other." We do this as a new people made up of every tribe and language and people and nation.

There are dangers in glocalization. Sugirtharajah warns of the commodification of local, contextual practices and theologies. When this happens they are "smoothed out of their primary contexts, concerns, and contestations, travel across borders and become objects of analysis and scrutiny within an alien secondary context."[27]

It's common for those of us who are Western to make mistakes when we wrestle with Majority World and indigenous ideas. Sugirtharajah mentions our tendency to commodify, reduce and institutionalize these ideas. We also risk doing these things: (1) We apply them in noncontextual, prescriptive ways. (2) We ignore their meanings in their original setting. (3) We glamorize or idealize their proponents or their contexts. (4) We demonize those persons or contexts. (5) We disregard them as irrelevant, rhetorical or minority discourse.

Kevin J. Vanhoozer says that we can fall into three traps when we glocalize theology: (1) We can underestimate the theological significance of local cultures. (2) We can homogenize cultures and theologies, exaggerating

---

[27]R. S. Sugirtharajah, "Textual Take-Aways: Third World Texts in Western Metropolitan Centres," *Black Theology in Britain: A Journal of Contextual Praxis* 2 (1999): 33, 37; Edward W. Said, *The World, the Text, and the Critic* (Cambridge, MA: Harvard University Press, 1983), 239.

"the one." (3) We can overemphasize cultural particularity, exaggerating "the many," and pursue "theological ethnification."[28]

My hope is that *GlobalChurch* does not fall into the traps Sugirtharajah and Vanhoozer describe. I hope that what unfolds in the following chapters is respectful and discerning. I hope it leads to further mutually enriching conversations between people of different cultures.

You, the reader, face the same challenges. You face them in your personal life, ministry context and missional engagements.

Will you treat the themes in this book as abstract, theoretical notions? Will this be a temporary infatuation, a flirtation with the "other" that dissipates as suddenly as it arrived? Or will glocal conversations become an enriching and formative *orientation* in your life? Will glocal conversations bring fresh approaches to theology, faith, mission, church and worship? Will conversations with other cultures and theologies become, for you, a compelling *way of life*?

My prayer is that glocal conversations will help the church be a global, visible, alternative "city set upon a hill": a truly *GlobalChurch.*

---

[28]Craig Ott and Harold A. Netland, *Globalizing Theology: Belief and Practice in an Era of World Christianity* (Grand Rapids: Baker Academic, 2006), 125.

PART TWO

LIGHT
Renewing Our Mission

CONTEXTUALIZING MISSION

*"Integral mission" has to do with the basic issue of the integrity
of the church's life, the consistency between what
the church is and what it proclaims.*

VINOTH RAMACHANDRA

When people think of the Australian landscape and outdoors, they often imagine sun, sand, ocean and surf. They picture superb summer days surfing at Bondi, swimming at Scarborough, snorkeling at Coral Bay or the Great Barrier Reef, and sunbathing at St. Kilda. There is something beautiful and spiritual about the Australian beach. These beaches have deep blue waters and long beautiful shores. Many Australians and overseas visitors find them irresistible.

The Australian bush has also shaped my nation's sense of our landscape and identity. Poets such as Banjo Paterson and Henry Lawson immortalize our feelings about the bush. Poets depict our outback's characters, beauties and harsh realities. Our outback has potential to evoke love, terror and fascination. Beaches, bushland and outback deserts shape our folklore and self-identity as Australians.

It isn't just people in rural areas who have been impacted by the spirituality and beauty of the Australian bush. National park surrounds the urban suburb where I live. I love walking through the bush admiring the glorious eucalypts. My family and I enjoy the laughter of the dignified kookaburras. We love throwing stones in the cool creek. And we enjoy listening to the screeching of the red-tailed black cockatoos. Only a few weeks ago my children squealed with delight as they watched an echidna shyly making its way down one of our local bush tracks. With wonder, they stirred up muddied waters full of tiny tadpoles.

Surrounded by the natural beauties of the Australian landscape, my suburb is a peaceful, comfortable place to live. It's an archetypal leafy, middle-class, contented Australian suburb.

My family loves living in such a beautiful setting. But my wife, Felicity, and I are concerned that our three daughters will grow too comfortable in these surroundings. They might too readily assume that this is the norm in Australia and in the Asia-Pacific region. The reality is that many people in my country and region live in poverty. Many are marginalized, exploited and in tremendous need.

To help my three daughters develop a passion for mission and service, my wife and I take our children on regular trips overseas. We take them to poorer Asian countries to think about justice and mission. We want them to spend time with Christians practicing contextual and integral mission among the urban poor.

In 2012, I travelled with my thirteen-year-old daughter Madison to Thailand, Cambodia and Malaysia. We spent time in urban slums and in Karen villages on the Thai-Burmese border. We served in a drug rehabilitation center in Cambodia. And we served among street children on the Thai-Cambodian border.

It was on this trip that Madison and I spent two days learning to cook Thai food with Saiyuud Diwong. Saiyuud is affectionately called "Poo." We experienced her contextual and integral mission in the Klong Toey Slum in Bangkok, Thailand. Early in the morning, Poo's team picked us up from our hotel in Sukhumvit. They took us to the local wet markets where they explained the astonishing array of local food. These included coconuts, garlics, chilies and pineapples as well as grasshoppers, silkworms, crickets, pig heads, cockroaches, worms, eels, frogs and ants. From there we went back to Poo's Helping Hands Cooking School in the Klong Toey slum. We learned to cook satay chicken, green Thai curry, sticky rice with pineapple, green curry fried rice and much more.

Helping Hands Cooking School is a ministry of Urban Neighbours of Hope (UNOH). Poo started the cooking school in her home in the Klong Toey Slum—a community of one hundred thousand people. Poo started the cooking school so that she and her family could earn a fair wage. It soon built a reputation among tourists and among expats living in Bangkok.

As the business grew, Poo employed twenty other poor slum residents. She began investing back into the slum for its development and renewal. Using her nickname to her advantage, Poo published a book of recipes called *Cooking with Poo*. It sold more than seven thousand copies. The BBC and a few American television stations have featured Poo's cooking school. The book also won the Diagram Prize for the oddest book title of the year at the Frankfurt Book Fair!

Poo now collaborates with the Urban Neighbours of Hope team. She trains others to develop their own businesses in the slums. These include a sushi service, a catering service, a Thai dessert business, Klong Toey Handicrafts, a recycling shop called Second Chance Bangkok and a sewing business called Fair Wear. They have developed youth clubs, cooking groups and employment projects. These businesses have brought hope and renewal into this urban slum.[1]

Urban Neighbours of Hope and Poo's cooking school are outstanding examples of mission. They show what contextual and integral mission can look like as it engages and transforms communities.

In this chapter, I consider why contextual mission is essential and biblical. Vision for the kingdom and mission of God shapes contextual mission. So does an emphasis on Jesus Christ's incarnation. Contextual mission must be both integral and transformational. There is a lot of theological jargon in those last few sentences. But I will explore the meanings of these ideas as we go. This chapter asks, *What can we learn from how Majority World Christians cultivate contextual mission?*

---

[1]Saiyuud Diwong, *Cooking with Poo* (Dandenong North: UNOH, 2011), 7-8, 96-106. See www .cookingwithpoo.com and www.unoh.org.

CONTEXTUAL MISSION IS ESSENTIAL AND BIBLICAL

Contextualization is a term coined by the Theological Education Fund of the World Council of Churches in 1972. Scott Moreau defines contextualization as "the process whereby Christians adapt the forms, content, and praxis of the Christian faith so as to communicate it to the minds and heart of people with other cultural backgrounds. The goal is to make the Christian faith *as a whole*—not only the message but also the means of living out of our faith in the local setting—understandable."[2]

It's important that we contextualize the gospel for particular cultures. We live in a time when the liberating themes of the gospel and the evolving concerns of our culture are poorly related, so we lose opportunities to build bridges of meaning. The result is miscommunication, retreat and mistrust. Yet the biblical and missional underpinnings of the gospel provide a solid basis for contextualization. The church needs to examine these underpinnings and the nature of biblical contextualization. The church also needs to consider the possibilities of contextual theology and transformational mission.

There are rich resources that exist for understanding and practicing contextual mission. We can learn much from contextual mission in the Majority World. And we can learn from their struggles with religious syncretism. Contextualization involves building a constructive and dynamic relationship between the gospel and culture. We should remember an important point: "Syncretism develops not because of contextualization but from a failure to contextualise."[3]

---

[2]A. Scott Moreau, *Contextualization in World Missions: Mapping and Assessing Evangelical Models* (Grand Rapids: Kregel, 2012), 36. Scott Moreau examines the work of Stephen Bevans and Robert Schreiter as he proposes various models and maps of contextualization in chapter 1. See Stephen B. Bevans, *Models of Contextual Theology*, rev. and expanded ed., Faith and Cultures Series (Maryknoll, NY: Orbis, 2002); Robert J. Schreiter, *Constructing Local Theologies* (Maryknoll, NY: Orbis, 1985). Dean Gilliland outlines models of contextualization in *The Word Among Us: Contextualizing Theology for Mission Today* (Dallas, TX: Word, 1989). Scott Moreau develops a schema of contextualization models (based on the work of Nicholls, Hesselgrave, Bevans, Schreiter, Gilliland and Van Engen) in "Evangelical Models of Contextualization," in *Local Theology for the Global Church: Principles for an Evangelical Approach to Contextualization*, ed. Matthew Cook (Pasadena, CA: World Evangelical Alliance Theological Commission, 2010), 165-93. Moreau writes, "Of the six schema listed, Bevans's is the most frequently cited by other missiologists as a viable way to map the entire field," 168.

[3]Craig Ott, Stephen J. Strauss and Timothy C. Tennent, *Encountering Theology of Mission: Biblical Foundations, Historical Developments, and Contemporary Issues*, Encountering Mission (Grand Rapids: Baker Academic, 2010), 266.

Orlando Costas of Costa Rica, Vinoth Ramachandra of Sri Lanka and René Padilla of Argentina have all written on contextual and integral mission. All three argue the importance of such mission for the transformation of individuals, societies and theology. Costas, Ramachandra and Padilla echo a global missional consensus. (Yet not all agree on definitions, models, methods and limits of contextualization.) I'll be drawing on their thought throughout this chapter.

Orlando Costas says that we must root our contextualization and contextual mission in Scripture and in the incarnation. Scripture, after all, is contextual. "The Scriptures are contextual from beginning to end." They show God interacting with people in context. He reveals himself contextually through their stories, worldviews, languages, situations and settings. "He reveals himself to concrete peoples in specific situations by means of particular cultural symbols and categories." This revelation "reaches its peak" when God takes on human flesh in the incarnation.[4] "The incarnation turns theology proper and anthropology into a Christological issue. It also makes contextualization an inevitable and indispensable process for a proper understanding and communication of the Christian faith."[5]

We must contextualize offshore models and theologies of church and mission if we are going to be faithful to the gospel and culture. We also need to catalyze first-level, homegrown theology and approaches to mission and church. To do this well, we had best examine Scriptures, traditions and cultures. As pastors and leaders, we must exegete culture. We ought to wrestle with the relationships between theology and Scripture and critical dimensions of our culture. And we need to empower our congregations to do the same.

The role of Christian leaders is to identify, develop and release contextual responses. Such responses are critical for mission and theology and church. Transplanting offshore, noncontextualized models and reasoning into cultural contexts is irresponsible and self-defeating.

And it is not enough to contextualize. As communities of faith, we must go on to develop indigenous ways of being church. We need to cultivate home-

---

[4]Orlando E. Costas, "Contextualization and Incarnation," *Journal of Theology for Southern Africa* 29 (1979): 25.

[5]Orlando E. Costas, *Christ Outside the Gate: Mission Beyond Christendom* (Maryknoll, NY: Orbis, 1982), 5, 12.

grown approaches to mission and foster indigenous forms of theology. When we do this, we open opportunities for meaningful engagement with culture and our contextualization has missional drive and direction.

Contextual Mission Is Kingdom Oriented and Incarnational

Contextual mission is rooted in missional theology. Contextualization is not always missional or kingdom oriented, but contextualization is best when it emerges from a passion for Jesus and his mission and kingdom. It is worthwhile when it emerges from a desire to be faithful to these three in our context.

Just as the missional God reaches out to humans in contextual ways, so Christians must pursue contextual mission. Orlando Costas says that Christian mission is rooted in "the missional dynamic of the Father, the Son, and the Spirit, in and for history. To understand the mission of Christians in any situation we need first and foremost to understand God's mission as it is revealed in his trinitarian history."[6] Costas is not interested in an abstract theology of the Trinity. He values the trinitarian actions of God in human history. And he cares about the pastoral and missional implications for the church. The concrete, trinitarian actions of God guide the church in its contextual mission and ministry.[7]

Contextual mission is not merely about proclamation or getting people to believe propositions. I am not saying that the truths of the gospel are unimportant! But a living encounter with Jesus Christ and the power of the Holy Spirit transforms people. The Spirit of Christ enables us to embrace the values and community and justice and transformation present in Christ's kingdom. He empowers us to do this individually and in community. "As a messianic community, the church is that fellowship of men and women, both liberated and in the process of liberation."[8]

The missional church embraces the proclamation and demands and priorities of Christ's kingdom. "The kingdom serves as the frame of reference

---

[6]Ibid., 88.
[7]Orlando E. Costas, *Liberating News: A Theology of Contextual Evangelization* (Grand Rapids: Eerdmans, 1989), 149.
[8]Costas, *Christ Outside the Gate*, 90.

for the mission of God. . . . The participation of the People of God in his mission will have to be directed, therefore, by the message of the kingdom."[9] Proclamation is not just propositional and verbal. We proclaim the gospel through contextualized and Spirit-empowered and liberating witness. Orlando Costas calls this witness "dynamic transforming witness."[10]

Contextual mission is best when it's kingdom oriented. René Padilla says, "Because the kingdom has been inaugurated in Jesus Christ, the mission of the church cannot be properly understood apart from the presence of the kingdom. The mission of the church is an extension of the mission of Jesus. It is the manifestation (though not yet complete) of the kingdom of God, through proclamation as well as through social service and action."[11]

The responsibilities of the kingdom of God reach beyond the personal and church-based dimensions of our lives. They reach into the social and public realms of the church's witness within societies. The church cannot avoid its political role; it cannot ignore the way in which Jesus calls it into a transforming relationship with cultures and with creation. The church must confront cultural powers and principalities. These include materialism, sexism, exploitation, lust, pride and greed. And it needs to confront these things when they are present *within* the structures and relationships of the church.

Our contextual mission is to individuals, groups, cultures and creation. Courage and suffering and hope characterize contextual mission. Contextual mission confronts violence and socioeconomic oppression. It affirms life and human dignity. It condemns torture and exploitation. And it calls for legal and political justice. Such mission affirms human solidarity across racial, religious, sexual, economic and other divides. Our churches will only witness to Jesus Christ in their specific contexts when they pursue unity and reject division.

We must root our contextual mission in the gospel. Contextual mission and theology need to take whole contexts and whole persons and whole communities seriously. The church's missional nature and activities are "grounded in the mission of God and will have to be steered by the message

---

[9]Ibid., 91.

[10]Ibid., 92.

[11]C. René Padilla, *Mission Between the Times: Essays on the Kingdom* (Grand Rapids: Eerdmans, 1985), 192.

of the kingdom."[12] God invites the church to be a *worshiping* and *missional* community within specific contexts.[13]

Contextual mission is incarnational. It patterns itself after the extraordinary fact that God took on human flesh in the incarnation of Jesus Christ. For Orlando Costas, the incarnation of Jesus Christ makes contextualization and contextual mission a "theological necessity." Contextualization is an "inevitable and indispensable process for a proper understanding and communication of the Christian faith." Costas locates contextual mission within a trinitarian frame.[14] From the beginning of history, the triune God reaches out to humanity for its redemption. The words and deeds of the Father, Son and Holy Spirit show us the ultimate form of contextual mission.

It's in the incarnation that contextual mission reaches its peak. The incarnation has missional implications for the church. It's critical for the church's mission among the marginalized, oppressed, impoverished, broken and "powerless majority. Indeed, it was out of the mystery of the incarnation, to which Jesus' resurrection and death bear witness, that the early Christian community began to understand its mission as participation in the continuing mission of Jesus Christ."[15]

Costas says that the incarnation directs and shapes our contextual mission. In the incarnation, Jesus Christ "humbled himself to the extent that he took the form of a servant and thus the identity of the poor, powerless, and oppressed." Jesus revealed himself "within the harsh reality of the hurt, destitute, and marginated of the earth." Moreover, he continues to be one with the marginalized, the outcast and the oppressed. Jesus shares their experiences and is present in their suffering. He assumes their broken identity and is one with them. "We can affirm, accordingly, that Christ today is a black South African, a Latin American peasant, a Cambodian refugee, a homeless Palestinian, a persecuted Russian Jew, an orphan and homeless child, a humiliated female person. He is all of these things because he is truly human and truly God, the one for others, *God of the oppressed*."[16]

---

[12]Costas, *Christ Outside the Gate*, 94-98.
[13]Orlando E. Costas, *The Church and Its Mission: A Shattering Critique from the Third World* (Wheaton, IL: Tyndale House, 1974), 40.
[14]Costas, *Liberating News*, 149.
[15]Costas, *Christ Outside the Gate*, 13.
[16]Ibid. Italics added for emphasis.

This doesn't mean that Jesus isn't present with those with financial, political and cultural power. It doesn't mean that he's absent from those who enjoy the privileges of a particular race, ethnicity or gender. However, he reveals himself uniquely through the ignorant, exploited, humiliated and subjugated. He calls his church to struggle against personal and systemic evil.

Samuel Escobar observes,

> Drive and inspiration to move forward and take the gospel of Jesus Christ to the ends of the earth, crossing all kinds of geographic and cultural barriers, is the work of the Holy Spirit. There is an element of mystery when the dynamism of mission does not come from people in positions of power or privilege, or from the expansive dynamism of a superior civilization, but from below—from the little ones, those who have few material, financial or technical resources but who are open to the prompting of the Spirit.[17]

The church's contextual mission involves struggle. It confronts sexism, racism, colonialism, imprisonment, sexual violence, war mongering, torture, exile and exploitation. This mission includes the visible demonstration of an alternative *polis*. The church is a "city on a hill." It reflects the values of Jesus' kingdom. In its contextual mission among specific groups, the church must reveal the countercultural values of Jesus' kingdom. Jesus Christ's people are to embody the incarnation in their humility. They witness to it in their service of the poor and powerless and silenced and oppressed.

The incarnation shows us the person of Jesus Christ and the shape of his contextual mission. In the incarnation we discover "who he is (the Lord and Savior of the oppressed)." We see "where he is to be found today (among the poor, the powerless, and the oppressed)." And we take part in "what he is doing (healing their wounds, breaking their chains of oppression, demanding justice and peace, giving life, and imparting hope)."[18] This informs and shapes the church's mission.

In the incarnation, we see Jesus present among and transforming the lives of the downtrodden and the oppressed. Jesus demonstrates the definitive form of contextual mission and holistic transformation. In the incarnation, Jesus enters people's contexts. And he transforms individuals and groups.

---

[17]Samuel Escobar, *The New Global Mission: The Gospel from Everywhere to Everyone*, Christian Doctrine in Global Perspective (Downers Grove, IL: InterVarsity Press, 2003), 19.
[18]Costas, *Christ Outside the Gate*, 15-16.

The church's contextual mission must confront systemic evil and oppression. It ought to engage in processes of transformation that lead to liberation, justice, healing and wholeness.[19] We can only do this if we build relationships with the oppressed and marginalized and forgotten and silenced. We need to collaborate with them as they seek transformation and freedom and justice. In the process, contextual mission not only transforms individuals and cultures—it transforms the church.

Theological speculation on the incarnation isn't enough. Nor it is good enough to be missionally aware because of the incarnation. We must move from theological speculation and missional awareness to concrete practices. These practices ought to be context specific and costly and inspired by prayer.

Orlando Costas says that the mission of the church is only authentic when it is concrete:

> The real issue is whether or not we as Christians are willing to be immersed in the concrete situations of the disenfranchised of our societies and witness to the lordship and saviorhood of Christ from within, a commitment that will have to be verified in our participation in the concrete transformation of these situations. Anything else is pure talk, and the kingdom of God "does not consist in talk but in power" (2 Cor. 4:20).[20]

Worthwhile mission isn't only contextual—it is concrete and integral and transformational.

CONTEXTUAL MISSION MUST BE INTEGRAL AND TRANSFORMATIONAL

I teach at Morling Theological College in Sydney. Our mission is to "equip the whole believer and whole churches to affirm the whole Bible and to take the whole gospel to the whole world." (This reflects the 1974 Lausanne Covenant.) Contextualization is transformational when we dedicate ourselves to the liberation, redemption, well-being and transformation of whole persons, entire families and total societies. This contextual and integral mission is a participation in the mission of the triune God. It is dependent on the power of the Spirit of Jesus Christ.[21]

---

[19]Costas, *Liberating News*, 30.
[20]Costas, *Christ Outside the Gate*, 16.
[21]Escobar, *The New Global Mission*, 94.

Our mission must be transformational. Transformation happens when our mission is holistic—to whole persons and whole communities. It also occurs when processes of critical contextualization shape our mission. Transformation occurs when believers contextualize the gospel to their settings and when they engage the gospel with their whole lives. New life occurs when individuals and groups embrace a transforming relationship with Jesus and his Spirit. Transformation happens when Jesus Christ renews individuals and communities in their totality. He does this by the power of the Spirit. Transformation occurs when the people of God are missional and courageous. It happens when we are more concerned about the extension of the kingdom, the glorification of Christ, and the well-being of people than the prosperity, power or reputation of the church.

What does it mean to say that contextual mission must be *integral*? *Integral mission* is an expression that developed within the Latin American Theological Fraternity (FTL). *Integral mission* means that the church's mission is to whole persons. It's to their mind and body and spirit. It also means that the church's mission is to individuals and people groups and whole cultures. Integral mission is transformational and contextual because it involves the transformation of whole persons and families and communities.[22]

This understanding reflects the mission of Jesus and the early churches. It is more about the nature of the church than the activities of the church. Integral mission arises out of the missional nature of the triune God. Since God is missional his church is also missional.

The church's integral, transformational mission is not primarily an action, program or strategy. It is a response to Jesus and his kingdom. It is about the missional nature and vocation of the church.

According to Costas, the church sometimes abandons this nature and call. It does this when it ignores issues of ethics and justice and reconciliation. The content of the gospel then becomes "a conscience-soothing Jesus, with an unscandalous cross, an otherworldly kingdom, a private, inwardly limited spirit, a pocket God, a spiritualized Bible, and an escapist church. Its

---

[22]Samuel Escobar, *A Time for Mission: The Challenge for Global Christianity* (Leicester: Inter-Varsity Press, 2003), 142-54. Note that *A Time for Mission* and *The New Global Mission* are the same book. The first is the IVP UK edition, and the second is the IVP US edition.

goal is a happy, comfortable, and successful life, obtainable through the forgiveness of an abstract sinfulness by faith in an unhistorical Christ."[23]

Contextual mission must be integral. If it is not integral it has no integrity. And it is distanced from the biblical picture of mission. Vinoth Ramachandra says,

> Integral mission has to do with the Church's *integrity*. Integral mission flows out of an integral gospel and an integrated people. There is a great danger that we transform the mission of the church into a set of special "projects" and "programs," whether we call them "evangelism" or "socio-political action," and then look for ways to integrate them methodologically. . . . The primary way the church acts upon the world is through the actions of its members in their daily work and their daily relationships with people of other faiths. . . . "Integral mission" has to do with the basic issue of the integrity of the church's life, the consistency between what the church is and what it proclaims.[24]

But it is not enough for contextual mission to be integral; it must also be transformational. Orlando Costas says that transformational mission has many expressions. These include proclaiming, discipling, mobilizing, growing, liberating and celebrating. These characteristics "make up the church's mission-in-life."[25] These aspects of mission express themselves best in local contexts.

Transformation, in the words of Vinay Samuel, "is to enable God's vision of society to be actualized in all relationships, social, economic, and spiritual, so that God's will may be reflected in human society and his love be experienced by all communities, especially the poor."[26] *Mission as transformation* constructs interdependent connections between evangelism and social action. Such transformation forges deep roots within the world. When we engage in such mission we choose not to stand apart from the world. This is why transformation is contextual.

Transformational mission aligns theory and practice. It elevates local communities and their specific concerns. It brings freedom from oppressive

---

[23]Costas, *Christ Outside the Gate*, 80.
[24]Vinoth Ramachandra, "Integral Mission: Exploring a Concept," in *Integral Mission: The Way Forward*, ed. C. V. Mathew (Kerala: Christava Sahitya Samithy, 2006), 57.
[25]Orlando E. Costas, *The Integrity of Mission: The Inner Life and Outreach of the Church* (San Francisco: Harper and Row, 1979), xiii.
[26]Vinay Samuel and Chris Sugden, eds., *Mission as Transformation: A Theology of the Whole Gospel* (Oxford: Regnum, 1999), ii.

use of power. It strives for reconciliation, justice and solidarity. It is especially concerned for the poor and marginalized.

Transformational mission seeks community transformation. It does this by working with groups on concrete issues. (These issues include violence, addiction, sexuality and poverty.) And transformational mission has a goal. It seeks to help groups experience the liberation of the gospel, the life of the kingdom of God and the redemption and lordship of Jesus Christ. And it always does this by working with people in concrete, particular, local settings.[27]

Transformational mission is always contextual. We shape transformational mission around context and culture. "Cultures are religio-linguistic entities. They provide people with a framework for understanding their reality and a means for integrating the transcendent into daily life. . . . One must look at how the gospel affects the whole of the communities' cultures, in value system, structures, and direction."[28]

Transformation is a long-term process. We cannot achieve it without the kind of integral commitments expressed in the Micah Declaration (see the final section of this chapter). Transformation involves enduring commitment to people in local contexts. It demands immersion in particular settings.

Samuel says that transformation is a long-term "commitment to community building." Transformation demands "the unity of the whole body of Christ." This recognizes the person in community and appreciates the centrality of social units. It discerns where God is present and at work in the community. It invites people to take part in what God is already doing. Transformation invests in contexts. It builds social bonds, social reconciliation, social community and social transformation.[29]

Transformational mission discerns where God is at work in the world. It notices where the values of the kingdom are flourishing—integrity, service, humility, peace and freedom. Transformational mission seeks to develop these values. It does this through mission, discipleship, community building and social action.

---

[27]Vinay Samuel and Chris Sugden, eds., *The Church in Response to Human Need* (Grand Rapids: Eerdmans, 1987), 229-31.

[28]Samuel and Sugden, *Mission as Transformation*, xii.

[29]Ibid., 227-35; Vinay Samuel and Albrecht Hauser, eds., *Proclaiming Christ in Christ's Way: Studies in Integral Evangelism* (Oxford: Regnum, 1989), 10-12.

Samuel says that the values of the kingdom of God are clear. These values shape the outlook and practices of mission as transformation. They always work themselves out in context. And we must contextualize these values. Samuel says the values of the kingdom of God that shape transformational mission are clear. And these values become practices. The first value is human dignity. The second is freedom of conscience without threat or control. The third is participation in decisions that affect one's life and community. The fourth is struggle against evil and injustice. And, finally, the fifth is the cultivation of hope, respect, dignity, humility, faith, love, equity and mutuality.[30]

The church must declare the whole gospel to the whole world. The church does this in word and action. It declares that the kingdom of God is manifest in the whole world. It announces that Jesus Christ reigns over this world and the entire cosmos. "The church in the power of the Spirit proclaims salvation in Christ and plants signs of the kingdom, always giving itself fully to the work of the Lord, knowing that its labor in the Lord is not in vain (1 Cor 15:58)."[31]

The church anticipates all things coming under the final rule and reign of Jesus Christ. It proclaims salvation and announces the kingdom in word and deed. The church embraces Jesus' concern for "justice and reconciliation throughout human society." It shares Jesus' passion for the liberation of all humanity "from every kind of oppression."[32]

The people of God engage in contextual mission in integral, transformational ways. We root these missional *practices* and *ways of being* in context. We can never divorce ourselves from context, *nor would we want to.*

Padilla writes that integral mission must be both contextual and evangelical. We should take care that our mission is "truly *evangelical*—rooted in the gospel and consequently bringing about transformation in society."[33]

Similarly, Costas affirms the emphasis placed on the *whole gospel* in the phrase *the whole gospel for the whole world.* He challenges us to explore what we mean by the *whole world.* Hence, "a vision of 'the whole world' is essential

---

[30]Samuel and Sugden, *Church in Response to Human Need,* 149-50.

[31]Padilla, *Mission Between the Times,* 209.

[32]Ibid., 186-99.

[33]C. René Padilla and Tetsunao Yamamori, eds., *The Local Church, Agent of Transformation: An Ecclesiology for Integral Mission* (Buenos Aires: Ediciones Kairos, 2004), 19-20.

for a faithful and relevant proclamation of the whole gospel."[34] According to Costas, the whole world is both the object and context of the whole gospel. Jesus gives his gospel to the world. "Hence, the whole world, the world of humans and the world of things, is the object of the gospel." The world is also the context of the gospel. "It is the context in which the good news of salvation was first given and received and is today proclaimed and heard. Outside the world there is no gospel and certainly no Christian mission."[35]

The world is not static, rigid or passive. It's dynamic and changing and multidimensional. It's a world of linguistic, ideological, political and ethnic diversity. The world is awash in myths and symbols. Connections exist between wildly differing cultures. The world is full of dynamic structures and institutions and collective identities.

The church must contextualize the gospel in this dynamic, "crowded, complicated, and captive" environment. This way the gospel is "made flesh in concrete situations. . . . Hence one basic requirement of Christian mission is the immersion of the community of faith in the various situations that make up the world." This is an "experiential knowledge of human society rather than an intellectual understanding of an abstract world."[36]

To engage in *mission as transformation* in local contexts, the people of God need missional passion for the world. We must embrace a desire for the redemption and liberation and well-being of individuals and groups. We need to commit to integral mission expressed through particular service in local settings. We need "analytical tools and communication skills." These help us fulfill the missional task in particular contexts. We require prophetic courage as we challenge demonic and oppressive powers, structures and principalities. God's people must cultivate spirituality adequate for contextual mission. We need an ability to assess the relationship between the gospel and cultures. And, finally, we need to form contextual responses, "incarnating the gospel in today's world."[37]

Jesus Christ died "outside the gate of the Holy City." So, the church must understand that salvation has "moved to the periphery." Our contextual

---

[34]Costas, *Christ Outside the Gate*, 163.
[35]Ibid.
[36]Ibid.
[37]Ibid., 164, 172.

mission is "outside the gates" of the edifices and institutions "that surround our religious compound and shape the structures of Christendom." Christ died outside the gate. So we understand mission as *going out to the periphery*.

Contextual mission leads to transformation when we identify with the suffering and alienation of the outsider. And when we share in Christ's suffering "by serving, especially, its lowest representatives: the poor, the powerless, and the oppressed."[38]

Outside the gate, we have a fuller understanding of the relationship between Jesus and the gospel and culture. Outside the gate, we can pursue a radical contextualization of the whole gospel for whole persons and the whole world. And we "become apostolic agents in the mobilization of a servant church toward its crucified Lord, outside the gate of a comfortable and secure ecclesiastical compound."[39]

CONTEXTUAL MISSION AND THE GLOBALCHURCH:
CONCLUDING REFLECTIONS

There has been a recent flood of books on missional theology and practice in the West. This is a welcome development. But much of the missional growth of the church has been in Asia, Africa and Latin America. Conversion rates in those contexts have been astounding. Missional passion in those settings is thrilling and humbling. And while mission in those settings has not always been contextual—especially because of the influence of colonialism, globalization and Western culture—many in those settings are demonstrating what contextual and integral mission looks like.

We can learn much from the contextual and integral mission among the churches of indigenous settings and the Majority World. We can especially learn from their focus on the kingdom of God. Their commitment to bring healing and justice and freedom and transformation to whole persons and whole communities is instructive. We can also learn from their focus on incarnational immersion among the poor and exploited and marginalized. And we can learn from their missional integrity.

Here are nine things we learn from how Majority World Christians cultivate contextual mission:

---

[38]Ibid., 172, 188, 190-91.
[39]Ibid., 194.

1. Contextual mission understands that mission is "a permanent and intrinsic dimension of the church's life."[40] The church is essentially missional. Mission is central and pivotal and constitutive of its nature. David Bosch writes that "the classical doctrine of the *missio Dei* as God the Father sending the Son, and God the Father and Son sending the Spirit was expanded to include yet another 'movement': Father, Son, and Holy Spirit sending the church into the world."[41] The church serves the mission of Christ. It is caught up in the missional purposes and "movements" of the triune God. The church exists because of that mission. We exist because of God's redemptive mission to all humanity and creation and history.[42]

Western missional thinkers often articulate this position. But many Majority World churches go further. They allow this conviction to soak every dimension of their theology and worship and prayer and mission. Will we do the same?

2. Contextual mission focuses on the missio Dei *and its consequences for the missional activities of the church.*[43] This includes the need for the church to stop focusing merely on the *activities* of mission. Instead, it should recognize that gospel proclamation, church planting, works of justice and compassion, and so forth, are all grounded in and directed toward the *missio Dei*. They are not so much missional activities as expressions of the essential missional nature of the church.

The mission of the church is essentially about the *nature* and *essence* of the church. Mission isn't merely about *adiaphora* (that is, a thing not regarded as essential to faith or to the actual nature of the church). Mission isn't only about *addresses* (that is, a message for proclamation) of the church. Mission isn't a contingent, peripheral or optional activity of the church. Instead, the church "is missionary by its nature" and "exists by mission, just as fire exists by burning."[44]

It's possible to speak of mission as a set of determining goals or aims (such as in a *mission statement*). We can also view mission through our *mis-*

---

[40]David J. Bosch, *Believing in the Future: Toward a Missiology of Western Culture* (New York: Trinity, 1995), 27-32.

[41]David J. Bosch, *Transforming Mission: Paradigm Shifts in Theology of Mission* (Maryknoll, NY: Orbis, 1991), 390.

[42]Graham Hill, *Salt, Light, and a City: Introducing Missional Ecclesiology* (Eugene, OR: Wipf and Stock, 2012), 153.

[43]Bosch, *Transforming Mission*, 391.

[44]Bosch, *Believing in the Future*, 31-32. Bosch is making his case with support from the Vatican Decree on Mission (paragraph 9) and from a quote attributed to Emil Brunner.

sional actions. But a missional understanding of the church prioritizes the *missional nature of the church.* Missional ecclesiology proceeds from there to missional actions, systems, strategies and structures. It's a theological vision shaped by the messianic mission of Jesus Christ.

3. *Contextual mission considers the missional "marks" of the church.* Since the Reformation, it's been common to speak of the *notae ecclesiae* (the "marks" of the true church).[45] The Reformation "marks" include true preaching, church discipline and administration of the sacraments. The Nicene "marks" are unity, holiness, catholicity and apostolicity. It's important that we consider how we can understand these "marks" missionally. How do the *notae ecclesiae* relate to the *notae missionis* (the missional "marks" of the church, or the marks of the church in mission)?

John Howard Yoder proposes four missional "marks" of the church. These are holy living, brotherly and sisterly love, witness and suffering.[46] He also describes the fruit of such *notae missionis.* These are the "five sample practices of the church before the watching world": (1) We practice healthy conflict transformation. (2) We release the whole body of Christ to mission and ministry. (3) We listen to each other and to the Spirit. (4) We are hospitable and we share our resources. (5) We practice inclusivity and the transcendence of prejudices.[47] Alan Roxburgh writes that the missional church has three primary themes: (1) All cultures and societies are mission fields. (2) Mission is about the *missio Dei.* (3) Missional church is about the church being a contrast society.[48]

Having read Majority World perspectives, it's important that we take time to consider two important questions: What do I believe to be the missional marks of the church? And, How will my church express these missional marks in my context?

The chapters of this book give a good starting point as you form your own missional "marks" of the church. The book chapters reveal the mis-

---

[45]Hill, *Salt, Light, and a City,* 161.

[46]John Howard Yoder, *The Royal Priesthood: Essays Ecclesiological and Ecumenical* (Grand Rapids: Eerdmans, 1994), 75-89; Hill, *Salt, Light, and a City,* 164.

[47]John Howard Yoder, "Sacrament as Social Process: Christ the Transformer of Culture," *Theology Today* 48, no. 1 (1991): 34-39.

[48]A. J. Roxburgh, *What Is Missional Church? An Introduction to the Missional Church Conversation* (Eagle, ID: Allelon, 2007), 5-8. I discovered this article by Roxburgh after developing my *notae missionis* and am delighted that he identifies similar themes.

sional "marks" that Majority World churches pursue. Here's some examples that emerge from these chapters: Missional churches cultivate glocal awareness and missional theology. They foster contextual and integral mission. They nurture indigenous expressions of church and theology and faith. Missional churches liberate the whole person. They welcome the stranger. They embrace the Spirit. And they care for creation. Missional churches are ethical communities. They transform neighborhoods and seek the welfare of the city. They devour Scripture. Missional churches reimagine theological education and ministry training, so that mission is central. They recover beauty—artistic, literary, natural, physical and other forms of beauty. Their leaders practice servantship. They recover authentic community. Missional churches develop missional spirituality and discipleship. Of course, you'll want to develop your own list of the missional "marks" of the church over time.

4. Contextual mission immerses itself "in the concrete situations of the disenfranchised of our societies and [witnesses] to the lordship and saviourhood of Christ from within." We verify this commitment "in our participation in the concrete transformation of these situations."[49] What does this involve? We commit to scriptural and gospel obedience and witness. We practice love, forgiveness, reconciliation, mutual accountability, hospitality and the embrace of "difference." We pursue the practices of justice, peace and mercy even when they cost us much. We embrace a kingdom-sized vision and purpose that includes, but is bigger than, the local church.

Immersed in the situations of the disenfranchised, we are a church of sinners and of grace. We stand as a positive contrast to racism, religious and ethnic violence, sexism, colonialism, warmongering, success orientation, manipulation and oppression.[50] Contextual and integral mission is transformational when the love and grace of Jesus Christ saturates it.

5. Contextual mission seeks to embody the gospel of Christ in all cultures. This includes cultivating indigenous forms of theology, mission, worship and discipleship. We should refuse to *merely* adapt other people's theology, mission and worship for our own setting. (We may do this from time to time, but it shouldn't be a regular practice.) Instead, we must form *our own, home-*

---

[49]Costas, "Contextualization and Incarnation," 23, 28, 30.
[50]Ibid.

grown, indigenous theologies and practices. This requires courage and innovation and passion.

Contextual mission must stay true to the core of the gospel message. But it must also contextualize its mission, proclamation, discipleship, training, service, worship and so on. We must shape the choices we make in contextual mission around four things: (1) Does this contextualization glorify God? (2) Does it communicate and translate the gospel to this culture? (3) Is this a faithful proclamation of the gospel? (4) Does this contextual mission lead to the salvation of children, women and men? Paul Hiebert and Scott Moreau provide us with useful resources for *critical contextualization.*[51] In another chapter of this book, I've provided many examples of how Majority World Christians contextualize and indigenize theology, church and mission. We can learn from these examples.

6. Contextual mission demands that we "place the totality of life under the lordship of Christ in [our] historical situation."[52] Missional theology focuses on obedience to the lordship and mission of Jesus Christ. It places Jesus and his mission at the center of its being and organization and ministries. It expresses this complete submission to Jesus in its historical situation. Moreover, Christ's incarnation, life, teaching, love and self-sacrificial death on the cross provide us with the ultimate example of contextual mission.

We need to ask ourselves a critical question: How do we concretely place the totality of life under the lordship of Jesus in this particular setting? How are your mission, worship, discipleship, ministry and fellowship under Jesus' lordship? Your politics? Your aspirations? Your ego? Your finances? Your family? Your career? Your time? Your sexuality? Your Internet use? Your relations with Muslims? Your identity? Your national allegiance or pride? Other areas not listed here?

7. Contextual mission translates and communicates the gospel "in the language and culture of real people in the particularities of their lives." Our goal is to see the gospel "transform them, their societies, and their cultures into what God intends for them to be." We should seek "to build the bridge between

---

[51]Paul G. Hiebert, "Critical Contextualization," *International Bulletin of Missionary Research* 11, no. 3 (July 1987); Moreau, *Contextualization in World Missions.*
[52]C. René Padilla, "The Contextualization of the Gospel," *Journal of Theology for Southern Africa* 24 (1978): 28-30.

Biblical revelation and human contexts." This involves removing "the gap between orthodoxy and orthopraxy, and between truth, love, and holiness."[53]

Let's take the United States as an example. Gallup says that in 2014, North Americans worried about weak government, the economy in general, unemployment/jobs, healthcare, immigration, the federal deficit/debt and ethics/moral decline. If you're in the United States, your responsibility is to translate and communicate the gospel to a culture worried about such things. In that setting, you reveal Jesus' truth and love and holiness. In a different culture you would, of course, translate the gospel in a way that deals with the concerns of that culture.

8. Contextual mission is shaped around the kingdom of God and the incarnation of Christ. Let's start with the kingdom of God. This kingdom is countercultural to many of the values, structures and ethical systems of this world. This has implications for our lifestyles, churches and practice of mission. While recognizing and celebrating the presence of the kingdom in this world, we must also renounce all that is not of the kingdom of God. We are to pursue righteousness, peace, justice and joy. We will be misunderstood, persecuted and even disowned at times.

That shouldn't surprise us—we're a countercultural messianic movement. "Today the church faces two big challenges: (1) how to make the kingdom of God understood in the different cultures of the world; and (2) how to live Jesus' own life principles of love, justice, and compassion in a world where the poor are getting poorer and the rich few are getting richer."[54]

The church is faithful to the mission of Christ and its missional nature when it's about the establishment of the kingdom of God. This involves the redemption of individuals and of entire peoples, systems, societies and cultures. "The objective of the mission is the establishment of the kingdom of God which is the reign of God over all the forces of death, the triumph of love over all the forces of hatred, the triumph of peace over all the forces of violence and warfare. The kingdom of God is the object of the mission, and the life of Jesus Christ continues to be manifest through the church as it witnesses to, embodies and proclaims the kingdom."[55]

---

[53]Tite Tiénou and Paul G. Hiebert, "Missional Theology," *Missiology* 34, no. 2 (2006): 225.
[54]J. Fuellenbach, *Church: Community for the Kingdom* (London: Orbis, 2002), xiii.
[55]J. M. Hull, *Mission-Shaped Church: A Theological Response* (London: SCM, 2006), 5.

The church needs to be both a "prophetic community and a sign of hope." The church serves as a sign and instrument of salvation while conducting a prophetic role in the world. It's not enough for churches to be places where Christians worship, gather and listen to preaching.[56] We need to practice justice, forgiveness, compassion, love, liberation, peace and reconciliation. We must love our neighbor and care for creation. We do this as a new creation. We're a sign, foretaste, herald and witness to the kingdom and reign of God.

We also shape contextual mission around the incarnation. This involves patterning our mission after God becoming flesh in Jesus Christ. And it means joining with the poor, powerless, conflicted, oppressed and marginalized. We do this for the sake of empowerment, peace, justice, healing, reconciliation and hope.

As I've already noted, this involves moving from distance to proximity, from power to weakness, from answers to questions, and from theological speculation to concrete and costly practices. Incarnational practices are always local, hands-on, costly, Spirit-dependent and saturated in prayer.

9. Contextual mission must also be integral mission. What does this mean? It means that the Spirit of Christ shapes us, if we'll let him, into a missional church with a transforming mission.

> When the church is committed to an integral mission and to communicating the gospel through everything it *is*, *does*, and *says*, it understands that its goal is not to become large numerically, nor to be rich materially, nor powerful politically. Its purpose is to incarnate the values of the Kingdom of God and to witness to the love and the justice revealed in Jesus Christ, by the power of the Spirit, for the transformation of human life in all its dimensions, both on the individual level and on the community level.[57]

Ramachandra reminds us that *integral mission* is less about the church's *actions*, and more about the church's *being*. Ramachandra says that integral mission "has to do with the church's *integrity*." The church has integrity when it brings together its public and private practices, its actions and

[56]Miroslav Volf, "The Church as a Prophetic Community and a Sign of Hope," *European Journal of Theology*, no. 2 (1993), 9.

[57]C. René Padilla, "What Is Integral Mission?," http://im.handsupstaging.com/wp-content/uploads/2011/10/WHAT-IS-INTEGRAL-MSSION.pdf.

preaching, and its passion for truth and compassion and justice.

> Integral mission is then a way of calling the church to keep together, in her
> theology as well as in her practice, what the Triune God of the Biblical nar-
> rative always brings together: "being" and "doing," the "spiritual" and the
> "physical," the "individual" and the "social," the "sacred" and the "secular,"
> "justice" and "mercy," "witness" and "unity," "preaching truth" and "practicing
> the truth," and so on.[58]

One hundred and forty Christian leaders ministering among the poor
in over fifty countries drew up the Micah Declaration on Integral Mission.
Its definition of *integral mission* prioritizes the contextual mission of the
local church.

> Integral mission or holistic transformation is the proclamation and demon-
> stration of the gospel. It is not simply that evangelism and social involvement
> are to be done alongside each other. Rather, in integral mission our procla-
> mation has social consequences as we call people to love and repentance in
> all areas of life. And our social involvement has evangelistic consequences as
> we bear witness to the transforming grace of Jesus Christ.
>
> If we ignore the world, we betray the word of God that sends us out to serve
> the world. If we ignore the word of God, we have nothing to bring to the world.
> Justice and justification by faith, worship and political action, the spiritual and
> the material, personal change and structural change belong together. As in the
> life of Jesus, being, doing and saying are at the heart of our integral task.
>
> The grace of God is the heartbeat of integral mission. God by his grace has
> given local churches the task of integral mission. The future of integral
> mission is in planting and enabling local churches to transform the commu-
> nities of which they are part. Churches as caring and inclusive communities
> are at the heart of what it means to do integral mission.[59]

As we cultivate contextual and integral mission, the words of Micah 6:8
will ring in our ears. "He has shown all you people what is good. And what
does the LORD require of you? To act justly and to love mercy and to walk
humbly with your God."

---

[58]Ramachandra, "Integral Mission," 45-46.

[59]Tim Chester, ed., *Justice, Mercy and Humility: Integral Mission and the Poor* (Carlisle: Paternoster, 2002), 19-21. See also Wonsuk Ma and Brian Woolnough, eds., *Holistic Mission: God's Plan for God's People* (Eugene, OR: Regnum, 2010).

LIBERATING PEOPLE

WHAT CAN WE LEARN FROM HOW MAJORITY WORLD
CHRISTIANS PURSUE SOLIDARITY WITH THE BROKEN,
OPPRESSED, EXCLUDED AND VULNERABLE?

*All the political theologies, the theologies of hope, of revolution,
and of liberation, are not worth one act of genuine solidarity
with exploited social classes. They are not worth one act of faith,
love, and hope, committed—in one way or another—in active
participation to liberate [people] from everything that dehumanizes
[them and prevents them] from living according to the will of the Father.*

GUSTAVO GUTIÉRREZ

During the last few decades, inequality in Western countries has increased. The themes of justice, race, gender, equality, liberation and concern for the poor, marginalized and oppressed are now more relevant in Western settings than ever before. These, of course, are themes that liberation theologians are passionate about. Economic, political and social forces have eroded many of the equalities and opportunities that Western countries enjoyed.

Stanford University's Center on Poverty and Inequality is a research and policy analysis institute. It asserts "that poverty and inequality constitute one of the gravest threats of our time."[1] On their website they have published "20 Facts About U.S. Inequality That Everyone Should Know."

---

[1] The Stanford Center on Poverty and Inequality, "About the Center," www.stanford.edu/group/ scspi/center_about_home.html.

Here are some of their troubling findings:[2]

Wage inequality: "Over the last 30 years, wage inequality in the United States has increased substantially. The level of inequality is now approaching the extreme level that prevailed before the Great Depression."

Homelessness: "There are 750,000 Americans who are homeless on any given night. One in five of them are chronically homeless. The ranks of the sheltered homeless include disproportionate numbers of males, blacks, middle-aged people (i.e., ages 31-50), veterans, and disabled."

CEO pay: "Recent decades have seen a clear increase in the difference between CEO compensation and that of the average worker in manufacturing or 'production.' CEOs in 1965 made 24 times more than the average production worker. But in 2009 they made 185 times more."

Gender pay gaps: "Throughout much of the 20th century, the average woman earned about 60% of what the average man earned. Starting in the late 1970s, there was a large increase in women's relative earnings. Women came to earn about 80% of what men earned. This historic rise plateaued in 2005. Since then, the pay gap has remained roughly unchanged."

Racial gaps in education: "High-school dropout rates are least among whites and highest among Hispanics. And college enrollment rates are least among blacks and highest among whites."

Racial discrimination: "Racial discrimination continues to be in the labor market. An experiment carried out in Chicago and Boston during 2001 and 2002 shows that resumes with 'white-sounding' names, whether male or female, were much more likely to result in call backs for interviews than were those with 'black-sounding' names (even though the resumes were otherwise identical)."

Child poverty: "In the United States, 21 percent of all children are in poverty. This poverty rate is higher than what prevails in virtually all other rich nations."

Discouraged workers: "Discouraged workers are persons not currently looking for work because they believe that there are no jobs available for them. The number of discouraged workers in the U.S. increased sharply during the current recession. It rose to 717,000 in the first quarter of 2009, a 70-percent increase from the first quarter of 2008. Relative to their share

---

[2]The Stanford Center on Poverty and Inequality, "20 Facts About U.S. Inequality That Everyone Should Know," www.stanford.edu/group/scspi/cgi-bin/facts.php.

of the labor force, young people, blacks, and, to a lesser extent, Hispanics and men were over-represented among discouraged workers."

Wealth inequality: "The ownership of wealth among households in the U.S. became somewhat more concentrated since the 1980s. The top 10% of households controlled 68.2 percent of the total wealth in 1983. They controlled 73.1% of the total wealth in 2007."

North Americans are struggling to come to terms with a downwardly mobile middle class. From childhood, many in the United States are taught that if you are industrious, disciplined, resolved, creative, resilient and patient, and if you go to college and get a good education, then you can get ahead. They're told that professional and social and financial successes are guaranteed. The downward mobility of middle-class families provides a challenge to that optimistic worldview. This is especially the case for families that have embraced all those virtues and more. The US education secretary recently lamented that "in the space of a generation" America's graduation rate had fallen from first place in the world to fourteenth. The Pew report *Downward Mobility from the Middle Class* suggests that almost a third of all middle-class Americans will fall out of the middle class during their lifetime.[3]

Recently, the *Economist* noted some factors that exacerbate inequality in America: (1) The downward mobility of the middle class. (2) The disappearance of many of the jobs that were once available to high-school dropouts. (3) Deteriorating family structures. (4) A diminishing concern for the poor.

In 2011, 46.2 million Americans (15.1% of the population) lived below the poverty line. This figure increased to over 16% of the population in 2012. 10% of whites and more than 25% of blacks and Latinos live in poverty. The child-poverty rate in America is higher, "according to a UNICEF report, than Japan, Canada or any European country other than Romania, and it blights lives."[4] In America, 40% of the population own 0.3% of the wealth. And the top 20% own close to 85% of the wealth.[5]

---

[3]Gregory Acs, *Downward Mobility from the Middle Class: Waking Up from the American Dream*, www .pewtrusts.org/~/media/legacy/uploadedfiles/pcs_assets/2011/MiddleClassReportpdf.pdf?la=en.

[4]"The Poor in America: In Need of Help," *Economist*, November 10, 2012, www.economist.com /news/briefing/21565956-americas-poor-were-little-mentioned-barack-obamas-re-election -campaign-they-deserve.

[5]Dan Ariely, "How Americans View Wealth and Inequality," BBC News, August 20, 2012, www.bbc .co.uk/news/business-19284017.

The challenge of liberation theology, then, is as pertinent for Western contexts as it is for the Majority World.

Liberation theology, as a technical theological term, dates from the mid-1960s. It began within Latin American Roman Catholicism. By 1970, Protestant theologians were becoming involved and influential. It is more correct to speak of *theologies of liberation*. This is because differences exist between writers and between regions. There are differences between Latin American and African theologians. And there are unique features in South African, Asian, Northern Irish, Native American, indigenous, feminist and womanist liberation theologies. Even so, there are common factors in the rise of the liberation theologies and many similarities in approach and theology and concern.[6]

Liberation theologies assert the value of context. The church must theologize in and serve among particular contexts. Theology needs to arise from reflection on and within the manifold contexts in which the church finds itself. Yet theology does more than reflect. It also becomes part of the process of transforming society, serving human liberation.

Liberation theologies arise as theology from the perspective of the poor, marginalized, powerless, silenced and oppressed. Gustavo Gutiérrez says this well: "The starting point of liberation theology is commitment to the poor, the non-person. Its ideas come from the victim."[7] Leonardo and Clodovis Boff say, "Liberation theology was born when faith confronted the injustice done to the poor."[8]

The churches in Western nations need to come to terms with their role in addressing poverty, injustice and inequality. So too, liberation theology arose as a response to these burdens in Latin American and African contexts. And it moved later to other cultures.

Liberation theologians felt compelled to confront the legacies of imperialistic colonial domination, totalitarian regimes, revolutions and indepen-

---

[6]Miguel A. De La Torre, *Handbook of U.S. Theologies of Liberation* (St. Louis, MO: Chalice, 2004); Isaac T. Mwase and Eunice Kamaara, *Theologies of Liberation and Reconstruction* (Nairobi: Acton, 2012); Stacey M. Floyd-Thomas and Anthony B. Pinn, *Liberation Theologies in the United States: An Introduction* (New York: New York University Press, 2010).

[7]Sinclair B. Ferguson, David F. Wright and James I. Packer, *New Dictionary of Theology*, The Master Reference Collection (Downers Grove, IL: InterVarsity Press, 1988), 388.

[8]Leonardo Boff and Clodovis Boff, *Introducing Liberation Theology* (Maryknoll, NY: Orbis, 1987), 3; Max Davidson and Graham Hill, "Liberation Theology" (lecture, Morling College, Macquarie Park, 2015).

dence. They considered the role of the colonial churches in the Majority World and indigenous cultures. They examined the responses made to the Latin American and African contexts by postconciliar Latin American and African Catholicism. They engaged the shape of faith, church and mission amid postcolonial deprivation. And they addressed the search for hope, justice and liberation in a world of poverty and oppression.

These liberation theologians considered the functions and demands of competing ideologies—capitalist, communist and Marxist. They scrutinized the role of politico-economic structures in causing social division, oppression and class struggle. They realized the importance of consciousness raising—helping people become aware of their situation and ways out. And they fostered the expansion and diversification of liberation theologies as they spread beyond Latin America and Africa. (Contextual forms of liberation theology emerged in Asia, Northern Ireland and Eastern Europe, and in First Nation, indigenous, feminist, womanist and Western contexts.)[9]

Liberation theology challenges Western churches and pastors to examine our unspoken assumptions. It calls us to scrutinize our associations with power. It invites us to increase our concern for the poor and powerless. It confronts our spiritual, political and social complacency.

Jesus Christ demonstrated a deep and responsive concern for the poor. He was passionate for the silenced, marginalized, vulnerable, forgotten and oppressed. The Bible is clear about God's special concern for the poor and the downtrodden. We must ensure that our theology and ministry are contextual, compassionate and lived. God calls us to act justly, love mercy and walk humbly with him (Mic 6:8).

We can express the principles and concerns of liberation theology in ways that are relevant to our context. We can develop these themes in fresh ways, ways that are responsive to biblical analysis and to the challenges of our time and culture. We must ask, Who is my neighbor? and act upon the answer (Lk 10:25-37).

Liberation theologies highlight the importance of mission among the margins of society. They show us ways that the church can express the priesthood of all believers (especially among the marginalized, broken and

---

[9]Ferguson, Wright and Packer, *New Dictionary of Theology*, 387-88.

excluded). Liberation theologies call the church to diversity and hospitality. How diverse and welcoming are our structures, language, cultures and leadership? Other Christian traditions can explore the insights of liberation theologies. Evangelicals, for instance, can explore themes to do with liberation, social justice, poverty, power and gender. The church must become a community of partnership, hospitality, justice, equality and welcome.

How are justice, liberation, hospitality and inclusion missional themes? Jesus calls his church to be a community of justice and liberation. We must stand for those marginalized or silenced by religion, politics and society.

Unfortunately, white, middle-aged, university-educated and ecclesiastically employed males still headline most Christian conferences in the West. And this isn't just true of conferences. This group dominates all kinds of events, seminars, publications and media. Where are the voices from the margins of this dominant culture?

In many aspects of the life of the church, race, social status, gender, education and theological and linguistic uniformity are central. These things shape the culture and leadership of gatherings. (This is the case even when the rhetoric suggests otherwise.) This form of structural complacency works against mission, hospitality, inclusion and diversity. It works against the culture of the kingdom of God. We need to examine the biblical text—and Majority World and indigenous witness—for guidance here. We need help in the midst of these challenges to authentic church and mission. Missional churches show solidarity with those oppressed, marginalized or excluded by societies and churches. The broken, oppressed, excluded and vulnerable make up missional churches. They are at the heart of the church. We must form missional practices and theology with attention to—and the participation of—the vulnerable and marginalized. Compassion and inclusion mark the missional church.

Missional churches need to be honest about who they are as they engage in mission. We need to be honest about our presumptions, assumptions, cultural biases, prejudices, theological convictions, brokenness and frailties. Understanding leads to repentance. Repentance leads to authentic and compassionate acts of justice and mercy and liberation.

In this chapter, I consider the themes of liberation theology. These include a focus on context, human liberation and solidarity with the oppressed. Liberation theologians emphasize the liberating person and work of Jesus Christ. I also outline the liberationist focus on base communities, spirituality, ecology and dialogue. Finally, I suggest where liberation theology is headed. This chapter asks, *What can we learn from how Majority World Christians pursue solidarity with the broken, oppressed, excluded and vulnerable?*

LIBERATING CONTEXTS: CONTEXTUAL THOUGHT AND MISSION

Liberation theology charges us to remember that theology's domain is the concrete situation. Particular situations and contexts are formative for worthwhile theology and mission and ministry.

If our theology is merely abstract, it's impoverished. Our theology is deficient when we remove it from concrete, genuine contexts. Liberation theology protests against the abstractness of European theology. It challenges the whiteness, maleness and parochialism of too much Euro American God-talk.

There can be no distinction between secular and sacred history. As Hugo Assman puts it, the history of salvation is "the salvation of history."[10] All history is the history of salvation. This is true of both the overarching histories of peoples and cultures, and the local narratives of particular contexts. Human beings experience salvation now, in the present, in this particular context. We need to see salvation as something more than personal and individual. Salvation is also sociopolitical. According to liberation theologians, it is as much about redeeming the world and its systems, structures and cultures as it is about saving individual human beings. Thus, the gospel is political. The gospel involves the redemption of the world community. The gospel leads to the radical transformation of particular contexts.

The biblical text is the ground and starting point for all evangelical theology. Otherwise, as René Padilla warns, we fall into a form of historical reductionism. When we do this, historical situations determine the shape and content of all our theology. This reductionism makes our vision of the kingdom of God narrow and selective. Yet we ignore historical and particular contexts to our detriment.[11]

---

[10]Hugo Assmann, *Teología Desde La Praxis De La Liberación: Ensayo Telogico Desde La America Dependiente* (Salamanca: Ediciones Sigueme, 1976), 25.

[11]C. René Padilla, "Liberation Theology: An Appraisal," in *Freedom and Discipleship* (Maryknoll, NY: Orbis, 1989), 44.

Leonardo Boff, Oscar Romero, Juan Luis Segundo and Jon Sobrino agree on many things. They all say, for example, that "the new context for theologizing" is among common people. The ideal, authentic setting for the church's mission, theology and ministry is the local and particular context. To do this well, the church needs an integral, holistic mission. It needs to make the kingdom of God central to its vision and mission and life together. And the church needs a commitment to peace, justice and the struggle for liberation.

Leonardo Boff says that the church needs to be the Good Samaritan. The church does this as it proclaims the gospel prophetically and contextually. The church is the Good Samaritan as it strives for the liberation and rights of the poor and oppressed in every context, as it stands against social injustice, as it defends and promotes decent standards of living, and as it reinvents itself as a grassroots movement.

At the heart of all this is a contextually shaped church that is, at the same time, faithful to Christ and his Scriptures. This is a church with a contextually relevant theology and mission. It's a church listening attentively to the poor. It's a people pursuing justice and liberation in the world.[12]

LIBERATING PRAXIS: CULTIVATING SUSPICION AND HOPE

Liberation theology is committed to leading transformational change in society. It sees itself as having a mission in the world. To bring liberation from oppression, we must scrutinize all values and presuppositions. We need to examine their contribution to liberation or oppression.

Co-opting Paul Ricoeur's language, Gustavo Gutiérrez and Juan Luis Segundo describe the role of Christian theology. They say that theology serves to cultivate a "critical openness" and a "hermeneutic of suspicion and hope."[13] All Christians read the Scriptures through their own particular culture. So we need to examine whether our culture's outlook, values and assumptions

---

[12]Leonardo Boff, *When Theology Listens to the Poor* (San Francisco: Harper & Row, 1988), 32-49; Oscar A. Romero and Arturo Rivera Damas, "The Church, Political Organisation and Violence," *Cross Currents* 29, no. 4 (1979); Juan Luis Segundo, "The Shift Within Latin American Theology," *Journal of Theology for Southern Africa* 52 (1985); Jon Sobrino, "Jesus of Galilee from the Salvadoran Context: Compassion, Hope, and Following the Light of the Cross," *Theological Studies* 70, no. 2 (2009); Jon Sobrino, "Awakening from the Sleep of Inhumanity," *Christian Century* 108, no. 11 (1991).

[13]Erin White, "Between Suspicion and Hope: Paul Ricoeur's Vital Hermeneutic," *Literature and Theology* 5, no. 3 (1991).

have "bound up" our reading of the Bible. Is our biblical interpretation culture-bound? Is it open to change?

Suspicion of hidden ideologies is necessary. For example, if the God of the Bible is for the poor, why are we so undisturbed as we live among the poor? How does our whiteness, wealth, gender, privilege or power prevent us from identifying with the humiliation of other people?

There is also hope. The Scriptures rephrase our questions. The Bible changes our understandings of life, death, society, power, relationships, liberation and so on. It draws us from suspicion and despair to faith and hope and love.[14]

Liberation theologies and approaches to biblical interpretation have striking features. We can learn much from them. This is true even as we adapt and contextualize them to our own cultural and theological settings.

Here are some features of liberation theology and interpretation:

Contextual. The starting point is *the experience and cause of the oppressed.* It isn't abstract notions of liberation, justice, integral mission, praxis and so on.[15] In the words of Gustavo Gutiérrez, it's "theology from the underside of history." It's a theology focusing on "God's preferential option for the poor."[16] Since that is the starting point, this theology is *concrete and contextual.*

Orthopraxic. Liberation theology roots itself in *tangible, particular orthopraxis*, not just orthodoxy. As we practice discipleship to Jesus among the poor, marginalized and oppressed (that is, as we engage in orthopraxis), orthodoxy emerges to complement this praxis. This praxis focuses on human dignity and liberation. It is about social transformation. It is a "liberative praxis."[17] Gustavo Gutiérrez says that theology is "done" as "critical reflection on praxis."[18] *Praxis* is a term borrowed and developed from Karl Marx. It means more than "practice." It is the dialectical process of action

---

[14]Juan Luis Segundo, *Liberation of Theology* (Maryknoll, NY: Orbis, 1976), 8-9; Alfred T. Hennelly, "Theological Method: The Southern Exposure," *Theological Studies* 38, no. 4 (1977); Harold Wells, "Segundo's Hermeneutic Circle," *Journal of Theology for Southern Africa* 34 (1981).

[15]Clodovis Boff, "Methodology of the Theology of Liberation," in *Systematic Theology: Prespectives from Liberation Theology: Readings from Mysterium Liberationis*, ed. Jon Sobrino and Ignacio Ellacuria (Maryknoll, NY: Orbis, 1996), 6.

[16]Gustavo Gutiérrez, *The Power of the Poor in History: Selected Writings* (London: SCM, 1983), 169-221; Gustavo Gutiérrez and James B. Nickoloff, eds., *Gustavo Gutiérrez: Essential Writings* (Maryknoll, NY: Orbis, 1996), 78-148.

[17]Boff, "Methodology of the Theology of Liberation," 10.

[18]Gustavo Gutiérrez, *A Theology of Liberation: History, Politics, and Salvation* (Maryknoll, NY: Orbis, 1988), 6; Jon Sobrino, *The True Church and the Poor* (Maryknoll, NY: Orbis, 1984), 21-24.

moving to reflection, to new action, to new reflection and so on. Christians can think their faith only as they live it. This includes the commitment to the alleviation of oppression and poverty. We cannot do this kind of reflection in the abstract. We do theology first and study it second. "It is a theology which is open—in the protest against trampled human dignity, in the struggle against the plunder of the vast majority of people, in liberating love, and in the building of a new, just, and fraternal society—to the gift of the Kingdom of God."[19]

Transformational. It is a theological method characterized by transformative "seeing, judging, and acting"—that is (to use more technical terms), by socioanalytic, hermeneutic and practical mediation. The *socioanalytic* mediation contemplates the world of the oppressed. It seeks to understand why the oppressed are oppressed. The *hermeneutic* mediation contemplates the Word of God. It attempts to see what the divine plan is with regard to the poor. Finally, the *practical* mediation contemplates the aspect of activity. It seeks to discover how we might overcome oppression in conformity with God's plan.[20]

Partnering. The features mentioned above need this theological method to form creative, constructive partnerships. These partnerships are with the social sciences and other disciplines. Liberation theology engages social analysis, sociology, politics, philosophy, economics and modern history.[21] The contexts of liberation theology push it into these partnerships. It is from these partnerships that it understands the world. Liberation theology's connections to Marxism are not philosophical as such.[22] But some liberation theologians do use Marxist social analysis. This is especially true of the Latin Americans. Other forms of liberation theology have been more reluctant to embrace Marxist social analysis. African American liberationists are an example. The demise of Marxism and the collapse of socialism have undermined much of this social analysis. I will discuss this later in this chapter.

Axial. Gustavo Gutiérrez says the axis of liberation theology is "the gratuitousness and exigence of love."[23] God calls the church to be a prophetic

---

[19]Gutiérrez, *Theology of Liberation*, 15.
[20]Boff, "Methodology of the Theology of Liberation," 11; Boff and Boff, *Introducing Liberation Theology*, 22-42.
[21]Gutiérrez and Nickoloff, *Essential Writings*, 42-49.
[22]This, of course, is open to debate.
[23]Gutiérrez and Nickoloff, *Essential Writings*, 149-83.

community. We are a community characterized by gratuitousness and the freedom of God's love. We are a people that embrace the neighbor and embody the Beatitudes. We are a family that reveals the freedom, love, truth and finality of God's kingdom. We are a people characterized by acts of love, mercy, peace, reconciliation, liberation and justice in a broken world.

Ecclesial. We must practice Christian faith and theology in community if we are to address the needs of the world. God calls his church to be a theologizing community. Professional theologians aren't enough. Faith communities ought to theologize together. "Theology is not an individual task; it is an ecclesial function."[24] Professional theologians must help pastors cultivate theologizing communities. Theologians need to do theology accountably. They should be accountable to—and located within—dynamic, questioning, theologizing, local faith communities. The community engages in the work of theology. And the professional theologian contributes, facilitates and practices accountable, community-shaped theology.

Liberation theologians cultivate suspicion of hidden ideologies and interpretive methods. They are especially suspicious of ideas and practices that foster oppression. And they complement this with hope. They hope for transformed societies, renewed church structures and fresh missional practices. They hope for gratuitous expressions of love and liberating theological methods. They hope for "seeing, judging, and acting" that results in liberation. They hope for genuine attention to the perspectives of the poor and oppressed. They hope that the church will indeed be the church envisaged by Jesus Christ.

LIBERATING ORIENTATION: SOLIDARITY WITH THE OPPRESSED

Western Christians have (at times) been far too complacent about issues of poverty, exploitation and oppression. We are wealthy, comfortable, passive and complacent. The Scriptures challenge us to be otherwise.[25]

---

[24]Gustavo Gutiérrez, *The Density of the Present: Selected Writings* (Maryknoll, NY: Orbis, 1999), 173.
[25]We have to be careful here not to overstate the complacency. It might be argued that Western cultures (and Western Christians in particular) were so concerned about poverty and so on that they built a civilization that addressed many forms of poverty, exploitation and oppression. That's an energetic and active response to these things over at least four hundred years. Western Christians live in societies where workers, women, children, minorities and other faiths are less poor, exploited and oppressed than anywhere else on earth or in history. It was preliberation theologians and their communities that built such values into a culture, along with the decrease of poverty, exploitation and oppression. It might be argued that Majority World Islam, Buddhism and atheism have been

Leonardo Boff describes how Christian convictions about God, Christ, Spirit, eschaton, apostolicity, church, faith, justice, love and mission compel the church. They compel the church to show a "clear and prophetic option expressing preference for, and solidarity with, the poor."[26]

Dietrich Bonhoeffer—who grew up in affluence and social privilege— wrote these words as he reflected on ten years under Hitler's tyranny: "There remains an experience of incomparable value. We have for once learnt to see the great events of world history from below, from the perspectives of the outcast, the suspects, the maltreated, the powerless, the oppressed, the reviled—in short, from the perspective of those who suffer."[27]

Liberation theologians concern themselves with the liberation of the oppressed. They care about God's preference for the poor and the marginalized. This solidarity begins where pain or subjugation is present. In Latin America, this begins with socioeconomic oppression. In Africa, it is with colonialism and dictatorships. In African American communities, it is with racism. Among indigenous peoples, it is with human rights. And among feminist and womanist thinkers, it is with gender equality. We must also begin where the needs are in our setting.

Liberating Christ: The Redeeming Liberator

Christology is a fertile source for Latin American liberation theology. Most liberation theologians deal with christological issues. They appeal to the Gospels and a theology of Jesus Christ when making a case for liberation.

Jon Sobrino exemplifies this. Sobrino offended the Vatican with his theology of Christ. He says that the poor "constitute the supreme, scandalous prophetic and apocalyptic presence of the Christian God." The poor confront all Christologies with this question: "Were you there when they

---

far too complacent about issues of poverty, exploitation and oppression—the evidence being the relatively high incidence of all those things in the spheres where their influence is most obvious.

[26]Boff and Boff, *Introducing Liberation Theology*, 44-46 and chap. 4. See also Oscar A. Romero and James R. Brockman, *The Violence of Love* (Maryknoll, NY: Orbis, 2004), chaps. 8-9; Gutiérrez, *Density of the Present*, chaps. 7-9; Sobrino, *True Church and the Poor*, chaps. 4-5; Sobrino and Ellacuría, *Systematic Theology*, chap. 2; Boff, *When Theology Listens to the Poor*, chap. 3; Leonardo Boff, *Saint Francis: A Model for Human Liberation* (New York: Crossroad, 1982), chap. 2; Leonardo Boff, Virgilio P. Elizondo and Marcus Lefébure, *Option for the Poor: Challenge to the Rich Countries*, Concilium 187 (Edinburgh: T&T Clark, 1986), ix.

[27]Dietrich Bonhoeffer, *Letters and Papers from Prison*, enlarged ed. (New York: Macmillan, 1972), 17, quoted in Gutiérrez, *Power of the Poor in History*, xvi.

crucified my Lord?" The poor especially ask this question of Christologies done at a distance from the poor and oppressed.[28]

According to Sobrino, the poor are the *locus theologicus* of Christology. They tell of Christ's "self-abasement, his *kenosis*, his concealment, his cross. . . . [As] locus of the current presence of Christ, they are a light illuminating all things, and specifically illuminating the truth of Christ . . . as Messiah, as Liberator, and as definitive mediator of the Reign of God."[29]

In *Jesus the Liberator*, Sobrino offers an examination of the relationship between the person, mission and faith of Jesus and the nature of the kingdom of God. For Jesus, the final reality was the kingdom of God—a kingdom of and for the poor, rejected and despised. The way of the kingdom is the way of liberation for the oppressed. It's the way of healing for the wounded. It's the way of victory over systemic and spiritual evil. It's the way of peace instead of the manifold forms of violence in this world. It's the way of welcome to sinners and hospitality toward strangers. And it's the way of liberation from selfishness, exploitation and marginalization.

Sobrino also considers what the death of Jesus tells us about the nature of salvation. His death shows us what it means to be his "crucified people." Following the Suffering Servant, the crucified people establish righteousness and justice. They embrace suffering and martyrdom. They bear the sins of the world. They are chosen for salvation. They serve as a light to the nations. They are the "martyred people." This doesn't mean that they will necessarily be martyred. They are the "martyred people" because "the essence of martyrdom is affinity with the death of Jesus."[30]

In his writings, Sobrino says that we must look at Jesus through the eyes of the poor. Looking at Jesus and Christology through the eyes and experiences of the poor, exploited, powerless, silenced and victims achieves one central thing: "It can open our eyes to the relationship between God and what is small."[31]

---

[28]Jon Sobrino, *Jesus the Liberator: A Historical-Theological Reading of Jesus of Nazareth* (Maryknoll, NY: Orbis, 1993), 28; Ignacio Ellacuria, "Discernir El 'Signo' De Los Tiempos," *Diakonia* 17 (1981): 58.

[29]Sobrino and Ellacuría, *Systematic Theology*, 142-44. I'm not convinced by Sobrino's argument. The *poor* don't tell of Christ's abasement, his kenosis—the *gospel* tells us of those things. No *class of people* are the locus of the presence of Christ—*Christ himself* is the locus of the presence of Christ.

[30]Sobrino, *Jesus the Liberator*, 267 and chaps. 4 and 10.

[31]Jon Sobrino, *Christ the Liberator: A View from the Victims* (Maryknoll, NY: Orbis, 2001), 294.

Like other liberation theologians, Leonardo Boff emphasizes the importance of the historical Jesus. Boff speaks of the implications of Jesus' priorities, practices and message about the kingdom. Jesus' values as revealed in the Gospels, must shape our churches and discipleship. Jesus' liberating practices are the yardstick or the measuring rod for the church. The church's attention to *Christopraxis* accompanies its *orthodoxy* and *orthopraxis*.[32]

Boff then turns to the cross. He reflects on its meanings for the suffering of the innocent and for Jesus' solidarity with the crucified of history. He also considers the power of the resurrection. Death and suffering no longer have the last word. We "die to be raised," and "the executioner shall not triumph over the victim."[33]

Oscar Romero was a bishop in El Salvador. He was famous for his liberation theology. He was known for his ministry among the poor and his denunciation of the persecution of the church. Romero was martyred in 1980 for the cause of Jesus Christ. He reminds us to trust in the Source of liberation:

Let us not put our trust
in earthly liberation movements.
Yes, they are providential,
but only if they do not forget
that all the liberating force in the world
comes from Christ.[34]

Liberating Community: Base Communities and the Church

Jesus calls his church to be a transformed and transforming community. We are to lead people into his liberating power and presence. This is true for all expressions of the church: large or small, institutional or independent, local or paralocal. This requires a renewal of the church. It demands a courageous examination of the church's systems and structures. It calls for reorientation of the church's purpose, structures, mission and ministries.

Transformed and transforming churches orient these things around Jesus' vision of the kingdom. The church requires a "radical revision" and a

---

[32]Leonardo Boff, *Faith on the Edge: Religion and Marginalized Existence* (San Francisco: Harper & Row, 1989), 134-38.
[33]Boff, *When Theology Listens to the Poor*, 135-36.
[34]Romero and Brockman, *Violence of Love*, 140.

"substantial transformation." It needs "courage and serenity." This is "the opposite of a facile emotionalism which leads to arbitrary measures, superficial solutions, or evasions, but avoids the search for radical changes and untrodden paths. At stake in all this is the Church's faithfulness to its Lord."[35] The church is in constant need of renewal. This is so that it can be "salt, light, and a city on a hill" in every cultural context in which it resides.

The true church is a church for all people, including the poor and the voiceless. It's a church that confronts the principalities and powers of this world. It is a scandalous church, a confronting church and a nonviolent church. It is a church characterized by the countercultural values of the kingdom of God.

As Gustavo Gutiérrez reminds us, "This is what always happens: it is easier to point out what must be done than to do it." So God calls us to examine the "meaning of the Church and its mission in the world."

Jesus leads us to openness to the "primordial and inescapable condition for fulfilling that mission." That condition is faithfulness to the mission of Jesus Christ. Faithfulness to that mission happens through the celebration of the Eucharist, through the authentic unity found in Christian *koinonia*, and through active mission in the world. We pursue God's mission through the "*denunciation* of every dehumanizing situation" that is contrary to unity, liberty and justice. And we pursue mission by *annunciating* the gospel that calls people to "union among themselves and communion" with Father, Son and Holy Spirit.[36] For Gutiérrez, "The mission of the church, as the community of Jesus' disciples, is to communicate and bear witness to this total liberation of the human being. The church's mission is, as I said, to proclaim an integral liberation, because nothing is left untouched by the saving work of Christ."[37]

Base ecclesial communities are commonly associated with liberation theology. Yet not all base communities identify with liberation social analysis. These grassroots ecclesial communities proliferate in the Majority World. They are small groups of self-reliant believers. They meet together for worship and to celebrate the Eucharist, and they engage in acts of justice and

---

[35]Gutiérrez, *Theology of Liberation*, 252.
[36]Ibid., 251-79.
[37]Gutiérrez and Nickoloff, *Essential Writings*, 259, 261; Gustavo Gutiérrez, *The Truth Shall Make You Free: Confrontations* (Maryknoll, NY: Orbis, 1990), 141.

mercy and consciousness raising among the poor and oppressed. René Padilla rejoices in the missional, liberating, educative and fellowshiping dimensions of these grassroots ecclesial communities.[38]

LIBERATING HOLISM: ECOLOGY, SPIRITUALITY AND LIBERATION

Leonardo Boff cares about human and ecological connections. He speaks
about the vital relationships between liberation, ecology, poverty and spirituality. Boff claims that it is impossible to separate three crucial things. These
are authentic Christian spirituality, concern for the poor and oppressed, and
ecological stewardship.

Liberation theology and eco-justice are partners. They join in responding
to the needs of the oppressed. They collaborate as they seek to bridge the
gap between the wealthy and the poor. They collaborate as they reclaim
dignity for the poor and the earth. The church needs an ecologically sustainable spirituality. It requires a spirituality that is deeply concerned for the
liberation of the earth and the poor. Christian spirituality must care about
the health of the planet while pursuing human freedom and dignity and
well-being.[39] Social injustice and environmental injustice are inextricably
connected, as are human and ecological liberation.

For Boff, "The earth is crying out and the poor are crying out, both victims
of both social and environmental injustice."[40] The answer to this problem
begins with theological reflection on ecology and violence. We need an eco-
social theology of liberation. We need new approaches to production. And we
need a socioenvironmental ethic that is attentive to the dignity and well-being
of humans and the environment. Boff says that there are connections between
politics, theology, ecology, poverty, oppression and spirituality. When we see
these, we can start addressing social and environmental injustice.

Boff turns to Saint Francis as a model for spirituality. Francis exemplified
concern for the poor. He sought the liberation of the oppressed. He practiced prayerful contemplation and a politically engaged spirituality. He was

---

[38]C. René Padilla, "A New Ecclesiology in Latin America," *International Bulletin of Missionary Research* 11, no. 4 (1987): 158. See Sobrino and Ellacuría, *Systematic Theology*, 184-91.

[39]Leonardo Boff, *Cry of the Earth, Cry of the Poor*, Ecology and Justice (Maryknoll, NY: Orbis, 1997), especially chaps. 5 and 10.

[40]Leonardo Boff and Virgilio P. Elizondo, *Ecology and Poverty: Cry of the Earth, Cry of the Poor*, Concilium (Maryknoll, NY: Orbis, 1995), xi.

welcoming and hospitable, inviting all into the life and ministry of the church. Francis was passionate about caring for humans, animals, nature and the planet.[41]

The church needs *political saints*. These are passionate for God. But they are also passionate for the poor, passionate for prayer and passionate for the environment.[42] Gustavo Gutiérrez describes a spirituality of liberation in this way:

> A spirituality of liberation will center on a *conversion* to the neighbor, the oppressed person, the exploited social class, the despised ethnic group, the dominated country. Our conversion to the Lord implies this conversion to the neighbor. Evangelical conversion is indeed the touchstone of all spirituality. Conversion means a radical transformation of ourselves; it means thinking, feeling, and living as Christ—present in exploited and alienated persons. To be converted is to commit oneself lucidly, realistically, and concretely to the process of the liberation of the poor and oppressed. It means to commit oneself not only generously, but also with an analysis of the situation and a strategy of action. To be converted is to know and experience the fact that, contrary to the laws of physics, we can stand straight, according to the Gospel, only when our center of gravity is outside ourselves.[43]

Liberating Futures: Women Extending the Conversation

Many women are expanding and revising liberation theologies, public theologies and missional theologies. These women bring a wide range of cultural and theological backgrounds to these tasks.

These women often criticize liberation theology's lack of engagement with women's issues. They highlight its patriarchal assumptions and outlook. Yet these women aren't only concerned with womanist questions. They absorb themselves in theological, ethical, justice, ecclesial and missional enterprises. Women develop these enterprises for and with their families, communities and societies. These women include Mercy Amba Oduyoye, Nana Amba Eyiaba, Elizabeth Amoah, Dianne Stewart Diakite, Rose Mary Amenga-Etego, Evelyn Parker, Brigalia Bam, Musimbi Kanyoro, Katie G.

---

[41]Boff, *Saint Francis.*

[42]Leonardo Boff, "The Need for Political Saints: From a Spirituality of Liberation to the Practice of Liberation," *Cross Currents* 30, no. 4 (1980).

[43]Gutiérrez and Nickoloff, *Essential Writings*, 288.

Cannon, Jacquelyn Grant, Letty Russell, Rosemary Ruether, Elisabeth Schüssler Fiorenza, Phyllis Trible, Rosalee Velloso Ewell, Elizabeth Petersen, Sallie McFague, Catharina Halkes, Anji Barker, Elisabeth Moltmann-Wendel and a host of others.

Recently, Ghanaian, Liberian, Nigerian and African American women gathered in Accra, Ghana. They met for the inaugural African and African Diasporan Women in Religion and Theology Conference. Mercy Amba Oduyoye hosted this conference at Trinity Theological Seminary's Talitha Qumi Institute of African Women in Religion and Culture in Legon, Ghana. Oduyoye founded and directs this institute. The conference focused on issues facing African cultures. It especially emphasized the need to address violence against African-descended women and girls.[44]

Mercy Amba Oduyoye inspires a younger generation of women and men to explore these issues afresh. Oduyoye says that women call liberationists and the broader church to account for patriarchal and antiwomen practices, hermeneutics and cultural sexism. She's leading the way in so many areas, setting an example for other women. Oduyoye champions theological and ministerial formation among women. She retrieves the narratives and experiences of women in church and society. Oduyoye catalyzes understanding and dialogue between genders. She addresses violence toward women and girls. She profiles women's theology. And she enhances the health, influence and power of women and girls.

Oduyoye and so many other women around the world are helping men, the church and liberation theology understand anew what it means to follow a just, merciful, transforming and compassionate Messiah.[45]

---

[44]Rosetta E. Ross, "An Historic Meeting: African and African Diaspora Women Convene in Ghana for First-Ever Religion Conference," *Religion Dispatches*, August 1, 2012, www.religiondispatches .org/archive/atheologies/6231/an_historic_meeting%3A_african_and_african_diaspora_women _convene_in_ghana_for_first-ever_religion_conference.

[45]Mercy Amba Oduyoye, *Hearing and Knowing: Theological Reflections on Christianity in Africa* (Maryknoll, NY: Orbis, 1986); Oduyoye, "The Passion Out of Compassion: Women of the Eatwot Third General Assembly," *International Review of Mission* 81, no. 322 (1992); Oduyoye, "Re-Imagining the World: A Global Perspective," *Church & Society* 84, no. 5 (1994); Oduyoye, "Calling the Church to Account: African Women and Liberation," *Ecumenical Review* 47, no. 4 (1995); Oduyoye, *Daughters of Anowa: African Women and Patriarchy* (Maryknoll, NY: Orbis, 1995); Oduyoye, "The Church of the Future, Its Mission and Theology: A View from Africa," *Theology Today* 52, no. 4 (1996); Oduyoye, *Introducing African Women's Theology*, Introductions in Feminist Theology (Cleveland, OH: Pilgrim, 2001).

LIBERATION AND THE GLOBALCHURCH: CONCLUDING REFLECTIONS

Western Christians can learn much from liberation theology. They can especially learn from its solidarity with the poor and vulnerable and its passion for justice.

It's time we became "liberating Christians." What does that mean? Liberating Christians join with the freeing power of Christ. They take part in his liberation of whole persons, whole communities and the whole of creation, from everything that oppresses, exploits or dehumanizes them. They strive to see people, communities and creation enjoy the freedom, hope and life offered by the Father, Son and Holy Spirit.

Here are ten things we learn from how Majority World Christians pursue solidarity with the broken, oppressed, excluded and vulnerable:

1. Liberating Christians have first enjoyed the liberation that only Jesus Christ can offer. We cannot help others find freedom unless we've experienced it. Before I join with God in liberating acts, I need to ask, What has Jesus liberated me *from* and *to*? How has Jesus liberated me *from* sin, oppression, lies, poverty, death, selfishness, burdens, legalism, prejudice and so forth? How has Jesus liberated me *to* forgiveness, hope, freedom, justice, life, love, faith, relationship and so on? How has he liberated me to join with him in bringing freedom to the world (individually and alongside others)? This doesn't mean that life is easy. It doesn't mean that life is completely free of suffering and discrimination and exploitation. Liberation is often an ongoing process. But even in the face of these challenges we know that Jesus Christ has liberated us and given us his hope.

2. Liberating Christians only offer the liberation found in the person and gospel of the Lord Jesus Christ. We do not offer our own liberation. We do not offer freedom and hope through other means. We recognize, in a spirit of dependency, "that all the liberating force in the world comes from Christ."[46] And we proclaim and live out the gospel of Jesus Christ confidently.

3. Liberating Christians examine themselves and how associations with power and privilege shape their lives. This is a challenge for those of us who've only known the privilege of our race, gender or birthplace. We must scrutinize our unspoken assumptions and our associations with power. We

---

[46]Romero and Brockman, *Violence of Love*, 140.

need to consider our concern for the poor and powerless. And it's time we repented of spiritual, political and social complacency.

We need to examine our perspectives on a wide range of issues. Do these views reflect the values of Jesus Christ and his kingdom? Does Scripture shape them? Or have we allowed the values of our culture, politics, race, class and gender to shape these perspectives? What forms our views on gender, ethnicity, the military, police brutality, race relations, money, property, immigration, healthcare and education (to name a few)?

Jayakumar Christian engages with the work of Walter Wink when he says that the world lies about the true nature of power.[47] Here are some of these distortions of truth: Power always belongs to the powerful. Force always prevails over ideas. (The victors are those with technological, military and economic strength.) Choice always belongs to the powerful. Power is truth. Assets are an all-important power base. (Power comes from the assets I own and the wealth I create.) Power is a zero-sum game. Powerful institutions are more important than people. And finally, God is the patron of the powerful.

These are all lies. These lies shape the way the world conceives, pursues, exercises and abuses power. It's why the power of Christ is either misunderstood or an affront. Sure, power influences all human relationships. It's dangerous to deny or fail to recognize this. But we need to recognize that power belongs to God (not power to the people or power to the powerful).

Power tempts us to play God in the lives of others—nurturing our god complexes. We must examine our associations with power and the way they shape our lives and points of view. And we need to speak truth about power. Power isn't found in resources, might, status, race and privilege. Power belongs to God alone. He "chose the weak things of the world to shame the strong" (1 Cor 1:27). And as Andy Crouch says, we can use power redemptively. As we examine our views and ourselves, we can decide to use what power we have for the well-being of others. We can use power in the way of Christ—enriching human life, addressing injustice, ushering in peace and enabling human flourishing.[48]

---

[47]Jayakumar Christian, *God of the Empty-Handed: Poverty, Power, and the Kingdom of God* (Monrovia, CA: MARC, 1999). See Walter Wink's list of "delusional assumptions" in *Engaging the Powers: Discernment and Resistance in a World of Domination*, The Powers (Minneapolis: Fortress, 1992).

[48]Andy Crouch, *Playing God: Redeeming the Gift of Power* (Downers Grove, IL: InterVarsity Press, 2013).

4. *Liberating Christians show an active concern for the poor, silenced, marginalized, vulnerable, forgotten and oppressed.* Liberating Christians acknowledge and respond to God's special concern for the poor and downtrodden. They respond in concrete ways. They seek hands-on solutions to the problems of poverty, injustice, inequality and suffering. The Spirit leads us to explore the ways in which conversion to Christ is conversion to the neighbor. We ask, "Who is my neighbor?" and we act on the answer (Lk 10:25-37). We act justly, love mercy and walk humbly with God (Mic 6:8). Sometimes we do this in concrete and ordinary ways. Sometimes we do it in extraordinary ways or on a larger scale.

We often think that poor and needy people are in settings *other* than our own. But poverty and vulnerability and disadvantage are close to home. In my country, Australia, one in eight people live in poverty (12.5%). In 2013, the U.S. Census Bureau reported that 46.5 million Americans (15%) live in poverty; 16.1 million (21.8%) American children under the age of eighteen live in poverty. "The overall poverty rate according to the Supplemental Poverty Measure is 16.1%. Compare this with the official poverty rate of 15.1%. Under the Supplemental Poverty Measure, there are 49.7 million people living in poverty. This is 3.1 million more than are represented by the official poverty measure (46.5 million)."[49]

Making a difference begins with building relationships. For most of us, friendships lead to solidarity, care and support. But Christians should also name and confront structural injustices. These enable poverty, oppression, exploitation and marginalization. Poverty is not merely an economic state. Systems, structures and social forces silence and dehumanize the poor. Poverty and oppression are scandalous and insidious forms of violence. They're a denial of the kingdom of God. They're an affront to the gospel and person of Jesus Christ. The oppressed must not give in passively to their tormentors. The church ought not sit idly by while oppression occurs.

As God's people, we must lead the way in confronting dehumanizing factors and in bringing change. The church needs to shape a "solid contem-

---

[49]From statistics provided at Feeding America, http://feedingamerica.org/hunger-in-america/hunger -facts/hunger-and-poverty-statistics.aspx. See Carmen DeNavas-Walt, Bernadette D. Proctor and Jessica C. Smith, *Income, Poverty, and Health Insurance Coverage in the United States: 2012* (U.S. Census Bureau, 2013); *The Research Supplemental Poverty Measure: 2011* (U.S. Census Bureau, 2012).

porary reflection on the witness of poverty."[50] This involves declaring the transformational power, presence and kingdom of God and doing this in word and action. It means moving beyond a *notional* concern for the poor and vulnerable. Instead, we become *actively* involved in their well-being. And we find ourselves transformed in the process.

5. Liberating Christians support the poor and marginalized and silenced as they form their own theologies and expressions of faith. The poor and oppressed are not the objects of the gospel, but the subjects. By the grace of God, they are calling the church back to gospel faithfulness. The theologian, pastor and missionary must identify with the oppressed in their struggle. Poverty and oppression are never neutral. We must always oppose and confront them. And we must support these groups as they form their own theologies and approaches to Christian faith.

6. Liberating Christians develop communities characterized by specific values and practices. These practices are always concrete, contextual, orthopraxic, transformational, collaborative and communal. They're characterized by extravagant love. (See the explanations in the section "Liberating Praxis.") Together, we shape communities passionate for Christ's liberating gospel and love. We embrace neighbors. We welcome the stranger. We practice hospitality. Together, we embody the Beatitudes. And we show the values of the kingdom of God through them. (The Beatitudes include humility, dependence, mourning, meekness, contentment, hunger for God, compassion, integrity, peacemaking, suffering and witness.) Together, we practice concrete and loving and costly deeds. These are works of mercy, peace, reconciliation, liberation and justice in a broken world.

7. Liberating Christians nurture contemplative-active spirituality that cares for humanity and the earth. Like Francis of Assisi, our spirituality must be contemplative and active. And it needs to care for the well-being of humans and the earth. We nurture the *contemplative* side of this spirituality through quiet meditation, communal prayer, immersion in Scripture and celebrating the Word and Eucharist together. We foster the *active* side through welcoming others, hospitality, peacemaking, creation care and serving the poor and marginalized. It involves helping oppressed people find freedom and justice. It

---

[50]Gutiérrez, *Theology of Liberation*, 287-302.

means healing the broken and wounded. It includes advocating on behalf of the silenced. And it's engaging in Christ-honoring political and social engagement. It's passionate care for individuals and humanity and the earth.

8. Liberating Christians take the Scripture's focus on mercy and justice and freedom seriously. More than two thousand passages of Scripture speak of God's attitude to poverty and injustice. Western Christians have ignored these passages too often. It's time to respond to God's passion for justice and mercy and healing and hope. It's time to take Scripture's focus on justice and poverty seriously.

9. Liberating Christians examine the claims of liberation theology and form their own conclusions. It's important to examine the claims of liberation theology. It's worth considering how we can contextualize its practices and theologies in our own unique settings. As we do this, it's worth listening to those who are renewing liberation theology today.

Some suggest that liberation theology is passé. They suggest that four things have diminished the influence of liberation theology. These are (1) the demise of socialism, (2) the marginalization of key liberation theologians by church authorities, (3) the familiarity with liberation theology in the West, and (4) the rising prosperity and middle classes in many parts of the Majority World.

These points are not groundless. Yet I do not believe that liberation theology is passé. Liberation theology has much to contribute to our understanding of the nature and mission of the church. This theology can enrich our appreciation of what it means for the church to express the kingdom of God. I have shown this significant, worthwhile contribution already in this chapter.

In a moment I turn to contemporary voices that are renewing and extending liberation theology. But before I do that, I want to identify a few difficulties with liberation theology. We need to be careful as we examine this theology. As Westerners, we are likely to look at liberation theology through the eyes of the affluent, the comfortable, the powerful and the privileged.

Building on the work of Max Davidson—an Australian systematic theologian—I've identified five problems with liberation theology.[51]

---

[51]Davidson and Hill, "Liberation Theology." These five points are adapted from the lecture notes developed by Max Davidson and Graham Hill. They were delivered at Morling Baptist Theological College in Sydney, Australia. They constitute a combination of Davidson's concerns and my own critiques of liberation theology.

First, liberation theology concentrates too much on sociopolitical issues. This focus is critical to liberation theology and is one of its assets. Yet on occasions it leads to loss of focus on biblical themes having to do with personal, spiritual and eternal need. Liberation theology protests against too little evangelical involvement in the needs of the oppressed. Liberationists refuse to spiritualize the biblical idea of "the poor." Yet the poor in the Bible are those who are not only oppressed but who also remain faithful to God and seek his deliverance (see Ps 34:6 and 40:17, for example). Commitment by God to the poor does not mean the poor are making a commitment to God.

Second, liberation theology locates sin and salvation in society. This is a reaction to much of Christianity's emphasis on the individual. Yet liberation theology too often bypasses the individual. This theology can, on occasion, reduce the gospel to a goad to action until the church makes the wrongs in society right.

Third, liberation theology identifies too readily with class struggle and socialism as the means of change, but such identification gives no ultimate reason for it. In contrast, Western evangelicals often leave the assumptions of capitalism and economics unchallenged. Marxism per se can provide no ultimate reason for change. The Bible sees history's great divisions as before and after Jesus Christ. The total perspectives of Jesus Christ—as revealed in Scripture—must determine praxis.

Michael Novak offers a scathing critique of liberation theology. He claims that it has been too prejudiced against capitalism and too favorable toward socialism. According to Novak, this has left liberation theology in a quandary since the "velvet revolution" in Eastern Europe.[52] It has also been too enamored by notions of peaceful revolution by throwing off the oppression of wealthy Western capitalists and their local cronies. Liberation theology didn't prepare for the rise of democratic ideals around the globe, including in Latin America. It is now left trying to figure out how its theology, social agenda and spirituality make sense in a different world. The world it is now in is postsocialist and mostly prodemocratic. Many Majority World nations are enjoying growing wealth, influence and power. They are pursuing hybridized, contextualized forms of democracy and capitalism.

---

[52]Michael Novak, "Will It Liberate? Questions About Liberation Theology," *Christianity and Crisis* 47, no. 10 (1987); Michael Novak, "Liberation Theology—What's Left?," *First Things* 14 (1991).

Liberation theology still has much to say to the church in a world torn by poverty and inequality. This is as true in Western as in Majority World and indigenous contexts. But it needs to examine its identification with socialism and find fresh ways to express its theology, concern for justice and vision for liberating mission.

Fourth, liberation theology sometimes fails to appreciate that the biblical kingdom of God provides the basis for analysis of society, not any one political analysis. Liberation theologians assume that the first step in theology is involvement in societal change processes. They base this assumption on a socialist analysis of structures and systems. Yet they too often take this position without biblical analysis. And as I have already mentioned, this socialist analysis has unraveled in the present global context. The kingdom of God is the biblical hermeneutic of society—not any one political analysis. As Christians, we must move Jesus Christ and his kingdom to the front of our worldviews and theologies. This way the biblical kingdom of God provides the basis for an analysis of society and a vision for social change. The biblical kingdom of God is our social program.

Fifth, liberation theology often reads Jesus and the Gospels selectively. For example, liberation theologians speak of the importance of Jesus. They often describe him as the poor and oppressed victim of his political system. But there are, of course, richer and more profound aspects to the centrality of Jesus Christ.

René Padilla says that we address the failings of liberation theology by developing a disciplined hermeneutical practice. This practice engages Scripture, the humanities, the church's praxis and the historical situation. And it puts these four things into critical, mutually enriching dialogue. None is adequate in isolation from the others.[53]

It is important that we inform this disciplined practice through an expansive, biblical vision of the kingdom of God.

How do we put Scripture, context and practices into conversation?

The alternative to both the "Theology of the Word" and the "Theology of Praxis" is a hermeneutical circulation in which a richer and deeper under-

---

[53]C. René Padilla, "Liberation Theology: An Evaluation," *Reformed Journal* 33, no. 6 (1983). Compare Boff and Boff's concerns and hopes for liberation theology: Boff and Boff, *Introducing Liberation Theology*, 64-65, 88-89.

standing of Scripture leads to a greater understanding of historical context, and a deeper and richer understanding of the context leads to a greater comprehension of Scripture from within the concrete situation and under the leading of the Holy Spirit.[54]

10. *Liberating Christians extend the conversation.* In this chapter, I showed how women are broadening and examining liberation theology. Besides these fresh perspectives offered by women, a new generation of liberation theologians is reframing liberationist thought for a globalized context. These thinkers tend to be Asian, Latin American, African, African American and Hispanic/Latino. These younger liberationists are communicating with each other in rigorous and intentional ways. This way they bridge the divides between the diverse expressions of liberation theology.

Ivan Petrella exemplifies this new generation of liberationists. He aims to refashion "liberation theology for a new century but an old challenge, the liberation of the poor."[55] Petrella and his peers are redefining the relationships between liberation theology, capitalism, democracy, globalization and neoliberalism.

Developing the work of Roberto Unger, Petrella says that "the task is no longer to counterpose two systems, such as capitalism/socialism or bourgeois democracy/participatory democracy, against each other but to find the gradual steps that will democratize access to political and economic opportunity."[56]

As we've seen, Western Christians can learn much from theologies of liberation. But we need to have the courage to extend the conversation. We ought to explore the connections between the ideas of liberation theology and other streams of thought. Such streams include politics, law, psychoanalysis, sociology, ethnology, poststructuralism, womanism, feminism, postcolonialism, systematic and biblical theology, missiology and so forth.[57]

Are there fresh ways that we can understand Jesus Christ's church as

---

[54]Padilla, "Liberation Theology," 18.

[55]Ivan Petrella, *The Future of Liberation Theology: An Argument and Manifesto* (Burlington, VT: Ashgate, 2004), vii.

[56]Ibid., ix.

[57]Ivan Petrella, *Latin American Liberation Theology: The Next Generation* (Maryknoll, NY: Orbis, 2005), xv. See Ivan Petrella, *Beyond Liberation Theology: A Polemic*, Reclaiming Liberation Theology (London: SCM, 2008); Ivan Petrella, Marcella Maria Althaus-Reid and Luiz Carlos Susin, eds., *Another Possible World* (London: SCM, 2007).

liberating and transforming? How can we join with Jesus in transforming democratic processes, political sciences, economic practices, ethno-religious conflicts, moral frameworks, civil societies, the consequences of globalization and so on? This involves renewing ecclesial structures. It includes challenging sociopolitical, religious and legal processes and structures. It means becoming *political saints*.[58] And it requires we do all this within the context of the global challenges of the twenty-first century.

Isaiah draws our attention to God's concern for justice, mercy and compassion:

> Is not this the kind of fasting I have chosen: to loose the chains of injustice and untie the cords of the yoke, to set the oppressed free and break every yoke? Is it not to share your food with the hungry and to provide the poor wanderer with shelter—when you see the naked, to clothe them, and not to turn away from your own flesh and blood? (Is 58:6-7)

---

[58]Boff, "Need for Political Saints."

SHOWING HOSPITALITY

What Can We Learn from How Majority World Christians Practice Hospitality and Welcome?

[Hospitality means] conversion from individualism to community,
from autonomy to interdependence, from idolatry to true worship,
from grasping to receiving, from oppressive dominion over creation
to loving care of it, from indifference to passionate, prayerful action,
from Western definitions of "development" to loving participation,
from competition to collaboration, from protagonism to service.

RUTH PADILLA DEBORST

Most in the Western world cannot imagine a scenario in which they might endanger their children or trust their family to the fate of strangers to avoid severe persecution, torture and execution for their faith. But that is Sarah's story. She, her husband (formerly a house church pastor in Iran) and their two sons were able to escape to Malaysia a year ago, before things came to such a grim impasse. Life in Malaysia has its own stresses. They face financial and political instability, and never knowing when the police might shake them down or when the local government might decide to ship them back home. Making ends meet from month to month when they can't legally work is also a huge strain. But they are grateful to be alive and together.

Malaysia is a major relay station on the refugee highway. Iranians are one of the groups coming to Malaysia in large numbers. Many arrive to seek asylum with the United Nations High Commission on Refugees (UNHCR).

This is a long, grueling process. They have to make an appointment to make their claim of asylum. Then they must go through a series of interviews where government and police and military officers question them about their claims. The whole process, if it goes without any hitches, takes about three years. In the meantime, they are stuck in a country in which they don't speak any of the main languages and cannot legally find employment. Unscrupulous employers force these refugees to work long hours for meager wages. And they know that they could lose their jobs at any time. For those with families, they have the added pressure of trying to continue their children's education.

One of the recurring themes among the refugees is the increased stress brought on by isolation in the midst of so many difficulties. They have low levels of trust for other people, especially for those from their own country. This cuts them off from any support networks they can find.

What they need is warmth, compassion and welcome—the loving hospitality of strangers.

Paul and Charis Wan are friends of mine who work with refugee groups in Malaysia. They have helped Sarah and her family find accommodation, employment and friendship in Kuala Lumpur. Paul and Charis try to help refugees and asylum seekers in tangible ways. But the best thing they offer is friendship, dignity, hospitality and a listening ear. So many refugees are dealing with their trauma and stress in isolation. They need genuine friendship and emotional support. They need to know someone cares, even when support groups can't fix all their problems. Refugee life is lonely and vulnerable. Their presence among us offers a perfect opportunity for us to love our neighbors.

The UNHCR recently released its *Global Trends 2012 Report—Displacement: The New 21st Century Challenge*. The report analyzes the trends among refugees, asylum seekers, returnees, stateless persons and groups of internally displaced persons (IDPs). The report estimated that in 2012 almost 50 million people were forcibly displaced worldwide. Persecution, conflict, violence and human rights violations caused these people to flee their homes. Developing countries hosted over 80% of the world's refugees. Children below eighteen years make up 50% of the refugee population.[1]

---

[1]*Global Trends 2012 Report—Displacement: The New 21st Century Challenge* is available at http://unhcr .org/globaltrendsjune2013. There are also photo images, press releases, video materials, graphics and audio recordings at that site. See www.unhcr.org.uk/about-us/key-facts-and-figures.html.

How should Christians respond to such need? In a word: hospitality.

Christian hospitality is broader than welcoming and caring for displaced persons. But it is no less than that.

Not all communities of the Majority World are hospitable. But since developing countries host over 80 percent of the world's refugees, it should not surprise us to find acts of extravagant, self-sacrificial hospitality in the Majority World.

Majority World and indigenous cultures have known their fair share of hostility, oppression and exclusion—within and between people groups and at the hands of colonial powers. A rich theology and practice of hospitality has developed within this context.

Authentic partnership and hospitality—in church and society—can act as an antidote to exclusion and domination. We see this hospitality demonstrated throughout Africa, Asia, Latin America, Eastern Europe and indigenous communities.

Scripture teaches us that God welcomes the oppressed, broken, outcast and excluded. The church needs to reflect God's hospitality.

God doesn't form a church of an elect and privileged and powerful few. Instead, he forms his church as a diverse and hospitable people. These people show authentic unity in diversity. Hospitality is the key to the formation of churches that are wonderfully diverse yet deeply unified.

Hospitality doesn't dominate others by demanding conformity. Hospitality "creates a safe and welcoming space for persons to find their own sense of humanity and worth."[2]

Many Majority World thinkers agree that hospitality is crucial for the mission of the church. Through hospitality and welcome, the church positions itself as an alternative culture, a culture that reveals Christ's kingdom. Such hospitality connects with the marginal, the broken, the rejected, the excluded and the despised. It fosters a spirituality of partnership, hospitality and inclusivity. It welcomes people into God's family. Hospitality demonstrates the extraordinary grace of Jesus Christ to the world.

To appreciate hospitality in Majority World and indigenous cultures, we need to consider its diverse expressions. These include its theology, sacra-

---

[2]L. M. Russell, *Church in the Round: Feminist Interpretation of the Church* (Louisville: Westminster, 1993), 173.

mentality, location, welcome, price, practices, reconciliation and witness. I proceed in that order. This chapter asks, *What can we learn from how Majority World Christians practice hospitality and welcome?*

Hospitality's Theology

Christine D. Pohl provides a comprehensive treatment of hospitality. She addresses its biblical foundations, theological themes and historical practices. Her book, *Making Room: Recovering Hospitality as a Christian Tradition*, is well worth reading. Amy Oden collects early Christian texts on hospitality and its practices—letters, sermons, instructions and community records. She presents these in her book, *And You Welcomed Me: A Sourcebook on Hospitality in Early Christianity*. In these two books, Pohl and Oden offer foundational treatments of Christian hospitality.[3]

I restrict myself here to briefly highlighting the theological themes shaping Majority World hospitality.

1. Biblical hospitality. Conservative biblical interpretation and passion for Scripture characterize Majority World churches. Their theology of hospitality has clear biblical commitments. These include the following: (1) They pay attention to the teachings of Jesus in Matthew 25, Luke 14 and elsewhere, and the example of his life. (2) They heed Old Testament narratives, including the stories of Abraham and Lot in Genesis 18–19 and Elijah in 1 Kings 17–18. They also take serious the texts dealing with welcoming and protecting the stranger and foreigner and dispossessed. (3) They follow the New Testament emphasis on hospitality toward Christians, those in need, strangers, the broader society and all creation. This includes Christ's call to welcome one another as he has welcomed them (Rom 15:7).

2. Trinitarian hospitality. Leonardo Boff defines the Trinity as "three Persons and a single communion and a single trinitarian community. . . . Speaking of God must always mean the Father, Son and Holy Spirit in the

---

[3]Six sources provide good introductions to ancient, biblical, historical and theological sources for hospitality: Christine D. Pohl, *Making Room: Recovering Hospitality as a Christian Tradition* (Grand Rapids: Eerdmans, 1999); Christine D. Pohl and Pamela J. Buck, *Study Guide for Making Room: Recovering Hospitality as a Christian Tradition* (Grand Rapids: Eerdmans, 2001); Diane C. Kessler, ed. *Receive One Another: Hospitality in Ecumenical Perspective* (Geneva: WCC, 2005); Matthew Carroll, "A Biblical Approach to Hospitality," *Review & Expositor* 108, no. 4 (2011); Amy Oden, *God's Welcome: Hospitality for a Gospel-Hungry World* (Cleveland, OH: Pilgrim, 2008); Amy Oden, *And You Welcomed Me: A Sourcebook on Hospitality in Early Christianity* (Nashville: Abingdon, 2001).

presence of one another, in total reciprocity, in immediacy of loving relationship, being one for another, by another, in another and with another."[4]

The church patterns itself, in a limited and creaturely way, after the social
relations of the Trinity. Community, difference-in-relationship, unity-in-
diversity, openness, reciprocity, mutuality, participation, and welcome and
hospitality characterize the trinitarian church.[5]

The trinitarian Persons fellowship in a free, loving, unified and differentiated way. The church is to reflect these relations in its community and
mission. Trinitarian theology shapes our hospitality so that it is unifying and
embracing and communing. If our hospitality does not have these characteristics, then it is not Christian or trinitarian.

3. Eucharistic hospitality. Hospitality relates to the sacrament of the Eucharist. Indeed, we need a sacramental hospitality. Eating and drinking,
food and wine, and fellowship around a meal table—these things are at the
heart of many Majority World cultures.

This should not surprise us, because these are at the center of many
Western cultures too. And of course, eating and drinking together was at the
heart of the biblical cultures and their hospitality. At the Last Supper, Jesus
shows us that eating and drinking are at the heart of our relationship with
him. We remember what he has done and anticipate his return. As the disciples partake in the last supper with Jesus, they also remember the many
years of eating and drinking and communing with him.

This theme runs throughout Jesus' ministry. Jesus invites disreputable
sinners, social outcasts, tax collectors, you and me and all who would come
to table fellowship. This is scandalous hospitality. It is divine welcome. He
eats and drinks with us. Jesus amazed the disciples through the way he embraced them. He welcomed them as family. He shared his life, food, Passover
meal and mission with them. He called them to image this divine hospitality.
And Jesus calls today's church to the same hospitality—to imitate him.

Majority World and indigenous cultures prioritize table fellowship. This
prioritization reminds us that eating together involves relationship,
friendship, thankfulness and welcome. It reminds us of the Last Supper and
all that it signifies. This table fellowship is a sign of the kingdom of God

---

[4]Leonardo Boff, "Trinitarian Community and Social Liberation," *Cross Currents* 38, no. 3 (1988): 287.
[5]Ibid., 306.

come among us. It is an anticipation of the age to come—of eating and drinking with our glorified Lord and each other. It is a sign of everlasting relationship. The resurrection of Jesus means that our table fellowship with him and each other will last forever. The meals that we share now—Holy Communion and enjoying food and fellowship around a meal table—anticipate the eternal feast.

We have responded to Jesus' welcome at the table. We are recipients of his divine hospitality. We offer this welcome and hospitality to the world.

The Eucharist reminds us of God's welcome to humanity. How we celebrate the Eucharist says much about Christian hospitality. The Eucharist must not only symbolize divine welcome and fellowship. Eucharistic welcome must spill over into the rest of the church's hospitality.

Angel Méndez says that the Eucharist has ethical implications for the church. The Eucharist reminds us of our contingencies and embodiment and complete reliance on God's nourishing grace. The Eucharist reminds us of God's generosity and superabundance and love.

The gospel demands, therefore, that the church address hunger, poverty, inequality and injustice. So does the Eucharist. It calls the church to address all forms of "violence, exclusion, and destruction." The gospel and the Eucharist call for hospitality toward Christians, strangers, other cultures, the vulnerable and creation. They remind us of divine hospitality.[6] And we extend this hospitality from our homes and lands and eschatological hope.

Hospitality's Welcome

Throughout successive generations, all over the globe human beings have recognized the intimate connections between humanity, cultures and the land. This theme runs throughout Majority World literature and indigenous oral traditions. It is a theme that emerges repeatedly in Western writings too.

We offer hospitality from our local soil, local culture and ultimate hope. We offer hospitality *from* a particular location—our soil, our home, our place, our culture, our relationships and our eternal hope.

Hospitality's location is often *the place that I love.*

---

[6]Angel F. Méndez, "Divine Alimentation: Gastroeroticism and Eucharistic Desire," in *Hunger, Bread and Eucharist*, ed. Christophe Boureux, Janet Martin Soskice and Luiz Carlos Susin (London: SCM, 2005), 14-20.

Sometimes we extend hospitality to others while *we ourselves* are foreigners or displaced or sojourners. More often, we welcome outsiders to our local culture and local soil. Frequently, if we are hospitable, we welcome strangers and neighbors from our own culture into our homes and lives.

We offer hospitality *from* this location and *to* this location. We welcome others *into* our location, relationships and place. We offer hospitality *to* that soil, that ecology, that location and those relationships.

Ruth Padilla DeBorst shows how Israel's condition as God's people was "intertwined with that of the people and place where God had situated them. *In its welfare you will find your welfare.*"[7]

We root our hospitality and well-being in our home and land and relationships and hope. God calls his people to be "hopeful home-builders." We nurture land, homes, gardens, children and earth. We show hospitality to these things. And we extend welcome to strangers with whom we share our lives. This requires many conversions: "Conversion from individualism to community, from autonomy to interdependence, from idolatry to true worship, from grasping to receiving, from oppressive dominion over creation to loving care of it, from indifference to passionate, prayerful action, from Western definitions of 'development' to loving participation, from competition to collaboration, from protagonism to service."[8]

Hospitality involves our relationship to our home, to the earth and to local place. It involves our connections to local relationships, local soil and local generosity.

Are we connected enough with these to be hospitable? Are we willing to offer strangers welcome into those places and relationships and lands we love the most? Are we willing to allow others to call our land their land and our homes their homes?

We need to take these things seriously to be welcoming and hospitable.

As we nurture local soils, cultures, homes and communities, we are able to offer hospitality. Our hospitality expresses itself in actions *toward* those things and *from* them.

DeBorst claims that this involves the following: (1) Building homes and

---

[7]Ruth Padilla DeBorst, "Living Creation-Community in God's World Today," *Journal of Latin American Theology* 5, no. 1 (2010): 58.
[8]Ibid., 60.

living sustainably in them. This means making these homes a refuge for the homeless, disposed, stranger, and rural and urban poor. (The idea of homes as refuge is truly terrifying for most people—myself included.) (2) Planting gardens, caring for creation and food sourcing. We must recover "our relationship to the earth in the creation-community." (3) Cultivating families and churches that provide "fertile ground for converted covenantal relations." We form these relationships through intimacy, simplicity, hospitality, collaboration and inclusion. (4) Seeking the welfare of the city. This includes its ecology, built environment, socioeconomic elements, human connections and marginalized persons.[9]

Hospitality is often richest in the context of *shared history* and *generous inclusion*. Such shared history with people and place and land is not always possible. But when it is possible and valued, it can provide a remarkable environment for hospitality and inclusion. What does it mean to enrich shared history through inclusion? It means welcoming others into our lovingly nurtured homes, lands, cultures and communities. It means recognizing the importance of shared history and the welcome of the outsider.

We open up this shared history so that the outsider can become an insider. It is an intentional openness to others entering our lives.

Our hospitality needs to be free and generous and active. John Chrysostom, fourth-century archbishop of Constantinople (in modern-day Turkey), charges the church to *be given* to hospitality.[10]

We welcome people into our homes in hopeful anticipation of our ultimate home. In welcoming them, we welcome Jesus Christ.

Hospitality will often disappoint us. People will wound us, use us and let us down. They will betray our trust and refuse to reciprocate in kind. Hospitality will be a "now/not yet" experience. Sometimes it will be as unpleasant as foot washing. Some will offer us hospitality in return, enriching our lives more than we could have imagined. It was like that for Jesus.

But hospitality makes us fuller, richer, more Christlike people. We welcome people into our homes and lives and lands in anticipation of the home and the

---

[9]Ibid., 62-69.

[10]John Chrysostom, "Homily 21 on Romans," in *Homilies on Acts of the Apostles*, ed. J. Walker and J. Sheppard, *Nicene and Post-Nicene Fathers of the Christian Church* (New York: Christian Literature Company, 1889), 505.

age to come. And in doing so, we are a foretaste of our ultimate home and of the age to come in Christ Jesus.

HOSPITALITY'S PRICE

Sometimes we think of hospitality as a soft, easy practice. Nothing could be further from the truth.

Churches that practice hospitality are courageous communities. Generous people fill these churches—practicing hospitality at personal cost.

The Asia-Pacific region is experiencing a dramatic rise in asylum seekers and refugees. This wave of displaced persons affects all countries in our Asia-Pacific region. Recently, a debate about asylum seekers has flared up in my country, Australia. Our main political parties are seeking to win votes through tough policies directed at refugees and asylum seekers. The United Nation's refugee agency, the UNHCR, and Amnesty International have criticized these policies. The concern is that Australia's harsh policies flout key articles of the Refugee Convention. This includes Article 31, which forbids discrimination against asylum seekers based on how they arrive.

Church groups have joined in the condemnation of Australian policies. Christian leaders and young people are in our news for showing love, welcome, generosity and practical support to asylum seekers. They are swimming against the tide of Australian opinion in response to the compassion and gospel of Jesus Christ. Two stories from my country illustrate hospitality and welcome.

During 2014, groups of Australian Christian leaders staged nonviolent sit-ins at the electorate offices of Australian politicians. These included the offices of Prime Minister Tony Abbott and opposition leader Bill Shorten. They were protesting the indefinite imprisonment of children in Australian immigration detention centers. They sat in the offices of these leaders, praying and reading Scripture, until police arrested them. These nonviolent protests made Australian news headlines.

Coco Knight is a twenty-two-year-old Australian Christian university student. Distressed by Australia's treatment of asylum seekers, she set up the Simple Love project. This project collects food, toiletries, clothing and household items for asylum seekers. Thirty-five churches now take part. During Christmas 2013, they collected 1,400 bags of food and many other items for asylum seekers. One of our national newspapers profiled the ministry of Coco Knight and the Simple Love project.

When we look around Africa, Asia and Latin America, we see countless stories of costly hospitality. Churches in indigenous and Majority World settings know about hospitality's *price* and *practices*.

Stephen Liggins, for example, tells of an experience he had while teaching in Africa: "I once travelled down into Rwanda for a couple of days after teaching in Uganda. By arrangement, I was met at the border by a Rwandan Christian. Making general conversation, I asked about his family, and how many children he had. His answer was something like: 'One of my own, and 35 others.'"[11] Hospitality is costly if we do it in the way of Christ.

HOSPITALITY'S PRACTICES

These stories cause us to consider hospitality's practices. What practices sustain such costly hospitality? What practices help us cultivate communities of hospitality, welcome and inclusion?

Wesley Ariarajah says the church needs practices that cultivate unity and harmony in diversity. This is especially true when we welcome people into our homes, lands and cultures. Ariarajah proposes six practices. I list these here and supplement them with fourteen other practices in Majority World and indigenous cultures.

We see extraordinary hospitality all over the Majority World. Malaysians welcome refugees from Myanmar. Tanzanians offer *Karibu* to foreigners. Brazilians deconstruct divisions on the Mexican border. Rwandans take in orphans after the Rwandan Civil War. Indigenous Australians seek reconciliation with their colonizers. And there are a multitude of other examples. Twenty practices emerge repeatedly.

These settings know their fair share of hostility, alienation, division, exclusion and prejudice. Amos Yong makes this clear in his Sri Lankan, Nigerian and North American case studies in *Hospitality and the Other*. Yong also shows how hospitality and reconciliation can emerge even in violent and conflicted contexts.[12]

---

[11]Stephen Liggins, "What We Can Learn from African Christians," *The Briefing*, April 8, 2013, http://matthiasmedia.com/briefing/2013/04/what-we-can-learn-from-african-christians/.
[12]Amos Yong, *Hospitality and the Other: Pentecost, Christian Practices, and the Neighbor* (Maryknoll, NY: Orbis, 2008), 1-37.

Here are twenty practices the church in Western settings must pursue if it is to reflect the best of hospitality in Majority World and indigenous cultures:[13]

1. Welcome plurality of "peoples, cultures, and ways of thinking." This means embracing "many-ness" as a blessing and promise.

2. Affirm the diversity of identities that contribute to plurality.

3. Embrace common commitments of respect and acceptance. "The communities that have successfully dealt with plurality have learned the art of weaving plurality into a coherent whole without, at the same time, abolishing, undermining or suppressing any of the elements that contribute to its richness."

4. Ensure justice for all. "Just relations, just ways of sharing power, and economic justice, are crucial in pluralist situations."

5. Construct mechanisms for reconciliation. These help address those times when conflict, misunderstanding and division will occur.

6. Reject violence—in all its forms—as a way of resolving conflict. Violence only "polarizes people, deepens grievances, and destroys community."

7. Nurture a spirituality of plurality and hospitality. This "equips us with the wisdom to deal with differences." Cultivate a spirituality of "inclusion of all, freedom for all, and participation of all."

8. Warmly greet and welcome people *as we receive* the other.

9. Move out of our comfort zones into other cultures and groups *as we go* to the other.

10. Welcome and advocate for the displaced, dispossessed, marginalized, needy, alienated, homeless, victimized, silenced and those with disabilities. Welcome them into our homes and churches and lives.

11. Wash feet and conduct other acts of humility and service.

12. Pray for the church, strangers, neighbors, foreigners and other cultures.

13. Reconstruct church small groups so that they are missional, outwardly focused and hospitable.

---

[13]S. Wesley Ariarajah, "The Challenge of Building Communities of Peace for All: The Richness and Dilemma of Diversities," *Ecumenical Review* 57, no. 2 (2005). The first seven points, including the quotes, come directly from Ariarajah's article.

14. Pursue interreligious dialogue as a demonstration of God's hospitality.

15. Invite people into the nucleus of our culture, soil and place—*the home*. Do we only invite friends and family into our homes? Do we invite strangers and foreigners into our homes?

16. Provide food, clothing, accommodation, protection, medical care, funds, sanctuary, advocacy and access into the host culture.

17. Allow Holy Communion to shape a lifestyle of table hospitality. This is one where we connect over food and drink. We welcome the stranger to our table. We evaluate our consumption. We address human hunger.

18. Reclaim spiritual friendship as a form of hospitality just as Jesus has made us his friends.

19. Cultivate hospitality as a *way of life* and a *way of being*, not just as a set of practices.

20. Revisit the structures that sustain or prevent hospitality. We must embed this list of practices in Christian community. This happens through institutional attention to practices. It also requires the renewal of our systems, structures, ministries and mission. We renew these so that they are truly hospitable—witnessing to Christ's astonishing, incomparable welcome.

These practices are crucial for the church's witness as a reconciling community.

HOSPITALITY'S RECONCILIATION

Amos Yong reminds us that practices of hospitality will vary according to context and the movement of the Spirit. Yong has distinguished himself as a leading Asian Pentecostal scholar. His basic thesis is that pneumatology—our theology of the Holy Spirit—is a point of contact with other religions.[14] Pneumatology opens up space for hospitality and reconciliation and understanding. Yong believes this is true for relationships in general and for interfaith relations in particular.

Yong develops a Spirit-centered theology of hospitality. He then makes

---

[14]Amos Yong, *Discerning the Spirit(s): A Pentecostal-Charismatic Contribution to Christian Theology of Religions* (Sheffield: Sheffield Academic, 2000); Yong, *Hospitality and the Other*; Amos Yong, "The Spirit of Hospitality: Pentecostal Perspectives Toward a Performative Theology of Interreligious Encounter," *Missiology* 35, no. 1 (2007).

Christian practices the key to understanding how the Spirit enhances hospitality. Yong says that Jesus Christ is the paradigmatic host and guest. He offers God's hospitality to humanity and comes to us as a guest.[15] The gift of the Holy Spirit "signifies the extension of God's abundant hospitality into the whole world."[16] And practices of hospitality embody trinitarian hospitality. "What is being given and what is being received is not any *thing*, but the triune God as manifest in the body of Christ and animated by the power of the Spirit."[17]

Practices of hospitality are participations in divine hospitality. God calls his people "to discern the Spirit's presence and activity so that we can perform the appropriate practices representing the hospitable God. Which tongues we speak and what practices we engage in will depend on where we are, who we are interacting with, and what the social, political, economic structures are that give shape to our encounter." Hospitality can take many forms. These include "signs and wonders and works of mercy and compassion and acts of social liberation. The hospitality of God is thus embodied in a hospitable church whose members are empowered by the Holy Spirit to stand in solidarity and serve with the sick, the poor, and the oppressed."[18]

According to Yong, the following things are all pneumatological practices: (1) interreligious dialogue, (2) Christian mission and (3) the pursuit of reconciliation and peace and justice. They demand that the church be both guest and host. They show the trinitarian hospitality of God. Hospitality is an indispensable foundation for many things. This includes interreligious dialogue and missional expressions of church. It also includes deeds of reconciliation, mercy, justice and peace. Hospitality is crucial to "keep[ing] in step with the Spirit" (Gal 5:25).

Yong claims, "Christian mission is nothing more or less than our participation in the hospitality of God."[19]

HOSPITALITY'S WITNESS

The trinitarian mission is a movement of extravagant hospitality. The church does not have its own mission. Instead, it participates in God's hospitality.

---

[15]Yong, "Spirit of Hospitality," 62.
[16]Yong, *Hospitality and the Other*, 126.
[17]Ibid., 127.
[18]Yong, "The Spirit of Hospitality," 63.
[19]Yong, *Hospitality and the Other*, 131.

Following the hospitality of God, the church must offer this hospitality to the most unlikely people and in the most unexpected places. DeBorst says that God calls his church to welcome "unexpected guests" at God's multi-cultural, multifaceted banquet table.

The church's witness is more than word or deed—it witnesses to Christ in its total life *together* and *toward* the world. It testifies to Jesus' passion and power and welcome in its *being*. The church *is* hospitable because God *is* hospitable. "In so doing, or rather in so *being*, the church—the multi-faceted community of Jesus' disciples, gifted in 'many tongues' by the Spirit—indwells God's story, she takes on God's mission in the midst of clashing and blending human cultures, and is used by God to weave those strands into meaning and life-granting wholes."[20]

The church's hospitality is a participation in the mission of God and an expression of its hopeful expectation. Hospitality gives us a taste of that which is to come. We are welcoming the stranger and neighbor to God's banquet table. This is a table where all socio-cultures, ethnicities, languages, genders and people groups are welcome. They are welcome to take part in the hospitality of God.

An inclusive church embodies this hospitality. More broadly, Jesus Christ reveals this hospitality wherever his inaugurated kingdom is present.

Tobias Brandner, who teaches at the Divinity School of Chung Chi College in Hong Kong and ministers among prisoners in that city, writes of "hospitality as an emerging paradigm in mission." Hospitality transforms the church into an "open church." The open church shares in "joint celebration and joint meals." It renews its language and liturgy so that communication and understanding and inclusion are possible. It welcomes the interruption of the guest and grows as a result. The "missionary encounter thus *transforms both sides, hosts and guest.*" We are at once both host and guest. There is only one true host, Jesus Christ. "Host-missionaries who keep their status as guest in mind will not be concerned about losing power or mastery. They will allow guest/strangers to become fellow citizens and part of the family."[21]

---

[20]Ruth Padilla DeBorst, "'Unexpected' Guests at God's Banquet Table: Gospel in Mission and Culture," *Evangelical Review of Theology* 33, no. 1 (2009): 74.

[21]Tobias Brandner, "Hosts and Guests: Hospitality as an Emerging Paradigm in Mission," *International Review of Mission* 102, no. 1 (2013): 102.

The church needs to develop "centripetal mission or evangelization by hospitality" if it is to reflect God's hospitality.[22]

Mortimer Arias writes that Latin Americans have a reputation for generous hospitality. But migration into that region, especially from Asia, has tested this in recent years. Human displacement has also tried this hospitality. "Need, oppression, repression, and persecution" have driven people from their lands. "What used to be 'lands of refuge' became hunting grounds of political prisoners, nonconformists and those suspected of independent ideas and wrong associations."[23]

Arias says that *centrifugal mission*—this term means radiating out from the church into the world—is necessary. But *centripetal mission* becomes especially important when groups of people move within and between nations. Centripetal mission means drawing people into the welcoming church. It means witnessing to Jesus by welcoming people into community. Centripetal mission is about being the hospitable people of God. It "has to do with quality, with authenticity, with being."[24]

HOSPITALITY AND THE GlobalChurch: Concluding Reflections

This chapter began with a discussion about asylum seekers and refugees. Arias says that such migrations provide opportunities for missional hospitality. They offer distinct occasions for the church to *be* the church. "Can we see in the faces of contemporary Asians, Latin Americans, and Africans, pushed from their lands and attracted to our shores, the potential glow of the angel of the Lord—the Lord of migrants who transforms and moves history through migrant peoples, and raises his own people as a pilgrim church among many diverse peoples?"[25]

But we're surrounded by opportunities to show hospitality. My family lives in a multicultural area. A high percentage of people in our area were born overseas (mostly in Asia). Recently, my daughters and I went around the neighborhood giving flowers and welcome cards to families who'd just moved into the area. I love the look of shock and delight on people's faces as you turn

---

[22]Mortimer Arias, "Centripetal Mission or Evangelization by Hospitality," *Missiology* 10, no. 1 (1982): 69.
[23]Ibid., 73.
[24]Ibid., 75.
[25]Ibid., 77.

up at their door with flowers and a warm welcome to the neighborhood. It's a small act. But it means so much to people. And what I hadn't anticipated was the constant gifts we'd get in return. For the next two weeks, people were turning up at our door with gifts. I discovered something afresh in this experience. People are longing for connection and community and welcome.

Orlando Costas says that when we show hospitality to others we also discover that the church has *come to us*. The church that welcomes the periphery discovers that the church is at the periphery. Consequently, we enjoy the renewal of the church.

> Black, Hispanic, Asian, and Native American churches and Christians, in partnership with a minority from the mainstream society that has identified itself with the poor, the powerless, and the oppressed of the land, are witnessing to the new world order announced in the gospel—outside the realm of economic wealth, military might, and political power, and inside the world of millions who are being wasted by numerous forms of social, economic, and political evils.[26]

It is time for us to learn from hospitality in Majority World and indigenous cultures. We need to consider hospitality's theology, sacramental dimensions, location, welcome, price, practices, reconciliation and witness.

Here are eight things we learn from how Majority World Christians practice hospitality and welcome:

1. Hospitality requires biblical and theological foundations. Our hospitality needs robust biblical and theological foundations. It needs them to meet the challenges posed by exclusion, violence, fear, indifference, idolatry, siege-mentalities and oppressive dominion. When a group moves into your neighborhood and threatens its homogeneity and sense of security and identity (let's say, for instance, a large Muslim group moves into your area), you need to ask yourself a question: Is my theology and practice of hospitality up to the task? In this chapter, I've outlined some biblical teachings and stories that undergird Christian hospitality. And I've shown how trinitarian and Eucharistic theology helps construct a theology of hospitality. These are starting points. It's up to you to build solid theological foundations—and personal commitments—that nurture and sustain Christian hospitality.

---

[26]Orlando E. Costas, quoted in ibid., 80.

I don't remember studying a theology of hospitality went I went to theological college. This is strange, given hospitality's prominence in Scripture and in the mission of God. The church needs "a radical theology of hospitality that might take the stranger and the poor into greater consideration." This theology is lived out in the world. We "live a radial hospitality." This includes daring to move away from the "rigidity of place, sacramental understanding, and liturgical practice." It means "venturing into a world that is yet to be created."[27]

Let's take our theology of the Eucharist (Holy Communion or the Lord's Supper) as *one* example. Latin American missional leaders saturate their theology of the Eucharist in a theology of hospitality. Cláudio Carvalhaes, for instance, says that the church should "welcome people in and around and through the Eucharistic sacrament." Through the Lord's Supper we "gather with one another to be with one another and issue this constant call of welcome to whomever wants to come and eat."[28]

Carvalhaes writes that when he was a child in Sao Paulo, Brazil, his family practiced constant hospitality. They welcomed neighbors, those in need and strangers. He carried this hospitality over into his pastoral ministry in the shantytowns of Sao Paulo. Later, he practiced hospitality among poor immigrants on the Mexico-US border. Carvalhaes says that on the Mexican border he discovered how the Eucharist reveals other "borders"—ecclesial, theological, socioeconomic and political borders. And Christ calls us to transcend them for his sake.[29]

2. Hospitality involves conversion. For most of us, when we made a decision to follow Jesus we didn't fully understand the breadth and depth of conversion. There's no such thing as a partial conversion. We're tempted to think that there is. We say, my Sundays are converted, but not my Mondays. My tithe is converted, but not the rest of my finances and spending habits. My reading is converted, but not my Internet use. My attire is converted, but not my consumerism and autonomy. My church building is converted into a welcoming place, but not my home. My singing of praise songs is con-

---

[27] All quotes in this paragraph are from Cláudio Carvalhaes, "Borders, Globalization and Eucharistic Hospitality," *Dialog* 49, no. 1 (2010): 54.

[28] Ibid., 45. Carvalhaes draws heavily on Jacques Derrida's notions of hospitality.

[29] Ibid., 46.

verted, but not my welcome of foreigners and strangers into my home and
land and nation. My Bible memorization is converted, but not my care for
creation or the most vulnerable in my neighborhood. My care for my home
is converted, but not my concern for the cries of the earth and the poor. My
hard work at my job is converted, but not my politics and nationalism. Am
I willing to let God convert my civil religion? This is a

> civil religion in which the main doctrine consists of God being on my side
> (and maybe a few others), a religion of empire in which God is served first
> and foremost by serving one's country (rather than one another) and obeying
> its leaders (rather than Jesus) who have been appointed by God himself.
> Colonialism is the new evangelism. Corporations are the new church. Con-
> sumerism is the new kingdom of Heaven. And the Constitution is the new
> Sermon on the Mount. Sadly, many Jesus-loving Christians have been con-
> vinced (or deceived) that they can live in both kingdoms, or worse yet, that
> they are one and the same.[30]

Jesus demands our complete conversion. We will only exercise his hospitality in the world when we allow him to fully convert us to himself and to
his hospitality. We need to be converted from "individualism to community,
from autonomy to interdependence, from idolatry to true worship, from
grasping to receiving, from oppressive dominion over creation to loving care
of it, from indifference to passionate, prayerful action, from Western definitions of 'development' to loving participation, from competition to collaboration, from protagonism to service."[31]

**3. Hospitality welcomes others into our homes and families and land
and churches and cultures.** We offer hospitality *from* this location and *to*
this location. We welcome others *into* our place, relationships, soil and
homes. And we do all this in hopeful anticipation of our ultimate home. As
we've seen, DeBorst encourages us to build homes and live sustainably in
them. We should make them a refuge for the homeless, disposed, stranger,
and rural and urban poor.[32] This includes planting gardens and caring for
creation. It means recovering "our relationship to the earth in the creation-

---

[30]Mike Rogers, during a Facebook conversation on Lance Ford's Facebook page on January 20, 2015.
   I don't usually quote Facebook comments—but this one was excellent.
[31]DeBorst, "Living Creation-Community," 60.
[32]In these next four points I'm quoting directly from DeBorst, ibid., 62-69.

community." We cultivate families and churches that provide "fertile ground for converted covenantal relations." We express these relations through intimacy, simplicity, hospitality, collaboration and inclusion.

Evelyn Parker, who calls herself an African of the Diaspora, writes of her experience of Tanzanian hospitality. African hospitality overwhelms her. Hospitality that is sacrificial and unconditional

> redefines what it means to welcome the stranger. As I reflect on the significance of my sojourn in Moshi, Arusha and other parts of northeast Tanzania . . . I realize [that the people of] Moshi modeled receiving the stranger unconditionally. . . . This [sacrificial] hospitality changes our priorities from self-serving and individualistic concerns to true *Koinonia*. . . . Persevering hospitality that the Moshi community modeled calls us to the responsibility of persistently pursing ways to compromise and reconcile so that all the world will see our oneness in Christ Jesus. Persevering hospitality fortifies our efforts for overcoming the sins of racism, classism, and sexism that hinder genuine visible Christian unity. This new meaning of hospitality as unconditional, sacrificial, and persevering, is captured in the phrase *incarnational hospitality*. This means the embodiment of divine practices for entertaining strangers. . . . The people of Moshi and northeast Tanzania call it *Karibu*.[33]

4. Hospitality cultivates a spirituality of embrace. Christian spirituality is welcoming, open, inclusive and embracing. This means welcoming people and demonstrating to the world the extravagant grace of Jesus Christ. A hospitable spirituality addresses hunger, poverty, inequality, injustice, "violence, exclusion, and destruction." We practice hospitality toward Christians, strangers, other cultures, the vulnerable and creation. We offer welcome to our homes and lands and relationships and churches and soil and eternal hope.[34] Together, we live out the twenty practices of hospitality. (See them listed under the heading "Hospitality's Practices" above.)[35] They shape a spirituality of welcome and embrace.

It's time to multiply the practices of hospitality and welcome. This includes "signs and wonders and works of mercy and compassion and acts of social liberation. The hospitality of God is thus embodied in a hospitable

---

[33]Evelyn L. Parker, "Karibu: A New Meaning for Hospitality," *Mid-Stream* 36, no. 1 (1997): 19.
[34]Mendez, "Divine Alimentation," 14-20.
[35]Ariarajah, "Challenge of Building Communities of Peace for All."

church whose members are empowered by the Holy Spirit to stand in solidarity and serve with the sick, the poor, and the oppressed."[36] A hospitable spirituality welcomes "unexpected guests" at God's multicultural banquet table. It witnesses to Jesus in our life *together* and *toward* the world. We *are* hospitable because God *is* hospitable.

5. Hospitality is courageous and costly. It takes courage to be hospitable when others are being hostile and exclusive. You risk being excluded too, or worse. True hospitality always comes at a price. It takes effort. We risk losing status and comfort. For a season, we may lose our sense of identity and belonging. Hospitality costs us our pride and control and dominance. And on some occasions, it costs people their homes and lives. What are you willing to do to show the hospitality of God? What are you willing to lose? What price are you willing to pay? And we pay this price in light of the treasure that is eternal.

6. Hospitality seeks the welfare of our immediate neighborhood and our broader town or city. Most of the time, I find it easy to pursue the well-being of my family and church. But do I seek the welfare of my neighborhood and town and city? Christian hospitality demands that I do. This includes their built environments, ethnicities, race relations, marginalized and impoverished persons, socioeconomics, human connections and ecologies. Love your neighbor. Seek the welfare of your city. Pray for your city. Bring peace and reconciliation. Know your neighbor's names. Welcome strangers. Care for creation and green space. Contribute positively to politics and community organizations. Support positive urban planning projects, local economic initiatives and neighborhood and community organizations. Help create "urban sanctuaries." (Urban sanctuaries are spaces for peace, recreation and community in urban centers: community gardens, green belts, nature corridors, recreation spaces and so on.) The Spirit calls us to actions that bring peace and well-being. Hospitality seeks human flourishing, healthy cities and the prosperity of nature.

7. Hospitality is essential to reconciliation and mission. Without hospitality there is no peace and reconciliation. Forgiveness and understanding and welcome require hospitality. Repeatedly, Australian Aboriginal com-

---

[36]Yong, "Spirit of Hospitality," 63.

munities have invited me into their lands and homes. They do this even though—as a white man—I symbolize the colonizer and invader. Through their generous hospitality they offer reconciliation, forgiveness, peace and warm welcome.

And hospitality is essential for mission. Just as God invites us into his love and kingdom and future, so we must be hospitable. Let me illustrate how hospitality relates to mission through a brief story. John Ong is a friend of mine who ministers among migrants, refugees and asylum seekers in Malaysia and surrounding countries. Twelve years ago, John established a network among churches of different denominations. This network ministers among refugees from eight nationalities. John set up a school for 250 refugee children aged five to seventeen. These children come from Myanmar (Chin, Rohingya and other tribal groups), Sri Lanka, Pakistan and Cambodia. This school comes under the supervision of UNHCR. It has a center that produces handmade soap and textiles. This employment helps refugee women support their families. It enables them to buy food, secure accommodation and enjoy education.

John's team also operates several drop-in centers. These enable displaced migrants who are in dispute with employers or property owners to find support. They have other centers for persecuted groups, for vulnerable, single, refugee women and for families with young girls. These refugee support centers are open to all regardless of ethnicity, religion or gender. Local churches and nonprofits support these centers. They are a demonstration of authentic Christian hospitality. This is mission inspired by God's extravagant hospitality in Jesus Christ.

8. Hospitality follows Jesus' example and teaching. Examples here are too numerous for this chapter. Jesus extolled the virtue of hospitality. He revealed God's hospitality in the incarnation. And he showed it in his embrace of the sinner, outcast, diseased, unclean and so on. Let's finish with Jesus' words:

> Then the King will say to those on his right, "Come, you who are blessed by my Father; take your inheritance, the kingdom prepared for you since the creation of the world. For I was hungry and you gave me something to eat, I was thirsty and you gave me something to drink, I was a stranger and you invited me in, I needed clothes and you clothed me, I was sick and you looked after me, I was in prison and you came to visit me."

Then the righteous will answer him, "Lord, when did we see you hungry and feed you, or thirsty and give you something to drink? When did we see you a stranger and invite you in, or needing clothes and clothe you? When did we see you sick or in prison and go to visit you?"

The King will reply, "Truly I tell you, whatever you did for one of the least of these brothers and sisters of mine, you did for me." (Mt 25:34-40)

EMBRACING THE SPIRIT

WHAT CAN WE LEARN FROM HOW MAJORITY
WORLD CHRISTIANS EMBRACE THE SPIRIT?

The Holy Spirit played a crucial role in every aspect of the kingdom mission of Jesus. At Pentecost the Spirit came on the early church in power so Jesus' mission could be advanced and completed. There is thus an indissoluble relationship between Pentecost and the missionary witness of the church. The witness of the church began at Pentecost, and in the power of the Pentecostal Spirit this witness continues to be carried forward. . . . The Holy Spirit's role is thus indispensable to the church's missionary enterprise.

IVAN SATYAVRATA

Spirit baptism has been a defining experience in my discipleship to Jesus Christ. I remember the night well. I was sixteen, angry, wounded and insecure. I had just attended a Pentecostal worship service. And I had responded to the pastor's invitation to receive Spirit baptism. Nothing happened to me when the pastor prayed.

That night, alone in my room, I cried out to God for his presence. Around midnight I experienced the Spirit's power and presence in an intense and overwhelming way. It wasn't "speaking in tongues" that impressed me. I felt overwhelmed by the direct experience of God's love. I felt his grace, for-giveness, healing, assurance, hope, joy and empowering presence. Since that time, *pneumatology* has interested me. Pneumatology is the study of the person and empowering presence of the Holy Spirit.

THE SPIRIT POURED OUT

Renewalist churches refer to Pentecostal, charismatic, neo-charismatic and "third wave" churches. These churches are broader than classical Pentecostalism but incorporate it. They are diverse. They often take on characteristics of their host culture.

These renewalist churches have grown and multiplied in the Majority World. This is especially the case in the Global South.[1] These churches emphasize baptism with the Holy Spirit. They also focus on divine healing, spiritual gifts and Spirit-empowered witness. They "agree on the presence and demonstration of the charismata [spiritual gifts] in the modern church, but beyond this common agreement there is much diversity as in all the other branches of Christianity."[2]

Since these renewalist churches are so diverse, it is not easy to measure their growth. In 1970, there was around fifteen million Pentecostals and sixty million other renewalists worldwide. Now researchers estimate that there are around 600 million people in renewalist churches worldwide.[3] Pew Research claims Pentecostal and charismatic Christians make up about 27% of all Christians. They make up more than 8% of the world's total population. Pew puts Pentecostal Christians at 279 million and charismatic Christians at 305 million.[4]

Recently, Gordon-Conwell's Center for the Study of Global Christianity (CSGC) released an important report. They called it *Christianity in Its Global Context, 1970–2020*. Their findings relating to renewalist churches are striking:

---

[1]Walter J. Hollenweger provides a comprehensive overview of Pentecostalism's origins and developments worldwide. He includes in-depth treatments of its African American, South African, Mexican, Korean and Chilean manifestations. See Hollenweger, *Pentecostalism: Origins and Developments Worldwide* (Peabody, MA: Hendrickson, 1997). Other useful treatments of Pentecostal and renewalist developments worldwide include Allan H. Anderson, *An Introduction to Pentecostalism: Global Charismatic Christianity* (Cambridge: Cambridge University Press, 2004); William K. Kay, *Pentecostalism* (Oxford: Oxford University Press, 2011); David Martin, *Pentecostalism: The World Their Parish*, Religion and Modernity (Oxford: Blackwell, 2002); Amos Yong, *The Spirit Poured Out on All Flesh: Pentecostalism and the Possibility of Global Theology* (Grand Rapids: Baker Academic, 2005).

[2]Hollenweger, *Pentecostalism*, 327.

[3]James D. G. Dunn, *The Christ and the Spirit*, vol. 2, *Pneumatology* (Grand Rapids: Eerdmans, 1998), 86.

[4]Pew Research uses data supplied by the Center for the Study of Global Christianity at Gordon-Conwell Theological Seminary.

Renewalists numbered 62.7 million in 1970. They're expected to grow to 709.8 million by 2020. In 1970, Renewalists were 5.1% of all Christians. But by 2010 they had grown to 25.8% (averaging 4.1% growth per year between 1970 and 2010). Looking forward to 2020, Renewalist movements will grow almost twice as fast as global Christianity as a whole. They'll represent 27.8% of all Christians. Renewalists grew the fastest in Asia and Latin America over the 40-year period. They'll grow most rapidly in Asia and Africa over the next 10-year period. In 1970, the three largest Renewalist populations were in the United States, Brazil, and the Democratic Republic of Congo. In 2020, the countries with the most Renewalists will likely be Brazil, the United States, China, and Nigeria. The growth of Renewalist Christianity in Asia, Africa, and Latin America has been astounding. They've grown from 18.8 million in 1970 to 226.2 million by 2020 in Africa, from 12.8 million to 203.1 million in Latin America, and from 9.3 million to 165.6 million in Asia.[5]

Patrick Johnstone says that at current rates of growth, renewalists will number one billion by 2050. That will be "one-third of all Christians and one-tenth of the world's population."[6]

Amos Yong is a Malaysian born, Asian American scholar. He writes that there are 400-plus million renewalists in the Majority World. This number is likely to grow to around 710 million by 2020 and one billion by 2050. Seventy-six percent of all renewalists are in Latin America, Asia and Africa.

Clearly, the most vibrant pentecostal communities are now in the Southern and Eastern Hemispheres, although traffic from South to North, from East to West, and vice versa is now busier than ever before, especially given the telecommunications revolution. . . . [Philip Jenkins] suggests that the coming Christendom will be radically pluralistic, centered not in Rome or Canterbury but variously in Seoul, Beijing, Singapore, Bombay, Lagos, Sao Paulo, and Mexico City.[7]

The Spirit is being poured out on all people (Joel 2:28; Acts 2:17).

These statistics show that Majority World Christians have much to teach

---

[5]Center for the Study of Global Christianity, *Christianity in Its Global Context, 1970–2020: Society, Religion, and Mission* (South Hamilton, MA: Gordon-Conwell Theological Seminary, 2013), 7, 8, 19.
[6]Patrick J. Johnstone, *The Future of the Global Church: History, Trends and Possibilities* (Colorado Springs, CO: Biblica, 2011), 125.
[7]Yong, *Spirit Poured Out on All Flesh*, 19-20.

the West. We can learn from them about ministry and mission in the power of the Spirit. Statistics measuring the growth of renewalist churches provoke us. They make us consider the *influence* of this mode of church. These statistics challenge the basic assumption that the Western church is the thriving church.

This focus on the Spirit and his role in mission isn't prominent in Western missional conversations. This must change. Charismatic and Pentecostal churches have much to teach missional movements, and vice versa.

The growth of Pentecostal Christianity in the Majority World has given these churches a global voice. But some issues have emerged. Some Western churches ignore God's empowering presence. But many Majority World renewalist churches overestimate the missional value of charismatic expressions. These churches are often missional yet may uncritically embrace elements of their host cultures. Similarly, the challenge for Western churches is their adoption of rational and secular assumptions.

The churches of the West, indigenous cultures and the Majority World can learn much from each other. This includes learning from each other about what it means for the Spirit to empower the mission of the church.

To date, the Western missional conversation hasn't prioritized pneumatology. It hasn't paid enough attention to the role of the Spirit's empowering presence and gifts in mission. This is strange since the Spirit empowers the church for mission and witness. Western missional conversations haven't focused enough on the role of the Spirit. They haven't prioritized the Spirit's role in the church's mission and discipleship and community.[8]

Missional theology needs to reclaim the role of the Spirit. Jesus Christ sends his church into the world for the glory of the Father. The Spirit empowers the church for faithful witness to the Father, Son and Holy Spirit. The Spirit enables the church to witness to the kingdom of God inaugurated by Jesus in the incarnation and at Pentecost.

The church needs a rigorous discussion about its role in Jesus' healing and reconciling mission. This demands greater attention to a theology of the Spirit.

---

[8]Two exceptions are worth noting. The first is my chapter, "The Spirit-Empowered Church: Responding to the Spirit's Power and Presence," in Graham Hill, *Salt, Light, and a City: Introducing Missional Ecclesiology* (Eugene, OR: Wipf and Stock, 2012), 205-29. The second is Michael Frost's chapter in *Following Fire: How the Spirit Leads Us to Fight Injustice*, ed. Ashley Barker (Springvale, Victoria: UNOH, 2008), 33-41.

This chapter considers the growth of Majority World renewalist and Pentecostal churches. It examines their emphases, worship, spirituality, contextualization, mission, challenges and future. This chapter asks, *What can we learn from how Majority World Christians embrace the Spirit?*

SPIRIT-CONSTITUTED CHURCHES

The rise of the Pentecostal-charismatic churches in the Majority World has been extraordinary. The growth of the churches in those cultures is a move of the Spirit. It is an expression of their dependence on the power, presence and provision of the Spirit.

In my book *Salt, Light, and a City*, I described the connection between the Spirit and mission.[9] A missional understanding of the church requires a deep commitment to the Spirit. A missional view of the church is only as good as its theology of the Spirit. The church needs a *missional pneumatology* and a *pneumatological mission*. A missional understanding of the church takes the Spirit seriously.[10]

The Spirit creates, fills and animates the church—he causes it to come into being. The church is the "people of God who are created by the Spirit to live as a missionary community."[11]

The Spirit creates and empowers the church so that it is a unique, spiritual community. It is the Spirit who "creates, leads, and teaches the church to live as the distinctive people of God."[12]

The Spirit is essential to the *being* of the church. "The church is and is visible because God the Holy Spirit is and acts."[13]

The Spirit creates the church and fills it with his grace and gifts. He empowers the church for the service of the messianic mission and the kingdom of God.

The Spirit is present in the church's sacraments, ministries, missions and structures. All these dimensions of the church are "conceived in the

---

[9]Hill, *Salt, Light, and a City*, chap. 16.

[10]Ibid., 205.

[11]Craig Van Gelder, *The Essence of the Church: A Community Created by the Spirit* (Grand Rapids: Baker, 2000), 25.

[12]Ibid., 31.

[13]J. B. Webster, "The Visible Attests the Invisible," in *The Community of the Word: Toward an Evangelical Ecclesiology*, ed. M. Husbands and D. J. Treier (Leicester: Apollos, 2005), 104; Hill, *Salt, Light, and a City*, 216.

movement and presence of the Spirit." The Spirit shapes all aspects of the church for the glory and mission of the Trinity.[14]

The Spirit renews the church as the triune God's ongoing creation. The Spirit forms the community of faith into a countercultural community embodying the reign of God. The Spirit is the advocate-helper of the church who helps it be faithful to the redemptive reign of God. He indwells it with his power and presence. The Spirit works in the church so that it is holy. The Spirit establishes the marks of the true church and enables its mission.[15]

Hans Küng says,

> If there is no Spirit, it does not mean that the community lacks its missionary commission, but that there is no community at all. . . . The church is filled and vivified, sustained and guided by his Spirit, the power and strength of God. The church owes to the Spirit its origin, existence, and continued life, and in this sense the church is a *creation of the Spirit*.[16]

The church is one, holy, catholic and apostolic, in the power of the Spirit. The Spirit uses these four attributes for the glory of Christ and his kingdom[17] and for the sake of the mission of God. He uses them to bring liberation, healing, justice, mercy and hope to the world.[18]

The Spirit fills the mission of God's people. This Spirit-empowered mission alerts people to the universal reign of God through Christ. The church in the power and presence of the Spirit exists for the mission of Christ. The Spirit empowers the church's mission. He does this for the sake of Christ's mission and the Father's glory. The Spirit empowers the church for Christ-honoring mission, service, love and compassion.[19]

Majority World churches are aware of this empowerment. They rely on the Spirit's renewal and remissionalization of the church.

Singaporean theologian Simon Chan says that our theology of the Spirit

---

[14]J. Moltmann, *The Church in the Power of the Spirit: A Contribution to Messianic Ecclesiology*, 2nd ed. (London: SCM, 1992), 289; Hill, *Salt, Light, and a City*, 206.

[15]Van Gelder, *Essence of the Church*, 42-44, 78-81, 86, 112-18, 142-62, 180.

[16]H. Küng, *The Church* (London: Search, 1968), 165, 172.

[17]Moltmann, *Church in the Power*, 337-38; Hill, *Salt, Light, and a City*, 207. Amos Yong provides a Pentecostal "re-reading" of the marks of the church in Amos Yong, "The Marks of the Church: A Pentecostal Re-Reading," *Evangelical Review of Theology* 26, no. 1 (2002).

[18]Moltmann, *Church in the Power*, 361.

[19]J. Moltmann, *The Source of Life: The Holy Spirit and the Theology of Life* (Minneapolis: Fortress, 1997), 55-69.

needs to be more communal and less individualistic. "To be baptized into Christ is to be incorporated into a Spirit-filled, Spirit-empowered entity. Spirit-baptism is first an event of the church prior to its being actualized in personalized Spirit-baptism."[20]

Chan develops what he calls an *ecclesial pneumatology*. He is talking here about a theology of the Spirit shaped around Christian community. Chan says that the Spirit forms the church. The Spirit does this in an ongoing way as the church worships, celebrates the Eucharist and joins with Christ in his mission. The Spirit enables the church to be a dynamic catholic, healing, truth-traditioning and eschatological community.

A dynamic catholic community: The Spirit of Christ makes the church *whole* and *one* in its local and universal expressions.

A healing community: The Spirit creates a church that transcends "all social, cultural, and historical boundaries." He forms a church "characterized chiefly by its work of reconciliation and healing."[21]

A truth-traditioning community: The Spirit "constitutes the church dynamically." He also "makes the church the place where truth exists dynamically." There is a profound connection between Christ the Truth and the action of the Spirit. This connection "makes possible the ongoing traditioning of Christ the Truth in the church." What does this mean? "Christ the Truth is made present in the church by the action of the Spirit in the preaching of the Word and in the sacrament."[22]

An eschatological community: The Spirit enables the church to join in historical events. These include the incarnation, the resurrection and Pentecost. The Spirit forms the church for present witness and for the age to come. The Spirit helps us to appropriate the inaugurated kingdom and the future reign of Christ in the present age. This is true even when we only have a foretaste and measure and glimpse of the age to come.[23]

Julie C. Ma and Wonsuk Ma claim the church and its mission are natu-

---

[20]Simon Chan, "Mother Church: Toward a Pentecostal Ecclesiology," *Pneuma: The Journal of the Society for Pentecostal Studies* 22, no. 2 (2000): 180. See also Chan, *Liturgical Theology: The Church as Worshiping Community* (Downers Grove, IL: IVP Academic, 2006), chap. 1; Yong, *Spirit Poured Out on All Flesh*, chap. 3.

[21]Chan, "Mother Church," 188.

[22]Ibid., 191.

[23]Simon Chan, *Pentecostal Theology and the Christian Spiritual Tradition* (Sheffield: Sheffield Academic, 2000), chap. 4.

rally renewalist. The church is "charismatic if left with little theological 'assistance.'" They argue,

> The church birthed in Jerusalem was highly charismatic. . . . Indigenous Pentecostal churches throughout the world are another sure proof of this contention. Completely unconnected with the modern Pentecostal tradition, there are countless number of "indigenous" churches, particularly in the non-Western world, that has made scholars revise the one-fountainhead theory of modern Pentecostalism. Healing, prophecy, miracles, exorcisms, and tongues are naturally practiced.
>
> In Asia, the Chinese house church movement provides another excellent example. After a generation without any outside "assistance," today's Chinese Christianity is strikingly charismatic. With this in mind, Pentecostals can encourage the churches to become closer to what has been intended for from the beginning.[24]

SPIRIT BAPTISM AND POWER

Majority World renewalist churches emphasize Spirit baptism—with varying definitions of this term. Spirit baptism is the hub of renewalist thought and praxis. They connect Spirit baptism with emphases on divine healing, spiritual gifts, demons, angels, deliverance, spiritual warfare and the Spirit's power.

Chan says that renewalist churches diverge on a range of issues. But "what comes through over and over again in their discussions and writings is a certain kind of spiritual experience of an intense, direct, and overwhelming nature centering on the person of Christ which they schematize as 'baptism in the Holy Spirit.'"[25]

Yong writes that renewalists don't understand Spirit baptism in a homogenous way. Even so, "it probably best symbolizes the distinctive orientation of the Pentecostal-charismatic imagination. . . . [Spirit baptism] has great theological import for the global movement . . . and brings us closest to what, if anything, can be termed the 'essence' of the Pentecostal-charismatic experience."[26]

---

[24]Wonsuk Ma and Julie C. Ma, "Jesus Christ in Asia: Our Journey with Him as Pentecostal Believers," *International Review of Mission* 94, no. 375 (2005): 503.

[25]Simon Chan, "Evidential Glossolalia and the Doctrine of Subsequence," *Asian Journal of Pentecostal Studies* 2 (1999): 196.

[26]Amos Yong, *Discerning the Spirit(s): A Pentecostal-Charismatic Contribution to Christian Theology of Religions* (Sheffield: Sheffield Academic, 2000), 165. Yong sees Spirit baptism as a "sacramental

Allan Anderson describes the various theologies of Spirit baptism. Classical Pentecostal, charismatic, neo-charismatic, "third wave" and Catholic charismatic views diverge. These groups debate how to understand Spirit baptism in the light of Scripture and experience. From this contested center come questions on the connection between Spirit baptism and conversion. For example, "What is normative about this experience and its expressions? And is 'speaking in tongues' inconsequential, normal, or normative?"[27]

David Yonggi Cho is the pastor of Yoido Full Gospel Church in Seoul, South Korea. This is the largest Pentecostal church in the world and has more than one million members. Cho typifies the classical Pentecostal view on Spirit baptism. For Cho, baptism in the Spirit is necessary. Spiritual power, supernatural gifts, effective prayer and church growth evidence Spirit baptism. The Spirit baptizes and gives spiritual gifts. There are many spiritual gifts. *Revelatory gifts* include knowledge, wisdom and discernment. *Vocal gifts* include tongues, interpretation and prophecy. *Power gifts* include faith, healing and miracles. Cho claims that established churches resist the Holy Spirit. He says they encourage wrong doctrines and persecute renewalist churches.[28]

Korean theologian Koo Dong Yun has a more open position than Cho. Yun undertakes a fascinating treatment of Spirit baptism. He notes the centrality of Spirit baptism to renewalist churches. He says, "The Classical Pentecostal view of Spirit baptism is characterized by (1) the Lukan orientation, (2) the vitality of experience, and (3) the verifiability of Spirit baptism."[29]

Yun goes on to examine nine divergent theologies of Spirit baptism. He does this to enrich doctrine and ecumenical understanding. Yun sees the essence of Pentecostalism in its pragmatic orientation. He contrasts this with Chan's articulation of Pentecostalism's essence; for Chan, this essence is a desire for the miraculous, surprising and unexpected. But according to Yun, pragmatism is at the heart of Pentecostalism. This pragmatism allows it to revise and

---

sign." He ties water baptism and Spirit baptism together closely. Spirit baptism witnesses to our regeneration in Christ.

[27] Anderson, *Introduction to Pentecostalism*, 192-95.

[28] Paul Yonggi Cho, *The Holy Spirit, My Senior Partner* (Milton Keynes: Word, 1989), 182. For recent developments in Cho's life, see Ruth Moon, "Founder of World's Largest Megachurch Convicted of Embezzling $12 Million," *Christianity Today*, February 26, 2014, www.christianitytoday.com /gleanings/2014/february/founder-of-worlds-largest-megachurch-convicted-cho-yoido.html

[29] Koo Dong Yun, *Baptism in the Holy Spirit: An Ecumenical Theology of Spirit Baptism* (Lanham, MD: University Press of America, 2003), vii.

expand its understanding and practice of Spirit baptism. This is good news. It allows global Pentecostalism to form a new theology of Spirit baptism. This theology will be holistic and open and ecumenical. An array of cultures and experiences and Christian traditions and biblical texts will inform it.[30]

Renewalist churches in the Majority World seek the power and presence and provision of the Holy Spirit. They long for the Spirit of Christ to fill them with power for faith and mission. Their experience of the spirit world convinces them of the necessity and power of the Holy Spirit. (Such experience includes exposure to animism, ancestral spirits, cults, magic, divination, demonic powers, "gods," miracles and traditional religions.)

Renewalist churches are not content with what they consider a powerless Christianity. These Majority World believers ask critical questions: "If God's Spirit is supreme, then why shouldn't healings, signs, wonders, miracles and supernatural gifts follow? Why shouldn't our experience of the Spirit mirror that of the early church—especially when our lives are like the lives of those in the Bible? Since we know the spiritual world is real and full of powerful spiritual beings, why shouldn't we expect the Holy Spirit to reveal Jesus Christ? And why wouldn't he reveal Jesus in holiness and power and wonder? Didn't Jesus Christ promise to fill us with the Holy Spirit and power?"

Malaysian theologian Hwa Yung says that these churches call the global church to "recover the supernatural." This includes "addressing the demonic at both the personal and cosmic levels." It means fitting "signs and wonders of the Holy Spirit" into our theological frameworks.

Yung arrives at clear conclusions. "A 21st-century reformation will demand reinserting the supernatural into the heart of Christianity. This will result not only in a sounder biblical theology but also a more powerful missional church. The world will then understand what Jesus meant when he said, 'But if it is by the Spirit of God that I cast out demons, then the kingdom of God has come upon you' (Matt. 12:28)."[31]

Spirit-constituted churches are attentive to the Spirit. They "recover the supernatural" together. They embrace the Spirit's power in culturally appropriate worship and mission.

---

[30]Ibid., 147-62; Koo Dong Yun, "Water Baptism and Spirit Baptism: Pentecostals and Lutherans in Dialogue," *Dialog: A Journal of Theology* 43, no. 4 (2004).

[31]Hwa Yung, "Recover the Supernatural," *Christianity Today* 54, no. 9 (2010), 32-33.

Spirit-Infused Cultures and Contexts

Many Majority World thinkers appreciate that aspects of their cultures and contexts are Spirit infused. The Spirit is present in these cultures, inspiring repentance and renewal, among other things.

These thinkers and practitioners also know that a theology of the Spirit must be contextual. It must be relevant to its setting if it is to align with what the Spirit of Christ is doing there.

Veli-Matti Kärkkäinen acknowledges this. He dedicates a third of his book *The Spirit in the World* to "The Spirit Among Cultures."[32] In that section, Asian and African thinkers describe the relationships between renewalist theology and practice and cultural diversity. Paulson Pulikottil considers native Pentecostalism in Kerala, India. Koo Dong Yun examines Minjung thought and Asian Pentecostalism. Deidre Helen Crumbley studies gender and Afro-Christian renewalist churches. Ogbu U. Kalu considers Pentecostalism and African cultural heritage. All these authors show how the Spirit is present in their cultures and how Christians are responding in context.

Let's consider Yun's treatment of Minjung liberation and Asian Pentecostal theology. Yun notes a recent shift in scholarship examining the origins of global Pentecostalism. Recent scholarship has questioned Americentric descriptions of the origins of Pentecostalism, which usually trace Pentecostalism's origins to the Azusa-related churches. Today it is becoming more common to trace Pentecostalism in Asia and Africa to different origins. Scholars note origins within those cultures that predate the arrival of the Azusa-related missionaries.

Westerners often entertain a flawed notion about the origins of global Pentecostalism by believing that America is the main birthplace of the global Pentecostal-charismatic movement. Yun writes, "I want to refute this kind of narrow, colonial, egotistical, Western definition of Pentecostalism and try to reinterpret Pentecostalism from an Asian *minjung* perspective. . . . From the very beginning, modern (or twentieth-century) Pentecostalism has been multicultural and global."[33]

---

[32]Veli-Matti Kärkkäinen, *The Spirit in the World: Emerging Pentecostal Theologies in Global Contexts* (Grand Rapids: Eerdmans, 2009). Kärkkäinen also deals with contextual pneumatologies in chap. 6 of *Pneumatology: The Holy Spirit in Ecumenical, International, and Contextual Perspective* (Grand Rapids: Baker Academic, 2002). He covers process, liberation, ecological, feminist and African contextual pneumatologies.

[33]Kärkkäinen, *Spirit in the World*, 91.

Minjung is a collective noun. It refers to a group of people who are marginalized, victimized, oppressed and exploited. Yun says it is difficult to translate the meanings of *minjung* well into English. Even so, "A theological translation of *minjung* refers to *the people of God* who do not possess political power, economic wealth, social status, and advanced education in contrast to the wealthy and dominant class."[34]

In that sense, minjung transcends culture, gender and nationality. We can apply the concept in non-Korean settings. For example, Yun considers the Azusa Revival in America a "black *minjung* movement." He shows how Pentecostalism took hold in poor and marginalized cultures across the globe. It had a natural home among minjung groups worldwide, including South Korea.[35]

There are many examples of contextually shaped theologies of the Spirit in the Majority World. I detail examples from Africa, Asia, Latin America and indigenous cultures in another chapter of this book.[36]

Western churches cannot duplicate these indigenous, contextualized expressions. As Western Christians, we need to find fresh, innovative ways to contextualize our theology of the Spirit. At the same time, we need to notice where the Spirit is already at work in our cultures and contexts. How is the Spirit meeting people in our context? How do we engage in Spirit-empowered mission?

SPIRIT-EMPOWERED MISSION

What is the shape of Spirit-empowered mission in Western contexts? How do we contextualize Western theologies of the Spirit for our own cultures? How do we contextualize these theologies for the sake of the mission of Jesus Christ?

---

[34]Ibid., 95.
[35]Ibid., 114.
[36]See for example Peter Olufiropo Awoniyi, "Charismatic Movements' Appropriation of Indigenous Spirituality in Nigeria," *Ogbomoso Journal of Theology* 13, no. 2 (2008); Henri Paul Pierre Gooren, "The Pentecostalization of Religion and Society in Latin America," *Exchange* 39, no. 4 (2010); Brian Grim, "Pentecostalism's Growth in Religiously Restricted Environments," *Society* 46, no. 6 (2009): 484; Akiko Ono, "You Gotta Throw Away Culture Once You Become Christian: How 'Culture' Is Redefined Among Aboriginal Pentecostal Christians in Rural New South Wales," *Oceania* 82, no. 1 (2012): 74; Malcolm Calley, "Pentecostalism Among the Bandjalang," in *Aborigines Now*, ed. Marie Reay (Sydney: Angus and Robertson, 1965); John Mansford Prior, "The Challenge of the Pentecostals in Asia: Part One, Pentecostal Movements in Asia," *Exchange* 36, no. 1 (2007); Prior, "The Challenge of the Pentecostals in Asia: Part Two, the Responses of the Roman Catholic Church," *Exchange* 36, no. 2 (2007).

These are not easy questions. But the answers are important for Spirit-empowered mission in Western settings. Why is Spirit-empowered mission important in the West? Today, many Westerners find spirituality and the spiritual world fascinating.

The religion and society think tank Theos recently released some important research. It indicated how interested the British are in the spiritual world. Spirit-empowered mission has never been more important. Here are some key findings from Theos's research:

> For all that formalized religious belief and institutionalized religious belonging has declined over recent decades, the British have not become a nation of atheists or materialists. On the contrary, a spiritual current runs as, if not more, powerfully through the nation than it once did. Over three-quarters of all adults (77%) and three fifths (61%) of non-religious people believe that "there are things in life that we simply cannot explain through science or any other means." A majority of people (59%) are believers in the existence of some kind of spiritual being. 30% believe in God "as a universal life force." 30% believe in spirits. 25% believe in angels. And 12% believe in "a higher spiritual being that can't be called God." More than half of people—52%—think spiritual forces have some influence either on earth, in influencing people's thoughts, events in the human world, or events in the natural world.

This research goes on to say,

> Two in five people (38%) think prayer could heal people. Compare this with 50% who think it cannot. Remarkably, a sixth, or 16%, of people say that they or someone they knew had "experienced what [they] would call a miracle." Younger respondents are consistently more likely to say this than older ones. Overall, spiritual beliefs are not the preserve of the elderly, who might be more inclined towards them on account of having grown up in a more religious culture. Such beliefs are to be found across the age ranges. Moreover, spiritual beliefs are clearly not the preserve of the "religious." Such beliefs are to be found across religious and non-religious groups. But those who consider themselves to belong to a religious group are more likely to hold such beliefs and practices.[37]

---

[37]Theos, "The Spirit of Things Unseen: Belief in Post-Religious Britain" (London: Theos, 2013), www.theosthinktank.co.uk/publications/2013/10/17/the-spirit-of-things-unseen-belief-in-post-religious-britain, 7-9.

Majority World, indigenous and Western cultures are spiritual contexts. Doing mission in them requires the power of the Spirit.

The Spirit *propels* the church into mission. He empowers it for the mission of God. The church is dependent on the Spirit's presence in its mission.

The Spirit *precedes* the church's mission. He is active and present in the cultures and peoples of the world. He is preparing the soil for the missional efforts and gospel proclamation of the church.

The Spirit is *present* in the mission of the church. He enables the church to take part in the *missio Dei*.

The Spirit *prevails* even where the church can no longer be present. He prevails even when the church has had to withdraw from a culture or people or when the church is not present anymore. The Spirit continues God's sovereign purposes in the world.

The Spirit *persists* in convicting hearts, transforming lives and confronting principalities and powers. He leads toward repentance and discipleship to Jesus Christ. The Spirit does this *before* the church arrives, *while* the church is on mission and even *after* the church has withdrawn.

A missional theology of the Spirit does not minimize the importance of the church in mission. But it does frame this mission with attention to the sovereign and powerful work of the Spirit.

The Spirit is the fulfillment of God's promise. The Spirit is his life-giving breath, power-in-weakness and personal presence. The Spirit is his assurance of what is to come. God empowers the church's proclamation and action through the Spirit. The Spirit guides the church into the kind of witness that is only possible through holiness, unity, catholicity and apostolicity. The Spirit distributes his supernatural gifts for the edification of the church. The Spirit gives these gifts for the glorification of Jesus Christ. And the Spirit pours out these gifts to enable bold and passionate and effective witness.

The church and its mission are dependent on the Spirit, who creates, fills and empowers it.[38]

What do we learn from Majority World churches about Spirit-empowered mission? What are the missional characteristics of these Majority World renewalist churches?

---

[38]Hill, *Salt, Light, and a City*, 226-27.

Ma and Ma provide the most thorough treatment of these questions. Stephen Bevans calls their book *Mission in the Spirit* a "*summa missiologiae pentecostalis.*"[39] These Korean scholars assert that empowerment, creation, eschatology and practices characterize Majority World Spirit-empowered mission.

1. Empowerment. "For Pentecostal theology, the most influential theological ground [for Christian mission] is its theology of empowerment, often anchored on the unique experience called baptism in the Holy Spirit."[40] Renewalist mission emphasizes supernatural empowerment. It seeks Spirit-emboldened witness and focuses on divine gifts of healing. It longs for the Spirit to provide supernatural power and deliverance and restoration.

2. Creation. A Spirit-empowered mission includes a theology of creation. This is because mission is the "restoration of God's creation." The Spirit of creation calls the church to a Spirit-empowered restoration of the whole creation. A theology of creation places mission at "the center of God's activity in human history." Creation theology shapes the church's mission, which must seek to restore all creation, and leads to a mission that addresses *anticreation* in human cultures. Anticreation includes injustice, poverty, oppression, exploitation and so forth. Creation theology sees mission as the restoration of human and divine/human community.[41]

3. Eschatology. Eschatology is the study of the "last or end times," when Jesus Christ returns and restores and reigns. All Spirit-empowered mission

> is an attempt to bring a "foretaste" of kingdom life through proclamation, serving, and miracles. . . . Pentecostals have an understanding that the advent of the Spirit in the modern times is the sign of the beginning of the end of the end of time, *vis-à-vis* the first outpouring of the Spirit being the beginning of the end. Consequently their mission engagement should be the expression of their eschatological conviction.[42]

4. Practices. Ma and Ma say that Majority World Christians express Spirit-empowered mission through a wide range of practices. What are some of those practices? Here's a snapshot. They democratize ministry—the whole

---

[39]Julie C. Ma and Wonsuk Ma, *Mission in the Spirit: Towards a Pentecostal/Charismatic Missiology* (Eugene, OR: Wipf and Stock, 2010), back cover.
[40]Ibid., 27.
[41]Ibid., 18-27.
[42]Ibid., 27.

community participates in mission and ministry. Their missional zeal and commitment is palpable—passion for mission is a primary characteristic of many of these churches. They are willing to suffer considerable personal loss for the sake of mission. They link mission with healing and miracles and the supernatural. Renewalist churches grow through missional planting and innovation. Gospel proclamation, power evangelism, indigenous leadership, prayer and continual reproduction characterize this church planting and missional innovation. Such reproduction happens through the multiplication of disciples and churches.

Other practices are evident in Spirit-empowered mission in the Majority World. Pastors expect Holy Spirit manifestations to go with their preaching. (This includes divine healing, speaking in tongues, miracles and wonders, prophecy and other manifestations.) Missionaries expect to have power encounters with angels and demons. Spirit-empowered mission has a particular focus on spiritual warfare and deliverance from evil. This mission prioritizes *both* inner change and societal transformation. It emphasizes *both* evangelism and social concern. Spirit-empowered mission in the Majority World adapts its expressions and mission to indigenous contexts. It often pursues ecumenical, interracial cooperation and leadership. It's characterized by local, regional and global networking in mission. It integrates Spirit-empowered mission into ministry training and theological curriculum. This integration is central to theological and ministry education in Majority World renewalist churches. And such Spirit-empowered mission engages with other religious, spiritual and secular worldviews. (In Asia, this is especially animism, Buddhism, Confucianism, Hinduism, Islam and secular perspectives.) It has also become more common for such mission to address the plight of women and girls in the Majority World. These face degeneration, violence, rape cultures and poor educational opportunities.

So much can be said about the practices of Spirit-empowered mission in the Majority World. It's mission that's characterized by enthusiastic, spontaneous, participatory, experiential and community-centered worship, prayer and spirituality. Yes, that's a mouthful. But this defining feature of renewalist churches is key to their missional vitality.[43]

---

[43]Ibid., 8-9, 49-58, 65-272; Julie C. Ma, "Pentecostalism and Asian Mission," *Missiology* 35, no. 1 (2007): 32-34.

Anderson examines Pentecostal-charismatic churches and missions in the Majority World and lists the missional practices of Spirit-empowered churches. He says that they practice Spirit-centered mission. They embrace dynamic and contextual missional forms, focus on evangelism and church planting, and shape contextualized missional leadership. They throw enormous energy into mobilization in (and for) mission. And often pre-millennial and dispensational eschatology goes with such mission—that is, a belief in the imminent return of Christ that inspires passionate mission. Mission among Majority World renewalist churches is often pragmatic and contextual, addressing issues like "sickness, poverty, unemployment, loneliness, evil spirits, and sorcery."[44]

What does all this mean for the global church?

Yong writes that the global church must develop a Spirit-centered theology and practice of mission. This missional theology and practice must (1) deal with its "social and political locations." This includes its relationship to Christendom, colonialism and Pentecostalism. (2) It must depend "on the church being a body of Spirit-empowered people who embody and invite an alternative way of being in the world." This is crucial—especially if this Spirit-centered theology and practice is to be post-Christendom, postcolonial and Spirit-focused. (3) And it must develop attention to the many cultural, ethnic and other voices and "practices of the Spirit-filled people of God." That way it remains dialogical, dispersed, multicultural and multivoiced.[45]

Ghanaian pastor Opoku Onyinah writes about the extraordinary growth of renewalist churches in Africa. He describes Spirit-centered and Spirit-empowered foundations for mission. Onyinah says that the Holy Spirit "is a missionary Spirit. He is the motivating force behind every activity that the believer undertakes. The climax of his work in the believer is baptism in the Holy Spirit, whose main purpose is to witness for Christ."[46]

We can learn from what these Majority World writers have to say about

---

[44]Allan Anderson, "Towards a Pentecostal Missiology for the Majority World," *Asian Journal of Pentecostal Studies* 8, no. 1 (2005); Anderson, *Introduction to Pentecostalism*, chap. 11.

[45]Amos Yong, "Many Tongues, Many Practices," in *Mission After Christendom: Emergent Themes in Contemporary Mission*, ed. Ogbu Kalu, Peter Vethanayagamony and Edmund Chia (Louisville: Westminster, 2010), 43-58.

[46]Opoku Onyinah, "Pneumatological Foundations for Mission: From a Pentecostal Perspective," *International Review of Mission* 101, no. 2 (2012): 334.

Spirit-empowered mission. This is a dynamic picture of mission. It's clearly Spirit-empowered. It's unmistakable that God is moving through this. And the Western church needs to listen and learn.

The role of the church is to join with the Spirit of Christ in his mission. This participation includes the liberation of individuals, people groups, societies and creation. We join with the Spirit in restoration and healing and salvation.

THE SPIRIT AND LIBERATION

Renewalist churches in the Majority World are not always interested in socio-political matters. Many focus on proclamation evangelism and personal salvation. But there is a growing global trend for renewalist Christians to focus on both evangelism and social action. These renewalists ask an important question: What might it mean to address issues of justice, liberation, poverty, and social action in the power of the Spirit?[47]

Chilean theologian Juan Sepulveda serves as an example. He compares indigenous Latin American Pentecostal communities and liberation theology. He especially focuses on Base Ecclesial Communities (BECs). Sepulveda describes how each may learn from the other. They both engage in Spirit-empowered service with and among the poor and are both at home among the poor and marginalized. They both encourage a direct encounter with the Spirit. And they both make the Christian Scriptures accessible to ordinary readers.

Both types of communities see the church as a healing presence in the world. They believe the Spirit empowers the church for mission, justice, restoration and healing. So while Pentecostalism tends to focus on the Spirit and BECs on liberation, there are many points of connection. The cross-pollination between the two is resulting in richer forms of mission and church and social action.[48]

---

[47]See, for instance, Hollenweger, *Pentecostalism*, 208; Anderson, *Introduction to Pentecostalism*, chap. 14; Douglas Petersen, *Not by Might, nor by Power: A Pentecostal Theology of Social Concern in Latin America* (Eugene, OR: Wipf and Stock, 2012); M. M. Thomas, "The Holy Spirit and the Spirituality for Political Struggles," *Ecumenical Review* 42, nos. 3/4 (1990); Katy Attanasi, "Getting in Step with the Spirit: Applying Pentecostal Commitments to HIV/AIDS in South Africa," *Political Theology* 9, no. 2 (2008); Marthinus L. Daneel, "African Independent Church Pneumatology and the Salvation of All Creation," *International Review of Mission* 82, no. 326 (1993): 153-58.

[48]Juan Sepulveda, "Pentecostalism and Liberation Theology: Two Manifestations of the Work of the Spirit for the Renewal of the Church," in *All Together in One Place: Theological Papers from the*

José Comblin describes the relationship between the Holy Spirit and liberation. Comblin was known throughout Latin America for his sharp theological mind and his service among the poor. Military dictatorships expelled him from Brazil and Chile for his views. He died in 2011 and was buried in a small town in the impoverished Brazilian state of Paraíba, which is also in the state of Bahía where he lived. Comblin was a passionate defender of human rights. He proclaimed Jesus' option for the poor and complemented his defense of liberation theology with his vigorous opposition to military dictatorships. Comblin served tirelessly among poor peasant communities in northeastern Brazil.

Comblin's best-known book is *The Holy Spirit and Liberation*. He argues that renewal in the Spirit leads to service among the poor and marginalized and oppressed. The outpouring of the Spirit can have many manifestations. This includes the renewal of worship, the charismatic gifts and proclamation of the gospel. But compassion, justice and mercy also flow from any true renewal in the Spirit.

The Spirit leads us into service among and with the poor, wounded, broken, forgotten and oppressed. In the words of Jesus, "The Spirit of the Lord is on me, because he has anointed me to proclaim good news to the poor. He has sent me to proclaim freedom for the prisoners and recovery of sight for the blind, to set the oppressed free, to proclaim the year of the Lord's favor" (Lk 4:18-19).

Comblin says the Spirit is liberating all creation—not just the church or individuals. The church's mission is to cooperate with the Spirit in his work of new creation. The Spirit invites us to join him in making new creations of all things. This includes persons, churches, cultures, creation and history. The church does this best when it is self-giving and dispersed and serving.

Brighton Conference on World Evangelization, ed. Harold D. Hunter and Peter D. Hocken (Sheffield: Sheffield Academic, 1993), 53-62. See the following on the similarities and differences and cross-fertilization between Latin American Pentecostalism and Base Ecclesial Communities: Charles E. Self, "Conscientization, Conversion, and Convergence: Reflections on Base Communities and Emerging Pentecostalism in Latin America," *Pneuma* 14, no. 1 (1992); Michael Bergunder, Ralph Woodhall and Allan H. Anderson, "The Pentecostal Movement and Basic Ecclesial Communities in Latin America: Sociological Theories and Theological Debates," *International Review of Mission* 91, no. 361 (2002); Adoniram Gaxiola, "Poverty as a Meeting and Parting Place: Similarities and Contrasts in the Experiences of Latin American Pentecostalisms and Ecclesial Base Communities," *Pneuma* 13, no. 2 (1991).

Comblin comes to the following conclusions about the Holy Spirit, justice and liberation:

The Spirit in focus: Western churches have given too little attention to the Spirit. "There was one Easter; there are millions of Pentecosts."[49]

The Spirit in the church: The global Pentecostal phenomenon is God's renewal of the church. It calls the church away from a materialistic, "rationalized, intellectualized, and institutionalized" existence. It calls the church to a living and transforming experience and community.[50]

The Spirit in the world: The Spirit is at work in the world. He calls the church to join with him. The Spirit is ushering in resurrection life, the kingdom of God, the new creation and "the birth of a new humanity." And we get to take part in this mission![51]

The Spirit and the poor: The Spirit is among the poor and their struggle and liberation. As the church recognizes and celebrates this it experiences a just and Christlike spirituality.

> The Holy Spirit lies at the root of the cry of the poor. The Spirit is the strength of those who have no strength. It leads the struggle for the emancipation and fulfillment of the people of the oppressed. . . .
>
> The signs of the action of the Spirit in the world are clear: the Spirit is present wherever the poor are awakened to action, to freedom, to speaking out, to community, to life. . . .
>
> A new spirituality is being born under the impulse of the Spirit, among elites placing themselves at the service of the poor, and among the poor themselves who are irrupting on to the stage of history.[52]

Many Majority World theologians challenge us to see the connection between our theologies of liberation, justice and Spirit. These include Sepulveda, Comblin, Marthinus L. Daneel, Katy Attanasi and M. M. Thomas. They do not minimize Spirit-filled worship and spirituality. After all, these

---

[49]José Comblin, *The Holy Spirit and Liberation*, Theology and Liberation Series (Maryknoll, NY: Orbis, 1989), 184. This shouldn't take away from the uniqueness of the first Pentecost. Reading Acts shows that Pentecost was itself a major unique point in salvation history and part of a "parcel" of unique events (cross-resurrection-ascension-pouring out) that pivot salvation history out into the Gentiles, with Pentecost unfolding in its threefold stages of Jerusalem, Judea/Samaria and all the earth (Acts 2; 8; 10).

[50]Ibid.

[51]Ibid., 185.

[52]Ibid., 184-86.

are hallmarks of Pentecostal-charismatic faith. But they do assert that a true experience of the Spirit leads to Spirit-empowered social action and concern.

SPIRIT-FILLED WORSHIP AND SPIRITUALITY

What can the Western church learn from renewalist worship and spirituality in the Majority World?

I'll begin with worship and move on to spirituality.

Certain features characterize renewalist worship in Asia, Africa, Latin America and indigenous settings. The importance and shape of each feature will vary according to context.

Many Majority World congregations embrace renewalist expressions as "normal Christianity." What Westerners consider "Pentecostal," "over the top" or "ecstatic" they see as ordinary faith.

Immediately following this chapter, I provide a detailed list of the features of Spirit-centered worship and renewalist spirituality. (See tables 6.1 and 6.2.) I encourage you to read through those two tables carefully. In them I provide a brief description and questions to help you explore the implications for your church and ministry.

Chan provides a thorough treatment of Pentecostal-charismatic worship and spirituality.[53] He shows how contemplative, social, Word-centered and charismatic spiritualities can come together. These four spiritualities come together in Spirit-graced dialogue and Spirit-enabled *practices*. These practices are many. They include contemplative and self-examining prayer. They incorporate the art of "practicing the presence of God." They also include spiritual reading, biblical meditation and spiritual friendship. To these we can add social action, spiritual direction and corporate and individual discernment.

The Spirit leads the church into complementary spiritual practices and dialogue.[54]

SPIRIT-GRACED CONVERSATIONS

Renewalist churches do not always value conversation with other groups.

---

[53]Chan, *Pentecostal Theology*; Chan, *Liturgical Theology*; Chan, *Spiritual Theology: A Systematic Study of the Christian Life* (Downers Grove, IL: InterVarsity Press, 1998), chap. 2; Chan, "Restoring the Foundation: A Trinitarian Spirituality," in *Burleigh Conference* (Adelaide: Burleigh Baptist Seminary, 2003).

[54]Chan, *Spiritual Theology*, part two.

Suspicion of other groups was a defining feature of the Pentecostalism I experienced in my twenties.

But renewalist churches have a long history of positive ecumenical and interreligious engagement. Walter Hollenweger outlines "four phases of ecumenical development" in Pentecostalism. Through these phases, Pentecostal churches return to their original ecumenical roots.[55]

Timothy Tennent describes how Latin American Pentecostals have rediscovered the value of ecumenical cooperation and notes their positive contribution to ecumenical spirituality and mission. "The term [ecumenical] has come full circle to refer to the emergence of global Christianity of which we (despite our various denominations) are all participants."[56]

This emerging unity is not based on an *identical theology*. Unity emerges through a *shared passion* for Jesus Christ and his body, mission, kingdom and Spirit.

Pentecostal-charismatic theologians and pastors are influencing the global ecumenical movement. The World Council of Churches (WCC) 2005 Athens conference is an example. The conference ran with the theme, "Come, Holy Spirit, Heal and Reconcile." This gathering considered global and ecumenical mission from a Spirit-centered perspective: "We call on God the Spirit to heal, reconcile and empower us so that, as individuals and communities, we may become and share signs of peace, forgiveness, justice and unity, and renounce hatred, violence, injustice and divisions."[57]

There is a growing ecumenical drive among Majority World renewalists. This involves conversation with other Christian groups and religious faiths and worldviews.[58]

Koo Dong Yun and Grace Si-Jun Kim are examples of this interreligious and ecumenical conversation. Yun constructs an elaborate ecumenical theology of Spirit baptism. He develops his theology of Spirit baptism in con-

---

[55]Hollenweger, *Pentecostalism*, 334-87; Allan H. Anderson and Walter J. Hollenweger, eds., *Pentecostals After a Century: Global Perspectives on a Movement in Transition* (Sheffield: Sheffield Academic, 1999), 186-88.

[56]Timothy C. Tennent, *Theology in the Context of World Christianity: How the Global Church Is Influencing the Way We Think About and Discuss Theology* (Grand Rapids: Zondervan, 2007), 184-89.

[57]Conference on World Mission and Evangelism, www.mission2005.org.

[58]This is illustrated in the writings of Grace Si-Jun Kim (Korean), Wonsuk Ma and Julie C. Ma (Korean), Amos Yong (Malaysian born Asian American), Koo Dong Yun (Korean), Hwa Yung (Malaysian) and others.

versation with nine theologians, including Karl Barth. Yun believes that a deep understanding and experience of Spirit baptism requires conversation. It requires dialogue with different cultures, spiritual experiences and theological traditions.[59] Kim believes that we need a "global understanding of the Spirit." This results from authentic conversation. Kim believes that we need to listen to others as we develop a theology of the Spirit.[60]

Yong is prolific on this topic. No one else makes such a contribution to "a Pentecostal-charismatic Christian theology of religions." Yong believes that the church, empowered by the Spirit, must engage other religions.

Here are seven of Yong's key assertions:

1. A pneumatological theology of religions. We need a "robust pneumatological theology of religions." How is a theology of religions robust and Spirit-graced? It is robust because of its systematic engagement with trinitarian theology and other worldviews. It is Spirit-graced through its attention to the Spirit in Christian faith and experience. It is robust through "the emergence of a new set of categories that may chart the way forward." It is Spirit-graced through its attention to the Spirit's voice in other faiths.

Yong writes, "In brief, a pneumatological theology of religions begins with the doctrine of the Holy Spirit as the universal presence and activity of God, and attempts to understand the world of the religions within that universal framework."[61]

2. Discernment. We must root our engagement with other religions in trinitarian thought. "The Pentecostal narrative of Acts 2" grounds our discernment. It takes into account all the ways the triune God reveals himself—manifesting his power and presence and voice. God pours his Spirit out "on all flesh" (including the world of religions). "Hence, the pentecostal narrative can be understood to redeem not only human languages and cultures, but also human religiosity. However, just as this does not mean that all human words and all aspects of human culture are holy without qualification, so also it does not mean that all human religiousness is sanctified."[62]

We must learn to discern the voice of the Spirit in those religious tradi-

---

[59]Yun, *Baptism in the Holy Spirit.*
[60]Grace Ji-Sun Kim, "A Global Understanding of the Spirit," *Dialogue & Alliance* 21, no. 2 (2007): 20-21.
[61]Amos Yong, "A P(new)matological Paradigm for Christian Mission in a Religiously Plural World," *Missiology* 33, no. 2 (2005): 175.
[62]Ibid., 177.

tions. This happens through developing sound trinitarian and biblical theology. This Christian theology serves as our foundation. And our discernment increases through prayerful attention to the Spirit in all cultures.
We also need thoughtful guidelines and categories.

3. Guidelines and categories. We need guidelines for discerning the voice of
the Spirit in other religions and cultures and theological traditions. This voice
may challenge our understanding of what the Spirit is doing in the world. Yong
offers guidelines and categories. I won't list them here, but I encourage you to
read his book. Yong says we need "dynamic categories for comprehending the
phenomena of religion and religiosity." We then see "the openness and unfinished character of religious traditions and human religiousness."[63]

4. Moving beyond exclusivism or inclusivism. We need to move beyond
exclusivism (we have the truth and no other religion does). And we need to
reject *inclusivism/pluralism* (everyone has the truth). Instead, we need a
pneumatological theology of religions. This is a discerning engagement with
other religions. The Spirit enables this engagement. And we must shape it
around clear guidelines and categories.

5. Attention to the other. It is important that we hear other religious faiths
on their own terms. We should listen to them as they "define themselves in
their own voices."[64]

6. The middle way. We need to "find a middle way between the Scylla of
subordinating the Spirit to the Word (the perennial failure of the classic
theological tradition) and the Charybdis of disengaging the Spirit from the
Word altogether (the perennial temptation of the tradition of enthusiasm)."[65]

7. Interreligious dialogue. "Christian mission should include both authentic dialogue and sincere proclamation as two sides of the one coin.
Dialogue and proclamation together constitute authentic interreligious engagement (i.e., authentic engagement between individuals from different
religious traditions)."[66] This dialogue, if it is authentic, will lead to "con-

---

[63]Ibid., 179; Yong, *Beyond the Impasse: Toward a Pneumatological Theology of Religions* (Grand
   Rapids: Baker Academic, 2003), 21. Yong defines those categories carefully in this book.
[64]Amos Yong, "Beyond Beyond the Impasse? Responding to Dale Irvin," *Journal of Pentecostal Theology* 12, no. 2 (2004): 281.
[65]Ibid.
[66]Yong, "P(new)matological Paradigm for Christian Mission," 182. This article is Yong's most
   concise summary of his thought.

version to the other." This does not mean abandoning Christ or his gospel. But it does mean that all dialogue partners open themselves up to the transforming, converting work of the Spirit.

As we discern the Spirit in this interreligious dialogue, he transforms us. He renews us spiritually, theologically, relationally and morally. Our Christian faith experiences the benefit of the cross-fertilization of religions.

The Spirit guides us into constructive conversations between various religious faiths. The Spirit leads toward constructive, healthy cooperation between Christian traditions.

People like Samuel Solivan are working to construct a Pentecostal approach to interreligious dialogue.[67] We may not embrace all the perspectives of people like Kim, Solivan, Yong or Yun. But they do give us a window into a burgeoning conversation in the Majority World and beyond. They show us the characteristics and concerns of this conversation.

Clark Pinnock writes, "One might expect the Pentecostals to develop a Spirit-oriented theology of mission and world religions, because of their openness to religious experience, their sensitivity to the oppressed of the Third World where they have experienced much of their growth, and their awareness of the ways of the Spirit as well as dogma."[68]

SPIRIT, ATONEMENT AND HEALING

In 2013, I presented at a Baptist theological conference focused on the Holy Spirit. The conference theme was *In Step with the Spirit*. The Baptist World Alliance held it in Ocho Rios, Jamaica. Participants came from all over the world. Presenters came from Australia, Canada, Jamaica, Nigeria, Romania, the Philippines and the United States. The organizers gave me the topic "The Atonement and Healing." They gave me this theme for a specific reason—the emphasis on atonement and healing in the Majority World.

I came to a personal faith in Jesus Christ in my late teens. Having grown up in a Reformed, Free Church, congregational church, I made a decision to follow Jesus in an Australian Pentecostal church. I embraced the biblical

---

[67]Samuel Solivan, "Interreligious Dialogue: An Hispanic American Pentecostal Perspective," in *Grounds for Understanding: Ecumenical Responses to Religious Pluralism*, ed. S. Mark Heim (Grand Rapids: Eerdmans, 1998).

[68]C. H. Pinnock, *Flame of Love: A Theology of the Holy Spirit* (Downers Grove, IL: InterVarsity Press, 1996), 274.

foundations of my childhood and the spiritual enthusiasm of Pentecostalism. Then in my early twenties, I experienced a spiritual crisis.

The Pentecostal church I attended taught that God guarantees physical healing in the atonement. God will heal all those who have enough faith. This church told me that the following things guarantee healing: (1) the personal faith of the sick person; (2) the faith of the believing congregation; (3) the spiritual gift of the charismatic leader; (4) the atoning work of Jesus Christ; and (5) the biblical guarantee of present physical healing. Even as a young person, I struggled with this theology. I could not reconcile this theology with Scripture, modern medicine and human experience.

Then in the early 1990s, two Pentecostal Christian leaders I knew died from cancer in the same year. Both of them were certain that God would heal them from their cancer in this life. I watched as their congregations tried to make sense of their deaths (which were at complete odds with their theology). And I decided that I would allow Scripture to speak for itself. I began to investigate the biblical relationship between the atonement and physical healing.

Some Pentecostal and neo-Pentecostal and Charismatic movements have linked physical healing with the atonement. They do this by appealing to Isaiah 53:4-6, Matthew 8:16-17 and 1 Peter 2:24. This is common in the Majority World. This theology has also influenced evangelical and Free Church and mainline Protestant churches. This is especially the case in the Majority World and among churches with charismatic leanings.

There have been rigorous debates around the associated theological and biblical and pastoral issues. On one end of the spectrum are those who believe that God guarantees physical healing in the atonement (e.g., A. B. Simpson, Kenneth Hagin and Kenneth and Gloria Copeland). At the other end are those who reject any such notion. This latter group focuses on the way the atonement deals with sin (e.g., B. B. Warfield, Merrill F. Unger, John MacArthur and Richard Mayhue).

There is, of course, a long tradition of linking *healing* with the *atonement* with variations on what groups mean by both terms. Roman Catholic theologians often have healing at the center of their view of atonement. The patristic era produced atonement theories that were healing based. (To call them theories may be overstating the case.) This is also true of Eastern

Orthodox theology—*theosis* being the key lens for such treatments. *Theosis* is the theology of spiritual and holistic healing and transformation. Christians experience this transformation in union with God and the attainment of his likeness. *Theosis* has three main stages: (1) purification of body and mind (*catharsis*), (2) spiritual contemplation and illumination (*theoria*), and (3) union with and likeness of God found in sainthood (*theosis*).

Other theologians link spiritual healing and the atonement. These include Athanasius, Clement, Irenaeus and Origen.

Why is this theology emphasized in renewalist churches in the Majority World?

The answer to this question resides in the physical sickness and impoverishment in so much of the developing world. Such an emphasis also emerges from the focus on divine spiritual encounter in Pentecostal-charismatic churches. There is a heightened attention to the spiritual, metaphysical realm in the Majority World. And the eschatology of these renewalist churches leads to a focus on present-day healings and deliverance. Finally, this theology grants some sense of control and influence to people who feel powerless.

So what do we make of the focus on the atonement and physical healing in many renewalist churches in the Majority World?[69] There isn't space here to examine the key passages (Is 53:4-6; Mt 8:14-17; 1 Pet 2:21-25). When we examine these texts, we arrive at a clear conclusion. The atonement includes the possibility of physical healing in the present. But we can't demand it "any more than we have the right and power to demand our resurrection bodies."[70] It is only in the age to come that we are completely healed and receive our promised resurrection bodies.

Inaugural eschatology affirms that the kingdom of God has *present* and *future* dimensions. The end is already here. The kingdom is already inaugurated through the life and death and resurrection of Jesus Christ. But we are yet to experience the final consummation. It is *now but not yet*. The person and work of Jesus Christ brought the ultimate future reality into the present. He demonstrated the *current presence* of the kingdom in his life and death

---

[69]I first published these thoughts on healing and atonement here: Graham Hill, "The Atonement and Healing: Wrestling with a Contemporary Issue," *The Pacific Journal of Baptist Research* 8, no. 1 (2013).

[70]Donald A. Carson, *Matthew*, The Expositor's Bible Commentary (Grand Rapids: Zondervan, 1995), 207.

and resurrection. But it is only in the *final consummation* that all disease, suffering, conflict and death end (Rev 21:4).

Because the kingdom is *present*, God heals believers from their sin and unrighteousness. He also heals them physically on occasion. Because the kingdom is *future*, our ultimate physical healing, like our resurrected bodies, awaits the final and decisive reality.

The life and message and resurrection of Jesus witnesses to this present and future healing. So we are "confidently restless." We wait for the final restoration of all things—including our bodies.

We can associate bodily healing with the atonement just as we can link every other blessing promised by God. People experience divine healing on occasions. We can relate this to Christ's atonement for our sins. But "God has not seen fit to shower us with all physical blessings now in the way he has with spiritual blessings (Eph 1:3); we await the final consummation of God's redemptive plan, and this is our 'blessed hope'—the glorious appearing of our great God and Savior, Jesus Christ (Titus 2:13)."[71]

THE SPIRIT AND THE GLOBALCHURCH: CONCLUDING REFLECTIONS

The Spirit of Christ is sovereign over the global church's past, present and future.

God has tied the future of the global church to the worldwide emergence of renewalist movements.[72] The West can learn much from the growth of the Pentecostal and renewalist churches in the Majority World. The West

---

[71]W. Kelly Bokovay, "The Relationship of Physical Healing to the Atonement," *Didaskalia* 3, no. 1 (1991): 37.

[72]These renewalist churches face many challenges. Vinay Samuel writes of their need to deal with questions of Christian unity, sociopolitical injustice, Christian ethics, religious plurality and faith in the public square. Other writers speak of the need for renewalist churches to address the issues associated with "health and wealth" doctrines (the "prosperity gospel"). Samuel, "Pentecostalism as a Global Culture," in *The Globalization of Pentecostalism*, ed. Murray W. Dempster, Byron D. Klaus and Douglas Petersen (Oxford: Regnum, 1999); Joe Maxwell and Isaac Phiri, "Gospel Riches: Africa's Rapid Embrace of Prosperity Pentecostalism Provokes Concern—and Hope," *Christianity Today* 51, no. 7 (2007); Ma Wonsuk, "David Yonggi Cho's Theology of Blessing: Basis, Legitimacy, and Limitations," *Evangelical Review of Theology* 35, no. 2 (2011); Milton Acosta, "Power Pentecostalisms: The 'Non-Catholic' Latin American Church Is Going Full Steam Ahead—but Are We on the Right Track?," *Christianity Today* 53, no. 8 (2009); Allan H. Anderson, "The Newer Pentecostal and Charismatic Churches: The Shape of Future Christianity in Africa?," *Pneuma* 24, no. 2 (2002); J. Kwabena Asamoah-Gyadu, "Did Jesus Wear Designer Robes? The Gospel Preached in Africa's New Pentecostal Churches Ends Up Leaving the Poor More Impoverished Than Ever," *Christianity Today* 53, no. 11 (2009).

can learn from renewalist emphases, worship, spirituality, contextualization, mission and challenges.

Here are ten things we learn from how Majority World Christians embrace the Spirit:

1. Spirit-empowered Christians depend on the power, presence and provision of the Spirit. In the West, we tend to rely too heavily on our resources and finances. We trust our programs, academic training, conferences and personalities. As I travel through Majority World and First Nation cultures, I notice a striking thing, repeatedly. They often have few resources and little money. But they depend on the Spirit for provision, empowerment and mission. Their dependency is evident in their corporate prayer and expectant worship. It shows in their confrontation of the principalities and powers of this world (Eph 6:12). It's revealed in their courageous witness. And the fruit is abundant—fruit that will last.

2. Spirit-empowered Christians develop their mission and attention to the Spirit simultaneously.[73] For too long, a focus on the way the Spirit forms the church and empowers it for mission has been (mostly) absent from Western missional conversations. And for too long renewalist churches have overestimated the missional value of charismatic expressions. They haven't been attentive to the insights of missiology.

It's time for this to change. We need a theology of the Spirit that's focused on the mission of God. And we need a theology of mission that's shaped through attention to God's empowering presence.

In the Majority World, Spirit-empowerment and mission are inextricable. Let's make this so in the West too. It's imperative that we live as Spirit-empowered missionary communities. We do this as we examine our theology and practices of empowerment, Spirit, mission, creation care, the end times, justice, peacemaking and so forth. As Yong says, Spirit-centered mission is conversational, dispersed, multicultural and multivoiced.[74]

Michael Frost challenges us to see the place of the Spirit in mission. It's time we rediscovered (1) the Spirit in dialogue, (2) the Spirit beyond the church, (3) the Spirit within the local congregation, (4) the Spirit and justice, (5) the Spirit and creation and (6) the Spirit and the world. Elsewhere I've

---

[73]We need a *missional pneumatology* and a *pneumatological mission*.

[74]Yong, "Many Tongues, Many Practices," 43-58.

written that the missional church recovers (1) its Spirit-constituted being, (2) its Spirit-filled structures, (3) its Spirit-formed communities, (4) its Spirit-shaped theology, (5) its presence within a Spirit-infused world and (6) its Spirit-empowered mission.[75]

3. Spirit-empowered Christians invite the Spirit to empower them for ministry, mission and life. The Spirit of Jesus moves us to foster spiritual expectation. He empowers us for ministry and mission and life. We must be open to "the invasion of the Spirit" and to encounter with him. Do we desire Jesus to reveal himself through the ordinary moments of life and through the miraculous, surprising and unexpected? Do we long for the Spirit of Christ to fill us with power for faith and mission? Do we expect Jesus to reveal his holiness, power, love and truth in every aspect of our lives, mission and gathered worship? Are we content with a powerless Christianity? Or are we actively seeking God's empowering presence?

4. Spirit-empowered Christians believe the Spirit fills their entire life together and on mission. And they recover the supernatural power of the Spirit. We should invite the Spirit's presence in our sacraments, ministries, missions and structures. More than that, we must see how the Spirit forms, animates and sanctifies these things for the glory of God the Father. Jesus promised to fill us with the Holy Spirit and power. And we should expect that in every dimension of our service, worship, mission and life together. (At the same time, of course, we recognize our frailties and faults.)

We must commit to the recovery of the supernatural in our worship and mission and prayer. This means inviting the signs and wonders of the Holy Spirit into our theological frameworks and ministry training and inviting this power into our gathered worship and organizational structures and mission in the world. We need to recover the supernatural power of the Spirit in our churches, worship and mission (with contextual and cultural sensitivity).

5. Spirit-empowered Christians bring liberation, healing, justice, mercy and hope in the power of the Spirit. Jesus leads us to seek Spirit-enabled reconciliation and healing in the world. When God pours out his Spirit he renews worship and empowers mission. And he releases the charismatic gifts and emboldens gospel proclamation.

---

[75]Frost in Barker, *Following Fire*, 33-41; Hill, *Salt, Light, and a City*, 205-29.

But he doesn't stop there. Compassion, justice, liberation and mercy also proceed from all true movements of the Spirit. The Spirit of Jesus Christ— the companion of sinners and outcasts—leads us into service with the poor, wounded, forgotten and oppressed. We look for signs of hope where the Spirit is already at work in our neighborhoods, families and cities. And we join with him in processes of healing and hope and reconciliation and justice and liberation and renewal.

6. Spirit-empowered Christians are attentive to the voice and presence of Jesus Christ in other Christian traditions and in the world. God is present in every expression of his church. This demands qualification. On the one hand, there is a sense in which God is present everywhere, outside as well as within the church. We need to look for signs of hope in cities and neighborhoods and churches. This way, we discern where God is already at work, and we join with him. But, as my colleague David Starling points out, there is the terrible possibility that some forms of the church and its mission can become apostate structures:

> They are edifices in which the form of godliness is present but the power has departed. These are places where the Spirit of Christ is no more present than he is at a football game or the shopping mall. For all the discontinuities and differences within the history of the last 2000 years of Christianity, the New Testament nevertheless reminds us that our identity as the church is created by our union with Christ, a union that we possess in common with believers of all times and places.[76]

Being attentive to the Spirit in other Christian traditions and in the world requires courage, humility, wisdom and discernment. I have offered Amos Yong's seven guidelines in this chapter. They're helpful. It takes courage to listen to others. It takes wisdom and discernment to know what to offer and receive.

7. Spirit-empowered Christians embrace particular practices in mission, worship and spiritual formation. We need to release the practices of Spirit-empowered gatherings and mission. (See these practices in the section "Spirit-Empowered Mission" above.) And it's vital that we cultivate Spirit-filled approaches to worship and spirituality. (See the descriptions in tables 6.1 and 6.2,

---

[76]David Starling, "Theology and the Future of the Church." Available for order online: www.case.edu .au/index.php/case_magazine/case_28_2011_theology_the_future/.

which describe *Spirit-filled worship and spirituality* in the Majority World.)

Not everyone attends a renewalist church. But I encourage you to look through the practices of Spirit-empowered mission offered by Julie C. Ma and Wonsuk Ma. I invite you to consider the two tables outlining the features of renewalist worship and spirituality. They have the power to transform congregations and their mission. What's missing from your setting? What can you contextualize to your church and its worship and mission?

8. Spirit-empowered Christians integrate Spirit-empowered mission into ministry training and theological education. It's common for theological colleges to speak of equipping heads (theology), hands (competency) and hearts (spirituality). Colleges often do well in the first and second areas and struggle to do the third. Repeatedly, I hear graduates lament that colleges don't prepare them to serve in the power of the Spirit. They go into mission and ministry and quickly discover that they're at war with principalities and powers. They need to rely on God's empowering presence in mission and service. Theological colleges and churches must put this theme back into the heart of ministry training.

9. Spirit-empowered Christians join with the Spirit wherever he is at work in the world. This involves preparing and ushering in resurrection life, the kingdom of God, the new creation and the birth of a new humanity. Stop behaving as though the Spirit was absent before we arrived. Start discerning his presence in the world. Start joining with him in bringing resurrection life, the new birth, the new creation and the kingdom of God. And courageously proclaim and live out the gospel of Jesus Christ.

10. Spirit-empowered Christians must think critically and biblically about their theology of healing and the atonement. The church needs to develop a broader understanding of healing and its relationship to the atonement.

Craig Keener writes, "Matthew informs his audience that healing was part of Jesus' mission, which God provided at great cost to Jesus (8:17)." And so we need to consider the various dimensions of healing associated with the atonement. Healing is also linked with Christ's empathy with our human condition. Jesus exemplifies this empathy and identification in his incarnation. But we must also recognize that ultimate healing is in the age to come.

What does it mean for humans to experience full healing? How is healing physical, emotional, relational and spiritual? How do the atoning life, passion, death and resurrection of Jesus Christ heal us?

We need to be careful here—very careful. Atonement is primarily about cancellation of guilt. It is about God's work in liberating individuals, the church and the created order from guilt and sin. But our theology of the atonement can expand our understanding of the nature and scope of healing. We can see the connections between the atonement, the incarnation and the resurrection.

We have seen that physical healing is available to all through the atonement. But thanks to the *already but not yet* nature of the kingdom, it is not available to all in this present life. It is only guaranteed in the age to come. Ultimate bodily healing is in the resurrection of our bodies, but God is able to heal bodily if he chooses to do so. So we shouldn't neglect to pray for those who are sick.

We also need to explore the nature of healing associated with the atonement in its broadest sense. How is healing liberation from sin? How is it restoration of relationships? How is it freedom from addictions and slavery? And how is it rejection of idolatries? How is healing, peace, freedom and joy in the emotional, psychological and spiritual dimensions of our lives?

The church joins in this healing ministry—as a sign, foretaste, herald and witness to the *now but not yet* kingdom. It participates in human healing for the sake of Jesus Christ and his mission in the world. God calls his church to express this healing it its corporate life and ethics and in its public witness and service. To be a healing presence in the world, the church must pursue the healing mission of God. It does this best with a mature and biblical view of the kingdom of God. Its grasp of the kingdom—and the kingdom's *present* and *future* aspects—enables healing ministries. The Spirit gives us a foretaste of the reign of Christ and of the church's future.

My proposal is that Western churches can learn much from renewalist churches in the Majority World. We cannot ignore the enormous growth of these churches in Latin America, Asia and Africa. They are having a global and local influence.

These churches are missional and empowered by the Holy Spirit. It is up to us to adapt these Spirit-centered commitments to our own setting. Adopting the lessons outlined above prioritizes the Spirit in our way of doing church. I don't want churches to conform to *this* image of church. Rather, I want the renewalist movement to challenge us to do church differently. We do this by adapting aspects of renewalist churches to our setting.

Thankfully, we are not alone in this task. And we can rest in the presence of the Spirit of truth.

Jesus said,

> And I will ask the Father, and he will give you another advocate to help you and be with you forever—the Spirit of truth. The world cannot accept him, because it neither sees him nor knows him. But you know him, for he lives with you and will be in you. I will not leave you as orphans; I will come to you. . . .
>
> These words you hear are not my own; they belong to the Father who sent me. All this I have spoken while still with you. But the Advocate, the Holy Spirit, whom the Father will send in my name, will teach you all things and will remind you of everything I have said to you.
>
> Peace I leave with you; my peace I give you. I do not give to you as the world gives. Do not let your hearts be troubled and do not be afraid. (Jn 14:16-18, 24-27)

Table 6.1. Features of renewalist (Charismatic and Pentecostal) worship in the Majority World

Feature	Description	Implication
Intense	Worship is lively and emotional and intense. Bodily movements often go with this worship. This includes hand clapping and raising, loud instruments, spiritual expectation and vocalizations (e.g., shouting "Hallelujah," "Amen," "Praise the Lord").	Is your worship lively and passionate? Does it provide space for emotion and physical expression? Is there room for full enjoyment of the five senses (sight, hearing, taste, smell and touch)?
Charismatic	Worship includes the use of charismatic gifts (e.g., speaking in tongues, interpretation, prophecy and prayer for healing).	Are the gifts used freely and passionately and wisely in your gatherings?
Participatory	Worship is participatory and experiential. There are key moments in the gathering for the involvement of the whole congregation.	How participatory and experiential and interactive is your worship? Is the whole congregation involved?
Communal	Worship is corporate. There is a focus on worshiping "together." This includes corporate prayer (e.g., the whole congregation praying together at once in "choral prayer").	Does your worship build community and relationships? Is it truly communal and corporate?
Spontaneous	Congregations worship with an expectation that God will surprise and astonish. This encourages spontaneity and improvisation.	Do you expect God to astonish you? Surprise you? Do new things among your congregation? Does your worship have space for spontaneity?
Pragmatic	Worship facilitates connection with God in the Spirit. Congregations and their leaders design forms and practices and venues for that purpose.	Do your forms and practices and venues facilitate worship and formation and connection with Jesus?

Feature	Description	Implication
Applicable	Worship, although mystical, affects ordinary life. Renewalist Christians pursue the practical implications of spiritual experiences. This means that they apply these experiences and Scripture to daily life. They apply these to poverty and wealth, oppression and justice, sickness and health, suffering and joy, oppression and freedom, persecution and vindication, corruption and morality, and so on. Worship shapes ethics and families and workplaces and finances.	How does your worship affect the ordinary lives of your congregation? Does it connect with the real issues that people face?
Mystical	Worship is mystical and transcendental. This is even true when renewalists apply it to daily life.	Does your worship lead to communion with Father, Son and Spirit? Does it lift people out of their circumstances to gaze on the beauty and love of Christ? Does it then empower them for service and everyday life?
Formative	Worship serves (as much as Scripture) to form and educate the congregation. Worship shapes its theology, spirituality, ethics and culture.	How does your worship shape your congregation's imagination and love? Ethics and spirituality? Theology and discipleship? Community and grace?
Personality centered	Worship is not only participatory. It is also personality centered. Pastors are often charismatic and large personalities. They are "anointed by God" to lead and speak with passionate enthusiasm.	Are leaders free to lead in your setting? Are they given authority, accountability, responsibility and grace? Is this balanced with communal leadership and discernment? And how are leaders developed to build up others?
Contextual	Worship often integrates indigenous practices, rituals, stories, myths, musical forms and so on. This raises the usual questions about religious syncretism. Recognition of such indigenization varies. African Independent Churches are proud of their incorporation of indigenous traditions and rituals. But many Korean Pentecostal churches deny such contextualization.	Is your worship relevant to your culture? Shaped by your culture? Prophetic within your culture?
Testimonial	Worship is often shaped around narrative. This includes the stories of individuals, communities, cultures and Scripture. Renewalist congregations locate individual testimonies within a narrative-shaped worship tradition. "Testimonies of healing, God's answer to prayers, or overwhelming sense of his presence and love . . . abound in the Pentecostal communities. Thus, God is understood as actively involved in human affairs that highlight the immanent presence of God."[a]	How do stories saturate and shape your worship? How do they shape your church's culture and imagination and faith and hope and love and grace?
Evangelistic	Renewalist churches saturate their worship with evangelistic themes and moments. These churches tend to take every opportunity to proclaim the gospel and a call to repentance.	Is your worship missional? Is the gospel proclaimed? Does it lead people to Jesus?

[a]Ma and Ma, "Jesus Christ in Asia," 497. Also see Wonsuk Ma, "Pentecostal Worship in Asia: Its Theological Implications and Contributions," *Asian Journal of Pentecostal Studies* 10, no. 1 (2007).

Table 6.2. Features of renewalist (Charismatic and Pentecostal) spirituality in the Majority World

Feature	Description	Implication
Spirit centered	Renewalists focus on the power and presence and provision of the Holy Spirit.	Are you depending on the Spirit? For witness to Christ? For spiritual growth? For healing and liberation? For multiplication and reproduction? For life-giving faith and transformed community?
Biblically conservative and courageous in biblical application	Renewalists couple conservative readings of the Bible with courageous applications of its message.	How is your congregation trusting in the authority, inerrancy and transforming power of Scripture? Are people learning to connect with God in Scripture and in other ways? Is Christ transforming them into his image? Does your engagement with Scripture make disciples?
Spiritually intense and expectant	Renewalists practice worship, preaching, healing and discipleship with a central purpose in mind: an encounter with the presence and power of God. This is an anticipation of encounter. It's an intense expectation that God will act. God will heal and liberate and empower and save.	Does your congregation expect an encounter with God in prayer and worship and everyday life? Do they rely on his inbreaking power to free and empower and fill them with love?
Restorationist and revivalist	There is a desire to restore the passion and power of the early church in the power of the Spirit.	How are you exploring the implications of the missional and gathered life of the early church? How are you adapting these insights to your church and culture?
Mystical and experiential	This experience includes an expectation of a direct encounter with the presence of God.	Is your Christian spirituality merely cerebral? Or also experiential? How do people in your church meet God in their whole life? Their emotions? Their minds? Their bodies? Their spirits?
Participatory and communal	Renewalists expect leaders to lead. But congregational gatherings also involve lots of participation and community.	Can people genuinely join in your worship and ministry and mission? Do these things build community? Are people transformed by serving together and by supporting each other?
Personality and charisma centered	Charismatic leaders and celebrity personalities shape renewalist church cultures. These churches are often focused on the "larger than life" leader. Ecstatic worship and a theology of anointing also play a role.	How is your church releasing leadership gifts? How are you dealing with the negative aspects of personality centeredness? How are charismatic leaders pointing beyond themselves to Jesus?
Pragmatic and mystical	Renewalist spirituality couples mysticism and pragmatism. This spirituality emphasizes both God's immanence and transcendence. Recently, renewalists have been seeking to integrate pragmatics and ecstatic experience with theology. This is a movement toward a holistic spirituality.	Is your worship both inspirational and applicable? How are people in your church growing in theological understanding, spiritual depth and practical skills for life? Is your spirituality meaningful to heads and hearts and hands? Is knowledge bifurcated in your church? Is it split between head knowledge (academics), heart knowledge (spirituality) and hand knowledge (competencies)? Or is your spirituality integrated and holistic?

Feature	Description	Implication
Focused on leadership development	There is a commitment to leadership identification and development and release.	Do leaders treat each other and the rest of the congregation with honor? Do people express mutual submission? Are emerging leaders identified and developed and released?
Interpersonal and ethically formative	Congregational worship and Spirit-focused disciplines shape people's ethical and relational practices.	How do we shape practices that form community? And that form people's relationships and theology and ethics?
Holiness centered	There is a conviction that God's Holy Spirit desires holy people.	Is your congregation moving by God's grace into holiness? Are you?
Land and place and territory centered	Including territorial spirits and God's purposes for lands and nations.	Are you aware of the spiritual forces that control your culture and particular place? What is God doing in your land, soil, nation and culture?
Materially and socially aspirational	This aspiration is especially, but not only, present in impoverished and oppressed settings.	How is your church helping people move toward fullness of life? Spiritual and material well-being? A critical assessment of the values within aspirational and materialistic cultures?
Eschatologically centered (focused on the end times)	The idea that "in the last days I will pour out my Spirit on all people" shapes renewalist spirituality (Acts 2:17).	How are the reign and kingdom and coming of Jesus shaping your congregation's spirituality?
Embodied and physical	Including healing, the laying on of hands, raising hands, hugging and dancing.	In your church, can people express their faith through their bodies?
Testimonial and narrative based	Including personal testimonies and narrative and story-based preaching.	Do stories shape key things in your church? Your missional imagination? Your biblical understanding? Your interpersonal relationships? Your connection with the story of salvation and the story of the triune God?
Contextually and culturally oriented	Renewalist spirituality is far from homogenous. Renewalists form it with attention to context and culture.	Is your Christian spirituality indigenous to your culture? Does it reflect the best parts of your culture and critique fallen aspects?
Evangelistic and missional	The dramatic spread of renewalist churches is largely due to their missional spirituality.	Is your spirituality missional? Does it focus on joining in the mission of God in the world?

CARING FOR CREATION

WHAT CAN WE LEARN FROM HOW MAJORITY
WORLD CHRISTIANS CARE FOR CREATION?

*We commit ourselves to be members of both the living community of
creation in which we are but one species, and members of the covenant
community of Christ; to be co-workers with God, with moral responsibility
to respect the rights of future generations; and to conserve and work for the
integrity of creation both for its inherent value to God and in order that
justice may be achieved and sustained.*

KEN GNANAKAN

The growth of many Majority World economies has been extraordinary (take
China, for example). This growth has often paralleled the growth of the Majority World churches. Majority World middle classes are as enthusiastic for
material accumulation as Western middle classes. Global growth in middle-
class consumerism results in increased pressure on the environment. Majority
World leaders are seeking solutions and responses. These leaders include economists, environmentalists, business people, religious leaders and politicians.

Recently, I attended a four-day summit of Asia-Pacific theologians. Sixty-
eight theological educators and church leaders participated in the summit.
These represented seventeen seminaries and churches from thirteen countries of the Asia-Pacific region. They gathered at Korea Baptist Theological
University, Daejeon, South Korea. The theological colloquium was on the

theme "Church and Environment."[1] These leaders wrestled with theological and practical questions relating to creation. Together they constructed a theology of environmental concern and care. They proposed a suite of practical responses for churches, leaders and populations.

Western churches can learn much from Majority World and indigenous thinking about ecology. We can learn from their eco-theology and eco-justice. Humanity faces terrible ecological challenges. These include global warming, climate change, deforestation and desertification. Pollution, water deterioration, habitat destruction and species extinctions are serious problems. Humans have depleted natural resources. Global population growth is putting the earth under pressure. It is time to learn from each other about creation care. And it is time to act.

This chapter considers Majority World ideas about eco-theology, eco-justice, eco-feminism, eco-indigenous movements and eco-practices. I proceed in that order. Churches and individual disciples need to take responsibility for the environment. We need to act for its well-being and for the sake of future generations.

We need to pursue constructive environmental solutions as proactive stewards of the earth. God has entrusted the earth to our care. This chapter asks, *What can we learn from how Majority World Christians care for creation?*

ECO-THEOLOGY

Indigenous writings contain substantial eco-theological reflections. It is not possible to treat such eco-theology in detail here. But it is possible to summarize some of the central proposals and considerations.

1. Eco-theology is a global, multivocal dialogue. David G. Hallman edited a volume called *Ecotheology*. In that book, he shows that we do the best and richest eco-theology in dialogue. Our eco-theology flourishes in dialogue between Majority World and indigenous and Western voices.[2] Hallman constructs a global and multivoiced and dialogical eco-theology. He considers the biblical witness—creation, covenant, prophets, Psalms, Gospels,

---

[1]Quotes are from the colloquium's handouts and summaries.
[2]David G. Hallman, ed., *Ecotheology: Voices from South and North* (Maryknoll, NY: Orbis, 1994). Conradie sets up a similar "intercontinental dialogue" on eco-theology in Ernst M. Conradie, "Towards an Agenda for Ecological Theology: An Intercontinental Dialogue," *Ecotheology* 10, no. 3 (2005).

Romans and eschatology. His eco-theology covers the theological challenges and the shape of eco-feminist theology. He unpacks indigenous perspectives and investigates ethical implications.

Hallman's book exemplifies the future of multivoiced and global eco-theology. All eco-theology is at its best when we construct it in a global and multifocal way. Why is this the case? Only a globalized approach is adequate for the vast challenges of climate change and environmental degradation. And Christians have done minimal work on eco-theology, so we need to get on with this and learn from voices from all over the globe. The globalized nature of the modern world demands a globally shaped eco-theology. And rich possibilities reside in a global eco-theological conversation.

This dialogue will not only be between individuals and cultures. It will also be between theological traditions, the sciences, the biblical witness and the humanities and will involve discussions and actions that deal with the crisis facing the environment.

2. Eco-theology is obedient to the biblical witness. In recent years, Christian scholars have examined Scripture for ecological themes. The Earth Bible is one example. This project examines Scripture for eco-justice themes, and it contributes to current debates on ecology and eco-theology and eco-ethics. Its interpretations range from brilliant to dubious. But it makes a valuable contribution to ecological hermeneutics (i.e., interpreting the Bible through an ecological lens).[3]

Ken Gnanakan is a theologian based in Bangalore, India. He writes books and articles on a biblical theology of the environment. These include pieces for the World Evangelical Alliance Theological Commission. Gnanakan calls evangelicals back to "responsible stewardship of God's creation." This stewardship responds to an eco-theology constructed upon a careful interpretation of Scripture.

The Bible testifies that the earth belongs to the Lord. Sin and the fall affect humans and all creation. The Bible also calls humanity to responsible stewardship of the earth. God gives us dominion over creation, but it is a role characterized by care and nurture and protection. It is an earth-enriching, "creation care" role. Christian must reject all forms of earth-destroying domination.

---

[3]See details about the Earth Bible at www.flinders.edu.au/ehl/theology/ctsc/projects/earthbible.

We must see ourselves as stewards of God's creation. God connects us intimately with creation. He charges us with nurturing and protecting it. We share our final redemption and healing and resurrection and renewal with creation.

As the resurrection community, we are called by God into a just and responsible and loving relationship with creation. We worship and witness and reveal true community and stewardship in our care for the earth. Commonality, love, responsibility, interdependence, servanthood, respect, worship, mission and eschatological vision characterize this stewardship.[4]

3. Eco-theology is connected with justice, liberation and spirituality. Leonardo Boff connects ecological justice with justice for the poor. He links the cries of the poor with the cries of the earth. Boff draws on elements of James Lovelock's *Gaia Theory* to construct an eco-theology.

Gaia Theory takes both rational and mystical forms. It suggests that all the geological, physical, chemical and biological dimensions of the earth interpenetrate each other. This interpenetration or interdependence regulates the planet and makes it an optimal habitat for life.

For James Lovelock, "We define Earth as Gaia, because it presents itself as a complex entity embracing the biosphere, the atmosphere, the oceans, and the land; in their totality, these elements constitute a cybernetic or self-sustaining system that provides an optimal physical and chemical medium for life on this planet."[5]

As I noted, Gaia Theory has both scientific and mystical forms. Science has verified some aspects of the theory, while other features remain untested or unverifiable. Leonardo Boff claims that this interdependency between humanity and the earth provides an ethical and spiritual challenge for Christians. Like Francis of Assisi, we are to recognize our interdependent responsibility for the earth and the terrestrial community—soil, subsoil, air, plants, animals, birds, fish, biodiversity and the rest of the planet. We have ethical and spiritual and practical responsibility for these things.[6]

---

[4]Ken Gnanakan, *God's World: A Theology of the Environment* (London: SPCK, 1999); Gnanakan, *Responsible Stewardship of Creation* (Bangalore: Theological Book Trust, 2004); Gnanakan, "Creation, Christians and Environmental Stewardship," *Evangelical Review of Theology* 30, no. 2 (2006).

[5]James Lovelock, quoted in Leonardo Boff, "Earth as Gaia: An Ethical and Spiritual Challenge," in *Eco-Theology*, ed. Elaine Wainwright, Luiz Carlos Susin and Felix Wilfred (London: SCM, 2009), 27.

[6]Leonardo Boff, *Ecology and Liberation: A New Paradigm*, Ecology and Justice Series (Maryknoll, NY: Orbis, 1995), 52-54.

Boff believes this "experience of radical communion with the Earth," united with an experience "of the Father of limitless love and goodness, will open us up to a more global and all-embracing experience of the mystery of God."[7]

To put it another way, all genuine eco-theology will lead to radical eco-justice and eco-ethics and eco-politics. True eco-theology leads to innovative eco-technologies. It results in constructive social and interpersonal approaches to ecology. We reveal authentic eco-theology in our eco-spirituality and eco-communities. Our daily habits show whether we mean the things we say when we do eco-theology.[8]

Boff's eco-theology is a form of Christian panentheism. Panentheism is the idea that God is greater than the universe and that he transcends nature—but God also interpenetrates every part of nature. God fills creation with his presence. He draws it into his divine and final purpose. Process (Whiteheadian) theology and creation spirituality are related to panentheism. Note that panentheism is not pantheism. Panentheism doesn't believe that everything is God. It acknowledges that God is distinct from—and revealed in—creation.

Like Jürgen Moltmann, Boff builds trinitarian dimensions into this panentheistic eco-theology. Boff proposes an ecologically active God. "The world, indeed, is complex, diverse, one, united, interrelated, because it is a reflection of the Trinity. God invades every being, enters into every relationship, erupts into every ecosystem."[9]

4. Eco-theology is multidimensional. Majority World eco-theology engages in a vast array of theological themes. These include creation, Christ, salvation, ethics, church, Spirit, Trinity, ecology and eschaton.

For example, Ferdinand Nwaigbo writes that the Trinity's communion provides a model for communion between humans and creation. How do we know what good "creation care" looks like? We turn to the trinitarian mutual indwelling and missional actions. Trinitarian relations guide us toward communion with creation. Trinitarian mission compels us to act for the sake of creation's well-being. The Trinity is our model and motivation.

---

[7] Boff, "Earth as Gaia," 31.

[8] Boff, *Ecology and Liberation*, 9-54.

[9] Ibid., 48.

The Trinity leads us toward "ecological-hearted community and inclusiveness." The Trinity inspires us to embrace ecological responsibility for persons, creation, societies and the planet.

Nwaigbo centers his eco-theology on Christ. His eco-theology highlights the power and presence of the Spirit in creation. Nwaigbo shapes his eco-theology with attention to the mission of God and his church and peppers it with African sociocultural and theological perspectives.[10]

Similarly, M. L. Daneel, Kok-Weng Chiang and Geoffrey Tan show that a theology of the Spirit must have ecological implications. This is because the Spirit participates in the work of creation. The Spirit heals and protects humanity and nature. The Spirit brings justice and liberation. All Spirit-human-creation relationships are a work of the Spirit. He leads toward a "Spirit-driven, human-responsible, earth-friendly" eco-theology. Such eco-theology is dynamic and multifaceted.[11]

ECO-JUSTICE

Eco-theology leads to ethical and just considerations and actions. Boff makes this case when he speaks of ecology and poverty being the cry of the earth and the cry of the poor. Liberation and ecology bridge the concerns of the Majority World and Western cultures, the North and South. This is because the destiny of the world's poor and the destiny of the world's climate and ecosystems affect us all.

The poor need liberation from oppression and marginalization. The earth needs liberation from exploitation and degradation. We all need liberation from "a paradigm that places us—against the thrust of the universe—over things instead of being with them in the great cosmic community."[12]

Jayapaul Azariah is an Indian marine scientist, bioethicist and theologian.

---

[10]Ferdinand Nwaigbo, "Cosmic Christology and Eco-Theology in Africa," *AFER* 53, no. 2 (2011); Ferdinand Nwaigbo, "Trinity and Ecology," *AFER* 53, no. 2 (2011).

[11]Marthinus L. Daneel, "African Independent Church Pneumatology and the Salvation of All Creation," *International Review of Mission* 82 (1993): 143-66; Daneel, "Earthkeeping in Missiological Perspective: An African Challenge," *Mission Studies* 13, nos. 1-2 (1996); Daneel, "African Initiated Churches as Vehicles of Earth-Care in Africa," in *The Oxford Handbook of Religion and Ecology*, ed. Roger S. Gottlieb (Oxford: Oxford University Press, 2006); Daneel, "Christian Mission and Earth-Care: An African Case Study," *International Bulletin of Missionary Research* 35, no. 3 (2011).

[12]Leonardo Boff, *Cry of the Earth, Cry of the Poor*, Ecology and Justice (Maryknoll, NY: Orbis, 1997), xii, 104-14; Boff, *Ecology and Liberation*, 131-36; Leonardo Boff and Virgilio P. Elizondo, *Ecology and Poverty: Cry of the Earth, Cry of the Poor*, Concilium (Maryknoll, NY: Orbis, 1995), xi-xii.

He writes passionately about the ethical management of natural resources. These include renewable and nonrenewable resources, natural eco-systems, human-produced resources and human resources. By human resources, Azariah means care for the health and dignity and well-being of humans. Azariah says that Christians should lead the way in the ethical care and management of creation.[13]

Paul G. Harris teaches at the Hong Kong Institute of Education. Harris examines the relationships between ethics, global justice, urban settings, built environments, international politics, poverty and climate change. Those who suffer most from climate change contribute the least to it. They have little ability to mitigate or adapt to its effects. Those who benefited the most from the practices that caused climate change have obligations. They have an obligation to care for those who suffer the most from climate change. They must protect the vulnerable. And they must commit themselves to "climate justice."

Economic globalization and environmental interdependence demand international environmental justice. Harris cites examples of such international ecological justice, including the *Stockholm Conference on the Human Environment*, the *Law of the Sea*, the *Montreal Protocol*, the *Earth Summit* and the *Biodiversity Convention*, as well as agreements such as the *1992 Framework Convention on Climate Change* and the *1997 Kyoto Protocol*. All nations and states have responsibility. But responsibility increases according to a nation's contribution to the problem. It also increases in relation to a nation's level of development. In other words, some nations have greater responsibility than others.[14]

Harris argues for "cosmopolitan justice." He doesn't discount nation-state organizations pursuing international justice. But he argues that the best approaches to global environmental justice happen at local and regional levels. This is true in both developed and developing nations.

Who should champion global eco-justice? Poorer people have a role to play. They show the effects of climate change to the rest of the world. They demonstrate generosity and contentment. They often exemplify creation care.

But wealthier people have a role to play too. Richer people have the fi-

---

[13]Jayapaul Azariah, "Ethical Management of Natural Resources," in Wainwright, Susin and Wilfred, *Eco-Theology*.

[14]Paul G. Harris, *World Ethics and Climate Change: From International to Global Justice*, Edinburgh Studies in World Ethics (Edinburgh: Edinburgh University Press, 2010), 26, 58, 68.

nancial means to make a difference and to contribute to solutions. They have the resources to help those that climate change has ravaged. Wealthier groups need to cultivate sufficiency, generosity, service, justice and contentment. They need to collaborate with the poor in climate justice and creation care.[15]

Gnanakan roots eco-justice in biblical theology. He shows how eco-justice, sustainable development and environmental sustainability develop from Scripture. Eco-justice emerges from biblical notions of creation, solidarity, equity, justice, Sabbath, Jubilee and restoration. It develops out of our theology of the nature and mission of God.[16]

As the Micah Challenge document on a "Theology of Climate Change" asserts, the people of God have a responsibility to pursue eco-justice. We must engage with politics and development and economics for the sake of the planet. God calls us to put faith into action. Now is the time to develop sustainable practices and lifestyles and churches. We must seek justice for those whom climate change and ecological degradation have ravaged. It is time to take responsibility for the implementation of the seventeen Sustainable Development Goals. We do this individually and collectively.[17]

1. Eradicating extreme poverty and hunger

2. Achieving universal primary education

3. Promoting gender equality and empowering women

4. Reducing child mortality rates

5. Improving maternal health

6. Combating HIV/AIDS, malaria, and other diseases

7. Ensuring environmental sustainability

8. Developing a global partnership for development

ECO-EQUALITY

Aruna Gnanadason is coordinator of the World Council of Churches team

---

[15]Ibid.

[16]Gnanakan, *Responsible Stewardship of Creation*, 115-16; World Council of Churches, 1990 Affirmation—VII.

[17]Micah Challenge, "Theology of Climate Change," May 2009, www.micahchallenge.org.au/assets/pdf/Theology-of-climate-change.pdf. The United Nations, "Sustainable Development Goals," 2015, www.un.org/sustainabledevelopment/sustainable-development-goals.

on Justice, Peace and Creation. She constructs a holistic theology of creation stewardship in her small but profound book *Listen to the Women! Listen to the Earth!*

Gnanadason exemplifies the environmental and social consciousness in postcolonial eco-feminist theology. She connects the liberation of women and creation and the poor. The bondage of one of these three always leads to the bondage of the others. We must seek the liberation of the *poor* from marginalization and oppressed. We need to work for the liberation of *creation* from degradation and exploitation. And we should ensure the liberation of *women* from patriarchal, abusive systems.

Gnanadason draws on stories of women and indigenous people who struggle on behalf of the poor and females and creation. She challenges her readers to learn from these *eco-systems peoples*. She notes the different concerns of Western and indigenous and Majority World eco-feminists. She says that Euro American eco-feminists make an important contribution. But they often indulge in psychospiritual issues. Gnanadason quotes Rosemary Radford Ruether here. Western eco-feminists fail "to make real connections between their own reality as privileged women, and racism, classism, and impoverishment of nature."[18]

In contrast, Majority World eco-feminism cares about "intentionally created poverty and wealth." It concerns itself with "poverty that afflicts whole communities (particularly women and children)," and seeks the recovery of precolonial and postcolonial "patterns of spirituality that connect them to their indigenous roots—a past that is still present in the lives of communities, as women care for the earth."[19]

Rosemary Radford Ruether's book *Women Healing Earth* contains the writings of sixteen Latin American, Asian and African eco-feminists. There are five from each continent, plus Ruether. Each contributor writes about the struggle for eco-justice. They construct fresh eco-theologies. This eco-feminism is not homogenous, so we need to differentiate "between women of different classes, castes, races, ecological zones, and so on."[20]

---

[18] Aruna Gnanadason, *Listen to the Women! Listen to the Earth!* (Geneva: World Council of Churches, 2005), 32; Rosemary Radford Ruether, ed., *Women Healing Earth: Third World Women on Ecology, Feminism, and Religion*, Ecology and Justice (Maryknoll, NY: Orbis, 1996), 5.

[19] Gnanadason, *Listen to the Women! Listen to the Earth!*, 32.

[20] Bina Agarwal, quoted in ibid., 35.

Such diverse, postcolonial, indigenous and Majority World eco-feminism asks a series of important questions: "Have women been colonized by patriarchy? Do women's bodies and labor function as the invisible substructure for the extraction of wealth? How does the positioning of women as caretakers in the family make this work inferior? And how does this identify women with the non-human world that is also given an inferior status?"[21]

Gnanadason builds an eco-feminist theology by developing an integrated theological understanding of grace. She incorporates ecological perspectives on grace—*green* grace, *red* grace and *brown* grace. This notion of green and red and brown grace draws on the work of Jay McDaniel and Indian eco-feminists.

Green grace is about the wisdom and healing and integrity of creation. It sees nature as an integral and self-organizing and beautiful gift from God.

Red grace is about the love of God demonstrated on the cross. It highlights the human and ecological responsibilities we share as the people of the resurrection.

Brown grace is about learning from the "traditions of prudent care." Indigenous peoples, who are almost always attentive to ecological systems, have handed down these traditions to humanity. Brown grace is about seeing these practices as a grace from God.[22] This brown grace does not idealize indigenous and first peoples as ecologists. Instead, it seeks to assess their contributions. It regards indigenous practices as a grace for our planet and our environmental stewardship.

Eco-feminist theology develops metaphors for God that inform and inspire creation care. For example, God's trinitarian communion helps us understand our connection with him and others and creation. We are able to build "a holistic vision" of the interdependence between all created things. All things are intimately connected—animate, inanimate, human and the rest of creation.[23]

Gnanakan claims that eco-feminism features the spirituality of indigenous communities. It also emphasizes the ecological perspectives in

---

[21]Ibid., 33.

[22]Ibid., 81-106; Jay McDaniel, "The Sacred Whole: An Ecumenical Protestant Approach," in *The Greening of Faith: God, the Environment and the Good Life*, ed. John E. Carroll, Paul Brockelman and Mary Westfall (Hanover, NH: University Press of New England, 1997), 114-15. See Aruna Gnanadason, "Yes, Creator God, Transform the Earth! The Earth as God's Body in an Age of Environmental Violence," *Ecumenical Review* 57, no. 2 (2005).

[23]Aruna Gnanadason, "Women, Economy and Ecology," in *Ecotheology: Voices from South and North*, ed. David G. Hallman (Maryknoll, NY: Orbis, 1994), 184.

Scripture. Eco-feminism calls the church to consider women's concrete and daily and local struggles. These are struggles for justice and wholeness and liberation and dignity. We need to learn from these women. Gnanakan provides examples from the Vacaia Project in Brazil, tribal women in Iran and the Chipko women of India.[24]

Eco-feminism calls the church to action. It invites people into just relationships with each other and creation. In the words of Ruether, "a healed ecosystem—humans, animals, land, air, and water together—needs to be understood as requiring a new way of life, not just a few adjustments here and there. . . . One needs pioneering ecological communities that demonstrate a new way of life in which the community as a whole lives in an ecologically sustainable way."[25]

ECO-INDIGENOUS CONTRIBUTIONS

In my country, Australia, there is an ongoing discussion about what we can learn from indigenous practices. What can Aboriginal and Torres Strait Islanders teach us about caring for the planet and its ecosystems? What can we learn from their sustainable practices and land care and conservation? A conversation is developing between indigenous peoples and contemporary models of land care and sustainability.

The Australian ecological landscape is fragile. My country needs to respond urgently. We face serious problems—environmental degradation, pollution, endangered ecosystems and extinction of species. The Australia Government's Threatened Species Scientific Committee (TSSC) claims that over the two hundred years since European settlement, hundreds of species— and many ecological communities—have become extinct or endangered. This is due to "loss, change, and fragmentation of habitat; the effects of invasive plants, animals, and diseases; and direct effects of human activities."[26]

In contrast to the ecological devastation and exploitation of European set-

---

[24]Gnanakan, *God's World*, 150-65.

[25]Rosemary Radford Ruether, "Religious Ecofeminism: Healing the Ecological Crisis," in *The Oxford Handbook of Religion and Ecology*, ed. Roger S. Gottlieb (Oxford: Oxford University Press, 2006), 373.

[26]Australian Government, Department of Sustainability, Environment, Water, Population and Communities, "Threatened Species and Ecological Communities in Australia," 2004, www.environment .gov.au/biodiversity/threatened/publications/overview.html.

tlement, Aboriginal and Torres Strait Islander people maintained a deep and spiritual connection with the land. They saw themselves as created, along with the land, by the Creator Spirit. This Spirit provided for them through nature's abundance. He gave them a sacred responsibility to nurture and protect and sustain the land. Indigenous Australians cultivated an understanding of the needs of local ecosystems. They only took from the land what they needed. For countless generations they cared for specific, local areas. They developed sustainable practices handed down from generation to generation.

Indigenous Australians developed a creation-based, nature-nurturing and ecologically attentive spirituality. They shaped this spirituality around sacred sites, ancestral lands, myths and rituals and hunting and farming. They fashioned all these around care for the land.[27]

Graham Harvey says that environmental concern is crucial to the construction of indigeneity. Sacred places and lands play an important role in the construction of indigenous environmentalism. It is true that indigenous peoples both damaged and sustained their environments. We need to remember this and avoid idealism or romanticism. But Harvey shows the ecological concerns embedded in indigenous cultures. Indigenous people shape their cosmologies, myths, narratives, sacred sites and communities around the earth. We cannot develop forms of holistic environmentalism without indigenous outlooks and practices. Jacob K. Olupona of Nigeria and George E. Tinker of the Osage-Cherokee make this point strongly.[28]

All over the globe, contemporary ecologists are conversing with indigenous communities. These ecologists aren't discarding modern eco-sciences or ecologically sustainable practices. They are enriching these through conversation with the wisdom of indigenous peoples.

Rob Cooper is a Maori of Aotearoa-New Zealand. He writes, "The coupling of technological, scientific, and indigenous experiences and skills is

---

[27]Vassills Adrahtas, "Perceptions of Land in Indigenous Australian Christian Texts," *Studies in World Christianity* 11, no. 2 (2005); Norman C. Habel, Garth Cant and Heather Eaton, "Voices and Silences—Ecotheological Perspectives from Canada, Australia and New Zealand," *Ecotheology: Journal of Religion, Nature & the Environment* 6 (2001).

[28]Graham Harvey, "Sacred Places in the Construction of Indigenous Environmentalism," *Ecotheology: Journal of Religion, Nature & the Environment* 7, no. 1 (2002); Harvey, "Environmentalism in the Construction of Indigeneity," *Ecotheology: Journal of Religion, Nature & the Environment* 8, no. 2 (2003); Jacob Obafemi Kehinde Olupona, "The Spirituality of Matter: Religion and Environment in Yoruba Tradition, Nigeria," *Dialogue & Alliance* 9, no. 2 (1995).

not merely desirable but essential. To achieve this will not be easy, but we must try. The whole earth is the Lord's, and we are called to be co-operators with this wonder in creation and re-creation."[29]

Boff invites his readers to learn from indigenous people. We learn from their ancestral wisdom and their love for nature. We're challenged by their approaches to work, production, sustainability, dance, community and celebration. Boff quotes the Villas-Boas brothers, who worked for fifty years among indigenous groups in the Amazonian rainforests: "If we want to be rich, accumulate power, and rule the Earth, there is no point in asking the native peoples. But if we want to be happy, combine being human with being [spiritual], integrate life and death, put the person in nature, connect work and leisure, harmonize relations between generations, then let us listen to the indigenous peoples. They have wise lessons to impart to us."[30]

George E. Tinker is an Osage-Cherokee scholar who writes extensive Native American theology. Tinker examines "missionary conquest" and Western categories of thought. He also calls the Christian church to eco-justice and concern for the integrity of creation. Tinker invites us to embrace responsible and balanced nurture of ecosystems. He calls the church to listen to indigenous environmentalism. He wants us to do this without succumbing to racism or romanticism. Racist views dismiss native perspectives. Romanticized and idealized acclaim of eco-indigenous practices is also unhelpful. We need to listen to indigenous perspectives on creation care without committing these errors.[31]

For Tinker, God calls human beings to *world-balancing* and *world-renewing* practices. Eco-balance and renewal occurs when we understand and respond to reciprocity, spatiality, connections, community, integrity and graces. Let me explain how these relate to ecological well-being.

Reciprocity: We recognize our reciprocity with the earth and each other and act accordingly. We care for the earth and its peoples.

---

[29]Hallman, *Ecotheology*, 212. See also Tui Cadigan, "Land Ideologies That Inform a Contextual Maori Theology of Land," *Ecotheology: Journal of Religion, Nature & the Environment* 6, no. 1/2 (2001).

[30]Boff, *Cry of the Earth, Cry of the Poor*, 123.

[31]George E. Tinker, "An American Indian Theological Response to Ecojustice," *Ecotheology: Journal of Religion, Nature & the Environment* 5, no. 3 (1997): 86; Tinker, "The Integrity of Creation: Restoring Trinitarian Balance," *Ecumenical Review* 41, no. 4 (1989); Tinker, "Native Americans and the Land: 'The End of Living, and the Beginning of Survival,'" *Word & World* 6, no. 1 (1986).

Spatiality: We focus on both temporality (time) and spatiality (place). This is an emphasis on historical and eschatological processes (time) and on our concrete location in a place. Place includes family, tribe, culture, land and ecosystem. We prioritize and nurture specific "animals, birds, plants, rocks, rivers, and mountains" in our place.

Connections: We see the connections between ecological, social, ethnic, class, gender and socio-economic injustices. We recognize the relationship between ecological injustice and the subjugation or extinction of cultures.

Community: We relinquish some dimensions of Western individualism. We embrace ecological solutions. We find these collectively, within community and in intercultural dialogue.

Integrity and graces: We honor the integrity of creation. We respect the spiritual and ecological gifts of indigenous peoples. These are graces to us amidst the current ecological crises.

ECO-PRAXIS

Our concern for the environment cannot remain merely theological or ideological. We must work it out in our practices. The Brazilian educator and philosopher Paulo Freire defined praxis as "reflection and action upon the world in order to transform it."[32]

We must express our eco-theology in our discipleship and spirituality and in our mission and witness.

1. Spirituality and discipleship. Boff has put a lot of thought into the shape of eco-spirituality. He believes that "a new spirituality, one adequate to the ecological revolution, is urgently needed."[33] This spirituality is less anthropocentric (i.e., it doesn't place human beings at the center of all things). It prioritizes eco-stewardship and the restoration of creation. It is a spirituality characterized by simplicity, by an active awareness of our ecological interdependency and by celebration and reverence and thankfulness for the wonder and beauty and sacredness of creation.

This spirituality doesn't replace Christ and the gospel with creation. Rather, it is a spirituality that sees Christ present in all creation. It understands creation's importance in Christ's redemptive plan and history.

---

[32]Paulo Freire, *Pedagogy of the Oppressed* (New York: Herder and Herder, 1968), 36.
[33]Boff, *Cry of the Earth, Cry of the Poor*, 189, and see 187-202.

It commits to creative ecological stewardship and the worship of the Creator God. It demonstrates the values of the kingdom of God through environmental care.

We need models of such spirituality and discipleship to Christ. Boff turns to St. Francis of Assisi as an exemplar of such spirituality. St. Francis exemplified "all the cardinal ecological virtues,"[34] and demonstrated the fusion of *outer and inner ecology*. He merged his compassion for the poor and the earth with his rich spiritual life. He cared about human and ecological liberation. He sought the health and well-being of creation. He proclaimed the gospel in prayer and word and action. He showed the world sustainable, earth-renewing, human-liberating, outwardly engaged Christian spirituality.[35]

Outer ecology is "harmony with nature and its rhythms" and concern for the well-being of humanity.

Inner ecology is a prayerful and spiritual and joyful integration of key aspects of our inner lives. These include our environmental concern, social compassion, intellectual curiosity and emotional and psychological wholeness.

This fusion of outer and inner ecology is displayed in St. Francis's "Canticle to Brother Sun."[36] It is never experienced in isolated contemplation, but it is always experienced in communion between humans and nature and God.

Affirming these ideas, Neil Darragh describes a "Christian Earth Spirituality" that values the sacramentality of all things. It views creation through eschatological eyes. And it participates in the redemptive work of the triune God in humans and nature.

It also seeks justice and righteousness in practical ways. "Christian Earth Spirituality" works toward *justice* for people and nature. It pursues the *common good* of all beings and eco-processes and eco-systems. It initiates *sustainable practices* that benefit humans and allow nature to regenerate. And it embraces *solidarity* with marginalized people and endangered species.[37]

The Guatemalan theologian Julia Esquivel Velasquez describes this spirituality. He says that it's "experiencing grace, gratitude, and free giving." It's

---

[34]Ibid., 203-20.
[35]Boff, *Ecology and Liberation*, 52-54.
[36]Boff, *Cry of the Earth, Cry of the Poor*, 216. (The final explanatory note is mine.)
[37]Neil Darragh, "An Ascetic Theology, Spirituality, and Praxis," in *Eco-Theology*, ed. Elaine Wainwright, Luiz Carlos Susin and Felix Wilfred (London: SCM, 2009), 80.

"healing and growing in order to assume our responsibility." And it's "praising and communing with all creation."[38]

David Hallman wrote *Spiritual Values for Earth Community*. He says that gratitude, humility, sufficiency, justice, love, peace, simplicity, faith and hope characterize eco-spirituality.[39]

Are we developing such disciples in our churches and seminaries and colleges? Do they show the *ecological virtues* and the *inner and outer ecology* of St. Francis of Assisi?

2. Mission and witness. Our theology and practices of creation care have direct influence on our witness before a watching world. Our societies and communities examine our engagement with human and ecological issues. Do Christians have a concern and theology and response to environmental issues? Are they disinterested and environmentally irresponsible? Are they developing sustainable practices? Are they leading the way in environmental innovation and responsibility? What does this say about the Christ they follow? How does it reveal his relation to humans and the planet?

Geevarghese Mor Coorilos is an Indian church leader and theologian. He develops a missiology that begins with creation and with postcolonial perspectives on mission.[40] Mor Coorilos says the church is guilty of colonizing people and dominating the earth. And it often does this while "on mission." He proposes a different missiology. "A missiology grounded in biblical creation theology, with creation as a harmonious act of God who brings about life in abundance and preserves it, will be a missiology that is life affirming." Furthermore, "Mission theology cannot ignore these concerns [i.e., climate change, global warming, deforestation, desertification, pollution and de-

---

[38]Boff and Elizondo, *Ecology and Poverty*, 58-66.
[39]David G. Hallman, *Spiritual Values for Earth Community* (Geneva: WCC, 2000), 33-124.
[40]Mor Coorilos develops the missiological themes identified in
    (1) the 1990 World Council of Churches (WCC) convocation on "Justice, Peace and the Integrity of Creation," held in Seoul, South Korea;
    (2) the 1991 Canberra Assembly's "Giver of Life: Sustain Your Creation";
    (3) the 1998 WCC Harare Assembly's "Theology of Life"; and
    (4) the theological debates of the 2006 WCC Porto Alegre assembly.
Coorilos is the moderator of the WCC Commission on World Mission and Evangelism. See Gnanakan, *God's World*, 186-207 for
    (1) the ten affirmations drawn up at the 1990 World Council of Churches (WCC) convocation on "Justice, Peace and the Integrity of Creation" and
    (2) the eco-theology, eco-practices and eco-ecclesiology developed by the 1992 WEF Theological Commission Study Unit on Ethics and Society.

struction of land and water and biodiversity] because *missio Dei* encompasses the entire creation of God."[41]

Mor Coorilos develops a missional theology and praxis of self-emptying. He calls Christians and churches to divest and empty and sacrifice themselves and to do this for the sake of humanity and creation. This is a *kenotic* and *creation-oriented* missiology. Our gospel proclamation must be "creative, affirming life, and encompassing the entire creation." We ought to shape our mission around an awareness of the trinitarian presence in creation (*perichoresis*). God calls us to be a peaceable kingdom. We are to direct our missional practices toward the redemption of human beings and the restoration and integrity of the entire created order.[42]

CREATION CARE AND THE GLOBALCHURCH: CONCLUDING REFLECTIONS

The earth is crying out for justice and healing. The church cannot stand on the sidelines as a neutral or disinterested observer. We must make fresh commitments to eco-justice and eco-theology and creation care.

Here are nine things we learn from how Majority World Christians care for creation:

1. Creation care nurtures a just and responsible and loving relationship with all creation. Our care for creation does this in recognition of our God-given stewardship. As outlined in the chapter, we have a biblical and theological mandate to act justly and conscientiously and lovingly toward all creation.

This includes taking environmental and climate-change science seriously. Naturally, this includes the IPCC reports and recommendations. I'm not advising we accept all science uncritically. But we must listen to the consensus from international scientific institutions. NASA reports the following: "97 percent or more of actively publishing climate scientists agree: Climate-warming trends over the past century are very likely due to human activities. In addition, most of the leading scientific organizations worldwide have issued public statements endorsing this position." NASA then provides a partial list of these organizations. They offer "links to their published state-

---

[41]Geevarghese Mor Coorilos, "Toward a Missiology That Begins with Creation," *International Review of Mission* 100, no. 2 (2011): 310, 315.
[42]Ibid., 321.

ments and a selection of related resources."[43] You can see the list and statements in the footnoted link I've provided.

But we don't stop at climate change. Our creation care also needs to address resource depletion, toxicants and environmental degradation. We tackle pollution and other environmental problems. And we pursue cleaner production and climate change mitigation. We support reforestation and the preservation of marine environments. We invest in industrial ecology, organic agriculture and restoration ecology. And we applaud waste minimization and sustainable consumption.

2. Creation care develops robust eco-theologies. These eco-theologies must also be fresh and courageous and biblically faithful. In this chapter, I've also outlined the ways in which these eco-theologies need to be glocal, biblical, liberationist, trinitarian, practical and public.

Recently, a group of Australian Baptists got together to summarize our position on climate change into a concise statement. Eco-theology needs to be more robust than this statement. But this statement does summarize our theological and biblical convictions. Here's what we concluded:

> Baptists believe the Bible is the primary authoritative guide to faith and life. The Bible declares that God created all things and that God's creation (i.e., the natural environment and its ecosystems) is good. Humans are not separate from but are part of this creation, although humans alone are made in the image of God (Gen 1:1-2:2). The creation teaches us about God (Rom 1:20; cf. Job 39:1-42:6). While all things belong to God, God has entrusted the care of creation to humans (Ps 24:1; Gen 1:28-29; 2:15).
>
> The relationship between humans and the rest of creation is therefore one of interdependence and stewardship. We are creatures shaped by the same processes and embedded in the same systems as those that sustain all other life. Yet as God's stewards we bear an ethical responsibility for the care of the Earth and the welfare of all living things.
>
> We bless God for his greatness and goodness, his mercy and grace, and his love and justice evident in the creation. We enjoy the beauty and pleasures of God's creation. We are sustained and satisfied by its provisions. We are amazed by what science reveals of its structure and systems. We are awed by the miracle of life that continues to unfold day by day.

---

[43]NASA Global Climate Change, "Scientific Consensus: Earth's Climate Is Warming," updated October 2015, http://climate.nasa.gov/scientific-consensus/.

We also acknowledge that humans have often denied our interdependence with the creation. We have abrogated our stewardship of the creation. One major result of this is the global environmental degradation and climate change we now face. Overwhelming scientific evidence shows that humans have caused much of the global warming occurring today.

Climate change is one of the most significant threats to our economic and social life. It is imperative that governments and corporations, as well as individuals and local communities, respond to the current global environmental crisis. Failure by national governments to respond to climate change in decisive ways may result in unmanageable cost blow-outs. And it may result in irreversible devastation to ecosystems and biodiversity. Further, failure to address climate change may ultimately contribute to the suffering and death of millions of the world's poorest and most vulnerable people. And it may lead to the forced migration of millions more to cooler and less physically threatening regions such as Australia.

We affirm that godly stewardship of the creation includes the following. (1) Respect for the creation and its ecosystems as gifts from God. (2) Teaching and learning about the creation and its ecosystems. (3) Wise allocation and use of the creation's finite natural resources. (4) Rejecting a lifestyle of overconsumption and greed-satisfaction in favor of simplicity. (5) An awareness that willful environmental degradation is sin and will attract God's judgment.

We deny certain things. (1) That the creation and its ecosystems are to be worshipped or venerated. (2) That humans have a right to exploit natural resources in permanently destructive ways. (3) That technological advances can be expected to solve global ecological problems "just in time." (4) That Christians have a responsibility to focus on "spiritual" or "heavenly" matters to the exclusion of godly stewardship of the Earth's resources and proper care of the creation. (5) That the present global warming is merely part of a natural cycle and does not warrant urgent action on a global scale.

We call on the Australian Government to take immediate action, in collaboration with other governments, corporations, community organizations, and faith communities to mitigate the effects of global climate change. We call on our government to do the following. (1) Reduce to a sustainable level human contributions to climate change. (2) Address the adverse environmental effects of climate change. (3) Address the human suffering and loss resulting from climate change. (4) Restore and replenish the ecosystems that humans have used or misused. (5) Pass on Earth's resources responsibly and faithfully to future generations.

We call on all Australian citizens to do the following. (1) Urge their political leaders to take steps to reduce global "greenhouse gas" emissions by 50 per cent by 2050. Spur them to encourage wider use of renewable energy sources. (2) Take steps to reduce their own "greenhouse gas" emissions. This includes using public transport or walking where possible. It means purchasing smaller vehicles and reducing household energy consumption (especially air conditioners). It involves reducing household water consumption and installing rainwater tanks where possible. And reusing and recycling household products.[44]

As you can see, the eco-theology we outlined—albeit briefly—is rooted in Scripture. And it speaks with prophetic passion to the world and humanity's treatment of creation. I encourage you to develop your own statement. Include a call to action for your nation's government, citizens, businesses, not-for-profits and churches.

3. Creation care takes action for the well-being of the planet and against climate change and environmental degradation. Eco-theology must lead to action. And action must inform eco-theology. Ideally, eco-theologies lead to radical actions against environmental degradation and climate change. These actions should facilitate eco-justice and eco-ethics. Preferably, these actions lead to innovative eco-technologies. And they result in social systems that nurture and protect the environment.

Some actions are small and everyday. But they make a difference if we all contribute. Use compact fluorescent bulbs. Turn off electronics at night. Plant a tree. Compost. Recycle glass, aluminum, paper and other products. Use a cloth or environmentally friendly disposable diaper. Hang-dry clothes. Use both sides of paper. Unplug devices when possible. Stop using bottled water. Eat less meat. Avoid fast food. Take shorter showers. Buy local. Buy secondhand. Turn off lights. Install skylights and solar tubes. Stop using electronic exercise equipment. Conserve water. Walk or cycle to work. Use public transport. Carpool. Buy a fuel-efficient car. Telecommute. Insulate exterior doors and windows. Install window treatments. Reduce junk mail. Stop using plastic bags. Pay bills electronically. Share and reuse. Start or join

---

[44]BUA National Council, "Statement on Climate Change by the Baptist Union of Australia," November 11, 2006, www.baptist.org.au/News/Articles_and_Statements/Statement_on_climate_change_by_the_Baptist_Union_of_Austral.aspx.

a community garden. Use renewable energies. Consume mindfully.

Other actions are corporate and demand the commitment of institutions. See the suggestions in this book's study guide.

And there are actions on behalf of the planet that are brave and costly. I'll illustrate this with a story from Brazil. It's a story of fearless and costly advocacy for eco-justice. It's an example of godly, ecological martyrdom.

They Killed Sister Dorothy is an enthralling, award-winning documentary. It considers the February 12, 2005, murder of the seventy-three-year-old Sister Dorothy Stang. Assassins murdered her on a muddy road in the Brazilian Amazon.[45] The film traces the life and work of Sister Dorothy. It examines who murdered her and why they committed this horrific act.

Sister Dorothy was a nun from Ohio and a naturalized Brazilian. She worked alongside indigenous peoples in the Amazon. Sister Dorothy supported sustainable agricultural projects. She advocated for the protection of native peoples and their cultures and assisted them in reclaiming land that others had taken through violence and force. The film considers Sister Dorothy's mission to protect the people and ecology of the Brazilian rainforests and follows the trials of her killers.

The Brazilian theologian Luiz Carlos Susin has written a book chapter called "Sister Dorothy Stang: A Model of Holiness and Martyrdom." Susin writes of the clash between the traditional way of life of the indigenous Brazilian forest peoples and the forces of globalized agri-business. This results in the possession of land through violence. It leads to the murder of countless innocents and the rape of the Brazilian rainforests and results in slave labor and the destruction of indigenous cultures. Christians and others are murdered when they oppose these forces. Martyrs include Sister Dorothy, Sister Adelaide Molinari and the young priest Josimo Tavares.

After receiving death threats, Sister Dorothy said, "I don't want to flee, nor do I want to abandon the battle of these farmers who live without any protection in the forest. They have the sacrosanct right to aspire to a better life on land where they can live and work with dignity while respecting the environment." Her assassins were paid the equivalent of twenty US dollars.

Following Sister Dorothy's murder, some influential Brazilians set up a

---

[45]Nigel Nobel, Henry Ansbacher and Daniel Junge, *They Killed Sister Dorothy*, Just Media, 2008, http://theykilledsisterdorothy.com.

"Dorothy Committee." These people came from a wide range of professions in Brazil. They dedicated themselves to the preservation of the rain forests and the survival and flourishing of the peoples and cultures of the Amazon.

Luiz Carlos Susin concludes that Sister Dorothy "loved the people and the forest, biodiversity and justice, with one and the same love, her love for God. She ended by helping to overthrow, or at least shake, the ranks of profiteers who desecrate [creation] and make the people desolate. And for that she was executed."[46]

Whether our actions are small and everyday, corporate and institutional, or brave and costly, we must all do our part for the sake of the planet. It's time to be good stewards of what God has given us.

4. Creation care fosters Christian eco-spirituality. This Christian eco-spirituality seeks the well-being of humans and creation. St Francis of Assisi models it for us. Ecological stewardship and creation care are intrinsic to a biblical, Christian spirituality. We sustain this passion for creation care through prayer and contemplation. We fuel it through theological inquiry and action in the world. And we seek to help people in our churches develop this conviction and associated practices. Our *inner and outer ecologies* witness to the Creator God who redeems and restores creation and humanity.

5. Creation care seeks justice for those displaced, disadvantaged or ravaged by climate change and ecological degradation. Creation care pursues eco-justice. It seeks *justice* for both people and nature. It works for the *common good* of all beings and eco-processes and eco-systems. It develops *sustainable practices* that benefit humans and allow nature to regenerate. It embraces *solidarity* with marginalized people and endangered species. And it works for their healing and justice and hope.[47] Such advocacy may come at a personal cost. But it's a price we must pay. And in the long-term, the cost of doing nothing is far greater. (That is, doing nothing always costs humanity, creation, discipleship and integrity.)

6. Creation care does its part, individually and collectively, toward the implementation of the seventeen Sustainable Development Goals. We aim for these goals for the sake of humanity and creation. Recently my friends and

---

[46]Luiz Carlos Susin, "Sister Dorothy Stang: A Model of Holiness and Martyrdom," in *Eco-Theology*, ed. Elaine Wainwright, Luiz Carlos Susin and Felix Wilfred (London: SCM, 2009), 112-13.
[47]Darragh, "An Ascetic Theology, Spirituality, and Praxis," 80.

I sat down together to plan how we'll contribute toward reaching these goals. We asked each other what we'll each do. And we asked what we'll do together and in our families and churches and organizations. You can do the same.[48]

7. Creation care practices green grace, red grace and brown grace.[49] As Aruna Gnanadason says, we need an integrated theology of grace. How is God's grace expressed in creation, cross, science and indigenous traditions of creation care? How can we join with him in these graces for the sake of humanity and the planet?

8. Creation care listens to indigenous and Majority World environmentalism. What can we learn from the environmental practices of indigenous and First Nations peoples? What can Westerners learn from ecological perspectives in the Majority World? I've summarized some eco-indigenous and Majority World contributions in this chapter. But we need to learn from these peoples without succumbing to either racist dismissal or romanticized acclaim.[50]

9. Creation care enhances the church's witness through its response to environmental issues. Creation care is missional. The world is watching. Do we exercise loving care of the planet? Are we concerned about those made vulnerable through environmental degradation and climate change? Do we engage in ecological responsibility and innovation? Do we cultivate sustainable practices and simple lifestyles? Do we testify to Jesus Christ through our caring relationship with humans and the planet? Our care for creation can witness to Jesus Christ, his gospel and kingdom, and his restoration of all things.

The Lausanne Movement and the World Evangelical Alliance recognizes the missional importance of creation care. They organized the Lausanne Global Consultation on Creation Care and the Gospel in Jamaica in November 2012. Fifty-seven women and men from twenty-six countries participated. These included theologians, church leaders, scientists and creation care practitioners. They came from the Caribbean, Africa, Asia, Latin America, Oceania, North America and Europe. After reflecting on Scripture and talking through the issues, the group formed two major convictions.

---

[48]The United Nations, "Sustainable Development Goals," 2015, www.un.org/sustainabledevelopment /sustainable-development-goals.

[49]See the section on eco-equality. Also see Gnanadason, *Listen to the Women! Listen to the Earth!*, 81-106; McDaniel, "The Sacred Whole," 114-15.

[50]Tinker, "American Indian Theological Response to Ecojustice," 86; Tinker, "Integrity of Creation"; Tinker, "Native Americans and the Land."

First, creation care is a

"gospel issue within the lordship of Christ" [quoting the Lausanne Cape Town Commitment]. Informed and inspired by our study of the scripture—the original intent, plan, and command to care for creation, the resurrection narratives, and the profound truth that in Christ all things have been reconciled to God—we reaffirm that creation care is an issue that must be included in our response to the gospel, proclaiming and acting upon the good news of what God has done and will complete for the salvation of the world. This is not only biblically justified, but an integral part of our mission and an expression of our worship to God for his wonderful plan of redemption through Jesus Christ. Therefore, our ministry of reconciliation is a matter of great joy and hope and we would care for creation even if it were not in crisis.

Second,

We are faced with a crisis that is pressing, urgent, and that must be resolved in our generation. Many of the world's poorest people, ecosystems, and species of flora and fauna are being devastated by violence against the environment in multiple ways, of which global climate change, deforestation, biodiversity loss, water stress, and pollution are but a part. We can no longer afford complacency and endless debate. Love for God, our neighbors and the wider creation, as well as our passion for justice, compel us to urgent and prophetic ecological responsibility.[51]

The group then outlined specific responses. These ten responses included a commitment to simple lifestyle and further theological work and a commitment to action to address climate change and its consequences. The group also recognized the need for leadership on this issue from the churches of the Majority World.

My prayer is that the global church will cooperate to confront climate change. I pray that the global church will advocate for the environment. I pray that it will commit to simplicity and sustainability. I pray that it will develop fresh and vigorous theologies of creation care.

This will involve cooperation between governmental, business, nonprofit, academic, scientific, religious and other groups. We can find solutions through

---

[51]Lausanne Global Consultation on Creation Care and the Gospel, "Consultation Statement," St. Ann, Jamaica, November 2012, www.lausanne.org/content/statement/creation-care-call-to-action.

collaboration. It will involve making a firm commitment to care for the world God has given us. We must work in harmony with each other and with God's creation.

In the words of the consultation,

> Each of our calls to action rest on an even more urgent call to prayer, intentional and fervent, soberly aware that this is a spiritual struggle. Many of us must begin our praying with lamentation and repentance for our failure to care for creation, and for our failure to lead in transformation at a personal and corporate level. And then, having tasted of the grace and mercies of God in Christ Jesus and through the Holy Spirit, and with hope in the fullness of our redemption, we pray with confidence that the Triune God can and will heal our land and all who dwell in it, for the glory of his matchless name.[52]

---

[52]Ibid.

LIVING ETHICALLY

*To talk about "ethical leadership" is to speak from experience, not because
you were a perfect leader, but because you were thrust into difficult
situations—stirring hatred or calling for cool heads, igniting a war or
enshrining peace, reaching out to the poor or assuming they will perish—
and maybe you helped to see humanity prevail.*

DESMOND TUTU

As I write this, the world is mourning the loss of Nelson Mandela. Mandela
was a remarkable ethical leader. He paid a high personal price for his fight
against injustice and discrimination and apartheid. Mandela was released
from prison in 1990. He won the Nobel Peace Prize in 1993 and became the
first democratically elected president of South Africa in 1994. Mandela's auto-
biography, *Long Walk to Freedom*, had a deep and lasting affect on me when
I read it in 1995.

Mandela advocated *ethical leadership* and called a generation of African
and world leaders to it. Leaders behave ethically when they pursue justice,
freedom, reconciliation, peace, equality and mercy:

> It was during those long and lonely years that my hunger for the freedom of
> my own people became a hunger for the freedom of all people, white and
> black. . . . The oppressed and the oppressor alike are robbed of their humanity.

When I walked out of prison that was my mission, to liberate the oppressed
and the oppressor both. . . . For to be free is not merely to cast off one's chains,
but to live in a way that respects and enhances the freedom of others.[1]

Archbishop Desmond Tutu is another well-known antiapartheid figure.
Tutu defended human rights during apartheid and continues to do so since
its demise. He received the Nobel Peace Prize in 1984. Since then, he has won
other international peace prizes.

Tutu also uses the term *ethical leadership* often and challenges world and
church leaders to it. Tutu says that ethical leaders stand *for* justice and peace
and reconciliation. They stand *against* violence, discrimination, disease,
poverty, racism, sexism and exploitation. They have ethical roles, including
the following: (1) advocating for the powerless and marginalized and silenced; (2) communicating ethical principles; (3) warning against war and
violence; (4) upholding human dignity; (5) seeking truth and reconciliation;
(6) foreseeing and naming ethical challenges; (7) standing with victims; (8)
demanding action; (9) respecting and enhancing human and animal and
ecological freedom; and (10) urging the pursuit of justice, truth, reconciliation and peace.[2]

Christian ethics is about what is *good* (virtuous, noble and worth valuing)
and what is *right* (right individual and corporate moral behavior). Arthur F.
Holmes says that Christian ethics "examines alternative views of what is
good and right; it explores ways of gaining the moral knowledge we need; it
asks why we ought to do the right; and it brings all this to bear on the practical moral problems that arouse such thinking in the first place."[3]

Christian ethics explores these questions about the good and right
through key sources. These include the Bible, Christian theology and tradition.[4] Christian ethics also consult philosophical, scientific, religious, cultural and other relevant sources (i.e., human knowledge and experience of

---

[1]Nelson Mandela, "Nelson Mandela Reflects on Working Toward Peace," 2008, www.scu.edu/ethics
/architects-of-peace/Mandela/essay.html.

[2]Desmond Tutu, "Who Will Lead Syria out of Crisis?," *The Elders*, October 30, 2013, http://
theelders.org/article/who-will-lead-syria-out-crisis.

[3]Arthur Frank Holmes, *Ethics: Approaching Moral Decisions*, Contours of Christian Philosophy
(Downers Grove, IL: InterVarsity Press, 1984), 10.

[4]Especially the creation narrative, the Decalogue, wisdom ethics, ethics of the prophets, the teaching
and practices of Jesus (especially on the kingdom of God and during the Sermon on the Mount),
the ethics of the apostles, eschatology and ethics, and Pauline, Petrine and Johannine ethics.

the world). And Christian ethics consults particular ethical traditions and fields. There are too many to name. But *virtue ethics* is a good example (how your character and virtues shape your behavior). And so is *bioethics* (the ethics of medicine and the biological sciences).

The West has much to learn from indigenous cultures and the Majority World about ethics. They can especially teach us about the cultivation of *applied ethics* (ethics associated with politics, power, war and peace, sexuality, family, criminal restoration, truth telling, religion, medicine, finance and economics, globalization and care of creation).

Majority World thinkers often link mission and ethics.

The missional church pursues the ethics of the kingdom of God and the Sermon on the Mount. The ethical church is missionally oriented. It stands for justice and liberation and peace.

Louise Kretzschmar of the University of South Africa writes, "Theological ethics is inescapably linked to the missio Dei, the mission of God in the world." She says that the task of ethics is, therefore, fourfold. It analyzes "the nature, extent, and causes" of global ethical problems. It proclaims salvation. It pursues human freedom and liberation. And it acts in ways that lead to the transformation of individuals and societies. "Theological ethics, therefore, adopts a world-transforming rather than a world-escaping approach to social and physical realities."[5]

This chapter considers how indigenous and Majority World writers approach these themes when doing ethics: biblical theology, culture, interreligious relations, church, personal integrity, politics, sexuality, medicine, commerce, ecology and ethical commitments. I proceed in that order. This chapter asks, *What can we learn from how Majority World Christians express the ethics of Christ and his kingdom?*

BIBLICAL ETHICS

Majority World thinkers and pastors often discuss applied ethics. But they pursue the specialized discipline of theological ethics less commonly. People like Vimal Tirimanna (Sri Lankan) and Nimi Wariboko and Samuel Waje

---

[5]As quoted in Charles Villa-Vicencio and John W. De Gruchy, *Doing Ethics in Context: South African Perspectives*, Theology and Praxis (Cape Town: David Philip, 1994), 22.

Kunhiyop (both are Nigerian) are exceptions to the rule.[6]

Most Majority World Christian leaders who examine ethical issues are not trained as ethicists. They have trained as biblical scholars, theologians or pastors. A level of expertise is lost when this is the case.

On the positive side, ethical reflection in the Majority World has many good qualities. It is often biblically faithful, culturally sensitive, prophetic and concretely applied. This is true even when theological and philosophical sophistication is lacking.

Recently, I spent a day listing the ethical concerns of Majority World Christian literature. I also listed the theological themes associated with those concerns. Imagine my surprise when a friend gave me a copy of Christopher Wright's *Old Testament Ethics for the People of God*. The ethical concerns I had listed, and their associated theological themes, basically appear in Wright's chapter headings.

Old Testament and Majority World ethics consider the *theological* ground for ethics, especially as found in God's actions, words, sovereignty and holiness. They treat the *social* location of ethics (how do we *together* think and act ethically?). They deal with the *economic* dimension of ethics (land, wealth, generosity, stewardship and so on). And they cover the *applied* scope of ethics (both bodies of literature focus on ethics relating to ecology, economics, poverty, justice, the land, truth telling, politics, war, violence, legal systems, culture, love, race, nation, marriage, family, divorce, domestic violence, sexuality, rape, prostitution, witchcraft, corruption, power and so on).[7]

In a sense, this is not news. Philip Jenkins, for instance, demonstrates how Old Testament themes and stories resonate with Christians of the Global South.[8] To my delight, I had discovered significant correspondence between

---

[6]Nimi Wariboko's book, *The Pentecostal Principle*, provides an especially sophisticated treatment of Pentecostal-theological method in social ethics. "This book argues that ethical methodology (engagement) must assume the mode of cultural criticism, social creativity, and political engagement in which we should resist commitment to any knowledge-machinery that only works to understand the world but not change it, and instead we must provoke moral development, and enact constituting and constituted social practices of human flourishing." For Wariboko, this is an "ethical methodology in a new [Pentecostal and theological] spirit." Nimi Wariboko, *The Pentecostal Principle: Ethical Methodology in New Spirit* (Grand Rapids: Eerdmans, 2012), ix, xii.

[7]Christopher J. H. Wright, *Old Testament Ethics for the People of God* (Downers Grove, IL: InterVarsity Press, 2004).

[8]Philip Jenkins, *The New Faces of Christianity: Believing the Bible in the Global South* (Oxford: Oxford University Press, 2006).

the ethical concerns of the Old Testament and those of the Majority World.

Of course, the New Testament deals with these themes too. Glen Stassen and David Gushee show us how the teachings and practices of Jesus deal with ethical themes. This is especially the case in Jesus' teaching on the kingdom of God and during the Sermon on the Mount.[9]

Samuel Waje Kunhiyop draws on theological themes in the Old and New Testaments to build a biblical foundation for African Christian ethics. He provides an example of how biblical and cultural themes can converse as we construct culturally appropriate ethics. He puts African ethics—based in African customs, stories, taboos, oral traditions and communities—into conversation with biblical ethics. He shows how community is central to both African and biblical ethics. We must root our biblical ethics in trinitarian and human community. African ethics are inconceivable outside of human community.[10]

I consider the importance of community in Majority World ethics later in this chapter.

But I want to make this point clear: the correspondence between the concerns of biblical and Majority World ethics is striking.

CULTURAL ETHICS

It should not surprise us that ethics shape, and are shaped by, their cultural context. We make individual and corporate ethical decisions by putting these things into conversation: Bible, theology, reason, experience, tradition, culture and the guidance of the Holy Spirit. Culture affects our interpretation of the Bible. And our application of Scripture to ethical problems is always sociocultural.

This is why we need to listen to many cultures as we construct Christian ethics.

M. Daniel Carroll is a Guatemalan theologian. He notes the importance of cultural conditioning for Christian social ethics. Quoting Lausanne, Carroll says that Christian social ethics must do three things: (1) recognize cultural conditioning; (2) appreciate cultural variety; and (3) put the Bible

---

[9]Glen H. Stassen and David P. Gushee, *Kingdom Ethics: Following Jesus in Contemporary Context* (Downers Grove, IL: InterVarsity Press, 2003).

[10]Samuel Waje Kunhiyop, *African Christian Ethics* (Nairobi: Hippo Books, 2008), 65-66.

and theology into conversation with these cultural values and behaviors and ethical challenges.[11]

Cultures wrestle with their own particular ethical issues. Particular ethical problems take center stage from culture to culture. Global ethical issues inform these particular cultural challenges, and vice versa.

For example, a team from the International Baptist Theological Seminary in Prague, Czech Republic, recently conducted a major research project: *A Comparative Mapping of Baptist Moral Concerns and Identity in Six Regions of Europe and Central Asia*. Their study considers how different cultures prioritize ethics to do with sexuality, marriage, church unity, war, violence, medicine, speech, poverty, justice and refugees and asylum seekers.

The findings are fascinating. Moldovan Baptists, for example, emphasize ethics having to do with divorce and remarriage. Bulgarian and Polish Baptists focus on ethics that have to do with poverty and justice. Baptists from Omsk Oblast (southwestern Siberia) believe the key ethical issue of our time is refugee and relief work.[12]

There is much to explore here. Why do these different Eastern European and Central Asian cultures prioritize certain ethical problems? It is clear that culture plays a major role in ethical consideration and prioritization. And these cultures and their ethics are almost always focused on community.

COMMUNITY-BASED ETHICS

In *African Christian Ethics*, Kunhiyop describes the role of church and community in African traditional and Christian ethics. It is one of the clearest treatments of the role of relationships, community and church in non-Western Christian ethics available.

Kunhiyop quotes John Mbiti when he describes the centrality of community in traditional cultures. Mbiti says that in traditional life people see themselves entirely within the context of community.

> In traditional life, the individual does not and cannot exist alone except corporately.... The community must therefore make, create or produce the individual;

---

[11]M. Daniel Carroll R., "The Relevance of Cultural Conditioning for Social Ethics," *Journal of the Evangelical Theological Society* 29, no. 3 (1986).

[12]Walter Wink, *Engaging the Powers: Discernment and Resistance in a World of Domination*, The Powers (Minneapolis: Fortress, 1992).

for the individual depends on the corporate group. . . . Whatever happens to the individual happens to the whole group, and whatever happens to the whole group happens to the individual. Therefore the individual can only say, "I am because we are, and since we are, therefore, I am."[13]

In this context, morality and ethics are completely social, even when practiced by an individual. Individuals practice morality within broader social contexts. These include families, groups, villages, tribes, clans, societies, nations and humanity.

Kunhiyop proceeds to construct a theology for Christian ethics. He places community and relationship at its core. He starts with the Trinity. When it comes to Christian ethics, God the Father is the *norm*. Jesus Christ is the *model*. And the Holy Spirit is the *power*. Furthermore, trinitarian relationships and actions shape our understanding of ethical community. Trinitarian relations exemplify love, service, sacrifice, reciprocity, mutuality and self-giving. The Trinity's love and mission show us the shape of real community and witness and ethics.

Kunhiyop says that our desire for community results from God creating us in his image. He places us within relationships and redeemed communities. We will enjoy community with each other and with the Trinity eternally. Relationships—human and divine—form our convictions about what is good and right. By the grace of God, we have entered an ethical community. Together we pursue the ethics of Christ's kingdom. Together we form ethical, Trinity-imaging relationships.[14] When the church is truly the church, it's an ethical community. The church reveals *kingdom ethics* as a foretaste of Jesus' inaugurated kingdom.[15]

This obedience to Jesus results in *lived ethics*. We are witnesses to Jesus and his kingdom and the new humanity. This means that our personal and corporate *integrity* supports our ethical positions. Our lives testify to the goodness and rightness and justness of the ethics we embrace: the ethics of the kingdom of God.

---

[13]Kunhiyop, *African Christian Ethics*, 21; John S. Mbiti, *African Religions & Philosophy* (London: Heinemann, 1969), 108-9.

[14]Kunhiyop, *African Christian Ethics*, 7-71.

[15]C. René Padilla and Tetsunao Yamamori, eds., *The Local Church, Agent of Transformation: An Ecclesiology for Integral Mission* (Buenos Aires: Ediciones Kairos, 2004), 33, 34, 49.

ETHICAL INTEGRITY

Ethical teachings and positions are meaningless without ethical integrity. If we contradict our teachings through our lives and behaviors, then our ethics lack credibility.

This principle is true in all cultures: the most persuasive moral voices live consistent moral lives. Their private and public integrity confirms their articulated ethics. They show ethical integrity. Many people see it and admire it and aspire to do the same (or it outrages them).

The lives of many Christian leaders illustrate this principle. Oscar Romero is a prime example. His moral voice was persuasive because of his integrity. Tod Swanson writes, "Romero had integrity as a public figure. He lived in such a way that his life, and especially his death, became an exemplary embodiment of the larger religious narrative that both grounded his ethics and gave meaning to the nation."[16]

Swanson describes how Romero's "moral reasoning resonated with Salvadoran identity." Romero's "moral judgments were timely." His ethical position on institutionalized, political and military violence was apt for San Salvador. Finally, his life was a public testimony to his ethic. Forces assassinated him because of his public message and his personal integrity and because of the alignment between his actions and his message. His ethical integrity cost him his life. This integrity drove home his message about peace and justice.[17]

This alignment between life and speech is a pressing issue for the global church.[18] It is one thing to speak about holiness and ethics. It is another to support this message through credible witness and ethical integrity.

Romero and others show us that our integrity must confirm our positions on applied ethics (politics, sexuality, family, biotechnologies, economics, the environment and so on). Our applied ethics are not merely theoretical or theological. We ought to align them with our personal and corporate ethical practices.

---

[16]Tod D. Swanson, "A Civil Art: The Persuasive Moral Voice of Oscar Romero," *Journal of Religious Ethics* 29, no. 1 (2001): 127.

[17]Ibid., 142-43.

[18]See Yee Tham Wan's article on the need for Pentecostals to align their theology of holiness with their moral integrity. He believes this is a pressing global issue for Pentecostals. Perry Shaw, *Transforming Theological Education* (Carlisle, Cumbria: Langham Partnership, 2014).

APPLIED ETHICS

Indigenous and Majority World Christians focus on applied ethics. Here I survey a few of the key themes in these practical ethics: (1) political ethics; (2) financial ethics; (3) scientific and biomedical ethics; (4) sexual and familial ethics; and (5) ecological ethics.

1. Political ethics. Political ethics are ethics involving states and governments and political agents. Political ethics includes these political agents' philosophies, actions, processes and policies. Christian political ethics is about the church's relation to these in the light of the rule and reign of Jesus Christ.

God is sovereign over the world. And he has charged human beings with its care. But we care for a world marred by sin. Sin has widespread consequences, including the corruption of human relations. These relations need external, human management because of sin. God allows governments to rule and to restrain or punish socially damaging expressions of sin. Governments exist for the benefit and good of human societies.

God charges Christians with challenging and supporting this governmental rule. We challenge this rule when it is oppressive, perverted, demonic, idolatrous and self-deifying. We will resist, and even die, when necessary. We resist governmental exploitation or neglect of the silenced and powerless. We call governments to care for the most vulnerable, neglected and invisible in their societies. We resist governmental injustice and violence.

Christians are also charged with supporting governments and their efforts toward peace, justice and law and order. We respect their limited and provisional rule. And we offer submission to all rule exercised within the scope of God's mandate for governments. We cultivate loving, just, peaceful and righteous relationships with each other and our societies. We support law and order. We pursue reconciliation and peace between peoples. We acknowledge the mistakes the church has made in the past and accept responsibility for them. We seek justice for those who have suffered at the hands of the church and its members and leaders. And we seek forgiveness for these mistakes and abuses. We recognize governments and their agencies as gifts from God.

And we embrace our prophetic role. This involves challenging the powers and principalities. It means keeping a vigilant eye on governmental behavior. And it involves witnessing to the rule and reign of Christ.

Christians witness to another kingdom. We prefigure and embody the reign of God in our love, justice, peace and righteousness. We find ways to advance this kingdom and proclaim the gospel as we await Christ's return. We fix our eyes on his final and total transformation of the world.

Christians must diligently protect their political independence. Our complete submission is only to the lordship and rule of Jesus Christ. And we ought to determine the best way to engage relevant political challenges. These include the relationship between church and state and our position on war and violence. We need to determine the nature of our political engagement, especially on contested moral and social issues.

Kunhiyop provides a detailed treatment on the relation between church and state. He outlines the historical positions on this question and examines these positions' expressions in Western and African settings. Kunhiyop concludes, "Three important principles should govern the relationship between church and state: separation, transformation, and involvement."[19]

Church and state must remain separate. The church needs to seek the transformation of the world, including its ethics and political systems. The church is to be deeply involved in the world for the sake of its healing and transformation.

Majority World and indigenous ethicists remind us that our involvement in political ethics is crucial. I briefly outline two areas here. The first is conflict, peace and reconciliation. The second is human rights and political oppression.

1. Conflict, peace and reconciliation. The church must address war, violence and ethnic and religious conflict. Consider the ongoing conflicts in Afghanistan, Pakistan, Syria, Sudan, Israel/Palestine, the Democratic Republic of Congo, the Korean Peninsula and Northern Mali. This is without counting the regions struggling for independence or the countless conflicts between militia-guerrilla, separatist, insurgent and anarchic groups. Between 794,000 and 1,115,000 people died in 2012 in 131 armed conflicts.[20] This requires the church to be about peacemaking and healing and reconciling.

The words of Jesus challenge us to be courageous peacemakers. "Blessed are the peacemakers, for they will be called children of God" (Mt 5:9).

Emmanuel Katongole and Chris Rice describe how reconciliation is at

---

[19]Kunhiyop, *African Christian Ethics*, 104-6.
[20]Amnesty International, *Annual Report 2013: The State of the World's Human Rights* (London: Amnesty International, 2013), www.amnesty.org/en/annual-report/2013.

the heart of the gospel. The church ought to recover "reconciliation as the mission of God." Christian reconciliation begins with God and is his "gift to the world."[21] It is primarily a theological and interpersonal journey. God's reconciliation of all things in the new creation is the final purpose of this ministry. Reconciliation requires lament for the conflicts of the past and the world's brokenness. It has eyes to see God's seeds of hope. Reconciliation requires memory, truth telling and forgiveness. It's served by the ability to imagine a better future. Reconciliation means conversion to God's reconciling grace.

Moreover,

> Reconciliation needs the church, but not as just another social agency or NGO. . . . To be a sign and agent of reconciliation, the church must inspire and embody a deeper vocation of hope in broken places. We do this through our presence in local places and in the everyday and ongoing practices of building community, fighting injustice and resisting oppression, while also offering care, hospitality, and service—especially to the alien and the enemy.[22]

Christian reconciliation "calls forth a specific type of leadership that is able to unite a deep vision with the concrete skills, virtues, and habits necessary for the long and often lonesome journey of reconciliation."[23]

2. Human rights and political oppression. Amnesty International says that in 2012, 112 countries tortured their citizens. One hundred one countries repressed their people's right to freedom of expression. Eighty countries conducted unfair trials.

Christians need thoroughly Christian responses to such abuses.

Vinoth Ramachandra of Sri Lanka says that Christians need to reclaim biblical perspectives on human rights. These must inform their actions. "A rigorous argument for human rights (as in a Christian theological perspective) will radically expose the hypocrisies and double standards of those powerful nations whose domestic and foreign policies run counter to their lip service to universal norms."[24]

---

[21]Emmanuel M. Katongole and Chris Rice, *Reconciling All Things: A Christian Vision for Justice, Peace and Healing* (Downers Grove, IL: InterVarsity Press, 2008), 147.

[22]Ibid., 150.

[23]Ibid.

[24]Vinoth Ramachandra, *Subverting Global Myths: Theology and the Public Issues Shaping Our World* (Downers Grove, IL: IVP Academic, 2008), 125.

Melba Maggay speaks of the church's role in confronting political oppression and violence: "Fresh in the memories of the peoples of the Philippines, Latin America, and Eastern Europe is the church as refuge, sanctuary to dissidents hunted down by repressive regimes, the last stronghold against the menace and madness of political powers gone haywire."[25]

2. Financial ethics. By *financial ethics*, I mean ethics to do with finances and economies. Financial ethics includes such things as poverty, aid, development, economics, markets, globalization and business. Majority World ethicists write a lot on financial ethics. They especially write about themes to do with globalization and poverty.[26]

Globalization has ethical implications[27] and raises many ethical problems. It affects economies, cultures, churches, politics and creation. It has the potential for good and for creating prosperity. But it also reinforces the negative dimensions of Western cultures. These include enthusiastic consumerism and individualism.

Samuel Escobar says that globalization has helped some impoverished societies prosper. But it has also accentuated existing social inequalities and disparities. Some have gotten rich through globalization. The middle classes of Asia, Africa and Latin America are growing at an astounding rate. Five hundred twenty-five million Asians are now middle class. Homi Kharas of the Brookings Institute says that by 2030, 64 percent of the world's middle class will live in Asia. By 2030, almost five billion people will be middle class.[28]

---

[25]Melba Padilla Maggay, *Transforming Society* (Oxford: Regnum, 1994), 36.

[26]I recommend the following books that deal with political and financial ethics (mostly Majority World thinkers): Ramachandra, *Subverting Global Myths*; Kunhiyop, *African Christian Ethics*; Jayakumar Christian, *God of the Empty-Handed: Poverty, Power, and the Kingdom of God* (Monrovia, CA: MARC, 1999); Villa-Vicencio and De Gruchy, *Doing Ethics in Context*; Amartya Sen, *Development as Freedom* (Oxford: Oxford University Press, 2001); Amartya Sen, *There Is a Better Way! An Introduction to the Development as Freedom Approach* (Winnipeg: International Institute for Sustainable Development, 2003); Katongole and Rice, *Reconciling All Things*; Jon Sobrino, "Redeeming Globalization Through Its Victims," in *Globalization and Its Victims*, ed. Jon Sobrino and Felix Wilfred (London: SCM, 2001); Maggay, *Transforming Society*; Vishal Mangalwadi, *Truth and Social Reform*, 3rd ed. (New Delhi: Nivedit, 1996).

[27]The International Monetary Fund (IMF) defines globalization, and its possibilities and challenges, here: *Globalization: Threat or Opportunity?*, April 12, 2000, www.imf.org/external/np/exr/ib/2000 /041200to.htm#II.

[28]David Rohlde, *The Swelling Middle*, Reuters, www.reuters.com/middle-class-infographic. This site allows you to track the growth of the middle classes around the world.

There is another side to this story. While many have been getting wealthier, a "proportion of people are being driven into extreme forms of poverty."[29] In 2013, the Asia Development Bank (ADB) reported that the gap between rich and poor is widening in Asia and across the globe. The Worldwatch Institute summarizes the ADB findings on the widening income inequality in Asia this way:

> Although poverty rates in Asia are declining and inequality rates in the region are lower than in parts of Latin America and sub-Saharan Africa, 15 of the 21 countries the ADB surveyed experienced a proportionate widening in people's incomes since the early 1990s. . . . Among the worst affected were Bangladesh, Cambodia, China, India, Laos, Nepal, and Sri Lanka. . . . Meanwhile, "absolute" inequality—the actual dollar differences in incomes—increased virtually everywhere in Asia between the 1990s and 2000s.[30]

The ADB calls on Asian governments to work against this inequality by investing in education, training and health care.

This is not just an Asian phenomenon. The inequality gap is also widening in countries like the United States and Australia.

Sobrino suggests that the victims of globalization can be its redemption. They summon the world to truth and solidarity and poverty.

The victims of globalization summon the world to *truth*. They call the world to the truth revealed in Jesus Christ. They reveal the way globalization has positive and destructive elements. They summon the world to acknowledge injustice, inequality and suffering. "This suffering is on a massive scale, unjust and cruel; it battens on innocent, defenseless people, and is a product of the world of power (economic, military, political, media, sometimes even church and university)."[31] By revealing the truth, the victims summon the world to mercy, compassion, justice and equality.

The victims of globalization summon the world to *solidarity*. Solidarity means identification, support and closeness to the weak, victimized, ignored and impoverished. The wealthy support the poor and the poor support the rich. "The victims can convert 'a globe' into 'a family,' 'a giant supermarket'

---

[29]Escobar, *A Time for Mission*, 61.
[30]Worldwatch Institute, *Inequality Gap Grows in Asia, United States*, www.worldwatch.org/node /5322.
[31]Sobrino, "Redeeming Globalization Through Its Victims," 110.

into 'a home.' They can also bring in something that, to our great detriment, is virtually absent from present-day civilization: grace."[32]

The victims of globalization summon the world to *poverty*. Sobrino does not mean the poverty typified by oppression and bondage and deprivation. He means a generosity and contentment and way of life that stands in contrast to a world obsessed with capital and wealth and individuality. He means a way of life that is humanizing rather than consuming and greedy and individualistic.

Majority World thinkers write so much on financial ethics that I could not cover it all here. They address poverty, wealth, corruption, employment, strikes, aid, development, economics and globalization.

Jayakumar Christian is one of the most articulate voices on matters to do with "poverty, power, and the kingdom of God." My thirteen-year-old daughter and I have just returned from Malaysia. We had the privilege of hearing Christian teach on serving among the urban poor. He offers seven themes on "developing a kingdom-based paradigm for responding to the powerlessness of the poor": a kingdom-based response (1) reverses the process of disempowerment; (2) confronts the god complexes; (3) heals persons in poverty relationships; (4) addresses inadequacies in worldview; (5) challenges principalities and powers; (6) establishes truth and righteousness; and (7) proclaims that all power belongs to God.[33]

Pope Francis has recently written on the church's missionary transformation. He describes the relationship between the church's mission and its social action. This Argentinian pope addresses social and financial and political ethics. He is a passionate advocate for the poor and powerless and for economic justice. He reminds the global church that it cannot ignore financial ethics.

Francis writes, "As long as the problems of the poor are not radically resolved by rejecting the absolute autonomy of markets and financial speculation and by attacking the structural causes of inequality, no solution will be found for the world's problems or, for that matter, to any problems."[34]

---

[32]Ibid., 112.

[33]Christian, *God of the Empty-Handed*, 212-13.

[34]Pope Francis, *Evangelii Gaudium*, www.vatican.va/holy_father/francesco/apost_exhortations /documents/papa-francesco_esortazione-ap_20131124_evangelii-gaudium_en.html.

3. *Scientific and biomedical ethics.* Scientific and biomedical ethics include ethical issues associated with science, medicine, healthcare, infertility, reproductive technologies, contraception, biomedical technologies, life and death responsibilities, genetically modified foods, and disease treatment and prevention.

These issues do not receive the same breadth of ethical consideration in the Majority World as they do in the West. But this is changing. Asian, African and Latin American ethicists provide fresh perspectives on bioethics.[35] And there are particular issues that receive substantial ethical treatment in those settings. HIV/AIDS is an example.

Ramachandra provides a fascinating treatment of the "myths of science." He shows how these myths have influenced humanity. He unpacks the political ideologies of science. Quoting Mary Midgley, Ramachandra says that science offers the world a value-laden system. This system serves as a "moral signpost that could take the place of religion."[36] Its values are rational observation, theory formation, clinical experimentation and intellectual respectability.

Ramachandra doesn't decry all these values. But he does say they are political ideologies. They are "dominant social myths" that compete with other perspectives and often squash alternative ways of seeing the world. Ramachandra describes the moral responsibilities associated with scientific research. He especially considers genetic engineering, eugenics, biomedical advances and artificial intelligence.

What is Ramachandra's main point? He wants us to realize that we don't have to choose between being "gods or nothings." We aren't *nothings* that have evolved in a vast, uncaring universe. We don't have to be nihilistic about our existence. But we are also not *gods*. We don't have "unlimited

---

[35]Catholic Theological Ethics in the World Church (CTEWC) organized a conference on bioethics in 2010. Almost six hundred theological ethicists from seventy-five countries attended. After the conference, Andrea Vicini reported that Asians, Africans and Latin Americans provided fresh insights into global ethical issues. Vicini's report summarizes interesting bioethical considerations happening in those settings. Graham Hill, ed., *Servantship: Sixteen Servants on the Four Movements of Radical Servantship* (Eugene, OR: Wipf and Stock, 2013). Also see the journal *Developing World Bioethics*: "*Developing World Bioethics* provides long needed case studies, teaching materials, news in brief, and legal backgrounds to bioethics scholars and students in developing and developed countries alike. . . . *Developing World Bioethics* is the only journal in the field dedicated exclusively to developing countries' bioethics issues." http://onlinelibrary.wiley.com/journal/10.1111/%28 ISSN%291471-8847.

[36]Ramachandra, *Subverting Global Myths*, 174.

capacity for self-design on the part of the technocratic magi of the future."
We aren't supreme over creation. Ramachandra concludes, "A Christian
theological anthropology recognizes the multidimensional nature of human
experience."[37] Christians believe that faith, theology, science, medicine and
ethics need each other. Together, they offer human well-being.

HIV/AIDS is a topic in this area that receives a lot of consideration. The
World Health Organization provides these key facts on the epidemic: "HIV
continues to be a major global public health issue, having claimed more than
36 million lives so far. . . . There were approximately 35.3 (32.2–38.8) million
people living with HIV in 2012."[38] HIV/AIDS has infected at least 10 percent
of the populations of Botswana, Lesotho, Malawi, Mozambique, Namibia,
South Africa, Swaziland, Zambia and Zimbabwe. The spread of the disease
has remained stable in most of Asia and Latin America. But there has been
a recent increase in Eastern Europe and Central Asia.

The AIDS epidemic, especially in parts of Africa, raises many ethical
questions to do with sexuality, medicine, poverty and society. A person's
lifestyle will determine whether they are at a high or low risk of infection
from the HIV virus. High-risk groups include homosexual and bisexual
men with many partners. They include intravenous drug users who indis-
criminately, frequently or even rarely share needles. People who receive
blood transfusions, such as hemophiliacs, are also at risk. The sexual
partners of those in high-risk groups are also at risk. And children born to
those infected with HIV, or born to parents who are in the high-risk groups,
are at risk.

There are many ethical issues associated with this disease. These include
ethics to do with sexuality, poverty, marginalized persons, social taboos,
access to medicines and care for the sick and dying.

Kunhiyop says, "The Christian response to HIV/AIDS must be multifaceted, focusing both on the church and the community." Pastors and congregations need to care for those living with and dying from the disease.
Educators need to help individuals and communities develop healthier
sexual and lifestyle practices. Spouses face ethical dilemmas. Can they con-

[37]Ibid., 213-14.
[38]HIV/AIDS, Fact Sheet no. 360, November 2014, www.who.int/mediacentre/factsheets/fs360/en/
index.html.

tinue to have sexual intercourse with an infected partner? A host of other ethical issues arise. Kunhiyop provides a moving example:

> I know of a young woman whose husband had died of HIV/AIDS and left her HIV positive. Another young man proposed to her and was told her HIV status, but insisted on marrying her all the same. Some pastors would refuse to officiate at such a wedding because it would likely lead to the untimely death of the groom. Others might be prepared to officiate, provided the couple were given full counseling about the risks they are running and about how to have the safest possible sex within marriage.[39]

There is often discrimination against those infected with the HIV virus. This is especially the case in the areas of employment, accommodation, education and provision of social services. Sufferers experience discrimination in everyday social interactions. Discrimination is often directed against men who are homosexual or who may appear to be homosexual. Discrimination affects those who live in the same household as these individuals. Some direct their discrimination toward hemophiliacs. And cultures may discriminate against ethnic minorities who suffer from the disease. And people may discriminate against health-care professionals who work with those infected with HIV.

The focus of the theological debate associated with the AIDS epidemic in parts of the Majority World has been fourfold. It has focused on a Christian response to homosexuality. It's emphasized a Christian view of marriage and sexuality. It's highlighted the relationship between poverty and societal problems and disease. And it's explored God's role in the AIDS epidemic (and in epidemics in general).

The incarnation and the cross reveal a compassionate God who identified with a suffering world. Jesus Christ shows supreme love, self-sacrifice and identification with the broken, suffering and stigmatized. He is our example. He reveals the ethical approach to HIV/AIDS.

The incarnation, cross and resurrection are about compassion, sacrifice, grace, mercy, reconciliation, truth, forgiveness and human value. They speak of our resurrection to new lives and bodies. These qualities must characterize our ethical response to those infected with HIV.

John Mary Waliggo of Uganda speaks of the loss of a whole generation

---

[39]Kunhiyop, *African Christian Ethics*, 328.

to HIV/AIDS. He then provides a wonderful plan of action for the church. The plan is too comprehensive for me to detail here. But I will summarize its main points. It focuses on the particular vulnerability of girls and women.[40] It develops the church's health and social and education services to respond to the epidemic. It advocates for those who are too poor to access treatment. It promotes partnerships between churches, governments, NGOs, businesses, the United Nations and so on (and doing this to provide collaborative solutions). Waliggo's plan addresses the damaging stigma and discrimination experienced by sufferers. It trains pastors and congregations to care for sufferers and their families. And it welcomes sufferers and their families into "warm, non-judgmental and compassionate" churches and homes.[41]

Musa Dube of Botswana calls the church to see this epidemic as more than a matter of medicine and individual morality. We must address issues of poverty and discrimination in this epidemic and in other global healthcare issues. We need to pursue a plan of action like the one outlined by Waliggo.

And we must develop churches that are able to interpret Scripture among and with sufferers. These churches and their leaders will help communities explore key biblical and social themes. These themes include suffering, justice, sexuality, discrimination, poverty, gender inequality, healing, hope and resurrection. And the church must learn to listen to sufferers as it interprets Scripture with them and develops its ethics.[42]

Kay Lawlor of Kitova Hospital in Uganda calls this ethic the "way of the cross." Using the Stations of the Cross, Kitova shows how we meet Jesus Christ as we minister with those who suffer. We encounter Jesus as we practice his compassionate ethic. We meet him at the cross. "We make the way of the Cross in the homes and at the bedsides" of those who suffer. In our care for them, we image the radical ethic of Jesus Christ.[43]

---

[40]See Musa Dube's article on the unique vulnerability of females in societies ravaged by HIV/AIDS. Musa W. Dube, "Reducing Women's Vulnerability and Combating Stigma," *Church & Society* 94, no. 2 (2003).

[41]John Mary Waliggo, "The Church and HIV/AIDS (a Ugandan Pastoral Experience)," *AFER* 46, no. 1 (2004): 29-34.

[42]Musa W. Dube, "Go Tla Siama. O Tla Fola: Doing Biblical Studies in an HIV and AIDS Context," *Black Theology: An International Journal* 8, no. 2 (2010).

[43]Kay Lawlor, *AIDS Way of the Cross*, Kitova Hospital, Masaka, Uganda, www.afriprov.org/index.php /african-stories-by-season/12-easter-stories/38-aids-way-of-the-cross-kitovu-hospital-masaka -uganda.html.

4. Sexual and familial ethics. Many Majority World cultures are changing. Globalization, Western media, economic prosperity and shifts in political and cultural power are influencing them. This effects perspectives on sexuality, gender and family. Cultures that were once sexually conservative—with clear gender roles and family cohesion—are now changing. This leads to much discussion about sexual and gender and family ethics.

Majority World ethics cover such issues as patriarchy and matriarchy, masculinity and femininity, feminism and womanism, misogyny and sexism, abortion and contraception, and parenthood and marriage.[44] They address culture and its relation to sex and gender and family. They tackle issues to do with pornography, rape, sexual exploitation, incest, predatory violence, human and sex trafficking, prostitution, female circumcision, and pedophilia.[45] These ethics explore the intersections of gender, religion, race, poverty and class. They cover sex education for young people. They address marriage as between a man and a woman (dominant Western view) or marriage as between families and families (common Majority World view).[46] They tackle monogamy and polygamy, divorce and remarriage, and widows and orphans. These ethics explore gendered division of labor and family responsibilities. They challenge systemic gender violence and propose intervention programs. They look at gender inequality and issues to do with human rights—especially the neglected or violated rights of women and children. They cover sexual orientation and homosexuality and bisexuality. These ethics address issues to do with political instability, war and violence and the unique vulnerability of women and girls. They examine HIV/AIDS and other epidemics and the way in which they affect families and genders. They consider the relationships between education, health care, employment and gender. They analyze the connections between gender and religious ideologies. And, importantly, these ethics deal with the church's role in perpetuating, challenging and healing these issues.

I cannot cover all these issues here. So I will just focus on ethics to do with the protection of women and children.

Writing from the Ugandan context, Waliggo and Benedict Ssettuuma

---

[44]Don Richardson, *Peace Child* (Glendale, CA: G/L Regal Books, 1974).
[45]Kunhiyop, *African Christian Ethics*, 271-311.
[46]Ibid., 190.

write about the plight of women and children in armed conflicts. After caring for women and children in African war zones, Waliggo describes "abduction, rape, defilement, forced marriages, brutal beatings, widowhood, loss of life, inability to provide for the family, displacement, mental and psychological torture, trauma, mistrust, feelings of revenge, sense of help-lessness, dehumanization, and constant fear."[47]

Waliggo calls African churches to joint action to address these issues. They must join with each other and with governments and other agencies in efforts to find solutions. He describes the actions of churches as they address issues such as children-soldiers and the rights of women and children. Waliggo shows how many African churches are peacemaking. These churches also address the rural-urban migration of vulnerable people.

In *The Rights of a Child*, Waliggo says the church has a role in protecting women and children and families. We must denounce "all policies, practices, and attitudes which undermine the full and holistic growth of children."[48] We must take practical actions to address war, violence, poverty, corruption and HIV/AIDS. We should address moral decline, environmental degradation and negative or exploitative cultural practices. Waliggo lists ways in which churches and societies must work together in this cause. These include supporting human rights, advocating for the victimized and providing pastoral care and healing programs. Churches and governments and agencies need to collaborate. Partnerships help develop constitutional, governmental, policing and community safeguards and protections.

June O'Connor gathers the stories of Latin American women. She details their experience of sexual violence, poverty, inequality, family and politics. "These women want us to see the ways in which our lives are implicated in theirs. In this lies the problem but also their hope: because we North Americans are part of their problem we can also be part of the solution."[49]

These and other solutions are not easy in societies ravaged by war and

[47]John Mary Waliggo, "The Plight of Women and Children in Areas of Armed Conflicts in Uganda," *AFER* 45, no. 4 (2003): 375. Also see Muriel Orevillo-Montenegro, *The Jesus of Asian Women*, Women from the Margins (Maryknoll, NY: Orbis, 2006), 199.

[48]Benedict Ssettuuma and John Mary Waliggo, "The Rights of a Child," *AFER* 52, nos. 4-1 (2011): 62.

[49]World Council of Churches, "Together Towards Life: Mission and Evangelism in Changing Landscapes: New Affirmation on Mission and Evangelism," September 5, 2013, www.oikoumene.org/en/resources/documents/commissions/mission-and-evangelism/together-towards-life-mission-and-evangelism-in-changing-landscapes, 290.

violence. But the church must take an active part in protecting and nurturing women and children. It must especially seek the welfare of the most vulnerable. The church ought to work within societies and in cooperation with governments and NGOs and other agencies. Our aim is to ensure all people receive "love and security, food, clothes, shelter, medical care, and education."[50]

5. Ecological ethics. I have dedicated a chapter of this book to indigenous and Majority World perspectives on care for creation.

Creation care raises many ethical issues. Members of the Micah Network met at Limuru, Kenya, July 13–18, 2009. They discussed creation stewardship and climate change. Participants came from thirty-eight countries from all five continents. Latin American theologian René Padilla published the resulting "Declaration on Creation Stewardship and Climate Change."[51]

The declaration covers the church's ethical responsibility to pursue faithful stewardship of creation. As the church, we need to confess and repent of our exploitation and abuse and neglect of creation—and our greed, arrogance and self-centeredness. We must "repent of our self-serving theology of creation, and our complicity in unjust local and global economic relationships." We should "acknowledge that industrialization, increased deforestation, intensified agriculture and grazing, along with the unrestrained burning of fossil fuels, have forced the earth's natural systems out of balance."[52] The Spirit calls us to change our lives so that we live sustainably—practicing God-honoring creation stewardship. This involves rejecting consumerism and greed and environmental exploitation. It means bearing witness to God's love for creation and his redemptive purposes for all creation and includes interceding on behalf of humanity and creation. The church must collaborate with governments, NGOs, other agencies and the United Nations in addressing climate change and ecological destruction. We have a responsibility to partner with those organizations to invest in solutions. We can advocate on behalf of the poor and the vulnerable, who are most likely to suffer from climate change. And finally, we must stop any further denial or delay in our

---

[50]Ibid., 61.

[51]C. René Padilla, "Micah Network Fourth Triennial Global Consultation on Creation Stewardship and Climate Change: Declaration on Creation Stewardship and Climate Change," *Journal of Latin American Theology* 5, no. 1 (2010).

[52]Ibid., 76-77.

ethical responsibilities. "We will labour with passion, persistence, prayer, and creativity to protect the integrity of all creation and hand on a safe environment and climate to our children and theirs."[53]

Korean theologian Jo Yong-Hun puts Hindu, Buddhist and Chinese views of nature into conversation. The goal is to show how Christian creation care can speak with other views of nature in Asian thought. Yong-Hun believes that cooperation between religions and worldviews and cultures is necessary for the preservation of nature: "Although Christianity cannot accept the Asian worldview without a critique, ideas from the Asian religions will be helpful in order to create a global environmental ethos for the preservation of the integrity of creation."[54]

Yong-Hun notes the significant differences between Christianity and Asian religions when it comes to nature. For example, Christianity has a theology of radical transcendence, but Buddhism does not. Christianity has a theology of God as Creator, but Confucianism does not. God is sometimes identified with the universe in Hinduism, but he is not in Christianity.

Still, dialogue and cooperation with other religions and worldviews is necessary, especially if we are to address the present climate and ecological crisis.

South African theologians John De Gruchy and David Field claim that Christian ethics must deal with Christianity's role in our present ecological crisis. Christianity had a role in the development of "modern science, technology, capitalism, and the ideology of progress." These "provided an environmentally devastating combination."[55]

But Christians have also valued and nurtured and protected creation.

Historically, Christianity has been ambiguous toward the environment. Some Christians oppose environmentalism, while others engage with environmental issues. De Gruchy and Field say that Christian ecological ethics must take into account Christianity's critique of the consumer society and of present inequalities. Such ecological ethics must consider Christianity's views on the ethical status of nonhuman life and ecosystems. And these ethics must consider Christianity's approach to reproductive responsibility.

---

[53]Ibid., 78.
[54]Andy Crouch, *Playing God: Redeeming the Gift of Power* (Downers Grove, IL: InterVarsity Press, 2013), 407.
[55]Mangalwadi, *Truth and Social Reform*, 203.

The exponential growth of the human population has had severe impacts on ecosystems and biodiversity. Finally, such ecological ethics ought to examine Christianity's understanding of the relationship between ecological ethics and Christian mission.

The last point is an especially important one. Creation care is integral to our "witness to the creative and salvific reign of God. As the church has been forced to reexamine its witness in relation to the oppression of human beings, so it is now called to do so in the light of the devastation of the environment. In doing so, the church needs to get its own house in order, as well as to issue a prophetic call to society."[56]

ETHICS AND THE GLOBALCHURCH: CONCLUDING REFLECTIONS

Christian ethics and community and mission are closely linked. Christ-honoring churches reveal the ethics of the Sermon on the Mount. These churches do this in their life together and their missional practices. Ethical churches witness to Jesus Christ. They do this through their commitment to justice, holiness, truth, love and peace.

Here are ten things we learn from how Majority World Christians express the ethics of Christ and his kingdom:

1. Christian ethics are based on Scripture, faith and the values of Christ's kingdom. Faith, not culture, is the primary source for Christian ethics. Christian faith submits to the authority of Scripture. Christian ethics embrace the values of the kingdom of God. (The Beatitudes, for instance, give us a window into these values.)

I have noted the complex relationship between faith and culture in ethics. But Paulinus Ikechukwu Odozor laments the common temptation to prioritize culture over faith and Scripture. All groups are tempted to do this. But this elevation of culture over faith can often occur when people feel that forces have marginalized or colonized their culture.

Odozor writes,

The Christian faith, not cultural pattern, should provide the theologian with the primary lens through which to view life and reality in general. Only in

---

[56]Villa-Vicencio and De Gruchy, *Doing Ethics in Context*, 208. See also R. S. Sugirtharajah, *Frontiers in Asian Christian Theology: Emerging Trends* (Maryknoll, NY: Orbis, 1994), chap. 19.

this way can the theologian perceive the strengths and the distortions and evil
in any culture. . . . The Christian story is not an arcane or exclusive source of
moral insight, even though, for the Christian, it should be the primary criterion for measuring the soundness of any other source.[57]

We must scrutinize all cultural ethics, practices and values in the light of
Scripture and the values of the kingdom of God revealed in Christ Jesus.
This takes courage and honesty. We don't usually like examining ourselves.
We often avoid scrutinizing what our culture has bequeathed us. It's hard
and uncomfortable work. But we need to scrutinize our ethics in the light
of Christian faith and Scripture.

Scripture and the values of the kingdom of God shape all true Christian
faith-based ethics. We need to put our culture's ethics into conversation with
biblical and kingdom ethics. This means that we will recognize our cultural
conditioning and appreciate cultural variety. We'll put Scripture into conversation with these cultural values and behaviors and ethical challenges.
And we'll courageously explore what emerges.

2. Christian ethics are inculturational. What do I mean by *inculturational*? Inculturation is the adaptation of Christian teaching and ethics for
cultures. And it's the subsequent influence of those cultures on these things.

This is important for much Majority World Christian ethics and theology.
Inculturation is an effort to form indigenous Christian ethics. It seeks to
evaluate colonial and Western legacies. It hopes to transform culture.

Odozor writes, "Inculturation is a continuous process of dialogue between
faith and culture." Its goal is a "symbiotic fusion, as it were, of culture and faith
into a new creation that is Christian because it is totally permeated by the
Spirit and teaching of Jesus Christ." Odozor proceeds to quote Pedro Arrupe
when he describes inculturation. Inculturation is not merely about adapting
theology and ethics to a culture. It is much more than that. It is "*a principle
that animates, directs, and unifies the culture, transforming it and remaking it
so as to bring about a 'new creation.'*"[58]

---

[57]Paulinus Ikechukwu Odozor, "An African Moral Theology of Inculturation: Methodological
Considerations," *Theological Studies* 69, no. 3 (2008): 601.

[58]Odozor, "African Moral Theology of Inculturation," 585. Emphases added. See also Alan J. Roxburgh, M. Scott Boren and Mark Priddy, *Introducing the Missional Church: What It Is, Why It
Matters, How to Become One*, Allelon Missional Series (Grand Rapids: Baker, 2009). A comprehensive list of African texts on inculturation can be found here: Don Richardson, *Peace Child*,

Take the HIV/AIDS epidemic in Africa as an example. Christians shape ethical responses to this outbreak with attention to culture and science and Scripture. But such responses should also lead to the animation, healing and transformation of the cultures affected by HIV/AIDS—that is, to the birth of a "new creation." Waliggo asserts that Christian ethics must engage specific cultural dynamics when responding to HIV/AIDS. As we form ethical responses to these cultural challenges, we engage in inculturation. I list some of these challenges here: (1) African traditional customs and practices ("funeral rites, traditional marriages, initiation, and circumcision rites"); (2) traditional healing, spiritual practices and attitudes to modern medicine; (3) social hierarchies, the exploitation of the vulnerable and the marginalization of the sick; (4) community, neighborliness and social cohesion; (5) a "sub-culture" of "defilement, incest, and rape"; (6) polygamy and polygyny; (7) the sex trade, human trafficking and pornographic consumption; (8) global attitudes to human sexuality, homosexuality, marriage and family; and (9) issues of justice, mercy, peace, forgiveness and reconciliation.[59]

What are the ethical challenges in your situation? What cultural dynamics undergird them? How will you adapt Christian teaching and ethics for your culture? And how will your culture positively influence your understanding of Christian ethics? Will you have the courage to form ethical views and responses that are both *indigenous* to your setting and *adequate* for your culture's ethical challenges?

3. *Christian ethics are political.* Christian ethics have political dimensions and repercussions. Christian ethics challenge the cultures and powers and systems of the world. They witness to an alternative politic. They testify to the kingdom of God.

People like Oscar Romero give us a marvelous example of Christian political ethics before a watching world. Romero was the former archbishop of San Salvador and was assassinated on March 24, 1980, for his Christlike political ethic.[60]

Solidarity with those on the periphery is at the center of such an ethic.

International Adventures (Seattle: Youth With A Mission Pub., 2003), 124-25.

[59]John Mary Waliggo, "Inculturation and the HIV/AIDS Pandemic in the Amecea Region," *AFER* 47, no. 4-1 (2006). See also Laurenti Magesa, *Christian Ethics in Africa*, Christian Theology in African Scholarship (Nairobi: Acton, 2002).

[60]Swanson, "A Civil Art."

When Christians form ethical positions on bioethics, the environment, economics, sexuality, family, human rights, war, and refugees and asylum seekers, they are always engaged in politics. This is even more so when the goal is social and structural transformation.

Jesus' life and work and teaching must shape our social and ethical behavior. When we take Jesus serious, we practice political ethics. This is because our ethics confront issues of power, freedom, justice, relations and status. We engage social and ethical and political issues in word and deed. We tackle them individually and corporately. We address such things as conflict, peace, reconciliation, human rights, political oppression, migration, persecution, displaced persons, economic systems, ethno-religious violence, racial discrimination, gender inequality, ecological responsibility, sexuality, family, scientific and biomedical advances, and the dynamics of globalization. So our ethics are inevitably political. And we witness to the resurrected Lord and his gospel and kingdom.

4. Christian ethics are transformational. Christian ethics have the power to transform people and cultures. So we must examine the nature and extent and causes of global and local ethical problems. We proclaim salvation. And we pursue justice, freedom, liberation and the transformation of individuals and societies. We adopt "a world-transforming rather than a world-escaping approach to social and physical realities."[61]

The Ghanaian theologian Simon Kofi Appiah calls on Christian ethicists to pay attention to Scripture, theology, culture and the human sciences. And he invites Christian ethicists to do this for the sake of cultural transformation. Christian ethics can help cultures "make sense of their past and present cultural, historical, religious, and anthropological experiences." But it can only do this if it calls cultures to "a radical renewal of memory." These cultures make sense of their past and present values and experiences and challenges in the light of the gospel. The gospel speaks to a culture's history and values and sins. The gospel reveals possibilities for renewal and conversion. Christian ethics need this transformational dimension. Otherwise, contextualized Christian ethics are "a masque that covers the concrete situation" of cultures.[62]

---

[61]Villa-Vicencio and De Gruchy, *Doing Ethics in Context*, 2-23.
[62]Simon Kofi Appiah, *Africanness, Inculturation, Ethics: In Search of the Subject of an Inculturated Christian Ethic*, Forum Interdisziplinäre Ethik (New York: Peter Lang, 2000).

Christian ethics must tackle the pressing issues that cultures face. Let's have a look at an example from Africa and one from Asia. And let's start with Africa.

Agbonkhianmeghe E. Orobator shows how Christian ethics must engage and transform the *big five* moral issues of Africa. The first issue is the "lion" of *governance* (ethical approaches to politics, law, policing, military, human rights, poverty, corruption, social inequality, displacement, peace, justice and reconciliation). The second is the "elephant" of *creation care* (ethical approaches to climate change, global warming, natural disasters and sustainable care for the earth). The third is the "rhinoceros" of *genetically modified foods* (ethical approaches to biotechnologies in the light of hunger and scarcity). The fourth is the "buffalo" of *resource extraction* (ethical approaches to mining, water use and the extraction of precious, mineral and natural resources). And the fifth is the "leopard" of *domestic justice* (ethical approaches to human morality—including marriage, sexuality and family life—and justice for the poor and exploited and voiceless).[63]

Now let's turn to an example from Asia. Muriel Orevillo-Montenegro shows how Christian ethics must have a transformational role. This is especially the case when Christian ethics address the marginalized women of Asia. She shows how Asian women are developing indigenous Christologies and associated ethical practices. These can have a transforming effect on women in India, Korea, the Philippines and Hong Kong.

For example, Orevillo-Montenegro writes of the plight of many young girls in the Philippines. Cartels traffic these girls for sex with foreign tourists. The legal and policing systems that should protect these girls ignore and abuse them. She writes how Filipino women's voices are rising. They are seeking justice.

Orevillo-Montenegro shows how Filipino women are exploring the person and work of Jesus afresh. They are meeting Jesus, the Wounded Healer, as wounded healers. "Filipino women must face the challenge to keep going, to embody Christ in accompanying the people in their journey out of the bondage of evil. Her prophetic ministry, her dances,

---

[63]Cf. Agbonkhianmeghe E. Orobator, *Theology Brewed in an African Pot: An Introduction to Christian Doctrine from an African Perspective* (Nairobi: Paulines, 2008).

her songs and rituals, must provide healing and inspiration to the wounded spirits out there."[64]

What are the pressing moral and social and political issues in your culture? How will you and your church provide ethical responses? Will these help lead toward the well-being, liberation, healing and transformation of people in your setting?

5. Christian ethics are dialogical. To engage cultures fully, Christian ethics must speak with their religions and worldviews. Interreligious dialogue is vital. It helps Christian ethics be relevant to cultures and their histories and experiences and values.

Comparative ethics—comparing ethics across religions and worldviews—is common in the Majority World. These cultural and religious melting pots lead to fruitful interreligious, comparative ethics. Majority World ethicists cannot ignore the Abrahamic, Taoic, Dharmic, Shamanic, Animistic, philosophical and secular traditions around them. Majority World Christian ethicists often engage these traditions. They do this to make an impact on their cultures for the sake of Christ.[65]

The same is now true in the West. We do Christian ethics in a pluralistic, global setting. This demands interreligious dialogue and comparison and learning. And it requires us to do this without surrendering, minimizing or apologizing for our distinctive Christian beliefs.

Michael Amaladoss and Peter Phan write much on comparative religious ethics and interreligious dialogue. They examine how religions might share insights on peace and justice and reconciliation. Both Amaladoss and Phan say that the events of September 11, 2001, demand more conversation between the world's major religions. We need more cooperative peacemaking and healing and reconciliation.

Hans Küng's famous dictum says, "No peace among nations without peace among the religions. No peace among the religions without dialogue between the religions. No dialogue between the religions without investi-

---

[64]Orevillo-Montenegro, *Jesus of Asian Women*, 157.

[65]In my opinion, the two best introductions to comparative religious ethics are Darrell J. Fasching, Dell deChant and David M. Lantigua, *Comparative Religious Ethics: A Narrative Approach to Global Ethics*, 2nd ed. (Malden, MA: Wiley-Blackwell, 2011); Joseph Runzo and Nancy M. Martin, eds., *Ethics in the World Religions* (Oxford: Oneworld, 2001). For comparative religions, see Huston Smith, *The World's Religions: Our Great Wisdom Traditions* (San Francisco: HarperOne, 2009).

gation of the foundation of the religions."[66] Phan expands Küng's dictum; he says, "Most importantly, no reaching the foundation of religions without a dialogue of life, action, theological exchange, and, above all, religious experience and prayer."[67]

6. Christian ethics are anamnestic. Bénézet Bujo describes how traditional African ethics are *anamnestic*. By this, he means that Africans shape their ethics around memory and solidarity with the past.

Bujo says, "The ancestors' words and deeds, the norms they set, are made available to the current generation so that it has life and continues to look after the deceased, and so that it prepares the future of the not-yet-born."[68]

I agree with Odozor when he says that all Christian ethics must be anamnestic. All Christian groups remember. We remember our unique cultural and Christian heritage. We also remember our Christian story (the stories and persons and drama of Scripture). We recall God's saving deeds. We remember Jesus' example, teaching, ethics, passion, resurrection and ascension. And we construct Christian ethics as we remember.[69]

7. Christian ethics are relational and community based. Majority World and indigenous ethics show us that Christian ethics must be relational and community based. Tutu and Mandela popularized the Nguni Bantu term *Ubuntu*. *Ubuntu* means that our bonds with others form and express our human nature.[70] Similarly, as Christians we must construct our ethics around notions of human and divine community.

Christian ethics are relationship centered. They're community based. As Kunhiyop says, Christian ethics must image trinitarian relations. They're loving, self-sacrificial, reciprocal and mutual. And Christian ethics are concerned for the well-being of the church, humanity and all creation. This

---

[66]H. Küng, *Global Responsibility: In Search of a New World Ethic* (New York: Crossroad, 1991), xv.

[67]Peter C. Phan, "Global Healing and Reconciliation: The Gift and Task of Religion, a Buddhist-Christian Perspective," *Buddhist-Christian Studies* 26 (2006): 105. See also Peter C. Phan, *Being Religious Interreligiously: Asian Perspectives on Interfaith Dialogue* (Maryknoll, NY: Orbis, 2004); Michael Amaladoss, "Religions for Peace," *America* 185, no. 19 (2001); Amaladoss, "Interreligious Dialogue: A View from Asia," *International Bulletin of Missionary Research* 19, no. 1 (1995).

[68]Bénézet Bujo, "Differentiations in African Ethics," in *The Blackwell Companion to Religious Ethics*, ed. William Schweiker (Malden, MA: Blackwell, 2005), 433.

[69]Odozor, "African Moral Theology of Inculturation," 609. For an expansive treatment of African moral traditions, see Laurenti Magesa, *African Religion: The Moral Traditions of Abundant Life* (Maryknoll, NY: Orbis, 1997).

[70]Desmond Tutu, "A Passion for Justice," *Third Way* 17 (1994): 17.

causes these ethics to emphasize such things as reconciliation and peace and love and freedom. And Christian ethics seek the transformation and well-being of local and global cultures. Majority World and indigenous Christians root their ethics in church and relationship and community. Western Christians must do the same.

8. Christian ethics are foundational for Christian ministry and leadership. We must cultivate *ethical leadership.* We need leaders who stand for justice and peace and reconciliation and oppose violence, discrimination, disease, poverty, racism, sexism and exploitation. It's time to foster "a specific type of leadership that is able to unite a deep vision with the concrete skills, virtues, and habits necessary for the long and often lonesome journey of reconciliation."[71] This includes dedicating ourselves to peacemaking and healing and reconciling.

9. Christian ethics are integral. Christian ethics are about living with integrity. Our private and public integrity needs to confirm our articulated ethics. Integrity must be present in all dimensions of individual and corporate life. This involves removing the distinctions between sacred and secular, physical and spiritual, private and public, evangelism and social action, and so on. It means cultivating individual and corporate integrity— being an *integral* people. We do this through complete submission to Jesus Christ. And we do this through discipleship, love, justice, holiness, reconciliation and peace. Our *lived* ethics must confirm our *proclaimed* ethics.

10. Christian ethics are holistic and glorifying. By *holistic*, I mean that Christian ethics seek the well-being of whole persons, whole families, whole churches, whole cities, whole cultures and the whole creation. More simply put, Christian ethics pursue the welfare of all humanity and all creation. What are some ways that we do this? We are compassionate and welcoming. We welcome sufferers and outcasts into "warm, non-judgmental and compassionate" churches and homes.[72] We make the way of the Cross with those who suffer. We stand with those who church and society shun or discriminate against. In our solidarity with them, we image the radical ethics of Jesus Christ. We are a countercultural people—salt, light and a city on a hill—showing the ethics of the kingdom to a watching world. And we care

---

[71]Katongole and Rice, *Reconciling All Things*, 150.
[72]Waliggo, "Church and HIV/AIDS," 29-34.

for creation. We change our lives so that we live sustainably. We practice God-honoring creation stewardship. We reject consumerism and greed. And we bear witness to God's redemptive purposes for humanity and all creation.

By *glorifying*, I mean that Christian ethics are about bringing glory to the Father, Son and Holy Spirit. Our upright and holy and ethical lives and communities exist to bring glory to the triune God.

As a glocal faith community, we choose to shape our ethics in such a way that we live as those made alive in Jesus Christ. We embrace these ethics in our life together and our service to Christ and his world. Through our individual and corporate ethics, we seek to bring praise and glory and worship to God.

TRANSFORMING
NEIGHBORHOODS

WHAT CAN WE LEARN FROM HOW MAJORITY WORLD
CHRISTIANS TRANSFORM NEIGHBORHOODS
AND ENGAGE IN PLACE MAKING?

*Transformation is to enable God's vision of society to be actualized in all
relationships, social, economic, and spiritual, so that God's will may be reflected
in human society and his love be experienced by all communities, especially
the poor. . . . Fundamentally, Transformation is the transformation of
communities to reflect kingdom values.*

VINAY SAMUEL

On July 18, 2009, the sounds of helicopters and sirens pierced the tranquility of our North Epping neighborhood. Our local newsagent Min Lin, his wife, Yun Lin, her sister Irene Lin and their two sons, Henry and Terry, had been brutally slain in their own home, overnight. The murders were so vicious that police needed to use forensics to identify the family members.

The Lin family was a popular and loved family in our neighborhood. The boys went to school with my children—Henry was twelve and Terry was nine. Terry was in my daughter Grace's class. Their fifteen-year-old daughter Brenda was on a school trip in New Caledonia at the time of the murders.

The violent murder of this family rocked our neighborhood to its core. North Epping is a small Sydney suburb of just over four thousand people. It's a quiet, leafy, middle-class, cul-de-sac suburb, with only one street leading in and out. It's surrounded by the spectacular bushland of the Lane Cove National Park. Community and trust and relational connection characterize our suburb. Families see it as a safe and quiet and neighborly place to raise children. Children and families develop their closest connections within the neighborhood. All my children's best friends live within a few streets from each other.

As you might imagine from this description, the Lin family murders had a shattering effect on our neighborhood. This vicious murder of a family in their sleep splintered our suburb's sense of safety and identity.

In the shadow of this horrendous event, something surprising happened. The neighborhood began to pull together, in a collective move toward healing and solidarity and community. Classmates, teachers, neighbors, friends, family, those who regularly visited their news agency and many others pulled together to provide support and care to each other and to the Lin's surviving fifteen-year-old daughter, Brenda.

Roger Green, the pastor of the neighborhood's Anglican church, took the lead in helping the community deal with its shock and grief. The church invited a registered clinical psychologist and a team of counselors to attend a community night. The night addressed what to expect when a tragedy like this occurs and how to respond as a community. Hundreds of people from our neighborhood attended this night at the church. The psychologist gave insights into how to best answer children's questions. She guided people on how to reassure children as they try to make sense of what happened. There was opportunity for adults and teenagers to ask questions and grieve together. There was also a chance to make commitments to work together to rebuild a wounded community. The church joined with the psychologists to develop a resource for families to use in talking through the tragedy with children. This church also joined with many other community organizations in holding a memorial service.

Children planted a tree in the school in memory of Henry and Terry Lin. The school also established a counseling service. Our local bank set up a support fund to help Brenda Lin. The bank also created two white "grief boxes" for Henry and Terry for anyone (especially children) to leave messages and photos for the boys or the family.

Our neighborhood came together to grieve and heal and support each other and Brenda. And the local church was at the center of this care. Neighbors connected in fresh and profound ways. They were God's grace to each other. Neighbors became a source of courage and transformation and community. Our neighborhood experienced healing and hope. People in our neighborhood engaged in *place making*. That is, they worked together to promote healing, wholeness and well-being.

In this chapter, I consider how the church can be God's instrument of transformation in neighborhoods. We need kingdom-oriented approaches to neighborhood transformation and community building. Our churches must address need, addiction, violence and racial tension. We need to be agents of change and reconciliation and transformation. This chapter invites the church and the reader to consider four important issues: What does it mean to be urban neighbors of hope? How can we be converted to the neighbor? How is the church God's instrument of transformation? And how can we be involved in kingdom-based struggles for justice?

Essentially, this chapter asks, *What can we learn from how Majority World Christians transform neighborhoods and engage in place making?*

BEING URBAN NEIGHBORS OF HOPE

Up until recently, Ash and Anji Barker and their children have lived in the largest urban slum in Bangkok, Thailand. Residents of Bangkok know the Klong Toey slum precinct well. It has a reputation for poverty and crime.

Ash and Anji are Australians. They've dedicated their lives to the transformation of impoverished urban communities and neighborhoods. They established Urban Neighbours of Hope (UNOH) in 1993. From mid-1993 to early 2002, Ash and Anji served within the multicultural Melbourne suburb of Springvale. They served among Pacific Islanders, East Timorese, Vietnamese, Cambodians, Burmese, indigenous Australians and communities of people with mental illness. They focused on church planting, leadership development, community and neighborhood transformation, and missional service.

Recognizing that by 2025 there will be "3 billion urban poor living in poor neighbourhoods," they moved to Klong Toey, Bangkok, in March 2002. They made the move in order to extend UNOH's work beyond Australia into the slums of the Asia Pacific.[1] Ash and Anji and their children have immersed themselves in this urban slum community. They've built deep relationships by loving families and children. They've forged friendships among the most broken and destitute. They've passionately pursued mission and community transformation in this urban slum.

UNOH teams bring the same passion for transformation shared by Ash and Anji Barker. These teams immerse themselves

> in the life of neighbourhoods facing urban poverty, joining the risen Jesus to seek transformation from the bottom up. Living and serving as small, responsive neighbourhood-based teams in urban Thailand, New Zealand, and Australia, [they] have a vision to multiply UNOH teams in cities across the world. . . . [In 2013] there are now 38 full-time UNOH workers who join hundreds of volunteers and neighbours in living and serving Christ in 9 of the neediest urban neighbourhoods in Melbourne, Sydney, Bangkok, Auckland, and Mae Sot (Thai-Burma border).[2]

UNOH's vision is to serve among impoverished urban neighborhoods in six Asia-Pacific cities by 2015. They are developing twenty neighborhood teams, sixty full-time workers and six thousand supporters. The teams are composed of people from the West and the Majority World.

UNOH workers and teams commit to the following covenant. They're a contemporary Protestant *missionary order* characterized by loving obedience, missional service, voluntary poverty and prophetic advocacy. They shape their mission around social justice, incarnational living, compassion and holistic mission. Missional discipleship and presence and small urban-mission teams characterize UNOH. Their vision is "to raise up followers of Jesus who help release neighbourhoods from urban poverty in Asian-Pacific cities." UNOH teams desire to be "neighbours seeking neighbourhood transformation." They commit to the following covenant to be "urban neighbours of hope."[3]

As Urban Neighbours of Hope we covenant with God and each other to

- Live out our passion for loving God and neighbour
- Focus on releasing neighbourhoods from urban poverty

---

[1]Ashley Barker, *Surrender All: A Call to Sub-Merge with Christ* (Springvale: UNOH, 2005), 111.
[2]Compiled from the UNOH website, www.unoh.org/.
[3]Barker, *Surrender All*, 105.

- Grow through equipping each other, neighbours and the broader church to radically follow Jesus and join God's Kingdom coming

To be true to these commitments we share the following common commitments and practices.

A. Loving obedience

Lifestyle commitment: To discern the will and heart-beat of our Lord together and respond faithfully

Personal practice: Have I met God afresh in my Sabbath day, common devotionals and mentoring this month and followed through on any challenges that emerged?

Communal practice: Have we met God afresh in our daily communion times and life together and followed through on any challenges that emerged?

B. Missional service

Lifestyle commitment: To seek God's Kingdom come through sharing Jesus in word, deed and sign

Personal practice: Have I spent at least a third of each work-day and week-end seeking to free my neighbours and neighbourhood from urban poverty?

Communal practice: Have we invited and supported neighbourhood-based discipleship and worship?

C. Voluntary poverty

Lifestyle commitment: To share our lives and resources in solidarity with those facing poverty and injustice

Personal practice: Have I limited my own freedom to seek my neighbour's freedom from poverty?

Communal practice: Have we found and invited Jesus as disguised among 'the least of these' into our lives and open homes?

D. Prophetic advocacy

Lifestyle commitment: To help the broader Body of Christ to take God's special concern for the poor as seriously as Jesus does

Personal practice: Have I discerned and shared what I've been learning and needing from God with the broader Body of Christ?

Communal practice: Have we invited, informed and inspired the broader Body of Christ to more radical responses to Jesus among the poor?

UNOH's book *Voices of Hope* is a ninety-eight-page collection of extraordinary stories of hope and renewal in (mostly) Majority World urban neighborhoods.[4] Similarly, the Mission Advanced Research and Communications Center (MARC) has a Cases in Holistic Ministry series. It covers inspiring case studies in holistic mission and neighborhood renewal and community transformation. These stories are from all over Africa, Asia, Latin America and other parts of the Majority World.[5]

Many neighborhoods desperately need healing and transformation. They need the liberation that only Jesus offers.

Transformation includes (1) individual/personal, (2) public/social and (3) fundamental worldview/cultural transformation. These are Harold Turner's *three levels of mission*.[6] Missional transformation reorients persons and communities and worldviews. It seeks to enable these to embrace the values and attitudes and behaviors of the kingdom of God.

Many churches in the Majority World don't just want the Spirit to renew and transform them. They want this conversion to lead to the transformation of their local, regional, national and global communities. This is a remarkable vision. It starts in local communities and embraces a regional and global vision. It is changing the face of global mission. It is challenging the shape of the global missional conversation. And it is putting the emphasis back on local neighbourhoods. By this I don't just mean urban slums like those UNOH works within. I also mean rural, urban, suburban and other types of neighborhoods.

Majority World missiology often places neighborhoods at the center of authentic mission.

I briefly deal with the theology and practice of *mission as transformation* in my chapter on *contextual mission*. This chapter focuses on local neighborhood transformation and *place making*. God calls his church to transformational engagement with local communities and neighborhoods.

---

[4]Ashleigh Newnham, ed., *Voices of Hope: Stories from Our Neighbours* (Dandenong: UNOH, 2013).
[5]Tetsunao Yamamori, Kwame Bediako and Bryant L. Myers, eds., *Serving with the Poor in Africa*, Cases in Holistic Ministry (Monrovia, CA: MARC, 1996); Tetsunao Yamamori, David Conner and Bryant L. Myers, eds., *Serving with the Poor in Asia* (Monrovia, CA: MARC, 1995); Tetsunao Yamamori et al., eds., *Serving with the Poor in Latin America* (Monrovia, CA: MARC, 1997); Tetsunao Yamamori, Kenneth L. Luscombe and Bryant L. Myers, eds., *Serving with the Urban Poor* (Monrovia, CA: MARC, 1998).
[6]Harold Turner, "The Gospel as Truth in a Secular Society: The Three Levels of Mission in New Zealand," *Evangelical Review of Theology* 18, no. 4 (1994): 348-53.

The Western missional conversation has often explored the shape of missional congregations. But it has only recently begun to examine the shape of missional *place-making* and engagement with neighborhoods. And it is now exploring this theme with enthusiasm. Notable Western examples include the Parish Collective (a collective of missional churches and practitioners and Christ-followers committed to neighborhood renewal) and Urban Neighbours of Hope. Like UNOH, InnerCHANGE is a Christian order serving among poor and marginalized neighborhoods.[7] The writings and ministries of Alan Roxburgh, Bruce Bradshaw, Bryant Myers, Dave Andrews, John Perkins, Michael Duncan, Robert Linthicum, Shane Claiborne, Simon Carey Holt and Viv Grigg also investigate the transformation of neighborhoods. These examples offer a sense of this Western conversation about neighborhood mission and renewal.

Majority World churches are also exploring transformation of local communities and neighborhoods. They're doing this creatively.

The Inhabit Conference is an example of the collaboration that can happen when Majority World and Western leaders come together. At this conference, leaders from all over the globe join to "discover the imaginative, redemptive, and courageous practices that stir up God's dream in particular places."[8] The focus of this multivoiced conference is courageous *practice*, transformational *presence* and local *place*.

The Spirit invites the church to ask, How can we cultivate churches that renew and heal neighborhoods? How can we engage in *place making*? How can we help churches do this in such a way that they are *both* transformed and transforming? How do we shape churches that join with Jesus in changing neighborhoods from the bottom up?

BEING CONVERTED TO THE NEIGHBOR

The church needs a *conversion to the neighbor* if it is to embrace *mission as transformation*.[9]

Vinay Samuel describes transformation like this: "*Transformation* is to

---

[7]Here are the websites for these three groups: http://parishcollective.org, www.unoh.org and www.innerchange.org.

[8]"Inhabit Conference: The Art of Parish Renewal," last modified March 7, 2013, www.nextreformation.com/?p=10598.

[9]Gustavo Gutiérrez, *A Theology of Liberation: History, Politics, and Salvation* (Maryknoll, NY: Orbis, 1988), 194.

enable God's vision of society to be actualized in all relationships, social, economic, and spiritual, so that God's will may be reflected in human society and his love be experienced by all communities, especially the poor. . . . Fundamentally, *Transformation* is the transformation of communities to reflect kingdom values."[10] The church mainly pursues transformation and its practices in local communities and neighborhoods.

Gustavo Gutiérrez claims that we encounter God in human relations. This encounter especially happens as we engage with human beings in church and community and society. God loves and reveals himself through our neighbor—so we need a "conversion to the neighbor, to social justice, to history."[11] To love God is to seek justice and healing and liberation for our neighbor. It is to join in God's ministry of reconciliation—bringing justice, salvation, beauty and wholeness. The incarnation of Jesus Christ compels us to embrace our neighbor. It moves us to enter our neighbors' lives and to seek their well-being and salvation and liberation.

Gutiérrez unpacks the parables of the last judgment (Mt 25:31-46) and the good Samaritan (Lk 10:29-37). He shows that "the neighbor was the Samaritan who *approached* the wounded man and *made him his neighbor*. The neighbor, as has been said, is not the one whom I find in my path, but rather the one in whose path I place myself, the one whom I approach and actively seek."[12]

Gutiérrez challenges those of us who know power, privilege, inclusion, access or wealth to make the difficult choice to be "converted" to the service and love of the poor, abused, needy, neglected, despised, wounded and marginalized neighbor:

> It is not enough to say that love of God is inseparable from the love of one's neighbor. It must be added love for God is unavoidably expressed *through* love of one's neighbor. Moreover, God is loved in the neighbor. . . .
>
> The conversion to the neighbor, and in him to the Lord, the gratuitousness which allows me to encounter others fully, the unique encounter which is the foundation of communion of men among themselves and of men with God, these are the source of Christian *joy*.[13]

---

[10]Vinay Samuel and Chris Sugden, eds., *Mission as Transformation: A Theology of the Whole Gospel* (Oxford: Regnum, 1999), ii, xii.

[11]Gutiérrez, *Theology of Liberation*, 205.

[12]Ibid., 198.

[13]Ibid., 200, 207.

Recently the government of the state I live in contracted an international corporation to widen a freeway, including major bridgework. This freeway runs parallel to my street. Our government informed us that this would mean two years of construction noise, often at night. The noise included jackhammering, concrete sawing and heavy machinery. The company erected a crane that leaned over our houses.

In response to this, I went door to door inviting neighbors to join a community action group. The purpose of the group was to demand consideration of how this construction affected our lives. Twenty families came together to represent our neighborhood. As chair of the community action group, I wrote letters on the group's behalf. I contacted local and state and federal politicians. I sought appropriate forms of relocation and compensation.

A Nepalese family live two doors up from us. Their teenage daughter was studying for her final year at high school during this construction. I raised their case before our state member for Parliament and our federal minister for transport and infrastructure. I also wrote letters to the chief executive officer of the contracted international corporation. Thankfully, the company relocated the family to alternative accommodation on the noisiest nights at no cost. This Nepalese Hindu family has welcomed my family into their lives as have many of the twenty families in our community action group.

Love for God is always expressed through love of our neighbor. Kōsuke Koyama speaks of *neighborology*. While our neighbors may not care about our theology, they are often interested in our neighborology. In Luke 13:11-16, we have the story of Jesus healing a sick woman on the Sabbath. The religious rulers are enraged that Jesus does this on the Sabbath. Jesus exposes their hypocrisy and misunderstanding of the Scriptures and the kingdom of God. Koyama writes, "The uncushioned neighborology of Christ cuts like a knife through the cushioned neighborology of the ruler of the synagogue." Jesus Christ is the "uncushioned *neighbor* to us all."[14]

The church needs to be present with people. For Koyama, "Christian presence, which is rooted in and participates in the crucified Christ, must demonstrate the quality of Christ's glory in suffering, his exaltation in rejection."[15] Koyama says that this presence among our neighbors—this per-

---

[14]Kōsuke Koyama, *Water Buffalo Theology*, 25th anniversary ed. (Maryknoll, NY: Orbis, 1999), 67.
[15]Ibid., 160-70.

sonal identification with the world—has at least three modes: it's a stumbling presence, a discomforted presence and an unfree presence.

Stumbling presence: "Can unstumbling Christians point to the shaking of the foundations caused by the crucified Lord? Can Christians bear witness to Christ's crucified lordship unless they themselves stumbled at it? Can a house unshaken bear witness to the earthquake which is going on?"[16]

Discomforted presence: "Can Christians who do not involve themselves in the great 'discomfort' of the nailed Christ point to the source of all comfort? Isn't it true that precisely because they are comforted by the crucified Lord, they are inescapably involved in the 'discomfort' of the crucified Lord?"[17]

Unfree presence: "We are called to participate in all situations of life as the Incarnate Lord fully did. Yet this participation must not lead them to 'drink the cup of demons.'"[18] We're not so free that we are free to sin.

Our conversion to the neighbor leads to transformation and hope when we practice Christ-centered presence.

BEING GOD'S INSTRUMENT OF TRANSFORMATION

At the Thai-Cambodia border near Poipet there is a one-kilometer-long gambling strip. This area has manicured lawns, luxury hotels, air-conditioned shopping centers, eight casinos and many brothels. Gambling kingpins, mobsters, drug and human traffickers, and corrupt officials and soldiers control much of the activities of this gambling strip. Thais and Cambodians gamble around three billion US dollars in casinos every year. Thailand bans casinos, so people gamble much of that money in this strip between Thailand and Cambodia. They also gamble at other border crossings. There are now thirty-two casinos located in Cambodia. These are mainly located at border crossings into Thailand and Vietnam.

Around two thousand Thais and Cambodians flock to these eight casinos every day to gamble and work and visit brothels. Many low-paid Cambodians and Thais work in this gambling precinct. Poverty and powerful criminal groups trap them in a debt cycle. The casinos have caused a population boom in Poipet. Many poor Cambodians move there to find work in

---

[16]Ibid., 163.
[17]Ibid., 166.
[18]Ibid., 170.

casinos but end up trapped in poverty or criminal activity. Or criminal organizations traffic them to other countries as illegal construction or sex workers. Child trafficking and prostitution is widespread in Cambodia. The social and human costs of the situation I am describing are incalculable. And the people living in and around the wild border town of Poipet suffer greatly from this situation.

Into this scenario, enter Sopern Pov, a Cambodian national, his Australian fiancé Pip Miner and a team of Cambodians and Australians committed to bringing hope and transformation to Poipet. Pip and Sopern lead a small nongovernment organization in Poipet called Christian Care for Cambodia (CCFC). This group collaborates with local churches to bring social change and healing. They do this through sport, education, development and ministry.

Recently, I had the privilege of spending a week with Sopern and the team in Poipet. My daughter and I rode around on motorbikes with members of the CCFC team, visiting their community projects. Pip and Sopern and their team connect with over two thousand people every week through activities like soccer, volleyball, tae kwon do and running. They conduct regular visits to drug detention centers, teach English and provide resources to local schools. They run kids clubs, give emergency relief and rebuild homes.

Their family and child development program provides educational support and economic empowerment to families in poverty. Their youth program, in partnership with churches, provides education and sports activities. They also have a program that assists tertiary students at the masters level.

Poipet is one of the rougher parts of Cambodia for young people. Many get involved in trafficking and drugs and crime. So Pip and Sopern spend a lot of time collaborating with local churches to help youth. The youth program involves sports ministry, creative arts, educational help and mentoring children and youth. This program enhances young people's potential for education and employment. It also develops their leadership capacities.

Pip, Sopern and their team teach English to youth and teachers at several small schools around Poipet. Some of these schools meet under a house or in a shed. The team also holds an annual English Camp or English Intensives, usually in conjunction with a visiting team. They also collaborate with a two-room community school that provides preschool and primary school education for over one hundred children. Through this school, the CCFC team and local churches develop relationships with Poipet parents and neighbors. They help these people identify the assets available within their own community.

The CCFC team and its partner churches are bringing hope and transformation into one of the most impoverished towns in the Asia-Pacific. They are agents of transformation, reconciliation, justice, beauty and hope in this wild, frontier neighborhood in Asia. God calls each of us to be instruments of transformation in our neighborhoods.

BEING INVOLVED IN STRUGGLES FOR JUSTICE

In *Transforming Society*, Melba Padilla Maggay challenges the church to take part in struggles for justice. She examines biblical and historical models for effective Christian involvement in social transformation. Maggay says the church has usually engaged in four approaches to social transformation.

The first is being an alternative, exemplary and *countercultural community*. This involves witnessing to the gospel and the kingdom by being "salt" and "light." The Anabaptists and Mennonites and Quakers exemplify this approach.

The second is being an *influence on power structures* and making an appeal to them through the promotion of Christian ideals and principles. Christian political parties take this approach, and it was the dominant approach in Western Christendom.

The third is being a *liberationist community* concerned for solidarity and freedom—being a church that seeks the liberation of the oppressed, marginalized, impoverished and powerless. Liberation theology embodies this approach.

The fourth is being a *compassionate presence* in the world. This involves bearing witness to Christ through compassionate care of the sick and wounded and broken. Catholic orders, like the one established by Mother Teresa, epitomize this approach. So do multinational Christian aid and development agencies.[19]

---

[19]Melba Padilla Maggay, *Transforming Society* (Oxford: Regnum, 1994), 46-67.

Maggay seeks to integrate these approaches through the metaphors of *prophet, priest* and *king*. The church has a prophetic role ("bringing the Word of God to the world," including the political arena). It has a priestly role ("bringing the need of the world to God and the power of God to the world" through compassion and liberation and care). And it has a kingly role ("managing the world under God" by taking part in technological and economic and developmental advancement).[20]

Whenever the church takes part in social transformation it finds itself going through a process of change. This change can be renewing or retrograding. And change occurs no matter what approach the church adopts. Maggay is careful to note this. So is Jayakumar Christian in *God of the Empty-Handed*. Christian examines the strengths and weaknesses of various Christian approaches to social transformation. He considers developmental, liberationist, countercultural and evangelical models. Christian then discusses a recent development in social transformation in the Majority World (especially in India). Megachurches, church plants, mainline churches, Pentecostal churches and parachurch groups are focusing on neighborhoods. They are putting enormous, concentrated effort into changing local neighborhoods and joining with community leaders and organizations to address their concrete needs. This includes poverty, crime, employment, infrastructure, housing, family, youth and so on. Christian notes the importance of carefully considering our approaches to social transformation—since in the process the church is both transforming and transformed.[21]

Maggay says that we shape the best responses around a theology of the cross. The cross leads us to a self-emptied, Christ-centered, obedient and sacrificial confrontation with powers and principalities. The way of the cross binds us to people and their needs and neighborhoods. We must develop approaches that focus on strategic minorities (i.e., those who influence their communities). And we need to address the practical needs and concerns and interests of local people. These strategies pay careful attention to personal and community flourishing and well-being. These responses practice

---

[20]Ibid., 68-75.
[21]Jayakumar Christian, *God of the Empty-Handed: Poverty, Power, and the Kingdom of God* (Monrovia, CA: MARC, 1999), 19-166.

"radical pessimism" (they take evil seriously). And they practice "radical hope" (they believe in the possibility of transformation as those who have an ultimate hope).[22]

René Padilla and Christian put it this way:

> The kingdom demands at this critical moment of history nothing less than a revolution of values for the fostering of justice and peace; a restructuring of the church as the community that exists for sacrificial service to the gospel of Jesus Christ, and a renewed spirituality that brings together worship and public life, evangelism and social responsibility, personal faith and kingdom service.[23]

> Kingdom-based response can reverse the process of disempowerment, confront the god complexes, heal persons in poverty relationships, set right inadequacies in the worldview of a people, challenge principalities and powers, establish truth and righteousness, and proclaim that all power belongs to God. . . . Mission is a response in which the kingdom community's involvement at the micro level influences macro-global dimensions at cosmic levels.[24]

PLACE MAKING AND THE GLOBALCHURCH: CONCLUDING REFLECTIONS

As God's people, we must seek a Christ-glorifying transformation of communities and neighborhoods. We do this through meaningful presence and practices and proclamation. And we make a commitment to place. Through these we witness to the hope, power, liberation, reconciliation, wholeness, love and beauty of God's kingdom. As we do this, we find that neighborhoods *and* the local and global church are renewed.

Here are eight things we learn from how Majority World Christians transform neighborhoods and engage in place making:[25]

1. Place making is key to transforming neighborhoods. Place making means immersing oneself in a local neighborhood or community for the long haul. It's about capitalizing on that place's assets, relationships, dreams, imagination and potential so that it becomes what God intends. It's about helping a neighborhood see where God is already at work bringing hope

---

[22]Maggay, *Transforming Society*, 78-108.
[23]Samuel and Sugden, *Mission as Transformation*, 449.
[24]Christian, *God of the Empty-Handed*, 223.
[25]More than a few of these are direct quotes from the UNOH covenant.

and peace and love and renewal. Place making seeks a place's welfare and transformation and flourishing.

Neighbors transform neighborhoods from the inside. That's why place making is key. Local people must cooperate for the renewal and future of their own area. Otherwise, change isn't long-term. Place making is about collaboration. It's people working together over an extended period for the well-being of a local community, and doing this through community-based and community-initiated strategies and relationships. Place making seeks "[his] kingdom come, [his] will be done, on earth as it is in heaven" (Mt 6:10).

2. *Place making nurtures local ecology, local economy, local community and local faith.* In many cities today, people are localizing their lives. They're tired of feeling disconnected. People are planting urban gardens and serving with community-based organizations. They're exploring sustainability and simpler lifestyles. They're buying, building or renting properties that facilitate shared lives and community living. Extended family and multifamily households are increasingly common. People are buying local. They're supporting neighborhood causes, organizations and sporting teams. They're getting rid of cars and catching public transport or walking and cycling to work. Many people in my Sydney suburb are urban homesteading. People are becoming *locavores*—growing, buying and consuming fresh, local produce. They're collecting rainwater, keeping urban livestock, canning and preserving foods, and growing household, street and community vegetable gardens. People are becoming increasingly passionate about living, working, spending, loving, serving and growing local.

God's people have a unique opportunity to be at the forefront of this. But we must prioritize local worship, mission, community, ministry and discipleship. Too many Christians commute out of their suburbs for church and ministry. Root yourself deeply in your suburb. Get to know the families, personalities, issues and hopes. Worship Christ locally. Serve Christ locally. Be discipled to Christ locally. Eat, love, produce, laugh, mourn, spend, grow and pray locally. And as stewards of God's creation, we need to nurture local ecologies. These include green spaces, community gardens and the plants and animals unique to our area. And finally, local churches need to invest in local economies. Encourage the well-being and prosperity of local establishments and the people who own them and work in them.

Place making is often wonderfully missional. But it demands a movement away from autonomy, disconnectedness and anonymity. Instead, we make the most of place making's missional potential through rootedness, stability, localization and deep, long-term relationships. *Staying is the new going.* We choose to stay in *this* local place and in *these* local relationships. And we see God's grace manifested in the change and transformation of local neighborhoods. In this local place, we grow in loving obedience, missional service, prophetic advocacy and generosity and contentment. A simpler, local lifestyle enhances our mission.

3. Place making is collaborative transformation. Place making involves *serving alongside* the people who live and work in our neighborhood. We collaborate with others to release neighborhoods from urban poverty. We join with them to facilitate healing from woundedness and dysfunction. We partner with others so that together we might move toward holistic prosperity. (By this I mean the well-being of whole persons and whole communities through the whole gospel.) This involves the collaboration of churches, governments, businesses, community organizations, developers and so forth. We work together for the well-being and transformation of neighborhoods.

We have a responsibility to help the body of Christ take God's special concern for the poor as seriously as Jesus does. We can never address poverty, oppression, exploitation and disadvantage alone. We need to collaborate. This involves inviting the broader church to mission and ministry with Jesus among the poor. And it means cooperating with other groups and organizations.

Seeking "God's kingdom come"—through sharing Jesus and his gospel in word and deed and sign—is a collaborative affair. We partner with each other, with our community and with Christ. This starts by asking the right questions and having the courage to respond to the answers. For example, how can we be Christians who engage missionally with our neighborhoods? How do we do this collaboratively, not colonially? How can we join with others in healing and renewing and transforming our neighborhood? How do we shape churches that join with Jesus in transforming and releasing neighborhoods from the bottom up? How do we pursue cooperative, kingdom-based responses that "reverse the process of disempowerment, confront the god complexes, heal persons in poverty relationships, set right inadequacies in the worldview of a people, challenge principalities and powers, establish truth and righteousness, and proclaim that all power belongs to God"?[26]

4. Place making serves as hope enfleshed.[27] What does it mean to say that the church needs to be *hope enfleshed?* The church witnesses to the new creation. It does this through its message, love, service, faith and hope. The church testifies—in word and deed and sign—to the hope of Jesus Christ. We root our hope in his incarnation, life, death, resurrection and glorification. As we immerse ourselves in our neighborhoods—collaborating with the Spirit's work, connecting deeply with people and witnessing to the new creation—we embody the hope of Christ. By the grace of God, we are *hope enfleshed.*[28]

Tetsunao Yamamori and René Padilla bring together a host of Latin American thinkers and practitioners in *The Local Church, Agent of Transformation.* These leaders address the ways in which churches can pursue integral mission and community transformation. The book establishes a theological basis for local churches as agents of transformation. God calls his church to be a transforming presence within neighborhoods and a sign of hope.

In that book, Padilla describes how the church he pastored sought transformation in its neighborhood. They became a sign of hope. In an urban slum, Padilla discovered that being hope enfleshed means being committed to the poor. It's being

> a sign of the new creation that burst into history in the person and work of Jesus Christ—a sign of hope in the midst of despair. So it is important that we should have a teaching ministry which combines theory with practice and is oriented toward creating, in the whole church and in each of its members, the Christian mind—a mind that conceives of the totality of human life as the locus of God's transforming work. We can find many good reasons to criticize the church. Far too often it has been the primary cause of people's turning their back on God, because they believe that the Christian faith has nothing

---

[26]Christian, *God of the Empty-Handed*, 223.

[27]Ashley Barker, *Slum Life Rising: How to Enflesh Hope Within a New Urban World* (Dandenong: UNOH, 2013), 21-22.

[28]See also Ashley Barker, *Make Poverty Personal: Taking the Poor as Seriously as the Bible Does* (Grand Rapids: Baker, 2009); Ashley Barker and John Hayes, *Sub-Merge: Living Deep in a Shallow World* (Springvale: UNOH, 1989); Ashley Barker, "Enfleshing Hope: Toward a Christian Response to the Rise of Urban Slum and Squatter Neighbourhoods" (MCD University of Divinity, 2011).

to offer them. Often that is true. But it also is true that whenever the church opens itself up to people who are marginalized and poor, God surprises it, making it a Good Samaritan who responds to the needs of the neighbor with the resources of the Kingdom of God: faith, hope, and love.[29]

5. Place making is welcoming and being welcomed. By *welcoming,* I mean that we find and invite Jesus, disguised as "the least of these," into our lives, homes, lands, families, friendships and churches.

By being *welcomed,* I mean that we're willing to let others welcome us into their lives. We're humble enough to be a guest. We don't always need to be the host. We're willing and eager for the people Jesus fellowships with to welcome us into their lives and homes. He communes with the powerful and the weak, the sober and the drunk, the dignified and the prostitute, and the religious leader and the tax collectors. But he prefers the humble, poor in spirit, meek, despised, foolish, weak and marginalized. Are we humble enough to let others receive and welcome us?

6. Place making is conversion to Christ and to the neighbor.[30] Jesus Christ converts us to himself. And he converts us to our neighbors. Jesus converts us to loving and serving our neighbors and seeking their well-being and relationship with him. This conversion leads us to pursue mission through the transformation of neighborhoods. It also involves allowing Jesus to convert us to the service and love of the poor, abused, needy, neglected, despised, wounded and marginalized neighbor. We also care for the prosperous, powerful and privileged neighbor.

People will judge the truth of the gospel by our love for each other, and our love for our neighbors and neighborhoods. They will especially notice our love for our unlovable, offensive, stigmatized or immoral neighbor. They will notice the love we show the neighbor who is different to us (class, ethnicity, politics, sexuality, religion, worldview and so on). Loving people who are like us, who share our values and beliefs and race, is easy. But can I love and serve that *particular person,* right there in front of me, who stands in contrast to my race or religion or values or politics or sexuality or beliefs? Can I really love and serve *that* person?

---

[29]C. René Padilla and Tetsunao Yamamori, eds., *The Local Church, Agent of Transformation: An Ecclesiology for Integral Mission* (Buenos Aires: Ediciones Kairos, 2004), 299-300.
[30]Gutiérrez, *A Theology of Liberation,* 194.

Vinay Samuel puts it this way:

> One sign and wonder, biblically speaking, that alone can prove the power of the gospel is that of reconciliation. . . . Hindus can produce as many miracles as any Christian miracle worker. Islamic saints in India can produce and duplicate every miracle that has been produced by Christians. But they cannot duplicate the miracle of black and white together, of racial injustice being swept away by the power of the gospel. . . . Our credibility is at stake. . . . If we are not able to establish our credibility in this area, we do not have the whole gospel. In fact, we have not got a proper gospel at all.[31]

Our conversion to the neighbor testifies powerfully to our conversion to Christ.

7. Place making develops neighborology and a theology of place.[32] Our theology is more appealing if we are loving neighbors. Hospitality is missional. Love for God and love of neighbor are inseparable. What price am I willing to pay for the well-being and transformation of my neighbor and neighborhood? Ridicule? Exclusion? Discomfort? Persecution? Poverty? Slander? What price did Jesus pay for his "uncushioned neighborology"?

And place making requires a theology of place. I don't have the space to develop a theology of place here. But I highlight some key themes. First, Christians and Jews have a long history of describing the sacred relationship between God and people and place. Second, place is important in Scripture. This theology of place is present in biblical notions of creation, covenant, exile, pilgrimage, land, Israel and holy places. Third, Jesus Christ was God incarnate in a particular body, time, culture and place. Fourth, God calls us to worship and serve with a particular people in a specific place—hence the importance of the local church. Fifth, the Eucharist is a remembrance of Christ's bodily death and resurrection in a particular place and time. And the sacraments are a celebration of his presence with us in this place now. Sixth, a theology of God's kingdom contributes to a theology of place. The kingdom of God is "God's people in God's place under God's rule."[33] It's

---

[31]Vinay Samuel, "Evangelicals and Racism: The Lausanne II Press Conference," *Transformation*, no. 7 (January/March 1990): 32.
[32]Koyama, *Water Buffalo Theology*, 160-70.
[33]Graeme Goldsworthy, *Gospel and Kingdom: A Christian Interpretation of the Old Testament* (Exeter: Paternoster, 1981), 53.

manifest in particular places as Christ reigns in human history, liberating people from sin and darkness and establishing the rule of God on earth. Lastly, our ultimate hope includes resurrection to a particular, physical place.

What does all this mean? Simply that we must root Christian place making in a theology of place. Consequently, our place making is rich in practice and theology.

8. Place making must be saturated in prayer. Immerse yourself in your neighborhood. And pray. Nurture that place's assets and relationships and imagination. And pray. Help people see where God is already at work in your neighborhood. And pray. Seek your neighborhood's welfare and transformation and flourishing. And pray. Collaborate with others for the well-being of your community. And pray. Champion justice, hope, faith and love in your local place. And pray. Serve with your neighbors. And pray. Promote a culture of peace. And pray. Celebrate and grieve with neighbors. And saturate every dimension of your place making in prayer.

As we engage in place making and transforming neighborhoods, Jesus' example and words chart our course:

> On one occasion an expert in the law stood up to test Jesus. "Teacher," he asked, "what must I do to inherit eternal life?" "What is written in the Law?" he replied. "How do you read it?" He answered, "'Love the Lord your God with all your heart and with all your soul and with all your strength and with all your mind'; and, 'Love your neighbor as yourself.'" "You have answered correctly," Jesus replied. "Do this and you will live." (Lk 10:25-28)

PART THREE

CITY
Revitalizing Our Churches

INDIGENIZING FAITH

WHAT CAN WE LEARN FROM HOW MAJORITY WORLD CHRISTIANS INDIGENIZE FAITH?

It boils down to this: Can an unevangelized world, caught up in a process of political, social, economic, and cultural awakening, be effectively evangelized by a church that is not indigenous?

ORLANDO E. COSTAS

I came to faith in my late teens and began attending a local Pentecostal church in a poor, working-class suburb of Sydney, Australia. This church practiced ecstatic worship. This included prophecy, tongues, demonstrative singing, dancing, playing tambourines, waving flags and people "falling over in the power of the Spirit."

Even in those days, I was a passionate missionary. I would bring many of my friends to church. But I encountered a problem. Each person I brought to church would refuse to return. Some would even walk out during the first few songs. My younger brother barely got through the second song before walking out of the service. He refused to return. The leaders of the church tried to reassure me. They said that my friends and family were not "open to the Spirit." But this explanation did not ring true for me.

I was eighteen when the truth dawned on me. There was nothing wrong with this kind of worship, but it would never be relevant or appealing to my friends. It was not *indigenous* to my culture.

Alan Tippett was an Australian missionary to the Fijian islands for more than twenty years. He then served as a professor of missiology at various universities in the United States. Tippett's work among Fijian peoples led him to a firm conviction: "The truly indigenous church is an ideal for which we strive—something truly a church and truly indigenous."[1]

What does it mean to say a church is *indigenous*? Tippett answers this question. "When the indigenous people of a community think of the Lord as their own, not a foreign Christ; when they do things as unto the Lord, meeting the cultural needs around them, worshipping in patterns they understand; when their congregations function in participation in a body which is structurally indigenous; then you have an *indigenous* church."[2]

I consider the terms *indigenization, inculturation* and *contextualization* to be (basically) synonymous and interchangeable. This is the case even though these terms have different nuances in meaning.[3]

There is an ongoing debate about the meaning of these three concepts and about which is better to use. Some prefer *indigenization* (e.g., James Buswell and Charles Kraft). Others prefer *contextualization* (e.g., Shoki Coe, Charles Taber and the Theological Education Fund).[4] Others prefer *inculturation* (e.g., Pedro Arrup, John Walligo and many Catholic theologians). Some use the terms interchangeably (e.g., Saphir Athyal, René Padilla and Daniel Von Allmen).

As you read the examples of theologies and practices in this chapter, you may prefer to think of them as examples of indigenization or inculturation or contextualization (or all three). I will leave it to you to come to your own

---

[1]Alan R. Tippett, *Introduction to Missiology* (Pasadena, CA: William Carey Library, 1987), 381.
[2]Ibid.
[3]For the range of terms given to "local theologies" and their nuances of meaning, see Robert J. Schreiter, *Constructing Local Theologies* (Maryknoll, NY: Orbis, 1985), 5. For an excellent documentary history of inculturation/indigenization/contextualization, see Robert A. Hunt, *The Gospel Among the Nations: A Documentary History of Inculturation*, American Society of Missiology Series (Maryknoll, NY: Orbis, 2010). Hunt gathers dozens of primary and secondary documents from Orthodox, Catholic and Protestant sources and from Western and Majority World contexts. His collection of documents spans the history of the church and includes documents from Majority World authors such as Choan-Seng Song, Kōsuke Koyama, Samuel Escobar, Segundo Galilea, Peter K. Sarpong, Manas Buthelezi and Lamin Sanneh. Hunt's book is one of the most comprehensive documentary histories of inculturation/indigenization/contextualization available today. For a comprehensive documentary history of church and mission in Asia, Africa and Latin America (1450–1990), see Klaus Koschorke et al., eds., *A History of Christianity in Asia, Africa, and Latin America, 1450–1990: A Documentary Sourcebook* (Grand Rapids: Eerdmans, 2007).
[4]It is worth noting that Charles Taber and Charles Kraft were anthropologists rather than theologians. This raises the issue of phenomenological contextualization as opposed to theological contextualization.

conclusions. As Bruce Nicholls says, "In the end it is not so much the word used as the meaning that grows up around it that is important."[5]

How are these three terms defined? I've dedicated an entire chapter of this book to *contextual mission*. It shows how Majority World and indigenous churches define and express such *contextualization*. Alan Tippett has defined *indigenization* for us already in this chapter. Pedro Arrup defines *inculturation* like this: "The incarnation of Christian life and of the Christian message in a particular cultural context, in such a way that this experience not only finds expression through elements proper to the culture in question (this alone would be no more than a superficial adaptation) but becomes a principle that *animates, directs, and unifies the culture*, transforming it and remaking it so as to bring about a 'new creation.'"[6]

This chapter considers what we can learn from indigenous expressions of faith in Africa and Asia and Latin America. We can learn from *what* Christians in those settings have to say to us. Indigenous theological perspectives enlarge our theological imagination. We can also learn from *how* believers in those settings indigenize their spirituality, worship, mission and churches.

In a chapter this size, it is impossible to survey indigenization in Africa, Asia and Latin America fully. Instead, I provide some *brief* examples of indigenous *theology* and *practices* from those settings. I don't have space to consider indigenization in Eastern Europe, in the Middle East, in Muslim settings and among indigenous peoples. On my website, TheGlobalChurch Project.com, I list books and articles dealing with Christian contextualization and indigenization in Africa, Asia, Latin America, Eastern Europe, Muslim settings, the Middle East, Western cultures and among indigenous peoples.

I am a little concerned that this chapter will feel like lists of indigenous theologies and practices in the Majority World. So how can you make the most of this chapter? Ask yourself, What can I learn from these theologies and practices? What can they teach me and my culture, and the global

---

[5]Bruce Nicholls, *Contextualization: A Theology of Gospel and Culture* (Downers Grove, IL: Inter-Varsity Press, 1979), 21.

[6]Pedro Arrupe, "Letter to the Whole Society on Inculturation," in *Other Apostolates Today: Selected Letters and Addresses of Pedro Arrupe*, ed. Jerome Aixala (St Louis: Institute of Jesuit Sources, 1978), 172. For a full treatment of "inculturation," see Gerald A. Arbuckle, *Earthing the Gospel: An Inculturation Handbook for Pastoral Workers* (Maryknoll, NY: Orbis, 1990).

church? What can these indigenous expressions teach us about Jesus, mission, worship, spirituality and the church?

Indigenous expressions of faith are present throughout the global church. They are reactivating the church. Ask yourself, How indigenous is my theology and my church? How can my church develop indigenous theology and homegrown practices? How can these grassroots theologies and practices develop "from below"? How can Christians indigenize their faith in their everyday lives?[7] How can our church and theology become indigenous to our particular culture at this particular time?

This chapter asks, *What can we learn from how Majority World Christians indigenize faith?*

1. INDIGENIZATION IN AFRICA

During the last sixty years, African Christian theologies and expressions of faith have multiplied. The African churches have sought to shake off colonial influences. They're forming indigenous churches and theologies. And they're innovating theologically and practically. Africans link this creativity to local concerns and indigenous expressions. This innovation is also associated with the (positive and negative) influence of globalization on indigenous cultures. Globalization shapes the prioritization and health and revival of indigenous cultures. This melting pot of theological and practical experimentation is diverse and astonishing.

African theologies. Diane Stinton teaches theology in Nairobi, Kenya. She highlights four features of African Christian theologies.[8]

The first is *formality and informality.* African theologies express a duality of "formal and informal expressions." Systemic, propositional theology is present in Africa. But Africans complement formal theology with informal theology. Such informal theologizing happens through art, dance, music, painting, liturgy, drama and oral traditions.

The second is *community.* African theologies focus on "the community of faith in their formulation." Theology is often done within community. An

---

[7]Stephen B. Bevans, ed., *Mission and Culture: The Louis J. Luzbetak Lectures,* The American Society of Missiology Series (Maryknoll, NY: Orbis, 2012), 115.

[8]Diane B. Stinton, "Africa, East and West," in *An Introduction to Third World Theologies,* ed. John Parratt (Cambridge: Cambridge University Press, 2004), 107-10.

entire community often theologizes together. Stinton provides many examples of this. The most striking is the work of Cameroon theologian Jean-Marc Ela. Ela calls for "shade-tree theology." This is a theology that, "far from the libraries and the offices, develops among brothers and sisters searching shoulder to shoulder with unlettered peasants for the sense of the word of God in situations in which this word touches them."[9] The theologian roots his or her role, then, in community and praxis and specific locations.

The third feature is *contextuality*. African theologies have a "contextual nature." Indigenous African theologies deal with contextual problems (social, political, sexual, economic and religious). These problems and contexts are often different from those faced by Western Christians. So contextual African theologies often take a different form.

The fourth is *plurality*. African theologies have "many articulations." Africa is a large and diverse continent, with many cultures. It should not surprise us that African theologies are many and diverse.

Kenyan theologian James Kombo takes a different approach. Kombo categorizes African theologies into four types:[10]

Identity theologies explore the continuities between biblical ideas about God and the perspectives of African primal religions. (See the work of Bolaji Idowu, John S. Mbiti, Gabriel M. Setiloane, Charles Nyamiti, Ajayi Crowther and Kwame Bediako.)

Incarnational theologies cultivate homegrown Christian theologies that are completely "African" and indigenous. (See the work of Placide Tempels, Alexis Kagame, John S. Mbiti, Kwame Bediako, Lamin Sanneh and Andrew Walls.)

African/world theologies shape theologies that are attentive to indigenous needs and primal religious connections. They're globally influential. These theologies commit to an African Christianity that isn't second-rate to Western forms or theologies. They see these theologies influencing and shaping a new, global, "world Christianity." Their conviction is that—given the explosive growth of the church in the Majority World—Christianity is now a religion of the Global South. They believe that a new era of Christianity is emerging—one

---

[9]Jean-Marc Ela, *African Cry* (Eugene, OR: Wipf and Stock, 2005), vi.
[10]James Kombo, "African Theology," in *Global Theology in Evangelical Perspective: Exploring the Contextual Nature of Theology and Mission*, ed. Jeffrey P. Greenman and Gene L. Green (Downers Grove, IL: IVP Academic, 2012), 134-47.

that the Global South is shaping. "What happens within the African churches in the next generation will determine the whole shape of Church history for centuries to come. . . . What sort of theology is most characteristic of the Christianity of the twenty-first century may well depend on what has happened in the minds of African Christians in the interim."[11] (See the work of Sanneh, Walls and Bediako.)

Contextual theologies contextualize African Christian theologies and expressions. Examples include apartheid-related theology, inculturation theology and South African black theology. African womanist and liberation theologies are also examples. The proponents of African contextualized theologies and practices are too many to name. Some notable persons include Desmond Tutu, Byang H. Kato, Jean-Marc Ela, Benezet Bujo, Mercy Amba Oduyoye, Emefie Ikenga-Metuh, Victor Chendekemen Yakubu, Laurenti Magesa, Isabel Phiri, Yvette Akle and Anne Nasimiyu-Wasike.[12]

As you can see, African theologies are many and diverse. So are the practical expressions of mission and church and worship that arise from them.

The late Byang H. Kato supported these developments, especially contextualization. But some developments in African indigenous theology and practice concerned him. These included the rise of universalism and the syncretistic elevation of primal religions and practices. Kato wrote that biblical perspectives were too often devalued in these settings.

To counter this, Kato developed ten principles for safeguarding biblical Christianity in Africa. I will not list them all here. But Kato called the African churches to adhere to the core tenets of historic Christianity. He challenged them to train African leaders in biblical exegesis and original languages. Kato acknowledged that culture and Scripture are mutually interpreting. But he maintained that Scripture has authority over culture.[13]

---

[11] Andrew Walls, quoted in Kwame Bediako, "The Significance of Modern African Christianity—a Manifesto," *Studies in World Christianity* 1, no. 1 (1995): 51. Bediako goes on to outline a manifesto for African Christianity and its influence on global Christianity.

[12] See, for instance, Emefie Ikenga-Metuh, "Contextualization: A Missiological Imperative for the Church in Africa in the Third Millennium," *Mission Studies* 6, no. 2 (1989); Victor Chendekemen Yakubu, "Contextual Theology: A Basic Need Within the Church in Africa Today," *AFER* 38, no. 3 (1996).

[13] Byang H. Kato, *Theological Pitfalls* (Kisumu: Evangel, 1975), 181-84. For a similar treatment of biblical approaches to contextualization in Africa, see Gwamna Dogara Je'adayibe, "A Contextual Consideration of the Church, Culture and the Gospel in Africa," *Ogbomoso Journal of Theology* 17, no. 1 (2012).

Indigenous Christian theologies and practices are best when they have a dynamic relationship with historic and global Christianity. These indigenous expressions also need deep biblical foundations.

There is not space here to deal with a wide range of indigenous forms of African theology. Instead, I highlight the indigenization of two areas. These are *Christology* (reflections on Jesus Christ) and *ecclesiology* (reflections on the church as extended family).[14] As you read them, I invite you to consider them in the light of Stinton's *four features* and Kombo's *four types* of African Christian theologies.

Let's start with Jesus Christ in African theology (*Christology*). Kwame Bediako lists some of the ways African Christians use indigenous ideas and analogies and metaphors to understand the person and work of Jesus.[15] Jesus is the "Grinding Stone," who sharpens us for service. Jesus is the "Sword Carrier" (the *nkrante brafo*). He's the "Hero Incomparable" (the *okatakyi birempon*). He's victorious in battle. Jesus is the "Hunter" who leads us deep in the dangerous forest and removes the heads of evil spirits. He kills the *sasabonsam* and the *mmoatia*, those evil spirits that haunt humans and forests. Jesus is the "Great God" (the *onyankopon*) to whom all lesser spirits and gods must submit. Jesus is the "Lion of the Grassland" who defeats Satan. He "tears out Satan's entrails and leaves them on the ground for the flies to eat." "Jesus of the Deep Forest" provides shelter, food, water, healing, wholeness and new life. Jesus is the "Fearless One" (the *tutugyagu*). He's the "Strong-armed One" (the *adubasapon*). He defeats our terrors. Jesus protects us from war, famine, illness and deadly beasts. He gives us courage in the face of these things. Jesus is the

---

[14]Key books on African Christian theology include Bénézet Bujo and Juvénal Ilunga Muya, *African Theology in the 21st Century: The Contribution of the Pioneers* (Nairobi: Paulines, 2003); Bujo, *African Theology in Its Social Context*, Faith and Cultures Series (Maryknoll, NY: Orbis, 1992); Agbonkhianmeghe E. Orobator, *Theology Brewed in an African Pot: An Introduction to Christian Doctrine from an African Perspective* (Nairobi: Paulines, 2008); Gwinyai H. Muzorewa, *The Origins and Development of African Theology* (Maryknoll, NY: Orbis, 1985); John Parratt, *African Theology: A Bibliography*, Sources for the Study of Religion in Malawi (Zomba: Dept. of Religious Studies, Chancellor College, University of Malawi, 1983); John Parratt, *A Reader in African Christian Theology*, North American ed. (London: SPCK, 2001); Parratt, *Reinventing Christianity: African Theology Today* (Grand Rapids: Eerdmans, 1995); John S. Pobee, *Toward an African Theology* (Nashville: Abingdon, 1979).

[15]Kwame Bediako, *Jesus in Africa: The Christian Gospel in African History and Experience*, Theological Reflections from the South (Carlisle: Paternoster, 2000), 1-33. For the sources of African contextual Christologies, see Victor I. Ezigbo, "Rethinking the Sources of African Contextual Christology," *Journal of Theology for Southern Africa*, no. 132 (2008).

"Savior of the Poor." He's the "Great and Dependable Friend" (the *damfo-adu*). We rely on him "as the tongue relies on the mouth." Jesus is the "Great Rock" whom we hide behind. He's the "Magnificent Tree" who shelters us and causes "luxuriant growth below." Jesus is the "Tall Mountain" (the *sekyere buruku*). He shows the nations his glory and points us to God. Jesus is the "King of the Nations" (the *amansanheme*). He's the "Chief of the Valiant" (the *owesekramo-fohene*). He "brings nations together, milk and honey flow in his vein."

In *Jesus of Africa*, Stinton provides a comprehensive survey of African Christologies and unpacks contemporary African images of Jesus. These images include Healer, Life-giver, Mediator and Ancestor. Other images include Loved One, Family Member, Friend, King/Chief and Liberator. Stinton examines the cultural origins of these metaphors and demonstrates their interconnections. She studies both their beneficial and controversial aspects. For example, there is division among African theologians about whether Africans should view Christ as "Ancestor."[16]

Now let's consider the church as *extended family* in African theology (*ecclesiology*). Besides reflecting on the person and work of Christ, Africans think a lot about the church. This consumes much of their theological energy. They're concerned about the church's community and mission.

Africans often view the church as an extended family (in theology and practice). African understandings of *church as family* resonate with trinitarian-communion ecclesiology. But just as importantly, Africans express church as family in the practical ways they do church. Africans prioritize community, union, intimacy and relationships. Relationship surpasses institution. Relationships lead to passionate mission.

John Waliggo writes,

> The *koinonia* practiced in the early church is nothing but familial relationship. Every believer is a brother or sister to the other. It was only through the subsequent development of the church that this relational and charismatic model became weak and was gradually substituted with the institutional model. One of the signs of the times in the church has been the reawakening of this familial model through small groups, charismatic groups, and others.[17]

---

[16]See also Tennent's chapter on "Christ as Healer and Ancestor in Africa," in Timothy C. Tennent, *Theology in the Context of World Christianity: How the Global Church Is Influencing the Way We Think About and Discuss Theology* (Grand Rapids: Zondervan, 2007), 105-34.

[17]John Mary Waliggo, "The African Clan as the True Model of the African Church," in *The Church*

Tite Tiénou examines African notions of the church as a family or clan. Tiénou is supportive of the image. He believes that it has biblical roots and favorable consequences for mission and community. But he is also critical of its emphasis on ancestors. He disagrees with its prioritization of "Christ as Ancestor" over biblical images.[18]

Tiénou, Waliggo and many other African theologians believe that Christian participation in the church as family should supersede ties to natural family. Christian communion and mission are dependent on deep, authentic relationships in the local church.

In Africa, as in many other contexts, local practices complement indigenous theologies.

African expressions and practices. There are a multitude of creative indigenous expressions in Africa. Some are innovative in the way they point Africans to Jesus and his gospel. These expressions allow Africans to worship in indigenous ways. Other practices are problematic. African evangelicals question the assumptions, validity and consequences of these practices.

I will not be scrutinizing the value of these expressions and practices. I will merely provide a taste of the breadth and creativity of indigenous worship and community and mission in Africa.

1. Relational expressions of church. As I mentioned earlier, Africans view the church as an extended family or clan. It is common for Africans to think of family as "extended" rather than "nuclear," so this is a natural development. Jesus Christ is the "ruler/chief/elder" or "protoancestor." Africans tend to pursue deep relationships. They see the church as an extended and prioritized family group.

Solidarity and unity and community characterize this *koinonia*. Natural families and the church as family celebrate communal feats and rites of passage together. These include births, deaths, marriages and coming of age.

Stinton quotes Mbiti and Anne Nasimiyu Wasike to illustrate this point. She shows the centrality of community in African culture and faith. "The

---

in *African Christianity: Innovative Essays in Ecclesiology*, ed. J. N. K. Mugambi and Laurenti Magesa (Nairobi: Initiatives, 1990), 125. For a biblical analysis of "clan ecclesiology" and the "church-as-family" model, see Paul J. Sankey, "The Church as Clan: Critical Reflections on African Ecclesiology," *International Review of Mission* 83, no. 330 (1994); Aidan G. Msafiri, "The Church as Family Model: Its Strengths and Weaknesses," *AFER* 40, nos. 5-6 (1998).

[18]Tite Tiénou, "The Church in African Theology," in *Biblical Interpretation and the Church: Text and Context*, ed. Donald A. Carson (Exeter: Paternoster, 1984), 162-63.

individual can only say: 'I am, because we are; and since we are, therefore I am.'"[19] "Community participation is a very prominent value among the African people. It permeates all life; it is the matrix upon which all the human and social values, attitudes, expectations, and beliefs are based, and it is the foundation of an African theology, catechesis, and liturgy."[20]

Since this is true, it is easy to see why relational expressions of church are the foundation for other indigenous expressions and practices. For example, Stinton notes the consequences of *church as family* for particular African understandings and practices. These include Jesus as family member and protoancestor, paternal and maternal images of Christ, and Eucharist as communal meal. *Church as family* influences the way that many Africans see other denominations as "true relatives in the wider clan." Moreover, they see Christian mission as social and communal and familial transformation.[21]

2. Liturgical innovations. Many African Christians experiment with indigenous forms of worship. They indigenize baptism, the Eucharist, penance, marriage, ordination and consecrations. Many African churches indigenize these liturgical and sacramental dimensions of the church.

For example, many Africans celebrate the Eucharist through dance and drama. The Eucharist focuses on caring for the environment. It draws the worshiper's attention to the ancestors and the Great Ancestor. Africans often celebrate the Eucharist within the context of food and wine and feasting. They associate the Eucharist with agricultural and hunting motifs, struggles with famine and drought, and rites of passage.

F. Kabasele Lumbala is a Congolese theologian. He describes how Africans innovate with a wide range of liturgies and sacraments. This innovation has a few key features. They indigenize liturgies, sacraments, blessings, prayers and rites to African cultures. They recognize the holiness of the "other" (humans, rituals, creation and spiritual beings). There's a desire for harmony with the universe and creation. They remember ancestors (who are the "living past"). Africans often celebrate the holiness of embodiment (bodily holiness).

---

[19]John S. Mbiti, *African Religions & Philosophy* (London: Heinemann, 1969), 107-8.
[20]Anne Nasimiyu Wasike, "Vatican II: The Problem of Inculturation" (PhD diss., Duquesne University, 1986), 258.
[21]Stinton, "Africa, East and West," 129-31.

They connect worship with social harmony and interpersonal connection. And they seek to release the power of human imagination and language.[22]

3. *Explosive growth of indigenous, independent churches.* Three groups are major forces in African Christianity today. The first are the "African Independent/Initial Churches" (henceforth AICs). The second are the Roman Catholic "Small Christian Communities" (henceforth SCCs). The third are the newer "Independent Pentecostal/Charismatic Churches" (henceforth (IPCCs).

Even though I focus on the AICs and IPCCs here, the Roman Catholic SCCs are important too. Catholic believers in Africa developed the SCCs as a pastoral priority to meet local needs. In the SCCs, local people determine who celebrates the sacraments. And there is space for polygamous and female leaders. The SCCs are self-governing, self-ministering and self-supporting. The parish is a communion of SCCs. As you might imagine, the Roman Catholic Church felt threatened by these developments. The priests and bishops set out to quash the SCCs. The result is that they are not as numerous or vibrant as they once were.[23]

The AICs and IPCCs have been much more successful. Harold Turner and Allan Anderson have written extensively on their characteristics and growth. Anderson writes, "Observers have long recognized that the AIC movement amounts to a fundamental reformation of African Christianity, a movement of such momentous significance that it can truly be called an African Reformation. It must be taken seriously by anyone interested in African Christianity and the globalization of Christianity."[24] The *World Christian Encyclopedia* puts the number of AIC participants in Africa at 83 million. It estimates IPCC participants at 126 million.[25]

---

[22]F. Kabasele Lumbala, *Celebrating Jesus Christ in Africa: Liturgy and Inculturation* (Maryknoll, NY: Orbis, 1998), ix-xiv.

[23]H. Mellor and T. Yates, *Mission and Spirituality: Creative Ways of Being Church* (Sheffield: Cliff College, 2002), 103-6.

[24]Allan H. Anderson, "Types and Butterflies: African Initiated Churches and European Typologies," *International Bulletin of Missionary Research* 25, no. 3 (2001): 107. See Anderson, "The Newer Pentecostal and Charismatic Churches: The Shape of Future Christianity in Africa?," *Pneuma* 24, no. 2 (2002); Anderson, "African Initiated Churches of the Spirit and Pneumatology," *Word & World* 23, no. 2 (2003); Anderson, "New African Initiated Pentecostalism and Charismatics in South Africa," *Journal of Religion in Africa* 35, no. 1 (2005); Harold W. Turner, *African Independent Church* (Oxford: Clarendon, 1967).

[25]Barrett, Kurian and Johnson, *World Christian Encyclopedia*, 1:13 (table 1-4).

Allan Anderson cautiously divides these churches up into three main types:[26]

The first type are the *African/Ethiopian churches.* The leaders of these groups shape them after European mission churches. They do not have the spiritualist and charismatic elements of other independent churches. In southern Africa, people often call them *Ethiopian* or *Ethiopian-type* churches. In Nigeria, people often call them *African* churches. They are older than other forms of AICs and are not as numerous.

The second type are the *spiritual/prophet-healing churches.* These are like Western Pentecostal/charismatic churches. But they have shaped their worship around African cultures. And they claim an indigenous Pentecostal heritage. They focus on spiritual power. Some are small. Others are huge.

Allan Anderson includes a broad range of AICs in this group.

> They are particularly difficult to describe, for they include a vast variety of some of the biggest of all churches in Africa—the Kimbanguists and the African Apostolics in central Africa; the Christ Apostolic Church, the Aladura churches, and the Harrist churches in West Africa; and the Zion Christian Church and the Amanazaretha in southern Africa. These are all churches with hundreds of thousands of members, and in at least the cases of the Kimbanguists and Zionists, several millions.[27]

These churches have sought to engage and express their indigenous cultures. There is a focus on healing, deliverance, prayer for the sick and miraculous works. These churches link these practices with "the use of various symbolic objects such as blessed water, ropes, staffs, papers, or ash." Members wear uniforms—often white robes with colored sashes. These AICs have "adapted themselves to and addressed the popular African worldview."[28] They portray Jesus as the suffering and healing chief. They emphasize story (rather than

---

[26] Anderson, "Types and Butterflies," 109-12. See the work of Marthinus L. Daneel for a thorough treatment of the theology and expressions of Africa Independent Churches: Marthinus L. Daneel, "African Independent Church Pneumatology and the Salvation of All Creation," *International Review of Mission* 82 (1993): 143-66; Daneel, "African Initiated Churches as Vehicles of Earth-Care in Africa," in *The Oxford Handbook of Religion and Ecology*, ed. Roger S. Gottlieb (Oxford: Oxford University Press, 2006); Daneel, *Quest for Belonging: Introduction to a Study of African Independent Churches* (Gweru: Mambo, 1987).

[27] Anderson, "Types and Butterflies," 109.

[28] Ibid., 110.

proposition). They enjoy song and dance and drama (rather than apologetics). They practice healing (rather than hermeneutical analysis). They embrace the prosperity gospel with its focus on health and wealth and general prosperity. Their leaders are frequently seen as apostles and prophets. These churches often equate these "big men" (and they're usually men) with the chiefs of African settings.

The third type are the *newer Pentecostal/charismatic/renewalist churches*. These also emphasize the power and gifts and healings of the Holy Spirit. But they refer to themselves as *charismatic* rather than *Pentecostal*. And they view themselves as "Evangelical" rather than "independent." These are growing rapidly. They tend to maintain strong connections with the West. Anderson includes the following churches in this group: "The Deeper Life Bible Church in Nigeria led by William Kumuyi, the Zimbabwe Assemblies of God led by Ezekiel Guti, and the Grace Bible Church led by Mosa Sono in South Africa."[29]

These newer charismatic/evangelical AICs have less indigenous expressions than the spiritual/prophet-healing churches. They seek to be relevant to their cultures. But they are more wary of African primal religion and practice than are the spiritual/prophet-healing churches. Africans lead them all. And while they connect with the West, they are fiercely independent and "African." They are critical of established African churches and denominations. These newer churches tend to see the established churches as nonindigenous and lukewarm. They see real connections between biblical cultures and their own (especially Old Testament cultures). They address these biblical themes by showing that African and biblical cultures deal with similar problems—war and violence, family and ancestors, genocide and rape, poverty and corruption, famine and disease, procreation and infertility, polygamy and marriage, widows and orphans, prostitution and sex trafficking, displacement and migration, sickness and oppression, witchcraft and substance abuse, and spirits and deliverance.

Indigenous theology, worship, community and mission in Africa is diverse. I find it inspiring. Stinton describes how African indigenous Christian theologies and practices are influencing the global church. She quotes John

---

[29]Ibid.

Pobee as she describes the prophetic voice of the African church in this area.

> The test of any cultural construct of the gospel is whether it enables growth, change, and transformation in and into the image and likeness of God through Christ. . . . The Akan have a saying, "The mother feeds the baby daughter before she has teeth, so that the daughter will feed the mother when she loses her teeth." The old church has lost her teeth. Evidence: empty churches. This new church, the younger church, is now the vibrant part. It owes it to the so-called mother churches to share its insights, so that together they may be renewed and transformed.[30]

2. INDIGENIZATION IN ASIA

Asia is a vast melting pot of cultures. There are almost fifty countries in Asia. Two-thirds of the world's six billion people live there (almost four-and-a-half billion people). Asians speak 33 percent of the world's living languages (more than two thousand languages). So Asian Christianity is diverse.

Two books illustrate this well. Peter Phan edits the first book, called *Christianities in Asia*. Each contributor traces the unique shape and development of Christianity in particular parts of South Asia, Southeast Asia, Northeast Asia and Southwest Asia. They show the unique expressions of Christianity in more than twenty countries. They consider major churches and denominations. They outline missionary figures and the role of women in Asian churches. They give us a window into Asian martyrs and persecution and into relations with other religions. They profile Asian theologians and theological trends. And they tackle church-state relations and future prospects for the Asian church. Finally, they reveal indigenous and contextualized expressions of mission and worship and spirituality.

Phan's book is the best treatment I have seen on "how Christians in Asia have received and transformed Christianity into a local or indigenous religion, with their own ecclesiastical structures, liturgy and prayers, spirituality, theology, art and architecture, music and song and dance, often in dialogue with Asian cultures and religions."[31]

---

[30]Diane B. Stinton, *Jesus of Africa: Voices of Contemporary African Christology*, Faith and Cultures Series (Maryknoll, NY: Orbis, 2004), 250-53.

[31]Peter C. Phan, *Christianities in Asia*, Blackwell Guides to Global Christianity (Malden, MA: Wiley-Blackwell, 2011), 4. Also, see Saphir Athyal, ed., *Church in Asia Today: Challenges and Opportunities* (Singapore: Asia Lausanne Committee for World Evangelization, 1996); John C. England, Jose

The second is by Muriel Orevillo-Montenegro (a Filipino theologian). The book's title is *The Jesus of Asian Women*. Orevillo-Montenegro considers how many Western Christologies imported into Asia were inadequate for Asian challenges. These Christologies were irrelevant to Asian cultures. She says that Westerners underestimated the diversity and complexity of Asian cultures and religions.

Orevillo-Montenegro then considers the diverse and indigenous Christologies developed by Asian Christian theologians. She is especially interested in those developed by Indian, South Korean, Filipino and Hong Kong Chinese women.

> Indian women's Christologies criticize Christianity's use of Jesus' maleness as a norm. These Christologies reveal these women's view of the cross in light of Indian women's experience of complex suffering at the intersection of caste, ethnicity, religion, gender, race, and poverty. Indian women also explore the meaning of Jesus the Christ in connection with the degradation of women and the exploitation of nature.[32]

South Korean women develop Christologies that converse with Korean indigenous religions. They value creation care. Filipino women develop Christologies in the context of political struggle and upheaval. These reflect Asian womanist liberation theologies. Hong Kong Chinese women are developing hybridized Christologies. These take into account Chinese and Western ideas and postcolonial theology.

Orevillo-Montenegro concludes with the following: "Overall, the Jesus of Asian women is the Asian Christ who accompanies them in their daily struggles

---

Kuttianimattathil and John Mansford Prior, eds., *Asian Christian Theologies: A Research Guide to Authors, Movements, Sources*, 3 vols. (Delhi: ISPCK, 2002). The Asia Lausanne Committee for World Evangelization commissioned *Church in Asia Today* (edited by Saphir Athyal). It outlines the trends in church and mission occurring in twenty-five Asian nations. It shows how the church in some parts of Asia is in real trouble (through persecution, decline or irrelevance). In other parts of Asia, the church's growth and indigenization has been inspirational. *Asian Christian Theologies* (edited by John C. England et al.) is a three-volume series on contextual theologies and indigenous movements in Asia. These three volumes consider South and Austral Asia (volume 1), Southeast Asia (volume 2) and Northeast Asia (volume 3). England also provides a selected annotated bibliography on contextual theology in Asian countries here: John C. England, "Contextual Theology in Asian Countries: A Selected Annotated Bibliography," *Missiology* 12, no. 4 (1984).

[32]Muriel Orevillo-Montenegro, *The Jesus of Asian Women*, Women from the Margins (Maryknoll, NY: Orbis, 2006), 7.

for liberation from all forms of oppression and suffering. This Christ seeks to engage with religions, cultures, and indigenous spiritualities to make life flourish for every living being."[33]

Indigenous Asian theologies and practices take many forms. Let's consider some examples and what we can learn from them.

Asian theologies. There have been various attempts to categorize indigenous Asian theologies. And Asian evangelicals have sought to analyze these theologies in the light of Scripture and evangelical convictions. See, for example, the 1982 *Seoul Declaration: Toward an Evangelical Theology for the Third World.*[34]

Bong Rin Ro provides the best-known categorization of Asian theologies. He lists four types. I list these types here and include the examples Ro provides as well as some of my own examples.[35]

The first type are *syncretistic theologies*: Asian theologies that have moved beyond indigenization and are syncretistic (e.g., Raimon Panikkar's *The Unknown Christ of Hinduism*).

The second type are *accommodation theologies*: Asian theologies that seek to accommodate good ideas from other religions, while preserving Christian belief (e.g., Kōsuke Koyama's *Waterbuffalo Theology* and Batumalai Sadayandy's *A Prophetic Christology for Neighborology*).

The third type are *situational theologies*: Asian theologies that arise from and speak to concrete situations in Asia (e.g., Kazoh Kitamori's pain of God theology, Kim Yong Bock's Minjung theology, liberation theologies in India and the Philippines, Minjung theology in South Korea, and Asian postcolonial, ecological and womanist theologies).

The fourth type are *biblically oriented Asian theologies*: Asian theologies that prioritize evangelical commitments (e.g., the 1982 *Seoul Declaration*, Bong Rin Ro and Ruth Eshenaur's *The Bible and Theology in Asian Contexts*, Ken Gnanakan's *Biblical Theology in Asia*, and Vinay Samuel and Chris Sugden's *Sharing Jesus in the Two-Thirds World*).

Let me introduce you to a few examples of creative indigenous Asian

---

[33]Ibid., 194.

[34]Bong Rin Ro and Ruth Eshenaur, eds., *The Bible and Theology in Asian Contexts: An Evangelical Perspective on Asian Theology* (Taichung: Asia Theological Association, 1984).

[35]Bong Rin Ro, "Theological Trends in Asia: Asian Theology," *Asian Theological News* 13 (October/ December 1987).

theologies. These are Dalit theology from India, "pain of God theology" from Japan, "water buffalo theology" from Thailand, Minjung theology from South Korea and "story theology" from China.

1. Dalit theology (India). Like liberation theology, Dalit theology is theology for and by the poor and oppressed. It seeks liberation from oppressive forms of the Indian caste and political system. Seventy percent of Indian Christians are lower-caste Dalits. But they have often felt marginalized and silenced by church and society.

Dalit theology does not draw on Marxist philosophy in the way that Latin American liberation theology does. Instead, it seeks inspiration from biblical motifs that resonate with the experience of the Dalits. These motifs include suffering, incarnation, service and freedom. Arvind P. Nirmal wrote that the suffering servant of Isaiah 53 reveals Jesus Christ as a Dalit. Jesus exists in solidarity with the downtrodden and suffering and oppressed.[36] Dalit theology is closely associated with *subaltern theology*—theology done by those at the margins of society. In Asia, this includes many women and groups like the Indian Dalits and the Japanese Burakumin.[37]

2. Pain of God theology (Japan). This grew out of Kazoh Kitamori's book, *Theology of the Pain of God.* Kitamori shows how God suffers. God roots his love in his pain, and draws us into communion with his pain. In doing so, he heals and transforms human suffering, and he makes it meaningful.

Kitamori draws on biblical and Japanese and Buddhist ideas of suffering to develop his theology. Kitamori wrote *Theology of the Pain of God* during World War II and published the book just after the Japanese defeat and the atomic bombings of Hiroshima and Nagasaki. It struck a cord with a world in terrible suffering and pain.[38]

---

[36]George Oommen, "The Emerging Dalit Theology: A Historical Appraisal," *Indian Church History Review* 34, no. 1 (June 2000); Arvind P. Nirmal and V. Devasahayam, eds., *A Reader in Dalit Theology* (Madras: Research Institute for Dalit Theology, 1990).

[37]See, for example, the chapters in R. S. Sugirtharajah, *Frontiers in Asian Christian Theology: Emerging Trends* (Maryknoll, NY: Orbis, 1994). Kirsteen Kim provides an overview of the many contextual theologies in India in chapter 3 of John Parratt's *An Introduction to Third World Theologies* (in chapter 4, Edmond Tang does the same for East Asia—China, Japan and Korea): John Parratt, ed., *An Introduction to Third World Theologies* (Cambridge: Cambridge University Press, 2004). For a detailed study of indigenous Indian theologies and key theologians, see Sunand Sumithra, *Christian Theology from an Indian Perspective* (Bangalore: Theological Book Trust, 1990).

[38]Kazoh Kitamori, *Theology of the Pain of God* (London: SCM, 1966).

3. Water buffalo theology (Thailand). This developed out of Kōsuke Koyama's book, *Water Buffalo Theology.* Koyama was a Japanese theologian who served as a missionary in Northern Thailand. Koyama rejected abstract, academic theology. He developed a way of talking about Jesus that he rooted in the experience of Thai peasants. He also sought to bridge Buddhist and Christian thought. Koyama called this blending Western Aristotelian theological "pepper" with Eastern Buddhist philosophical "salt."

Koyama rooted his theology in Thai history and Asian Buddhist culture. He believed that "neighborology" was as important in Asian mission as proclamation or apologetics. Christians do mission best in Asia through intimate, self-sacrificial, honest and neighborly relationships.[39]

4. Minjung theology (South Korea). Ahn Byung-Mu was the best-known proponent of this theology. Minjung is a movement seeking social justice for the poor and marginalized and silenced members of Korean society. It is a movement for the people and of the people. Jesus' experience is not only the hope of the Minjung—it is the experience of the Minjung. Minjung's popularity has waned since Korea became democratic and economically prosperous.[40]

5. Story theology (Chinese). Choan-Seng Song typifies this theology. Drawing on Chinese ideas, Song shows how the imagination and relationships and stories birth theology. Song says that theology must have four ingredients:

> (1) It is the power of *imagination* given to us by God who created us human beings in the divine image. (2) It is the *passion* that enables us to feel the compassion of God in us and in others. (3) It is the *experience of communion* that makes us realize we are responsible for one another and for God. (4) It is the *vision* of God's redeeming presence in the world, enabling us to envision a new course for theology.[41]

---

[39]Kōsuke Koyama, "From Water Buffaloes to Asian Theology," *International Review of Mission* 53, no. 212 (1964); Koyama, "The Asian Approach to Christ," *Missiology* 12, no. 4 (1984); Koyama, "'Extend Hospitality to Strangers': A Missiology of Theologia Crucis," *Currents in Theology and Mission* 20, no. 3 (1993); Koyama, "My Pilgrimage in Mission," *International Bulletin of Missionary Research* 21, no. 2 (1997); Koyama, *Water Buffalo Theology;* Koyama, "Creation, Space and Time," *Svensk missionstidskrift* 90, no. 1 (2002); Koyama, *No Handle on the Cross: An Asian Meditation on the Crucified Mind* (Maryknoll, NY: Orbis, 1977); Koyama, *Three Mile an Hour God: Biblical Reflections* (Maryknoll, NY: Orbis Books, 1980).

[40]For a good evaluation of Minjung theology, writings and practices, see Yung Suk Kim and Jin-Ho Kim, eds., *Reading Minjung Theology in the Twenty-First Century* (Eugene, OR: Pickwick, 2013).

[41]Choan-Seng Song, *Theology from the Womb of Asia* (Maryknoll, NY: Orbis, 1986), 3. See Song,

Song claims that indigenous Asian theology is always rooted in story; it must be *story theology*. Good theology emerges out of the intersection between *my* story, *our* story, *Christ's* story, *our culture's* story and *countless* life stories. "In the beginning were stories, not texts."[42]

Asian Christians often complement theological creativity with indigenous Christian practices.

Asian expressions and practices. Each of the five Asian theologies mentioned above have associated practices. These theologies lead to concrete Christian expressions. All over Asia, Christians are shaping indigenous expressions of church, worship, mission and spirituality.

Balinese Christianity serves as an example. Christianity has struggled to get a foothold in Bali. Hinduism has been extraordinarily successful in winning over the Balinese. Some say this is because Hinduism presented itself as an Asian religion. It adapted itself to indigenous Balinese animism. I. Wayan Mastra writes, "The success of the Hindus in winning Balinese for Hinduism was the result of their efforts in introducing Hinduism not in the form of a foreign religious and cultural invasion, but as a seed planted in Balinese soil and growing up in its own way."[43]

During the last few decades, many churches have sought to move Christianity away from its perception as a foreign religion. These Christians have done this through indigenization. This includes building churches in Balinese style. Balinese art and color and architecture and symbols and paintings and decorations adorn the churches. The worship services have incorporated Balinese dance and dramatic opera (*tembang*). Church leaders dress in Balinese clothes and wear colors that speak of life and freedom and joy in Balinese culture. Churches engage in social action and cultural enhancement. This includes supporting Balinese agriculture, fishing, medicine, families and education.[44]

Third-Eye Theology: Theology in Formation in Asian Settings, rev. ed. (Maryknoll, NY: Orbis, 1991); Song, *The Believing Heart: An Invitation to Story Theology* (Minneapolis: Fortress, 1999); Song, *And Their Eyes Are Opened: Story Sermons Embracing the World* (St. Louis: Chalice, 2006); Song, *In the Beginning Were Stories, Not Texts: Story Theology* (Eugene, OR: Cascade, 2011). For a valuable collection of essays by many of the Asian theologians mentioned in this chapter, see Douglas J. Elwood, *What Asian Christians Are Thinking: A Theological Source Book* (Quezon City: New Day, 1976).

[42]Song, *Theology from the Womb of Asia*, 3.

[43]Robert T. Coote and John R. W. Stott, *Down to Earth: Studies in Christianity and Culture. The Papers of the Lausanne Consultation on Gospel and Culture* (Grand Rapids: Eerdmans, 1980), 265-66.

[44]Ibid., 269-72.

We see similar approaches to indigenization in Japan. In *Developing a Contextualized Church*, Mitsuo Fukuda shows how Japanese Christians are attempting to put Christianity into conversation with the Japanese worldview and its religious rituals. Building on Japanese supernaturalism, ritualism and groupism, many Japanese churches are redefining themselves as "divine families" and "holy places." Japanese culture values form and mysticism and ritual and relationship. So indigenous Japanese churches are prioritizing these in their worship. They are also emphasizing these in small groups, mentoring, rituals and ceremonies. These Christians are keeping church buildings open in the way of Shinto shrines and Buddhist temples.

Mitsuo Fukuda calls this *Japanese ethno-ecclesiology.* "Seeking indigenous church forms for the Christian church in Japan is a pioneering work. . . . Our conviction is that through working with the Holy Spirit, we can discover God's redemptive gift within Japanese culture and employ it for a better church ministry."[45]

Another example is the Mukyokai Non-Church Movement, which began in Japan. Founded by Uchimura Kanzō, it now boasts thirty-five thousand participants across Japan and Taiwan and South Korea. The movement has no church buildings, clergy, liturgy or sacraments. Groups meet in homes, and people with pastoral gifts continue full-time secular work. The movement practices scholarship, social criticism and sophisticated theological conversations. It speaks out against Japanese nationalism and militarism. It also seeks harmony between Asian cultures.

Mukyokai believe that the church and Christian faith should be spiritual and relational and life affirming. Mukyokai hold that Christianity shouldn't be institutional or structural. Christians experience *koinonia* in deep community. All believers are ministers. The whole congregation teaches and leads. The church is a dynamic and living organism, not a static institution. It is forever being reborn and renewed. "The church is forever constructed and forever destroyed."[46]

---

[45]Mitsuo Fukuda, *Developing a Contextualized Church as a Bridge to Christianity in Japan* (Gloucester: Wide Margin, 2012), 240.

[46]William H. Norman, "Kanzo Uchimura—the Church," *Contemporary Religions in Japan,* December 1964, 358, 360.

In China, many Christians are contextualizing the Chinese New Year Festival. They are adapting their Christian practices at this time of the year. This way, Christian New Year festivities are indigenous. Christian Chinese New Year Festivals involve valuing kinship groups and elders and extended families. They include honoring the ancestors (Christian and otherwise). And they entail culturally appropriate greetings, visitations and exchanging of gifts.[47]

What does a truly indigenous Asian Christianity look like? The Federation of Asian Bishops offered a description when they met in Samphran, Thailand, in 2000. While they are only one group in Asia (albeit a major group—there are 137 million Catholics in Asia), they do highlight salient features of an Asian indigenous church. They examined what the Spirit has been saying to their churches over a thirty-year period. And they desired to be faithful to Christ through an indigenous Asian vision of a renewed church. This is instructive for us in our own settings.

So what did they conclude? They observed "eight movements that as a whole constitute an Asian vision of a renewed Church." A renewed Asian church is a church of the poor and the young. It's a truly local church with a deep interiority. It's an authentic community of faith with an active and integral mission. It empowers men and women. It serves and generates life. And it enters into dialogue with other faiths, with the poor and with Asian cultures.[48]

What will a truly indigenous church look like in your setting? Will it be a church of the poor and young that is indigenous to its culture? Will it practice deep interiority and authentic community? Will it embrace active integral mission and empowerment of women and men? Will it confront your culture's sin? Will it promote creation care, religious dialogue and ethnic harmony? Will it value human dignity and life and peace and solidarity? Or will a genuinely indigenous church be evident through other distinctives and characteristics?

---

[47]Betty O. S. Tan, "The Contextualization of the Chinese New Year Festival," *Asia Journal of Theology* 15, no. 1 (2001).

[48]Franz-Josef Eilers, ed., *For All the Peoples of Asia: Federation of Asian Bishops' Conferences. Documents from 1997 to 2002*, vol. 3 (Quezon City: Claretian, 2002), 3-4.

3. Indigenization in Latin America

Like Africa and Asia, indigenization in Latin America is widespread and diverse. Latin Americans have found innovative ways to meet the challenges and opportunities of their cultural contexts.

Latin American theologies. I have devoted an entire chapter to liberation theology—and associated Latin American Christian perspectives—in this book. (See the chapter called "Liberating People.") In that chapter, I demonstrated that liberation theology has a range of recognizable features. These qualities are often shared with other expressions of Latin American contextual theology.

Liberation theology shares many features and perspectives with other Latin American theological movements. But it isn't the sum total of indigenous Latin American theology.[49] We must avoid caricaturing Latin American theology into one homogenous type. In Latin America, *liberation* theology, *Pentecostal* theology, *mujerista* theology, *base ecclesial* communities, *integral mission* movements and *evangelical* groups are all unique. Each has a particular form of worship and theology and leadership.

There are also unique forms of theology developing among Latino Jewish Christians, Afro-Latinos and Amerindians (to name a few). But even though these theologies are unique, they also share certain features and perspectives. They're committed to Scripture and social transformation. They combine evangelistic passion and integral mission. They enjoy deep personal spirituality and countercultural lifestyles. They cultivate private piety and immersion in community. And they embrace contextual theology and grassroots missional practices.

---

[49]For a range of ecclesiastical, academic and practical critiques of liberation theology, see Lee M. Penyak and Walter J. Petry, eds., *Religion in Latin America: A Documentary History* (Maryknoll, NY: Orbis, 2006), part XVIII. Good introductions to Latin American contextual theologies (and liberation theology in particular) include Parratt, *Introduction to Third World Theologies*, chap. 2; Christopher Rowland, *The Cambridge Companion to Liberation Theology*, 2nd ed., Cambridge Companions to Religion (Cambridge: Cambridge University Press, 2007); Hans Schwarz, *Theology in a Global Context: The Last Two Hundred Years* (Grand Rapids: Eerdmans, 2005), chap. 14; David J. Hesselgrave and Edward Rommen, *Contextualization: Meanings, Methods, and Models* (Grand Rapids: Baker, 1989), chap. 7; Roger Haight, *An Alternative Vision: An Interpretation of Liberation Theology* (New York: Paulist, 1985); Sharon E. Heaney, *Contextual Theology for Latin America: Liberation Themes in Evangelical Perspective* (Milton Keynes: Paternoster, 2008); Mark Lau Branson et al., *Conflict and Context: Hermeneutics in the Americas; A Report on the Context and Hermeneutics in the Americas Conference* (Grand Rapids: Eerdmans, 1986).

There is theological diversity here but also commonalities.

Here are some features of Latin American contextual theologies (not merely what we have come to know as "liberation theology"):

Liberating Scripture and theology. There's a focus on renewing theology and theological method. Theologizing practitioners, pastors, congregations and missionaries do theology together. They prefer this to outsourcing theology to "professional theologians." And the whole community does theology together. The powerful and wealthy do theology alongside the marginalized and poor. Latin American contextual theologies are, of course, culture specific. They recognize their social location and theologize within particular contexts. They immerse themselves in human community.

Liberating contexts. There's an emphasis on transforming concrete situations. Contextual theologies form theology and mission and church that's specific to particular contexts.

Liberating praxis and interpretation. There's a suspicion of oppressive ideologies. Certain practices complement this suspicion. These include seeking social transformation and renewing church structures. They confront unjust political and social systems. They parallel suspicion of ideologies with innovation in church and mission. Later in this chapter, I provide examples of Latin American indigenous innovations in such areas. Juan Luis Segundo speaks of the hermeneutical circle. This circle involves at least three steps: (1) scrutinizing received interpretations with holy suspicion, (2) being open to paradigmatic and interpretive upheaval and change and (3) practicing circumstance-defying hope.[50]

Liberating orientation. There's solidarity with the poor and marginalized and oppressed.

Liberating mission. There's an emphasis on mission. They see mission as participation in the *missio Dei*. Mission is liberation to fullness of life. It is participation in the extension and proclamation of Christ's inaugurated kingdom. Mission is healing and redemption and liberation of whole persons and whole cultures and the whole world. Mission is *integral*. This means that mission involves holistic transformation and social responsibility.

---

[50]Leif E. Vaage offers a collection of subversive Latin American biblical interpretations in *Subversive Scriptures: Revolutionary Readings of the Christian Bible in Latin America* (Valley Forge, PA: Trinity, 1997).

It means that mission calls people to personal conversion and discipleship. And it means that mission places everything within the context of the liberating mission and love and kingdom of God.

Liberating Christ. These contextual theologies focus on Jesus. They form indigenous Christologies that are true to Scripture and relevant to the culture.

Liberating Trinity. There's an aversion to dry, abstract academic doctrine. Instead, trinitarian theology provides meaning and impetus for fresh theological understandings and fresh explorations of Christian community, mission, faith and praxis. Segundo and Boff show how trinitarian perspectives give these things deeper foundations.

Liberating Spirit. Pentecostalism has grown exponentially in Latin America. Latin American liberation and Pentecostal and evangelical theologies are especially focused on the Spirit. They emphasize the person and work and empowerment of the Spirit (pneumatology).

Liberating kingdom. There's an effort to understand faith and church and mission in the light of the kingdom of God. God inaugurated this kingdom in the incarnation, life, death, resurrection and glorification of Jesus Christ.

Liberating community and church. There's a desire to reactivate the church. This includes grassroots communities that worship together. They do mission together. And they engage in justice and mercy and consciousness raising among the poor and oppressed.

Liberating holism. There's a focus on holistic practice and theology. This involves describing the connections between liberation, eco-theology, poverty, economics and spirituality. It also means pursuing appropriate actions.

Liberating dialogue. There's an effort to put key things into critical and enriching dialogue. These include Scripture, theology, the humanities, the church's practices and the historical situation.

Liberating futures. There's a focus on meeting the present challenges within Latin America. This involves listening to the voices of women and children. It also involves paying attention to a younger generation of theologians. These emerging thinkers are influencing global conversations. They come from many settings—Asian, Latin American, African, Eastern European, Middle Eastern, indigenous and more. They don't ignore Western voices. But Western voices have been dominant for so long. And Latin

American thinkers know that it is time to pay attention to voices and practices from the Majority World.

Almost all forms of indigenous Latin American theology contain a common feature. They integrate theology and practice in Christian social action and community and mission.

Latin American expressions and practices. I consider four indigenous expressions of Latin American faith here: *mujerista* theology, basic ecclesial communities (BECs), autochthonous Pentecostal churches (LAAPs) and integral mission movements.

1. Mujerista theology (Latina/Hispanic womanist theology). Mujerista theology emerges from the life experiences and theologies of Latin American and US Hispanic women. It sees itself as womanist, not feminist. *Mujerista* theology integrates Latin American liberation theology, Latin American and US Hispanic womanist theology, and cultural studies.

Mujerista is a grassroots Latina ecclesiology. It seeks the liberation of the church and its mission from forms of oppression based on gender. It has a communal focus. *Mujerista* prefers the theological perspectives of black and Hispanic/Latina women (*mujeres*). It encourages Latina women to rediscover the Bible for themselves in small reading groups.

Mujerista is also characterized by (1) a preferential option for women and the poor; (2) the pursuit of justice and liberation for women and the poor; (3) the development of a unique Latina theology; and (4) practices outworked through community.[51]

2. Basic Ecclesial Communities (BECs). These are small, basic, grassroots, autonomous, self-reliant, rural and urban Christian groups.

BECs emerged in Brazil in the 1960s. They spread throughout Latin America and Asia and Africa. They are often associated with liberation theology. BECs focus on solidarity with the marginalized and poor. They enjoy participatory forms of ministry and decision making and governance. Liberation theologians

---

[51]Ada María Isasi-Díaz, "Mujeristas: A Name of Our Own," *Christian Century*, May 24–31, 1989, 560. See Ada María Isasi-Díaz and Yolanda Tarango, *Hispanic Women—Prophetic Voice in the Church* (Scranton, PA: University of Scranton Press, 2006); Isasi-Díaz, *La Lucha Continues: Mujerista Theology* (Maryknoll, NY: Orbis, 2004); Isasi-Díaz, *Mujerista Theology: A Theology for the Twenty-First Century* (Maryknoll, NY: Orbis, 1996). Bird collects a broad range of female interpretations of scripture from Africa, Asia and Latin America in Phyllis A. Bird, ed., *Reading the Bible as Women: Perspectives from Africa, Asia, and Latin America* (Atlanta: Scholars, 1997).

popularized BECs, and the 1968 meeting of the Latin American Council of Bishops (CELAM II, Medellín, Colombia) brought them to the attention of the world. These BECs sought fellowship within the Roman Catholic churches of Latin American after Medellín. Post–Vatican II modernizing impulses helped this shift. The vision for renewal expressed in the Vatican II documents *Lumen Gentium* and *Gaudium et Spes* provided further momentum for these basic communities.

Boff is an enthusiastic supporter of BECs. Boff encourages new forms of church "from below"—hence his book *Ecclesiogenesis: The Base Communities Reinvent the Church*. These churches "from below" are autonomous and multivoiced and self-governing. They're *of* the poor and *for* the poor. Boff says that particular ecclesiologies must replace universal ecclesiologies. And our vision for the kingdom of God must be greater than our commitment to the institutional church.

For Boff, BECs are reinventing the church. They're forging new ways of being church, and they're growing beyond current church structures. They give space for oppressed people to organize for liberation. And they encourage people to question the institutions of the church. A layperson can coordinate the celebration of the Lord's Supper as "an extraordinary minister of the Lord." And BECs open up possibilities for women's priesthood.[52]

Occasionally, Catholic Church leaders have criticized the theology, deinstitutionalization and practices of BECs. But in *Redemptoris Missio*, Pope John Paul II affirmed BECs:

> BECs are centers for Christian formation and missionary outreach. They are
> a sign of vitality within the Church, an instrument of formation and evan-
> gelization, and a solid starting point for a new society based on a "civili-
> zation of love." BECs decentralize and organize the parish community to
> which they remain united. They take root among the less privileged. They
> become a leaven of Christian life, care for the poor, and commitment to the
> transformation of society. . . . They are a means of evangelization and of initial

---

[52]Leonardo Boff, *Ecclesiogenesis: The Base Communities Reinvent the Church* (Maryknoll, NY: Orbis Books, 1986). For an introduction to the theology and practices of BECs, see Margaret Hebblethwaite, *Base Communities: An Introduction* (Mahwah, NJ: Paulist, 1994); Guillermo Cook, *The Expectation of the Poor: Latin American Base Ecclesial Communities in Protestant Perspective*, American Society of Missiology Series (Maryknoll, NY: Orbis, 1985); C. René Padilla, "A New Ecclesiology in Latin America," *International Bulletin of Missionary Research* 11, no. 4 (1987).

proclamation of the Gospel—a source of new ministries. They are a true expression of communion and a means for the construction of a more profound communion. They are a cause for great hope for the life of the Church.[53]

Writing to the *13th Interecclesial Meeting of the Basic Ecclesial Communities* (December 17, 2013, Brazil), Pope Francis expressed support for BECs. He said they "bring a new evangelizing fervor and a new capacity for dialogue with the world whereby the Church is renewed." And he challenged them to pursue fellowship with the rest of the church. He exhorted them to be "missionary disciples who walk with Jesus, proclaiming and witnessing to the poor the prophecy of a new heaven and a new earth."[54]

Basic ecclesial communities have not received much attention recently. They have suffered from the rise of neoliberalism and the decline of socialism in Latin America. They have also struggled under the resurgence of conservatism during the pontificates of John Paul II and Benedict XVI.

This does not mean that BECs are insignificant—millions of people are members of them in Brazil alone.[55] It will be interesting to see whether they make a comeback during Francis's pontificate.

3. Latin American Autochthonous Pentecostal Churches (LAAPs). These are Pentecostal churches that originated in Latin America. They're *autochthonous*. This means they're not missionary, and they're not transplanted from elsewhere. They're typically independent from denominations or mission agencies. Like the BECs, they are Christian communities formed "from below." They are grassroots, locally led, self-supporting and indigenous. Unlike most of the BECs, they are Pentecostal.

The LAAPs are fringe to Latin American denominational Pentecostalism. They're separate from Western-planted and Western-led Pentecostal movements. LAAPs are more resistant than BECs to Protestant and Catholic denominational cultures and institutions. LAAPs are restorationist. They value Pentecostal holiness and biblical primitivism and literalism. They elevate nonprofessional leadership. And they practice solidarity with the poor. They've

---

[53]Pope John Paul II, *Redemptoris Missio* (December 7, 1990), 51.

[54]Pope Francis, *Letter to Participants in the 13th Meeting of the Basic Ecclesial Communities in Brazil* (December 17, 2013).

[55]There is some debate about the numbers of people associated with BECs and about their place and contribution to the church in Latin America. Phillip Berryman, *Religion in the Megacity: Catholic and Protestant Portraits from Latin America* (Maryknoll, NY: Orbis, 1996), 63-70.

been more successful than missionary-led, Western forms of Latin American Pentecostalism. They often view Western Pentecostalism as foreign, professionalized, elite and dependent on Western support.

Clayton L. Berg Jr. and Paul E. Pretiz are missionary researchers in Latin America. Their book *Spontaneous Combustion* considers the explosive growth of LAAPs in Latin America.[56] These LAAPs correspond to the African Independent Churches (AICs). They're especially like the Independent Pentecostal/Charismatic Churches (IPCCs).

In 1980, LAAPs constituted around 40 percent of Protestants in Latin America. Today, more than 50 percent of Latin America Protestants are in LAAPs. Berg Jr. and Pretiz say that LAAPs are breaking the nonindigenous stereotype of Latin American Protestantism. They are revealing fresh and indigenous and contextual forms of Protestant Pentecostalism in Latin America.

Occasionally, researchers compare Latin American Pentecostal churches with BECs. The stereotype is that Latin American Pentecostalism is "otherworldly" and tied to the West. It is portrayed as disinterested in the plight of the poor or in social transformation. BECs are stereotyped as the opposite to this.

But LAAPs are challenging the stereotypes. LAAPs are Pentecostal churches committed to indignity and independence and solidarity with the poor. They pursue social transformation and political activism. LAAPs break the stereotype of "otherworldly" or "materialistic" or "Western-dependent" Latin American Pentecostalism.[57]

4. Integral mission movements. I have discussed integral mission in the chapter "Contextualizing Mission." The chapter contains the definition, key personalities and characteristic practices of integral mission.

This *approach to* and *theology of* mission is often associated with liberation theology. But many others practice and embrace and advocate integral

---

[56]Clayton L. Berg Jr. and Paul E. Pretiz, *Spontaneous Combustion: Grass Roots Christianity, Latin American Style* (Pasadena, CA: William Carey, 1996).

[57]Bergunder challenges these stereotypes and shows how Latin American Pentecostalism is evolving into a movement for social transformation, in Michael Bergunder, Ralph Woodhall and Allan H. Anderson, "The Pentecostal Movement and Basic Ecclesial Communities in Latin America: Sociological Theories and Theological Debates," *International Review of Mission* 91, no. 361 (2002). See Clayton L. Berg Jr. and Paul E. Pretiz, "Latin America's Fifth Wave of Protestant Churches." Located online at www.thefreelibrary.com/Latin+America%27s+fifth+wave+of+Protestant +churches.-a018826941.

mission—both in and outside Latin America. Many who do not self-identify with liberation theology do practice and support integral mission. This is as true in Latin America as it is elsewhere. And integral mission is always best practiced in indigenous and contextual ways.

In *Serving with the Poor in Latin America*, C. René Padilla, Tetsunao Yamamori and others provide examples of integral mission in Latin America. Here are five examples. First, the *Evangelical Hospital* in Honduras doesn't just provide hospital services. It offers economic contributions to the local community. And it assists with the transformation of the national health system. Second, the *Redeemer Project* in Brazil works in the major cities. It cares for homeless people, prostitutes, addicts, adolescents, trafficked persons and battered women. Third, the *Child Well-Being Project* in Brazil helps disadvantaged children through holistic measures. These initiatives address poverty, illiteracy, crime, gangs, addiction and family breakdown. Fourth, the *Assemblies of God* in Nicaragua engage in soil regeneration and environmental conservation enterprises. These have positive social consequences. This group invests in soil conservation and enrichment and in reforestation. They build family and communal gardens. They improve traditional and non-traditional crops. And they rebuild local communities by supporting connections between people and lands and Christ. Finally, the *Christian Office for Social Advancement and Development* in Colombia is getting women and men out of poverty and the drug trade. They invest in microenterprise and education. And they help churches serve their communities. This NGO encourages churches to invest in local businesses, families, social networks and education.

Padilla and Yamamori offer other case studies in integral mission in their book. In each case, local people are finding indigenous ways to *be* church and *do* mission. Local Christians are helping transform their particular locations.[58]

INDIGENIZATION AND THE GLOBALCHURCH: CONCLUDING REFLECTIONS

In this chapter, I've outlined the diverse indigenous expressions of faith in Africa and Asia and Latin America. I've examined what we can learn from

---

[58]Tetsunao Yamamori et al., eds., *Serving with the Poor in Latin America* (Monrovia, CA: MARC, 1997), 11-84.

their unique and indigenous theologies. I've considered what we can learn from how they indigenize their faith. I've shown how they indigenize their spirituality, worship, mission and church. And I've asked the reader to take note of these things and learn from them.

These examples of indigenous theology and practice should inspire us. And they should especially motivate us to shape *our own* indigenous ways of being God's people in our particular setting. How can your church be indigenous? How will you and your Christian community develop a grassroots and indigenous theology? What forms of church and mission and theology will emerge in your setting? And how will they be relevant and indigenous to your culture?

Here are thirteen things we learn from how Majority World Christians indigenize faith:

1. Indigenous churches evidence the six marks of indigenization. Alan Tippett's six marks of a truly indigenous church are helpful. He developed these while doing mission among the Fijian islands. The first is *self-image*. An indigenous church knows that it's *the* church of Jesus Christ in its local situation. It knows that it's not a poor imitation of the true church located elsewhere or in another culture.

The second is *self-function*. Indigenous people *take part in* and *lead* the ministries and mission of the church. They *own* those ministries and missions and expressions of church under the lordship of Jesus Christ.

The third is *self-determination*. An indigenous church makes its own decisions and determines its own structures. It forms its own theology. It shapes its own ministries. It develops indigenous expressions of worship. It leads its own process of *self-contextualization* or *self-indigenization*. It does all these things in a way that is indigenous to its culture so that its witness and worship make sense to that culture.

The fourth is *self-support*. An indigenous church raises and administers its own finances. It carries its own financial burdens. It funds its own local ministries, service projects and missions.

The fifth is *self-propagation*. An indigenous church multiplies itself through church planting and raising up its own missionaries. It does not rely on missionaries from elsewhere but becomes a missional movement.

The sixth is *self-giving*. Indigenous people seek to transform their own cultures. They engage the political, social and relational challenges of their setting. They serve their own cultures in ways that are indigenous and transformational.[59]

How do you know if your church is indigenous to your culture? Ask yourself whether it displays these six qualities.

2. Indigenous churches fuel theological imagination. As you've read this chapter, you may have noticed the theological creativity in Asia and Africa and Latin America. Theological originality is a hallmark of indigeneity. Duplicating the theology of others never leads to indigenous churches. Truly indigenous churches throw fuel on the fire of theological imagination. This theological experimentation listens to history and tradition. It respects the authority of Scripture. It pays close attention to the interpretations of other cultures and groups. But it's still theologically imaginative. It strives for theological innovations and interpretations and explorations. These challenge *and* communicate to its culture. It gives fresh meaning to cultural narratives, images, rituals, rites, myths and practices. And it puts these into a dynamic conversation with a Christian worldview. This way we understand and reshape *both* Christian theologies and cultures. And we do this in fresh and mutually enriching ways.

3. Indigenous churches are relevant and prophetic. They do worship and mission in ways that are indigenous to their culture. They're relevant. Their language and practices and analogies are meaningful to their culture. But they're also confrontational and prophetic. They proclaim the gospel in word and deed without compromise. They pursue Christ-honoring worship, preaching, service, mission and discipleship that call their culture—and individuals within that culture—to repentance and discipleship.

In my early twenties, I did a youth ministry course with a local megachurch. They geared their church services to youth culture, drawing thousands of young people. But the backup singers were mostly young and

---

[59]Tippett, *Introduction to Missiology*, 377-81. Evangelical Christianity and Democracy in the Global South is a fascinating series edited by Timothy Samuel Shah on the way evangelical Christianity has engaged (and transformed) politics and democracy in Africa, Asia and Latin America. See Paul Freston, ed., *Evangelical Christianity and Democracy in Latin America* (Oxford: Oxford University Press, 2008); Terence O. Ranger, ed., *Evangelical Christianity and Democracy in Africa* (Oxford: Oxford University Press, 2008); David H. Lumsdaine, *Evangelical Christianity and Democracy in Asia* (Oxford: Oxford University Press, 2009).

beautiful women, dressed in tight and skimpy clothing. I asked the youth pastor whether this was appropriate. She replied, "Well, don't complain, it brings the young boys to church." The church also watered down the gospel message, removing references to sin and repentance. The youth pastor explained, "After all, we don't want to scare people away." I left the course convinced that this church was doing many good things. And it was clearly indigenous to youth culture. But it was compromising. Truly indigenous churches don't make such compromises. They are relevant and prophetic and committed uncompromisingly to the gospel. Indigenous forms and analogies can be countercultural but only when they witness to the values, holiness, faith, hope, love, gospel and person of Jesus Christ. They stand within culture but witness to the One who transcends all cultures and persons, calling them to faith and repentance.

4. Indigenous churches engage the hearts and minds and hands of local people. I've seen too many churches and theological colleges around the world that expats start and lead and fund. Recently, I spoke at a large church in Malaysia. Westerners (I won't say which nationality) planted the church. And after twenty years of operation, these non-Malaysians still filled almost all senior positions in that church. That makes no sense to me. Here's another example. Six months ago, I spent a few nights staying with friends in a Cambodian village. These Cambodian Christians serve among the poorest of the poor. They live among slum dwellers whom the Cambodian government had forcibly removed into a rural area. These Cambodian Christians collaborate with this poor community to develop its educational, health-care, employment and microenterprise opportunities. They also partner with the community to grow its spiritual capacities and receptivity to Christian faith. But recently a rich church from another Asian nation "planted a church" in that village. They built an expensive building and started paying people to come to church. They offered food and clothing and money to people who turned up to church services. The leaders of the poor community went to the Cambodian Christians in distress. They said, "What are these Christians doing? They're turning Cambodians into beggars. Our people are losing all self-respect."

Local people form and lead indigenous churches. These locals ensure that other local people *take part in* and *lead* the ministries and mission of the church. They help them *own* these ministries and missions and expressions of the church—under Christ's lordship. Indigenous churches engage the hearts and minds and hands of local people. We must entrust the indigenous church to them. This includes its theology, leadership, funding, identity, governance, propagation and so forth.

5. Indigenous churches proclaim the gospel in indigenous ways. We must use indigenous ideas and metaphors and analogies to help all people understand the person and gospel of Jesus Christ. And the best people to determine and shape these are indigenous to the receiving culture.

The classic story missionaries use to illustrate this point is the story of the peace child.[60] Don Richardson was a missionary among the tribes of New Guinea, Indonesia. He lived among the Sawi tribe, who were cannibalistic headhunters. For a long time he tried to communicate the gospel with them. But cultural barriers prevented its reception. This tribe considered betrayal advantageous. So they saw Judas as a clever hero and Jesus as weak. That was until Richardson stumbled upon the image of the "peace child." During times of tribal warfare, warring sides would sometimes exchange children to make peace. A fierce chief would offer up his son to another tribe as an ultimate sacrifice. He would offer his precious child as a peace offering. This image presented a window for the Sawi people into the substitutionary atonement of Jesus Christ. Richardson called it a "redemptive analogy." And he proposed that such redemptive analogies exist in all cultures. We can use them to illustrate the meaning of the gospel of Jesus Christ to people groups.

Don Richardson found a "redemptive analogy" that made sense to the Sawi. But once the Sawi became Christian, they needed to explore their own cultural analogies. Only this way would they shape their own indigenous faith. This is always the case. What redemptive analogies exist in your culture and in the cultures around you? How will you empower "cultural insiders" to use indigenous stories and analogies and ideas to shape their own theologies?

The goal isn't indigenization. The goal is the reception of the gospel and person of Jesus Christ. The Balinese theologian I. Wayan Mastra outlines the role indigenization plays:

---

[60]Don Richardson, *Peace Child*, 4th ed. (Ventura, CA: Regal, 2005).

Let us be clear that "indigenization" is not the goal of the church. We are not embarked on an effort to make an indigenous church just for the sake of making an indigenous church, nor for the sake of preservation of the culture. . . . No, the process of making an indigenous church is undertaken for the sake of making the Gospel relevant to the people in a certain place at a particular period. It is a strategy of its mission, so that Christianity can have a home base and be rooted in the soul of a society, so that the Christians will not be foreigners in their own country, so that then Christ can be truly felt by all people to be the Savior of all the nations of the world.[61]

6. Indigenous churches experiment with forms of liturgy and sacrament. They shape indigenous prayers and liturgies. They cultivate indigenous forms of baptism, the Lord's Supper, ordination, blessings, consecrations and other Christian rituals. We need to indigenize these and other liturgical and sacramental dimensions of our churches.

7. Indigenous churches import critically. They refuse to blindly import theologies, church models, governance structures, mission programs, preaching guides and worship expressions. Sometimes these resources can help us. After all, that's one of the benefits of glocalization. We gain from a mutual exchange of ideas and resources and practices. Glocalization means that the global is in the local, and the local is in the global. But we make a grave mistake when we adopt these things uncritically and without contextualizing them.

Instead, we must make our own local and indigenous decisions. We determine our own structures. We form our own theologies. We shape our own ministries. We set our own curriculum. We choose our own analogies and metaphors. We develop our own expressions of worship. And we seek to make these dimensions of our churches relevant and transforming for our contexts. We make them truly indigenous to our cultures.

8. Indigenous churches take a long-term view. They scrutinize what the Spirit has been saying to their churches and culture over a long period. Earlier in this chapter, I showed how Asian bishops explored what the Spirit had been doing among their churches over thirty years. The goal was to discern what Jesus was doing in their Asian cultures and to join with him.

---

[61]I. Wayan Mastra, "Christianity and Culture in Bali," *International Review of Mission* 63, no. 251 (1974): 399.

We also need to take a long-term view. What has Jesus been doing in your church over the past ten, twenty or thirty years? How will you join with him? And how will you respond in obedience—developing indigenous theologies and practices that lead to renewed churches?

9. *Indigenous churches make holistic commitments.* We need to proclaim the gospel in word and deed and sign. We should reject dualisms and instead pursue holism in our unique settings. This means seeking indigenous expressions of holistic commitments. What do I mean by this? I mean that we must find indigenous ways to combine these kinds of things: (1) gospel proclamation and social transformation; (2) evangelistic passion and integral mission; (3) cultural relevance and countercultural lifestyle; (4) private piety and public witness; (5) personal spirituality and immersion in community; (6) contextual theology and attention to history and tradition; (7) national political action and grassroots mission; and (8) passion for Scripture and reliance on God's empowering presence.

10. *Indigenous churches seek the transformation of their cultures and societies.* They seek to transform and heal and liberate and unify their culture. Of course, this usually starts with individuals and families and small groups within a society. Indigenous churches don't pursue transformation in their own strength. And they don't do this through their own clever plans and initiatives. Instead, they seek to bring transformation through the power and gospel and Spirit of Jesus Christ. Yes, we must plan and strategize and work wisely within the systems of this world, but transformation can't rely on such things. Regeneration and renewal isn't by might or power but by the Spirit of Christ.

11. *Indigenous churches test their indigenous forms.* They test them according to John Pobee's criteria: "The test of any cultural construct of the gospel is whether it enables growth, change, and transformation in and into the image and likeness of God through Christ."[62] Here are other important tests. Does this cultural construct proclaim the true gospel of Jesus Christ? Does it lead to the glory of the Father and Son and Holy Spirit? Does is look like the Beatitudes? Does it cause people to seek first the kingdom of God and his righteousness? Does it inspire them to love the Lord their God with

---

[62]Stinton, *Jesus of Africa*, 250.

all their heart and soul and mind and strength and love their neighbor as themselves?

12. *Indigenous churches care about the local and global.* In one of the first chapters of this book, I discussed the importance of the glocal church. Healthily indigenous churches understand the importance of the exchange between the local and the global. They pursue the well-being of both expressions of the church. They invest in the welfare of their own church and culture. And they look for ways to enrich the global church and contribute positively to the whole world.

13. *Indigenous churches are flowerpot breakers and seed sowers.* In summary, how do we know if our church and theology are truly indigenous? Here are the signs. First, we know that Jesus is the Lord and Savior of our culture and church (and not some imported God from another context). Second, we fashion churches and missions and services that meet the needs of our culture. Third, we worship in ways that are indigenous to our culture. This worship makes sense to believers and nonbelievers alike. This is the case even when our worship contains elements that challenge our culture. Fourth, our congregations are places where local people *take part in* and *lead* the ministries and mission of the church. They *own* these ministries and missions and expressions of the church (under Christ's headship). Fifth, we refuse to blindly import theologies, church models, governance structures and worship expressions. Instead, we make our own decisions and determine our own structures. We form our own theologies and shape our own ministries. We develop our own expressions of worship. We seek to make these dimensions of our church relevant and transforming for our context. These things are truly indigenous to our culture. Sixth, we carry our own financial burdens and multiply indigenous churches and ministries. Seventh, we seek to transform, animate, direct and unify our own culture. (And we do this through the power of the gospel and the Spirit of Christ.) Eighth, we do all these things not only for the sake of our own culture but also for the sake of the whole world. We seek to enrich the local and global church.

Lastly, our churches are flowerpot breakers and seed sowers. The Sri Lankan preacher and evangelist Daniel Thambyrajah Niles put it this way:

> The gospel is like a seed and you have to sow it. When you sow the seed of the gospel in Palestine, a plant that can be called Palestinian Christianity grows.

When you sow it in Rome, a plant of Roman Christianity grows. You sow the gospel in Great Britain and you get British Christianity. The seed of the gospel is later brought to America and a plant grows of American Christianity. Now when missionaries came to our lands they brought not only the seed of the gospel, but their own plant of Christianity, flowerpot included! So, what we have to do is to break the flowerpot, take out the seed of the gospel, sow it in our own cultural soil, and let our own version of Christianity grow.[63]

Will you and your Christian community do this? "Break the flowerpot, take out the seed of the gospel, sow it in your own cultural soil, and let your own version of Christianity grow."

---

[63]Niles is quoted in Emilio Antonio Núñez, *Crisis and Hope in Latin America: An Evangelical Perspective*, rev. ed. (Pasadena, CA: William Carey, 1996), 332-33.

DEVOURING SCRIPTURE

WHAT CAN WE LEARN FROM HOW MAJORITY WORLD CHRISTIANS DEVOUR AND INTERPRET SCRIPTURE?

A xeroxed copy of a theology made in Europe or North America can never satisfy the theological needs of the Church in the Third World. Now that the Church has become a world community, the time has come for it to manifest the universality of the Gospel in terms of a theology that is not bound by a particular culture but shows the many-sided wisdom of God.

C. RENÉ PADILLA

Twenty-five years ago, I spent time studying at a Bible college in Hyderabad, India. I was twenty-one years old. Most of the students were my age or younger. Bible study, memorization, application and proclamation were central to our studies. We would rise at 4:30 a.m. for two hours of prayer. Then we would have breakfast at 6:30 and study and memorize Scripture until lunchtime. We spent the afternoons preaching in the villages and cities and planting churches. During the evening, there would be further biblical studies and prayer.

Lecturers expected the students to memorize all sixteen chapters of Romans as well as other large portions of Scripture. The college tested them on this memorization. And students saturated their preaching with biblical references and stories. They believed Scripture literally. And they applied Scripture with an expectation of signs, wonders, miracles, deliverance and spiritual gifts to follow.

I discovered in India an enthusiasm for Scripture—and a belief in its power and authority—that I had rarely seen in my own country, Australia. Passion for Jesus Christ and his Scriptures typifies belief in Majority World contexts. This passion is at the center of the renewal of church and mission in those cultures.

As the church grows in the Majority World, it will need to wrestle with its *multivoiced* and *multipeopled* nature. This global and diverse nature is reshaping its understanding of mission and church and biblical interpretation. Western cultures no longer define how Christians should understand and believe and interpret the Bible. Interpretive approaches in the West are now part of a global conversation. This conversation is broadening and enriching the way Christians believe and apply Scripture. This global exchange is heralding a transformation of the church. Christians in the Majority World are believing and interpreting the Bible in fresh, dynamic ways. And they're influencing the Western and the global church.

Global ethnic diversity is dewesternizing the global church. Global and local conversations about biblical interpretation are dewesternizing hermeneutics. *Hermeneutics* is the branch of theology that deals with the interpretation of Scripture. The way the church interprets and applies Scripture in global situations will witness to the power of the gospel. Biblical belief will determine the shape and missional vitality of the church to come.

Majority World and indigenous voices can teach the global church further practices of biblical faithfulness. They can help the worldwide church discover further multivoiced and multipeopled approaches to interpreting and believing the Bible. What characterizes these approaches? People believe in the absolute authority of Scripture. They passionately apply the Bible to everyday life. They put their interpretations into a living conversation with their cultures. And they identify personally with the biblical text and its stories.

How can we nurture communities characterized by dynamic biblical interpretation and belief? What can we learn from Christians in the Majority World and indigenous cultures about reading the Bible? How can they help us interpret Scripture missionally and faithfully and expectantly?

This chapter considers how many Majority World believers complement conservative readings of Scripture with innovative applications. I look at the many contextual, popular and communal readings of Scripture in the

Majority World. From there, I consider a wide range of other approaches to interpreting Scripture in those cultures. These include sociopolitical, active, supernaturalist and Pentecostal readings. This chapter asks, *What can we learn from how Majority World Christians devour and interpret Scripture?*

CONSERVATIVE READINGS—RADICAL APPLICATIONS

Philip Jenkins describes the conservative approach to Scripture in the Global South. He contrasts this with liberalizing tendencies in Anglo-European contexts. Majority World Christians tend to see Scripture as inspired, infallible, authoritative and sacred text.

Liberal Majority World scholars don't tend to represent belief and interpretation in the churches. The writings of such academics may give a distorted view of belief and practice in those churches. Jenkins writes that average Asian, African and Latin American believers have particular views on Scripture: (1) They respect "the authority of Scripture, especially in matters of morality." (2) They honor "the Bible as an inspired text" and tend toward literalism. (3) They have "a special interest in supernatural elements of Scripture, such as miracles, visions, and healings." (4) They believe "in the continuing value of prophecy." (5) And they venerate "the Old Testament, which is considered as authoritative as the New."[1]

Fernando Segovia surveys Asian biblical hermeneutics, including the way ordinary Asians read the Bible. He describes a high regard for the Bible as the Word of God. "The biblical texts are regarded as a locus of unquestionable truth and liberation."[2]

These Majority World believers are redefining terms like *liberal* and *conservative*. Their faith in the authority of Scripture doesn't prevent "a creative and even radical exegesis." These Christians often apply biblical texts "to contemporary debates and dilemmas."[3]

Many Majority World believers complement their trust in Scripture's authority with imaginative applications. They believe in the authority of Scripture, and they apply Scripture creatively to sociopolitical and postcolonial issues.

---

[1]Philip Jenkins, *The New Faces of Christianity: Believing the Bible in the Global South* (Oxford: Oxford University Press, 2006), 4.
[2]Fernando F. Segovia, "The Emerging Project of Asian Biblical Hermeneutics: Reading Asian Readers," *Biblical Interpretation* 2, no. 3 (1994): 372.
[3]Jenkins, *New Faces of Christianity*, 12.

They also apply the Bible in innovative ways to moral, supernatural, sexual and environmental issues. We see this throughout the Majority World. Sherron Kay George says that Latin American Pentecostals exemplify this. For them, the Bible is "a constant companion and identifying sign." Scripture "provides models, examples, and solutions for the contemporary Christian. It is used extensively in church services, healing, exorcism, testimony, daily witness, street-preaching, problem-solving, and vehement apologetics."[4]

It's like a breath of fresh air to read of those who trust and use the Scriptures so trustingly. How will Western evangelicals react? We will probably applaud the adherence to Scripture's authority, but we'll probably also be wary of what we would label "superstitious" uses of the Bible and passages. But is that just two centuries of critical scholarship affecting our thinking unawares?

Religious plurality sharpens this biblical interpretation in the Majority World. Social and political upheaval sharpens it too. Anglo-European Christians have often underestimated the ability of conservative exegesis to address contemporary issues. Such conservative readings can lead to transforming applications. We'll see this as this chapter unfolds. These readings can lead to naming and confronting the principalities and powers in societies. These innovative readings of the Bible are often carried out with careful attention to culture and context.

Contextual and Inculturational Readings

Contextualization and inculturation characterize Majority World interpretations of Scripture. *Contextualization* means shaping an idea or practice for a particular context. *Inculturation* is about the adaptation of ideas and practices and teachings for particular cultures. And it is about the influence of these cultures on the evolution of these aspects of the church.

Majority World readers often contextualize their reading of Scripture for their own setting. Those cultures in turn shape Majority World biblical interpretation and theology and practice.

What are some examples of contextual, inculturational readings of Scripture? In his writings, R. S. Sugirtharajah puts Majority World and indigenous

---

[4]Sherron Kay George, "From Liberation to Evangelization: New Latin American Hermeneutical Keys," *Interpretation* 55, no. 4 (2001): 367.

contextual interpretations into five rough groups. These are subaltern, post-colonial, intertextual, popular and numerous readings.

Subaltern readings are those of the rejected, subservient, oppressed, lowly and marginalized. These groups are not homogenous. So they develop a contextual reading for their own circumstances. The Dalit peoples of India, for example, have cultivated a contextual reading that is distinct from that of HIV/AIDS sufferers in Uganda.

Postcolonial readings are those from former colonial contexts. These include Australia, Brazil, Congo, Guinea, Hong Kong, India, indigenous peoples, Indonesia, Jamaica, Macau, Mozambique, Philippines, Sri Lanka and Taiwan. These postcolonial readings ask questions about "empire, religion, and the role of the Bible in the imperial cause." They also examine "the colonial and neo-colonial power operating in biblical interpretation."[5]

Intertextual readings seek to compare the Christian Scriptures with the sacred texts of Judaism, Hinduism, Buddhism and Islam.

Popular readings are those of the ordinary reader. Truly contextual interpretation puts biblical scholarship into conversation with local issues and voices. It regards the "religio-spiritual interests and aspirations of the grassroots and their communitarian readings."[6] Sugirtharajah provides examples from Latin American Pentecostal congregations. He also considers African nonliterate communities. And he offers examples from postapartheid black nonacademic women and Southeast Asian rural churches. These nonacademic groups read the Bible in fresh, grassroots and relational ways. And they normally do this within local communities and congregations.

Numerous readings refers to the breadth of contextual interpretations in the Majority World. We see Latin American, Asian, Palestinian, indigenous, womanist and many more interpretations. I only have space here to give a few examples. In *An Introduction to Third World Theologies*, John Parratt draws together thinkers from across the globe. Latin Americans, Indians, Asians, Africans and Caribbeans unpack unique contextual theologies from their settings. They describe the unique ways they interpret and apply Scripture in their cultures. Edmond Tang's chapter on East Asia is an

---

[5]R. S. Sugirtharajah, *Voices from the Margin: Interpreting the Bible in the Third World*, rev. and expanded 3rd ed. (Maryknoll, NY: Orbis, 2006), 8.
[6]Ibid., 9.

example of the rich contextual theologies growing in each continent. Tang writes of the relationship between biblical interpretation and the support of Confucian virtues in Chinese churches. He explores the relationship between biblical interpretation and cultural notions of human suffering in Japan. And he shows how storytelling and "the reconstruction of history from below" shapes biblical interpretation among the Minjung of South Korea.[7] In a different book, Nestor Miguez analyzes the wide range of Latin American approaches to interpreting Scripture. He writes of the diverse interpreters of the Bible. These include "African descendants, aboriginal peoples, mestizos, women, campesinos, and so on." These show that "there is no 'simple poor,' but a complexity of reading locations."[8]

Contextual Bible reading involves rereading the Bible through the lens of our own culture. It is not about ignoring perspectives from other cultures and societies. We critically engage those perspectives. But we develop forms of interpretation relevant for (and shaped within) our own culture.[9]

In the Majority World, people who closely identify with the Bible also do contextual theology. They identify with biblical stories and concerns. They interpret Scripture in community. They identify with the world of the Bible together.

POPULAR AND COMMUNAL READINGS

Jenkins describes how Majority World Christians identify with biblical themes and stories. The Bible describes a world they know well. It's a world of poverty and wealth, injustice and reconciliation, evil and good, demons and angels, sickness and healing, exorcism and deliverance, suffering and liberation, famine and plague, war and sexual violence, occupation and colonialism, persecution and vindication, corruption and integrity, privileged and marginalized, holy sites and pilgrimage, and rituals and sacred texts.

This identification with the Bible leads to rich *popular* or *ordinary* readings.

---

[7]John Parratt, ed., *An Introduction to Third World Theologies* (Cambridge: Cambridge University Press, 2004), 74-104.

[8]Néstor O. Miguez, "Latin American Reading of the Bible: Experiences, Challenges and Its Practice," *Expository Times* 118, no. 3 (2006): 126. For a scholarly introduction to numerous, global readings, see Craig S. Keener and M. Daniel Carroll R., eds., *Global Voices: Reading the Bible in the Majority World* (Peabody, MA: Hendrickson, 2013).

[9]Justin S. Ukpong, "Rereading the Bible with African Eyes: Inculturation and Hermeneutics," *Journal of Theology for Southern Africa*, no. 91 (1995): 5.

This identification with the ancient world and stories of the Bible is more *communal* than individual. These themes resonate with entire communities. They touch their beliefs and concerns and experiences.[10]

How does personal and communal identification with Scripture shape biblical interpretation in much of the Majority World? How does trust in the Bible's absolute authority influence interpretation? It leads to communal, relevant, Christ-centered, Spirit-oriented, obedient, practical, literal and multivoiced readings.

Here I use African churches as an example. In four separate articles, Zablon Nthamburi, Daniel Waruta, Fergus King, Gerald West and Fidon Mwombeki list the assumptions and practices of popular African Bible reading.

Let's start with a group of popular African convictions that Nthamburi and Waruta notice:

> The Bible is a document which shapes communities, not just individual faith. The meaning of the Bible is both historical and contemporary. The Bible presents a message that is to be obeyed. The Bible is practical and involving. The Bible gives news of salvation from all kinds of catastrophes, physical, political, and spiritual. The Bible gives counsel and enlightenment. The Spirit of God speaks directly to us from Scripture. The Bible's message is clear and to the point. The literal sense is a necessary precursor of any allegorical interpretation. The Bible's message is not always positive: it can warn, condemn, curse, and threaten, as well as bless.[11]

Mwombeki adds that African interpretation has key features.[12] (1) Africans see the Bible "as a symbol of God's presence and protection." (2) They read the Bible for its practical use. "It is a book of life, neither a book of fiction nor one of history. It is not read for curiosity or fun. In this book, the reader listens to God speaking: giving comfort, instruction, exhortation, even condemnation." (3) The Bible "does not always have to be understood rationally." Many Africans appropriate their biblical reading "spiritually,

---

[10]Jenkins, *New Faces of Christianity*, 68-69. See Jenkins, "Liberating Word: The Power of the Bible in the Global South," *Christian Century* 123, no. 14 (2006).

[11]Zablon Nthamburi and Daniel Waruta, "Biblical Hermeneutics in African Instituted Churches," in *The Bible in African Christianity: Essays in Biblical Theology*, ed. Hannah Kinoti and John Waliggo (Nairobi: Acton, 1997), 48 (points 1–10).

[12]Fidon Mwombeki, "Reading the Bible in Contemporary Africa," *Word & World* 21, no. 2 (2001): 121-23.

emotionally, and mystically. The historical setting of the text is not significant, and even less the identify of its author." Often, many Africans appropriate the Bible worshipfully: "by heart, not necessarily by mind." (4) Many Africans apply the Bible to contemporary problems through communal discussion. (5) "There is strong affinity between the religious and cultural context of the Bible and that of contemporary Africa." (This includes issues surrounding poverty, famine, child mortality, begging, prostitution, fishing, exclusion of women and children, demon-possession and so on.)

King describes other qualities of popular African biblical interpretation.[13] The "Christocentric interpretation of the Old Testament is often seen as standard" (i.e., many Africans prefer a Christ-centered interpretation over the historical meaning of the text). Additionally, many Africans memorize and quote the Bible directly. "Instead of paraphrases or explanations, the interpreter will encourage a reading of the text itself." This comes with the assumption that "there is an authority in the words of Scripture themselves, and they must be used accurately." And many Africans change their interpretations according to their context and setting. They subject the Bible to a "plurality of interpretations" depending on the needs of the situation. They give Scripture "fresh layers of meaning within new circumstances."

Many Africans interpret the Bible for personal and societal transformation. "Biblical interpretation is always about changing the African context. This is what links ordinary African biblical interpretation and African biblical scholarship." It is "a common commitment to 'read' the Bible for personal and societal transformation."[14] Often, local African congregations hold African biblical interpreters accountable. These theologians interpret within community. Their churches hold them accountable for their accuracy and application and spiritual vitality.

Identification with the Bible extends beyond Majority World scholarship into popular readings. These are readings by ordinary local believers. They are often conducted within congregations and families and communities.

For example, Miguez describes how many Latin American Christians

---

[13]Fergus King, "Across the Great Divide: Higher Criticism, the Writers of the New Testament, and African Biblical Interpretation," *Mission Studies* 15, no. 2 (1998): 20.
[14]Gerald West, "Biblical Hermeneutics in Africa" (Natal: University of Kwa-Zulu Natal, 2008), 2, 9.

developed popular, communal readings of the Bible within the context of repression. Their readings emerged as a response to persecution and torture and harsh repression. This resulted in contextual and complex readings within Latin America. These developed at both popular and critical levels.

Musimbi Kanyoro says this identified, literal, communal reading has strengths and challenges. A literal reading will often mean an unwillingness to challenge the cultures of the Bible. Readers may consider doing this sinful.

> This points to a central task for those who read the Bible in cultures whose practices closely mirror those of Bible times. We can easily justify our behavior simply because we think we are in good company with the biblical culture. On the other hand, those cultures that are far removed from biblical culture risk reading the Bible as fiction. Cultural hermeneutics scrutinizes every culture with the intention of testing its liberative potential for people.[15]

Identification with the Bible can be as risky as distance from the Bible. Both have possibilities for interpretation and application. But we need to examine ourselves, the text and our context. Both distance and proximity from the world of the Bible require us to examine our reading and using Scripture.

Sociopolitical and Active Readings

Sociopolitical and active readings are common in the Majority World and indigenous cultures.

By *sociopolitical*, I mean reading the Bible to transform social and political realities. I also mean interpreting the Bible in the light of those realities. This is a dynamic engagement between Scripture and social factors. It involves appropriating the Bible in social and political contexts.

By *active*, I mean a *dialogue* between key things: reason and action; interpretation and application; theology and praxis; thought and social transformation; biblical interpretation and mission; and scholarship and congregational practices.

Our actions interrogate our use of Scripture. This includes our mission, ministry, politics and service. And our interpretation of Scripture scrutinizes our actions.

---

[15]Musimbi Kanyoro, "Reading the Bible from an African Perspective," *Ecumenical Review* 51, no. 1 (1999): 20.

In Majority World theology, sociopolitical and active readings are prophetic and creative and many. Let's look at four examples. These are liberationist, feminist/womanist, postcolonial and subaltern/marginal interpretations. These four are often woven together in sociopolitical readings in the Majority World.

1. Liberationist readings. I deal with liberation theologies in another chapter of this book. Liberationist readings focus on liberation from all forms of oppression. They seek freedom from economic, social, political, religious, colonial, sexual and racial domination.

Some liberation theologians are well-known. These include Gustavo Gutierrez, Juan Luis Segundo, Jose Porfirio Miranda, Jose Miguez Bonino and Fernando Belo. They have particular commitments when it comes to interpreting and applying Scripture. This is perhaps best articulated in Segundo's "hermeneutic circle." But here I've tried to summarize their combined thought on biblical interpretation.[16]

Suspicion. Good interpretation begins with *suspicion*. We are skeptical of our inherited narratives, interpretations, theologies, ideologies and traditions.

Praxis. The Bible is always interpreted in *context*. And we study Scripture in the context of *praxis*. Praxis is the outworking of our theories in customs, practices, habits and applications. The relationship between praxis and interpretation is complex and critical. It is also mutually informing.

Transformation. The Bible is best interpreted alongside a commitment to personal and social *transformation*. The Scriptures are best studied within the context of transforming practices. These include efforts to address poverty and injustice and conflict. And the church can learn much from the readings of oppressed people who struggle for liberation and justice. We form liberating interpretations in the context of struggle and mission and praxis. Our readings transform individuals and churches and societies when they are committed to liberation.

Examination. We must *examine* all interpretations in relation to their context. All readings emerge from contexts and cultures and practices. This is true of the *biblical* socioeconomic and theological and historical contexts.

---

[16]Juan Luis Segundo, *Liberation of Theology* (Maryknoll, NY: Orbis, 1976), 9.

And it is just as true for the *contemporary* contexts and practices in which people interpret and apply the Bible.

New orthodoxy and orthopraxis. The Bible interprets our contemporary praxis. Our praxis interprets Scripture. And this exchange leads to new belief and praxis. This results in new *orthodoxy*—right, liberative interpretation and belief. And it leads to new *orthopraxis*—right, liberative praxis. This ongoing exchange anticipates renewal of interpretation and belief and practice.

2. Feminist/womanist readings. Women are not immune from exploitation and oppression in the churches of the Majority World. Repressive cultures often find expression in oppressive churches. Repressive, unjust cultures may seek to fashion conservative interpretation in their own image.

But conservative biblical interpretation is not always the culprit. Often conservative, complementarian Bible readings challenge repression. They support distinct gender roles in society. But they emphasize the care, nurture, protection and flourishing of women. The picture is complex. We need to be careful not to read Western assumptions into our examinations of the cultures of the Global South.

Having said that, Majority World Christianity has nurtured the rise of distinct female voices. These voices challenge the political, economic, gender and religious status quo. They are paving the way for the global church. They are tackling the big issues that have to do with society and gender. And they are doing this courageously. These women include Maricel Mena Lopez, Mercy Amba Oduyoye, Kwok Pui-lan, Elsa Tamez, Saroj Nalini Arambam Parratt, Yuko Yuasa, Virginia Fabella, Elina Vuola, Ruth Padilla Deborst, Azza Karam, Yong Ting Jin, Pauline Hensman, Denise Ackermann and Musa Dube. They are forging ahead with innovative and distinct forms of biblical interpretation. They are pursing gender equality and social justice. And they are leading the way with missional and ministry practices.[17]

Kwok writes about how these women challenge the church's patriarchy. They disciple both women and men. And they call for the equal partnership of women. These women develop distinct sociopolitical readings of the Bible from the perspective of women. They interpret colonial and patriarchal repression through the experience of women. They address issues

---

[17]Mercy Amba Oduyoye, "Feminist Theology in an African Perspective," in *Paths of African Theology*, ed. Rosino Gibellini (Maryknoll, NY: Orbis, 1994), 179.

surrounding the cessation of the exploitation of women and children. They call for the abolition of sexism and discrimination. And they seek the rise of grassroots, participatory movements. They dream of a church that represents God's liberative reign, and they work for a church that pursues peace, antimilitarization and justice. They describe and create churches characterized by intercultural and interfaith and intergender shalom.

Kwok describes how Majority World womanists often distance themselves from Western feminists. They are uncomfortable with the views and hermeneutics of Euro American feminists.[18] She describes the breadth of women's theology in Asian, African, Latin American, African American and indigenous settings.[19]

3. Postcolonial readings. These are biblical interpretations from former colonies. They "emerge out of liberation hermeneutics, or extra-biblical Postcolonial Studies."[20] Postcolonial literature is massive and growing and contested.

Postcolonial biblical interpretation is "diverse and hybrid."[21] These interpretive readings examine the relationship between empire, power, religion and biblical interpretation. They do this in matters that are diverse, yet interwoven. These include gender, liberation, race, ethnicity, marginality, power, geopolitics, social theory, church-state relations, globalization and exclusion of the "other."

Sugirtharajah is probably the most widely read postcolonial theologian. He has written much on postcolonial biblical reading. So I will focus briefly on his thought here. Sugirtharajah defines postcolonial biblical interpretation:

> Postcolonialism is roughly defined as scrutinizing and exposing colonial domination and power as these are embodied in biblical texts and in interpretations, and as searching for alternative hermeneutics while thus overturning and

---

[18]There is, of course, a broad spectrum of feminism in the West. Kwok is referring to the perception (among some) of Euro American feminism in Asia, rather than the actual state or breadth of Euro American feminism. She does recognize the diversity of feminism in the West. She then goes on to explore the diversity of feminist/womanist theology in Asia, which is fascinating given the range of Asian cultures.

[19]Kwok Pui-lan, *Introducing Asian Feminist Theology* (Sheffield: Sheffield Academic, 2000), 112.

[20]Stephen D. Moore and Fernando F. Segovia, eds., *Postcolonial Biblical Criticism: Interdisciplinary Intersections*, The Bible and Postcolonialism (London: T&T Clark, 2005), 5-6.

[21]Ibid., 6.

dismantling colonial perspectives. What postcolonialism does is to enable us to question the totalizing tendencies of European reading practices and interpret the texts on our own terms and read them from our specific locations.[22]

This project is about rejecting colonial, Western interpretations of Scripture. Or it is at least about modifying Western readings for the Majority World. Postcolonial theologians cultivate specific and local and postcolonial readings. The kind of postcolonial interpretations Sugirtharajah champions include those by outcast, subaltern groups in the Majority World (e.g., the Dalits of India). They include the interpretations of indigenous cultures and First Nations. They include the interpretations of oppressed, silenced or marginalized women and children. They incorporate Majority World and indigenous postcolonial interpretations of Scripture (e.g., *A Postcolonial Commentary on the New Testament Writings*).[23] And they encompass the work of Majority World scholars pursuing intertextual interpretations. These put non-Christian sacred and secular texts into postcolonial conversation with the Christian Scriptures. Additionally, some postcolonial theologians develop indigenous and Majority World images and understandings and contextualizations of Jesus (e.g., relevant images of Christ for Buddhist, Islamic, Hindu, Sikh, pluralistic and indigenous contexts).

Having put together this list, one has to be careful. Sugirtharajah addresses the dangers associated with exoticism and reception and power.

The issue of exoticism: "The practice of treating American and European interpretation as *the* interpretation and labeling the enterprise of others 'Asian,' 'African,' and so on, or of using gender or ethnic terms persists. Those who work on the margins are unable to shake off the exotic tag attached to them."[24]

The issue of reception: "Those who act as the interpreters of minority communities find themselves in the strange situation of working with a troubled

---

[22]R. S. Sugirtharajah, *The Postcolonial Bible* (Sheffield: Sheffield Academic, 1998), 16. See Sugirtharajah, *Asian Faces of Jesus*, Faith and Cultures Series (Maryknoll, NY: Orbis, 1993); Sugirtharajah, *Frontiers in Asian Christian Theology: Emerging Trends*; Sugirtharajah, *The Bible and the Third World: Precolonial, Colonial, and Postcolonial Encounters* (Cambridge: Cambridge University Press, 2001); Sugirtharajah, *Postcolonial Criticism and Biblical Interpretation* (Oxford: Oxford University Press, 2002); Sugirtharajah, *Exploring Postcolonial Biblical Criticism: History, Method, Practice* (Chichester: Wiley-Blackwell, 2012).

[23]Fernando F. Segovia and R. S. Sugirtharajah, *A Postcolonial Commentary on the New Testament Writings*, The Bible and Postcolonialism (London: T&T Clark, 2009).

[24]Sugirtharajah, *Voices from the Margin*, 1.

awareness that their productions will be less appreciated by the minorities themselves than by the outsiders who want to know about the 'other.'"[25]

The issue of power *and* the center: "Do we want to replicate the colonial game of occupation and capture the center in the name of the oppressed, or do we want to demolish the center itself and redraw its parameters? The next set of questions will be: How many centers should we have? Who will provide the parameters? And whose resources will we draw upon to redesign them?"[26]

4. Subaltern/marginal readings. *Subaltern* readings are those by groups and cultures and subcultures that have been marginalized. Within their settings, they are considered outsiders, subservient, undesirable and on the margins.

As I indicated earlier, these groups are numerous and diverse. They live in many Majority World and indigenous contexts. These include poor, rural, illiterate women; small-scale agrarian workers; HIV/AIDS sufferers; indigenous and aboriginal groups; asylum seekers and refugees; immigrant laborers; the Dalit in India; the Burakumin in Japan; the Roma in Europe; the Baekjeong in Korea; the Midgan in Somalia; the Al-Akhdam in Yemen; homeless people and alcoholics and prostitutes on the streets of major cities; the incarcerated; and those with skin or sexual or other diseases.

Christians among these groups often grow biblical interpretations and applications for their situations. And these can have significant implications for the global church and humanity. They often challenge the sociopolitical, religious, economic and racial status quo. And they foster unique understandings of the message of Jesus. They grasp a vision of the kingdom of God rarely seen in less marginal groups.

One example will need to suffice. Joel Van Dyke lives in Central America. He directs a grassroots training initiative called *La Estrategia de Transformacion.* This involves ministering among gang members and prostitutes and their families. His organization works in some of the most notorious men's prisons in Central America. He writes of the lonely, marginalized girlfriends, wives, mothers and sisters of these prisoners. These women sleep on the hard, concrete floors of the prisons. They are often abused and violated and treated like property by the prisoners and authorities.

---

[25]Ibid., 9.
[26]Ibid.

In one prison, his team decided to lead a conversation with these women centered on the story of Hagar in Genesis 16. "The women quickly applied the story personally." In Hagar's story, "the women found their story. Reading the Bible with those we serve means we learn to take the stained glass off the text of Scripture and begin reading from the perspective of those who have been crushed by life. It's an adventure in mining good news out of the holes in Scripture that the church typically refuses to climb down into."[27]

Hagar calls God *El Roi*, "the God who sees me." The women in the prison were so gripped by the idea that God "sees them"—forgotten, rejected, violated and invisible—that they painted a mural of Hagar's story on a prison wall. They made the focal point of the mural the words *El Dios Que Me Ve* (The God Who Sees Me).

> The larger missional implication is that Hagar grasps something about God that Abraham is not able to confess until six chapters later. In Genesis 22:14, Abraham names Mount Moriah *Jehovah Jireh* ("the God who provides"), using the verb *ra'ah*, the same one that Hagar used in naming God. This leads us to marvel that perhaps the Hagars of the world are able to recognize the gospel long before the Abrahams do.[28]

Supernaturalist, Mystical and Pentecostal Readings

Majority World and indigenous cultures identify closely with the world of the Bible. Its supernatural and spiritual dimensions ring true with their experience. They're familiar with a world of healings, demons, exorcisms, angels, witches, shamans and cults. They believe in the power of prayer, dreams, visions and spiritual warfare. They've experienced charismatic renewal and Pentecostal power.

This means that their interpretations of Scripture are often *supernaturalist*. They shape these interpretations around an experience of the spiritual world. They form them around their identification with the spiritual world of the Bible's cultures. This is especially true of ordinary, popular interpretations in grassroots congregations.

By *mystical*, I mean that ordinary Majority World readings are mystically

---

[27]Joel Van Dyke and Kris Rocke, "Asking the Beautiful Question: Reading the Bible Through the Eyes of Outsiders Can Awaken the Church from Numbness," *Christianity Today* 54, no. 4 (2010): 46.
[28]Ibid.

oriented. They are often saturated in prayer and spiritual fervor. And an expectation of Pentecostal experiences and power go with these readings of Scripture. This mystical, prayerful, charismatic reading engages and anticipates these supernatural realities.

These churches believe in supernatural agencies that intervene in the natural world. They find support for this belief in the narratives and themes of Scripture. Their experience of these supernatural forces corresponds with those of biblical cultures. So the biblical witness does not surprise them at all.

Jenkins has made much of this supernaturalist tendency in the Global South. "The supernatural approach certainly harks back to the ancient roots of Christianity." For millions of Majority World believers, "proclaiming the power of Jesus means declaring his victory over conquered forces of evil."[29]

An example of such readings comes from Kenya. John Mbiti writes of the encounter between biblical ideas and traditional beliefs among the Akamba of Kenya. He also draws on material from other parts of Africa. The Akamba see the spirit world as pervasive. They consider distinctions between the visible and invisible as inconsequential. "Magic, witchcraft, and sorcery play a prominent role in Akamba life. The people are saturated with beliefs, fears, and superstitions connected with these practices. Every Mukamba, whether Christian or otherwise, has a dormant or active share of these beliefs."[30]

The Akamba believe in the active presence of *Mulungu* or *Engai* the Creator God. They fear demonic and angelic spirits and magic and sorcery. They look for the "living-dead" (those who have died up to three or four generations ago). And they revere the *Aimu* (spirits of ancestors who have died many generations ago, whom none remember). These beliefs pervade Akamba life, language, social relations and churches. They demand a response from Christianity—its spirituality and eschatology and biblical interpretation.[31]

Mbiti constructs such a response. He shows the divergences and similarities between Akamba and biblical views of the spirit world:

[29]Philip Jenkins, "Believing in the Global South," *First Things*, no. 168 (2006): 16.
[30]John S. Mbiti, *New Testament Eschatology in an African Background: A Study of the Encounter Between New Testament Theology and African Traditional Concepts* (Oxford: Oxford University Press, 1971), 9.
[31]Ibid., 9-10.

> As the Akamba feel themselves surrounded by innumerable "spirits" (the living-dead and the Aimu), so do the Christians with their great cloud of witnesses (Heb. 12:1), angels, the Church of the firstborn, and the spirits of just men (12:22ff.). But whereas the spirit world of the Akamba is conceived physically and anthropocentrically, the N.T. view is 'spiritual' and Christocentric.[32]

Mbiti shows how Akamba Christians appropriate these understandings. They then express their Christianity responsively. Cultural and biblical views of the spiritual world enter into dynamic conversation. Akamba Christians expect the spirit world described in the Bible to infuse their prayer, worship, miraculous works and mission. This is because they've seen the nearness of the spirit world in pre-Christian Akamba culture.

Pentecostal hermeneutics is another example of supernaturalist interpretation. Pentecostalism is enormous and diverse in the Majority World.[33] Amos Yong notes that Pentecostal theology has a biblically grounded hermeneutic and a deep respect for the authority of the Bible. It also has a reliance on the Spirit in the interpretive task. It seeks Spirit-empowered application. It expects many things to go with faithful biblical application. These things include signs, miracles, wonders, hearings, manifestations, dreams and visions.

According to Yong, Pentecostal readings of Scripture have three features. They have a Lukan interpretation, a pneumatological framework and an experiential and practical base.

Lukan interpretation. Pentecostal interpretation of Scripture is "informed explicitly by Luke-Acts." This Pentecostal hermeneutic "is animated by the conviction that the accounts in the book of Acts (especially) are not merely of historical interest but an invitation to participate in the ongoing work of the Holy Spirit."[34]

Pneumatological framework. Pentecostal interpretation of Scripture is pneumatological. This means that it focuses on the power and presence of the Holy Spirit. It relies on God's empowering presence for ministry and theology. It seeks to rethink "traditional theological loci from the starting

---

[32]Ibid., 154.
[33]Amos Yong, *The Spirit Poured Out on All Flesh: Pentecostalism and the Possibility of Global Theology* (Grand Rapids: Baker Academic, 2005), 19-20.
[34]Ibid., 27.

point of pneumatology." Whereas pneumatology "provides the orienting dynamic for this theology, Christology provides the thematic focus."[35]

Experiential and practical base. Pentecostal interpretation of Scripture is rooted in the experience of the Holy Spirit. Conversation between theology, praxis, prayer and spiritual experience shapes these interpretations of the Bible.

Many Majority World and indigenous Christians identify with the spiritual world of the Bible. They expect the Spirit to act with signs and wonders. They complement their reading of Scripture with passionate prayer and spiritual fervor. They expect the Bible to open up a world of supernatural revelation and Pentecostal power.[36]

SCRIPTURE AND THE GLOBALCHURCH: CONCLUDING REFLECTIONS

Typically, Christians in the Majority World are passionate about Scripture. Conservative readings of the Bible are often complemented by innovative applications. Clearly, we can learn much from the love for Scripture in the Majority World. But these believers don't just love the Bible. They're passionate for Jesus Christ revealed in Scripture.

Here are ten things we learn from how Majority World Christians devour and interpret Scripture:

1. The Bible must be devoured as a means to know and love and serve and glorify Christ. As I serve among churches in Australia, North America, Europe and the United Kingdom, I'm struck by a trend. Western Christians seem to have a declining passion for memorizing and contemplating and interpreting and applying Scripture. I find this deeply concerning. When I serve in Asia and Africa and Latin America, I see the opposite. People are passionate for Scripture. They devour and honor and memorize it. They interpret it contextually while maintaining a conservative bias. And they

---

[35]Ibid., 28. *Pneumatology* is theology concerned with the Holy Spirit. *Christology* is theology concerned with the person and work of Jesus Christ.

[36]For a fuller treatment of Pentecostal hermeneutics see Kenneth J. Archer, *A Pentecostal Hermeneutic for the Twenty-First Century: Spirit, Scripture, and Community*, Journal of Pentecostal Theology Supplement Series (London: T&T Clark, 2004). For an overview of global Pentecostalism, historical developments within the Pentecostalism of different parts of the world and the role of Scripture in Pentecostalism, see Allan H. Anderson, *An Introduction to Pentecostalism: Global Charismatic Christianity* (Cambridge: Cambridge University Press, 2004); Allan H. Anderson and Walter J. Hollenweger, eds., *Pentecostals After a Century: Global Perspectives on a Movement in Transition* (Sheffield: Sheffield Academic, 1999).

apply it creatively and bravely. This is instructive for those of us in the West. We need a revival in our enthusiasm for Scripture. This isn't so that we "fall in love" with Scripture. Rather, we devour Scripture as a means of knowing and adoring and following and magnifying our Lord Jesus Christ.

2. *The Bible must be interpreted glocally.* The local is in the global, and the global is in the local. We can't confine biblical interpretation to local contexts, thereby ignoring global trends. Nor can we do it in such a way that ignores the insights and applications of local interpretive communities. Instead, we must seek to interpret Scripture glocally. There is a beneficial mutual exchange between local and global interpretations.

For those of us in the West, we must learn from the passion for Jesus Christ and his Scriptures in other cultures. We need to wrestle with the *multivoiced* and *multipeopled* nature of the church and biblical interpretation. Western cultures no longer define how Christians understand and believe and interpret the Bible. As the church, we must put Western interpretive approaches into glocal conversation. This broadens and enriches the way we believe the Bible. It heralds a transformation of the church as Christians believe and interpret the Bible in fresh ways.

It's time we acknowledged that global ethnic diversity is dewesternizing the global church. And it is dewesternizing glocal biblical interpretations. This is a good thing. It enhances our understanding of Scripture as we listen to indigenous and Majority World interpretations. We need to get better at hearing and heeding the Scriptural interpretations of other cultures and Christian theological traditions. The church needs to interpret Scripture glocally. Let's multiply forums that enable glocal interpretations of the Bible and glocal theological constructions.

3. *The Bible is to be believed and obeyed and identified with and applied.* The Spirit of Christ is calling us to deepen our belief in the authority of Scripture. Christians need a high concept of the Bible as Scripture and Word of God. We must grow a deep regard for Scripture "as a locus of unquestionable truth and liberation."[37]

While we must have a high regard for the authority of Scripture, we still need to deal with questions around how we know that Scripture is authoritative

---

[37]Segovia, "Emerging Project of Asian Biblical Hermeneutics," 372.

and true. And we need to tackle questions about the relationship between objectivity and subjectivity in our biblical interpretations.

I tend toward *critical realism*. N. T. Wright says that we need critical awareness as we approach Scripture and history. There's no "god's eye view . . . available to human beings." We interpret everything from the world "through a grid of expectations, memories, stories, psychological states, and so on." This is "peculiar in terms of my worldview." The way we understand the world is shaped by our belonging "to a particular human community. . . . Every human community shares and cherishes certain assumptions, traditions, expectations, anxieties, and so forth, which encourage its members to construe reality in particular ways." I agree with N.T. Wright's form of *critical realism*:

> This is a way of describing the process of "knowing" that acknowledges the *reality of thing known, as something other than the knower* (hence "realism"), whilst also fully acknowledging that the only access we have to this reality lies along the spiraling path of appropriate *dialogue or conversation between the knower and thing known* (hence "critical"). This path leads to critical reflection on the products of our enquiry into "reality," so that our assertions about "reality" acknowledge their own provisionality. Knowledge, in other words, although in principal concerning realities independent of the mind of the knower, is never itself independent of the knower.[38]

We must complement this *critical realism*—which has a high view of the authority of Scripture—with risky and innovative and radical forms of application. We need to shore up our application of the Bible to everyday life. I've outlined how Majority World and indigenous Christians do this. They apply Scripture to familial, political, postcolonial, interfaith and a host of other settings. What creative applications and interpretations can you construct for your location?

And as they do in the Majority World, we must reactivate our personal identification with the biblical text and its stories. Our cultures are often different from biblical ones. But biblical stories and images and analogies and instruction can still speak to us in fresh and transformative ways.

---

[38]N. T. Wright, *The New Testament and the People of God*, Christian Origins and the Question of God (Minneapolis: Augsburg Fortress, 1996), 35-36.

4. The Bible needs to be contextualized. Worthwhile biblical interpretation is *both* contextual and committed to the authority of Scripture. C. René Padilla claims, "A xeroxed copy of a theology made in Europe or North America can never satisfy the theological needs of the Church in the Third World. Now that the Church has become a world community, the time has come for it to manifest the universality of the Gospel in terms of a theology that is not bound by a particular culture but shows the many-sided wisdom of God."[39] But contextualization isn't enough. Padilla says that contextualized biblical theology must have a high view of the authority and relevance of Scripture. It is "based *on* Biblical revelation, *in* the life context, and *for* obedience to Christ today. . . . The *basis* of theology is the Word of God. . . . The *context* of theology is the concrete historical situation. . . . The *purpose* of theology is obedience to Christ."[40] Such readings are faithful to Jesus Christ. They have a high regard for Scripture. We construct and apply these readings locally. And we engage with the processes of *critical contextualization.*[41]

It's imperative we cultivate contextual readings in our own settings. This involves asking these kinds of questions: How do we identify and nurture diverse and contextual readings of the Bible in our culture? How do we do this with a high regard for the inspiration and authority of Scripture? How do we do this within community and life context? How can these contextual readings of Scripture lead to obedience to Christ? How can they enable mission, ministry, fellowship, worship and discipleship?

5. The Bible can be interpreted by ordinary believers in community. Often in the West we act as though only pastors and theologians can interpret the Bible well. And then we wonder why people don't read their Bibles! But the Bible and its interpretation aren't for the ivory tower. Ordinary believers often come up with the most creative readings and courageous applications. Churches must encourage ordinary, local believers to interpret Scripture together. This involves helping them make sense of its themes and message in their own context. It's empowering people to move from interpretation to

---

[39]"The Contextualization of the Gospel," *Journal of Theology for Southern Africa* 24 (1978): 28.
[40]Ibid. Italics added for emphasis.
[41]See Paul Hiebert's work on the stages and concerns of critical contextualization. Paul G. Hiebert, "Critical Contextualization," *International Bulletin of Missionary Research* 11, no. 3 (July 1987).

formation and application. People do this best in groups, including marriages, families, ministry teams, congregations and communities.

6. *The Bible confronts and transforms cultures and principalities and powers.* Are we allowing Scripture to address the issues that are relevant to our culture? In the Majority World, this is poverty, injustice, reconciliation, spirits, sickness, deliverance, suffering, famine, war, sexual violence, colonialism, persecution and corruption. What are the issues in your culture? Do you need to confront ethno-religious violence, gender discrimination, rampant consumerism or strident individualism? Or are there other issues? Why have so many Western Christians lost confidence in the transforming power of the Word of God for individuals and whole nations? How will you and I access Scripture to confront and address the issues of our culture and time?

Recently, some friends of mine have been protesting Australia's treatment of refugees and asylum seekers. International humanitarian organizations and the United Nations have condemned Australia's behavior. As my friends read Scripture, they concluded that the Bible calls for compassion and hospitality and welcome and justice. So they arranged peaceful "sit-ins" at the offices of high-profile politicians. This included the office of our prime minister. Together, they traveled to these politicians' offices. They refused to leave until police arrested them. They asked these politicians to change our national laws. Australia must meet its international humanitarian obligations and act with mercy and compassion and justice. Police have arrested them many times. Politicians have taken them to court. But judges refuse to charge them. Australia hasn't yet changed its laws. It hasn't reversed its offshore processing and resettlement of asylum seekers. It continues to detain vulnerable and traumatized men and women and children in appalling conditions. It continues to resettle people in dangerous third countries where their well-being and lives are at risk. But these friends continue to protest. They believe that the truth and love of Christ can transform cultures, politics, principalities and powers. As Christians, we must read and apply the Bible in ways that lead to the transformation of social and political realities. This may cost us dearly. And change may not happen quickly. But we must be strong and do the courageous and right thing.

7. *The Bible is understood by the oppressed and marginal and weak and despised.* This shouldn't surprise us. Majority World and indigenous writers regularly develop this theme. The foolish things of the world shame the wise. The weak things embarrass the strong. God chooses to reveal himself in the most unlikely places. He reveals his truth to the least "deserving" and least qualified and most marginalized people. So we must listen to the biblical interpretations of marginalized, disregarded and silenced groups. What is the Spirit saying to us through them? How do they help us understand the truths of Scripture, the gospel and the kingdom of God?

8. The Bible is key in pluralist settings. Sometimes we're timid about biblical truth in pluralist and multifaith settings. But we don't need to be faint-hearted. It's possible for us to be *confident* in the truth of Scripture and in the power of the gospel and in the uniqueness of Christ, even in pluralist settings. And such conviction doesn't preclude dialogue. Dialogue can enhance our assurance.

David Bosch, writing from the South African context, discusses three interfaith approaches. These are exclusivism, Christianity as fulfillment of other religions, and relativism. He dismisses these three. Bosch calls for Christians to dialogue with other religions.

What commitments must we make to do this well? Bosch maps these out for us.[42] We need to be confident in the gospel and in the truth revealed in Scripture. We need a willing acceptance of religious coexistence and pluralism.[43] We must be open to dialogue, which we root in a certain and deep commitment to the gospel of Jesus Christ. We should desire to see where God is already working in other cultures and convictions and religions. We need a commitment to conducting dialogue with humility and grace. And we must recognize the diversity of religions and within religions. (The Christian gospel relates differently to Islam, Buddhism, Hinduism and so on, and to groups within those religions.)

We also need a passion for mission: "Dialogue is neither a substitute nor a subterfuge for mission. . . . They are neither to be viewed as identical nor as irrevocably opposed to each other." (The same is true of biblical interpretation. Such interpretation must always serve the mission of God.) But we

---

[42]David J. Bosch, *Transforming Mission: Paradigm Shifts in Theology of Mission* (Maryknoll, NY: Orbis, 1991), 474-89.

[43]We need to accept pluralism as a social fact. But religious pluralism isn't desirable if we believe in the uniqueness of Christ and the gospel. Our desire is for a world without any religion other than that which honors Jesus Christ.

must focus our dialogue on more than "eternal salvation." It must have a vision of lives and communities transformed with Jesus Christ as their center and Lord. It must lead to "cleansing, forgiveness, reconciliation, and renewal in order to become a participant in the mighty works of God."[44]

Finally, we must be willing to wrestle with the tension between mission and dialogue. There's a tension between the uniqueness of Jesus Christ and his presence in other religions and in the world.

Bosch expresses the heart of an emerging Christian missional perspective. The debate over the relationship between Bible interpretation and mission and dialogue will remain heated. But many Majority World thinkers are helping the global church navigate this important relationship. We must elevate Scripture whenever we enter into dialogue with other faiths. We must be confident in its truth and power. And *critical realism* helps us be humble and willing to learn. The Bible plays a key role in Christian faith and apologetics in pluralist cultures.

9. The Bible must be interpreted in community. Westerners tend to read and interpret the Bible individualistically. Individual devotion and spiritual discipline are good. But there's greater transforming power in communal reading and interpretation and application. Community magnifies the power of Scripture to change lives. Community amplifies our ability to understand and contextualize and proclaim Scripture. And as the analogy goes, if you take a coal out of the fire, it quickly goes cold. But if you leave it in with the other red-hot coals and continue to throw fuel on it, then watch it blaze! Our discipleship is the same. To burn red hot for Christ, we need others and fuel. We must saturate our Bible reading and application in corporate prayer and worship and mission.

10. The Bible needs to be read and applied with spiritual expectation. When you and I read and apply the Bible, do we do so in a spirit of expectation? Majority World and indigenous readers do. God reveals himself. He transforms lives. He overcomes evil with good and darkness with light. He heals, forgives, liberates and transforms. We should read Scripture expecting to experience the power and presence and provision and protection of the Holy Spirit.

---

[44]Bosch, *Transforming Mission*, 483, 489.

A few years ago, I had the opportunity to visit a prison in Poipet, Cambodia. Cambodia's prisons are among the most overcrowded in the world. The conditions in this particular prison are harsh and many of the men are hardened, violent criminals. Food is scarce, clean water is nonexistent and living quarters are cramped. It is hot and humid. In the summer it's almost one hundred degrees Fahrenheit everyday. Guards and prisoners are violent. Prisoners who fail to follow minor rules or routines are beaten with batons.

I was there just before Christmas and had the opportunity to share the Christmas story with groups of prisoners. I used a children's Bible to share the story. I hoped the colorful illustrations would enhance the presentation and discussions. After sharing the story with the prisoners, I had discussions with them about the relevance of Christmas for their lives. We then prayed together. It was clear that the story was alive to them. The Christmas themes and narratives rang true with their experiences of life and the spirit world. The story spoke of sin and shame and violence. It spoke of divine intervention, forgiveness, hope, resurrection and transformed lives.

As I was leaving the prison, a prisoner approached me. His body was heavily muscled and covered in gang tattoos.

"Sir, can I please have that Bible?" he asked. "I want to follow this Jesus and learn more about serving him."

I told him I needed to ask the prison guards. After getting their permission, I brought the Bible back to him. His face beamed radiantly as he walked back to his prison cell with his new Bible under his arm.

RENEWING EDUCATION

WHAT CAN WE LEARN FROM HOW MAJORITY WORLD CHRISTIANS ARE RENEWING THEOLOGICAL AND MINISTRY EDUCATION?

The mission of the church on earth is to serve the mission of God, and the mission of theological education is to strengthen and accompany the mission of the church. . . .

Those of us who provide theological education need to ensure that it is intentionally missional, since its place within the academy is not an end in itself, but to serve the mission of the church in the world. . . .

We urge that institutions and programs of theological education conduct a "missional audit" of their curricula, structures, and ethos, to ensure that they truly serve the needs and opportunities facing the church in their cultures.

THE LAUSANNE *CAPE TOWN COMMITMENT*

In 2013, the Arab Baptist Theological Seminary (ABTS) in Beirut, Lebanon, ran an important conference. It was "Your Rights and My Responsibilities: Biblical and Islamic Perspectives on Human Rights." It addressed human rights in the Middle East, including human trafficking and ethno-religious violence in the region. Many Christians keep their heads down when there is political conflict. But there's so much political unrest in parts of the Middle East. Consider the number of MPs in Lebanon who have lost their lives through car bombs. Christians need to be peacemakers during political unrest. ABTS is a seminary that gets involved in making a valuable contribution in this setting and to the wider region.

> In 2009, ABTS launched a new curriculum focusing on formation through multidimensional learning. The curriculum integrates four main areas during three years of study. The areas are: biblical, historical-theological, sociological-cultural, and personal-ministerial. This culminates in an integrative project.[1]

The ABTS integrative model embraces key values. They value authentic worship, missional church, Christlike leadership, empowerment, reflective practice, community cohesion and personal and spiritual development.

This model has been so successful that ten other Majority World seminaries are now following suit. Once these ten seminaries have done this, the plan is to roll out this model to another two hundred seminaries in the Majority World (in a contextualized way).[2]

This is just one example of contextualized and creative theological education in the Majority World. Theological and ministry education has been expanding in many parts of the Majority World. We see this all over Africa, Asia, Latin America and the Pacific. But theological education also faces challenges.

Southeast Asia serves as an example of the growth and challenges for theological education in the Majority World. The Association for Theological Education in South East Asia (ATESEA) was established in 1957. It began with sixteen Protestant schools. "ATESEA was the first formal regional association of theological schools in the non-Western world. Today, it is the largest theological education association outside of North America."[3] Based in Manila, the Philippines, ATESEA now has 102 member institutions and schools in sixteen countries. It has more than twenty thousand students and 1,500 faculty members. These institutions are evangelical, Pentecostal

---

[1]See details and diagrams on the Arab Baptist Theological Seminary website: www.abtslebanon.org.

[2]Perry Shaw, *Transforming Theological Education: A Practical Handbook for Integrative Learning* (Carlisle, UK: Langham Global Library, 2014), 95. A good overview of regional developments is provided in Dietrich Werner et al., eds., *Handbook of Theological Education in World Christianity: Theological Perspectives—Regional Surveys—Ecumenical Trends*, Regnum Studies in Global Christianity (Oxford: Regnum Books International, 2010), part 2; and World Council of Churches, "Global Survey on Theological Education," *World Council of Churches 10th Assembly, Busan, 30 Oct—8 Nov, 2013*, www.globethics.net/web/gtl/research/global-survey.

[3]Gerald H. Anderson, "Developments in Theological Education in South East Asia," *International Bulletin of Missionary Research* 30, no. 2 (2006): 96.

and Adventist. Twenty-six of these institutions are in the Philippines, seventeen in Indonesia and seventeen in Myanmar.[4]

But it is not all good news or smooth sailing. Dietrich Werner writes of the challenges and prospects facing theological education in Asia. These are many. There is "unequal allocation of resources" and "unbalanced accessibility to theological education." There are discrepancies between standards in "different national contexts and regions within Asia." There's "the unfinished work of contextualizing theological education in Asia." Seminaries are still not good at relating theological education to today's multireligious Asian setting. There's the need to overcome "the ecumenical/evangelical divide" and explore "possibilities for state recognition." Seminaries face increasing "public visibility" and scrutiny. There's the need to ensure quality in standards and delivery and to strengthen theological associations. And there's the challenge of "deepening the movement to do theology with Asian resources."[5]

Similarly, Huang Po Ho writes of the rapid growth of theological education in Asia over the last fifty years. For Ho the challenges reside in quality control and contextualization. There are also challenges for curriculum renewal and faculty development. Asian education must grapple with rapidly changing Asian cultures. And it must deal with globalization and unpredictable political systems. It needs to cultivate association and networking. And it needs to foster organizational health. Not least, Asian theological colleges grapple with the expectations, needs and demands of churches and denominations.[6]

This chapter considers the nature of Majority World theological education. It is multidimensional: contextual, grassroots, postcolonial, liberating, engendered, missional, transformational, Spirit-empowered and biblically focused. And it equips people practically for ministry and mission. I explore these themes in Majority World theological education in that order. This chapter asks, *What can we learn from how Majority World Christians are renewing theological and ministry education?*

---

[4]See http://atesea.net.

[5]Dietrich Werner, "Memorandum on the Future of Theological Education in Asia," *The Ecumenical Review* 26, no. 2 (2012): 209-22.

[6]Huang Po Ho, "Theological Education in the Changing Societies of Asia," *Ministerial Formation* 109 (2007): 6-13.

CONTEXTUAL AND INTERCONTEXTUAL EDUCATION

Western churches can learn much from theological education in the Majority World. Contextualization is a clear example. Majority World institutions believe in the contextualization of curriculum and delivery and methods. This includes accountability and dialogue with students in contextualization processes. Students need tools for diagnosing their particular and societal and contextual needs. They also need opportunities to plan the best integration of theory and practice to address those needs. This includes forums to check their progress in missional and ministry skills. Training bodies need to show reciprocal, democratic, enabling and participatory styles of leadership. This way graduates can reflect such a style in their future ministries.

Majority World theologians have long advocated for contextualized churches and mission. And they've called for contextual approaches to theology and theological education.[7]

Contextualization can carry many nuances of meaning. There is more than one model of contextualization. The meanings we assign it depend on our theological tradition and cultural background.[8]

Tite Tiénou writes about the contextualization of theology. "Contextualization is the inner dynamic of the theologizing process. It is not a matter of borrowing already existing forms or an established theology in order to fit them into various contexts. Rather contextualization is capturing the meaning of the gospel in such a way that a given society communicates with God. Therein theology is born."[9] Tiénou and Shoki Coe both argue that we must contextualize both theology *and* theological education.[10]

How does contextualization express itself in the Majority World?

An example from Asia illustrates this. ATESEA member seminaries developed the Critical Asian Principle (CAP). They also formed "Guidelines for Doing Theology in Asia." The CAP uses "the common spiritual and socio-economic context of Southeast Asian countries as the point of reference for

---

[7]C. René Padilla, "The Contextualization of the Gospel," *Journal of Theology for Southern Africa* 24 (1978): 30.

[8]A. Scott Moreau, *Contextualization in World Missions: Mapping and Assessing Evangelical Models* (Grand Rapids: Kregel, 2012).

[9]Tite Tiénou, "Contextualization of Theology for Theological Education," in *Evangelical Theological Education Today: Agenda for Renewal*, ed. Paul Bowers (Nairobi: Evangel, 1982), 51.

[10]Shoki Coe, "Contextualizing Theology," in *Mission Trends, No. 3: Third World Theologies*, ed. Gerald H. Anderson and Thomas F. Stransky (New York: Paulist, 1976), 22.

biblical reflection and theologizing." These seminaries developed critical principles for doing Asian theology. These principles engaged Asian contexts, interpretations, missions and education.

ATESEA seminaries then developed "Guidelines for Doing Theology in Asia." These guidelines grew in response to the many challenges facing the region. These challenges include religious fundamentalism, gender issues, ecological problems and natural disasters. The region is also coming to terms with globalization and colonization. And one must not forget the Asian search for spirituality and meaning and identity. The region is dealing with political upheavals and power struggles and indigenous issues. So these Asians formed guidelines for doing theology in Asia—with its opportunities and challenges.

The guidelines call Asians to contextualize Asian theological education so that it does the following: It promotes "responsive engagement with the diverse Asian contexts." It fosters "critical engagement with indigenous cultures and wisdom for the preservation and sustenance of life." It encourages "reflective engagement with the sufferings of the Asian people in order to provide hope for the marginalized, women, indigenous people, children, differently-abled people, and migrant workers." It challenges students to "restore the inter-connectedness of the whole creation." It nurtures "interfaith dialogue as well as intrafaith communion and communication for the fullness of life and the well-being of the society." It enhances "capacity building in order to serve people experiencing disaster, conflict, and disease as well as those people who suffer physical, emotional, and mental disabilities." It inspires "prophetic resistance against the powers of economic imperialism." And it equips "Christians for witnessing and spreading the gospel of Jesus with loving care and service to fulfill the Christian mission of evangelism."[11]

GRASSROOTS EDUCATION

Evaluations of traditional, extractional forms of theological education are common in the Majority World. Ross Kinsler researches educational trends in those cultures. He has identified six reasons why many people

---

[11]Association for Theological Education in South East Asia, "Guidelines for Doing Theology in Asia," *International Bulletin for Missionary Research* 32, no. 2 (April 2008): 77.

in those cultures are reassessing traditional, residential models of ministry training.[12]

Theological. "What is the ministry?" Traditional theological education
may create an unhealthy distinction between graduates and congregations.[13]
The gifts and talents within congregations are then poorly developed and
used. This is because people form a dependency on professional ministers.
Moreover, missiology is often marginalized in the curriculum. Before long,
there is little evidence "that mission is the mother of theology."[14]

Historical. "Can the people participate fully in theological study and
ministry?" Viewed historically, traditional forms of theological education
equip people poorly for mission. They don't often provide effective practical
or theological training for missional contexts. Students become consumed
with their studies and academic commitments. And they often don't have
the time to apply what they are learning. Residential seminaries often extract
key leaders from their local churches and missional contexts. This model
reduces local discipleship, mission, ministry and church planting.

Sociological. "Who are the leaders?" Traditional theological institutions
often select young people who haven't proven themselves in society. They
place them in artificial academic and spiritual surroundings. And these settings are rarely missional or local. Residential seminaries exclude them from
the normal processes of indigenous leadership development and selection.
After graduation, denominations often place these young people in authority
over their elders and contemporaries. Local apprenticeship models of
training are often more useful for ministry and missional formation.

Educational. "How can leaders be trained?" Educational institutions,
both secular and theological, often create elite groups within cultures. These
institutions may not integrate theory and practice in leadership development. Such integration is critical in the formation of missional church
leaders. Furthermore, technical competencies are often taught instead of

---

[12]F. Ross Kinsler, *The Extension Movement in Theological Education: A Call to the Renewal of the
Ministry* (Pasadena, CA: William Carey, 1977). I'm summarizing Kinsler in these six points—I
don't share all his opinions.

[13]Ibid., 4.

[14]Martin Kähler, *Schriften zu Christologie und Mission* (Munich: Chr. Kaiser Verlag, 1971), 189;
David J. Bosch, *Transforming Mission: Paradigm Shifts in Theology of Mission* (Maryknoll, NY:
Orbis, 1991), 489.

necessary ministry and missional skills. Seminaries and teachers need to redesign their curriculum. They must emphasize the integration of theory and practice. Curriculum and methods need a missional focus. They must develop missional leaders for congregations in pluralistic cultures.

Financial. "What kind of theological education can we afford?" The church needs to use its financial resources wisely. This is especially true in poorer cultures. When it comes to finances, do extractional residential colleges make sense? Do educational programs based in local churches make more financial sense? Professional graduates from seminaries often demand higher salaries. They expect full-time ministry positions that average congregations have difficulty affording. The movement from "pedagogue to professional" hasn't helped the mission of the church. This professionalization of ministry is hurting the church in the West and in the Majority World. We need to return to grassroots—and more affordable—ministry training models.[15] And training for bivocational ministry will become more important and useful.

Missional. "What are the goals of our training programs?" Theological education must serve the mission of God. It must enable the church to meet its missional mandate. It must develop a passion for mission and ministry within students. Traditional theological institutions are often too introverted to pursue this goal. And denominational seminaries often foster competition and criticism and rivalry between denominations. To help rectify this, theological education must operate in partnership with local churches. It must collaborate with grassroots missional initiatives. It must place the mission of God at the center of everything it does—curriculum, methods and goals. Pastors, churches and missional leaders should collaborate with seminaries in shaping and delivering training.

Ross Kinsler builds an argument for grassroots ministry education. He draws on case studies from Africa, Asia, Latin America and the West. He advocates *Theological Education by Extension* (TEE). And he champions *Diversified Theological Education* (DTE). TEE is a decentralized, church-based form of theological and ministry education. DTE seeks to bridge the gap between TEE and traditional, residential theological education. DTE emphasizes a diversity "of methods, models, and concepts of theological

---

[15]Darrell L. Guder and Lois Barrett, *Missional Church: A Vision for the Sending of the Church in North America*, The Gospel and Our Culture Series (Grand Rapids: Eerdmans, 1998), 194-95.

education." DTE doesn't just focus on one approach to training. It often combines "centralized and decentralized elements."[16] It acknowledges this global diversity in theological education. But it is especially interested in developments in the Majority World.

Some criticize TEE. They're critical of the quality of curriculum and educators. And they question whether it is sufficiently contextualized and administered and funded. Yet forms of TEE now operate in Africa, Asia and Latin America. TEE is also popular in the Pacific, Eastern Europe and among indigenous peoples. DTE, which is more flexible and difficult to define, is a global phenomenon. It will only expand as theological education becomes increasingly diverse and multidimensional.

Grassroots theological education is broader than TEE. Hence, Kangwa Mabuluki says TEE is a form of DTE. He says that grassroots theological education needs to maintain academic standards and foster deep contextualization. It needs accreditation and oversight. It must collaborate between diverse models. It needs to be aware of gender issues. It should use technologies cleverly. Grassroots theological education must shape head and heart and hands. And it must be owned and sustained by local churches.[17]

The global church needs to be a learning community. And it needs to be one characterized by grassroots participation and global dialogue. TEE and DTE offer clues about the shape of a local-global (glocal) learning community.

POSTCOLONIAL AND LIBERATING EDUCATION

Postcolonial and liberationist concerns are growing in theological education in the Majority World. These are concerns for the liberation and education of the poor. The powerless, oppressed, voiceless, marginalized and colonized need freedom and education.

Postcolonialism is hard to define. It is an evolving field of research. Basically, it is the study of how humans dominate and control each other. It is also the study of how we experience and respond to this oppression. Colonizing forces oppress others because of their race, gender, class, age,

---

[16]Ross Kinsler, ed., *Diversified Theological Education: Equipping All God's People* (Pasadena: William Carey, 2008), 2.

[17]Kangwa Mabuluki, "Diversified Theological Education: Genesis, Development, and Ecumenical Potential of Theological Education by Extension (TEE)," in Werner et al., *Handbook of Theological Education in World Christianity*, 251-62.

poverty, religion and sexuality. Postcolonialism is a conversation arising from the abusive behavior of colonialism, and now influences learning all over the globe.

Namsoon Kang notes that old binaries of "oppressor-oppressed," "victimizer-victimized" or "colonizer-colonized" are redundant. They're no longer accepted in postcolonial theory or theology. Postcolonial theology doesn't depose the "West-as-center" and set up the "Majority-World-as-center." Such binaries are expressions of the "politics of domination." They express colonialism's oppressive core. All cultures should be self-critical. Kang says there isn't just a "colonialism-out-there." There's also a "colonialism-in-here." One can be the oppressor and the oppressed at the same time.[18]

This means that postcolonial theology is a discourse of resistance and liberation. As a *discourse of resistance*, it resists oppressive and dominating structures and relationships. As a *discourse of liberation*, it seeks to liberate people from such experiences. It tries to free them from the mentalities and systems and practices that support subjugation.[19]

Postcolonial theological education resists perspectives and practices that promote control and domination. How do power relations work in our institutions? How do our seminaries "colonize" people on the basis of race, gender, knowledge, disability, education, medical condition, class, theology, language and so on? Are we resisting such attitudes and actions? And are we practicing opposite, liberating behaviors?

EN-GENDERED EDUCATION

Men tend to fill most pastoral ministries. This is true in Western, indigenous and Majority World settings. This shouldn't surprise us given the cultural and historical and theological influences.

The Hartford Institute for Religion Research reports that a third of all seminary students in the United States are women. The percentage of women entering seminary and ministry is increasing. But women tend to drop out of seminary in their last year. They do this when they realize how difficult it is for them to secure pastoral positions. Women also find it hard

---

[18]Namsoon Kang, "Envisioning Postcolonial Theological Education: Dilemmas and Possibilities," in Werner et al., *Handbook of Theological Education in World Christianity*, 33.
[19]Ibid., 34.

to get senior positions.[20] African American, Asian, Hispanic, Latino, indigenous and First Nation women face even greater hurdles.

Majority World contexts tend to be conservative. This conservatism extends to biblical interpretation, societal expectations and gender roles. In the West, women face greater challenges than men when entering seminary and ministry. This varies between Majority World cultures depending on cultural and historical and theological factors. Gender inequality is a major issue in many parts of the Majority World.

Some seminaries and educators are seeking to address this inequality. Beverley Haddad writes from the South African context. She argues for the transformation of theological education so that it is relevant to the lives of women. This can only happen when poor and marginalized women collaborate in that transformation.

Gender equality must be a value and an organizational goal. This is as true in the West as it is in Majority World and indigenous settings. Discussions about gender are not discussions about "women's issues." They are about men and women. It's about both genders and how they relate to each other, the church and the world. These discussions must move from the margins to the center. They need to move from the few to the mainstream. This is true regardless of our position on women in ministry.

Haddad notes the links between gender and poverty in Africa. She argues that theological education has a role to play in delinking these realities. Theological education must become *en-gendered*. "The role that gender plays in the transformation process should not be an afterthought to transformation, but lies at the heart of the process."[21]

MISSIONAL AND TRANSFORMATIONAL EDUCATION

Mission and transformation are significant themes in Majority World theology and practice. Theological education reflects this. Western theology and theological education can learn much from these emphases.

By *missional*, I mean education that prioritizes the missional nature of

---

[20]Hartford Institute for Religion Research, "Fast Facts About American Religion," http://hirr
.hartsem.edu/research/fastfacts/fast_facts.html#health.

[21]Beverley Haddad, "Engendering Theological Education for Transformation," *Journal of Theology for Southern Africa*, no. 116 (2003): 65-66.

God and church and ministry. It equips leaders and churches to take part in the mission of God. Missional education teaches mission theory and practice. It forms people *in* and *for* and *through* mission. It shapes its curriculum around missional theology and practices. And it teaches people to interpret and apply Scripture through a missional paradigm.

By *transformational*, I mean education that transforms individuals, churches, families and cultures. Transformational education is about

> the change from the condition of human existence contrary to God's purpose to one in which people are able to enjoy fullness in harmony with God (John 10:10; Col. 3:8–15; Eph. 4:13). This transformation can only take place through the obedience of individuals and communities to the Gospel of Jesus Christ, whose power changes the lives of men and women by releasing them from guilt, power, and consequences of sin, enabling them to respond with love toward God and towards others (Rom. 5:5), and making them "new creatures in Christ" (2 Cor. 5:17).[22]

Theological education that is missional and transformational focuses on the mission of God. Such education pursues *transformational mission*. It seeks stewardship of creation, equality between human beings and reconciliation of peoples. It pursues social justice and mercy. It equips people to lead socioeconomic and political and spiritual freedom. It values the mission and transformation at the heart of the gospel of Jesus Christ.

In 2010, the Third Lausanne Congress on World Evangelization brought together 4,200 leaders from 198 countries. They met in Cape Town, South Africa. The *Cape Town Commitment* was the fruit of that gathering. Here is what they declared about the missional nature of theological education:

> The mission of the church on earth is to serve the mission of God, and the mission of theological education is to strengthen and accompany the mission of the Church. . . .
>
> Those of us who lead churches and mission agencies need to acknowledge that theological education is intrinsically missional. Those of us who provide theological education need to ensure that it is intentionally missional, since its place within the academy is not an end in itself, but to serve the mission of the church in the world. . . .
>
> Theological education stands in partnership with all forms of missional

---

[22]Vinay Samuel and Chris Sugden, eds., *The Church in Response to Human Need* (Grand Rapids: Eerdmans, 1987), xi.

engagement. We will encourage and support all who provide biblically faithful theological education, formal and non-formal, at local, national, regional and international levels. . . .

We urge that institutions and programs of theological education conduct a 'missional audit' of their curricula, structures and ethos, to ensure that they truly serve the needs and opportunities facing the Church in their cultures.[23]

Writing from South Africa, Steve de Gruchy says theological education requires missional practice. And mission needs theological education. Missional practice orients theological education toward the world. It focuses education on the mission of God, provides theological education with a direction and purpose, aligns such education with God's redemptive purposes and forces theological reflection into engaged practice. Such practices enrich theology and church and the world. And missional practice demands theology be interdisciplinary.

Conversely, theological education ensures that missional practice is reflective and self-critical. It emphasizes the importance of a robust theology of the mission of God. Theological education recognizes the role that various doctrines play in the mission of God and the church. These include our theologies of the *missio Dei* and the *missiones ecclesia*. Trinitarian theology is another an example. And theological education deconstructs colonial missionary legacies. Finally, when seminaries do theological education well, it's an example of missional vitality. Students take part in local mission and efforts to transform particular groups. Mission, ministry, societal engagement and theological education go hand in hand. Theological education must "assist the missional practice of the church to stay on the cutting edge of what God is doing in the world."[24]

Tite Tiénou, Samuel Escobar and Ken Gnanakan write about missional and transformational emphases in theological education. They're writing from African, Latin American and Asian perspectives. They suggest that such education has certain characteristics.[25] I summarize their ideas here,

---

[23]The Lausanne Movement, *The Cape Town Commitment: A Confession of Faith and a Call to Action* (Lausanne Library: 2011), www.lausanne.org/en/documents/ctcommitment.html.

[24]Steve de Gruchy, "Theological Education and Missional Practice: A Vital Dialogue," in Werner et al., *Handbook of Theological Education in World Christianity*, 50.

[25]Tite Tiénou, "The Training of Missiologists for an African Context"; Samuel Escobar, "The Training of Missiologists for a Latin American Context"; Ken R. Gnanakan, "The Training of Missiologists

and add a few of my own. In the final chapter, I explore global missional theological education further.

Biblical. It is faithful to Scripture. It values the missional themes running through the entire biblical narrative.

Contextual. It develops a language, curriculum and method for mission and theology that is local, contextual and indigenous. It trains people for mission and ministry within their own context.

Transformational. It prepares people for the moral, spiritual, political and economic transformation of their contexts. It promotes transformation through the liberation offered in the gospel. It values active participation in social, political, ecclesial and economic arenas.

Holistic. It develops the whole person for transformational mission. This includes the *head* (theological and theoretical knowledge). It incorporates the *heart* (character and spirituality). And it trains the *hands* (competencies).

Spiritual. It cultivates a spirituality that sustains mission and transformational leadership.

Action-reflection. It trains people for reflective practice. It uses an action-reflection model of training.

Theological. It ensures theological reflections both critical and systematic. This includes reflection on Scripture, history, context, culture, classics and social sciences.

Integrative. It encourages an integrative learning environment. Students engage in interdisciplinary study and spiritual formation. They develop competencies through praxis and academic rigor. They learn through public engagement, serving in churches and missional activities.

Mobilizing. It mobilizes people for mission and ministry and transformational leadership. It equips for service inside and outside the church. It mobilizes all the ministry gifts. It develops the apostolic, prophetic, evangelistic, teaching and pastoral gifts. And it shapes and releases many other types of gifts.

Multidimensional. It has a diverse set of characteristics that help missional reflection and formation. These include, but aren't limited to, (1) action-reflection learning; (2) decentered and missionally focused training;

---

for Asian Contexts," all in *Missiological Education for the Twenty-First Century: The Book, the Circle, and the Sandals: Essays in Honor of Paul E. Pierson,* ed. J. Dudley Woodberry, Charles Van Engen and Edgar J. Elliston (Maryknoll, NY: Orbis, 1996).

(3) postcolonial and trinitarian theology; (4) conversational and dialogical approaches; (5) discernment in seminary and church and local community; and (6) high-trust, low-control models of leadership.

Engaged. It takes engagement seriously. This includes engagement with pluralism, globalization, other religions and new religious movements. It involves wrestling with colonialism and postcolonialism and secular humanism.

Purposeful. It shapes curriculum and methods and goals around the gospel. It shapes its educational approaches and values around God's mission. And it's purposeful about its role in social transformation.

Interpretive. It teaches a missional reading of Scripture.

Formational and praxeological. It forms students with focused attention to missional and transformational practices.

SPIRIT-EMPOWERED EDUCATION

The growth of Pentecostalism in the Majority World and globally has been astonishing. Some put the total number of Pentecostals and charismatics at between 500 and 600 million. A large percentage of these are in the Majority World.

Pentecostal-charismatic and neo-Pentecostal groups put emphasis on Spirit-empowered ministry education. The breadth of the terms *Pentecostal-charismatic* and *neo-Pentecostal* show the diversity of Pentecostal groups. David Barrett and Todd Johnson catalogue twelve general forms of Pentecostalism.[26]

Wonsuk Ma has written a book chapter on this topic: "Theological Education in Pentecostal Churches in Asia." Ma studies the growth of Pentecostal and charismatic churches in Asia, focusing on South Korea, the Philippines, Malaysia, Singapore and India. He describes how theological education has developed in those contexts. The expansion of such education relates to the growth of Pentecostal and charismatic groups. Ma says that in Asia, "Pentecostals began training programs for church work from the start of their missionary operation, and these schools have been the main contribution to the growth of the Pentecostal church."[27]

---

[26]David B. Barrett, George T. Kurian and Todd M. Johnson, *World Christian Encyclopedia: A Comparative Survey of Churches and Religions in the Modern World*, 2nd ed., 2 vols. (New York: Oxford University Press, 2001), 13-15.

[27]Wonsuk Ma, "Theological Education in Pentecostal Churches in Asia," in Werner et al., *Handbook of Theological Education in World Christianity*, 733.

The West has much to learn from such Pentecostal and charismatic learning communities. Ma claims that Pentecostal and charismatic theological education is missional, pneumatological, democratized, mobilized, educational, networked and adaptational.

Missional. It dedicates its training to the mission of God. It seeks the transformation of society. And it values the missional health and expansion of the church.

Pneumatological. It values the ways the Holy Spirit empowers men and women for ministry.

Democratized and mobilized. It mobilizes the whole church for mission and ministry. This includes laity, church planters, pastors and missionaries.

Educational. It helps people access education and develop advanced critical and research competencies. It allows disadvantaged persons and communities to access education.

Networked. It provides opportunities for students, faculty and Christian leaders to build strong connections. It facilitates beneficial exchanges with other parts of the Majority World. Theological consortiums have an important role.

Adaptational. Ma says these Pentecostal and charismatic churches and seminaries face challenges. They must adapt. These challenges include relevance to modernizing cultures and globalization and its implications. They're coming to terms with the potential distance between academic programs and societal needs. They're dealing with heresies and divisions. They're teaching future leaders to embrace biblical servant leadership (rejecting authoritarian leadership). They're shaping new missional models for contemporary cultural challenges. And they're cultivating a vital public witness.

THEOLOGICAL EDUCATION AND THE GLOBALCHURCH: CONCLUDING REFLECTIONS

What's the future of theological education and ministry training in the West? What's its future in indigenous cultures and in the Majority World? How will this education adapt to rapidly changing cultures?

This chapter offered reflections on theological education in the Majority World. It considered what the West can learn from such education. The Majority World can help Western educational institutions become learning communities. It can show us how to shape education characterized by contextualization, grassroots participation, missional vitality, ministry competency and deep spirituality.

Here are seventeen things we learn from how Majority World Christians are renewing theological and ministry education.

1. Renewed education is Christ centered and gospel focused and biblically grounded. It's easy for us to focus on secondary issues in theological education. Teaching methodologies and academic programs grab our attention. Staff shortages and limited finances weigh on our shoulders. We spend time designing curriculum and allocating resources and marking papers. We worry about government legislation and student numbers. We're concerned about keeping denominations and churches happy and about getting accredited. Many secondary issues demand attention in our classes. For instance, when I teach pastoral studies, do I use a psychotherapeutic, managerial, pastoral or other paradigm? Theological educators manage competing roles. They are teachers, administrators, pastors, researchers, writers, public speakers and leaders in local churches.

All these things are important. But they can distract us from our primary purpose. As theological educators, we often get bogged down in all this. But we must stay focused on the main thing—forming women and men as disciples of Jesus Christ. And shaping them to love and serve Jesus and his church and his world.

To do discipleship well, our training needs to be Christ centered and gospel focused and biblically grounded. Everything we do must glorify Christ. We need to ensure that we place Jesus Christ and his gospel at the center of our teaching, formation, research, writing and everything else we do. And we place Scripture at the heart of our theological education and ministry training. We evaluate our training and formation through the lens of Scripture. We teach students to be disciples of Jesus who read and interpret and communicate Scripture accurately, contextually, skillfully and clearly.

2. Renewed education equips the whole believer to take the whole gospel to the whole world. The Lausanne Theology Working Group brought together sixty people from all continents to consider the three themes of the Lausanne slogan, "The whole church taking the whole gospel to the whole world." You can find an excellent outline of their conclusions at lausanne.org.

Listening closely to this global conversation, my theological college has developed the following emphases. Morling College's vision is to provide quality and biblically grounded education and training. We aim to equip "the whole believer to take the whole gospel to the whole world."[28] Morling pursues this aim through eight strategic objectives: We mobilize people for mission and ministry. We cultivate discipleship and personal and spiritual formation. We pursue excellence and innovation in education and research. We foster community. We facilitate worldview engagement. We provide ongoing training to pastors and missionaries and people serving outside ministry roles. We support and resource congregations and pastors and Christian organizations. And we collaborate with like-minded bodies.

I'm certain that "equipping the whole believer to take the whole gospel to the whole world" begins with our values. At Morling, we've spent a lot of time pondering what these values must be. We've concluded that they should be fivefold: *transformational discipleship*, *unity in diversity*, *evangelical conviction*, *missional focus* and *educational excellence*.

Here's how we describe these values at Morling College:

Believers who take the whole gospel to the whole world must pursue *transformational discipleship*. We long to be people who love God with all our heart and soul and mind and strength. So we will pursue a balance between academic study, practical training and spiritual formation. We know that such integration transforms us as whole persons.

Believers who take the whole gospel to the whole world must foster *unity in diversity*. We welcome a diversity of theological opinion and ministry practice on secondary issues. We do this within a framework of shared evangelical conviction. And we delight in the diversity of cultures, genders, backgrounds and gifts represented within our college community. We seek to give practical expression to the unity we have in Christ.

Believers who take the whole gospel to the whole world must embrace *evangelical conviction*. We are committed to the centrality of the gospel of Jesus Christ in the life and mission of the church and in prayerful dependence on the power of the Spirit, to the glory of God. And we gladly submit to the authority of Scripture as God's infallible word. We seek to honor the

---

[28]Morling College, "Beliefs and Vision," www.morlingcollege.com/about-morling/beliefs-and-vision.

trustworthiness of God's Word in our teaching. We aim to combine intellectual rigor and integrity with a humble and gracious orthodoxy.

Believers who take the whole gospel to the whole world must commit to
missional focus. We aim to equip men and women to take the whole gospel
to the whole world with vision, courage, wisdom and creativity. We recognize the crucial importance of both evangelistic proclamation and active
social concern. We affirm the centrality of the church within the purposes
of God for the world. And we train pastors and teachers and evangelists to
serve the church and its mission in the world.

Believers who take the whole gospel to the whole world must seek
training in a context of *educational excellence*. We are committed to ad-
vancing knowledge and understanding through dedicated involvement in
scholarly activities. We enable individuals to grow and learn throughout
their lives through personal and character formation and the enhancement
of lifelong learning. We are committed to quality education and professional
formation of students. We value professional development, ministry training,
missional equipping and academic contribution.

"Equipping the whole believer to take the whole gospel to the whole world"
requires us to develop clear values and strategies. I encourage you to develop
those that are suitable for your setting.

3. Renewed education develops learning communities. Students and
educators pursue learning together. Lecturers may have more knowledge in
a particular area. But it isn't that some are "experts" and others "novices."
Rather, theological education happens best in learning communities. This
kind of education is experiential, participatory, interactive and communal.
Together we explore faith and theology and curriculum and mission and
ministry. Together we shape learning communities characterized by contextual theology and glocal conversations and grassroots participation. This
is a move from hierarchy to equality. It's a change from monological trans-
mission of information to participatory learning. It's a shift from mere intellectual stimulation to the formation of whole persons in life and community.
Learning communities focus on the formation of the whole person in whole
community. They do this so that they might equip whole believers to take
the whole gospel to the whole world. Learning communities build shared
educational experiences. They invite contribution by educators, students,

families, churches and others. Learning communities consult with students, churches, educators and pastors when shaping and evaluating curriculum and methods. They foster emotional authenticity, interpersonal connection, active teaming, spiritual depth, community vitality and interaction between students and educators.

4. Renewed education grows through **glocal** *conversations.* I've described glocalization and glocal theology in another chapter. The best kind of theological education introduces students to glocal conversations. It expands their worldview beyond Western theologies and personalities. It introduces students to theological themes, ministry models and missional experiments in Majority World and indigenous settings. And it invites students to put their local, contextual experiences and theology into conversation with global voices. It teaches students the value of glocal. And it trains them to hear and cultivate glocal conversations.

5. Renewed education shapes its vision of ministry training around Scripture. I've noted that Majority World contexts usually practice conservative biblical interpretation. They carry this into their expectations for ministerial education and practice. A conservative reading of Scripture informs their approaches and expectations.

Majority World churches expect their pastoral leaders to be above reproach. Theological institutions in the Majority World pay careful attention to Scripture in pastoral formation. Key texts include Matthew 5:1-12, 6:33, 10:26-33; Mark 10:35-45; Acts 20:17-35; Romans 12:1-13; 1 Corinthians 12–13; 2 Corinthians 4–5; Galatians 5:16-26; Ephesians 4:1-16; Philippians 3:7-17; Colossians 1:28-29; 1 Timothy 3–4; Titus 1; 1 Peter 5:1-11; and Jude 20-23.

Here are some pastoral qualities sourced from these passages. They are exemplary rather than exhaustive. They surface repeatedly in Majority World writings and are often the goals of Majority World ministry education. They inform their aims in ministry training, and they must inform ours too. These may feel like a random group of exhortations, but they are biblical instructions for Christian leaders, and they must shape our ministry training and formation.

So what does Scripture say to graduates and to colleges that engage in their formation? Be poor in spirit and willing to mourn or be persecuted for the sake of righteousness. Be merciful, meek and pure of heart. Be peacemakers who hunger and thirst after righteousness. Seek first the kingdom and God's righteousness. Boldly and fearlessly proclaim the gospel. Demonstrate the characteristics and qualities of a servant. Serve the Lord with humility. Faithfully proclaim the gospel. Obey God's leading. Consider one's life worth nothing save obedience to Christ. Keep watch over oneself and the flock as faithful shepherds. Offer one's body as a living sacrifice. Be transformed by the renewing of the mind. Use one's gifts enthusiastically. Never lack in zeal. Keep one's spiritual fervor. Serve the Lord. Honor all members of the body of Christ and their unique spiritual gifts. Demonstrate the qualities of divine love. Set forth the truth plainly. Preach the Lord Jesus Christ. Persevere under trials. Fix one's eyes on what is unseen and eternal. Live by faith, not by sight. Make it one's goal to please the Lord in view of his return. Commit to the ministry and the message of reconciliation through Christ Jesus. Live by the Spirit rather than gratifying the desires of the sinful nature. Demonstrate the fruit of the Spirit—love, joy, peace, patience, kindness, goodness, faithfulness, gentleness and self-control.

Other biblical exhortations are important for us as we design ministry training that emphasizes formation. Here are some examples. Crucify the sinful nature with its passions and desires. Live by the Spirit, while keeping in step with him. Live a life worthy of God's call. Be humble and gentle and patient. Maintain unity in the church. Humbly use one's gifts and ministry to prepare God's people for works of service. Build up the body of Christ toward maturity and the whole measure of the fullness of Christ. Speak the truth in love, with a view to the whole body growing up into Christ. Consider everything loss compared to the surpassing greatness of knowing Christ, for whose sake you have lost all things. Seek to be found in Christ. Have a righteousness that comes by faith. Strive to know Christ and the power of his resurrection, the fellowship of sharing in his sufferings, becoming like him in his death and attaining the resurrection from the dead. Press on to take hold of that for which Christ Jesus took hold of you. Forget what is behind. Strain toward what is ahead. Press on toward the goal to win the prize for which God has called you in Christ. Follow the example and pattern of those who have exemplified this life.

What other biblical qualities and competencies should our ministry graduates show? They should proclaim Christ. Admonish and teach with all wisdom in order to present everyone perfect in Christ. Struggle with all Christ's energy, which so powerfully works in you. Be above reproach and faithful in marriage and exemplify an honorable family life. Be temperate, self-controlled, respectable, hospitable, able to teach and not given to drunkenness. Don't be violent, but be gentle. Don't be quarrelsome. Don't be a lover of money. Have a good reputation in the world. Keep hold of the gospel with a clear conscience. Hold firmly to and teach consistently the truth of the gospel. Train oneself in godliness. Set an example in speech, life, love, faith and purity. Faithfully serve through one's spiritual gifts. Watch your life and doctrine closely. Be blameless. Don't be quick-tempered, drunk, violent or a pursuer of dishonest gain. Be hospitable. Love what is good. Be self-controlled, upright, holy, disciplined and gospel-focused. Be a shepherd who is eager to serve and self-controlled. Resist the devil. Stand firm in the faith. Be an example to the flock, a servant leader and one clothed with humility. Build yourself up in your most holy faith. Pray in the Holy Spirit. Practice mercy. Be passionate for the gospel and salvation. Hate sin.

As we seek to form hearts and hands and heads, these biblical instructions to Christian leaders must play a pivotal role.

6. *Renewed education forms hearts and hands and heads.* Theological education must be *student focused*, not *student led*. Student-focused education is a formative process. Theological educators need to shape student-focused learning around the holistic formation of students' hearts and hands and heads. And they must invite the active participation of students in their education and formation. Student-led education is a consumeristic enterprise. It shapes education around the tastes and choices of students. It rarely asks whether these choices positively contribute to student formation. This is why I prefer a student-focused approach over a student-led approach to theological education.

We need theological colleges that form the whole person in collaboration with students and churches. These colleges prioritize ministry competency, theological insight, missional enthusiasm and spiritual passion.

To do this well, we need to develop specific outcomes for our pastoral and other graduates. By *outcomes* I mean "the qualities and skills and commitments we're hoping to see in our graduates." These outcomes should be biblically based. And they should be appropriate to a student's area of study and chosen ministry. Colleges might shape these outcomes around these areas: Bible and theology, communication and preaching, pastoral and ministry competencies, leadership, ethics, spirituality, character, church life, worship, interpersonal skills, mission, apologetics and cultural analysis.[29]

Majority World theological colleges and churches expect certain outcomes from theological training. They expect graduates to grow in particular ways. Wilson Chow writes that ministry education must integrate many important things. This includes Bible, theology, pastoralia, spirituality, church life, ministry fieldwork, worship and mission. Keith Ferdinando says that theological education must follow apprenticeship and whole-of-life patterns. Jesus modeled these in the way he trained his disciples.[30] Integrated theological education needs to be about the whole of a person's life. And it needs an intentional and integrated approach. This "covers the academic, spiritual, and practical formation of leadership in one whole."[31]

Ministry education in the Majority World usually does all it can to see graduates develop in the ABCs (Affective and Behavioral and Cognitive domains). The first is the *heart* (maturation of attitudes, values, faith and spirituality). The second is the *hands* (achievement of practical competencies). The third is the *head* (cognitive development, acquisition of knowledge and intellectual progress). This is especially the case for pastoral and missionary graduates (but not only that group). Those of us in the West must also focus on student formation so that they evidence these ABCs.

Affective (heart). This is about our theological education and ministry training forming students and graduates who value and develop Christian

---

[29]Ministry education strives for these outcomes in other settings too. But these characteristics are noticeable in Majority World theological education. While I was working through the literature on Majority World ministry and theological education, I was asked to form a taskforce to develop such *outcomes* at my own seminary, Morling College, Sydney, Australia. We at Morling have developed a document listing these objectives for pastoral and other graduates (called *Morling College Outcomes*). I draw on that document here. I am grateful for all the hard work our faculty put in to developing this outcomes document as we listened to each other and to global voices. We now shape our pastoral and "lay" training strategies with these outcomes in mind. It has been well received by pastors and students and denominational leaders. And it keeps us on track as we provide theological and ministry education—through *outcomes* shaped by a *global conversation*. Graham Hill et al., "Morling College Outcomes" (Sydney: Morling College, 2015). See also Ken Clendinning, "Readiness for Ministry Assessment Guidelines" (Sydney: Morling College, 2013).
[30]Keith Ferdinando, "Jesus, the Theological Educator," *Themelios* 38, no. 3 (2013).
[31]Wilson W. Chow, "An Integrated Approach to Theological Education," in *Evangelical Theological Education Today: An International Perspective*, ed. Paul Bowers (Nairobi: Evangel, 1982), 60.

character. It's about forming graduates who embrace personal and spiritual formation. In Majority World theological education, spiritual formation "is not simply a goal among others, but a permeation of all educational goals."[32] This includes forming Christlike qualities of character and integrity that reflect scriptural standards.

What else should be sought in our formation of students' hearts? What personal and spiritual qualities are we seeking? There are many things. Here are some examples: We want them to shape priorities around the mind of Christ. Embrace ethical standards and personal integrity in obedience to the imperatives of Scripture. Conduct themselves in a way consistent with Christian teaching and values. Maintain sexual purity, especially—but not only—in relationships in ministry. Willingly observe ministerial ethics, including loyalty to peers and colleagues. Cultivate thinking reflective of a clear understanding of biblical values. Be above reproach as reflected in the passages listed in the previous section of this chapter. Be emotionally mature, including healthy self-awareness and self-acceptance. Be emotionally stable over time and under difficult and various circumstances. Foster awareness of behavioral patterns, motivations and growth areas. Respond well to difficulty and anxiety and conflict. Develop self-discipline in ministry and life. Cultivate spiritual disciplines (including prayer, reflection, Bible reading and other personal encounters with God). Apply biblical truth to self and life and ministry. Take devotional time to bring their lives into line with God's Word. Align theology with personal application, ministry praxis and spiritual growth. Demonstrate a vital personal faith in every area of life (private life and ministry). Live in a Spirit-filled way. Live according to the prompting and fruit and guidance of the Spirit. Consistently make space to commune with God. Demonstrate a love for time with God and in the Scriptures. Cultivate a rich devotional life, including regular prayer and biblical study. Strengthen and deepen a relationship with God. Respond to the call of God revealed by the Spirit in the Word. Seek God's call on their lives, through the church, Scripture, mission, reflection and prayer. Cultivate an attitude toward ministry that reflects a sense of obedience to the leading of God. Be consistently and authentically immersed in a local church and ministry. Be

---

[32]Marilyn Naidoo, "Spiritual Formation in Protestant Theological Institutions," in Werner et al., *Handbook of Theological Education in World Christianity*, 193.

committed to the local expression of the body of Christ. Meet with Christians in a local church regularly. Submit to appropriate discipline. Be committed to corporate worship. Have an authentic spiritual fervor and passion for God's kingdom and his righteousness.

Behavioral (hands). This is about our theological education and ministry training forming graduates with competent mission and ministry skills. We want to see them embrace an authentic commitment to the local church. Be an active participant in a local church community. Explore their ministry vocation in local churches and in other opportunities. Encourage evangelism in organized missionary work and through personal encounters and relationships. Support mission through announcement (proclamation) and demonstration (social concern and action). Understand themselves as Christians called to world mission. This includes local, regional, national and global mission. Be ready for appropriate Christian ministry and mission and service. Show a commitment to ministerial and missional formation. Be competent interpreters and teachers and proclaimers of Scripture. Demonstrate a solid understanding of hermeneutics, exegesis and homiletics. Be able to accurately exposit the Scriptures. Apply Scripture to their own and others' lives. And communicate these truths effectively. Be able to preach and teach capably in the context of their ministries.

What other expressions of behavioral formation must we seek? We desire students and graduates to interpret the cultural context for the purposes of ministry and mission. Apply principles that will promote church growth and mission by the whole congregation. Actively seek to lead others to a personal relationship with God. Know how to help various kinds of unbelievers move toward a commitment to Christ. Practice hospitality and welcoming the stranger. Demonstrate a capacity to relate to people from cultural backgrounds significantly different from the one they know best. Adapt well to changing and unpredictable and new ministry settings. Apply the insights of missiology to the whole life and outreach of the church. Be able to articulate their Christian faith, especially with respect to other belief systems and worldviews. Show and communicate *publicly* what it means to be a Christlike Christian leader.

Effective pastoral and leadership and interpersonal skills are also vital. We hope that our formation will lead to students and graduates with competent interpersonal relationships. They'll know how to give and receive love and respect. Be able to form healthy relationships with the opposite sex. Identify, develop, equip and release others to ministry and mission with integrity. Value the equipping role of Christian ministry. Disciple others. Develop a culture of discipleship in their ministries. Demonstrate competent empowerment of others for service. Understand how to lead change and transition in their ministries. Learn how to manage and resolve conflict. Understand and demonstrating the skills of servant leadership (servantship).[33] Pay attention to developing the next generation of leaders, who can likewise build up and develop others. Seek to equip others for ministry (Eph 4). Be able to lead through sound administrative and management capabilities. Embrace prayerful and compassionate care of others. Demonstrate skills in spiritual care giving. Be competent in pastoral care and visitation. Develop and oversee systems and structures of pastoral care (appropriate to the context). Nurture persons and families and congregations through crisis and change and difficulty. This involves using pastoral competencies and personal integrity and biblical wisdom.

Graduates also need skills in cultural engagement. They need to be able to put theological and ministry learning into conversation with cultures and contexts and do this for the sake of salvation and liberation and mission. Applying this principle to the African context, James Amanze says that African spirituality has enriched the church. And the church has deepened Africa's spirituality. Future and current church leaders need to find creative ways to put theology and faith and spirituality into conversation with local cultures.[34]

Gnana Robinson calls for the "re-orientation of theological education for a relevant ministry." Ministry education in indigenous and Western and Majority World settings needs constant renewal. It needs a reorientation to the outcomes I've detailed. This is vital for a relevant ministry. "Changing socio-economic and political situations in countries like Asia, Africa, and Latin America call for relevant ministries which, in turn, demands a change in the traditional pattern of ministries. . . . Re-orientation of theological education thus demands reorientation to our culture, our understanding of

---

[33]Graham Hill, ed., *Servantship: Sixteen Servants on the Four Movements of Radical Servantship* (Eugene, OR: Wipf and Stock, 2013).

[34]James N. Amanze, "Contextuality: African Spirituality as a Catalyst for Spiritual Formation in Theological Education in Africa," *Ogbomoso Journal of Theology* 16, no. 2 (2011): 19.

God, the world, the people of God, the pattern of ministry we want, and spirituality."[35]

Cognitive (head). Our theological education and ministry training must form graduates with competent theological skills. We want to see them demonstrate key competencies. Here are some examples. Develop in biblical passion and knowledge. Interpret the Bible accurately for themselves. Demonstrate an understanding of the Word of God, including appreciating the big picture and plotline of Scripture. Understand the Christian gospel and be able to share it with others. Be able to convey and apply the truths of Scripture to their own and others' lives in effective ministry. Have a keen interest in Bible and theology. Be able to grow and feed themselves in understanding and skills beyond study at theological college. Hold to a trinitarian orthodoxy (one God exists in one substance and in three persons: Father, Son and Holy Spirit). Uphold the historicity of the crucifixion and resurrection. Preserve the centrality of the person and work of Christ and his divine/human nature. Proclaim Jesus' saving work on the cross as the only means for salvation and the forgiveness of sins. Affirm the Bible as authoritative. Believe that it's God's revelation to humanity. Know that it's the supreme source of authority in matters of faith and practice. Understand their beliefs in the light of Christian history. Appreciate their particular Christian heritage and tradition. Develop a sound basic understanding of Christian history and historic Christian faith. Evaluate current theology and practices in the light of that history. Pursue a robust understanding and theology of ministry, leadership, church, worship, mission, training and discipleship.

This list of affective and behavioral and cognitive graduate outcomes may give the impression we're reaching for the perfect graduate. That's not the case. Graduates come in all shapes and sizes. They have unique skills and passions and callings. But having clear graduate outcomes for hearts and hands and heads keeps our theological education and ministry training focused. Our training is then student focused, not student led. It seeks to take graduates through a holistic formation process. And it desires that they glorify God the Father and witness to Jesus Christ and serve in the Holy Spirit's power in their lives and ministries.

---

[35]Gnana Robinson, "Re-Orientation of Theological Education for a Relevant Ministry," *East Asia Journal of Theology* 4, no. 2 (1986): 46.

7. Renewed education is contextual and intercontextual. It's important that we contextualize our curriculum, delivery, theology and methods. As we've seen already, Coe and others outline the significance of contextualization for education and theology. Paulo Freire says that skills in contextualized education include *problemization* and *conscientization*.[36] These have become core values in many educational institutions in the Majority World. They are also popular in Western education. They may be instructive for Western seminaries and churches.

Problemization. This is the encouragement of critical, analytical, perceptive, free, open and uninhibited dialogue between teachers and students. Teachers encourage students to mirror this process in their ministries. And students teach congregations to embrace these practices. Problemization aims to develop students into critical, expressive thinkers and leaders and change agents. It helps them wrestle with issues in their context. It encourages students to practice critical, imaginative thinking and problem solving in ministry. And it's a vital skill set for mission.

Conscientization. This is about enabling students to develop a "deepening awareness both of the socio-cultural reality which shapes their lives and of their capacity to transform that reality."[37] The message of the gospel relates to the whole of a person's life. This, of course, includes every aspect of their context. Theological education must reflect this truth. It must help leaders develop missional congregations that engage their cultures. It must give students an awareness of the realities of their context. And most importantly, it must help them embrace their "capacity to transform that reality."[38]

Contextualization is not adequate in isolation from intercontextual, global reflection. Huang Po Ho spells this out from an Asian perspective. Contextual theology is not subsumed into intercontextuality but enriched by it. Intercontextuality is about different groups sharing the things they are learning in their own contexts. This way they enrich each other's contexts.

Ho writes, "To emphasize contextuality does not mean to isolate a single particular context or to neglect the inter-relations in which a context is involved with other contexts. Accordingly, a genuine contextual theology must

---

[36]Paulo Freire, *Pedagogy of the Oppressed* (New York: Herder and Herder, 1968).
[37]Paulo Freire, *Cultural Action for Freedom* (Middlesex: Penguin, 1970), 51.
[38]Ibid.

be a theology that not only delves into the depth and nature of a given context, but that also explores its connectedness with other wider contexts." Ho still prioritizes context. A "particular context is not only the starting point of any contextual theological endeavor, but also remains the subject of the project as well as the object of all the concerns of that theology."[39]

M. Thomas Thangaraj says that robust contextual theology follows the formula: *Local + Global = Contextual.* Contextual theology needs intercontextual, global theology to flourish. So too contextual theological education is at its best when it engages both local and global issues.[40]

Paul Hiebert speaks of *critical contextualization.* The church is a global "hermeneutical community." It tests "the contextualization of cultural practices as well as theologies." Critical contextualization isn't monocultural. Nor is it "premised upon the pluralism of incommensurable cultures."[41] It takes global and cultural and historical contexts seriously.

Theological colleges must contextualize their curriculum and methodologies. This contextualization should consider a range of questions: What are the educational and experiential entry levels of the students? What are the contexts of the local supporting churches and the local community? What are the national and denominational and ecumenical contexts? What are the motivations of the students to undertake the program? (This includes their interests and values, and their expectations of the course.) How will this study relate to the conceptual and cognitive styles of the students? What's the best way to determine the objectives of the program? (Ideally, seminaries should develop these objectives in consultation with students and their local churches.) How will we relate these objectives to the development of the three key areas (head and heart and hands)?

To contextualize our curriculum and methodologies, we need to ask even more questions: What resources are available (space, time, books, human, materials and so on)? What cultural restrictions and norms and taboos exist?

---

[39]Huang Po Ho, "Contextualization and Inter-Contextuality in Theological Education: An Asian Perspective," in Werner et al., *Handbook of Theological Education in World Christianity,* 127.

[40]M. Thomas Thangaraj, "A Formula for Contextual Theology: Local + Global = Contextual," in *Contextualizing Theological Education,* ed. Theodore Brelsford and P. Alice Rogers (Cleveland: Pilgrim, 2008), 107.

[41]Paul G. Hiebert, "Critical Contextualization," *International Bulletin of Missionary Research* 11, no. 3 (July 1987): 100.

What are the external, physical, geographical and organizational constraints? Are there any cost and administrative considerations? Are there pressing local and global realities that influence this culture? What are the relevant historical, cultural and political factors influencing the status, function and accessibility of education? What access is there to technologies? What are the preferences, abilities, experiences, training, attitudes and styles of lecturers? What are the requirements of accrediting agencies? And how do we design and apply an appropriate grading system? (This needs to consider the local culture's view of competition, achievement and so on.)

Theological colleges and churches need to contextualize theological education—both content and methods. We do this to be faithful to the gospel in particular settings. And we do this to form men and women for service.

Contextualization helps theological education influence cultures. It helps to uphold and preserve appropriate values in cultures. It challenges sin in cultures. And it can reverse the colonizing forces within and beyond cultures. Contextualization honors what God is doing at the grassroots of cultures.

8. Renewed education places mission at the center of curriculum and methods. Most theological education isn't missional. Sure, it may have a few mission courses. And it may even have a mission faculty or institute. But to be truly missional, theological education must shape its entire curriculum around missional theology and practices.

The doctrine of the *missio Dei* has revolutionized the way we understand theology and mission and church. And it must reshape our theological education and ministry training. We need to teach all subjects from a missional perspective. This includes pastoral, systematics, preaching, biblical interpretation and so on. Colleges must form students *for* mission and *in* mission and *through* mission. Theological reflection is *for* mission and *in* mission. Since discipleship is participation in the *missio Dei*, theological education must also be participation in the *missio Dei*. It should prioritize the missional nature of God and church and ministry. Theological reflection and spiritual formation should happen in the context of mission, not only in the context of academy or church.

Theological education must equip leaders and churches to take part in the mission of God. It should be *outwardly oriented*. It equips people to engage fully in God's mission in the world. It should be *incarnational*. It's located in the lives and contexts and cultures of our world. It should be *discipleship focused.* It enables people to follow Jesus Christ and his mission in the world. It should be thoroughly *missional.* It reshapes its curricula, structures, faculty, assessment and ethos through missional paradigms, theologies and experiences. And it should be *formational.* It forms the whole person to serve the whole mission of Christ.

Moreover, our theological education must teach people to interpret and apply Scripture through a missional paradigm. To use technical terms, they need a *missional hermeneutic.*

Last, such missional education integrates the fourteen characteristics described by Tiénou, Escobar and Gnanakan. I outlined these earlier in this chapter.

Remissionalizing theological education takes courage. It takes time. It's risky to those leading the charge since it threatens existing educational models and curriculum design. But it's imperative if we take the *missio Dei* seriously.

9. Renewed education equips the whole body of Christ. It doesn't just train pastors and missionaries. These are important gifts to the church. But they're not the only gifts. If theological education is going to train all the fivefold gifts and more, then it must serve the whole church. It must develop and release apostles, pastors, teachers, evangelists, prophets and a host of other gifts. Theological education should equip moms and dads and entire families. It should train mechanics, lawyers, plumbers, doctors, hairdressers, teachers, counselors, carpenters and so on. Worthwhile theological education mustn't have an unnatural, Christendom-formed focus on one or two ministry gifts. Instead, worthwhile theological education and ministry training must equip the whole body of Christ.

10. Renewed education models and cultivates servantship. It's time we demonstrated a reciprocal, servanthood, enabling and participatory style of leadership as theological educators. This means modeling Christ-honoring spiritual leadership to our students. It means rejecting hierarchical and corporate models of leadership.

Servantship is following Jesus Christ, the servant Lord, and his mission. It's a life of discipleship to him. It's patterned after his self-emptying, humility, sacrifice, love, values and mission. Servantship is humbly valuing others more than yourself. It's looking out for the interests and well-being of others.

Servantship is the cultivation of the same attitude of mind as that of

Christ Jesus. It's making yourself nothing. It's being a servant and humbling yourself. And it's submitting yourself to the will and purposes of the triune God. Since servantship is the imitation of Christ, it involves an unreserved participation in his mission. Servantship recognizes in word and thought and deed that Christian leaders are servants. "Whoever wants to become great among you must be your servant, and whoever wants to be first must be slave of all. For even the Son of Man did not come to be served, but to serve, and to give his life as a ransom for many" (Mk 10:43-45).

11. Renewed education applies instruction-action-reflection models of learning. We need *instruction-action-reflection* approaches to education. Students receive *instruction*, undertake specific *actions* and *reflect* on their experiences and learnings. Here are the four stages: (1) Instruction leads to new experiences in ministry. (2) These lead to new observations and reflections. (3) Students then develop new skills and concepts and characteristics. (4) Further experimentation is then integrated with more instruction. This four-stage cycle continues repeatedly. This approach helps form people for discipleship and ministry and mission. This model integrates action, theory and reflection. It combines theology, formation and fieldwork. Educators must provide opportunities for reflection on new theologies and skills and experiences.

This model integrates at least six things. The first is theological and biblical reflection. The second is theoretical perspectives on ministry practice. The third is spiritual formation. The fourth is personal and relational and emotional growth. The fifth is ministry praxis and competency. And the sixth is missional theology and development.

The aim of *instruction-action-reflection* is to develop students holistically as disciples and for mission and ministry. And the goal is to do this in their contexts. It does this by allowing those trainees to develop within the context of their local churches and communities. And it makes sure they have competent supervision and guidance. The *instruction-action-reflection* cycle requires students to integrate theory and practice and spiritual formation in concrete settings. It's an apprenticeship and whole-of-life pattern to theological and ministry education. And it uses the way Jesus trained his disciples as a model.[42]

12. Renewed education offers diversified approaches to learning. It offers

---

[42]Ferdinando, "Jesus, the Theological Educator."

diversified theological education (DTE) by combining modes of education. Examples include residential and online, part-time and full-time, and on-campus and in-church education. Education is no longer a "one size fits all" affair. It needs to be flexible. During their studies, students will most likely combine a variety of modes of education. For many colleges, it's now difficult to talk about discrete online, full-time or part-time groups. They blend. And when we're focused on formation, such diversification can enhance our education.

13. Renewed education resists colonizing people. The best kind of theological education rejects "colonizing" people because of their race, gender, knowledge, disability, education, medical condition, class, theology and language. It's not blind to these things. But it doesn't colonize. And it refuses to use a "cookie-cutter" approach to training. Instead, it practices the opposite: liberating behavior. Even though we must practice theological education in community, we must still encourage unique, particular and even "eccentric" contributions. These are a gift to education and the church. Some are revolutionary and prophetic. All are a grace from God.

14. Renewed education addresses issues of access and power. Who can access our theological education? Are we addressing the gendered dimensions of power relations? Can both women and men fully take part in our theological and ministry education?

This is not just about women. It is about men *and* women. And it's about their relations before Jesus Christ. Gender is often about power relations, and theological institutions have a responsibility to address these dynamics. Theological institutions need to evaluate how "gender issues are being incorporated into the process of transformation. An engendered process of transformation comes about through organizational change, programme development, and collaboration with poor and marginalized women."[43]

Isabel Apawo Phiri, Esther Mombo, Limatula Longkumer and Ofelia Ortega call for en-gendered theological education. They do this from African and Asian and Latin American perspectives. They speak prophetically into local and global ministry education. I'm indebted here to their perspectives.

The church needs to address some critical questions if women are to fully take part in theological education.[44] Here are some examples: What are

---

[43]Haddad, "Engendering Theological Education for Transformation," 66.
[44]Ofelia Ortega, "Women and Theology: A Latin American Viewpoint," *Ministerial Formation*

women's socioeconomic status and roles in our society? How do we feel about this? How do we respond to women's long histories of subordinate roles in church and society? Do we want "separate" or "specialized" forms of women's ministry? What's our position on the ordination of women? What are the challenges facing women who want to attend residential colleges? What are the unique contributions of women to theology and church and education? Have we developed a biblical theology of gender and addressed the associated interpretive challenges? Do we have inclusive language in liturgy and training and theology? What do we do about the shaping of theological curriculum and structures by (mostly) men? What access do women have to shaping theological methods and curriculum and institutions? Do we value integrative approaches that incorporate theology and praxis and formation?

And other important questions emerge. Do we have interdisciplinary courses that empower people for life and service, enriching learning experiences? Have we offered special scholarships and opportunities for women? Do we encourage innovative forms and patterns of ministry led by women? Have we considered the importance of needs-based curriculum? Does our curriculum address gender, race, environment, class, health, human trafficking, poverty and so forth? Are our faculties and seminaries and churches and their leaders willing to address these issues?

En-gendering theological education takes courage and conviction. Beverley Haddad says,

> Engendering theological education is critical to transformation. Courage is needed, particularly by male educators, to get involved in this complex process that requires attention on a number of different levels. It requires long-term institutional change. It requires thoughtful and deliberate programme development. And perhaps, most difficult of all, it requires profound personal change so that we can better see, hear, and include our sisters who will never grace the doors of the academy, and yet are key subjects in the engendering process.[45]

---

110 (2008); Limatula Longkumer, "Women in Theological Education from an Asian Perspective," in Werner et al., *Handbook of Theological Education in World Christianity*; Isabel Apawo Phiri and Esther Mombo, "Women in Theological Education from an African Perspective," in Werner et al., *Handbook of Theological Education in World Christianity*.

[45]Haddad, "Engendering Theological Education for Transformation," 80.

15. Renewed education is Spirit empowered. We need to learn from Pentecostal and charismatic approaches to theological education in the Majority World. We can learn from their dependency on the Spirit to empower women and men for ministry. Too many theological institutions focus on academic learning and ministry competence, but neglect discipleship and formation and Spirit empowerment. People go into ministry and discover they're in a spiritual battle for which they're unprepared. The Holy Spirit empowers us for ministry and for the spiritual battle we're engaged in. He regenerates, sanctifies, guides, unifies and empowers us. We dare not neglect Spirit empowerment in ministry or in our training for ministry.

16. Renewed education seeks a global "renaissance" in theology and training. Timothy Tennent describes global shifts in theology. He says that these arise from the stunning growth of Majority World Christianity. He then explores four ways in which the rise of the Majority World church might help theology. These ways also have a positive influence on emerging forms of theological education. This rise of Majority World theology and education will lead to a "renaissance in Western theological scholarship."[46] This renaissance Tennent envisages won't stop in the West. It will be a global renewal of theological discourse and education.

First, this renaissance will mean the "reintegration of the theological disciplines." The disciplines of systematic theology, biblical theology, applied theology, missiology, apologetics and so on are more integrated in the Majority World. They must become more integrated in the West.

Second, it will lead to a "renaissance in systematic theology." Systematic theology in the Majority World tends to converse with contextual and spiritual and missional themes. Those themes shape systematic theology. This is also necessary in the West. "It is this reconnection between theological scholarship and the church's mission that is so vital to the future of a truly robust Christian movement."[47]

Third, it will result in the "particularization of theological discourse." Theological reflection and learning in the Majority World is often concerned with local needs. It addresses local concerns and challenges. Majority World, indig-

---

[46]Timothy C. Tennent, *Theology in the Context of World Christianity: How the Global Church Is Influencing the Way We Think About and Discuss Theology* (Grand Rapids: Zondervan, 2007), 250.
[47]Ibid., 251.

enous and Western theologies need to engage in local and global conversations. In this chapter, for instance, I have sought to listen to educational themes in Africa and Asia and Latin America. "If we engage in this kind of sustained cross-cultural theological discourse with the church around the world, the sheer diversity of global Christianity will help free the church from any one particular cultural bias."[48]

Fourth, it will inspire "theological engagement with ideologies of unbelief and with non-Christian religions."[49] Majority World theology and theological education tends to engage with its pluralistic context. It seeks to talk with other ideologies and worldviews and religions. It pursues engagement with Islam, Hinduism, atheism, Confucianism, Buddhism, religious sects, new spiritualities and religious movements, and so forth. The West is also becoming pluralistic. It needs theology and theological education capable of thriving in diverse, pluralistic settings.

17. Renewed education integrates the three "publics" of academy and church and society. Global conversations are important. Majority World, indigenous and Western theologies and education can renew each other. But they will only do this through robust dialogue. These conversations can contribute to the renewal of the global church. They can enhance its participation in God's mission in the world.

David Bosch says that theology and theological education must renew themselves. And they do this by integrating the three "publics" of academy and church and society. Theology (and theological education) mustn't only be relevant to these three "publics." It must engage with them critically. A critical conversation between theology, academy, church and society is necessary. This critical conversation enables theology (and theological education) to contribute to the well-being and renewal of academy and church and society. It helps both theology and theological education take part fully in the mission of God in the world.

> Theology and theological education, then, involve a dynamic interplay and a creative tension between *theoria, poiesis* and *praxis*, between head, heart and hand, between faith, hope and love, between the cognitive, the constitutive and the critical, between the intellectual, the relational and the intentional. It

---

[48]Ibid., 265.
[49]Ibid.

combines knowing, being and doing and seeks to communicate what is true, what is of God, and what is just.

Unless theological education succeeds—however inadequately—to embody these dimensions, it will not be credible to any of its three publics. In the world of *academia* it will be viewed as an atavistic enterprise, a throw-back to a bygone era. The *church* will regard it as peripheral to its life, as diffuse and cafeteria-like, lacking a unifying vision. *Society* will perceive it as pedantic, irrelevant and doctrinaire. In each of these instances our students will, in their search for an integrating world- and life-view, feel obliged to look elsewhere for help in respect of what really matters, even if they comply formally with our degree requirements.[50]

May theological educators and institutions have the courage to embody *theoria* and *poiesis* and *praxis* in the three public spheres of academia and church and society. May theological and ministry education serve the mission of God. In the words of the Lausanne *Cape Town Commitment,* may it enable the mission of God and his church. May theological educators have the courage to "conduct a 'missional audit' of their curricula, structures, and ethos, to ensure that they truly serve the needs and opportunities facing the church in their cultures."[51]

---

[50]David J. Bosch, "The Nature of Theological Education," *Theologia Evangelica* 25 (1992): 23.
[51]The Lausanne Movement, *The Cape Town Commitment: A Confession of Faith and a Call to Action* (Lausanne Library: 2011), www.lausanne.org/en/documents/ctcommitment.html.

PRACTICING SERVANTSHIP

*We are called to serve Jesus via the Broken Ones. They keep us
accountable for living our call with integrity and authenticity.*

ELIZABETH PETERSEN (PARAPHRASED)

There are many examples of great and good and bad leadership in the Majority World. There are as many examples of virtuous and flawed leadership in the Majority World as there are in the West.

Let's consider an example of great Christian leadership. Samuel Lamb (Lin Xiangao) was a gospel preacher and a leader of the Chinese house-church movement. Chinese authorities imprisoned him for these ministries for more than twenty years. He was tortured, starved, imprisoned and repeatedly beaten for his ministry in China. While imprisoned, Lamb was forced to do hard labor in the dreaded Shanxi Taiyuan coal mine. But Lamb continued to preach the gospel of Jesus Christ. He made disciples. And he baptized believers.

Once released, Lamb refused to take part in the Chinese state-controlled "Three-Self Patriotic Movement" churches. He suffered relentless persecution by Chinese authorities for that stance. But the church he planted quickly grew to five thousand worshipers. To the consternation of authorities, each time they arrested and imprisoned Lamb, his church grew. Lamb went on to publish two hundred booklets called "The Voice of the Spirit." Lamb died in 2013, and thirty thousand mourners attended his funeral in Guangzhou, China.

Some estimate that there are now close to 100 million house-church Christians in China. Lamb, and a generation of Chinese Christian leaders like him, made a remarkable contribution to this growth of the Chinese church. And his spiritual leadership was exemplary.

When we consider excellent Christian leadership in Asia, Africa, Latin America, Eastern Europe, First Nations and indigenous cultures, what do we see? This chapter unpacks the key leadership themes that emerge. These themes are servantship and culturally specific and crosscultural leadership. Other themes include disciple-making, church-multiplying, missional and spiritual leadership.

This chapter asks, *What can we learn from how Majority World Christians practice servantship?*

SERVANT LEADERSHIP (SERVANTSHIP)

Imagine the impact of Christian leadership shaped around service. This servant leadership has no selfish ambition or vain conceit. It humbly esteems others above itself. It looks to the interests and needs of others. Servant leadership cultivates the same attitude of mind as that of Christ Jesus. It doesn't grasp after its own advantage. And it humbles itself obediently to the will and mission of God in human history.

I am describing a leadership that seeks to witness to Christ Jesus. It depends on the power of the Holy Spirit. And it brings glory to God the Father. Picture the eternal legacy of Christian leadership shaped around the service of God. Serving God means wholeheartedly serving his mission and church and world.

It would be wrong to suggest that most Majority World leadership is servant leadership. In many places, it is the opposite. But there has been a move among Majority World thinkers to *reconceive leadership as servantship*. This shift involves allowing a theology of service to shape our understanding and practice of Christian leadership.[1]

---

[1]Some of this material was first published in Graham Hill, "The Theology and Practices of Self-Emptying, Missional *Servantship*," in *Servantship: Sixteen Servants on the Four Movements of Radical*

Here is my definition of *servantship*:

Servantship is following Jesus Christ the servant Lord and his mission. It's a life of discipleship to him. It's patterned after his self-emptying, humility, sacrifice, love, values and mission. Servantship is humbly valuing others more than yourself. It's looking out for the interests and well-being of others. Servantship is the cultivation of the same attitude of mind as that of Christ Jesus. It's making yourself nothing. It's being a servant and humbling yourself. And it's submitting yourself to the will and purposes of the triune God. Since servantship is the imitation of Christ, it involves an unreserved participation in his mission. (By this, I mean the *missio Dei*—the trinitarian mission of God.) Servantship recognizes in word and thought and deed that Christian leaders are servants. "Whoever wants to become great among you must be your servant, and whoever wants to be first must be your slave—just as the Son of Man did not come to be served, but to serve, and to give his life as a ransom for many" (Mt 20:26-28).

Elizabeth Petersen's perspectives on servantship among "the Broken Ones" serve as an example.[2] She's led an extraordinary servant ministry as the founder and executive director of SAFFI, which is short for the South African Faith & Family Institute. Petersen established SAFFI in 2008 to address violence against women and children in South Africa. Her ministry deals with sexual violence, domestic abuse, neglect and the exploitation of children. And she addresses the systemic structures and biblical misinterpretations that support such violence. SAFFI seeks to address faith issues and root causes of violence against women by being a resource to religious leaders, their faith communities, and secular domestic violence advocates to advance comprehensive coordinated culturally informed strategies and interventions.[3]

SAFFI's strategies include educational seminars and perpetrator intervention programs. They conduct gender reconciliation workshops and do research and advocacy. They offer technical support to community-based domestic violence initiatives. And they run interfaith forums on how to prevent and deal with violence against women.

Servantship, ed. Graham Hill (Eugene, OR: Wipf and Stock, 2013). Used by permission of Wipf and Stock Publishers, www.wipfandstock.com.

[2]I capitalize *Broken Ones* throughout this chapter because that is Elizabeth Petersen's practice.
[3]"About SAFFI," South African Faith & Family Institute, www.saffi.org.za.

SAFFI also challenges patriarchal theological traditions that condone or excuse such violence. SAFFI promotes "the promotion of Scriptural and theological teachings that encourage intimate relationships that set people free to live their full potential in supportive unions."[4]

Petersen provides perspectives on the nature of Christian servantship "via the Broken Ones." This is a servantship shaped by humility and service and sacrifice. This servantship collaborates with those whom society has "stripped of their human dignity." She shows us a servantship that "co-suffers and co-creates" with "the Broken Ones." Petersen says these broken people "keep me accountable for living my calling with integrity and authenticity." For Petersen, "the Broken Ones are Christ and the broken others in our society."[5]

Petersen shares how she came to realize that Christian servantship is about serving with broken people. She discovered Jesus present among them.

> I began to realize that these women and children were going to help me find my voice and that I needed them to help me find the expressions for my calling as a social worker. The Broken Ones became those who kept me accountable for living my calling with integrity and authenticity. I began to find God in and through the voices and stories of those who have been stripped of their human dignity through sexual, physically violent, and other forms of abuse. I began to discover the life-giving presence of God in the midst of my engagement with these women . . . co-suffering and co-creating with us all.[6]

Petersen helps us understand the nature of servantship. She does this through her personal reflections and writings and ministry among abused and broken women and children in South Africa.

Servantship stands in contrast to many of the leadership principles and practices of the global political and corporate age. Christians shape their servantship after the humility and sacrifice and values of the suffering servant, Jesus Christ. We need a servantship formed by the imitation of Jesus Christ. We show this servantship through a lifestyle of service. We shape a

---

[4]Ibid.

[5]Elizabeth Petersen and Jannie Swart, "Via the Broken Ones: Towards a Phenomenological Theology of Ecclesial Leadership in Post-Apartheid South Africa," *Journal of Religious Leadership* 8, no. 2 (2009): 12. In this YouTube clip (*I Am Woman*, season 2, episode 21), Elizabeth Petersen describes her call to minister among and with the "Broken Ones": www.youtube.com/watch?v=2lXbv1V5CF0.

[6]Petersen and Swart, "Via the Broken Ones," 9-10.

life of servantship through love, hope, faith and self-sacrifice. "Whoever wants to become great among you must be your servant" (Mt 20:26).

William F. Kumuyi founded Deeper Life Bible Church, Nigeria, in 1982. Kumuyi's church has planted close to nine thousand churches throughout Africa. The main church (in Lagos, Nigeria) has 120,000 attendees every Sunday. Some estimate that in Nigeria alone, 800,000 people worship in the Deeper Life Bible Church family of churches every Sunday. In April 2013, *Foreign Policy* named Kumuyi one of the "500 most powerful people on the planet."[7]

In spite of this success and acclaim, Kumuyi practices a deep commitment to servantship. He writes, "What Africa needs for its redemption is servant leadership, instead of the self-serving governance that the continent is famed for. Our leaders should add the servanthood attitude to their attributes and demonstrate that their primary motivation for seeking to lead the people is rooted in a deep desire to serve and help others."[8] Concerned about Africa's future, Kumuyi says that servantship is the rejection of leadership that's "a money-spinning business venture; or a rare opportunity to feather one's nest and bequeath material security to one's offspring."[9]

Kumuyi calls for reform to African political, military, corporate and church leadership. He calls for a systematic reform of African governance based on servant leadership. "In spite of the extensive damage that colonialism has done to Africa's capacity for holistic development, the continent can re-invent itself by effective leadership shorn of graft."[10]

Africa is not the only continent crying out for servantship. Western Christianity obsesses over leadership. And domineering and hierarchical leadership personalities and forms plague Western churches. But Jesus called his disciples to service. He modeled servantship and called his disciples to be servants. Societies practice leadership in culturally specific ways. Even though this is the case, all Christian leadership has service and

---

[7]Alicia P. Q. Wittmeyer, "The FP Power Map: The 500 Most Powerful People on the Planet," April 29, 2013, *Foreign Policy*, www.foreignpolicy.com/articles/2013/04/29/the_500_most_powerful _people_in_the_world.

[8]William Folorunso Kumuyi, "The Case for Servant Leadership," *New African*, no. 467 (2007): 18.

[9]Ibid., 19.

[10]William Folorunso Kumuyi, "The Functions of a Servant-Leader," *New African*, no. 468 (2007): 30. See also William Folorunso Kumuyi, "Why Serious Visioning and Visioners Are Strangers in Africa," *New African*, no. 470 (2008).

humility and love at its heart. You cannot be a Christian leader without being a servant.

CULTURALLY-SPECIFIC AND CROSSCULTURAL LEADERSHIP

Recently, significant research has been conducted into how different cultures *conceptualize* and *practice* leadership. This research deals with how cultures affect leadership expectations, preferences, models and styles. It also considers how leadership adapts to multicultural and crosscultural settings.[11]

The GLOBE study of how sixty-two cultures conceptualize, value and practice leadership is a fascinating example.[12] This major study involved 170 researchers, almost two-thirds of whom were from the Majority World. They designed the research instruments and collected and interpreted the data. The researchers asked how different cultures conceive and practice leadership. They also asked how culture is related to societal and organizational and leadership effectiveness.

The GLOBE researchers "tested 27 hypotheses that linked culture to interesting outcomes, with data from 17,300 managers in 951 organizations" in sixty-two cultures worldwide.

> They measured the variables with cultural sensitivity, developing instruments in consultation with members of the relevant cultures. By using focus groups, and by heavy dependence on the previous literature, the investigators developed instruments that tapped local meanings that were appropriate for each level of the data and also had equivalence across cultures.[13]

The research sought to answer these questions:

---

[11]See, for instance, Lewis's text on managing and leading successfully across cultures: Richard D. Lewis, *When Cultures Collide: Leading Across Cultures; A Major New Edition of the Global Guide*, 3rd ed. (London: Nicholas Brealey International, 2005). For an overview of the literature on leadership in crosscultural contexts, see Marcus W. Dickson, Deanne N. Den Hartog and Jacqueline K. Mitchelson, "Research on Leadership in a Cross-Cultural Context: Making Progress, and Raising New Questions," *The Leadership Quarterly* 14 (2003).

[12]The GLOBE study builds on the pioneering work of Geert Hofstede into the cultures and values of nations and people groups. Geert H. Hofstede, *Culture's Consequences: International Differences in Work-Related Values*, Cross Cultural Research and Methodology Series (Beverly Hills, CA: Sage, 1980); Geert H. Hofstede, *Culture's Consequences: Comparing Values, Behaviors, Institutions, and Organizations Across Nations*, 2nd ed. (Thousand Oaks, CA: Sage, 2001); Geert H. Hofstede, Gert Jan Hofstede and Michael Minkov, *Cultures and Organizations: Software of the Mind; Intercultural Cooperation and Its Importance for Survival*, 3rd ed. (New York: McGraw-Hill, 2010).

[13]Robert J. House et al., eds., *Culture, Leadership, and Organizations: The Globe Study of 62 Societies* (Thousand Oaks, CA: Sage, 2004), xv.

Are there leader behaviors, attributes, and organizational practices that are universally accepted and effective across cultures? Are there leader behaviors, attributes, and organizational practices that are accepted and effective in only some cultures? How do attributes of societal and organizational cultures affect the kinds of leader behaviors and organizational practices that are accepted and effective? What is the effect of violating cultural norms relevant to leadership and organizational practices? What is the relative standing of each of the cultures studied on each of the nine core dimensions of culture? Can the universal and culture-specific aspects of leader behaviors, attributes, and organizational practices be explained in terms of an underlying theory that accounts for systematic differences across cultures?[14]

The research proposed nine cultural attributes. It related these to leadership styles and practices in the cultures. In the words of the researchers, these nine are the following:

Uncertainty Avoidance is the extent to which members of an organization or society strive to avoid uncertainty by relying on established social norms, rituals, and bureaucratic practices.

Power Distance is the degree to which members of an organization or society expect and agree that power should be stratified and concentrated at higher levels.

Collectivism I, Institutional Collectivism, is the degree to which organizational and societal institutional practices encourage and reward collective distribution of resources and collective action.

Collectivism II, In-Group Collectivism, is the degree to which individuals express pride, loyalty, and cohesiveness in their organizations or families.

Gender Egalitarianism is the degree to which an organization or a society minimizes gender role differences.

Assertiveness is the degree to which individuals in organizations or societies are assertive, confrontational, and aggressive in social relationships.

Future Orientation is the degree to which individuals in organizations or societies engage in future-oriented behaviors such as planning, investing in the future, and delaying individual or collective gratification.

---

[14]Robert J. House et al., "Cultural Influences on Leadership and Organizations: Project Globe," *Advances in Global Leadership* 1, no. 2 (2013): 171-233; House et al., *Culture, Leadership, and Organizations*, 10.

Performance Orientation is the degree to which an organization or society encourages and rewards group members for performance improvement and excellence.

Humane Orientation is the degree to which individuals in organizations or societies encourage and reward individuals for being fair, altruistic, friendly, generous, caring, and kind to others.[15]

Researchers identified ten cultural clusters. These are Anglo cultures, Arab cultures, Confucian Asia, Eastern Europe, Germanic Europe, Latin America, Latin Europe, Nordic Europe, Southern Asia and Sub-Sahara Africa.[16] Researchers also identified six styles/theories of leadership. They correlated these with the nine cultural attributes and ten cultural clusters detailed above. They called these styles "culturally endorsed implicit theories of leadership":

1. Charismatic/values-based leadership. Characterized by vision, inspiration, self-sacrifice, integrity, decisiveness and performance orientation. (Flip side: can be dictatorial and inattentive to relationships.)

2. Team-oriented leadership. Characterized by collaborative team orientation, team integration, diplomacy and administrative competency. (Flip side: can use these traits malevolently to achieve own ends.)

3. Participative leadership. Characterized by participative behavior and gender egalitarianism and attention to relationships. (Flip side: can be indecisive and unassertive.)

4. Humane-oriented leadership. Characterized by humility and modesty and altruistic compassion for others. (Flip side: can fail to develop high-performing organizations.)

5. Autonomous leadership. Characterized by individualism, independence, autonomous initiative and unique contributions. (Flip side: can ignore the importance of institutional collectivism and humane behaviors.)

6. Self-protective leadership. Characterized by attention to procedures and, at times, positive forms of "saving face." (Flip side: can be self-centered, negatively "face saving," status conscious, conflict inducing, poor performing, gender discriminating and overly procedural.)[17]

So what did the research find? So much! The study concluded that there

---

[15]House et al., *Culture, Leadership, and Organizations*, 11-13.
[16]Ibid., 32.
[17]Ibid., 45-48.

are correlations between the nine cultural attributes and the ten cultural clusters and the six leadership styles/theories. The study also found that what cultures *value* is more closely aligned with their preferred *leadership style/theory* than what they actually *practice*.

In other words, *cultural values shape leadership preferences*. This is true even when other things are shaping leadership practices (e.g., other cultures or globalization). And *cultural values determine preferences for leadership styles*. This is true even when those cultures are practicing leadership styles that are at odds with their values.

How do *cultural values* affect preferences for *leadership styles*?

Performance orientation in cultures is positively correlated with all leadership styles except self-protective leadership.

Uncertainty avoidance in cultures is a positive predictor of self-protective and team-oriented and humane-oriented leadership. It's a negative predictor of participative leadership.

Future orientation and *humane orientation* in cultures are positive predictors of humane-oriented and team-oriented and charismatic/values-based leadership.

In-group collectivism in cultures is a positive predictor of charismatic/values-based and team-oriented leadership. It's a negative predictor of self-protective leadership.

Gender egalitarianism in cultures is a positive predictor of participative and charismatic/values-based leadership. It's a negative predictor of self-protective leadership.

Institutional collectivism in cultures is a negative predictor of autonomous leadership.

Power distance in cultures is a positive predictor of self-protective leadership. It's a negative predictor of charismatic/values-based and participatory leadership.[18]

In terms of total support across *all* cultures, here's the progression from the *most* to the *least* supported leadership style/theory: (1) charismatic/values-based, (2) team oriented, (3) participative, (4) humane oriented, (5) autonomous and (6) self-protective.

---

[18]Ibid., 45.

Charismatic/values-based leadership receives the most support in Anglo, Latin American, Latin European, Nordic European, Southern Asian and Germanic European cultures. (It receives the least support in Middle Eastern cultures.) Nevertheless, this style of leadership is *enormously* valued across *all* cultural clusters. (It is valued more highly across all cultures than any other style.)

Team-oriented leadership receives the most support in Latin American, Confucian Asian and Southern Asian cultures. (It receives the least support in Middle Eastern and Germanic European cultures.) But again, this style of leadership is *highly* valued across *all* cultural clusters.

Participative leadership receives the most support in Germanic European, Nordic European and Anglo cultures. (It receives least support in Middle Eastern, Eastern European, Southern Asian and Confucian Asian cultures.) Nevertheless, this style of leadership is *mostly* valued across *all* cultural clusters. (But it is less valued across all cultures than charismatic/values-based styles and team leadership styles.)[19]

Humane-oriented leadership receives the most support in Southern Asian, Sub-Sahara African, Anglo and Confucian Asian cultures. (It receives the least support in Nordic European and Latin European cultures.) This style of leadership only receives *moderate* support across all cultures.

Autonomous leadership receives the most support in Eastern European and Germanic European cultures. (It receives the least support in Latin American, Latin European and Sub-Sahara African cultures.) This style of leadership receives *minimal* support in most cultures.

Self-protective leadership receives the most support in Southern Asian, Confucian Asian, Middle Eastern, Latin American and Eastern European cultures. (It receives the least support in Nordic European, Anglo and Germanic European cultures.) This style of leadership receives *hardly any support* in most cultures.[20]

The GLOBE research found that across all cultures people are looking for the following things from leadership: integrity, inspiration, vision, per-

---

[19]It is also interesting to note how much *participatory leadership* is discussed in African publications. For example, Benjamin Kiriswa, "African Model of Church as Family: Implications on Ministry & Leadership," *AFER* 43, no. 3 (2001).

[20]House et al., *Culture, Leadership, and Organizations*, 42-45.

formance, collaborative team building, decisiveness, administrative competence, diplomacy, communication, self-sacrifice, humility and modesty. All cultures value visionary and empowering and transformational leadership. (This is also called charismatic/values-based leadership.) But culture determines how such leadership is demonstrated—whether it is participative or autocratic or something in-between.[21] And individual leaders within those cultures determine whether transformational leadership is damaging or enriching, controlling or liberating, self-centered or self-serving, and autocratic or serving. Leaders provide vision and transformation and empowerment best when they serve people—putting the organization and its people above their own ego.

There has also been a recent surge of publications in the West on multiethnic and crosscultural leadership. Much of this is being writing by first, second and third generation Asian Americans, Hispanic Americans and African Americans. (And those who minister within these communities are writing these books too.) Like the GLOBE research, these authors agree that today's leaders must be servant leaders. And they must do this across cultures and ethnicities and people groups. We now live in multiethnic and multicultural cities. Culturally responsive servantship is more important than ever.[22]

DISCIPLE-MAKING, CHURCH-MULTIPLYING AND MISSIONAL LEADERSHIP

A clear theme comes through in Majority World and indigenous writings on Christian leadership. This is the need to develop indigenous, mission-focused, servant leaders through home-grown means. In most of the Majority World, this usually occurs through *disciple making*. And it also happens through *church-multiplying* and *missional movements*.

---

[21]Marcus W. Dickson et al., "Conceptualizing Leadership Across Cultures," *Journal of World Business* 47 (2012): 491.

[22]For further reading see Jim Plueddemann, *Leading Across Cultures: Effective Ministry and Mission in the Global Church* (Downers Grove, IL: IVP Academic, 2009); Manuel Ortiz, *One New People: Models for Developing a Multiethnic Church* (Downers Grove, IL: InterVarsity Press, 1996); Efrain Agosto, *Servant Leadership: Jesus and Paul* (St. Louis: Chalice, 2005); Mark Lau Branson and Juan F. Martínez, "A Practical Theology of Leadership with International Voices," *Journal of Religious Leadership* 10, no. 2 (2011); Mark Lau Branson and Juan F. Martínez, *Churches, Cultures and Leadership: A Practical Theology of Congregations and Ethnicities* (Downers Grove, IL: IVP Academic, 2011).

Disciple-making movements and leadership. Mitsuo Fukuda of Japan describes indigenous disciple-making movements of Asia. These movements pass on the baton to future generations of Christians. Disciple-making movements focus on *compassion* for the lost. They seek *obedience* to the Great Commission and the Great Commandment. And they pursue the *multiplication* of homegrown disciples who multiply homegrown disciples.

Mitsuo Fukuda says these disciples embrace distinct emphases that help them multiply more disciples. These include praying for "persons of peace" and connecting through food and hospitality. They also focus on healing the sick and proclaiming the coming of Jesus Christ. New converts learn "to listen to God, to reach the world, and to catalyze organic fellowships."[23]

This grassroots disciple making and leadership development must be indigenous to its culture. In Japan, for example, this means that the training must be family focused and group oriented. Indigenous disciple-making movements do not just multiply disciples. They multiply indigenous churches. And these churches have indigenous leaders. These leaders minister to the needs of local cultures and people groups. These disciple-making movements are also church-multiplication movements.

Church-multiplying movements and leadership. David Lim is from the Philippines. He says that *church-multiplication movements* have made indigenous leadership training successful in Asia. These movements focus on transformational mission and indigenous leadership development.

The rapid multiplication of churches—usually through church planting—characterizes Asian Christianity. These church-multiplication movements are sometimes called *insider movements*. This is because the multiplied churches are indigenous to their setting. So are their leaders.

David Garrison provides a comprehensive account of these church-planting movements. Here is a snapshot of his findings (this is in his own words):[24]

---

[23]Mitsuo Fukuda, "Empowering Fourth Generation Disciples: Grassroots Leadership Training in Japan and Beyond," in *Developing Indigenous Leaders: Lessons in Mission from Buddhist Asia*, ed. Paul H. De Neui (Pasadena, CA: William Carey, 2013), 61-62.

[24]The following is quoted directly from David Garrison's research, as presented in David Garrison, *Church Planting Movements: How God Is Redeeming a Lost World* (Richmond, VA: Wigtake, 2003) 35, 49, 65, 99, 123.

In Madhya Pradesh, a Church Planting Movement produces 4,000 new churches in less than seven years. In the 1990s, nearly 1,000 new churches are planted in Orissa with another 1,000 new outreach points. By 2001, a new church was being started every 24 hours. . . .

A Church Planting Movement in a northern Chinese province sees 20,000 new believers and 500 new churches started in less than five years. In Henan Province Christianity explodes from less than a million to more than five million in only eight years. Chinese Christians in Qing'an County of Heilongjiang Province plant 236 new churches in a single month. In southern China, a Church Planting Movement produces more than 90,000 baptized believers in 920 house churches in eight years time. In 2001, a newly emerging Church Planting Movement yields 48,000 new believers and 1,700 new churches in one year. . . .

During the decade of the nineties, Church Planting Movements in Outer Mongolia and Inner Mongolia produce more than 60,000 new believers. A Church Planting Movement transforms Cambodia's killing fields into fields of new life with more than 60,000 new Christians and hundreds of new churches planted over the past ten years. Despite government attempts to eliminate Christianity, a Church Planting Movement in one Southeast Asian country adds more than 50,000 new believers in five years. . . .

More Muslims have come to Christ in the past two decades than at any other time in history. A Central Asian Church Planting Movement sees 13,000 Kazakhs come to faith in Christ over a decade and a half. Up to 12,000 Kashmiri Muslims turn from jihad to the Prince of Peace. In an Asian Muslim country, more than 150,000 Muslims embrace Jesus and gather in more than 3,000 locally led Isa Jamaats (Jesus Groups). . . .

Every Saturday night, 18,000 youth line up to enter a stadium for worship in Bogotá, Colombia. Each week another 500 youth commit their lives to Christ and the core values of prayer, fasting, and holiness. During the week, they gather in 8,000 youth cell groups. Among the Kekchi people in remote Guatemala, evangelical Christianity grows from 20,000 believers to more than 60,000 in three decades. During the decade of the 1990s, Christians in a Latin American country overcame relentless government persecution to grow from 235 churches to more than 4,000 churches with a further 40,000 converts awaiting baptism.

Increasingly, these church plants focus on transformational mission. This involves the proclamation of the gospel. But it also involves the transformation of local communities through the pursuit of justice. This justice is often sought in the midst of oppression. It involves a distinct commitment to community development. And it also involves strengthening families and building better societies. These church plants are also focused on multiplying indigenous leaders. Such leaders dedicate themselves to multiplying churches and transforming local communities.

David Lim says that leadership development within church-multiplication movements is transformational. This is because it expresses servant leadership in three ways—it is holistic and contextual and empowering. By *holistic*, he means that this leadership development commits to transforming whole persons and whole families and whole communities. By *contextual*, he means that these movements shape leadership development around cultural forms of faith and leadership. By *empowering*, he means that it commits to equipping and releasing indigenous leaders. These homegrown leaders are empowered to transform communities and multiply churches.

These indigenous leaders experience "simple, people-centered, practical, contextual, and participatory" training. Even though the training is simple, the goals are extraordinary. For example, "The Filipino mission movement seeks to mobilize a million tentmakers to do this type of mission and [transformational leadership development] by 2020."[25]

The West can learn much from these indigenous disciple-making and church-multiplication movements. It is important that we learn from their simple and contextual approaches. Their whole-of-life approaches to *transformational leadership development* can guide us.

Missional movements and leadership. Recently, I spent time in Seoul, South Korea. I was ministering with All Nations Church. As I listened to the way this church multiplies disciples and churches throughout Asia, I felt like I was listening to stories from the book of Acts. The stories of people who had given up everything for the sake of mission in China, India, Russia, Myanmar, Thailand and Japan astonished me. I knew that I was witnessing a missional movement that's developing the next generation of global missional leaders.

---

[25]David S. Lim, "Developing Transformational Leaders for Church Multiplication Movements in the Buddhist World," in De Neui, *Developing Indigenous Leaders*, 101.

All Nations Church is pursuing a missional strategy soaked in prayer and discipleship and sacrifice. It's moved by a dream to see Asia won for Jesus Christ. Every day of the year, even in mid-winter when it is snowing and bitterly cold, teams of evangelists go out into the streets and from home to home. From a church that started ten years ago in a home with seventeen people, it now has over one thousand members. This is largely because of its missional endeavors. All Nations Church believes that God desires to bring revival to the nations. This is because he is a missionary God. They believe that this means that they must be a missionary community. They must multiply missional disciples and churches and leaders.

After sending hundreds of full-time missionaries throughout Asia, they have decided to go further afield in their mission. They now send missionaries to nations that once sent missionaries to Korea. Instead of summer camps, young adults go on annual short-term mission trips. These youth pray about whether God is calling them into full-time mission. All Nations Church has a vision to send another thousand full-time missionaries into these countries over the next decade. They want to have as many missionaries on the field as people currently attending their Sunday worship services.

All Nations Church in Seoul is a good example of a *missional church* that has become a *missional movement*. It releases thousands of *missional leaders* throughout the world.[26] And it is only one story among countless others across Asia, Africa, Eastern Europe and Latin America.

Roger D. Ibengi of the Democratic Republic of Congo calls pastors to missional leadership. He says that it is time for the church to reexamine its missional passion and practice. The church must know if these line up "with God's mission of reconciling all of humankind to himself. God has raised up leaders for the purpose of equipping and empowering the church to engage in mission. We need to see the world as God sees it and help others embrace the same vision of reaching the whole world with the gospel of Jesus Christ."[27] Ibengi says that leaders will never be missional until they become spiritual leaders with Christlike character. And only servant leadership

---

[26]See http://yulbang.or.kr/ and Graham Hill, *Salt, Light, and a City: Introducing Missional Ecclesiology* (Eugene, OR: Wipf and Stock, 2012), xv.

[27]Roger Ibengi and Richard L. Starcher, "Missional Leadership for the African Church," *Global Missiology English* 1, no. 9 (2011). No page numbers.

can be missional since our Messiah himself is a servant. We express spiritual leadership through integrity, prayer, mission and service.

SPIRITUAL LEADERSHIP

Ajith Fernando embodies spiritual leadership. *Christianity Today* recently ran a story on Fernando's life and ministry. He serves as the national director of Youth for Christ in Sri Lanka. Amid the poverty, drug abuse, violence, hatred and hostility of war-torn Sri Lanka, Fernando is a spiritual giant. He speaks to thousands in conferences around the world. But Fernando lives a simple life of service and mission among the wounded, impoverished and needy in Sri Lanka and other parts of Asia.

Tim Stafford of *Christianity Today* writes, "Everything Ajith Fernando writes and teaches is forged on the anvil of poverty, suffering, ethnic strife, and war—and tedious, patient administration. . . . Though he speaks all over the world, he carefully limits that to 20 percent of his time, with half in Asia. Where he lives and breathes and theologizes is Sri Lanka, with all its pain."[28]

Fernando says that we develop infectious passion and spiritual leadership as we travel down the road of frustration and suffering and pain.[29] He asserts that Christian spiritual leadership has distinct qualities. And he deals with these themes often in his books, articles, seminars and sermons. At its core, spiritual leadership is servant leadership. And spiritual leaders commit to the supremacy of Christ and his gospel. They identify with people (especially the broken, vulnerable, suffering and poor). The Holy Spirit empowers their ministries (the Spirit gives power and fullness for service). They regularly retreat from activity (for times of solitude, prayer, study and fasting). Spiritual leaders embrace servantship instead of drivenness, dominance, power and control (servanthood is a regular theme in his writings). They saturate themselves in Scripture (the Scriptures are our authority, strength, security, qualification and delight). They commit to bearing good news (Ajith Fernando says this is a whole-of-life enterprise—the scope of which I have outlined in the footnotes[30]).

---

[28]Tim Stafford, "The Choice," *Christianity Today* 56, no. 9 (2012): 44.
[29]Ajith Fernando, *Jesus Driven Ministry* (Wheaton, IL: Crossway, 2002), 25-26.
[30]For Fernando, *bearing good news* includes such things as (1) preaching the gospel, (2) relating to those of other faiths, (3) witnessing to Jesus Christ in our whole lives, (4) participating in God's mission in the world, (5) sharing the truth in love and (6) engaging in social justice, compassionate service and community development.

Spiritual leaders have other qualities. They grow in community and team and build deep spiritual friendships. They disciple the next generation of leaders. They launch disciples into ministry. They minister to the sick, demon-possessed, powerless, oppressed and silenced. Spiritual leaders speak truth to secular and religious powers. They grow through suffering, frustration, pain, grief and loss. They find spiritual and vocational fulfillment in service and sacrifice and difficulty. They cultivate a life of prayer. And spiritual leaders understand that prayer is a source of power in ministry, a prevention to burnout, a spring of spiritual vitality and "the basic feature of the ministerial life."[31] They commune with the suffering servant. And Jesus empowers spiritual leaders to serve him and his church and his world.

SERVANTSHIP AND THE GLOBALCHURCH: CONCLUDING REFLECTIONS

We have seen that servant leadership (servantship) has many dimensions. It's culturally specific and crosscultural. It's disciple making and church multiplying. It's missional. And its deep spirituality relies on the power and presence and provision of the Holy Spirit.

Here are six things we learn from how Majority World Christians practice servantship:

1. Servantship is biblical and it glorifies Jesus Christ. Hierarchical and domineering leadership is unbiblical. It pollutes and corrupts and erodes the church. It points away from Christ. And it degrades the church's worship and ministry and fellowship and witness. Autocratic and ego-driven leadership never brings glory to God.

Servantship is the imitation of Jesus Christ. It is imitation through love and service. Servantship does not dismiss notions of *leadership* or *servant*

---

[31]See Ajith Fernando, *Leadership Lifestyle*, Living Studies (Wheaton, IL: Tyndale House, 1985); Fernando, *Spiritual Living in a Secular World: Applying the Book of Daniel Today* (Grand Rapids: Zondervan Pub. House, 1993); Fernando, *Reclaiming Friendship: Relating to Each Other in a Frenzied World* (Scottdale, PA: Herald, 1993); Fernando, *The Supremacy of Christ* (Wheaton, IL: Crossway Books, 1995); Fernando, *Sharing the Truth in Love: How to Relate to People of Other Faiths* (Grand Rapids: Discovery House, 2001); Fernando, *Jesus Driven Ministry*; Fernando, *The Call to Joy & Pain: Embracing Suffering in Your Ministry* (Wheaton, IL: Crossway Books, 2007); Fernando, "To Serve Is to Suffer: If the Apostle Paul Knew Fatigue, Anger, and Anxiety in His Ministry, What Makes Us Think We Can Avoid Them in Ours?," *Christianity Today* 54, no. 8 (2010); Fernando, *Reclaiming Love* (Grand Rapids: Zondervan, 2013); Fernando, *An Authentic Servant: The Marks of a Spiritual Leader* (Peabody, MA: Hendrickson, 2012).

leadership altogether. But it does evaluate and reshape these concepts. It examines and reconceives notions of power and authority and influence.[32] Servantship cultivates a biblically-informed and practical theology of leadership. This theology engages our understandings of church, servanthood, discipleship, Jesus and mission.

Darrell Jackson is right when he says that Jesus reconceives status in the kingdom of God as bonded service.[33] Such service is "accompanied by the forfeiture of social status and personal freedom, and characterized by utter reliance on the one to whom bonded service was being rendered."[34] Servantship reflects the Spirit of Jesus Christ. This is especially true when servantship evidences the characteristics of servanthood revealed in Philippians 2:1-11 and other Scriptures. The metaphor of servanthood—and the servant mission and ministry of Jesus—must shape our practices of Christian servantship. Only then will it be Jesus-centered and outwardly focused Christian servantship.

In Philippians 2:7, we read that Jesus "made himself nothing." He emptied himself. True Christian service is movement away from selfish ambition and pride and self-centeredness. Such service is movement toward the same attitude as that of Jesus Christ. It's emptying oneself of pride, status and control over others. It's being a servant. And it's humbling oneself. Self-emptied discipleship is submission to the love, will and mission of God. "The ultimate characteristic of servantship is love leadership. I can serve people but not love them. However, I cannot love people and not serve them. The central point of the incarnation was love."[35]

We practice and reveal servantship through love. And it must be the kind of love demonstrated in the incarnation and at the cross. Servantship isn't an abstract or idealized love. It's concrete and embodied and tangible love. Petersen says that we must put our theology of the cross into practice. We do this by serving the poor and broken and marginalized and silenced and

---

[32]See the excellent treatment of servant leadership by Puerto Rican American theologian Efrain Agosto in *Servant Leadership*.

[33]Darrell Jackson, "For the Son of Man Did Not Come to Lead, but to Be Led: Matthew 20:20-28 and Royal Service," in Hill, *Servantship*, 28.

[34]Ibid.

[35]Roger Helland, "Nothing Leadership: The Locus of Missional *Servantship*," in Hill, *Servantship*, 36. Helland coined the terms *downward missional leadership* and *nothing leadership* to describe Christian leadership.

oppressed. Only then can we say that we love as Jesus loved. "God is present and active *in the midst of the Broken Ones*."[36] And such loving service is costly. You cannot practice loving service without heartbreak, suffering and loss. But our eternal joy is greater.

Why do Christian leaders embrace unbiblical, self-serving or controlling models of leadership? Sometimes they do this because of pride. And sometimes they do this because they've traded theology for pragmatics. Servantship demands biblically grounded and self-reflective theology. It demands ministry practices rooted in Trinitarian theology. It requires us to nourish our ministry practices with theologies of church and mission and ministry. *Servantship is only possible when it's rooted in the dynamic theological imagination of the people of God.* In other words, it thrives in an environment of theological thought and relational connection. It flourishes where God's people take Scripture seriously—including Christ's call to service and humility and love. This theological imagination is not restricted to the academy. It finds its fullest expression in a living conversation. This conversation must include scholars, leaders, churches, the gospel narrative, traditions, theologies and cultures. This theological imagination finds its fullest expression in conversation with the needs and challenges of specific contexts.

How do we move toward servantship? By truly wanting to glorify Christ and not ourselves. By exalting him and making ourselves nothing. By rejecting self-seeking and self-serving and domineering forms of leadership. By embracing the servanthood exemplified by Jesus Christ. By reflecting theologically on Scripture. And by meditating on passages like Philippians 2 and on the four Gospels. And by putting our biblical observations and convictions into practice.

Jesus described himself as a servant. So did the apostle Paul. Repeatedly, Scripture commands us to serve Jesus and his church and his world. Jesus drives us from control to service, from competition to love, from a scarcity mindset to a generous spirit, from pride to humility, from ambition to self-denial, from drivenness to servanthood, from ego strength to interdependent vigor, and from identification with the powerful to servantship "via the Broken Ones." "Whoever wants to become great among you must be

---

[36]Petersen and Swart, "Via the Broken Ones," 20. Italics added for emphasis.

your servant, and whoever wants to be first must be slave of all. For even the Son of Man did not come to be served, but to serve, and to give his life as a ransom for many" (Mk 10:43-45; cf. Mt 20:26-28).

Examining the biblical material, my friend and colleague Darrell Jackson forms a powerful conclusion:

> By redefining the concepts of greatness and status within the kingdom of God with reference to the hallmarks of service and humility, Jesus initiates a revolution of ruling and leadership. This is a vital insight for those who lead churches and Christian organizations. . . . Far from the throne-rooms and boardrooms, the "scum" of the earth (1 Corinthians 4:13) are exercising a ministry of service and humility that is frequently regarded with contempt, is typically accompanied by sacrificial suffering, yet which is capable of a revolution on a cosmic scale, for it is a call to royal service in a kingdom against which the gates of Hades will not prevail (Matthew 16:18).[37]

This biblical servantship is revolutionary. It redefines ruling and status and leadership. It glorifies our Lord Jesus Christ. Through poverty, tears, humility, righteousness, mercy, purity, peacemaking, suffering, love for enemies and the service of all, servantship witnesses to the kingdom of God among us (Mt 5–7). And it joins in Jesus' mission to heal and transform and redeem the world.

2. Servantship is sustained by a dynamic theology and lifestyle of service. This flows from the previous point. We need to develop a biblical theology of servantship. And we must shape this in a multifaceted and multivoiced way. We do this in conversation with theology, Scripture, contexts, traditions, cultures and so forth. And we do this in dialogue and service with "the least of these." My book *Servantship* makes a start on this theology of service and servantship. But much more work needs to be done.

Those of us in Christian leadership are rarely comfortable with service. We want to be "leaders," not "servants." So we try to soften the radical demands of servanthood with a hyphenated term like *servant-leadership*. That way we can still talk about servanthood, but take on the posture of leaders. We can wax lyrical about service, but pride ourselves on being leaders. We can avoid the revolutionary outlook and demands of servantship. "Over the

---

[37]Jackson, "For the Son of Man Did Not Come to Lead," 30-31.

past forty years the ides of servant leadership entered the church leadership discussion. But leaders could not bear the concept of 'servant-ship' as a stand-alone term. 'Leadership' had to be added to the equation. Being a servant is the form of leadership urged upon us by Jesus [and] the ethos of leadership is not a posture but a result."[38]

We bolster our servantship through a vibrant theology *and* lifestyle of service. We need to be careful not to turn a theology of servantship into a rigid ideology. When we do this, we grasp after ideological control and power. Instead, we will integrate our theology of servantship with a lifestyle of sacrificial service, gratuitous love, Spirit-empowered grace, deep relationships and genuine humility.[39] We will let our theology of servantship emerge from our lifestyle of service. And we will enrich our service through a vigorous theology of servantship.

3. Servantship is "shaped via the Broken Ones."[40] Remember that the Broken Ones "are not mere objects to be ignored, manipulated, and denigrated, but are the significant partners for an incipient understanding of leadership, shaped *via* an engagement with the Broken Ones in the midst of their circumstances of brokenness."[41]

Our servantship must transcend "typical center/edge stereotypes in the power relations of engagement with broken people." This way we learn what it means to serve as Christian leaders "via the Broken Ones." In other words, we will learn to serve via their courage, brokenness, resilience, voices and stories.[42] The people whom the world scorns and despises and sidelines teach us to serve. Who are those people in your culture?

Servantship is *soul work*. It's a process of personal transformation that we embrace as we serve with Jesus Christ and the Broken Ones in our society. Jesus transforms us as we become cocreators, cosufferers and coservers with him and his Broken Ones. "It is leadership formation via the presence of the Broken One in the midst of the Broken Ones."[43] It's time we saw the Broken

---

[38]Lance Ford, *Unleader: Reimagining Leadership . . . and Why We Must* (Kansas City: Beacon Hill, 2012), 85-86.
[39]Petersen and Swart, "Via the Broken Ones," 26.
[40]Ibid., 18.
[41]Ibid., 19.
[42]Ibid., 12.
[43]Ibid., 22.

Ones as gifts and graces to our communities and theologies and formation as servants.

4. Servantship is expressed in culturally sensitive and culturally contradicting ways. The GLOBE study of sixty-two cultures helps us understand how different societies conceive and practice leadership. Cultural attributes affect leader behaviors and organizational practices. Culture shapes what people value in their leaders' traits and behaviors and attitudes.

All cultures value certain things in leaders. These include integrity, vision, collaboration, diplomacy, communication, self-sacrifice, humility and modesty. Servantship enhances these things. This is because it makes us less ego driven and selfish and domineering. Servantship involves joining with Jesus Christ as he empowers and transforms people and organizations. It involves inviting people to join with Jesus in his vision for their lives, their organizations and the world. When we are servants of Christ and his church, we are able to provide Christ-honoring vision and transformation and empowerment. We put people before programs, service before ego, love before demands, well-being before results and human flourishing before productivity. We empower people and organizations to allow Christ's vision for their lives and the world to transform them.

The challenge is to express servantship in culturally sensitive ways. We need to respect culture. We don't want to be unaware of culture norms and expectations. Let me use an example. My Australian culture is individualistic and egalitarian. People treat leaders as friends. Australians have little regard for titles and honors and formal positions. So Australian Christian leaders need to build credibility with Australians over a long period based on character and competency. But when I minister in South Korea, for example, I don't want to offend people by my egalitarian ways. Korea is a collectivist, hierarchical and harmony-oriented culture. I need to respect that when I minister and serve there. I tailor my service to the people and church of Korea according to their culture.

But we also need to show servantship qualities that contradict the way that leadership is usually done. Jesus told his disciples not to act like the rulers of the Gentiles. Instead, he expected them to be servants. So what are the leadership behaviors and postures in your culture that the gospel calls you to contradict? Some things emerge in most cultures (e.g., ego, dominance, and self-seeking and self-serving behaviors). But there may be particular leadership expectations, behaviors and postures in your culture that you will challenge through your life as much as your words. The good news is that in all cultures people want their leaders to show qualities that servantship enhances.

5. Servantship multiplies missional leaders and congregations. We see this repeatedly in the Majority World. I've provided examples in this chapter. These missional leaders and congregations have key characteristics. They're homegrown and indigenous to their cultures. And they're committed to disciple making and church multiplication and mission. What's the result? We see the astonishing growth in Majority World churches. We see an extraordinary multiplication of churches. And we see missional movements multiplying throughout Asia, Africa, Eastern Europe and Latin America.

6. Servantship is at the heart of Christian spirituality, and Christian spirituality is essential to servantship. Petersen, Fernando, Ibengi and other Majority World leaders make it clear that servantship is at the heart of Christian spirituality. Jesus makes this clear in the Gospels too. Servantship enriches and enlarges Christian spirituality. As we serve Jesus and his church and his world, our spiritual lives expand. In John 13, Jesus washes his disciples' feet. He shows them what discipleship and Christian spirituality looks like. It's a life of service. "Now that I, your Lord and Teacher, have washed your feet, you also should wash one another's feet. I have set you an example that you should do as I have done for you" (Jn 13:14-15).

Conversely, Christian spirituality is essential to servantship. The two are synergistic. They're the two sides of one coin. They're mutually sustaining and enriching.

I've arrived at a conviction. It emerges from reading biographies about (and books by) indigenous and Majority World spiritual leaders. I'm convinced that we cultivate Christian spirituality through *practices*. These practices give us internal and external resources that enable us to serve Jesus and his church and his world. We work out these practices individually and in community. These are practices in the world (such as when we are serving) and in the "secret place" of prayer and reflection.

Here are some of the practices I've formed in my life. These deepen my servantship. You'll form your own practices. I don't list these to suggest that

I've "arrived" spiritually. Far from it. But hopefully this list will provide an initial guide for you as you develop your own practices that enhance your life of service.

Engaging with God in service and mission. For me, this means making a clear commitment to living a missional lifestyle within a missional community. It means actively seeking to serve Christ's church—local and global. Here's an example: I look for opportunities to take my children with me into Asia to serve among the world's poorest communities. And I look for opportunities to connect with people in my local neighborhood. And I seek to share my faith with my nonbelieving family members and friends.

Worshiping in community, keeping a Sabbath and getting adequate rest. Genuine spiritual formation happens in community. It is not a solitary affair. We must share our lives with others to grow spiritually. This involves prayer, fellowship, service, worship and doing mission together. How many pastors and leaders neglect a Sabbath? How many neglect a day off? How many get adequate rest, and take time for *re-creation*? I take a Sabbath every week. No ministry happens on this day. My mentor and wife and ministry peers keep me accountable for this.

Accountability relationships. I meet once a fortnight with another pastor who is my accountability peer. We keep each other accountable in the areas of spirituality, sexuality, finances, ministry struggles and so on.

Spiritual mentoring. Spiritual growth requires help and guidance. I meet with a spiritual mentor six times per year. He asks me tough questions about my spiritual life and family relationships and ministry.

Prayer with a partner. If you are married, engaged or dating, it is important to pray daily with your partner. Praying together encourages personal and relational and spiritual growth. I also pray with my children.

Small group accountability. I meet once every six weeks with a group of pastors for accountability. We ask each other direct questions about our spiritual lives and our ministry and personal integrity. We also keep each other accountable in the areas of sexuality, marriage, finances, rest, recreation, personal and professional growth, and so on. My wife and I are also in a monthly home group with eight other couples.

Prioritizing family. It is too easy to neglect our families in ministry. Far too easy. And far too common. Like most other Christian leaders, I fall into this trap. Because of this, I am committed to prioritizing my family. This means blocking out quality time each day for my marriage and children.

Daily prayer. I shut my door for an hour every day to pray—either at home or in my office. I pray and reflect on Psalms and other Christian Scriptures. I also pray while reading spiritual classics and devotional works. My great-grandfather was a missionary to Sydney. When I was six years old, I remember staying at his house. He would get up at five o'clock every morning for at least an hour of prayer. His example has stayed with me for life.

Daily reading. Spiritual growth involves a commitment to daily reading. My commitment is to read at least an hour per day. Eugene Peterson has a useful list in his book *Take and Read.*[44] I read a lot of Christian writing coming out of Asia and Africa and Latin America. I want other cultures—and spiritual leaders from other contexts—to stretch my thinking and practices. See suggested reading in the study guide.

Regular spiritual retreats. I retreat once every six months, even if only for a day. Weekend retreats of silence and prayer are refreshing and challenging. My favorite retreat setting is the Benedictine Abbey in Jamberoo, Australia.[45]

Accumulate spiritual mentors. These can be living mentors and spiritual leaders from the past. Some of my mentors include Teresa of Avila, John of the Cross, Augustine, Thomas á Kempis, John Calvin, Jonathan Edwards, John Bunyan, William Gurnall, C. S. Lewis, Ignatius of Loyola, Thomas Merton, Walter Brueggemann, Dallas Willard, Eugene Peterson, Henri Nouwen, Gregory the Great, Hans Urs von Balthasar and Karl Barth. For non-Western Christian mentoring I turn to *The Philokalia* (three volumes). I also consult Ajith Fernando and Gregory of Nyssa and Edmund Chan.

Financial generosity. I include this as a spiritual discipline. It keeps me spiritually fit in an important area of spirituality—generosity and stewardship and contentment. This includes a commitment to living simply and giving more away.

Spiritual journaling. I keep a journal that records my journey with God. I record what he is saying to me and how he is leading and changing me. This is an avenue to open my soul to his grace and guidance and love.

---

[44] Eugene H. Peterson, *Take and Read: Spiritual Reading; An Annotated List* (Grand Rapid: Eerdmans, 1996).

[45] See the Jamberoo Abbey website, www.jamberooabbey.org.au.

Bodily exercise and fasting. Neglect of these areas is common in ministry. I walk our dog for thirty minutes to an hour most days. My wife and I go to the gym together a few times each week. I fast regularly for health and prayer (at least one day per month).

Servantship is crucial to Christian spirituality. And Christian spirituality is vital to servantship. These are interdependent. One cannot exist without the other.

As we seek to be servants, we remember the example and words of Jesus:

> You call me "Teacher" and "Lord," and rightly so, for that is what I am. Now that I, your Lord and Teacher, have washed your feet, you also should wash one another's feet. I have set you an example that you should do as I have done for you. Very truly I tell you, servants are not greater than their master, nor are messengers greater than the one who sent them. Now that you know these things, you will be blessed if you do them. (Jn 13:13-17)

RECOVERING COMMUNITY

*The [church is] the community of the faithful in communion with the
Father, through the incarnate Son, in the Holy Spirit, and in communion
with each other. . . . The trinitarian vision produces a vision of the church
that is more communion than hierarchy, more service than power, more
circular than pyramidal, more loving embrace than bending knee before
authority. . . . Then the church would in fact be "a people made one with
the unity of the Father, the Son, and the Holy Spirit."*

LEONARDO BOFF

The photo agency Majority World is more than just an innovative business
enterprise. And it's more than an international gathering of talented photographers. It's a social enterprise that brings together photographers from
Asia, Africa, Latin America and the Middle East. It invests in these artists
and provides them with a global platform. These photographers take extraordinary pictures. They photograph "local cultures, development issues,
environments, and contemporary lifestyles in these diverse continents."[1]

Through photography, these artists and communities tell their stories.
They break Western stereotypes and address Western blindness to the

---

[1]Shahidul Alam, "Headers and Snippets," *ShahidulNews* (blog), www.shahidulnews.com; see also
www.majorityworld.com.

creativity and talent in non-Western contexts. Through their artistic works, they contribute toward economic development in the Majority World. They also show intriguing dimensions of their cultures. Their photography spans culture, indigenous peoples, environment, business and industry. The pictures cover architecture, sanitation, festivals and religion. They also document daily life, health, education, agriculture, fisheries and travel.

The themes of community and relationship run through these photographs. This is also true of Majority World theological literature, ministry training and church contexts. For example, Mmutlanyane Stanley Mogoba says that community and relationships are central to an African worldview. They are the key features of African theology, philosophy, society, political theory and church.[2]

The pictures on the Majority World website show people in vibrant cultures and communities and relationships. The relationships are central and diverse and complex and manifold. These are relationships with the environment, architecture, culture, religion, communities, families and the sacred.

Relationship is the dominant theme in these pictures. It infuses and permeates this exquisite photography. Here are examples. An ethnic Hazara girl carries her younger sibling on her back in Bamyan Province, Afghanistan. A young Afghan girl cradles her siblings in her arms in the same province. Children play in a mustard field in Singair, Bangladesh. Children frolic in a timber yard in the Amazon region, Bolivia. A Guatemalan Indian woman and her daughter grind coffee together in Chichicastenango. Mothers in Plaza De Mayo, Argentina, gather to demand justice for relatives abducted and murdered by the military dictatorship. A Naga family gather on a hillside for a simple meal in Nagaland. A large Thai family run a food stall in the floating markets of Bangkok. Floodwaters trap a family in Dhaka, Bangladesh, while dozens of other families canoe down the same flooded river looking for a new place on the riverbank to call home. Family members of a Palanquin porters group huddle together, eating and laughing and waiting for the next wedding. Kashmiri college girls rally to demand environmental and social justice in Kashmir,

---

[2]Mmutlanyane Stanley Mogoba, "Christianity in a Southern African Context," *Journal of Theology for Southern Africa* 52 (1985): 9-10.

India. A group of conservationists and wildlife officers and indigenous Acehnese collaborate to check on the health of Sumatran tigers in Aceh Province, Indonesia.

In one of my favorite pictures, hundreds of ethnic Karen gather in villages on the Thai-Burmese border. They feast, wear colorful traditional outfits, celebrate Christmas, worship Christ and enjoy community. And they do this every night from the first of December to Christmas day. I remember spending time in those villages with my daughter Madison. We were amazed how these strong social relationships sustained them through persecution and displacement.

The photography is beautiful. The relationships depicted are vital and profound. Western churches and families need to rediscover such community. We need to recover *relationship* as the heart of human fullness and well-being. "The person is a being with a heart, one who has the capacity to be open to attraction by another, to be in communication and interpersonal communion with another, others, and God. This is what distinguishes us as persons: The capacity to be toward others in a relation of one, mutual Love."[3]

In this chapter, I discuss the need to shape churches characterized by community. I show how Christian theology helps us grasp the relationship between human nature and community. And I indicate how trinitarian theology helps us grasp the relationship between God's nature and the church's mission and community. From there, I consider lessons for Western churches. This chapter asks, *What can we learn from how Majority World Christians value community and relationship?*

THEOLOGY, HUMANITY AND COMMUNITY

Communion is a theme that runs through Majority World and indigenous writings on the church. The church is not made up of autonomous and independent individuals. God calls the church to communion. This communion is among humans. And it's with the Father and Son and Holy Spirit. Gustavo Gutiérrez, for example, develops the theme of community in his writings. He associates interpersonal and human-divine communion with key theological themes:

---

[3]Michael Downey, *Altogether Gift: A Trinitarian Spirituality* (Maryknoll, NY: Orbis, 2000), 70.

Salvation—the communion of human beings with God and among themselves—is something which embraces all human reality.[4]

In the final analysis, to set free is to give life—communion with God and
with others—or, to use the language of Puebla, liberation for communion
and participation.[5]

Liberation . . . is a journey toward communion. Communion, however, is
a gift of Christ who sets us free in order that we may be free, free to love; it is
in this communion that full freedom resides.[6]

Christian theology emphasizes the communion of human beings with
God and each other and associates such communion with the nature of
humans and God and the church. In Christian theology, humans are created
beings. God creates us in his image. We're sexual, physical, embodied and
relational beings. We're not self-sufficient. We're profoundly relational. We
are essentially and completely *persons-in-relationship*—from and for God
and others (Gen 1:26-27). In Christian anthropology, to be an integrated and
authentic self is to be in relationship. The person doesn't simply have relationships. The person *is* relationship. God forms us from "dust"—not as a
closed historical event, but as a relational process (Gen 2:7). We're fashioned
from clay by our Creator at our conception. And our entire lives are a testimony to the relational process of renewal and creative Divine genius. To
be a creature is to be shaped by God from nothing. It's to be birthed into a
process of being. God calls and creates us. He does this so that we might
fulfill our God-ordained purpose. Our purpose is to glorify him through
our relational being and capacities.

God continually and lovingly creates human beings. We're firmly located
within creation. And the created order is a relational order. Nicholas Lash, in
Believing Three Ways in One God, writes, "What makes the doctrine of createdness good news is the discovery that God makes the world 'parentally.'"[7]
We experience the parental nurture, interpersonal communion and love of

[4]Gustavo Gutiérrez, *A Theology of Liberation: History, Politics, and Salvation* (Maryknoll, NY: Orbis, 1988), 85.

[5]Gustavo Gutiérrez, *We Drink from Our Own Wells: The Spiritual Journey of a People* (Maryknoll, NY: Orbis, 1984), 92.

[6]Gustavo Gutiérrez, *The Truth Shall Make You Free: Confrontations* (Maryknoll, NY: Orbis, 1990), 103.

[7]Nicholas Lash, *Believing Three Ways in One God: A Reading of the Apostles' Creed* (Notre Dame: University of Notre Dame Press, 1993), 43.

God. We experience these in our createdness and our embodiment. (Here I am referring to our experience of these in our creation, through the person and work of Christ and a myriad of other ways.) God continually forms and sustains creation parentally. Human beings, as part of creation, enjoy the filial care and concern of the Creator Father.

We're often deluded by visions of grandeur, independence, control and self-sufficiency. Western understandings of self often encourage us to view ourselves this way. But we aren't self-made. We're not independent. We're not in control. We're continually created out of the abundance of God's immeasurable love and grace and power. We're connected with God and others as relational and created and interdependent beings.

The incarnation affirms humans as created, relational beings—as persons-in-relationship. In the incarnation, God elevates the created order by his grace. He comes into our context to redeem and heal. The incarnation affirms the value of creation and humanity and relationship. In the incarnation Jesus Christ reveals his ongoing relationship to creation and to humanity. Christ willingly and lovingly immerses himself in creation. He engages time and space and flesh and matter. He takes on human form. And he lovingly meets, touches and values persons, each one created in his relational image to be essentially, utterly relational. Christ's incarnation shows his passion for the trinitarian relations. And it shows his desire for relationship with us. Human beings yearn for relationship with each other and God. Christ has enabled this through creation and incarnation and death and resurrection.

God's ongoing creative activity and incarnational presence sustain a Christ-dependent world. This world is in real, dependent relationship with the triune God. (This is the case even though the Creator is distinct from the world and though the world is in rebellion from him.) God is in ongoing relationship with creation, which includes humanity. He reveals creation's future—a kingdom of glory and praise and relationship with him. Humanity, as part of creation, glorifies God along with the rest of creation. Our glorification of the triune God is an interpersonal outpouring of love and communion. This is the movement toward self-transcendence to which personal development models refer. Communion with God and others draws us away from self-centeredness. It enables us to focus on the God who is beyond us. It liberates us to connect with other human beings and with creation.[8]

We open ourselves to God to live in his creative love, to put off self and to make him the new center of our beings. We desire his life to flow through us. We want this divine life to express itself in the newness and wholeness of our lives. We grow personally, then, when we let go of self. We grow as we embrace God and others. Through relationship with God and others, we grow in love, compassion, humility and interdependence.

The doctrines of creation and incarnation, then, tell us much. They show us that human beings have relationship at the center of their beings. "Relationships are constitutive of who and all that we are. We are unthinkable outside of relationship. Outside of the God relationship, and relationships with others, we are nothing. We are no-thing. We would not exist."[9] In one sense, our divine purpose to glorify God and experience union with him is beyond the world. Yet we're now completely and relationally in the world. So being human means that we express our bodiliness and sexuality and relationality in the world. That's why we're responsible for (and influenced by) families, relationships, ecologies, societies and creation. Embodiment, personhood, world and history are relational concepts. They're knit together in the interdependent web of all created things. They take shape after their relational Creator God and are interconnected whether they're beautiful or mundane or horrifying.

This interpersonal and mutually responsible relatedness means that we aren't only located in creation. We have a responsibility to nurture and heal and restore it (after God's will and kingdom). We follow the mission of Christ. We seek the restoration of creation, persons, bodies, cultures, societies and communities. We do this in dependent communion with God and interdependent relationship with others. And we do this for the glory of the Father and Son and Holy Spirit.

Consider the brilliant photography, social contribution and economic impact of the Majority World photographers. What do we see here and in

---

[8]W. Norris Clarke, "To Be Is to Be Self-Communicative: St. Thomas' View of Personal Being," *Theology Digest* 33 (1986): 450-53.
[9]Michael Jackson, "Th568 Lecture Notes: The Christian Understanding of Person in the Light of the Doctrines of Creation and the Trinity," course notes (The University of Notre Dame, Fremantle, Australia, 2002), 4.

other such enterprises? We notice that we can shape our lives and communities by taking part in what God is doing around us. This is an important and relational dimension of the hopeful expectation of human existence. We take part in God's loving and restoring activity in creation—in bodies, families, social systems, the world and human history.

Ultimately, we take part in God's redemption—and experience wholeness—in relationship with him and others. Our theologies of creation, incarnation, the Trinity, humanity, mission, salvation and the church tell us that we are fundamentally *persons-in-relationship*.

TRINITY, MISSION AND COMMUNITY

Trinitarian theology is popular in the East and in other Majority World settings. For many Majority World theologians, it shapes their understanding of the church. Theologians who exemplify this include Jung Young Lee, James Henry Owino Kombo, Nozomu Miyahira, Miroslav Volf, John Zizioulas, Ricardo Barbosa de Sousa, Simon Chan, Leonardo Boff, Damon So, Athanasius, Gregory of Nazianzus and Basil the Great (see the Cappadocian Fathers).[10]

What do we learn from these authors about trinitarian and human community? Unity and oneness permeate the Trinity. The triune God *is* relations.[11] The people of God are the beneficiaries of the relationship of love and intimacy and communion between the persons of the Godhead. Jesus' redemptive mission springs from his love for the Father. It flows from his longing to fulfill his Father's will. In the Godhead, we see the highest example of self-sacrifice and mutual dedication. Three divine Persons exist in perfect harmony and unity. They share the same divine faculties and power and holiness and perfection and love.[12]

To be human is to be in the grip of God's grace. God moves us toward union with him. He draws us to interpersonal communion with him. In the Trinity, we see a dynamic process of self-giving and self-communicating and

---

[10]Whether Miroslav Volf is Western or not is debatable. Although he's Eastern European (Croatian), he trained very much in a Western tradition from his early days. Peter Kuzmic and Jürgen Moltmann have influenced Volf's trinitarian theology. John Zizioulas has spent much of his life in Western settings too, but his Eastern Orthodox theology distinguishes it from Western trinitarian thought.

[11]David S. Cunningham, *These Three Are One: The Practice of Trinitarian Theology* (London: Blackwell, 1997), 71.

[12]Graham Hill, *Salt, Light, and a City: Introducing Missional Ecclesiology* (Eugene, OR: Wipf and Stock, 2012), 233-35.

self-reciprocating love. This love penetrates the essence and relations of the Trinity. And this trinitarian love draws us in as beneficiaries and participants. This love shapes our being and personhood. And it makes us essentially relational and dependent on divine and human relationship.[13] It's the reason for our yearning for the other. It's the source of our desire for God. It's the cause of our hopelessness (or struggle for meaning) outside loving communion and community.

The intradivine communion within the person of God gives rich meaning and theological depth to the idea of *person-in-relationship*. God is a dialogical, communing being. He exists in intradivine relationship. This understanding of the nature of God uncovers the true nature of humanity. We are relational and interdependent. The trinitarian relationships reveal human nature. They explain our profound yearning for others and our desire for the triune God.

Human beings do not consist of a closed self. We exist in relation to others and God. Our interior lives reflect the nature of the Trinity. Moreover, the whole human self corresponds to the divine substance. (There are, of course, limitations to the correspondence.) The whole of our being is relational. We reflect (imperfectly and in a creaturely way) the Trinity.[14] Where do we see human yearnings for divine-human communion and grace and relationship? We see it in the desire for deeper relationship and community. We see it in the frustration about the inadequacy of everything acquired and achieved. We see it in modern and ancient spiritual quests. We see it in the radical protest against loneliness and death. These urges are relational urges. Much human suffering is the direct result of alienation and isolation.

At our core, we're interpersonal, relational and intersubjective. The triune God creates us in his relational image. He enjoys perfect relationship and love and communion. He invites us into this divine communion and into relationship with others. Communion with the Divine and with other persons is the means of salvation. There is no gospel, no saving truth, outside of a relationship with the Trinity and his people. And relationship is the means of fulfilled and authentic and integrated living and selfhood. "The

---

[13]Ibid., 257-60.
[14]Joseph Ratzinger, "Retrieving the Tradition: Concerning the Notion of Person in Theology" *Communio* 17 (1990): 444.

core of our integration as a person requires union with the God who is the ground of our being. Integration and spiritual wholeness involves living out of that union. Firstly, it's union with the Trinity. Then it's union with others."[15]

We shape missional churches and practices with attention to two things: First, we allow the interior life of the Trinity—*the social or immanent Trinity*—to shape our imagination and aims and relations. Second, the acts, roles and purposes of the trinitarian Persons in history—*the economic Trinity*—define our theology and gospel and mission. I put some focus on this in the seventeenth chapter of my first volume on missional ecclesiology, *Salt, Light, and a City*. The social reality of the Trinity has potential for helping us appreciate the social community of the church. The correspondence is important. But as Croatian theologian Miroslav Volf reminds us, the analogy has both benefits and limitations.[16]

Likewise, the functions of each member of the Trinity in the mission of God help us understand the missional nature of the church. The Trinity allows us to take part in "creation, re-creation, and final consummation."[17] The sending activity and the missional nature of the triune God are the source of the church's mission. The Father sends the Son. The Father and Son send the Spirit. And the Trinity sends the church into the world. "This perspective helps us understand the creation of a church in light of God's being, God's social reality as a Trinity, and the work of all three persons. The ministry of the church, in turn, must reflect all three aspects of the Godhead."[18]

Leonardo Boff has written extensively on this. He describes the relationship between the Trinity and the church's mission and community and structures and liberative actions. For Boff, the Trinity is the model of perfect community and of social liberation. Through the doctrine of the Trinity, Boff dismantles authoritarian notions. He deconstructs ideas that support centralized power. He attacks nontrinitarian monotheistic models of church. Instead, in trinitarian theology Boff finds resources for diversity in communion. He also finds inspiration for liberating relationships and missional passion.

---

[15]Jackson, "Th568 Lecture Notes," 5.

[16]Miroslav Volf, *After Our Likeness: The Church as the Image of the Trinity* (Grand Rapids: Eerdmans, 1998), 198-200.

[17]Craig Van Gelder, *The Essence of the Church: A Community Created by the Spirit* (Grand Rapids: Baker, 2000), 35, 97.

[18]Ibid., 130.

First, trinitarian communing with others involves *presence one to another.* This is a communicative and relational openness. Second, it requires *reciprocity.* This is generous and self-sacrificial giving and receiving. Third, it demands *immediacy.* This is "intimacy, transparency of intention, union of hearts, and convergence of interests," as well as forming "bonds of communion." Fourth, trinitarian communing with others needs *community.* By that, I mean the formation of a communing people. Fifth, it involves *being-in-openness.* "Only a being open to others can communicate with, relate to, and build up a community with other, con-natural beings." Sixth, trinitarian communing with others includes *being-in-transcendence.* This is reaching beyond oneself for the sake of communion with others and doing this to establish "bonds of interdependence." Lastly, trinitarian communing with others enables *being-us.* This means allowing communing to create real community. This isn't just visible community—it's "a mode of being." Through this community, we choose to become differentiated but also "part of a single whole."[19]

This leads us to the trinitarian ground of mission. It takes us to the trinitarian foundations of the missional and liberating life of the church. The communion and mission of the Trinity are inextricably linked. We cannot consider them as separate dimensions of God. Nor can we consider communion and mission to be separate realities shaping disconnected dimensions of the church. This is because the mission of the triune God is to bring humanity back into communion with the Father and Son and Holy Spirit.

Moreover, the communion within the triune God is the source or wellspring of his divine mission. And the triune God directs his mission toward his divine communion. In other words, *the communion of the triune God is the mission of the triune God. And the mission of the triune God is the communion of the triune God.* Again, God's being-in-communion is God's being-on-mission. And God's being-on-mission is God's being-in-communion. A missional understanding of the church claims that the church reflects this trinitarian dynamic. The church's being-in-communion is the church's being-on-mission, and vice versa.

---

[19]Leonardo Boff, "Trinitarian Community and Social Liberation," *Cross Currents* 38, no. 3 (1988): 293-95. See also Boff, *Trinity and Society* (Maryknoll, NY: Orbis, 1988); Boff, *Holy Trinity, Perfect Community* (Maryknoll, NY: Orbis, 2000).

For the church, there's no true communion without mission and no true mission without communion.

Scripture doesn't allow for a mission that is separate from a community on mission. And it doesn't allow for a community that is separate from a missional community.[20] Moreover, a truly participative community, modeled after the trinitarian relations, must be vivified and empowered by the Spirit. The Spirit shapes a communing and missional people in the image of the Trinity.[21]

This leaves us with an important question: How can we cultivate a community of Trinity-imaging relationships? I've discussed the importance of shaping churches characterized by meaningful relationships. I've talked about how crucial it is that our churches show Trinity-imaging mission and communion. I now turn to the concrete lessons Majority World thinkers teach us.

COMMUNITY AND THE GLOBALCHURCH: CONCLUDING REFLECTIONS

Building community is not easy. Individualism is deeply entrenched in Western cultures. Our churches are often embroiled in conflict and division. Yet we must *be* communities of faith that enrich lives and nurture relationships and show Jesus' love. We must witness to Jesus through our love and humility and unity.

The church will experience community and engage in effective mission when it practices *koinonia*. *Koinonia* is the deep, intimate, participatory and communing fellowship believers experience with each other and with God. The word appears nineteen times in the Greek New Testament. We can translate it as "fellowship," "sharing," "joint participation," "contribution" or "communion."

Here are eight things we learn from how Majority World Christians value community and relationship:

1. **Koinonia** *churches emphasize relational discipleship and spirituality.* Western cultures are individualistic. Western Christians absorb this individualism. It permeates Western Christian spirituality. But humans are inherently social, and Christian spirituality thrives in deep communion with God and others.

---

[20]Hill, *Salt, Light, and a City*, 233-35.
[21]Miroslav Volf, "Community Formation as an Image of the Triune God: A Congregational Model of Church Order and Life," in *Community Formation: In the Early Church and in the Church Today*, ed. Richard N. Longenecker (Peabody, MA: Hendrickson, 2002), 235.

Jesus confronts unhelpful and destructive forms of spirituality. These are individualistic and independent. They're vain and privatized. They're disembodied and self-justifying. They're legalistic. They're immoral and idolatrous. They're hostile and given to bitter conflict. They're jealous and enjoy disunity. They're conceited and envious.

True discipleship builds relationships up. It fosters community. It glorifies Christ. It enjoys faith and hope and love. Alone or in relationship, Christian spirituality shows love and joy and peace. It's patient, kind and good; it's faithful, gentle and self-controlled (Gal 5:13-26). It values and nurtures relationships and communities.

Authentic spirituality desires communion with God and others. It's located and nurtured in authentic and local community. Within community, authentic Christian spirituality experiences personal growth and integration. In community, it grows in Christlikeness and holiness and love. Through community, it grows in compassion, faith, hope and conversion. The primary forum for these things is relationship. Relationship is the hub of this spiritual expression of growth and development.

2. Koinonia churches embark on "a journey toward communion." Gustavo Gutiérrez reminds us that communion with God and others is a divine gift. Such communion is "a gift of Christ who sets us free in order that we may be free, free to love; it is in this communion that full freedom resides."[22] God frees us by his grace—in all areas of life—so that we can embark on a "journey toward communion" with him and others.[23] Our communion with God and other human beings is often less than ideal. But we need to remember that communion is a grace. And we are on a journey. We'll know complete and perfect communion with God and others at the end of the age. Our responsibility now is to keep in step with the Spirit on this journey toward communion.

3. Koinonia churches emulate the trinitarian relations. Many Majority World theologians assert that the church must imitate the trinitarian communion. We need to allow the mission, love, intimacy, community and unity of the Trinity to be a model for our mission and fellowship.

Craig Van Gelder claims that "a trinitarian understanding is now the common starting point for thinking about God's people in the world, about

---

[22]Gutiérrez, *Truth Shall Make You Free*, 103.
[23]Ibid, 106.

the church, and about how the church participates in God's mission in the world."[24] I agree with Van Gelder when he asserts that ecclesiology and missiology aren't only "interrelated and complementary." They're both grounded in the doctrine of the Trinity. They both find their source in "the Triune God in mission to all creation."[25]

The interior life of the Trinity can help us understand the nature and potential of communion among God's people. The love, intimacy, unity and embrace of the members of the Trinity provide a model or analogy for the church. Here I'm referring to the notion of the immanent (ontological) Trinity.

Volf reminds us that there are ways in which ecclesial communion corresponds to trinitarian communion. And there are limitations to the analogy. Volf's trinitarian ecclesiology affects his understanding of communion within local churches. It shapes his understanding of human personhood. It defines his theology of ecclesial relationships. The Trinity is his determining analogy for the nature and structures and relations and ministries and mission of the church. I believe that Volf is right when he says that that the trinitarian analogy should shape the church. It can shape our church's self-understanding and life together. It can deepen our love. It can help us navigate the complexities and paradoxes of unity and multiplicity as we seek to *image the Trinity*.[26] The love and communion between Christians and churches should correspond, as far as possible, to the trinitarian relations.

4. **Koinonia** *churches embrace distinctive qualities.* Boff outlines the qualities of churches that imitate the trinitarian relations. Individual Christians can cultivate these virtues too. These churches nurture presence, reciprocity, immediacy and community. What does this mean? Boff says that Trinity-imaging Christians (1) are present to one another. (They do this through communicative and relational openness.) (2) They embrace reciprocity. (They do this through generous and self-sacrificial giving and receiving.) (3) They pursue immediacy. (They do this through "intimacy, transparency of intention, union of hearts, convergence of interests," and "bonds of communion".) (4) And they develop authentic community. They are singularly focused in their formation of a communing and missional people.

---

[24]Van Gelder, *Essence of the Church*, 11.
[25]Ibid., 31.
[26]Volf, *After Our Likeness*, 194-97.

What other qualities do we observe? (5) Trinity-imaging churches cultivate *self-in-relationship*. There is no self without relationship. These churches recognize this, so they prioritize and nurture deep relationships. (6) They nurture *being-in-openness*. This means being truly open to others. (7) They foster *being-in-transcendence*. This involves reaching beyond themselves for the sake of communion with others. They establish "bonds of interdependence." (8) They encourage *being-us*. This means being differentiated but also "part of a single whole."[27]

5. Koinonia *churches practice extravagant welcome and hospitality.* Ruth Padilla DeBorst drives this point home. We must be churches and homes and families "at which immigrants, people of diverse cultural backgrounds and different languages are welcome, not as oddities or welfare cases, but as fully fledged members."[28] We replace exclusion with embrace, hostility with love, prejudice with respect, judgment with grace, greed with generosity, envy with contentment, fear with hope, rejection with welcome, frigidity with warmth, and isolation with community and hospitality. We do this *in response* to the extravagant grace and welcome offered to us by Jesus Christ. And we do this *as witnesses* to Christ and the coming age. He's our peace. He reconciled us to God and to each other.

> Consequently, you are no longer foreigners and strangers, but fellow citizens with God's people and also members of his household, built on the foundation of the apostles and prophets, with Christ Jesus himself as the chief cornerstone. In him the whole building is joined together and rises to become a holy temple in the Lord. And in him you too are being built together to become a dwelling in which God lives by his Spirit. (Eph 2:19–22)

On the final day, Jesus Christ will gather a great multitude from "every nation, tribe, people, and language" to worship him (Rev 7:9-17). The welcome and hospitality we practice now reflects what he has already done and what he is going to do in the age to come.

6. Koinonia *churches generate* communitas. *Communitas* is a significant term for understanding Christian community. It's an anthropological idea that has implications for the church and its community and mission.

---

[27]Boff, "Trinitarian Community and Social Liberation," 293-95.
[28]Ruth Padilla DeBorst, "'Unexpected' Guests at God's Banquet Table: Gospel in Mission and Culture," *Evangelical Review of Theology* 33, no. 1 (2009): 75-76.

Victor and Edith Turner developed their understandings of *communitas* while studying groups and rites of passage in indigenous and Majority World cultures. Victor Turner was a cultural anthropologist studying indigenous people groups. He described *communitas* as the profound community spirit, social solidarity and togetherness felt by groups going through change and transition. This is a *liminal* experience. Groups experience *liminality* when they're going through transition. Liminality is the disorienting and ambiguous stage between *what a group was* and *what it is becoming*. Liminality alters their social relationships. Their sense of meaning and identity shifts. The experience enriches their spirituality, community and shared identity. During the phases of transition, these groups experience uncertainty and fear, fresh courage, revived rites of passage, new meanings, common mission, and deep interconnectedness. They experience community in fresh and profound ways. They experience a renewal of social cohesion, shared values and fresh group identity.[29]

In 2012, Edith Turner produced a full treatment of *communitas*. She provided fascinating examples from all over the world.[30] Victor and Edith Turner suggest that Western cultures can learn much from liminality and *communitas* in Majority World and indigenous cultures. I believe that this is especially true for the church during periods of change and upheaval and transition. God draws his church into sacred covenant and intimate communion through periods of liminality. He leads his church into *communitas* and *koinonia*. God then sends the church into the world as a sign and foretaste and witness to the gospel, to the kingdom and to trinitarian communion.

7. **Koinonia** *churches cultivate spiritual friendships.* Ajith Fernando believes that we need to retrieve the Christian tradition of spiritual friendship. Such friendship builds authentic community. We need to develop spiritual friendships marked by love, prayer, vulnerability, commitment, forgiveness, mission and respect.

In *Reclaiming Friendship*, Fernando claims that real friendship is often alien to our culture and churches. We must shape such friendship around trinitarian relations and the values of the kingdom of God. The presence and

---

[29]Victor Turner, *The Ritual Process* (Ithaca, NY: Cornell University Press, 1969); Victor Turner, *Dramas, Fields, and Metaphors* (Ithaca, NY: Cornell University Press, 1974).

[30]Edith L. B. Turner, *Communitas: The Anthropology of Collective Joy*, Contemporary Anthropology of Religion (New York: Palgrave Macmillan, 2012).

power of the Spirit enables true friendship. Genuine spiritual friendship is a
rare gift. Even though it's rare, it's essential for Christian community. Christian
morality and virtue is crucial to successful friendships. Friendship is about
relational and personal holism. This is because deep and true friendships
demand much from us. They need commitment and love and honesty and
loyalty and respect. We discover spiritual friendship through shared lives,
dreams, worship, love, mission and respect. Fernando says that we need to
reclaim spiritual friendship for the sake of discipleship and community and
mission and personal wholeness.[31]

Aelred of Rievaulx's *Spiritual Friendship* portrays a friend as a guardian
of love and the spirit. A friend is a companion of one's soul from whom we
hide nothing. A friend is the medicine of life that we choose and test with
care and caution, and one with whom we can trust our affections and deepest
secrets. For Aelred, the goal of friendship is Jesus Christ, and "he that abides
in friendship abides in God and God in him."[32] Friendship can lead to union
with Christ and points the way to him. Aelred believed that the stages
toward perfect spiritual friendship are selection, probation, admission and
harmony. Union with a spiritual friend can lead to union with Christ. The
culmination of spiritual friendship is union with God in Christ.

Fernando says that deep spiritual friendship involves lingering with others.
It involves telling them the truth in a spirit of grace and love. Spiritual friendships require the wise choice of friends. We nurture spiritual friendships
through vulnerability, openness, redeemed egos and unselfish commitment.
We care for spiritual friends through gracious forgiveness and healthy communication and covenant love. We encourage their spiritual life and discipline. And they foster ours. We enrich spiritual friends through prayer,
presence, the healing of wounds and the control of our tongues. We provide
spiritual friends with comfort during grief and loss and celebration during
joy and success.[33] Our relationship with God enables us to pursue healthy
spiritual friendships.

Our modern world tends to exalt individualism and autonomous human

---

[31] Ajith Fernando, *Reclaiming Friendship: Relating to Each Other in a Frenzied World* (Scottdale, PA: Herald, 1993).

[32] Aelred of Rievaulx, *Aelred of Rievaulx: Spiritual Friendship*, trans. Lawrence C. Braceland, ed. Marsha L. Dutton, Cistercian Fathers Series (Collegeville, MN: Cistercian, 2010), 1:69-70.

[33] Fernando, *Reclaiming Friendship*.

existence and rights. Radical individualism leads people into a life of personal and social fragmentation. But healthy community can lead toward wholeness.

Much Majority World and indigenous thought challenges deep-seated individualism. It challenges an individualism that sees humans as standing outside traditions or communities. Human beings are individuals within community. Social networks and communities are integral and indispensable to human existence. We form worldviews and spiritualities and personal identities within community. We find meaning, virtues, morals, identity, vocation and personal formation within community. These themes find their peak in a theology of the social Trinity and of Christian *koinonia*.

8. Koinonia *churches reactivate* koinonia. How can the church reactivate *koinonia*? I will answer this by engaging some of the thought of five Majority World theologians. These are S. Wesley Ariarajah, Ruth Padilla DeBorst, Samuel Escobar, Izunna Okonkwo and M. M. Thomas. These five thinkers show us that we reactivate *koinonia* through eight practices:

First, we build *koinonia* on trinitarian and Christological foundations.

As we have seen already in this chapter, true Christian community is trinitarian in theology and practice. It's participatory, reciprocal, decentralized, mutual and so on. Such *koinonia* is Christ centered. It shapes its being, ministries, structures and mission around the person, gospel and mission of Jesus Christ.

Second, we enhance *koinonia* as we release all believers to ministry.

Contribution and participation are at the heart of *koinonia*. Liberating and nonmanipulative pastoral ministry seeks to identify and develop and release all God's people to ministry. It enables them to discover their God-given contribution to community and mission. Karl Barth puts it well: "There can be no 'ecclesiastics' and 'lay people,' there cannot be one church that simply 'instructs' and another that is 'under instruction,' because no member of the church exists who is not all of that in their own right." Jürgen Moltmann says, "The power behind unity is love. The power behind diversity is freedom."[34]

---

[34]Samuel Escobar, "The Church as Community," in *The Local Church, Agent of Transformation: An Ecclesiology for Integral Mission*, ed. C. René Padilla and Tetsunao Yamamori (Buenos Aires: Ediciones Kairos, 2004), 142-51. (Barth and Moltmann are quoted by Alberto Fernando Roldan on 151.)

Third, we foster *koinonia* by engaging pluralities.

Diversities and pluralities bring richness, possibilities, conflicts and quandaries. Today, diversity and plurality characterize the global and local church. Furthermore, the church is located in pluralist and multicultural and multireligious societies. We foster *koinonia* in the midst of such diversity. We nurture *koinonia* by cultivating a Christian "spirituality for plurality" and "communities of peace" for all peoples. Ariarajah suggests we do this by nurturing a positive and enthusiastic attitude to plurality, affirming ethnic and cultural identities, and embracing justice and peace as the bases for building community. We need mechanisms for reconciliation and communication. We need to reject violence.[35]

I agree with much that Ariarajah proposes. But let me be clear. I'm committed to diversity and peace without diminishing the uniqueness of the Christian gospel. God has a "multicultural kingdom table."[36]

Fourth, we unlock *koinonia* through liturgy and sacraments and worship.

The sacraments help reveal God to humanity. They make us receptive to him. They develop bonds of intimacy and communion. We aren't only bonded to God through the sacraments of baptism and Eucharist. We're also bonded to each other. "An individual receives a sacrament as an integral member of a believing community that awaits the second coming of her Lord and Master in glory. As such, though the sacraments are given to each member of the church one-by-one, they (sacraments) are 'experiences' which go beyond a particular individual, and involve the entire church."[37]

Fifth, we integrate *koinonia* with our theology and practice of mission.

"In the apostolic teaching about the life and mission of the church, a correlation between the fullness of Christian living and the complexity of integral mission can be established."[38] Real community and mission happen when the *centrifugal* (moving outward and away from the center in mission) and *centripetal* (moving inward and toward the center in fellowship) dimensions

---

[35]S. Wesley Ariarajah, "The Challenge of Building Communities of Peace for All: The Richness and Dilemma of Diversities," *Ecumenical Review* 57, no. 2 (2005).

[36]DeBorst, "'Unexpected' Guests," 65.

[37]Izunna Okonkwo, "The Sacrament of the Eucharist (as *Koinonia*) and African Sense of Communalism: Towards a Synthesis," *Journal of Theology for Southern Africa*, no. 137 (2010): 91-93. See also Izunna Okonkwo, "Eucharist and the African Communalism," *AFER* 52, nos. 2–3 (2010).

[38]Escobar, "Church as Community," 136.

of the church are in harmony. They enrich each other in profound ways. *Koinonia in Christ* has social, political, missional and ecological effects. There is a "widespread search by churches, Christian social action groups, and Christian peace movements throughout the world for a corporate spirituality and political theology for their participation in the struggles for justice, peace, and the protection of creation." The Eucharist is "a Sacrament of Love that unites all the recipients with Christ, strengthens them and makes 'holy' their relationship with fellow Christians, and other human beings." The church needs to rediscover the *koinonia* present in the sacraments. The sacraments can inspire and nurture love and unity and sharing and community.[39]

Koinonia is the effective infrastructure of mission. Deep and authentic and communing relationships provide the basis and infrastructure of mission. The New Testament, church history and the contemporary growth of the Majority World church witnesses to this. "The story of the relationship between Paul, Epaphroditus, and the Philippians is a telling illustration of this Christian attitude. Such human integration in Christ makes mission possible."[40]

Sixth, we revolutionize *koinonia* through our apostolic practices of discipleship.

Apostolic practices of discipleship integrate community experiences with missional endeavors in the discipleship process. And they always do this in the context of deep immersion in the communing life of the church. "Middle class evangelicals generally have not experienced the full healing force of this sense of belonging. But the socially marginalized, especially those in the cities, experience this life in the church as a consolation, a refuge, and a place of integration. And this experience has the power to transform and reorient their existence."[41]

Seventh, we broaden *koinonia* with an emphasis on creation community.

Koinonia and radical conversion are about restored relationships with God and creation and others. DeBorst makes this point: "Caring, faithful, truthful relationships are at the core of any hope for a better world. And these are gifts of grace, granted by the God-who-is-community."[42] We

---

[39]M. M. Thomas, "Will *Koinonia* Emerge as a Vital Theological Theme?," *Ecumenical Review* 41, no. 2 (1989): 182.

[40]Escobar, "The Local Church, Agent of Transformation," 142.

[41]Ibid., 139.

[42]Ruth Padilla DeBorst, "Living Creation-Community in God's World Today," *Journal of Latin American Theology* 5, no. 1 (2010): 61.

experience many conversions during life by the grace of God. He calls us to restored relationships through these conversions—restored communion with himself and his earth and his people. We can't ignore creation in this mix. "Care of the earth is a spiritual matter, and rampant destruction of it is blasphemy, an offense to our Creator."[43] The church is the *creation community*. It is *relational and holistic* koinonia. God calls his church to "converted covenantal relations." These are with all creation and with God himself—to the glory of the Creator God.[44]

Lastly, we enrich *koinonia* through *third-culture lifestyles and mission.*

DeBorst challenges churches to develop disciples and fellowships that are *third culture*. By this, she means that Christians must embrace the particular culture of the Christian faith. But they must also engage "meaningfully, and with a sense of belonging, with people from very diverse cultural backgrounds." (She uses third-culture children as an example. These grow up with two cultures. They find meaningful and creative ways to put these cultures into dialogue.)[45] God calls us individually and communally to this task. It's vital to the reactivation of *koinonia* and the fulfillment of mission.

DeBorst puts it well:

> God's kingdom is not some amorphous, supra-cultural, other-world milieu. Rather, it is a space of vibrant, life-giving, God honoring encounter of spice and colour, smell and sound, here and now, in the complex entanglement of human relations. As third-culture people, followers of Jesus are called to live today in the light of the completion of God's story, with daily expectation of Christ's imminent return. They are called to express in their daily interactions the confident belief that one day the triumphal choir before God's throne will be composed of a great multitude from every nation, tribe, and people, proclaiming, on bended knee, God's sovereignty in their own distinct languages. . . . In as far as Christian communities the world over live together in light of God's grace-full story, they become historically visible and culturally alternative out-workings of God's mission and localized expressions of the bountiful banquet of God's kingdom.[46]

---

[43]Ibid., 65.
[44]Ruth Padilla DeBorst, "God's Earth and God's People: Relationships Restored," *Journal of Latin American Theology* 5, no. 1 (2010); DeBorst, "A New Heaven and a New Earth: Community Restored," *Journal of Latin American Theology* 5, no. 1 (2010).
[45]DeBorst, "'Unexpected' Guests," 73.
[46]Ibid., 75-76.

DEVELOPING SPIRITUALITY AND DISCIPLESHIP

WHAT CAN WE LEARN FROM HOW MAJORITY WORLD CHRISTIANS PRACTICE CHRISTIAN SPIRITUALITY AND DISCIPLESHIP?

To take head on oppressive structures like consumerism, technology, militarism, multinational capitalism, international communism, racism, and sexism, we need a spirituality of missional engagement. . . . Mission without spirituality cannot survive any more than combustion without oxygen.

ORLANDO E. COSTAS

Recently, I attended a conference in Manila in the Philippines. To save money, I stayed at a backpacker's hostel. The room I was staying in had eight beds. Only one other man was staying in that room. He was an elderly Vietnamese man. I'll call him Tien. At five o'clock on the first morning, the sound of sobbing woke me. Tien was on his knees before an open Bible. He was praying for Southeast Asia with tears and loud cries. This continued until seven o'clock. Over that week, I discovered that this was his daily two-hour prayer vigil.

Tien told me how thirty years ago he had planted a house church of ten people in Vietnam. He now spent his time traveling Vietnam, encouraging and teaching house churches that his original church planted. Close to thirty thousand people now attended this single network of house churches.

He told me stories of persecution and suffering and martyrdom in communist Vietnam. Vietnamese security forces had arrested and imprisoned his brothers many years ago. These brothers were pastoring in this network of house churches at the time. He believed that authorities had murdered them. Yet this network of house churches had exploded in numbers. It had grown from ten people in one home to thirty thousand people across the country in thirty years.

Tien showed me how a deep spirituality and discipleship sustained his ministry. He exemplified this in his daily prayer vigil. Discipleship to Jesus Christ, and a community-centered spirituality sustained these Vietnamese churches and their leaders in persecution and suffering. These churches are hotbeds of missional outreach, fervent faith, spiritual formation and authentic discipleship.

Without attention to discipleship and spirituality, the church is in a fatally weakened state. It is time to draw indigenous and Majority World thinkers into this conversation. We need to pay careful attention to discipleship and spiritual formation as it occurs in these emerging global settings.[1]

We can understand Majority World and indigenous discipleship and spirituality through key themes. These are theology, Jesus, Spirit, culture, tradition, community, disciplines, creation, suffering and mission. This chapter proceeds in that order. This chapter asks, *What can we learn from how Majority World Christians practice Christian spirituality and discipleship?*

WHAT ARE SPIRITUALITY AND DISCIPLESHIP?

At its heart, *Christian spirituality is a life of communion with God in Jesus Christ*. It's expressed through a living and committed discipleship to Jesus. It's participation in the triune God's community, life, love, holiness, kingdom and mission.[2]

How do *spirituality* and *discipleship* relate to each other? My suspicion is that we conflate and confuse these terms even when we are not clear about what we mean by them. Everyone (Christian or not) has a "spirituality."

---

[1]Segundo Galilea, *The Way of Living Faith: A Spirituality of Liberation* (San Francisco: Harper & Row, 1988), 20.

[2]By "communion with God" I mean "communion with the triune God" (i.e., the Spirit-enabled participation in the Sonship of Jesus, along the lines of Rom 8, Gal 4 and so on).

Spirituality is people's "way of relating to God" (which is one way I define spirituality in general, although my culture thinks "spiritual" is anything that's not material). So spirituality differs highly from person to person. I would say the inner life and how people relate to God in many Western settings is governed by their Internet and media life. Whatever they plug into "forms" their inner life or perhaps their life with God. *Discipleship* is optional, however. It's an intentional choice to relate one's whole life to God through the life, death and resurrection of Jesus Christ.

So what are the characteristics of Christian spirituality and discipleship? And how do they relate to each other? When we consider the minor differences between spirituality and discipleship, we see that the two overlap. And they're integrated.

Spirituality seeks participation in God's being. Discipleship learns participation in God's doing.

Spirituality relates to our responses to meaning, persons, creation, sacred things, transcendence and, most importantly, God. Discipleship is the whole gamut of disciplined life in response to the call of Jesus.

Spirituality is relationship to God, others, self and creation. It's about how those relationships manifest themselves in our Christian faith. Discipleship is about the practices of following Jesus Christ. It's about integrating the concrete practices of those spiritual relationships into the whole of our lives as we seek to be Jesus' disciples.

Spirituality isn't necessarily Christian. But when it is Christian, we manifest it as faith in, and relationship with, the triune God revealed in Jesus Christ. Discipleship is the outworking of that relationship in conformity to Christ Jesus.

Spirituality, when it is Christian, is defined by discipleship to Jesus Christ. Discipleship isn't simply doing what Jesus commanded or following his example. Discipleship is becoming like him. This involves engaging in the spiritual reality of the kingdom of God and seeing that reality become manifest in the world.

Again, while there are some differences between spirituality and discipleship, there is substantial overlap. Jeffrey Greenman defines Christian spiritual formation as "our continuing response to the reality of God's grace shaping us into the likeness of Jesus Christ, through the work of the Holy

Spirit, in the community of faith, for the sake of the world."[3] When this is the case, Christian spiritual formation and discipleship integrate. And they have *trinitarian* and *relational* and *missional* orientations.

Both Greenman's and my definitions of Christian spirituality focus on *Trinity, community* and *mission.* I value Greenman's focus on the *ongoing process* of formation as we respond to God's gracious work in our lives. To these emphases, my definition adds a *kingdom* focus. Christian spirituality and discipleship reveals that God the Father inaugurated the kingdom in the incarnation of the Son and in the eschatological outpouring of the Spirit.

We must pursue spiritual formation and discipleship through a focus on (at least) these five things: Trinity, community, mission, process and kingdom.[4]

Unfortunately, post-Enlightenment dualism shapes the majority of books on Christian spirituality. It separates the *phenomenal* from the *noumenal.* The phenomenal are things perceptible by the senses or through immediate experience. The noumenal are things like ideas that we know as true or real without the need for perception, the senses or experience. This dualistic separation is unhelpful. It leads to approaches to "spirituality" that are not complementary to authentic Christian discipleship. It leads to concepts of devotional life and piety that have nothing to do with justice or mercy or subverting a fallen status quo. Spiritual dualism prevents people from living out the lifestyle of the inaugurated kingdom. It leads to concepts of truth where people can talk theology but never engage in praxis (especially beyond individual and family life) and to concepts of spirituality where pietism shapes the evangelical world. Then evangelicals are tempted to be accusers of the world rather than motivated by God's love.[5]

---

[3] Jeffrey P. Greenman, "Spiritual Formation in Theological Perspective," in *Life in the Spirit: Spiritual Formation in Theological Perspective,* ed. Jeffrey P. Greenman and George Kalantzis (Downers Grove, IL: IVP Academic, 2010), 24.

[4] Dallas Willard demonstrates the connections between spirituality, spiritual formation and discipleship in *The Great Omission: Reclaiming Jesus's Essential Teachings on Discipleship* (San Francisco: HarperSanFrancisco, 2006). Willard shows that when spiritual formation and discipleship are understood and practiced correctly they do not need to be pulled apart.

[5] Simon Chan writes of "new directions in evangelical spirituality." His tentative conclusion is that "the new evangelical spirituality does involve a major paradigm shift from individual to ecclesial formation." Chan concludes that these new directions involve an attempt "to recover their 'catholic' identities, that is, to recover what they hold in common with the church universal and the larger Christian spiritual direction, is a hopeful sign of a maturing evangelical spirituality." Chan, "New Directions in Evangelical Spirituality," *Journal of Spiritual Formation & Soul Care* 2, no. 2 (2009): 237.

This post-Enlightenment dualism shapes much contemporary Western Christian spirituality. It arises out of individualism. It leads to discipleship where people's lives and desires and the way they spend their time and money are no different from their neighbors. It fails to understand that a wise view of walking in the Spirit arises from good trinitarian theology. (This is *contra* those who say that trinitarian theology is just Greek.) Good trinitarian theology helps us understand what it means to be a person and a disciple. The last Adam shows what it means to be truly human. He was truly human in the power of the Spirit. So as we follow in his way, we'll understand biblical and theological categories that won't allow us to think or act in the dualism that exists in post-Enlightenment spirituality.

Jesus' incarnation and the eschatological outpouring of the Spirit leads to a view of discipleship that is *spirituality shaped by the inbreaking of God's kingdom*. It's a discipleship that stands in contrast to post-Enlightenment dualism. It's a holistic and integrated spirituality. It transforms the whole life of the whole person with the whole gospel in whole community.

With the incarnation and the eschatological outpouring of the Spirit, two astounding events occurred. One was that the Creator covenant God of Israel unveiled God's being as Father and Son and Spirit and invites us into the fellowship life of the triune Creator. Second, the kingdom was inaugurated in the incarnation and the eschatological outpouring of the Spirit. Those two amazing events have too little influence on how the majority of Protestant Christians in the West live. But they must encounter and transform our faith and discipleship and spirituality and mission. And Mortimer Arias says, "Discipleship is both an end and an instrument. It is for mission, it is for the Kingdom, to give witness to the Kingdom. . . . Discipleship includes formation and mission, formation for mission, formation in mission. So, discipleship was the model created by Jesus to make real and to announce the Kingdom of God."[6]

SPIRITUALITY AND THE TRINITY

What does it mean to say that Christian spirituality and discipleship must be trinitarian?

---

[6] Bp. Mortimer Arias, "Announcing the Kingdom as Challenge: Discipleship Evangelization," *Impact*, no. 8 (1982): 4.

First, we must shape discipleship and spiritual formation around the truth that the Creator covenant God of Israel unveiled God's being as Father and Son and Spirit and also around the joy that this triune Creator invites us into his fellowship life.

Second, our discipleship and spiritual formation must reveal that the kingdom was inaugurated in the incarnation of Jesus Christ and in the eschatological outpouring of the Holy Spirit.

These two astonishing events are our bedrock. They are the source of all authentic Christian discipleship and spirituality and spiritual formation.

How do Majority World thinkers articulate these truths? How are they foundational for Majority World writing on spirituality?

Two Brazilians provide us with good examples. These are Leonardo Boff (*Holy Trinity, Perfect Community*) and Ricardo Barbosa de Sousa (*The Trinity and Spirituality*).

Boff constructs an elaborate theology of the Trinity. He then speaks of the implications for churches and Christian faith and spiritual formation:

> The trinitarian mystery is reflected in each human person, in the family, and in society. But it is in the church that this august mystery of communion and life finds its most visible expression in history. The church is inherently the community of faith, hope, and love seeking to live the ideal of union proposed by Jesus Christ himself: " . . . that they may all be one. As you, father, are in me and I am in you, may they also be in us" (Jn 17:21).[7]

The church is essentially community. It images the trinitarian union. The church fosters spiritual formation through inclusion and participation and interpersonal communion. We grow into discipleship within communities that image the love, fellowship, inclusion, embrace and unity of the Trinity. We are welcomed into the trinitarian fellowship life of God and the church. In that community, we become disciples.

Barbosa de Sousa writes that Christian spirituality is inconceivable without a trinitarian framework. He says that the trinitarian relations must shape the church's understanding of human nature, community, love, happiness, freedom and creativity. Trinitarian thought isn't mere abstraction. It has concrete implications for our churches, spirituality, worship and life in the world.

---

[7]Leonardo Boff, *Holy Trinity, Perfect Community* (Maryknoll, NY: Orbis, 2000), 43.

Barbosa de Sousa says the doctrine of the Trinity has implications for Christian spirituality. Trinitarian theology helps us rediscover richer theologies of personhood, vocation, mission, spiritual friendship, relationship, discipleship, spirituality and love.

Rediscovering personhood: "The Trinity establishes the meaning and significance of being a person. Based on this doctrine, people see themselves as beings in relationship, and it is precisely in this relationship with others [and with God] that they discover their personhood."[8]

Rediscovering vocation: "Christian vocation is essentially relational. The invitation to discipleship is an invitation to personal communion with God and with the family of faith. . . . The only way to know myself is to open myself up to relationship of love with another person."[9]

Rediscovering mission: "Christian mission is, above all, an invitation to life in community."[10]

Rediscovering spiritual friendship: "Communion and friendship within the people of God becomes an external and visible sign of the life within the Trinity."[11]

Rediscovering relationship:

> Spirituality born from the trinitarian experience has a meaning that is absolutely revolutionary for our generation. This spirituality does not inspire us to seek power and control or anything else except personal and affective relationships with God and with our neighbors. . . . To rediscover the Trinity is to rediscover the way of personal and affective relationships, both with God and with our neighbor. It is to rediscover the way of love and of genuine friendship as the greatest expression of our spirituality and devotion.[12]

Rediscovering discipleship and spirituality: The Trinity is central to our spirituality and mission. "Without an adequate understanding of God's [trinitarian] nature, we can have no significant comprehension or grasp of our faith. Modern consumerism and utilitarian individualism completely deny the Trinity and compromise the church's entire spirituality." We need

---

[8]Ricardo Barbosa de Sousa, "The Trinity and Spirituality," *Journal of Latin American Theology* 1, no. 2 (2006): 31.
[9]Ibid., 35.
[10]Ibid., 39.
[11]Ibid., 43.
[12]Ibid., 58-59.

to allow the triune God to transform our churches. They must be places where "countercultural experiences take place, where the Trinity provides meaning and freedom."[13]

Rediscovering love: "To rediscover the triune God is to rediscover the essential secret of Christian faith and devotion. God, before everything else, is love."[14]

We turn now to the way in which Christian spirituality must reveal that the kingdom was inaugurated in the incarnation of Jesus Christ and in the eschatological outpouring of the Holy Spirit.

SPIRITUALITY, JESUS AND THE SPIRIT

Christian spirituality that witnesses to the inaugurated kingdom centers on Jesus. It focuses on his incarnation, life, death and resurrection. These events have ushered in the inaugurated kingdom. Therefore, they are at the center of Christian spirituality.

I have said that *Christian spirituality is a life of communion with God in Jesus Christ. It is expressed through a living and committed discipleship to Jesus.* Following Jesus—discipleship to him—is at the heart and definition of all authentic Christian spirituality.

Gustavo Gutiérrez writes much on how the person of Jesus Christ and his inaugurated kingdom shape Christian discipleship.[15] Jesus' teaching on the kingdom shapes our discipleship. This kingdom is countercultural. It stands in contrast to the oppressive and exploitative systems of this world. This kingdom demands that disciples renounce materialism, violence, competition, immorality, oppression, pride and social evil.

Disciples reject all that is not of the kingdom of God. They embrace all that is. Disciples pursue righteousness and peace. They do this even when it comes at a personal cost. And the cost might be misunderstanding, persecution, marginalization and suffering. Discipleship to Jesus in the way of his kingdom is countercultural. Disciples are willing to sacrifice ambition, reputation, relationship and security. They'll even sacrifice life. And they do this for the sake of Jesus and his kingdom.

---

[13]Ibid., 68.
[14]Ibid., 69.
[15]Gustavo Gutiérrez and James B. Nickoloff, eds., *Gustavo Gutiérrez: Essential Writings* (Maryknoll, NY: Orbis, 1996), 173-74.

The kingdom is a grace. But it demands the whole person. Sacrifice and suffering are characteristic of the kingdom. But so are love, joy, peace, hope, justice and reconciliation. In the words of Jesus, "Whoever wants to be my disciple must deny themselves and take up their cross daily and follow me" (Lk 9:23).

Richard Shaull and Waldo Cesar consider the rise of Pentecostalism in Brazil. They arrive at a compelling conclusion: *spiritual formation is growth toward the reign of God.*[16]

Pedro Casaldáliga (Brazilian) and Jose-Maria Vigil (Nicaraguan) distinguish between two types of spirituality. The first is a *basic, ethical-political spirituality*. All people, regardless of whether they follow Christ, can share it. "This level of spirituality, though it comes in the final analysis from the source of the Spirit of God, drinks from the sources of life: history, social conditions, praxis, reflection, wisdom, contemplation—all that feeds the heart and mind."[17] People express this first type of spirituality in many ways. This includes ethical indignation and spiritual contemplation, radical faithfulness to others, solidarity with the poor and oppressed, and in purposeful and positive action. They show it through hospitality and openness and passion for life. There are many ways that humans show this basic, ethical-political spirituality.

The second type of spirituality is a *religious, evangelical-ecclesial spirituality*. It's available to Christians through "the liberating Spirit of Jesus Christ."[18] It's a spirituality of discipleship to Jesus. This Christian spirituality witnesses to the kingdom of Christ, testifies through word and action and orientation, and announces the liberating reign of Christ. This is a spirituality patterned after Jesus. It reveals Jesus' kingdom. It's devoted to Jesus' reign. It subverts other kingdoms. This spirituality serves with the poor and embraces persecution. And it lives with integrity in prosperity and in suffering. Its hallmark is discipleship to Jesus and in the way of Jesus.

True discipleship is not merely Jesus centered. It's trinitarian. Therefore, Christian spirituality and discipleship witnesses to Christ and his kingdom in the power of the Holy Spirit to the glory of the Father.

---

[16]Richard Shaull and Waldo A. Cesar, *Pentecostalism and the Future of the Christian Churches: Promises, Limitations, Challenges* (Grand Rapids: Eerdmans, 2000), 219-26.

[17]Pedro Casaldáliga and Jose-Maria Vigil, *Political Holiness: A Spirituality of Liberation*, Theology and Liberation Series (Maryknoll, NY: Orbis, 1994), 14.

[18]Ibid.

Christian spirituality is possible because of God's empowering presence. What does it mean to follow Jesus in the power of the Spirit?

Some of my favorite writers on this subject are Casaldáliga, Vigil, Kōsuke Koyama, Anthony Bloom (Anthony of Sourozh), Frank Laubach, Simon Chan and José Comblin.

These writers tell us that following Jesus in the power of the Spirit shapes our Christian spirituality. How do we express Christian spirituality when we are disciples of Jesus? We're prophetically indignant about injustice and oppression. We show solidarity and generosity with the poor, outcasts, marginalized, silenced and exploited. We're in constant communion in prayer with Father, Son and Holy Spirit. We're persons of prayer—patterning our prayers and prayer lives after Jesus. We leave aside "ties and interests, security and status, comfort and consumerism, good name and prestige."[19] We have "courage to take up our cross every day, without fearing conflict and without saving up even our own lives." We're passionate about developing a discipling community, "always socializing our spiritual experience."[20] We show self-sacrificial action: putting love into costly, self-sacrificial practice. And we embrace political holiness: being "salt, light and a city on a hill" as an alternative culture. We're a people who witness to Jesus Christ through justice, peace, liberation, hope, equality, love, mercy and so on.

What are other ways in which discipleship to Jesus shapes Christian spirituality?

Liberation. Discipleship to Jesus inspires us to cultivate a spirituality of liberation. This is a spirituality characterized by focus on Christ's reign and kingdom. We focus on discipleship to Jesus and pursing his justice, peace, truth, love, freedom and so forth. We root a spirituality of liberation in the real world, in history, in place, among the poor and in politics. We're critical of oppressive structures and systems and powers. We're committed to liberating action. We pursue wholeness without reductions or dichotomies. This means we get rid of the divisions between sacred and secular, material and spiritual, "us" and "others," and so on.[21]

---

[19]Ibid., 100. The first ten points are developed by Casaldáliga and Vigil.
[20]Ibid.
[21]Casaldáliga and Vigil devote a chapter to these themes: ibid., 203-7.

Movement. Disciples take part in the "movement" of the Trinity. They especially join in the movement of the Spirit of Christ. "All attributes of the Spirit denote movement: the Spirit is giving, loving, living. The Spirit comes at the end of the movement of God, but the beginning of God's going-out to creation. It is the start of creation's road back to the Father."[22] Discipleship to Jesus means keeping in step with his Spirit and going where he wants us to go. It's about moving with him in mission and worship and fellowship and discipleship and ministry.

Power and holiness. The Spirit of Jesus is with his disciples as his empowering and sanctifying presence. When the Spirit fills us, he fills us with his power and holiness. "Pentecostal power and passion mean nothing if they do not issue from a life filled with the Spirit of holiness."[23]

Crucified minds. Disciples have minds captivated by "the foolishness and weakness of God." This means forming attitudes and hearts upon the mind of Jesus Christ. "The mind which has decided to live by the power of the crucified Lord is the crucified mind."[24]

Risen minds. Disciples of Jesus enjoy and proclaim the risen Christ as victor and Lord! Anthony Bloom rejoices, "The resurrection is the only event of the Gospel which belongs to history not only past but also present. Only in the light of the Resurrection did everything else make sense to me."[25] Discipleship to Jesus means embracing crucified and risen minds. The Spirit enables us to be dead to self but alive to the resurrected Lord and his power and regeneration.

Spirit-filled discipleship isn't divorced from history or culture. These always influence our Christian spirituality and discipleship.

Spirituality and Culture

Culture affects the shape of spirituality and discipleship. No spirituality is meaningful (or possible) apart from its cultural background and context.

---

[22]José Comblin, *The Holy Spirit and Liberation*, Theology and Liberation Series (Maryknoll, NY: Orbis, 1989), 186.

[23]Simon Chan, *Pentecostal Theology and the Christian Spiritual Tradition* (Sheffield: Sheffield Academic, 2000), 70.

[24]Kōsuke Koyama, *No Handle on the Cross: An Asian Meditation on the Crucified Mind* (Maryknoll, NY: Orbis, 1977), 8-12; Frank C. Laubach, *Prayer: The Mightiest Force in the World* (Old Tappan, NJ: Spire, 1956), 98-102.

[25]Quoted in Koyama, *No Handle on the Cross*, 119; William Barclay and Rupert E. Davies, *We Believe in God*, Unwin Forum (London: Allen & Unwin, 1968), 26.

Culture and spirituality are mutually forming. This is true whether they are in harmony or confrontation. Many forms of spirituality have evolved within and for their particular Western cultural context. This is also true of the many approaches to spirituality and discipleship that have developed within Asian, African, Latin American, indigenous and other contexts.

Our goal, then, is not to reproduce these forms. We don't want carbon copies of them in our own setting. We need to adapt them to our culture and context. Successful application of these forms of spirituality and approaches to discipleship in our culture will mean reconceiving and transforming them for our setting.

The West can learn much from the spirituality of Christians in other cultures. In my own country, Australia, nonindigenous Christians are finally beginning to learn from the spiritual contributions of our indigenous sisters and brothers.

In Australian Aboriginal spirituality, creation and holism and relationship are important.

Creation: "The land is the basis of all realities—human selfhood and identity. [Aboriginal culture] perceives all realities from creation perspectives" (rather than from human-centered thinking).[26] God is beyond creation but also in creation. He is perceived in creation (more so than in human history). Religious activities are focused on the earth and soil and on our relationship to these things.

Holism: There are no sharp dualisms. "There is no clear cut distinction between sacred and secular, religion and non-religion, and so on." Aboriginal spirituality is "holistic in thinking." Australian Aboriginal spirituality values ritual and ceremony, earth and soil, land and sea, welcome and hospitality, family and community, generosity and contentment, art and music, story telling and dancing, and balance and harmony with the whole cosmos. There's no dualism between the natural and the spiritual.

---

[26]Ibid., 36-41. For ways in which Western Christians can learn from indigenous and Native American spiritualities, see John W. Friesen, *Aboriginal Spirituality and Biblical Theology: Closer Than You Think* (Calgary: Detselig, 2000); Anne Pattel-Gray, *Aboriginal Spirituality: Past, Present, Future* (Blackburn: HarperCollins Religious, 1996); George E. Tinker, "Native Americans and the Land: 'The End of Living, and the Beginning of Survival,'" *Word & World* 6, no. 1 (1986); Tinker, "Spirituality, Native American Personhood, Sovereignty and Solidarity," *Ecumenical Review* 44, no. 3 (1992); Philip Jenkins, *Dream Catchers: How Mainstream America Discovered Native Spirituality* (Oxford: Oxford University Press, 2004); María Chávez Quispe, "Transformative Spirituality for a Transformed World: Contributions from the Indigenous Perspective," *International Review of Mission* 98, no. 2 (2009).

Relationship: Spirituality is person and community oriented. "Relationship between individuals in society is more important than the simple performance of tasks." Cooperation and community is valued. Generosity is more important than saving money or building riches. Aboriginal spirituality values interdependent connection with God and others and all creation.[27]

Let's have a brief look at some culturally formed approaches to Christian spirituality and discipleship in Africa and Asia. We need to reshape these, of course, for our own culture.[28] Africa and Asia, of course, are enormous continents. They have a multitude of cultures and religions and Christian traditions. Euro American Christianity has influenced African and Asian Christian spiritualities. But local cultures and spiritual traditions have also resulted in the indigenization (or contextualization) of spirituality and discipleship in the many cultures of Africa and Asia.

African Christian spiritualities are characterized by an awareness of the spiritual world. There's a focus on angels, demons, spirits, the Holy Spirit and Satan. Africans often work this out in the context of hunger and plenty, illness and health, suffering and healing, poverty and wealth, and death and life.

Africans value a concrete and whole-of-life spirituality. John S. Mbiti provides a collection of African prayers offered within the concrete experiences of African life. These are prayers for health, healing, prosperity, protection, harvest, peace, fertility, rain, joy and blessings.[29] Such prayers are a part of traditional African spirituality. Africans are as likely to develop Christian

---

[27]NATSIEC, Gabrielle Russell-Mundine, ed., *Christ and Culture: Christ Through Culture* (Ballina: National Council of Churches in Australia, 2010), 36.

[28]Space does not permit a treatment of culturally formed spiritualities in Latin American, First Nations and other contexts. For treatments of spirituality and discipleship in the cultures of those contexts, see Philip Sheldrake, *The New Westminster Dictionary of Christian Spirituality* (Louisville: Westminster John Knox, 2005), 398-400, 474-76; Glen G. Scorgie et al., *Dictionary of Christian Spirituality* (Grand Rapids: Zondervan, 2011), 568-69, 139-45; Michael Downey, *The New Dictionary of Catholic Spirituality* (Collegeville, MN: Liturgical, 1993), 318-30, 697-700; Arthur G. Holder, *The Blackwell Companion to Christian Spirituality*, Blackwell Companions to Religion (Malden, MA: Blackwell, 2005), 156-74; Gordon S. Wakefield, ed., *A Dictionary of Christian Spirituality* (London: SCM, 1983), 283-85, 343-45; K. C. Abraham and Bernadette Mbuy-Beya, eds., *Spirituality of the Third World: A Cry for Life* (Maryknoll, NY: Orbis, 1994); Gary H. Gossen and Miguel León-Portilla, *South and Meso-American Native Spirituality: From the Cult of the Feathered Serpent to the Theology of Liberation*, World Spirituality (New York: Crossroad, 1993); William Cook, "Spirituality in the Struggles for Social Justice: A Brief Latin American Anthology," *Missiology* 12, no. 2 (1984); Ernest W. Ranly, "Latin American Spirituality," *Cross Currents* 39, no. 4 (1990).

[29]John S. Mbiti, *The Prayers of African Religion* (Maryknoll, NY: Orbis Books, 1975).

spirituality in a large urban metropolis (e.g., huge cities like Lagos, Kinshasa, Johannesburg-Ekurhuleni, Khartoum, Mogadishu or Nairobi) as in a small, rural village. In the future, most Africans and Asians will live in cities—many of them in megacities.

Madge Karecki and Celia Kourie describe how Africans express their Christian spirituality. They are spiritually sensitive. They connect their faith to creation, the body, the land and physicality. They desire deep human connection, especially in family and church and local community. They develop a theology of ancestry and heritage, including Jesus Christ as the Proto-Ancestor. They embrace public demonstrations of faith (e.g., boisterous worship services and passionate evangelistic rallies). And they pursue zealous mission and evangelism.[30]

Ghanaian theologian John S. Pobee says that African spirituality emphasizes joy and celebration. It focuses on the power and presence of the Spirit. And it identifies with Old Testament "textures" and "orientations." African Christians feel connected to the values and themes and motifs within Old Testament cultures. These include family, hospitality, corporate personality, imagery, symbolism, the exodus motif, priests, holy leaders and sacred sites.[31]

African Independent Churches emphasize community and engagement with the spirit world. They pursue dramatic encounters with the Holy Spirit. They use symbolism to aid spiritual formation. Symbols include colors, water, garments, rings, oils, candles, crosses and so forth. "They easily blend and integrate African culture and tradition with that of Christian doctrine. . . . The symbols help both the leadership and membership of the [African Independent Churches] to be spiritual in all spheres of their Christian journey. They have, thus, used symbols to contribute immensely to the level of spirituality in African Christianity."[32]

Emefie Ikenga Metuh says that African Christian spirituality has distinct features: (1) African Christians are passionate in prayer; (2) they pursue mystical experiences; (3) they have a deep sense of the holy; (4) they desire

---

[30]Sheldrake, *The New Westminster Dictionary of Christian Spirituality*, 92-93.

[31]John S. Pobee, *Skenosis: Christian Faith in an African Context* (Gweru: Mambo, 1992).

[32]Thomas Oduro, "Symbolisms in African Independent Churches: Aides to Spirituality and Spiritual Formation," *Ogbomoso Journal of Theology* 16, no. 1 (2011): 82.

spiritual power (e.g., healings, miracles, prophecy and tongues); (5) they love the land; and (6) they have a commitment to community.[33]

The spiritual religious traditions of Asia influence Asian Christian spiritualities. So do Western spiritualities imported and adapted for Asia. Christian spiritualties derived from (or influenced by) the spiritual religious traditions of Asia often focus on three things. These are contemplation, interreligious dialogue and care for creation.

Sundar Singh of India is an example of an Asian spiritual leader who focused on these three things. Singh was the "wanderer for Christ." He embraced poverty and chastity and homelessness for the sake of mission among the poorest of India. Singh "chose the disciplined life of a mendicant preacher, living in caves and jungles and devoting himself to the remote hill peoples." He entered into conversation with the other religious traditions of India. Singh devoted himself to contemplation. He challenged Christians to care for the earth. And he did all this while proclaiming the uniqueness of Christ and the gospel. Singh's eight devotional books are now considered spiritual classics.[34]

Homegrown Asian Christian spiritualities often focus on liberation from oppression. (Examples include Minjung theology in Korea, Dalit theology in India and "theologies of struggle" in the Philippines.) These spiritualities develop an indigenous shape with contextual concerns. Meanwhile, imported varieties struggle to do the same.[35]

Aruna Gnanadason says a "spirituality of struggle" is "not an ephemeral, other worldly, private, esoteric reality. It is earthy, grounded in the grim realities of living and surviving in an inhumane, exploitative world." Gnanadason writes that this type of Asian spirituality forces people to dig deep into their spiritual heritage. It compels them to recover the heritage they've often lost to oppressive and colonial traditions. This kind of spirituality supplies people with the resources to challenge issues of "race, caste, gender, religion, and culture." It's a "spirituality of new life, of hope and of a future where justice and peace will reign—a spirituality wherein the Holy Spirit will

---

[33]Emefie Ikenga Metuh, "The Revival of African Christian Spirituality: The Experience of African Independent Churches," *Mission Studies* 7, no. 2 (1990).

[34]Timothy Dobe, "Wanderer for Christ," *Christian History and Biography*, no. 87 (2012).

[35]Sheldrake, *The New Westminster Dictionary of Christian Spirituality*, 133-35.

empower those ground to the dust to rise up and dance the dance of freedom and liberation—it is this spirituality that sustains us in our struggles."[36]

As in Africa, many Asian Christians are developing forms of spirituality and approaches to discipleship in huge and globally significant cities (e.g., Tokyo, Seoul, Shanghai, Karachi, Beijing, Mumbai, Jakarta, Delhi, Osaka-Kobe-Kyoto, Manila, Bangkok, Singapore, Hanoi or Yangon). Like Westerners, Asians and Africans are working out what it means to be disciples in a global world where the majority of people live in cities.

A huge shift is happening in our generation. It has significant implications for the shape and importance of urban mission and spirituality (especially among the poorest of the poor). The shift is toward cities. More than that: it's toward megacities. Quartz reports that "almost all the world's biggest cities will be in Africa and Asia by 2030. New York, Osaka, and Sao Paulo will no longer make the top 10. And Mexico City will barely hang on as the sole representative outside of Asia and Africa." The top ten megacities in 2030 will be Tokyo, Delhi, Shanghai, Mumbai, Beijing, Dhaka, Karachi, Cairo, Lagos and Mexico City.[37]

Even in these huge megacities, community and relationship are common themes in Majority World approaches to spirituality and discipleship.

SPIRITUALITY AS COLLECTIVE ADVENTURE

Individualism distorts much Western spirituality. We need a *spirituality of community*.

Christian spirituality is *relational*. It cannot occur outside of communion with others and with God. The Trinity is perfect community.[38] By grace, the Father and Son and Spirit invite the church into that community. The church participates in the fellowship and mission of the Trinity. As we engage in communion and mission with the Trinity and the church, we become disciples.

Argentinian pastor Juan Carlos Ortiz places relationship at the center of

---

[36]Aruna Gnanadason, "A Spirituality That Sustains Us in Our Struggles," *International Review of Mission* 80, no. 317 (1991): 37-41.

[37]Adam Pasick, "Almost All of the World's Biggest Cities Will Be in Asia and Africa by 2030," *Quartz*, July 11, 2014, http://qz.com/233334/almost-all-of-the-worlds-biggest-cities-will-be-in-asia-and-africa-by-2030/.

[38]Boff, *Holy Trinity, Perfect Community*.

discipleship. Ortiz says, "The oxygen of the kingdom is love. . . . Darkness is individualism, selfishness. Light is love, communion, fellowship."[39] Love for God, love for neighbor and love for our sisters and brothers in Christ characterizes discipleship. Discipleship flourishes in divine love. "Jesus wants us to be one. Just as the Trinity is one—Father, Son, and Holy Spirit—so he wants us to be one. He wants this not only in evangelistic efforts and in fellowship meetings; He wants us to love one another."[40] Ortiz says that this love and unity is the center of authentic discipleship.

Gutiérrez says that discipleship is *collective walking in the Spirit*. Discipleship is a *collective adventure*. "The following of Jesus is not, purely or primarily, an individual matter but a collective adventure. The journey of the people of God is set in motion by a direct encounter with the Lord but an encounter in community: '*We* have found the Messiah.'"[41]

Together we develop as disciples and learn the spiritual disciplines of discipleship.

SPIRITUAL DISCIPLINES AND DEVELOPING DISCIPLES

Much has been made of the spirituality of the Argentinian pope of the Catholic Church, Jorge Mario Bergoglio (Pope Francis). He chooses simpler papal attire. Instead of living in the official papal residence in the Apostolic Palace, he lives in the Vatican guesthouse. He ministers in the slums.

In November 2013, Francis made headlines. He embraced, kissed and prayed with Vinicio Riva. Riva is a Christian horribly disfigured by neurofibromatosis, a skin disease. Francis is widely acclaimed for his humility, love for the poor, desire to dialogue with other worldviews and practice of spiritual disciplines. He is compassionate, humble, open, prayerful and Christlike. *Time Magazine* named Francis the 2013 Person of the Year for these qualities.

Elizabeth Tenety wrote an opinion piece for the Washington Post titled "Like Pope Francis? You'll Love Jesus." In that piece, Tenety shows how Jesus is the source of Pope Francis's spirituality. She says that if people like the

---

[39]Juan Carlos Ortiz, *Disciple* (Carol Stream, IL: Creation House, 1975), 40-41.

[40]Juan Carlos Ortiz and Jamie Buckingham, *Call to Discipleship* (Plainfield, NJ: Logos International, 1975), 136.

[41]Gustavo Gutiérrez, *We Drink from Our Own Wells: The Spiritual Journey of a People* (Maryknoll, NY: Orbis, 1984), 42.

humility and compassion of Francis, they will love Jesus. Jesus inspires and amplifies these traits.[42]

This fresh Latin American servantship and spirituality is revitalizing the Catholic Church. Francis's spirituality focuses on and is nurtured by spiritual disciplines, encounter with Christ and witness in the world.[43] Spiritual disciplines are important for our development as disciples. These spiritual practices enable spiritual formation. They nourish authentic discipleship.

Richard Foster and others have written useful guides on spiritual disciplines.[44] Westerners write most of these guides. Francis shows the importance of learning about spiritual formation from the non-West.

Majority World and indigenous thinkers emphasize the following spiritual disciplines. This is not an exhaustive list, but just a few disciplines that stand out.

1. Disciplined, upside-down discipleship. The spiritual discipline of holding our values, beliefs, practices and desires up to the scrutiny of the gospel. And allowing Jesus to turn these upside-down. Anthony of Sourozh (Russian theologian) challenges the gospel he encounters in the West:

> The Gospel is a harsh document; the Gospel is ruthless and specific in what it says; the Gospel is not meant to be re-worded, watered down and brought to the level of either our understanding or our taste. The Gospel is proclaiming something which is beyond us and which is there to stretch our mind, to widen our heart beyond the bearable at times, to recondition all our life, to give us a world view which is simply the world upside-down and this we are not keen to accept.[45]

2. Disciplined prayer (ascesis). We need a disciplined life of prayer. Such prayer isn't only practiced in the spontaneous, suffering, ecstatic or

---

[42]Elizabeth Tenety, "Like Pope Francis? You'll Love Jesus," *The Washington Post*, December 11, 2013, www.washingtonpost.com/opinions/like-pope-francis-youll-love-jesus/2013/12/11/cf2d4fd8 -610d-11e3-8beb-3f9a9942850f_story.html.

[43]Matthew Bunson, *Pope Francis* (Huntington, IN: Our Sunday Visitor, 2013), 189-90.

[44]Richard J. Foster, *Celebration of Discipline: The Path to Spiritual Growth*, 20th anniversary ed. (San Francisco: HarperSanFrancisco, 1998); Richard J. Foster and Emilie Griffin, *Spiritual Classics: Selected Readings for Individuals and Groups on the Twelve Spiritual Disciplines* (San Francisco: HarperSanFrancisco, 2000); Adele Ahlberg Calhoun, *Spiritual Disciplines Handbook: Practices That Transform Us* (Downers Grove, IL: InterVarsity Press, 2005).

[45]Anthony Bloom, "Can Modern Man Believe?," sermon preached at Great St. Mary's, the University Church, Cambridge, March, 5, 1978.

enthusiastic moments. It's also practiced during the ordinary, drab, mundane or routine times of life. We need resources to persevere in prayer even when God seems absent or remote. Anthony of Sourozh says that we nurture this kind of *ascesis*—a disciplined life of prayer—through a rich variety of prayer practices. These practices include meditation on Scripture, liturgical prayer, the prayer of silence, praying the Lord's Prayer and so on.[46]

Simon Chan talks about the need to develop a *rule of life*—regular practices of prayer like those develop by Benedict of Nursia. Chan says spiritual direction and Christian mentoring nurture this.[47] He offers spiritual disciplines that focus on God and self (e.g., self-examining and contemplative prayer practices).[48] He suggests practices that focus on the Word (e.g., meditating on Scripture, spiritual reading and biblical memorization). And he outlines disciplines directed toward the world (e.g., spiritual friendship, meditation on creation, spiritual discernment and a spirituality of social involvement and liberation).[49]

3. Disciplined acts of liberation, justice, and mercy. Majority World spiritual disciplines are not typically interior and mystical and otherworldly. Many write about the spiritual discipline of intentionally practicing justice and dissent and liberation. This is fasting as loosing the chains of injustice. Untying the cords of the yoke. Setting the oppressed free. Breaking every

---

[46]Anthony Bloom, *Living Prayer* (Springfield, IL: Templegate, 1966); Bloom, *Beginning to Pray* (New York: Paulist, 1970); Bloom, *The Essence of Prayer* (London: Darton, Longman and Todd, 1986); Anthony Bloom and Gillian Crow, *Metropolitan Anthony of Sourozh: Essential Writings*, Modern Spiritual Masters (Maryknoll, NY: Orbis, 2010); Anthony Bloom and Georges Lefebvre, *Courage to Pray* (Crestwood, NY: St. Vladimir's Seminary, 2002).

[47]For treatment of spiritual direction in Africa, Asia, Latin America and multicultural contexts, see Susan Rakoczy, *Common Journey, Different Paths: Spiritual Direction in Cross-Cultural Perspective* (Maryknoll, NY: Orbis, 1992).

[48]Watchman Nee and Sadhu Sundar Singh are two examples of Asian Christian contemplative authors: Sadhu Sundar Singh and Charles E. Moore, *Sadhu Sundar Singh: Essential Writings*, Modern Spiritual Masters (Maryknoll, NY: Orbis, 2005); Watchman Nee, *The Normal Christian Life*, The Essential Christian Library (Uhrichsville, OH: Barbour, 1999); Nee, *The Complete Works of Watchman Nee* (Richmond, VA: Christian Fellowship, 2004); Nee, *Spiritual Exercise: Simplified Version of the Basic Lessons on Practical Christian Living* (New York: Christian Fellowship, 2007); Nee, *The Secret of Christian Living* (New York: Christian Fellowship, 2008); Nee, *Sit, Walk, Stand: The Process of Christian Maturity* (Fort Washington, PA: CLC, 2009); Watchman Nee and Randal W. Kulp, *Secrets to Spiritual Power* (New Kensington, PA: Whitaker House, 1998).

[49]Simon Chan, *Spiritual Theology: A Systematic Study of the Christian Life* (Downers Grove, IL: InterVarsity Press, 1998), part 2.

yoke. Sharing food with the hungry. Clothing and providing for the poor. Sheltering the homeless and stateless. Spending ourselves in behalf of the hungry. And satisfying the needs of the oppressed (Is 58). Writing about these spiritual disciplines is prolific in Asia and Africa and Latin America.[50]

4. Disciplined care for creation. Spiritual practices that are liberative must include justice for both humanity and the creation. I will not say much about this because I have dedicated a chapter to eco-spirituality in Majority World thinking. Leonardo Boff writes extensively on eco-spirituality. Boff believes that "a new spirituality, one adequate to the ecological revolution, is urgently needed."[51] The practices of this spirituality include simple living and celebrating ecological interdependency. It includes thankfulness for the wonder and beauty and sacredness of God's creation. Boff demonstrates how St. Francis of Assisi is an exemplar of "all the cardinal ecological virtues." He demonstrates the spiritual disciplines that exemplify creation-care.[52]

George E. Tinker is an Osage Christian theologian. Tinker reveals the extent to which Westerners can learn from Native American love for the land. We can learn from their sense of deep connection to and dependency on the land. Tinker says that Westerners must learn spiritual practices that respect and nourish the land. They must learn these practices from First Nations—from "indigenous prophets":

> The whites, too, shall pass—perhaps sooner than other tribes. Continue to contaminate your bed, and you will one night suffocate in your own waste. When the buffalo are all slaughtered, the wild horses all tamed, the secret corners of the forest heavy with the scent of men, and the view of the ripe hills

---

[50]See, for example, Virginia Fabella, Peter K. H. Lee and David Kwang-sun Suh, eds., *Asian Christian Spirituality: Reclaiming Traditions* (Maryknoll, NY: Orbis, 1992); Juan Carlos Ortiz, *Cry of the Human Heart* (Carol Stream, IL: Creation House, 1977); Ortiz, *Disciple*; Ortiz and Buckingham, *Call to Discipleship*. Boff invited his readers to "be a contemplative in liberation." We do this by synthesizing desire for God, fervent prayer, passion for the impoverished and zeal for justice and liberation: Boff, *Faith on the Edge: Religion and Marginalized Existence* (San Francisco: Harper & Row, 1989), chap. 4.

[51]Leonardo Boff, *Cry of the Earth, Cry of the Poor*, Ecology and Justice (Maryknoll, NY: Orbis, 1997), 189. Also see Boff, *Holy Trinity, Perfect Community*, part 10; Boff, *Ecology and Liberation: A New Paradigm*, Ecology and Justice Series (Maryknoll, NY: Orbis, 1995); Boff, *Saint Francis: A Model for Human Liberation* (New York: Crossroad, 1982).

[52]Boff, *Cry of the Earth, Cry of the Poor*, 203-20. Amos Yong says that we need a Spirit-centered theology of the environment. "Life in the Spirit is ultimately about life in this world, our world, God's world." Yong, *The Spirit Poured Out on All Flesh: Pentecostalism and the Possibility of Global Theology* (Grand Rapids: Baker Academic, 2005), 299.

blotted by talking wires, where is the thicket? Gone. Where is the eagle? Gone. And what is it to say goodbye to the swift and the hunt, the end of living and the end of survival?[53]

Randy S. Woodley is a Keetoowah Cherokee teacher, poet, activist, pastor, missiologist and historian. In *Shalom and the Community of Creation*, Woodley avoids romanticizing Native American relations with the land. Instead, Woodley shows how a Christian theology of creation resonates with native traditions. He also shows how Christian practices of creation care—let's call them eco-spiritual disciplines—can complement and integrate with native earth-keeping traditions. Woodley invites the church to move away from imperial metaphors like *the kingdom of God*. Instead, he'd prefer we embrace a metaphor like *the community of creation*.[54]

I'm sympathetic to Woodley's concerns. I appreciate his concern to deal with images that may be oppressive to some. But my problem with this replacement of metaphors is that the Lamb who was slain is victorious. He sits on the throne. He overthrows powers and principalities and rulers and kingdoms. So is it right to do away with this metaphor? Can we afford to throw it away? To take *kingdom* and *rule* out of the metaphor strips it of its ability to overthrow the enemy and the kingdoms of darkness and the world.

Having said that, when Woodley refers to the community of creation he has several things in mind: First, the replacement of the imperial side of Christendom. So Woodley uses the term *Shalom Kingdom*, tying the metaphor of kingdom into shalom. (This is a peaceable and reconciling and healing kingdom. It's a kingdom characterized by these other notions associated with the metaconstruct of shalom.) Second, Woodley wants to move into a less human-centered spirituality and worldview. Jesus Christ incarnates, lives, dies and resurrects for the whole of creation—not just humanity. We need to reflect this in our spiritual practices and in our disciplined care for creation.

---

[53]Tinker, "Native Americans and the Land," 74. See Tinker, "Spirituality, Native American Personhood, Sovereignty and Solidarity"; Tinker, "The Basileia of God: The Alternative to Violence," *Church & Society* 85, no. 3 (1995).

[54]Randy S. Woodley, *Shalom and the Community of Creation: An Indigenous Vision*, Prophetic Christianity (Grand Rapids: Eerdmans, 2012), 39. See Woodley, "Dream Catchers: How Mainstream America Discovered Native Spirituality," *Missiology* 35, no. 1 (2007); Woodley, "Following Jesus in Invaded Space: Doing Theology on Aboriginal Land," *Missiology* 38, no. 2 (2010).

Suffering is a common human experience. First Nations and poorer countries know it well. We turn now to Christian spirituality and discipleship in suffering.

SPIRITUALITY AND SUFFERING

A recent Pew Research Forum report showed that "more than 2.2 billion people—nearly a third (32%) of the world's total population of 6.9 billion—live in countries where either government restrictions on religion or social hostilities involving religion rose substantially over the three-year period studied [mid-2006 to mid-2009]." Christians are persecuted in 131 countries. It is hard to get an exact figure, but close to one hundred thousand Christians are martyred every year.[55]

Andrew F. Walls provides a moving account of the life and martyrdom of the African Christian leader Gudina Tumsa. Derg soldiers murdered Tumsa in 1979. He's been called the Dietrich Bonhoeffer of Africa. Walls shows how Tumsa's murder follows a pattern of persecution, suffering, martyrdom and witness in the African church and describes earlier episodes of witness and martyrdom in Africa. (These include the martyrs of Scilli, the life of Takla Haymanot of Ethiopia, the Ugandan martyrs and the murder of Christians in the Sudan today.) "The test of discipleship is suffering; and Africa, which has known so much suffering, has often been a furnace for the testing of Christian quality. . . . The word *martyr* has come to mean one who dies for the sake of Christ, but the basic meaning is simply *witness*."[56]

Majority World literature reminds us "to serve is to suffer." Discipleship comes at a cost. As Leonardo and Clodovis Boff remind us, Christians often suffer because of their solidarity with the suffering and oppressed and silenced. Christian spirituality and discipleship is forged in suffering. Ajith Fernando says, "If the Apostle Paul knew fatigue, anger, and anxiety in his ministry, what makes us think we can avoid them in ours?"[57]

---

[55]Pew Research, "Rising Restrictions on Religion: One-Third of the World's Population Experiences an Increase," *Pew Research Religion and Public Life Project*, August 9, 2011, www.pewforum.org /2011/08/09/rising-restrictions-on-religion2/.

[56]Andrew F. Walls, "The Cost of Discipleship: The Witness of the African Church," *Word & World* 25, no. 4 (2005): 434.

[57]Ajith Fernando, "To Serve Is to Suffer: If the Apostle Paul Knew Fatigue, Anger, and Anxiety in His Ministry, What Makes Us Think We Can Avoid Them in Ours?," *Christianity Today* 54, no. 8 (2010): 31.

René Padilla links discipleship and mission and suffering: "Christian mission and Christian discipleship are two sides of the same coin. Both derive their meaning from Jesus, the crucified Messiah, who even as Lord remains crucified. The Christian mission is the mission of those who have identified themselves with the Crucified and are willing to follow him to the cross. Mission is suffering."[58]

SPIRITUALITY AND THE MISSION OF GOD

Recently, there has been an upsurge of interest in missional spirituality in the West. Dwight J. Zscheile, for example, released a collection of essays in missional spiritual formation. Roger Helland and Leonard Hjalmarson have released a book called *Missional Spirituality*. In that book, they identify some of the practices of missional spirituality, which include reflection on missional theology and union with Christ and practicing humility. They include surrendering to God's will, love for God and neighbor, and reading Scripture missionally.[59]

Spirituality and discipleship and mission are linked in Majority World thinking and practice. As Padilla claims, discipleship and mission are two sides of the one coin. Asian and African and Latin American thinkers and churches challenge the West with a profound truth: *There's no true mission without discipleship. And there's no authentic discipleship without mission.*

Latin American thinkers cast a compelling vision for missional spirituality.[60] Samuel Escobar, for example, puts the interdependence between spirituality and mission like this: "Spirituality without involvement in social, economic, and political concerns is mere religiosity."[61] Mission and service form Christian spirituality and discipleship. Just as mission forges Christian theology, "the

---

[58]C. René Padilla, "Bible Studies," *Missiology* 10, no. 3 (1982): 338.

[59]Roger Helland and Len Hjalmarson, *Missional Spirituality: Embodying God's Love from the Inside Out* (Downers Grove, IL: InterVarsity Press, 2011); Dwight J. Zscheile, ed., *Cultivating Sent Communities: Missional Spiritual Formation*, Missional Church Series (Grand Rapids: Eerdmans, 2012).

[60]See, for instance, Joseph Davis, "The Movement Toward Mysticism in Gustavo Gutiérrez's Thought: Is This an Open Door to Pentecostal Dialogue?," *Pneuma: The Journal of the Society for Pentecostal Studies* 33, no. 1 (2011); Robert L. Gallagher, "Mission from the Inside Out: An Integrative Analysis of Selected Latin American Protestant 'Writings' in Spirituality and Mission," *Missiology* 40, no. 1 (2012).

[61]Rodger C. Bassham, *Mission Theology, 1948–1975: Years of Worldwide Creative Tension—Ecumenical, Evangelical, and Roman Catholic* (Pasadena, CA: William Carey, 1979), 237.

same is true for piety, for prayer, and the spiritual disciplines."[62] Jose Miguez
Bonino says that this means "evangelism, prayer, worship, and private devo-
tions do not have to be abandoned. They have to be converted to Christ."[63]

Orlando Costas describes a spirituality of missional engagement:

> To take head on oppressive structures like consumerism, technology, mili-
> tarism, multinational capitalism, international communism, racism, and
> sexism, we need a *spirituality of missional engagement*: a devotional attitude,
> a personal ethic, a continuous liturgical experience that flows out of and ex-
> presses itself in apostolic obedience. Prayer, Bible study, personal ethics, and
> worship will not mean withdrawal from the world but *immersion in its suf-
> fering and struggles*. Likewise, participation in the struggles of history will not
> mean an abandonment of piety and contemplation, but an experience of God
> from the depths of human suffering.
>
> *Mission without spirituality cannot survive any more than combustion without
> oxygen.* The nature of the world in which we live and the gospel that we have
> been committed to communicate therein demand, however, *that it be a spiritu-
> ality of engagement, not of withdrawal.* Such a spirituality can only be cultivated
> in obedience and discipleship, and not in the isolated comfort of one's inner self.
> By the same token, it can only be verified in the liberating struggles against the
> principalities and powers that hold so many millions in bondage.[64]

Costas does not stop there. A spirituality of missional engagement means
that worship and mission are inseparable. It is misleading to say that we
grow spiritually through worship *and* mission—as though the two are separate. Costas says that as we experience redemption through Christ's mission,
we worship. We respond by participating in Christ's mission as an act of
worship. Our spiritual formation testifies to the inseparability of mission
and worship and community.

> There is no dichotomy between worship and mission. Worship is the gath-
> ering of the people sent into the world to celebrate what God has done in
> Christ and is doing through their participation in the Spirit's witnessing
> action. Mission is the culmination and anticipation of worship. In worship

---

[62]Samuel Escobar, "Recruitment of Students for Mission," *Missiology* 15, no. 4 (1987): 543.
[63]Jose Miguez Bonino, "The Present Crisis in Mission," in *Mission Trends No. 1: Crucial Issues in
    Mission Today*, ed. Gerald H. Anderson and Thomas F. Stransky (New York: Paulist, 1974), 41.
[64]Orlando E. Costas, *Christ Outside the Gate: Mission Beyond Christendom* (Maryknoll, NY:
    Orbis, 1982), 171-72. Italics added for emphasis.

and mission, the redeemed community gives evidence to the fact that it is a praying and witnessing people.

Liturgy without mission is like a river without a spring. Mission without worship is like a river without a sea. Both are necessary. Without the one, the other loses its vitality and meaning. Put in other terms, the test of a vigorous worship experience will be a dynamic participation in mission. The test of a faithful missional involvement will be a profound worship experience.[65]

Leonardo Boff claims that the church needs a new spirituality. It needs one that makes prayer, politics, liberation, community and mission inseparable. This spirituality is evidenced by "prayer materialized in action." This is especially action with and among the suffering and oppressed. We come together as a community to share our missional experiences and liberative actions and prayers for the world. This is a movement from individual to corporate prayer and action. Furthermore, Boff says that liturgy must be a "celebration of life." As we pray together we celebrate our freedoms, hopes, cultures and life. This prayer is also "critical prayer." As we pray together we challenge each other to fuller expression and integration and integrity in discipleship and mission.[66]

Such spirituality requires "political holiness." As we pray together we *cultivate* a holiness characterized by justice and mercy and righteousness. And we *stand together against* poverty, oppression, exploitation and the destruction of people and cultures and creation.[67] And this spirituality also demands "prophetic courage and historical patience." Our spirituality must give us courage in mission and justice and peace making. "This attitude springs from a contemplative vision of history, whose only sovereign is God."[68]

Boff says that we need "an attitude of Easter." A missional spirituality will involve hardship and suffering and martyrdom. We suffer along with our Crucified Lord, triumph along with our Resurrected Christ and anticipate the fullness of his final triumph.[69]

---

[65]Orlando Costas, *The Integrity of Mission: The Inner Life and Outreach of the Church* (San Francisco: Harper and Row, 1979), 91.

[66]Leonardo Boff, "The Need for Political Saints: From a Spirituality of Liberation to the Practice of Liberation," *Cross Currents* 30, no. 4 (1980): 377-78.

[67]Pedro Casaldáliga and Jose-Maria Vigil provide a comprehensive treatment of political holiness in *Political Holiness*.

[68]Leonardo Boff, "Spirituality and Politics," in Curt Cadorette et al., *Liberation Theology: An Introductory Reader* (Eugene, OR: Wipf and Stock, 2004), 243.

[69]See M. M. Thomas, "The Holy Spirit and the Spirituality for Political Struggles," *Ecumenical Review*

CHRISTIAN SPIRITUALITY AND THE GLOBALCHURCH:
CONCLUDING REFLECTIONS

Being a disciple of Jesus is a thrilling and demanding adventure. A life of *communion with God in Jesus Christ* involves discipleship to him, intimacy with God and others and participation in his mission. It's participation in his community, life, love, kingdom and mission.

Here are eleven things we learn from how Majority World Christians practice Christian spirituality and discipleship:

1. Christian spirituality cultivates a life of communion with God in Jesus Christ. We express this life of communion with God through discipleship to Jesus. Communion with God brings love, joy, rest and peace. But it also brings change and discomfort and suffering. When we enjoy communion with God, we embrace his community, life, love, holiness, kingdom and mission.

While it may be possible to entertain a spiritual life in a variety of ways, Christian spirituality as a specific pathway develops through discipleship to Jesus Christ. It's living in and for the kingdom of God, with the people of God, in communion with God the Son, by the power of God the Spirit. It's living the resurrection life and its personal and community transformation and restoration. Christian spirituality is radical communion and union with Father and Son and Holy Spirit. The Holy Spirit empowers Christian spirituality. He enables us to be disciples of Jesus Christ for the glory of God the Father. Christian spirituality is a lived experience of faith in Jesus Christ. We develop it through relationship with others and union with the triune God.

2. Christian spirituality explores the concrete implications of trinitarian theology. We've seen how Leonardo Boff and Ricardo de Sousa place trinitarian theology at the heart of Christian spirituality. Chan also understands spiritual formation as participation in trinitarian and human fellowship. He demonstrates how a deep spirituality doesn't just focus on the whole Trinity. It also focuses on the individual members of the Trinity.

Spirituality *focused on the Father* emphasizes creation and covenant and life. It's a *sacramental spirituality*. It presupposes "an indirect working of grace through created things."

Spirituality *focused on the Son* stresses the inauguration of the kingdom

---

42, nos. 3/4 (1990). See also the writings of another Indian theologian, Aruna Gnanadason: "Spirituality That Sustains Us in Our Struggles."

in the incarnation. It also underlines "the gospel-events of Jesus' life, death, resurrection, ascension, and coming again." It's an *evangelical spirituality*. It's "marked by a warm and intimate relationship with Jesus Christ as Lord, Savior, friend, and so on."

Spirituality *focused on the Spirit* emphasizes God's empowering presence. It focuses on the eschatological outpouring of the Spirit. It's a *charismatic spirituality*. It's "open to the direct workings of the Spirit coming from 'beyond history' (Zizioulas) in surprising ways, such as prophecies and healings."[70]

We need each of these emphases—Father and Son and Holy Spirit—to develop a full spiritual life. And we must explore the concrete implications of trinitarian theology for the church and our discipleship. For example, what does the doctrine of the Trinity mean for our practices of prayer and worship and community? And how does it shape our practices of mission and friendship and discipleship? And how do we form churches that tap into the best of the sacramental and evangelical and charismatic traditions?

3. Christian spirituality follows Jesus in the power of the Spirit. In this chapter, we've seen that we follow Jesus in the power of the Spirit in a variety of ways. Such Spirit-empowered discipleship pursues holy indignation, self-sacrificial action and political holiness. It desires the gifts and fruit of the Spirit. Spirit-filled discipleship shows solidarity with the poor and powerless. It cultivates crucified and risen minds. It receives the power and presence and provision of the Spirit. It's holy and loving and righteous. It joins in the *missio Dei*. And it witnesses to the gospel in word and action and presence.

4. Christian spirituality learns from First Nation and indigenous faith. As Christians, we need to learn from the expressions of Christian spirituality in other cultures. As I travel throughout Asia, Africa and Latin America, I'm constantly challenged about what it means to be a disciple of Jesus Christ.

We also need to be open and responsive to what indigenous and First Nations peoples teach us about Christian discipleship and spirituality. This is especially true of the people who are indigenous to our area. For me, this is the Eora people of the Sydney Basin. While nonindigenous people have lived in Sydney for just over two hundred years, the Eora people have lived here for sixty thousand years. We can learn so much from indigenous and First

---

[70]Simon Chan, "Spiritual Theology" in Scorgie et al., *Dictionary of Christian Spirituality*, 53; Chan, *Spiritual Theology*, chap. 2.

Nations peoples. We can learn from their creation care and earth keeping, their welcome and hospitality, their family and community, their generosity and contentment, and their denial of any distinctions between the natural and the spiritual. We can learn from their courage, faith, forgiveness and spirituality in the face of invasion and occupation and colonialism. We do the same in response to other cultures that are different from our own.

5. Christian spirituality engages culture critically. In this chapter, I've outlined some culturally formed approaches to Christian spirituality and discipleship. I've especially focused on Africa, Asia, indigenous cultures and First Nations. As Christians, we must examine how our culture has shaped our discipleship, and vice versa. For example, when you consider Christian approaches to money, sex, work and family, how much of your conclusions are formed by Scripture or by your culture? Our spiritual life cannot flourish without a critical engagement with culture and its influence on us.

Part of that critical process is putting our expressions of faith into conversation with other forms of discipleship from other cultures.[71] This shows us how culture influences our faith, and how our faith can embrace fresh expressions.

6. Christian spirituality moves from individualism to community. Christian spirituality is a collective adventure. We must relinquish spiritual individualism and pursue spirituality in community.

Relationship is the hub of authentic human personhood. Relationship is central to personal growth and integration—with God and then with others. Psychosocial theories back up this theological claim. These theories say that we achieve fuller psychological and emotional wholeness when we go through crises with others. These relationships don't just sustain and support us through crises. They help make us more mature and integrated persons. Psychosocial theories say that this is human nature. Relationships enrich us as we interact with "a widening radius of significant individuals and institutions."[72] We should put weight on the meaning people attach to significant relationships in life. These relationships are crucial for personal growth and well-being and integration.

---

[71]For a fascinating example of how this might be done, see this collection of articles that put South African spirituality into conversation with Old Testament spirituality: Christo Lombaard, "The Old Testament and Christian Spirituality: Theoretical and Practical Essays from a South African Perspective," *Society of Biblical Literature, International Voices in Biblical Studies* 2 (2012).

[72]Michael Jackson, "Pastoral Theology Foundations: Unit Guide," course notes (The University of Notre Dame, Fremantle, Australia, 1991), 95. Jackson is citing Erik Erikson.

Psychosocial and socio-phenomenological theories emphasize the importance of relationship. Relationship is key to our discipleship and wholeness and personhood. Relationship is the key to the movement toward—or away from—authentic personhood and integration. Our interpersonal experiences—and our interpretations of them—shape the assumptions we build from these experiences. They lead to authentic personhood and growth and integration. (Or these interpersonal experiences lead away from these things. This is especially the case when relationships are damaging or when we respond to them in unhealthy ways.)

The movement of faith development through various stages is an example. (See the work of Robert Kegan and James Fowler.) This is a movement from no faith to self-surrender and self-transcendence. It is the movement from intuitive faith to self-transcending and self-sacrificing faith. Relationship is the hub of this growth. How do we manifest authentic selfhood? How do we grow as spiritual beings? Through loving relationship with God and others. This wholeness and spirituality is impossible apart from community.

The movement from self-centeredness to self-transcendence is as important to Christian spirituality as it is to developmental psychology. It's about growth in personal integrity, wholeness, faith, hope, love and Christlikeness. Both traditions speak of this phenomenon. But they use different terms and reference points.

The whole psychological self is *the loving self in relationship*. But in Christian terms, what is the whole spiritual self? It's *the trusting, interdependent, loving self in relationship (from and for God and others)*.

7. Christian spirituality is shaped through practices. As Christians, we need to develop spiritual disciplines and practices that allow Jesus to turn our values, practices, priorities and desires upside down. This includes scrutinizing these things in the light of the words and example of Jesus Christ. He wants to turn our worldview and values and lifestyle upside down.

Jesus shapes our Christian spirituality through his grace. But he also uses our practices. So we need prayer, meditation, fasting, spiritual reading and biblical memorization. And we need spiritual friendship and worship in community. We nurture Christian spirituality through our engagement in social justice. We enlarge it through our involvement in mission. We earth Christian spirituality through our care for creation. And we enrich it through our earth-keeping practices. (Among other things, earth-keeping practices include planting gardens, tending trees, growing vegetables, recycling waste, conserving energy, producing and consuming locally, and campaigning for ecological well-being and justice.)

8. Christian spirituality welcomes pleasure and suffering. This is hard. And it's too easy for me to make such a statement from the safety and comfort of my Australian home. Just this week, the terrorist group Islamic State brutally murdered twenty-one Egyptian Christians for being "people of the cross." As Christians, we welcome liberation, joy, faith, love, peace and hope as the fruit of discipleship and divine grace. But we will also welcome fatigue, persecution, hardship, martyrdom and suffering as the fruit of discipleship and witness to Jesus Christ and his gospel and kingdom.

The book of Job reminds us that suffering isn't always cleansing, educational, testing or edifying. Job's friends make the mistake of offering theological clichés and complicated explanations to the sufferer. Job needed comfort, presence and solidarity, not clichéd answers. Life is full of contradictions and pain. The righteous and innocent sufferer may find hope and peace in trusting God. This can be the case even if they can't find satisfactory answers to their painful questions.

The Bible shows us that God is not distanced from human suffering. He suffers greatly. Jesus experienced profound suffering: *physical* (from hunger, weariness, flogging and crucifixion), *emotional* (he wept for Lazarus) and *mental* and *spiritual* (such as his agony in the garden and his torment on the cross). Jesus identifies with the innocent sufferer because he was an innocent sufferer. We are not alone in our pain. When we suffer, he suffers with us. Sadhu Sundar Singh tells us that Jesus says, "Since I bore the cross I am able to deliver and keep in perfect safety all who are cross-bearers. Even when they walk through the fires of persecution, I am there."[73]

Since God enters our suffering, he is able to work through it for our good (even though suffering is never good in itself). God is with us when we suffer. He may use suffering to draw us to Christ and lead us to Christian maturity (he *uses*, not *causes*, suffering for his people). We grow spiritually as we hold on to the promise that God is with us in our suffering and as we cling to the

---

[73]Sadhu Sundar Singh, *At the Feet of the Master* (London: Hodder and Stoughton, 1985), 74; Singh and Moore, *Sadhu Sundar Singh*, 81-90.

hope of eternal healing. We show others compassion and solidarity in their suffering or persecution. We refuse simplistic or clichéd answers. We engage in prayer for healing and ministry among those who suffer. We stand in solidarity with those who suffer. We remember the cross. It is the cross and resurrection that show us that God suffers and shares our pain, that resurrection life is ours and that we have an eternal hope. We are in radical union with a suffering and crucified and resurrected Lord.

God forges our discipleship in the midst of suffering. This has been the way for millennia. As witnesses to the mission of God through Jesus Christ, we endure suffering. The Spirit enables us to be suffering and vindicated witnesses to the gospel of Jesus Christ.

9. *Christian spirituality rejects religiosity.* As disciples, we reject mere religiosity. We refuse the "form" of godliness that denies the power of God (2 Tim 3:5). Instead, we embrace a spirituality of personal transformation, immersion in community and conversion to the neighbor. We involve ourselves in the political, economic, ecological, moral and social struggles of our generation (and of our particular location). We seek authentic conversion to the gospel of Christ and the will of the Father and the power of the Spirit. We love the Lord our God with all our heart and soul and mind and strength. And we love our neighbor as ourselves (Lk 10:27).

10. *Christian spirituality is holistic and integrative.* Christian spirituality in the West is often dualistic. Sacred is separated from secular. Body is separated from spirit. Individual is separated from communal. Event is separated from process. Evangelism is separated from social action. Public is separated from private. Objective is separated from subjective. But as Christians, we must seek integrative spiritual formation. We must break down these divisions. We do this by nurturing a discipleship that's holistic and integrative. What do we integrate? Mission and discipleship. Rejoicing and suffering. Body and spirit. Prayer and political holiness. Evangelism and social action. Bible and Spirit. Worship and liberating action. Contemplation and selfless service. And that's just the start.

11. *Christian spirituality is inseparable from mission.* Christian spirituality and discipleship grow in mission. They provide resources for mission. They're inseparable from mission. They're the oxygen for mission. They need mission to flourish. The great South African missiologist David Bosch says we don't have to choose between spirituality and mission:

> Spirituality is not contemplation over against action. It is not a flight from the world over against involvement in the world. . . . The involvement in this world should lead to a deepening of our relationship with and dependence on God, and the deepening of this relationship should lead to increasing involvement in the world. Pouring out our love on people in selfless dedication is a form of prayer. . . . Spirituality is all-pervading.[74]

In conclusion, we shape our Christian spirituality around the truth that God unveiled his being as Father and Son and Spirit. And this triune God invites us into his fellowship life. God calls us to witness to the astonishing inbreaking of the kingdom of God in this world. Our Christian spirituality and discipleship witness to the kingdom inaugurated in the incarnation of Jesus and the outpouring of the Spirit. We offer this witness by the grace and will of God the Father. Christian spirituality is a life of communion with God in Jesus Christ.

---

[74]David J. Bosch, *A Spirituality of the Road*, Missionary Studies (Scottdale, PA: Herald, 1979), 13-14.

GLOBALCHURCH

Embracing a New Narrative

It is as if the globe had been turned upside down and sideways.

MARK NOLL

Mark Noll makes a striking observation:

> It is as if the globe had been turned upside down and sideways. A few short decades ago, Christian believers were concentrated in the global north and west, but now a rapidly swelling majority lives in the global south and east. If Rip Van Winkle wiped a half-century of sleep from his eyes [after awaking this past week] and tried to locate his fellow Christian believers, he would find them in surprising places, expressing their faith in surprising ways, under surprising conditions, with surprising relationships to culture and politics, and raising surprising theological questions that would not have seemed possible when he fell asleep.[1]

The Spirit of Christ is causing a fascinating and thrilling shift in global Christianity. Western Christians can no longer claim to be the center or heartbeat of the global church. The shift toward the Majority World is undeniable. Majority World churches are booming in numbers and growing at an exponential rate. Many scholars have documented this growth, and I've described it in this book. "By 2025 fully two-thirds of Christians will live in Africa, Latin America, and Asia."[2] "A century ago, the Global North (commonly

---

[1]Mark A. Noll, *The New Shape of World Christianity: How American Experience Reflects Global Faith* (Downers Grove, IL: IVP Academic, 2009), 19-20.
[2]Stephen B. Bevans, Roger Schroeder and L. J. Luzbetak, "Missiology After Bosch: Reverencing a Classic by Moving Beyond," *International Bulletin of Missionary Research* 29, no. 2 (2005): 69.

defined as North America, Europe, Australia, Japan, and New Zealand) contained more than four times as many Christians as the Global South (the rest of the world). Today . . . more than 1.3 billion Christians live in the Global South [61% of all Christians live in Asia, Africa and Latin America], compared with about 860 million in the Global North (39%)."[3] The Spirit enabled this astonishing shift to happen in only one hundred years.[4]

At the same time, the churches of the West are declining. The West is in desperate need of remissionalization. Patrick Johnstone observes that Europe's Christian growth rate "turned into absolute decline by 1980. This has rapidly accelerated and is likely to far exceed even the general population decline." Secularization and other forces have eroded North America's churches. They're likely to experience "a reduction of the Christian growth rate to almost zero in 2050."[5]

Western societies have shifted away from Christendom. They have mostly become post-Christendom cultures. Christendom took many forms in the West. But it's now finished in these cultures. *Christendom* was that period in Western history when church and state were closely aligned. During the Western experience of Christendom, Christianity became the majority religion in many nations. Christianity forged close connections with those nations. It often aligned itself with their politics and political goals. And it often supported their institutions and instruments of power. Philip Jenkins has demonstrated that some parts Asia and Africa and Latin America are experiencing *new Christendoms*.[6] But Western cultures and contexts are going in the opposite direction. They are moving away from Christendom settings and into post-Christendom dynamics.

What is *post-Christendom*? Stuart Murray defines it clearly: "Post-Christendom is the culture that emerges as the Christian faith loses coherence within a society that has been definitively shaped by the Christian story and

---

[3]Pew Research Center, *Global Christianity: A Report on the Size and Distribution of the World's Christian Population,* December 19, 2011, www.pewforum.org/2011/12/19/global-christianity-exec.

[4]See David B. Barrett, George T. Kurian and Todd M. Johnson, *World Christian Encyclopedia: A Comparative Survey of Churches and Religions in the Modern World,* 2nd ed., 2 vols. (New York: Oxford University Press, 2001), 12-15, and www.globalchristianity.org.

[5]Patrick J. Johnstone, *The Future of the Global Church: History, Trends and Possibilities* (Colorado Springs, CO: Biblica, 2011), 99.

[6]Philip Jenkins, *The Next Christendom: The Coming of Global Christianity,* 3rd ed. (Oxford: Oxford University Press, 2011).

as the institutions that have been developed to express Christian convictions decline in influence."[7] Many Western churches find themselves on the margins of post-Christendom cultures. A post-Christendom recalibration of the church and its mission is necessary. This includes a missional recalibration of mission, ministry, worship, discipleship and community. Western churches need to be more missional. Mission is a defining characteristic of the booming churches of the Majority World. The Western church faces its own cultural captivity. It must recalibrate itself in the light of the gospel and the *missio Dei* (the mission of God). This recalibration is necessary for the Western church to be missional in post-Christendom cultures. It's crucial if the church is to pursue missional approaches to theology, ministry, service and servantship. Missional recalibration is vital if the Western church is to stop its decline.

There's been a recent surge of books considering the mission of the church. These examine how we might remissionalize the church and reevangelize the West.[8] But North Americans have written most of these books. Australian, European and British authors have written many of these books too. And I recently heard a leading missional thinker make a claim. He said, "The future of Western cultures and churches rest with the North American church. North American Christian experiments and innovations hold the key for winning the West for Christ."[9]

I believe he's appealing to the dominant narrative in North America. But he's wrong. It's time that we embraced a new narrative. The future of the global church isn't found in the United States. How could we even think that when all the exponential growth of the church is in the Majority World? Western churches and theology and mission aren't the future. We're a *part* of the future. But we're not *the* future. The future of the global church exists in dynamic and global conversations. We need to move from a Eurocentric and Americentric view of mission and the church to one that prioritizes, respects, includes and hears the whole global church. These conversations must be multivocal, multicultural, multipeopled, missional and glocal (global and local). They must involve people from the Majority World, First

---

[7]S. M. Murray, *Post-Christendom: Church and Mission in a Strange New World* (Carlisle: Paternoster, 2004), 19.
[8]For examples of such books, see the *NextReformation Missional Reading List: Top 50,* http://nextreformation.com/?p=11081.
[9]I'm intentionally not naming this person.

Nations, indigenous cultures and the West. The global church needs a thrilling glocal exchange. We need one that we characterize by mutuality, respect, partnership and interdependence. Such exchange helps Majority World, First Nation, indigenous and Western churches learn from each other. It enables them to pursue missional theology and practice in their own contexts with attention to global exchanges. As Christians, we need to replace Eurocentric and Americentric worldviews with a global missional worldview. See table 16.1.

Table 16.1. A Eurocentric and Americentric worldview versus a global missional worldview

Eurocentric and Americentric Worldview	Global Missional Worldview
Western	Global
Monocultural	Multicultural
Superior	Meek
Independent	Interdependent
Isolationist	Collaborative
Monological	Conversational
Colonial	Mutual and Postcolonial
Parochial	Glocal
Insular	Multivoiced and Multipeopled
Myopic Mission	Local and Global Mission
Preservationist	Renewalist
Closed	Open
Uninterested and Dismissive	Interested and Attentive
Divisive	Holistic and Unifying
Oppressive	Liberating
Racist	Respectful
Nationalistic	Kingdom Focused
Exceptionalist	Equality
Nostalgic	Visionary
Centralized	Dispersed
Narcissistic	Humble
Westernized History and Theology	Localized and Globalized History and Theology

We need a contrary narrative to the one that dominates. I want the global church to embrace a new narrative. Here it is: Christ's global missional church needs a global missional worldview. Western Christians need to pay careful attention to the future of the church as it emerges from the Majority World, and vice versa. The truth is that the future isn't emerging from any *one* context. It's emerging globally. And it's especially emerging from the Majority World. (We see this in mission, worship, theology, spirituality, hermeneutics, the reading of church history and more.) The future is emerging from the kind of multivoiced and multipeopled conversations I've described. Western Christians can learn so much from their sisters and brothers in Majority World and indigenous cultures. We can learn from their contextual mission, servantship, ethics, hospitality, creation care, education and Spirit-empowerment. And we can learn from how they prioritize Scripture, discipleship, mission, beauty and relationships.

A note on *global Christianity* versus *glocal Christianity* and on *global Christianity* versus *world Christianity*. First, I wrestled with whether to call these sections glocal rather than global. For example, should I speak of "glocal missional theology" or "global missional theology"? I decided to use the descriptor *global*. When I use the word *global* to describe global missional theology, global missional worship and so on, I mean something broader than glocal. Glocal usually means a conversation between the local and global. Or people use it to describe something that reflects both local and global considerations. I'm convinced that such a conversation between local perspectives and global themes is crucial for church and mission and theology. But when I use the word *global* in this chapter, I mean something that's more extensive. I mean a worldwide conversation that seeks to include all cultures, contexts, theologies and traditions. This includes a glocal dialogue between local perceptions and global ideas, but it's more panoramic than that. For example, we construct "global missional theologies" by facilitating worldwide conversations between global themes, local considerations, glocal dialogues, diverse cultures, multiple confessions, many theological traditions, both genders and so on. This includes local-global (glocal) dialogues, but it's broader and richer than just that.

Second, Lamin Sanneh prefers the term *world Christianity* over *global Christianity*. He says the former is more indigenous and local and spontaneous, and the latter is more colonial and extraneous. Personally, I think the distinction is artificial in practice. As Philip Jenkins says, Lamin

Senneh's "distinction is difficult to draw in practice. Even when we can distinguish between 'global' and 'world' Christianity—in his sense—the two forms often mutate and merge into each other. I will therefore continue to use 'global' Christianity in a broad and nonjudgmental sense."[10] I agree with Jenkins's conclusion.

In this book, I've introduced you to theology and church and mission in the Majority World and indigenous cultures. My hope is to encourage the new narrative I've described. And I want to stimulate global conversations. Many themes in Majority World theology and practice are, of course, present in the Western literature too. But global voices and perspectives enrich them. This includes conversations between persons of different cultures, ages, genders, traditions and theologies—at both local and global levels.

In this chapter, I wrap things up by addressing an important question: In light of all the material covered in this book, what would it now look like to engage in global missional theology, ecclesiology, interpretation, history, pneumatology, spirituality, worship and education? In this chapter, I proceed in that order.

So let's start by considering the nature of global missional theology.

GLOBAL MISSIONAL THEOLOGY

Global missional theology puts indigenous and Majority World and Western voices into conversation. This results in a robust missional theology.

There are excellent books on Western missional theology (and the theology of mission).[11] I especially value David Bosch's *Transforming Mission* and Christopher Wright's *The Mission of God*. In *Transforming Mission*, Bosch shows how a theology of mission is necessary and relevant. He discusses paradigm shifts in it and unpacks New Testament models and historical paradigms of mission. He outlines thirteen key "elements of an

---

[10]Jenkins, *Next Christendom*, xiii.

[11]Foundational Western books in this area include David J. Bosch, *Transforming Mission: Paradigm Shifts in Theology of Mission* (Maryknoll, NY: Orbis, 1991); Francis M. DuBose, *God Who Sends: A Fresh Quest for Biblical Mission* (Nashville: Broadman, 1983); Ross Hastings, *Missional God, Missional Church: Hope for Re-Evangelizing the West* (Downers Grove, IL: IVP Academic, 2012); A. Kirk, *What Is Mission?: Theological Explorations* (Minneapolis: Fortress, 2000); Lesslie Newbigin, *The Open Secret: An Introduction to the Theology of Mission* (Grand Rapids: Eerdmans, 1995); Christopher J. H. Wright, *The Mission of God: Unlocking the Bible's Grand Narrative* (Downers Grove, IL: IVP Academic, 2006).

emerging ecumenical missionary paradigm": Mission is grounded in the *missio Dei*. Mission is church with others, mediating salvation and a quest for justice. Mission is evangelism, contextualization, inculturation and liberation. Mission is common witness and theology. Mission is ministry by the whole people of God and action in hope. And mission is witness to people of other faiths. Bosch believes that a robust theology of mission will awaken within us a fresh passion to serve Christ. It will inspire us to take part in Christ's mission in the world. But he warns us to "beware of any attempt at delineating mission too sharply."[12] In *The Mission of God*, Christopher Wright shows how theological themes are missional. These include Scripture, the Trinity, the church, creation, humanity, the kingdom of God and the nations. Wright also looks at the missional implications of ethical and ecological and social challenges.

Global missional theology broadens out this conversation. It includes the insights of Majority World and indigenous people. Many Majority World thinkers and themes speak into this space. Tite Tiénou, for example, calls for a movement from systematic and biblical theology to missional theology. "Missional theology is at the heart of the church's call to live in the world, but not to be of it, and to bear witness to God's transforming power in individuals and societies."[13] Emma Wild-Wood and Peniel Rajkumar gather a large group of Majority World thinkers to examine the experiential and biblical and theological foundations for mission.[14] They called the book *Foundations for Mission*. It examines twenty-first-century missional theology from many cultures and Christian traditions across the globe.

All churches—Majority World and indigenous and Western—should be self-governing and self-financing and self-reproducing.[15] Furthermore, they should be self-theologizing.[16] That's challenging for the Western

---

[12]Bosch, *Transforming Mission*, 9.

[13]Tite Tiénou and Paul G. Hiebert, "From Systematic and Biblical to Missional Theology," in *Appropriate Christianity*, ed. Charles H. Kraft and Dean S. Gilliland (Pasadena, CA: William Carey, 2005), 117-33.

[14]Emma Wild-Wood and Peniel Rajkumar, eds., *Foundations for Mission*, vol. 13, Regnum Edinburgh Centenary Series (Oxford: Regnum, 2013).

[15]Alan R. Tippett, *Introduction to Missiology* (Pasadena, CA: William Carey Library, 1987), 381.

[16]Jeffrey P. Greenman and Gene L. Green, *Global Theology in Evangelical Perspective: Exploring the Contextual Nature of Theology and Mission* (Downers Grove, IL: IVP Academic, 2012), 9.

church. We can feel very insecure when we realize that the rest of the world has a stake in the doing and shaping of Christian theology. The global church reminds us that so much of our theology is Eurocentric and Americentric. It's been largely framed within a Western philosophical and historical context. Global missional theology challenges that historical and inherited way of doing theology. It challenges its dominance and myopia and cultural superiority. It challenges the assumption that our inherited Western so-called canons of theology are universal and true for all times and all places. That assumption is false. The voices of the global church—its communities and leaders and theologians—challenge these Western theological canons and assumptions. They highlight their shortcomings. They emphasize the need for global theological conversations.

Global missional theology requires that we learn from indigenous and Majority World theologies. Steven Studebaker and Bradley Broadhead make this point strongly:

> Engaging with theology from diverse sources can correct the myopia that can occur from drawing one's theological sources from a singular cultural context. Theology can and must speak to a local context, but it must also engage with the concerns of the worldwide church and be willing to engage in mutually edifying and corrective dialogue. . . . Neither Western presuppositions and theologies nor local theologies are above being called into account. If Western theology can act as an antidote to syncretism in the Global South, so too can the theologians of the Global South call into question Western theology influenced by the powerful forces of Western secular culture. Humility and open ears are both required to reap the benefits of the mutually correcting and edifying voices of global theology.[17]

Putting Majority World and Western themes into conversation, global missional theology has certain features. First, it looks at the missional basis of the gospel as revealed throughout Scripture. The Bible has a missional basis, and mission has a biblical basis. As Christopher Wright says, "Mission is what the Bible is all about; we could as meaningfully talk of the missional

---

[17]Steven M. Studebaker and Bradley K. Broadhead, "Globalization, Christendom, Theology, Ministry, and Mission," in *The Globalization of Christianity: Implications for Christian Ministry and Theology*, ed. Gordon L. Heath and Steven M. Studebaker (Eugene, OR: Pickwick, 2014), 7-8.

basis of the Bible as of the biblical basis of mission."[18] We use biblical texts and themes to construct a biblical basis for mission. And our missional theology and practice helps us interpret those same biblical texts. Moreover, the Bible is a missionary document. God has shaped the biblical text and story in the crucible of mission from Genesis to Revelation. We conclude that all biblical theology is missional theology.

Second, global missional theology considers the missional nature of the trinitarian God. It ponders the way he shapes and sends his missional church. The mission of the Father and Son and Holy Spirit moves out to become the mission of Israel and Jesus and the church.[19] Third, global missional theology examines the missional nature of the church. The church serves the mission of Christ. The Spirit constitutes the church in mission. The church is missional at its core. It's caught up in the missional purposes and "movements" of the triune God. The church exists because of that mission. It joins in God's eschatological mission as he redeems humanity and creation and history. Fourth, global missional theology explores the relationships between various branches of theology. These include systematic theology, missiology, Christology, trinitarian theology and biblical theology. Fifth, global missional theology is attentive to the missional theology and actions of Jesus Christ, the apostles and the early church. And it learns from the missional theology and practices of the church throughout the ages and cultures and traditions. Sixth, global missional theology cultivates a vibrant eco-theology. It does this because all genuine mission must be about the redemption of all humanity and creation. Eco-theology and earthkeeping practices are essential to the mission of the global and local church. Seventh, global missional theology shapes a confident theology of beauty. This asks, How can we be the community of the beautiful who glorify the beautiful one?

Global missional theology is passionate about the practical implications of missional theology. It's dissatisfied with abstract theories. We need to apply its insights concretely and locally. A theology of mission is vital for our ministry. It's crucial for our mission in the world. Missional theology is critical for the structures, offices, ministries, worship, discipleship and mission of the church.

---

[18]Wright, *The Mission of God*, 29.
[19]Ibid., 29-69.

Majority World and indigenous perspectives enhance global missional theology in many ways. What do we learn from these cultures? So many things! Global missional theology focuses on the *missio Dei*. God is missional. He shapes the missional nature and forms and activities of the church. The church doesn't have its own mission: it joins in God's mission. Furthermore, Vinoth Ramachandra challenges us to see that global missional theology must be *integral*. It must seek to bring together the church's being and doing, theory and practice, spiritual and physical, evangelism and social action, individual and social, sacred and secular, and justice and mercy.[20] And global missional theology examines its associations with power and privilege and "the center." It's concerned for the poor, silenced, marginalized, vulnerable, forgotten and oppressed. It constructs a theology of hospitality and welcome and embrace.

Western missional theology rarely explores the relationship between the Spirit of Christ and the mission of the church. This is problematic given the trinitarian basis of mission. It's troubling given the crucial role of the Spirit in constituting and empowering the church. It's time missional theology considered the relationship between the Spirit and the missional church. As I've shown in the chapter "Embracing the Spirit," Majority World Christians explore a theology of Spirit-empowered mission. They're shaping a *missional theology of the Spirit* that goes hand in hand with a Spirit-empowered mission. Global missional theology is attentive to the voice and presence of Jesus Christ in the church, in other Christian traditions and in the world. And it engages crucial issues that relate to both mission and Spirit. These include healing, deliverance, atonement, empowerment and the presence of Christ in culture. In 2013, the World Council of Churches released a statement on mission and evangelism.[21] This statement assumes a trinitarian underpinning to missiology, but it formulates and applies this missiology with heavy reference to pneumatology (the work and person of the Spirit). In that statement, the World Council of Churches is taking account of the contribution of the

---

[20]Vinoth Ramachandra, "Integral Mission: Exploring a Concept," in *Integral Mission: The Way Forward*, ed. C. V. Mathew (Kerala: Christava Sahitya Samithi, 2006), 45-46.

[21]World Council of Churches, "Together Towards Life: Mission and Evangelism in Changing Landscapes: New Affirmation on Mission and Evangelism," Sept. 5, 2013.

churches of the Majority World. These churches are now influencing global missional theology. And they've rediscovered something of the role and person and work of the Holy Spirit that churches of the West have too often downplayed. The emergence of global missional theology brings with it a much greater emphasis on global missional pneumatology. I hope that Western churches and theologians will learn to appreciate this global pneumatological emphasis and that the West will engage critically with global missional pneumatology. This way we can move forward together, discovering fresh ways of being Christ's Spirit-empowered church.

We shape global missional theology in conversation with other theologies. These include biblical, historical, systematic, womanist, liberationist, interfaith, trinitarian, postcolonial, renewalist, sacramental and ecological theologies. We refuse to do missional theology in isolation from other theologies and cultures. We enrich our missional theology through ecumenical and interfaith discussions. After all, many of us live in pluralist contexts. We ground our missional theology in New and Old Testament scholarship. And we do this because of our passion for Scripture. We construct a missional theology that engages cultural and communication theories. We interact with postliberal, neo-Reformed, neo-Anabaptist and contemporary renewalist thought.

Let me be clear. We need to rethink our theology of mission. We need to do this in global and glocal conversation. And we must do this in the light of indigenous and First Nation and Majority World thought. This must be an authentic conversation. It must not be token, dismissive, colonial or superior. And it must not be a mere fascination with the "other." Tiénou quotes Frans Wijsen as he challenges us to genuinely embrace global missional theology: "Often European theologians eagerly take up contextual theologies from Asia, Africa, and Latin America, but they do not change their Western outlook and view of theology. They treat third world theologies as if they are exotic fruit to supplement their traditional European dishes."[22] Global missional theology is a multicultural banquet that does not preference one cuisine. (At times, it will privilege the voices of silenced

---

[22]Craig Ott and Harold A. Netland, eds., *Globalizing Theology: Belief and Practice in an Era of World Christianity* (Grand Rapids: Baker Academic, 2006), 45.

and marginalized people because of the church's historical neglect.) Global missional theology helps us understand Christ's hope and plan for his worldwide missional church.

Global Missional Ecclesiology

Ecclesiology is the study of the nature and structure of the Christian church. *Missional ecclesiology* is the study of the missional nature, structures, ministries and purposes of the church. First, we ground our missional ecclesiology in the missional nature of the triune God (the *missio Dei*). The church is missional because the triune God is missional. Second, we shape our missional ecclesiology around God's mission in the world and in human history. The church joins with God in his mission. Third, we express our missional ecclesiology according to the missional nature, structures, ministries and purposes of the church.

Global missional ecclesiology places mission at the center of the church's essence and identity and activities. We can never appreciate our missional identity without a robust global missional ecclesiology. We grow this ecclesiology out of global and glocal conversations. We root missional ecclesiology in the gospel and Scripture. This means we must value global dialogue and learning. And we must be careful to embrace the biblical relationship between the nature of God, the truth of the gospel, the missional thrust of the biblical story and the shape of the global missional church. Together as the church we take part in God's mission. We understand our mission in the light of the biblical narrative. We have an urgent and communal mission. While there are points of continuity and discontinuity, we continue the mission of Israel and Jesus and the early church. We do this as we recognize God's missional nature and the missional nature of the church. We take part in God's mission to humanity. God outworks this mission in human history. And he invites our participation.

The doctrine of the *missio Dei* tells us that God is missionary (in his very nature). The missionary, triune God sends the global church in mission to the whole world. The whole church joins in the whole mission of God. It proclaims and lives out the whole gospel in the whole world (i.e., locally and globally). Consequently, the church pursues global missional theology, global missional worship and so on. (See figure 16.1.)

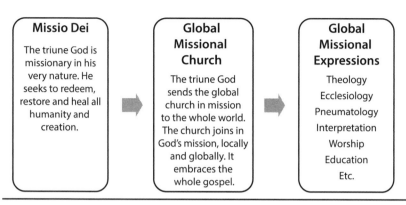

Figure 16.1. The *missio Dei* leads to global missional expressions

There are a few excellent Western books on missional ecclesiology.[23] We should enjoy these books. But in my book *Salt, Light, and a City*, I note the lack of a substantial theology of the church in the missional conversation. Missional writings often deal with the practical dimensions of the church. They ask, How do we help the church be more missional? But we also need a robust missional theology of the church. I began to correct this deficiency in the missional conversation with my first book. Missional theologians need to see the urgency of this issue and do more. This lack of a systematic missional ecclesiology is problematic. Lesslie Newbigin claims that congregations are the "only hermeneutic of the gospel." All missionary efforts "have power to accomplish their purpose only as they are rooted in and lead back to a believing community."[24] In *Salt, Light, and a City*, I construct an introductory missional ecclesiology. I do this in conversation with twelve theologians from the four main streams of the church. The book is foundational for missional ecclesiology. It examines the key theological themes that

[23]See Graham Hill, *Salt, Light, and a City: Introducing Missional Ecclesiology* (Eugene, OR: Wipf and Stock, 2012); Johannes Blauw, *The Missionary Nature of the Church: A Survey of the Biblical Theology of Mission* (Grand Rapids: Eerdmans, 1974); J. Driver, *Images of the Church in Mission* (Scottdale, PA: Herald, 1997); Michael W. Goheen, *A Light to the Nations: The Missional Church and the Biblical Story* (Grand Rapids: Baker Academic, 2011); Darrell L. Guder and Lois Barrett, *Missional Church: A Vision for the Sending of the Church in North America*, The Gospel and Our Culture Series (Grand Rapids: Eerdmans, 1998); Alan J. Roxburgh, M. Scott Boren and Mark Priddy, *Introducing the Missional Church: What It Is, Why It Matters, How to Become One*, Allelon Missional Series (Grand Rapids: Baker, 2009).

[24]Lesslie Newbigin, *The Gospel in a Pluralist Society* (London: SPCK, 2004), 227; Hill, *Salt, Light, and a City*, xvii.

undergird missional ecclesiology. These themes include a theology of mission, community, Jesus Christ, the Holy Spirit and the Trinity. "These interlocking themes offer foundations for a worthwhile, dialogical, theological, and systematic missional ecclesiology."[25]

The few Western books available on missional ecclesiology are excellent. Yet global missional ecclesiology puts these Western perspectives into conversation with Majority World and indigenous voices. My hope is that my first book and the one you're now reading will inspire the development of global missional ecclesiology.

Global missional ecclesiology examines the ontological ground of the church's missional nature (i.e., the Trinity's missional nature and purposes). It studies the relationship between the *missio Dei* and the church's nature, structures, community, ministries and mission. It explores the relationship between the church and the kingdom and reign of God. It considers the correspondence between the trinitarian mission and the church's mission. (And it notes the limits of the analogy.) It proposes missional models and practices and images of the church. Global and local developments inform these missional practices.

Western thinkers and leaders need to stop assuming they have all the answers. Global missional ecclesiology learns from Majority World innovations and movements. It celebrates ecclesial diversity. It examines, "What makes the church the church?" And it revisits the classical marks of the church so that they become missional marks. (I began to outline the missional marks of the church in my book *Salt, Light, and a City*.) Naturally, global missional ecclesiology includes Majority World and indigenous voices. But it avoids the false idea that any one culture "has it all together."

What other themes shape global missional ecclesiology? (1) We learn from Majority World renewalist movements. This means inviting the Spirit to empower and fill our worship and liturgy and mission. (2) We learn from Latin America autochthonous Pentecostal churches (LAAPs) and other lay-led groups in the Majority World. These are grassroots, locally led, self-supporting, restorationist and biblically primitive. Nonprofessional pastors

---

[25]Hill, *Salt, Light, and a City*, xix-xx.

lead them. This means that we increase the participation of the whole body of Christ. We reject the clergy-laity division. We cast off the sacred-secular divide. We seek to release the whole body to mission and ministry and service. (3) We learn from womanist ecclesiologies. These seek liberation from male-dominated structures and systems (e.g., the *mujeristas*). (4) We integrate the poor and oppressed and powerless. We stand in solidarity with the marginalized. This way we choose to become the church Christ had in mind. We develop new ecclesiologies "from below," which are *of* the grass-roots and *for* the grassroots. The Latin American Base Ecclesial Communities (BECs) and the LAAPs provide models for us here. We'll need to adapt these grassroots forms for our contexts. (5) We learn from the indigenous ecclesiologies of the African Initiated Churches (AICs). This "indigenous" and "lived" ecclesiology is attentive to the needs and hopes and desires of local neighborhoods. It's shaped around the culture and language of local people. It's *integral* and *holistic*. This means that it focuses on the well-being and whole life of people and communities. (6) We learn from the vast array of Asian ecclesiologies. Two examples will suffice. Subaltern ecclesiologies teach us to hear the voice of Jesus among the despised and rejected (e.g., Dalit theology). Cell-group ecclesiologies teach us the importance of small groups for the mission and vitality of the church. (A classic example is the Yoido Full Gospel Church in Seoul, South Korea.)

Missional churches interpret and proclaim the gospel in particular settings. So let's turn to the character of global missional interpretation.

GLOBAL MISSIONAL INTERPRETATION

Biblical hermeneutics is the study of the interpretation of biblical texts. *Missional hermeneutics* privileges mission in the interpretation of Scripture. Missional hermeneutics has core convictions. George Hunsberger describes these convictions this way:

> In a set of recent conversations among biblical scholars, missiologists, and scholars in other theological fields, four distinct emphases can be observed for defining a missional hermeneutic: the *missio Dei* as the unitive narrative theme of the Bible, the purpose of biblical writings to equip the church for its witness, the contextual and missional locatedness of the Christian community, and the dynamic of the gospel's engagement with human cultures. In their

convergence, these streams of emphasis provide foundations for the continuing development of a robust missional hermeneutic.[26]

Missional hermeneutics have matured and thrived during the last couple of decades.[27] This literature seeks a missional interpretation of the nature, formation, message and application of Scripture. Missional interpretations of Scripture pursue sophisticated approaches to biblical interpretation. They show the relationship between the missional Trinity, the missional Scriptures, the missional kingdom and the missional church. This isn't just gathering biblical proof texts for the church's mission. This is tracing the missiological themes and narratives that run throughout Scripture.

David Bosch (*Transforming Mission*) asserts that the Scriptures are a "missionary document." Christopher Wright (*The Mission of God*) agrees here. They want to move away from superficial missional interpretations. These include such things as "biblical foundations for mission."[28] Wright cautions that "in searching the Scriptures for a biblical foundation for mission, we are likely to find what we brought with us—our own conception of mission, now comfortingly festooned with biblical luggage tags."[29] Ouch!

Wright goes on to outline the ways in which mission produced the Bible. He shows how mission redefines our understanding of biblical authority. A missional interpretation of Scripture leads us to reading biblical imperatives and indicatives together. "God with a mission" is our interpretive starting point. This has missional implications for our theologies of church and

---

[26]George R. Hunsberger, "Proposals for a Missional Hermeneutic: Mapping a Conversation," *Missiology* 39, no. 3 (2011): 309.

[27]See H. Dan Beeby, *Canon and Mission*, Christian Mission and Modern Culture (Harrisburg, PA: Trinity, 1999); Arthur F. Glasser and Charles Edward van Engen, *Announcing the Kingdom: The Story of God's Mission in the Bible* (Grand Rapids: Baker Academic, 2003); Goheen, *Light to the Nations*; Johannes Nissen, *New Testament and Mission: Historical and Hermeneutical Perspectives*, 3rd ed. (New York: P. Lang, 2004); Howard Peskett and Vinoth Ramachandra, *The Message of Mission: The Glory of Christ in All Time and Space*, The Bible Speaks Today (Downers Grove, IL: InterVarsity Press, 2003); Christopher J. H. Wright, "Mission as a Matrix for Hermeneutics and Biblical Theology," in *Out of Egypt: Biblical Theology and Biblical Interpretation*, ed. C. Bartholomew (Grand Rapids: Zondervan, 2004); Wright, "Truth with a Mission: Towards a Missiological Hermeneutic of the Bible," *Southern Baptist Journal of Theology* 15, no. 2 (2011); James V. Brownson, *Speaking the Truth in Love: New Testament Resources for a Missional Hermeneutic*, Christian Mission and Modern Culture (Harrisburg, PA: Trinity, 1998).

[28]Bosch, *Transforming Mission*, 15; Wright, *The Mission of God*, 34.

[29]Wright, *The Mission of God*, 37.

mission. "God with a mission" shapes our biblical interpretation. It forms our expressions of faith, church and mission.[30]

In his historical analysis, Bosch draws on the work of Martin Hengel and Martin Khalif. Bosch shows how missionary zeal and problems shaped early Christian theology and history. Early Christians forged their theology "in the context of an 'emergency situation,' of a church which, because of its missionary encounter with the world, was *forced* to theologize."[31]

So what does global missional hermeneutics look like? First, it is a multivoiced and multipeopled hermeneutic. This missional hermeneutic draws on the voices of many cultures and theologies and traditions. And it becomes a pluriform collection of missional hermeneutics—not a single or uniform approach. Johannes Nissen puts it well:

> A missiologically relevant reading of the Bible will not lead to any universal missiology but (as in the New Testament itself) to a variety of missiological perspectives. Different theologies of mission do not necessarily exclude each other, "they form a multicolored mosaic of complementary and mutually enriching as well as mutually challenging frames of reference." Instead of trying to formulate one uniform view of mission we should rather attempt to chart the contours of a pluriverse of missiology in a universe of mission.[32]

Second, global missional hermeneutics scrutinize historical and cultural approaches to biblical interpretation. It questions the influence of modernity, Christendom and Western prejudices (among other things). It approaches biblical interpretation through at least three key lenses. These are (1) the whole of Scripture, (2) the broad experiences of God's people across the globe and (3) the diverse contexts and cultures in which the gathered and sent church exists. Global missional hermeneutics refuses to domesticate the Scriptures according to the values and logic and worldview of one culture. It doesn't prioritize Western methods and worldviews over others. Domestication often occurs when we read Scripture through one, exclusive interpretive approach. When we do this, we consider that approach superior to all others. Global missional interpretation demands a broader and more open and courageous approach. It must be multivoiced and multicultural to be worthwhile.

---

[30]Ibid., 61-69.
[31]Bosch, *Transforming Mission*, 17.
[32]Nissen, *New Testament and Mission*, 16-17.

Third, global missional hermeneutics complement global missional theologies. Bosch speaks of the "theologies of mission" present in the New
Testament.[33] Today there are a multitude of "theologies of mission" around
the globe. We must complement these theologies of mission with many missional interpretations of Scripture. We need to stay open to fresh possibilities and perspectives, especially in a globalized and multivocal context.

Fourth, global missional hermeneutics extend the Western conversation. I
quoted George Hunsberger at the beginning of this section. He notes four
differing streams of emphasis in Western missional hermeneutics that in-
tersect and enrich each other. No one stream is adequate without the others
if we desire a vibrant and substantial missional hermeneutic. The first stream
emphasizes the missional *direction* of the biblical story. It focuses on the *missio
Dei* as the unifying theme in the entire biblical narrative. The second stream
emphasizes the missional *purpose* of the Bible. It considers how the biblical
texts equip the church for witness. The third stream emphasizes the missional
locatedness of the readers. It shows how Christians can read the Bible faithfully
in their contexts and locations. The fourth stream emphasizes the missional
engagement with cultures. It examines how the mission-shaped gospel of Jesus
Christ serves as an interpretive matrix. We use this interpretive matrix as we
put the biblical tradition into critical conversation with our human context.[34]

What does a global missional hermeneutic add to these four streams?
Like each of the four streams, a global missional hermeneutic intersects and
synergizes with the other streams. It's inadequate without the other streams.
And they're insufficient without it. It needs the other four streams to produce
a robust missional hermeneutic. And they need it to generate the same. This
fifth stream emphasizes global missional *conversations*. A global missional
hermeneutic asserts that the global and local church must interpret the Bible
glocally. We only achieve robust missional hermeneutics through global
conversations. And these conversations must incorporate global themes,
local considerations, glocal dialogues, diverse cultures, multiple confessions,
many theological traditions, both genders and so on.

Here's my main assertion. God is a missionary God (in his very nature)
who shapes a global missional church (in its very nature). The missional

---

[33]Bosch, *Transforming Mission*, 16.
[34]Hunsberger, "Proposals for a Missional Hermeneutic."

God calls his global missional church to global missional conversations. These conversations include the formation of global and local missional theologies. We form such global missional theologies with close attention to global and local missional interpretations of the missional Christian Scriptures. Furthermore, we shape these missional theologies and interpretations in the context of hands-on global and local mission. See figure 16.2.

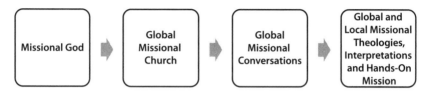

Figure 16.2. The shape of global missional interpretation of Scripture

This fifth stream of missional hermeneutics compels us to wrestle with the *multivoiced* and *multipeopled* nature of the church and missional interpretation. None of the other streams demand this. Western cultures no longer define how Christians understand and believe and interpret the Bible. As the church, we must put Western, indigenous and Majority World interpretive approaches into global conversation. This broadens and enriches the way we believe and obey and interpret the Bible. It heralds a transformation of the church as Christians believe and interpret the Bible in fresh ways. Global ethnic diversity is dewesternizing both the global church and glocal biblical interpretations. This is something we can celebrate and embrace. It enriches our understanding and practice of Scripture and mission. This fifth stream calls us to hear and regard the missional interpretations of other cultures and Christian theological traditions. And it helps us understand the Bible's missional narrative more fully. Let's multiply occasions that enable global missional interpretations of the Bible. Let's pursue global and local missional witness.

We don't just interpret texts and cultures and theologies. We also interpret history. So let's consider the shape of global missional history.

GLOBAL MISSIONAL HISTORY

When I studied church history at theological college, we didn't really study the history of the church. We studied the history of the European and North

American churches. And we briefly looked at the early history of the church in the Mediterranean. Most recountings of church and mission history is profoundly Eurocentric. They describe "church history" as a Western story, locating this story primarily in Europe and North America. And they depict "mission history" as the story of Europeans and North Americans taking mission outside of the West.

It's time for a global church history and a global history of mission. Global missional history is polycentric, not Eurocentric. It dismantles the divide between "church history" and "mission history." This division is usually a Eurocentric narrative. It covers the history of the church in mission and worship in all six continents over the past two thousand years. Global missional history paints a worldwide and polycentric picture. It examines the unique expressions of mission, church and worship in each culture, tribe and language. It shows how Jesus' global church has joined in the *missio Dei* in every continent throughout the ages. This isn't one linear chronological storyline. This is a plurality of stories that emerge simultaneously and influence each other profoundly. This polycentric story spans Africa, Asia, Latin America, the Middle East, Eastern Europe, First Nations, indigenous cultures and more.

Patrick Johnstone notes that three of the top four missionary-sending countries in 2010 were Asian.[35] The fifth largest missionary-sending country was African. Many Asian, African and Latin American churches are now sending missionaries into the West. Their aim is to see the West won for Christ. But the recent astonishing growth and mission of the Majority World churches isn't the beginning of their story. And it isn't a consequence of Western church history. Only Eurocentric and Americentric perspectives would claim that. We need a truly global and polycentric history of the church and its mission. This spans all ages, cultures, continents, traditions and so forth.[36] The Spirit of God empowers the church for mission in every place and time.

---

[35]Johnstone, *Future of the Global Church*, 233.
[36]A few books have made a start at such a global history. My favorites are Adrian Hastings, *A World History of Christianity* (Grand Rapids: Eerdmans, 1999); Diarmaid MacCulloch, *Christianity: The First Three Thousand Years* (New York: Viking, 2010). Johnstone traces the development of the church across the globe from the first to the twenty-first centuries in *Future of the Global Church*, 21-160.

GLOBAL MISSIONAL PNEUMATOLOGY

In the chapter "Embracing the Spirit," I described the incredible growth of renewalist churches in the Majority World. Amos Yong says there are 400-plus million renewalists in the Majority World. This number is likely to grow to around 710 million by 2020 and 1 billion by 2050. Seventy-six percent of all renewalists in the world live in Asia, Africa and Latin America.[37]

Clearly, the Spirit is empowering the global church for mission. We see this most clearly in the Majority World. It's time we developed global missional pneumatology. This allows us to learn from each other about what it means to embrace God's emboldening and missional presence. Not everyone will self-identify as Pentecostal, charismatic or renewalist. But we should all seek the power and presence of the Holy Spirit. The Spirit enables us all—regardless of the Christian tradition to which we belong—to witness to Jesus Christ and his gospel.

Pneumatology is the study of the nature and work of the Holy Spirit. *Missional pneumatology* is the study of how the Spirit empowers the church for mission and witness. Global missional pneumatology learns from what the Spirit is doing in his worldwide church. It listens to the Spirit as he inspires the church to join with God in his mission in the world.

Global missional pneumatology refuses to sideline the baptism, fruit, gifts and empowerment of the Holy Spirit. It highlights the importance of God's Spirit as he releases the church into effective mission. It practices Spirit-centered mission. It develops Spirit-focused missiology. Global missional pneumatology emphasizes supernatural empowerment. It seeks Spirit-emboldened witness. It releases the gifts of the Spirit. It joins with the Spirit as he restores humanity and all creation. In this way, it confronts ecological destruction, social evils, moral decay, political injustice, crippling poverty, war and violence, economic and social oppression, and human exploitation. And it seeks to cooperate with the Spirit as he brings peace, restoration, love, faith and hope. Global missional pneumatology focuses on the release of the whole body of Christ to mission and ministry. It invites the Spirit's power in gospel proclamation and power evangelism. It invites the Spirit's presence in indigenous leadership and grassroots ministry and

---

[37]Amos Yong, *The Spirit Poured Out on All Flesh: Pentecostalism and the Possibility of Global Theology* (Grand Rapids: Baker Academic, 2005), 19-20.

passionate prayer. It invites the Spirit's provision and enabling as it repro-duces disciples and churches. It integrates Spirit-empowered mission into ministry training and theological curriculum. And it engages with other religious and spiritual and secular worldviews for the sake of Christ. It's confident that the Spirit enables effective, bold and appropriate witness.

Yong writes that the worldwide church needs a global missional pneuma-tology. It requires a Spirit-centered theology and practice of mission. This must deal with its "social and political locations." (These include post-Christendom, neocolonialism, postcommunism and so on.) It must depend "on the church being a body of Spirit-empowered people who embody and invite an alter-native way of being in the world." And it must develop attention to the many cultural and confessional and other "practices of the Spirit-filled people of God." That way it remains polycentric, dialogical, multipeopled and multivoiced.[38]

I like what Michael Frost says about Spirit-empowered mission. Global missional pneumatology rediscovers the Spirit in ecumenical and multicul-tural and interreligious dialogue. It sees the Spirit beyond the church. It celebrates and releases the Spirit within the local congregation. It joins with the Spirit as he brings justice, peace, hope and mercy. It enjoys the Spirit in creation and it looks for—and points toward—the Spirit in the world. As I wrote in my first book, the Spirit-filled missional church recovers its Spirit-constituted being. It reactivates its Spirit-filled structures. It longs for Spirit-formed communities, which evidence the fruit and gifts and mission of the Spirit. It forms Spirit-attentive theologies. (Too many theologies pay little attention to the nature and power and work of the Spirit.) The Spirit-filled missional church seeks to be salt, light and a city on a hill within a Spirit-infused world. It recovers its Spirit-empowered mission.[39]

Global missional pneumatology can never be a solitary, abstract or dis-embodied affair. The Spirit won't allow that. It's "lived out" in global conver-sations and authentic local communities. It's expressed in hearts and minds and hands open to the Spirit. It's embodied in our love for our neighbor, in our rigorous thought, in our missional practices, in our passionate prayer,

---

[38]Amos Yong, "Many Tongues, Many Practices," in *Mission After Christendom: Emergent Themes in Contemporary Mission*, ed. Ogbu Kalu, Peter Vethanayagamony and Edmund Chia (Louisville: Westminster, 2010), 43-58.

[39]Hill, *Salt, Light, and a City*, 205-29; Michael Frost in *Following Fire: How the Spirit Leads Us to Fight Injustice*, ed. Ashley Barker (Springvale, Victoria: UNOH, 2008), 33-41.

in our care for creation, in our political holiness, in our personal ethics, in our commitment to justice and in our Christian spirituality.

GLOBAL MISSIONAL SPIRITUALITY

Global missional spirituality has the features outlined in chapter fifteen. It's a life of communion with God in Jesus Christ (individually and corporately). It's rooted in Scripture. It's trinitarian, Spirit-empowered, relational, practiced, pleasurable, suffering, holistic, integrative and missional. It rejects religiosity. It's open to learning from other cultures while being appropriately critical of the influence of culture.

We shape global missional spirituality as we learn from how other cultures read Scripture and pray. There are many ways we can do this. One way is by redesigning the manner in which we prayerfully read Scripture. We need to move from *lectio divina* to global *lectio missio*. Let me explain. *Lectio divina* is an ancient practice of reading and prayer. We can trace its roots back to Origen in the third century. The desert fathers practiced *lectio divina* in the fourth century. Benedict of Nursia prescribed it for monastics early in the sixth century. *Lectio divina* is about reading Scripture, devotional works and other spiritually edifying books prayerfully. It's reading slowly and with attention to the Spirit and voice of Jesus Christ. It's not about gaining knowledge. It's about reading for spiritual formation. It's about listening reverently and lovingly and prayerfully and silently to Jesus' voice. He is speaking to us through our reading. It's about savoring Scripture and devotional reading. And it's doing this for the sake of prayer, intimacy with God and spiritual formation.

Lectio divina has four movements. These are *lectio, meditatio, oratio* and *contemplatio*: (1) *Lectio* (reading) involves reading a passage slowly and prayerfully. As you read, wait for a word, concept or phrase to catch your attention. (2) *Meditatio* (meditation) involves savoring that word, concept, or phrase. How is God speaking to you through this? How is he touching your thoughts, desires, passions, memories, hopes, fears and experiences? How is he trying to get your attention in this moment? (3) *Oratio* (prayer) involves responding to God in prayer. This heart response can be a spoken prayer, or it can be prayer through journaling, artistic works or something else. (4) *Contemplatio* (contemplation) involves resting silently in the presence of Christ. Be grateful that God has spoken to you and is changing

you. Journal how he wants you to respond—repentance, restored relationships, fresh commitments, new habits or whatever it may be. These four
movements of *lectio divina* interlock and overlap. They're a conversation, a
dance and an intimate communion with God.

I have enjoyed practicing *lectio divina* for almost twenty years. But I'm
concerned that the four movements aren't enough for missional vitality or
for learning from the global church. I've expanded and modified the practice.
I put greater attention on Jesus Christ, global conversations, other spiritual
practices, missional life, transformational action and Christian community.
Missional spirituality needs more than *lectio divina*. It needs, among other
things, a global *lectio missio*. This is a practice of prayerful reading that especially focuses on the spiritual writings of Majority World and indigenous
Christians. (We include Western spiritual writings too, of course, but listen
carefully to the voices that we've too often ignored, so that we can begin to
form a global missional spirituality.)

A globalized *lectio missio* has eight movements. These are *adspecto, lectio,*
meditatio, oratio, imitatio, missio, communio and *contemplatio*. It's a mistake
to see these eight movements as discrete and separate stages. While they are
a movement, they are also interlocking and overlapping. It's more a dance
than a linear progression. Don't get caught up in rigidly following the steps.
They're a guide, but you should follow the leading of the Spirit as he shapes
you for discipleship and mission.

The eight movements aren't just a *dance*, a movement in response to the
leading of Jesus' Spirit. They're also a *cycle*. They begin with gazing upon
Jesus Christ, and they lead into another cycle as we gaze upon him. Figure
16.3 depicts the eight movements. I then provide a description of each.

Stage 1: **adspecto (gaze).** Begin by gazing upon Jesus Christ (especially as
revealed in the four Gospels). Read a gospel passage slowly and prayerfully
and attentively. Adore Jesus. Worship him. Commit to serving him and his
mission and kingdom. Commit to imitating him—his life, ethics, holiness,
compassion, justice, prayer and so on. Gaze on his person, message, example,
practices, life, death, resurrection, kingdom, mission and gospel. See his
mission as part of the *missio Dei*: the mission of the Father, Son and Holy Spirit
to redeem the world. His mission ushers in his rule and reign and kingdom.
Meet Jesus. Love Jesus. Adore Jesus. Gaze upon him. And listen to his voice.

Stage 2: **lectio** *(read).* Read Scripture and books prayerfully and slowly and attentively. Intentionally include books from other cultures and traditions. Aim to develop a global palate as you learn from Christian spiritual writers from all over the globe. Read Western Christian spiritual writers. But, more importantly, make a special effort to prayerfully read the spiritual writings of Majority World and indigenous Christians. (I provide a list of such books and writings on my website, TheGlobalChurchProject.com.) How should you read these Christian spiritual works? Perhaps read a passage or page several times waiting for a word, concept or phrase to catch your attention. Savor the reading. Don't be in a rush. It's okay to try to understand a reading (and to ponder the meaning of a difficult text). But more importantly, focus on spiritual growth and renewal. Be attentive to the Spirit and voice of Jesus Christ.

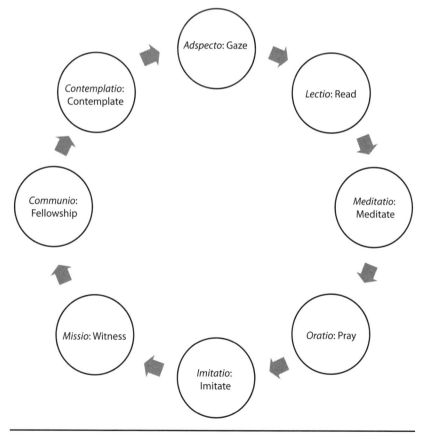

Figure 16.3. *Lectio missio:* a resource for developing a global missional spirituality

Stage 3: **meditatio** *(meditate).* Meditate upon and ponder the reading. Allow the Holy Spirit to reveal meaning and transform your heart. Savor the impression, word, concept or phrase that caught your attention as you read. How is God speaking to you? How does he want to transform you? How is he inviting you into his mission? Is he touching your thoughts, desires, passions, memories, hopes, fears and experiences? Is he expanding your missional imagination? How is he trying to get your attention in this moment? How does he want you to shape your Christian spirituality so that it's rooted in local community and shaped by the voices of God's global community?

Stage 4: **oratio** *(pray).* Respond to God in prayer. Enter loving conversation with him. Make this a dialogue, not a monologue. Verbalize and, if you desire, journal your prayers. Learn from (and practice) the prayers of other cultures (especially those from the Majority World and indigenous cultures). Express your prayers through the spoken word, journaling, artistry or any other way you want.

Stage 5: **imitatio** *(imitate).* Walk out into life imitating Christ. Imitate his love, justice, grace, hope, faith, mercy and so on. And imitate godly exemplars, especially as you've met them in your readings. Embody and live out the readings. I might have called this step *operatio* (action). It's about taking your readings and prayers into your everyday life. But it's more than *action.* It's the *imitation of Christ.*

Stage 6: **missio** *(witness).* *Lectio missio* has mission at its core. Join with the Father and Son and Holy Spirit in the *missio Dei.* Seek first the kingdom of God and his righteousness. Express mission afresh in response to your reading and prayer. Allow a global *lectio missio* to shape your theology and practice of mission as you listen to global voices on spirituality and mission. Go individually. But more importantly, go in community. Practice mission that is informed by local experiences and by global themes and voices. *Missio* and *communio* are interdependent. Our mission is in communion with the triune God and his people (local and global). And mission makes our communion real and rich and dynamic.

Stage 7: **communio** *(fellowship).* Immerse yourself in community. Move from reading individually to reading and learning in community. This communion is with God and others and creation. Seek community with other cultures and people groups (locally and globally). The whole process of global *lectio missio* is communal and relational, not individualistic. It's global, not parochial. You can practice parts of *lectio missio* alone. But the whole process is only missional and transformational when you practice it in community and with attention to global voices. Together we announce and demonstrate and embody the kingdom of God. Together we join in the mission of God as his body. Together we join in the *missio Dei*, for the sake of the world, to the glory of God the Father.

Stage 8: **contemplatio** *(contemplate).* Rest in the presence of God. Be thankful. Contemplate discipleship. Contemplate new missional actions, habits, practices, commitments and theology. Do this individually and, preferably, with others. Respond. Embrace repentance and change and restored relationships. Pursue fresh commitments, new missional outlooks and practices, and so on. *Contemplatio* must lead to *adspecto.* Contemplation must lead to gazing on Jesus Christ. So this is not the end of a process, but the beginning of a new cycle of *lectio missio.*

Lectio missio is a useful resource for developing a global missional spirituality. A global *lectio missio* is a process, a cycle and a dance that will reactivate your missional vitality. It'll help you listen and learn from other cultures and from global voices. When practiced together, it can also inspire your friends, family, team and church to join in the global mission of God. It's also a resource that enriches global missional worship.

GLOBAL MISSIONAL WORSHIP

The church often engages in worship wars. People debate about worship styles and lyrics and theology. But it's time we constructed a more mature discussion about worship. We need approaches to worship that are both missional and global. In other words, global missional worship incorporates the worldwide insights of diverse cultures, creative arts, languages, styles, liturgies and theologies. A mosaic of worship forms enriches global missional worship. But it doesn't flatten these out into a monolithic or universal worship form. Instead, it celebrates the diversity and plurality of these cultures and forms and expressions. And it integrates worship with the gospel proclamation and missional vitality of the church.

There are, of course, specific forms and occasions for worship. But the truth is that all Christian life is worship.[40] Global missional worship shapes worship practices for the gathered and dispersed people of God. These worship practices enrich the church's life together and their mission in the world. As I've suggested, global missional worship celebrates particular worship styles shaped *in* and *for* specific contexts. But for the sake of enhanced mission, it also blends many things. These include Scriptures, sacraments, liturgies, creeds, confessions, languages, images, hymns, charismatic gifts, contemporary styles, narrative messages, poetry, the creative arts, literature, labyrinths, bodily movement, contemplative prayer practices and hybrids of ancient and contemporary music (for example, Gregorian chants mixed to techno beats). To enhance mission and enrich worship, global missional worship blends many forms of biblical, historical, contemporary, experiential, participatory, interactive, communal, multisensory, multicultural, multivoiced and cultural worship experiences. The goal is to glorify Christ and join with him in his mission in the world.

Majority World thinkers teach us that we must integrate mission and worship. Worship magnifies God and equips people for mission. Mission glorifies God and releases people to worship. Worship and mission are two sides of the same coin. They're synergistic and integrated. To act as though one can exist without the other is false thinking. It's corrupted and corrupting theology. True worship is inseparable from the *missio Dei*. It glorifies God and enriches people and congregations as they join with God in his mission in the world.

Recently, Olive Fleming Drane presented a paper on the relationship between worship and mission in which she wrote the following:

> Jesus offers a holistic model of discipleship that should also be a model for worship: loving God with heart, soul, mind, and strength (Mark 12:29–31). Worship that engages every part of our being—physical and social as well as internal and personal—is what today's spiritual searchers are looking for, along with very many Christians. John Wesley regarded communion as a "converting ordinance"—for the saint as well as the sinner. I wonder how yours might measure up to that? Authentic worship and authentic mission really do go hand in hand.[41]

---

[40]Craig Van Gelder, *The Essence of the Church: A Community Created by the Spirit* (Grand Rapids: Baker, 2000), 148-52.

[41]Olive M. Fleming Drane, "What's the Relationship Between Mission and Worship?," in *Morling College Seminar on Missional Church* (Sydney: Morling College, 2011).

Global missional worship embraces the Spirit and his gifts. It cultivates Christian discipleship as it shapes minds and hearts and hands. It recovers community as people eat, create, sing, laugh and mourn together. It elevates artistic, natural, creative and theological beauty. It indigenizes expressions of faith. It enjoys singing, liturgies, sacred spaces, Scriptures, prayers, music, sacraments and so on. It draws on unique cultural expressions, contemporary music forms, mystical Christian traditions, the richness of specific languages and so on. But it isn't exclusively focused on the gathered people of God. As Avery Dulles says, "The Church's existence is a continual alternation between two phases. Like systole and exhalation in the process of breathing, assembly and mission succeed each other in the life of the Church. Discipleship would be stunted unless it included both the centripetal phase of worship and the centrifugal phase of mission."[42]

Global missional worship reactivates congregational mission and releases missional discipleship. Such discipleship grows "out of prayer, study, dialogue, and worship by a community learning to ask the questions of obedience *as they are engaged directly in mission.*"[43] Global missional worship welcomes immigrants and refugees and asylum seekers as neighbors. It worships God through extravagant generosity, hospitality and welcome. It glorifies God through its service to neighbors and communities and the poor. It gets out of its comfort zones. It glorifies God through its service of different cultures and people groups. It engages in earthkeeping practices as it cares for humanity and all creation. It worships as it seeks the liberation of people and creation from all forms of exploitation and oppression. Global missional worship tells the big story of God's historic and eschatological mission in the world. It does this through loving actions, Scripture, song, Eucharist, storytelling and self-sacrificial service. Through testimonies, it shows how God's big story intersects with our little stories. It reveals how God's redemptive story meets the stories of our neighbors. The multivoiced and multicultural people of Christ worship through mission. They worship God as they embody the gospel in their love, compassion, service, hope and witness. They worship God as they confront principalities and powers that

---

[42]Avery Dulles, *Models of the Church* (New York: Doubleday, 1987), 220.

[43]Alan J. Roxburgh, *The Missionary Congregation, Leadership, and Liminality* (New York: Trinity, 1997), 66 (italics in original).

hold people in bondage. They magnify him as they serve as peacemakers. They glorify Christ through their ministry of reconciliation. We need to educate and train God's people for confident missional worship.

GLOBAL MISSIONAL EDUCATION

Most Western theological education is neither global nor missional. It doesn't place missional theology and practices and equipping at its core. It tends to sideline mission to a faculty, course or institution. And it fails to help faculty and students hear and respond to global theologies and voices. Outdated Christendom perspectives characterize Western theological education. Furthermore, it's mostly Eurocentric and Americentric.

My friend J. R. Rozko recently released a paper called "The Missiological Future of Theological Education."[44] In that paper, Rozko makes important assertions and recommendations:

> To the extent that our current systems of theological education have been shaped by Christendom presuppositions, they have lost their missiological bearings and are wholly inadequate to prepare Kingdom leaders. Incremental changes and clever adaptations to these current systems only serve to distract from the opportunity we have before us to develop a Kingdom, and therefore missional, vision of theological education. At the heart of this vision is the conviction that the proper telos of theological education is an "accreditation" of students based not merely on the degrees they earn, but on the development and fit of their character and competency for life and leadership in the Kingdom of God. To this end, we argue that a missional vision of theological education will be praxeological—aimed at training reflective practitioners, mobilizational—aimed at training missionary leaders, and spiritual—aimed at training Kingdom citizens.[45]

I agree with Rozko that current Western theological education embraces Christendom assumptions. It's mostly lost its missional bearings and passion. It doesn't prepare leaders for missional leadership, nor does it stimulate missional theology and imagination. I also think that it's parochial—it's Eurocentric

---

[44]J. R. Rozko and Doug Paul, "The Missiological Future of Theological Education: A Whitepaper: A Joint Venture of 3DM and the Order of Mission," 2012, www.academia.edu/4148055/The _Missiological_Future_of_Theological_Education.
[45]Ibid., 3.

and Americentric, not globalized. Rozko proposes that we train reflective practitioners. We do this *through* elongated and contextualized programs of theological formation. We do this *by* missionary theologians. And we do this *in* diversified learning environments and communities. Rozko recommends that we train missionary leaders through affordable, local, accessible and mission-focused education. We need to help these leaders prepare as catalysts and pioneers. They need to be competent disciple makers and mobilizers and missionaries. Rozko asserts that we need to train kingdom citizens and leaders. These citizens and leaders love the church, but they also have a broader vision for the kingdom of God. They reject Christendom presuppositions. They embrace kingdom convictions and priorities and values. They impart spiritual knowledge, depend on the Spirit and reframe their relationship to Scripture. This way, they're reading and responding to the Bible missiologically. Rozko makes excellent suggestions here. He's my good friend and an avid supporter of my GlobalChurch Project video series.

I'd like to make one strong suggestion. I think we can enrich Rozko's missional proposal for theological education. We do this through an increased focus on global theologies and practices.

Global missional education takes a completely different approach to most systems of theological education. It considers the mission of God to be *the organizing principle* for all theological education and ministry training. It places missional theology and practice *at the center* of all theological and ministry education. Global missional education prioritizes missional and globalized theology. It does this as it develops its spirituality, ethics, people, structures, systems, curricula, buildings, fieldwork, ethos, pedagogy, methods and mission.

In the chapter "Renewing Education," I engaged Majority World sources as I painted a picture of the future of theological education. What do these teach us? They show us that we must shape global missional education that's focused on joining with God in his mission. It equips students and the church for mission. It equips the whole believer to take the whole gospel to the whole world. It's Christ centered and gospel focused and biblically grounded. It develops learning communities. It grows through glocal conversations and by engaging global theologies and voices. It shapes a vision of ministry training around Scripture. It forms hearts and heads and hands. It's contextualized. It equips the whole body of Christ. Global missional education models and cultivates servantship. It offers diversified approaches to learning. It resists colonizing people. It addresses issues of power and access. It relies on the Spirit. It seeks a global "renaissance" in theology and training as it reintegrates theological disciplines and listens to global voices. It engages with ideologies of unbelief, post-Christendom cultures and non-Christian religions. And it integrates the three "publics" of academy and church and society.

Theological colleges that are serious about mission invite students and pastors and churches to help them shape education. They foster accountability and dialogue with their students and churches. People training for globalized missional leadership need tools that help them diagnose and engage their particular, individual, societal and contextual needs. They also need opportunities to plan the integration of theoretical and practical experiences. Such integration helps them address the needs they have diagnosed. And it enables them to form relevant missional responses. Students need forums to test their individual and collective progress in missional tasks. They need to form missional and globalized theologies that sustain local missional practices. Training bodies need to show a reciprocal, democratic, enabling and participatory style of leadership. I call this servantship. This way graduates learn to reflect this servantship in their own ministries and in missional contexts.

Global missional education requires an *instruction-action-reflection* approach to education.[46] This involves integration. Colleges need to integrate theology and practice with fieldwork. They need to integrate local and global perspectives. Opportunities should exist for students to integrate multicultural and crosscultural competencies with biblical, systematic, pastoral and missional theologies. They need to integrate spiritual and personal growth with ministry and mission skills. The aim is to equip students to be competent local missional theologians and skilled glocal missional leaders. This leadership equipping is for local and broader contexts and framed in a glocal and a globalized conversation and setting. Students must develop within their local churches and communities. They need competent mentoring and

---

[46] Alan Hirsch, *The Forgotten Ways: Reactivating the Missional Church* (Grand Rapids: Brazos, 2006), 124; Michael Frost and Alan Hirsch, *The Shaping of Things to Come: Innovation and Mission for the 21st-Century Church* (Peabody, MA: Hendrickson, 2003), 218-22.

supervision. They need coaching and apprenticeship. They need crosscultural and multicultural skills. They need a missional and globalized imagination. As they integrate theology, theory, practice, mission and spirituality, they become competent globalized missional leaders.[47]

What should we focus on when we train global missional leaders? I think it starts with theology students doing more units in theology and missiology with more praxis built in. This is better than focusing on older models of pastoral training, which reinforce old methods. Global missional leaders need training in learning from other cultures. We want them to delight in the multivoiced, multipeopled, multitraditioned and multicultured people of God. They need training in listening to *local narratives* (the stories of their local area and neighbors). They need help to learn from *global discourses* (on theology, mission, church and so on). They need equipping in servant evangelism and servant mission. We must help them engage with comparative religions, new atheisms, crosscultural relationships, emerging urban demographics, new spiritualities and contemporary social and ethical problems. They need experience working among the poor, marginalized, disabled and stigmatized. They need experience of "difference." This includes practicing care for those who are outside of our "world" (those of a different sexual orientation, race, culture, socioeconomic situation and so on). We should help them learn to exegete culture. This includes reading newspapers, movies, the arts and so on with open eyes. They need to learn how to lead organizational change and transformation. This includes experiencing effective missional communities and remissionalizations.

Then there are the implications for theological colleges. Are your faculty and senior leaders mostly white, male, monocultural, middle-aged and monolingual? Go get global. Are your curricula and programs mainly aimed at equipping people for your context? Go get global. Are you focused on training pastoral leaders at the expense of the whole church? Go get global. Do you mainly train men? Go get global. Are your classes and programs in only one language? Go get global. Are your students mainly from one country or culture or language group? Go get global. Do you discourage your faculty from serving the global church beyond your own country? Go get global.

---

[47]L. Y. Barrett, *Treasure in Clay Jars: Patterns in Missional Faithfulness* (Grand Rapids: Eerdmans, 2004), 59-73.

Many theological colleges now offer training in missional leadership and theology.[48] This includes postgraduate awards, ministry cohorts and research programs. Sometimes these are pastoral leadership programs with a missional flavor. My hope is that these programs will teach more than missional leadership and theology from Eurocentric or Americentric perspectives. I hope they'll reshape their entire theological and educational curricula, ethos, courses and methods from a globalized missional perspective. This means placing global missional theology at the center of all these things. It's about making the *missio Dei* the organizing principle in theological education. I hope theological colleges will truly teach global missional education. I pray they'll help the people of God develop global missional theologies and practices.

Space prevents me from exploring more global missional practices. The chapters of this book represent some of them. The worldwide church needs global missional servantship, global missional spirituality, global missional communities, global missional justice, global missional earthkeeping and so on. I intend to explore these in a future book.

CONCLUSION

In 2014, I travelled with my thirteen-year-old daughter Grace to Malaysia and Cambodia. We served with friends in urban slums and among the poorest of the poor.

One of the highlights of the trip was attending the 2014 International Society for Urban Mission (ISUM) Summit in Kuala Lumpur, Malaysia. This summit was, without doubt, the most significant conference I've attended. It was a gathering of hundreds of Christians who are engaged in urban mission. These Christians pursue "God's Shalom in cities, and especially Majority World cities, through active reflection, solidarity and leadership

---

[48]Examples include Asbury Theological Seminary, KY; Cliff College, UK; Durham University, UK; Fuller Theological Seminary, CA; George Fox University, OR; Houston Graduate School of Theology, TX; Luther Seminary, MN; Morling Baptist Theological College, Sydney, Australia; Multnomah University, IL; Northern Seminary, IL; Northwest Nazarene University, ID; Northwest University, WA; Princeton Theological Seminary, NJ; Redcliffe College, UK; Regents Theological College, UK; Ridley Theological College, Melbourne, Australia; Rochester College, IN; Seattle School of Theology, WA; Springdale College, UK; Stirling Theological College, Melbourne, Australia; Wales Evangelical School of Theology, UK; Wheaton College, IL; Whitley Theological College, Melbourne, Australia; Wycliffe College, Canada.

development."[49] These came from all over the globe. Most were from the Majority World.

For me, one of the highlights of the summit was exposure to innovative theology, mission, worship and approaches to church and social justice coming out of Majority World and indigenous cultures. Another highlight was seeing indigenous and Western and Majority World leaders collaborating in creative ways. Together, we explored global theologies and practices.[50]

The summit illustrates my hope for this book and for the global church. I pray that indigenous and Western and Majority World Christians will learn from each other. I hope that we'll enrich each other's worship, theology, mission, faith and expressions of church. I hope that, together, we'll explore global missional theologies and practices.

In this book, I've explored how Christians can be the *salt* of the earth, the *light* of the world and a *city* set on a hill. I've considered how we do this locally and as Jesus Christ's global missional church. We do this by listening to others. We do this by learning from each other. We do this through local, national, regional and global collaborations. And we do this through brave and contextual applications of our mutual, global and missional discoveries. Majority World and indigenous voices help Westerners grow in our understanding and practice of mission, church and theology. They stir us to think in fresh ways about what it means to be *salt, light and a city*. We've too often ignored these voices. But we can't do this anymore. We mustn't do this anymore. We need to embrace a new narrative—one that's global and missional. We need to reshape our conversations, renew our mission and revitalize our churches. We must truly become a *GlobalChurch*.

---

[49]"About ISUM," International Society for Urban Mission, http://newurbanworld.org/about.
[50]Ibid.

GLOBALCHURCH PROJECT
VIDEO SERIES

The GlobalChurch Project films fifty-plus inspiring Christians from Asia, Africa, Latin America and more on mission, love, church, faith and theology.

The films are hosted at TheGlobalChurchProject.com.

The GlobalChurch Project seeks to do the following:

1. Find out what the astonishing shift in Christianity means for the church. (I'm talking about the shift toward Africa, Asia, Latin America and so on.) What does it mean for how we understand and practice mission, discipleship, theology and so on? What does it mean for the future of the global and local church?

2. Show what we can learn about mission, church, faith, discipleship and theology from Christians from Asia, Africa, Latin America, indigenous cultures and so on.

3. See churches all over the world transformed.

4. See global conversations catalyzed, glocal mission renewed and churches revitalized.

5. Help the global and local church truly witness to the transforming truth and power of Jesus Christ.

6. Make these films freely available to the worldwide church.

STUDY GUIDE

Reflection Questions, Practical Applications and Further Reading

You'll get the most out of this book by asking questions, engaging in practices and pursuing Further Reading You can do these alone. But they are best done with others. To help you get started, I've provided the following for each chapter:

1. *Reflection Questions*: Questions to help you reflect on the chapter's material.

2. *Getting Started*: Initial practices to get you started as you shape your own practical responses.

3. *Further Reading*: Readings to help you dig deeper into the themes in the chapter. (I've offered a mix of academic and nonacademic readings.)

My prayer is that the Holy Spirit will be with you and your church as you work through this guide. I pray that your heart will be thrilled and expanded as you explore global Christianity and the future of the church.

CHAPTER 1: INTRODUCTION: BEING SALT, LIGHT AND A CITY

Reflection Questions

- What does the growth of the Majority World churches mean for the mission and theology and worship and communities of the church worldwide?

- What does this shift in world Christianity mean for Western churches and theology?

- Why do we embrace a Eurocentric and Americentric view of the world? How do we change this?

Getting Started

- Spend time in prayer. Ask God to help you find ways to listen to (and join in) a global conversation that reshapes your theology, renews your mission and revitalizes your church.

- I released the *GlobalChurch Project* video series at the end of 2015. In these videos, I film fifty-plus inspiring Christians from Asia, Africa, Latin America and more on mission, love, church, faith and theology. The films are hosted at TheGlobalChurchProject.com. Watch one or more of the videos individually and with others (e.g., in a college class or ministry team). After each video, discuss what you can learn from this Majority World Christian leader.

- Look at the other resources at TheGlobalChurchProject.com. These include videos, reading lists, important links, a glossary and other resources. Use the material as needed. I've also provided ways that you can contact me.

Further Reading

Jenkins, Philip. *The Next Christendom: The Coming of Global Christianity*. 3rd ed. Oxford: Oxford University Press, 2011.

Noll, Mark A. *The New Shape of World Christianity: How American Experience Reflects Global Faith*. Downers Grove, IL: IVP Academic, 2009.

Ott, Craig, and Harold A. Netland, eds. *Globalizing Theology: Belief and Practice in an Era of World Christianity*. Grand Rapids: Baker, 2006.

CHAPTER 2: GLOCALIZING CONVERSATIONS

Reflection Questions

- Who are the downtrodden and silenced in your church, ministry or local community? How are they treated as invisible nonentities? How will you confront, expose and challenge this situation?

- John Macionis defines prejudice as "a rigid and irrational generalization about an entire category of people." Stereotypes, which are a form of prejudice, are "an exaggerated description applied to every person in some category."[1] Which races, ethnicities, socioeconomic groups or cultures stimulate your prejudices or stereotypes? What are you going to do to address and change this?

---

[1]John J. Macionis, *Sociology*, 13th ed. (Boston: Prentice Hall, 2012), 357, 359.

- Can you think of ways that people from your area involved in church, business, education, health, welfare and industry are providing input into local, city-wide, state-wide, national, regional or global forums? Try to discern the interdependence between the local and the global in your context.

Getting Started

- Find practical and tangible ways to collaborate with Christians from a variety of backgrounds. Do this in your local community. Serve with Christians from different ethnicities, denominations, theological traditions, ages, approaches to mission and witness, and so on. Now expand this out to collaboration with non-Christian groups that are trying to make a difference in your community. Such groups include social, welfare, religious, governmental and so on. Make sure the collaboration is practical and rooted in your local community. Then get your group to ask questions about their discoveries. What have they learned about mission, partnership, social action, grace and embrace in these tangible acts of collaboration?

- Once every four to six weeks visit a worship service, bible study, discipleship-training event, prayer meeting or mission program conducted by Christians from a different ethnicity than your own. Mix it up over a two- or three-year period. This way you've experienced these things in as many ethnic contexts as possible—African American, Arabic, Caucasian, Chinese, Greek, Hispanic, Indigenous Australian, Native American, Pacific Islander, Serbian, South Korean and so on. Or commit to spending twelve months immersed in a neighborhood and church of any ethnicity other than your own. Ask questions about what you can learn from these ethnicities and cultures other than your own.

- Start *Listen and Learn* nights at your church or in your organization. During these nights, invite someone from a different faith, ethnicity, theological perspective and so on to come and share. Invite them to share their story and their views in an attentive, nonthreatening environment. Your aim is not to criticize or debate them. It is to listen and learn. It is to reflect together on your learning as a group. Your group may never share all the perspectives or theologies of your visitor—especially if they contradict your biblical convictions. But you will grow together as you listen, and especially as you listen with respect, humility, prayer, grace and attention to the Spirit.

Further Reading

Sugirtharajah, R. S. *Voices from the Margin: Interpreting the Bible in the Third World.* Maryknoll, NY: Orbis, 1991.

Thangaraj, M. Thomas. "A Formula for Contextual Theology: Local + Global = Contextual." In *Contextualizing Theological Education*, edited by Theodore Brelsford and P. Alice Rogers. Cleveland: Pilgrim, 2008.

Tizon, Al. *Transformation After Lausanne: Radical Evangelical Mission in Global-Local Perspective.* Eugene, OR: Wipf and Stock, 2008.

Chapter 3: Contextualizing Mission

Reflection Questions

- Is the mission of your church, parachurch organization or denomination visible, demonstrable and verifiable? And is this evident through tangible acts of service, social reform and liberation?

- Does your church's missional life do these three things? (1) Does it *proclaim* the gospel? (2) Does it *make fully committed disciples* of Jesus Christ? (3) Does it *take part* in political, sexual, social, racial and economic liberation? And is your mission integral? Does it integrate all three of these missional dimensions in a comprehensive, dynamic, *and consistent* witness?

- Does your church or ministry engage in *critical* contextualization and *integral* mission? Is this leading to concrete expressions of personal, church and societal *transformation*?

Getting Started

I have shaped many of the "Getting Started" bullet points for this chapter around the chapters of Orlando Costas's book on integral mission. The book's title is *The Integrity of Mission*. Costas emphasizes six key areas of integral mission: preaching, disciple making, mobilization, integral growth, liberation and celebration.

- Expand the themes of your church's proclamation. Include more of the meanings associated with the names of God, the kingdom of God and the themes of conversion and repentance. Proclamation includes preaching, but isn't limited to it. Proclamation is verbal and nonverbal. It includes all the ways in which we declare the gospel. It's "a dynamic act that affects the whole life of the missionary."[2]

- Evaluate your church's missional faithfulness through the following three dimensions of Christian discipleship. As you do this, consider the words of Orlando Costas: "Disciple-making is an indispensable criterion for evaluating missional faithfulness. . . . Following, participating, and obeying. These are marks of authentic discipleship and of a faithful Christian mission."[3]

  - Are people following Jesus in every aspect of their lives?

  - Are they participating in God's mission in the world?

  - Are they obeying Jesus unreservedly?

Design a local church integral mission mobilization program. Follow the guidance provided by Orlando Costas in chapter three of *The Integrity of Mission*.[4] Costas provides the outline of a mobilization program that motivates, recruits, organizes and guides people into integral mission. It declericalizes mission and enables an analysis of church and culture. The program facilitates integral mission. This is mission focused on holistic transformation, sacrificial action, comprehensive faith and biblical faithfulness.[5]

Read chapters fourteen and eighteen of my book *Salt, Light, and a City: Introducing Missional Ecclesiology*. Chapter fourteen is called "The Mission-Forged Church." Chapter eighteen is called "The Courageous and Future Church." What do those chapters say about the shape of missional churches and missional leadership?

Further Reading

Costas, Orlando E. *Christ Outside the Gate: Mission Beyond Christendom*. Maryknoll, NY: Orbis, 1982.

Ma, Wonsuk, and Brian Woolnough, eds. *Holistic Mission: God's Plan for God's People*. Eugene, OR: Regnum, 2010.

---

[2]Orlando Costas, *The Integrity of Mission: The Inner Life and Outreach of the Church* (San Francisco: Harper and Row, 1979), 2.
[3]Ibid., 24.
[4]Ibid., 25-36.
[5]Ibid., 84-93.

Padilla, C. René, and Tetsunao Yamamori, eds. *The Local Church, Agent of Transformation: An Ecclesiology for Integral Mission.* Buenos Aires: Ediciones Kairos, 2004.

Samuel, Vinay, and Chris Sugden, eds. *Mission as Transformation: A Theology of the Whole Gospel.* Oxford: Regnum, 1999.

CHAPTER 4: LIBERATING PEOPLE

Reflection Questions

- What does it mean practically for your church to be the *good Samaritan*? How do you proclaim the gospel prophetically? How do you strive for the liberation and rights of the poor and oppressed in every context? How do you stand against social injustice?

- Ask yourself, if the God of the Bible is for the poor, why am I too often undisturbed as I live among the poor? How does my ethnicity, gender, wealth, privilege or power prevent me from identification with the humiliation of other people? How do these things shape prejudices in me that do not honor Jesus Christ? More importantly, how can Scripture change my understandings of society, power and relationships? How can Scripture make me a more compassionate servant of the broken, silenced, exploited and humiliated?

- What does liberation look like in your neighborhood, town, suburb or city? How is God calling you, your family and your church to take part in liberative actions?

Getting Started

- Gather up-to-date information on social issues in your town, suburb or city. Include wage inequality, homelessness, gender discrimination, gender pay gaps, racial discrimination, racial gaps in education, child poverty, unemployment, wealth inequality, difficulties among indigenous and First Nations peoples, and downward mobility from the middle class. Get your church and leadership team to plan ways in which your church can be a solution to these issues. Seek to address these issues with practical and compassionate action. Have your congregation ask, "Who is my neighbor?" Act upon the answer (Lk 10:25-37).

- Organize a spiritual retreat for your congregation. Contemplate the following quote as a group. Encourage people to leave the retreat with a renewed commitment to serving with and among the disadvantaged, forgotten, poor and marginalized in their neighborhoods.

- Gustavo Gutiérrez says, "All the political theologies, the theologies of hope, of revolution, and of liberation, are not worth one act of genuine solidarity with exploited [and poor and marginalized people]. They are not worth one act of faith, love, and hope, that's committed—in one way or another—to liberate [people] from everything that dehumanizes [them and prevents them] from living according to the will of the Father."[6]

- Lead a series of studies with your congregation on the environmental mandates outlined in the 2011 Lausanne *Cape Town Commitment*. (You may prefer to get an outside facilitator to lead these studies. Please see the text online for a fuller treatment of the theological and biblical themes.) *The Cape Town Commitment* encouraged Christians worldwide to

   A) adopt lifestyles that renounce habits of consumption that are destructive or polluting;

   B) exert legitimate means to persuade governments to put moral imperatives above political expediency on issues of environmental destruction and potential climate change; and

   C) recognize and encourage the missional calling both of (i) Christians who engage in the proper use of the earth's resources for human need and welfare through agriculture, industry and medicine, and (ii) Christians who engage in the protection and restoration of the earth's habitats and species through conservation and advocacy. Both share the same goal for both serve the same Creator, Provider and Redeemer.[7]

Further Reading

Boff, Leonardo, and Clodovis Boff. *Introducing Liberation Theology*. Maryknoll, NY: Orbis, 1987.

---

[6]Gustavo Gutiérrez, *A Theology of Liberation: History, Politics, and Salvation,* 15th anniversary ed. (Maryknoll, NY: Orbis, 1988), 308.
[7]The Lausanne Movement, *The Cape Town Commitment: A Confession of Faith and a Call to Action,* (Lausanne Library, 2011), www.lausanne.org/en/documents/ctcommitment.html.

Gutiérrez, Gustavo. *A Theology of Liberation: History, Politics, and Salvation*. 15th
    anniversary ed. Maryknoll, NY: Orbis, 1988.
Padilla, C. René. "Liberation Theology: An Appraisal." In *Freedom and Disci-
    pleship*, 34-50. Maryknoll, NY: Orbis, 1989.

CHAPTER 5: SHOWING HOSPITALITY

Reflection Questions

- Hospitality involves our relationship to our home, to the earth and to local
  place. We invite people to share our local relationships, our local lives, our
  local soil and our local faith. Are you connected enough with these to be
  hospitable? Are you willing to offer strangers welcome into those places
  and relationships and lands you love the most? Are you willing to allow
  others to call your land their land and your homes their homes?

- Is your family and church *given* to hospitality? Are you? Or is it an inci-
  dental, peripheral and optional activity?

- Look at the twenty practices of hospitality. Western churches must embrace these if they are to reflect the best of hospitality in the Majority
  World. How will your church, ministry and family practice these over the
  next few years and beyond?

Getting Started

- Choose a month to read the UNHCR *Global Trends 2012 Report* as an
  entire church.[8] Gather at the end of that month to consider ways you will
  respond in your city and country and region. Develop a concrete plan to
  keep this on your church's agenda.

- Collect stories of individuals and groups in your church and city that are
  demonstrating hospitality. Don't just collect churchy or in-house stories. Include stories from outside the walls and ministries of the church. Make sure
  the collection of stories is diverse. Share these stories at every opportunity.

- Ask your family and church leadership to develop cultures of hospitality
  and practical "hospitality plans." Consider framing those plans around

---

[8]*Global Trends 2012 Report—Displacement: The New 21st Century Challenge* is available at http://
unhcr.org/globaltrendsjune2013/.

Ruth Padilla DeBorst's advice (see this chapter's section on "Hospitality's Welcome" for more details):

- Building homes, living sustainably in them and making them a refuge
- "Recovering our relationship to the earth in the creation-community"
- Cultivating families and churches characterized by intimacy, simplicity, hospitality, collaboration and inclusion
- Seeking the welfare of the city[9]

Further Reading

DeBorst, Ruth Padilla, "Living Creation-Community in God's World Today." *Journal of Latin American Theology* 5, no. 1 (2010).
———. "'Unexpected' Guests at God's Banquet Table: Gospel in Mission and Culture." *Evangelical Review of Theology* 33, no. 1 (2009).
Yong, Amos. *Hospitality and the Other: Pentecost, Christian Practices, and the Neighbor.* Maryknoll, NY: Orbis, 2008.

CHAPTER 6: EMBRACING THE SPIRIT

Reflection Questions

- How can your congregation use the *spiritual gifts* as *missional gifts*?
- Is God's empowering presence enabling your mission?
- How do we recognize the presence of the Spirit beyond the walls of the church? Where is he present in popular spirituality, contemporary spiritual quests, consumer culture, film and media, and sports and recreation? How do we join with what the Spirit is already doing in those places?[10]
- How will you increase your spiritual expectation? How will you foster your openness to "the invasion of the Spirit" and to encounter with God? How will you help your congregation increase in spiritual intensity and expectation?

---

[9]Ruth Padilla DeBorst, "Living Creation-Community in God's World Today," *Journal of Latin American Theology* 5, no. 1 (2010): 62-69.
[10]Graham Hill, *Salt, Light, and a City: Introducing Missional Ecclesiology* (Eugene, OR: Wipf and Stock, 2012), 229.

Getting Started

- Consider the Alpha Holy Spirit weekend (http://alpha.org and http://
  alphausa.org). Develop a version of this weekend suitable for your church
  and Christian tradition. Run this weekend with an anticipation of the
  presence and power of the Spirit of Christ.

- Have your ministry team consider the list of characteristics of worship
  and spirituality in Asia, Africa and Latin America. (See tables 6.1 and 6.2.)
  Plan to modify your worship and spiritual development to reflect these
  characteristics. Do this in a contextual way. For instance, how will you
  develop Spirit-filled worship and spirituality that is participatory and
  communal and missional?

- As an entire congregation, discuss how you will practice the seventeen
  Spirit-centered commitments.

Further Reading

Anderson, Allan H. *An Introduction to Pentecostalism: Global Charismatic Chris-
   tianity*. Cambridge: Cambridge University Press, 2004.
Chan, Simon. *Spiritual Theology: A Systematic Study of the Christian Life*. Downers
   Grove, IL: InterVarsity Press, 1998.
Samuel, Vinay. "Pentecostalism as a Global Culture." In *The Globalization of
   Pentecostalism*, edited by Murray W. Dempster, Byron D. Klaus and
   Douglas Petersen, 253–58. Oxford: Regnum, 1999.
Yong, Amos. *The Spirit Poured Out on All Flesh: Pentecostalism and the Possibility
   of Global Theology*. Grand Rapids: Baker Academic, 2005.

CHAPTER 7: CARING FOR CREATION

Reflection Questions

- Consider the Micah Challenge document on a "Theology of Climate
  Change."[11] Discuss the following in small groups, as an entire congregation or with your leadership team. How can your congregation pursue
  eco-justice? How does creation care involve an engagement with politics
  and development and economics? How will your congregation address
  ecological degradation in your local area?

---

[11]"Theology of Climate Change," May 2009, www.micahchallenge.org.au/assets/pdf/Theology-of
  -climate-change.pdf.

- Read about the earthkeeping practices of the African Initiated Churches (AICs).[12] What do these earthkeeping practices teach your church and denomination?

- How can your church listen and learn from indigenous environmentalism (especially from groups indigenous to your area)? How do you listen without dismissing indigenous perspectives? How do you learn without romanticizing indigenous practices?

Getting Started

Recently, twelve leading seminaries joined as founding partners in the US-based Seminary Stewardship Alliance (SSA). This is a consortium of theological schools dedicated to reconnecting Christians with the biblical call to care for God's creation.

Here I adapt their Seminary Stewardship Alliance (SSA) Covenant so that it's relevant for local churches. Please use it as a starting point, as you develop your own commitments and practices.[13]

> As the people of God, charged with stewardship of the planet, we do publicly, and with God as our witness, covenant together that we will:
>
> 1. Teach creation care as the outworking of God's command that humans steward the created order. We will show its relation to Christian life, family, ministry, mission, individual calling, and congregational vocation.
>
> 2. Model sustainable practices in key areas of our church. These areas include facilities, missions, recycling, travel, community gardens, and use of water, energy, and other resources.[14]
>
> 3. Integrate creation care teaching across the congregation. Encourage the development of opportunities for living out what people are learning. Show how creation care develops from biblical notions. These include Creation,

---

[12]Marthinus L. Daneel, "Earthkeeping in Missiological Perspective: An African Challenge," *Mission Studies* 13, nos. 1–2 (1996); Daneel, "African Initiated Churches as Vehicles of Earth-Care in Africa," in *The Oxford Handbook of Religion and Ecology*, ed. Roger S. Gottlieb (Oxford: Oxford University Press, 2006); Daneel, "Christian Mission and Earth-Care: An African Case Study," *International Bulletin of Missionary Research* 35, no. 3 (2011).

[13]Adapted from the SSA Covenant, by Matthew Sleeth, Timothy Tennant and Richard Mouw, 2012, available at "Covenant," Seminary Stewardship Alliance, http://seminaryalliance.org/covenant.

[14]Tony Campolo and Gordon Aeschliman, *50 Ways You Can Help Save the Planet* (Downers Grove, IL: InterVarsity Press, 1992).

solidarity, equity, justice, Sabbath, Jubilee, and restoration. And it includes our theology of the nature and mission of God.

4. Take a leadership role in all facets of creation care. Pay particular attention to those that are distinctive to followers of Christ. These include simplicity, humbleness, love, forgiveness, retreat, forbearance, faith, prayer, and compassion.

5. Facilitate spiritual formation through biblically based creation care principles. These include sabbatical practices, self-control, sacrifice, and prayer with *eyes open* to creation.

6. Conduct a spiritual retreat based on the *inner and outer ecology* of exemplars such as St. Francis of Assisi.

7. Hold special worship services shaped around eco-theological, eco-justice, eco-liturgical, and eco-spirituality themes. There are many liturgies and orders of service developed around environmental stewardship and creation care online. See, for example, the liturgy of the European Christian Environmental Network at http://www.ecen.org/content/liturgy.

8. Form an active partnership with local and regional existing environmental organizations. How can we provide these with cooperation and support?

9. Establish a specific and strategic plan for creation care through our congregation. Identify creation care goals. Report our progress on an annual basis.

10. Develop our own congregation's eco-covenant. Ken Gnanakan provides a sample congregational eco-covenant with the following commitments. (1) Keep the first Sunday of June as the Lord's Environmental Day. (2) Pray for all the suffering creatures. (3) Deliver sermons reminding people of God's creatures. (4) Publish all printed documents on recycled paper. (5) Create a committee for environmental activities in the church. (6) Read the Bible in the view of God's creation. (7) Budget for environmental protection. (8) Cut down on unnecessary events and extravagant consumption. (9) Reduce heating and air-conditioning. (10) Work together with the regional community and local churches for environmental protection.[15] Every chapter of Gnanakan's book *Responsible Stewardship of God's Creation* has excellent action plans, discussion questions, prayers, and meditations.

11. Hold each other accountable for our efforts toward faithful creation care. Celebrate and encourage those who excel according to their gifts and means.

---

[15]Ken Gnanakan, *Responsible Stewardship of Creation* (Bangalore: Theological Book Trust, 2004), 129-30.

Further Reading

Boff, Leonardo. *Cry of the Earth, Cry of the Poor*. Ecology and Justice. Maryknoll, NY: Orbis, 1997.

Gnanakan, Ken R. *Responsible Stewardship of Creation*. Bangalore: Theological Book Trust, 2004.

Hallman, David G., ed. *Ecotheology: Voices from South and North*. Maryknoll, NY: Orbis, 1994.

Tinker, George E. "The Integrity of Creation: Restoring Trinitarian Balance." *Ecumenical Review* 41, no. 4 (1989).

CHAPTER 8: LIVING ETHICALLY

Reflection Questions

- How does the Bible relate to social justice, action and concern?

- How do people's roles in institutions affect their ethical decisions and character? What are the implications of this for your organization?

- Can we speak of sinful social structures and political systems or do only persons sin?

- What are the great ethical challenges facing your culture and family and congregation? How will you help others deal with these challenges? How are you helping them face these prayerfully, thoughtfully, courageously, biblically and ethically?

- I claim that Christian ethics are faith based, inculturational, political, transformational, dialogical, anamnestic, integral, holistic, glorifying, community based and foundational to Christian leadership and ministry. Does this describe your ethics?

Getting Started

- Have your family, friends, church or ministry team consider Desmond Tutu's characteristics of *ethical leadership*.[16] What practical things will you start doing to display ethical leadership? How will you advocate for the powerless, marginalized and silenced? How will you

---

[16]Desmond Tutu, "Who Will Lead Syria out of Crisis?," *The Elders*, October 30, 2013, http://theelders .org/article/who-will-lead-syria-out-crisis.

commit to ethical principles in your mission, relationships, finances and so on? How will you uphold human dignity and seek truth and reconciliation? How will you protect vulnerable persons, stand with victims and demand justice and action? How will you respect and enhance human, animal and ecological freedom? How will you urge the pursuit of justice, truth, reconciliation and peace? In summary, how will your family, friends, church or ministry team show ethical leadership?

- Do the following over a twelve-month period: (1) Make time for your church, family or small group to list the most important ethical issues faced by you and your culture (e.g., ecology, economics, poverty, justice, the land, truth telling, politics, war, violence, legal systems, culture, love, race, nation, marriage, family, divorce, domestic violence, sexuality, refugees and asylum seekers, corruption, power and so on). (2) Discuss why these ethical issues are important in your setting. (3) List the biblical passages and theological themes that relate to these ethical issues. (4) Brainstorm practical ways in which your church, family or small group might get involved in these issues. (5) Make commitments to concrete action. Hold each other accountable. Review these commitments together regularly.

- Register for a free End Exploitation church kit from World Vision, which inlcudes *A Church's Guide to Ethical Purchasing*. Work through the guide's modules as a church.[17]

Further Reading

Christian, Jayakumar. *God of the Empty-Handed: Poverty, Power, and the Kingdom of God*. Monrovia, CA: MARC, 1999.

Kunhiyop, Samuel Waje. *African Christian Ethics*. Nairobi: Hippo Books, 2008.

Magesa, Laurenti. *Christian Ethics in Africa*. Christian Theology in African Scholarship. Nairobi: Acton, 2002.

Ramachandra, Vinoth. *Subverting Global Myths: Theology and the Public Issues Shaping Our World*. Downers Grove, IL: IVP Academic, 2008.

---

[17]"End Exploitation," World Vision, accessed October 9, 2015, www.worldvision.com.au/get -involved/advocacy/end-exploitation.

CHAPTER 9: TRANSFORMING NEIGHBORHOODS

Reflection Questions

- Do you know your neighbors? What are their *particular and specific* concerns, joys, fears, hopes and dreams? What concrete things can you do to get to know your neighbors and be a *genuine* part of their lives?

- After reading through UNOH's covenant on pages 218-19 of this book, ask, What would it mean for our church to do the following?

  1. Live out our passion for loving God and neighbor.

  2. Focus on releasing our neighborhood from poverty or some other bondage or ailment.

  3. Grow through equipping each other, neighbors and the broader church to follow Jesus and join God's kingdom coming.

- How is your church seeking God's kingdom come in your neighborhood through word and deed and sign?

- Has your church experienced a *conversion to the neighbor*? How can you, together, *seek out* the wounded and *make them your neighbors*?

- How can you get involved in *place making* in your neighborhood?

Getting Started

- As a congregation and leadership team, design your own mission covenant. Develop one that seeks the transformation of your neighborhood. Prioritize place making. Make sure the covenant has concrete lifestyle commitments and personal and communal practices like those in the UNOH Covenant. Use the UNOH Covenant presented in chapter nine and the following *Baptist Churches of NSW and ACT Mission Covenant* to stimulate your thinking as you design your own church's mission covenant. Once you have designed a mission covenant, implement it as an entire congregation. Implement it in concrete, specific, attainable, relevant and measurable ways. Evaluate your progress at regular intervals. Seek the help of reputable external missional and church consultations.

Baptist Churches of NSW and ACT Mission Covenant.[18]

Christian mission is the announcement and demonstration of the Lordship of Jesus Christ, in the way of Jesus, to our world, both locally and globally. We acknowledge the Lordship of Jesus Christ and recognise that it extends over all creation and all aspects of human life and society. We believe that through his death and resurrection, Jesus is the Savior of all those who accept him as such by faith through grace. It is as our resurrected Savior that we acknowledge him as our Lord. We believe his Lordship extends to all people, and therefore it is his Lordship that gives us our mission. We embrace our calling to be committed to both its verbal announcement and its demonstration through acts of compassion, generosity, hospitality, and justice.

As a community of faith . . . we therefore commit to live out the following marks of a mission-shaped church:

1. A mission-shaped church **ANNOUNCES** the Lordship of Jesus locally and globally.

    This will be evidenced by:

    a. Regular opportunity for response to the gospel within the life and mission of the church;

    b. Regular opportunities for members to hear of evangelistic projects and needs they might commit to;

    c. A regular assessment of the needs of our immediate neighbourhood/ locality to determine whether certain ethnic, demographic or sub-cultural groups are not hearing the announcement of the Lordship of Jesus;

    d. A corporate commitment to at least one local and one global evangelistic focus;

    e. Active and prayerful consideration as to how we can be involved with planting a new congregation;

    f. A commitment to regularly pray as a whole church for non-Christians to turn to Jesus whether they are found locally or globally.

2. A mission-shaped church **DEMONSTRATES** the Lordship of Jesus locally and globally.

    This will be evidenced by:

    a. The way we prioritize *place-making*—immersing ourselves in local

---

[18]"Baptist Churches of NSW and ACTD Mission Covenant," www.nswactbaptists.org.au/images /directions%20missions%20poster.pdf. I was a part of the group that designed this mission covenant.

neighborhoods for the long haul, and collaborating with others for the well-being of those local communities;

b. The fostering of a community life that models compassion, generosity, hospitality and justice as expressions of the love of Jesus;

c. Regular opportunities for members to hear of effective community development projects and needs they might commit to;

d. A regular assessment of the needs of our immediate neighbourhood/ locality to determine whether certain ethnic, demographic or sub-cultural groups are not benefiting from the demonstration of the Lordship of Jesus;

e. A corporate commitment to at least one local and one global initiative aimed at addressing injustice, alleviating suffering or showing practical love in Jesus's name;

f. An annual review of our budget and the degree to which our missional priorities are reflected in our financial commitments;

g. A commitment to regularly pray as a whole church for the needs of our world, locally, regionally, nationally, and globally.

3. A mission-shaped church does mission **IN THE WAY OF JESUS.**

This will be evidenced by:

a. Regular teaching from the Gospels about the missional priorities, lifestyle and message of Jesus, and the fostering of a faith community that reflects this;

b. Regular opportunities for members to discern their own missional vocation;

c. Regular training and resourcing for members to be able to inculturationally develop friendships and share their faith in culturally and relationally effective ways;

d. Active reliance on the empowering Spirit in the announcement and demonstration of Jesus' Lordship;

e. Regular assessment of the time commitments of pastoral staff and lay leaders to determine that too much of their time is not spent on "in-house" church activities and that they are freed to engage regularly with unchurched people;

f. Regular teaching on the needs of our world and ways members can become actively involved.[19]

---

[19]This *Mission Covenant* was also reproduced in my first book, *Salt, Light, and a City,* 269-70.

Further Reading

Maggay, Melba Padilla. *Transforming Society*. Oxford: Regnum, 1994.

Newnham, Ashleigh, ed. *Voices of Hope: Stories from Our Neighbours*. Dandenong: UNOH, 2013.

Samuel, Vinay, and Chris Sugden, eds. *The Church in Response to Human Need*. Grand Rapids: Eerdmans, 1987.

Yamamori, Tetsunao, et al., eds. *Cases in Holistic Ministry Series*. 4 volumes. Monrovia, CA: MARC, 1995–1998.

CHAPTER 10: INDIGENIZING FAITH

Reflection Questions

- Investigate the meanings associated with the terms *indigenization, inculturation* and *contextualization*. Which do you prefer? Do you agree that they are (basically) synonymous? How do you arrive at your conclusion?

- What are examples of indigenous ministries and mission and theology and worship in your setting? Why do you believe that these are *authentically* indigenous?

- Has your church or denomination blindly imported theologies, church models, governance structures and worship expressions? How successful have these been (both in terms of *relevance for* and *mission to* people in your particular setting)?

- Is your church shaping your own forms of theology, church structure, ministry, worship and mission? How will you move toward homegrown, indigenous theologies and innovations?

- How would the forms and practices of your church change if you do the following? "Break the flowerpot, take out the seed of the gospel, sow it in your own cultural soil, and let your own version of Christianity grow"?[20]

Getting Started

- Do you have any songwriters in your church? Anyone interested in songwriting? Pay for them to go to songwriting workshops so they can develop songs for your church.

---

[20]Niles is quoted in Emilio Antonio Núñez, *Crisis and Hope in Latin America: An Evangelical Perspective*, rev. ed. (Pasadena, CA: William Carey, 1996), 332-33.

- Consider Kwame Bediako's list of African metaphors and analogies for the person and work of Jesus in the section "Indigenization in Africa." Now develop a list using ideas, media, stories, images, metaphors and analogies from your culture. Use music, film, fashion, television, advertising, sports, social media, novels and other forms of expression and identity in your culture. If you are finding this hard, ask yourself why that is.

- Ask your small group or ministry team to read C. René Padilla and Tetsunao Yamamori's *Serving with the Poor in Latin America*.[21] Discuss the nine case studies in that book. What can you learn from them? How will you practice indigenous forms of mission in your setting?

Further Reading

Isasi-Díaz, Ada María. *Mujerista Theology: A Theology for the Twenty-First Century*. Maryknoll, NY: Orbis, 1996.

Koyama, Kōsuke. *Water Buffalo Theology*. 25th anniversary ed. Maryknoll, NY: Orbis, 1999.

Orevillo-Montenegro, Muriel. *The Jesus of Asian Women*. Women from the Margins. Maryknoll, NY: Orbis, 2006.

Phan, Peter C. *Christianities in Asia*. Blackwell Guides to Global Christianity. Malden, MA: Wiley-Blackwell, 2011.

CHAPTER 11: DEVOURING SCRIPTURE

Reflection Questions

- How are you developing your love for the Bible? Are you growing in your trust in its authority and relevance? Are you being obedient to its commands? Are you understanding its content in and for your context?

- Are you applying your Bible reading to your life, relationships, service and mission?

- How are you teaching people in your congregation to love and trust the Scriptures and the Christ they reveal? Are you helping them interpret Scripture for themselves?

---

[21]Tetsunao Yamamori et al., eds., *Serving with the Poor in Latin America* (Monrovia, CA: MARC, 1997).

- What does it mean for your congregation to develop contextualized readings of Scripture? How is your congregation reading Scripture in and for your context?

- How is your congregation reading Scripture missionally? How are you perceiving and responding to the missional themes and narratives of Scripture? How is Scripture shaping your understanding and practice of mission?

Getting Started

- Choose your favorite passage of Scripture or one that defines your church or movement. Now, with your family, church or ministry team, read interpretations of that passage from other cultures or theological traditions. Discuss what can you learn from these other voices.

- After spending time in prayer and fasting as a ministry team, draft an initial preaching and teaching plan for your church for the coming year. Now consider the twenty assumptions and practices of African Bible reading. Discuss how each of these twenty points will affect the content, delivery and location of your proposed preaching and teaching plan. Reshape your draft plan in the light of those twenty points.

- Develop a version of this yearlong Bible reading plan for your context:

  - Buy a copy of Daniel Patte's *Global Bible Commentary.*[22]

  - Invite all the members and families of your church to do the Scripture Union Australia E100 Bible Reading Challenge in the coming year. This is "an effective Bible reading plan built around 100 carefully selected short Bible passages—50 from the Old Testament and 50 from the New Testament." It enables people in your church to get the "big picture of God's Word and in the process develop a daily Bible reading habit."[23]

  - During that year, provide quotes on those hundred Bible passages from the contributors to the *Global Bible Commentary.* (These contributors are mostly from the Majority World.)

  - Invite people from different theological and cultural backgrounds to

---

[22]Daniel Patte, ed., *Global Bible Commentary* (Nashville: Abingdon, 2004).
[23]Scripture Union Australia, "What Is the E100 Challenge?," The E100 Challenge, 2015, www
 .e100challenge.org.au/e100c.htm.

come to your church during that year. Have them share their readings of those hundred Bible passages.

- Over the course of that year, find other ways to help your congregation hear the perspectives of readers from other cultures.

Further Reading

Jenkins, Philip. *The New Faces of Christianity: Believing the Bible in the Global South.* Oxford: Oxford University Press, 2006.

Keener, Craig S., and M. Daniel Carroll R., eds. *Global Voices: Reading the Bible in the Majority World.* Peabody, MA: Hendrickson, 2013.

Segovia, Fernando F., and R. S. Sugirtharajah. *A Postcolonial Commentary on the New Testament Writings.* The Bible and Postcolonialism. London: T&T Clark, 2009.

Sugirtharajah, R. S. *Voices from the Margin: Interpreting the Bible in the Third World.* Rev. and expanded 3rd ed. Maryknoll, NY: Orbis, 2006.

CHAPTER 12: RENEWING EDUCATION

Reflection Questions

- Is your church or organization developing and using the gifts and talents in your setting? Are you mobilizing people for mission and ministry and transformational leadership? Are you equipping them for service *inside* and *outside* the church?

- Are you mobilizing *all* the ministry gifts (of which the apostolic, pro-phetic, evangelistic, teaching and pastoral gifts are only the start)?

- How are you training people's *heads* (knowledge), *hearts* (character) and *hands* (competencies)? Are you equipping them well for ministry and mission and church planting? What are the goals of your training programs?

- Are you *collaborating* with theological institutions, denominations, secular organizations, churches and missional initiatives to train people for ministry and mission?

- Are you preparing people for the moral, spiritual, political and economic *transformation* of their contexts? Do you promote transformation of lives and groups through the liberation of the gospel? Do you seek it through active participation in social, political, church and economic arenas?

Getting Started

- Write a list of things that you and others need to change in your context for women to take part more fully in ministry training and theological education. List and pursue concrete actions that redress these things. Do this in collaboration with both women and men in your setting.

- Look through the list of fourteen characteristics of missional theological education in this chapter. Take practical sets to incorporate these characteristics into your local church ministry training.

- Read J. R. Rozko's *The Future of Theological Education* (see the link in the footnote).[24] Consider the discussions at Fuller's *Seminary of the Future*: http://future.fuller.edu. Read Perry Shaw's *Transforming Theological Education*. After doing all that, take an audit of your curriculum and methodologies. What do you need to change to make these more relevant and missional and transformational?

Further Reading

Shaw, Perry. *Transforming Theological Education*. Carlisle, Cumbria: Langham, 2014.

Werner, Dietrich, et al. *Handbook of Theological Education in World Christianity: Theological Perspectives—Regional Surveys—Ecumenical Trends*. Oxford: Regnum, 2010.

Woodberry, J. Dudley. *Missiological Education for the Twenty-First Century: The Book, the Circle, and the Sandals: Essays in Honor of Paul E. Pierson*. Maryknoll, NY: Orbis, 1996.

CHAPTER 13: PRACTICING SERVANTSHIP

Reflection Questions

- Who are the *Broken Ones* in your community that you are serving? Are they leading you toward deeper healing and transformation and spiritual insight?

- What does it mean for you to *practice servantship* in your setting? What does it mean for you to be a servant?

---

[24] J. R. Rozko and Doug Paul, "The Missiological Future of Theological Education: A Whitepaper: A Joint Venture of 3DM and the Order of Mission," 2012, www.academia.edu/4148055/The _Missiological_Future_of_Theological_Education.

- Is your form of leadership culturally relevant? And *not* only for your church culture?

- How are you making disciples? Is your church, denomination or parachurch agency multiplying churches? How will it do this? Are you on the road to being a missional leader?

- What practices are you forming that sustain your *spiritual* leadership?

Getting Started

- Develop your own spiritual practices. Allow these to change and grow over time. Practice them in a joyful and grace-filled way. Ask people who love you to keep you accountable.

- As a small group or ministry team, consider Ajith Fernando's list of *the distinct qualities of spiritual leadership*. These are detailed in this chapter. How will you develop these qualities individually and as a group? How will you cultivate them in your church, family, small group, ministry team or personal discipleship?

- Do you want to think more about the connection between servantship and missional leadership?

- Read my book *Servantship: Sixteen Servants on the Four Movements of Radical Servantship*.

Further Reading

Agosto, Efrain. *Servant Leadership: Jesus and Paul*. St. Louis: Chalice, 2005.

Fernando, Ajith. *An Authentic Servant: The Marks of a Spiritual Leader*. Peabody, MA: Hendrickson, 2012.

Hill, Graham, ed. *Servantship: Sixteen Servants on the Four Movements of Radical Servantship*. Eugene, OR: Wipf and Stock, 2013.

CHAPTER 14: RECOVERING COMMUNITY

Reflection Questions

- Do you agree that in the church there is no true communion without mission *and* no true mission without communion? If this is the case, what does it mean for the fellowship and mission of your church in the coming year?

- Consider Leonardo Boff's list of the seven features of churches that reflect the trinitarian life. (These are listed in this chapter as presence one-to-another, reciprocity, immediacy, community, being-in-openness, being-in-transcendence and being-us.[25]) Then look at Jeffrey Pugh's corresponding list of ten features. (See the link in the footnote. These features are polycentricity, unity, multiplicity, fluidity, reciprocity, generativity, interpenetration, witness, collegiality and freedom.[26]) How are your congregation and leadership team doing in these areas? How could you grow into these?

- How can you cultivate deep and spiritual friendships in your personal life and among your congregation?

- How can your congregation practice and reactivate *koinonia*?

Getting Started

- Take time over the next few months to read Lesslie Newbigin's *The Open Secret*. Under three headings, list practical ways that your church can do the following trinitarian actions: (1) Proclaim the kingdom of the Father ("mission as faith in action"). (2) Share the life of the Son ("mission as love in action"). (3) Bear the witness of the Spirit ("mission as hope in action").[27]

- Is your church experiencing *communitas* and liminality? (Victor and Edith Turner developed these concepts in their work among indigenous tribes.) Ask your leaders to read Alan Roxburgh's *The Sky Is Falling* and *The Missionary Congregation, Leadership, and Liminality*. (Or read these books together in your local pastor's network.) Spend time reflecting together on the nature of *communitas* and liminality. Consider the implications of these concepts for your church.[28]

---

[25]Leonardo Boff, "Trinitarian Community and Social Liberation," *Cross Currents* 38, no. 3 (1988): 293-95.

[26]Jeffrey Raymond Pugh, "Symbols of Dysfunction, Strategies for Renewal" (PhD diss., Flinders University, 2006), 457-58. Explanations for each of these ten features can be found in Pugh's PhD thesis online: http://theses.flinders.edu.au/public/adt-SFU20060227.150043/index.html.

[27]Lesslie Newbigin, *The Open Secret: An Introduction to the Theology of Mission* (Grand Rapids: Eerdmans, 1995), v.

[28]Alan J. Roxburgh, *The Sky Is Falling: Leaders Lost in Transition; A Proposal for Leadership Communities to Take New Risks for the Reign of God* (Eagle, ID: ACI, 2005); Roxburgh, *The Missionary Congregation, Leadership, and Liminality* (New York: Trinity, 1997).

- Consider the features of churches that practice *koinonia*. (I outline these in the latter part of this chapter.) Work through these as a church over the next six to twelve months. Ask how you will practically and concretely respond to the following questions.

How are we cultivating *koinonia* in our church that

- builds community upon trinitarian and christological foundations?

- releases all believers to ministry, service and contribution?

- cultivates a spirituality for diversity and plurality?

- unlocks the community-building power of the sacraments?

- integrates community life with mission?

- fosters *koinonia* as the affective infrastructure of mission?

- recovers the apostolic practices of discipleship?

- embraces creation community?

- develops *koinonia* as radical conversion to restored relationships?

- nurtures third-place lifestyles and community?

Further Reading

Boff, Leonardo. *Holy Trinity, Perfect Community*. Maryknoll, NY: Orbis, 2000.

DeBorst, Ruth Padilla. "God's Earth and God's People: Relationships Restored." *Journal of Latin American Theology* 5, no. 1 (2010).

Escobar, Samuel. "The Church as Community." In *The Local Church, Agent of Transformation: An Ecclesiology for Integral Mission*, edited by C. René Padilla and Tetsunao Yamamori, 125–50. Buenos Aires: Ediciones Kairos, 2004.

Fernando, Ajith. *Reclaiming Friendship: Relating to Each Other in a Frenzied World*. Scottdale, PA: Herald, 1993.

CHAPTER 15: DEVELOPING SPIRITUALITY AND DISCIPLESHIP

Reflection Questions

- How are you enjoying a life of communion with God in Jesus Christ?

- Are spiritual formation and discipleship prioritized in your church? Are they at the center of your life together? Are they connected to your mission together in the world? What needs to change?

- Are you following Jesus in the power of the Spirit? In this chapter, we have seen that this includes indignation, solidarity, communion, relinquishment, courage, community, prayer, self-sacrificial action, political holiness, social action, holiness and crucified and risen minds.

- Is Christian spirituality a collective adventure for you? Or a privatized and individualized experience?

- How is your prayer materialized in missional witness, gratuitous love, just actions, political holiness and prophetic courage?

Getting Started

- Does your country have aboriginal, indigenous or First Nations peoples? If so, learn about their cultures and spiritualities. When appropriate, attend their churches, gatherings and conferences. Get to know them personally, as friends. Ask them what nonindigenous Christians can learn from their approach to life, faith, creation, family, community, art, identity, music, story, history and so on. If you find Christians among them, ask those people what you can learn about their indigenous approach to discipleship.

- Does your country have a refugee and asylum seeker population? Have you met refugees and asylum-seekers in your setting? Take time to learn about their cultures and spiritualities. Visit immigration detention centers. Get to know these displaced people personally, as friends. Discover how many of them are Christians. Get to know their approaches to discipleship and mission and Christian spirituality.

- Order the *Moved* video series for your church. (This includes DVDs, resource guides and small group guides. See globalinteraction.org.au/resources /multimedia/moved.) Show the series to your congregation. Have your congregation respond by defining what it means to be *missional disciples* and list the *characteristics of missional spirituality*. Have them outline individual and corporate characteristics. Make concrete commitments to put these into action. (Again, make these individual and corporate actions.)

Further Reading

Bosch, David J. *A Spirituality of the Road*. Missionary Studies. Scottdale, PA: Herald, 1979.

Casaldáliga, Pedro, and Jose-Maria Vigil. *Political Holiness: A Spirituality of Liberation*. Theology and Liberation Series. Maryknoll, NY: Orbis, 1994.

Galilea, Segundo. *The Way of Living Faith: A Spirituality of Liberation*. San Francisco: Harper & Row, 1988.

CHAPTER 16: GLOBALCHURCH: EMBRACING A NEW NARRATIVE

Reflection Questions

- If you're in a Western country, how does post-Christendom express itself in your setting?

- Do Eurocentric or Americentric attitudes arise in your setting? What can you do about this?

- How does listening to other cultures help you as you deal with the problems in your own culture? For instance, how might intercultural understanding help North American churches respond to the issues surrounding the death of Michael Brown and the unfolding events in Ferguson, Missouri?

- In groups, discuss the following: "Mission is what the Bible is all about; we could as meaningfully talk of the missional basis of the Bible as of the biblical basis of mission."[29] Do you agree or not? Why?

Getting Started

- In groups, discuss the following: What are the practical implications for your church or college of global missional theology, global missional worship and global missional education? As a church or college, how will you apply these insights in your local setting?

- Consider the way you interpret Scripture. Are you applying a *global missional hermeneutic*? If not, how are you going to change your approach to biblical interpretation? Make practical commitments to do this.

- Make plans to attend the next Urbana Conference, preferably in a group. During the conference, have each person take notes about what impacts them during the sessions they attend. Then, as a group, discuss the impli-

---

[29]Christopher J. H. Wright, *The Mission of God: Unlocking the Bible's Grand Narrative* (Downers Grove, IL: IVP Academic, 2006), 29.

cations of these (global) ideas for your church and college and life together. (See https://urbana.org.)

Further Reading

Adeney, Miriam. *Kingdom Without Borders: The Untold Story of Global Christianity.* Downers Grove, IL: InterVarsity Press, 2009.

Greenman, Jeffrey P., and Gene L. Green, eds. *Global Theology in Evangelical Perspective: Exploring the Contextual Nature of Theology and Mission.* Downers Grove, IL: IVP Academic, 2012.

Johnstone, Patrick. *The Future of the Global Church: History, Trends, and Possibilities.* Downers Grove, IL: InterVarsity Press, 2011.

Tennent, Timothy C. *Theology in the Context of World Christianity: How the Global Church Is Influencing the Way We Think About and Discuss Theology.* Grand Rapids: Zondervan, 2007.

WHO ARE THESE MAJORITY WORLD AND INDIGENOUS THINKERS?

Here are the leading Majority World and indigenous thinkers that I engage in this book. Many live and serve and write from Majority World and indigenous contexts. (This is the bulk of the persons on this list.) Others have moved to Western settings.

Those who live in Majority World and indigenous societies bring invaluable perspectives from their cultural settings. Those who have moved to Western contexts bring the value of hybrid or bicultural perspectives. I do not engage each thinker equally. Instead, I deal with them according to their relevance to the particular themes of the chapters of this book.

In this book, I could have consulted the work of many thousands of thinkers and writers and practitioners. But I have limited myself to a sample of those who speak directly to its themes.

These African, Asian, Eastern European, Latin American and indigenous thinkers inspire us to think in fresh ways about the kingdom of God. They challenge us to renew the worship and community and mission of Jesus Christ's church.

Ahn Byung-Mu (South Korean)—Ahn Byung-Mu laid the theological and biblical foundations for Minjung theology. He founded the Korean Theological Study Institute.

Rubem Azevedo Alves (Brazilian)—Alves was one of the founders of liberation theology. His particular interests lay in the relationship between liberation and philosophy and education and politics and psychoanalysis.

Michael Amaladoss (Indian)—Amaladoss is a Jesuit theologian. He is especially interested in interreligious and ecumenical dialogue and spirituality and mission.

Simon Kofi Appiah (Ghanaian)—Appiah is a West African priest and moral theologian. He is interested in the relationship between culture and psychology and ethics. He studies how these emerge in processes of inculturation.

S. Wesley Ariarajah (Sri Lankan)—Ariarajah writes about issues to do with the intersection between church and gospel and culture. He considers peacemaking, reconciliation and interfaith dialogue.

Mortimer Arias (Bolivian)—Arias calls the church to recover the biblical perspective of the kingdom for the mission of the church. This perspective must shape evangelistic witness.

Saphir Athyal (Indian)—Athyal is a retired Indian Orthodox theologian. He works closely with World Vision International in Asia.

Kwame Bediako (Ghanaian)—Bediako was a key figure in the African theology movement. (This movement develops theology characterized by distinct African features.)

Jorge Mario Bergoglio (Pope Francis) (Argentinian)—Francis is the first Latin American pope, the first pope from the Southern Hemisphere and the first non-European pope since Gregory III in 741.

Anthony Bloom (Spent his childhood in Russia and Iran and adult years in France)—Bloom was a spiritual theologian. He wrote on prayer and the Christian life. He was a monk and metropolitan bishop of the Russian Orthodox Church. He is also known as "Anthony of Sourozh."

Clodovis Boff (Brazilian)—Boff is a liberation theologian. He shares some convictions with his brother Leonardo Boff, but he criticizes the roots and outlook of much liberation theology.

Leonardo Boff (Brazilian)—Boff is interested in liberation theology, politics, ecology, community, justice issues, globalization, ethics, gender and education. He is a professor of religion and ecology at Rio de Janeiro State University.

José Míguez Bonino (Argentinian)—Bonino was a liberation theologian. He focused on political ethics, justice and liberation for the poor and the defense of human rights.

Bénézet Bujo (Congolese)—Bujo is a moral theologian. He is interested in African theological ethics and African theology in its social context.

Simon Chan (Singaporean)—Chan is a Pentecostal theologian. He writes about Pentecostal and liturgical and spiritual theologies.

Paul (or David) Yonggi Cho (South Korean)—Cho is senior pastor of one of the world's largest congregations—Yoido Full Gospel Church in Seoul, South Korea. This church has a membership of more than one million.

Jayakumar Christian (Indian)—Christian is national director of World Vision India. He ministers among the poor in India. He writes on development, economics, politics and child development.

Shoki Coe (Taiwanese)—Coe grew up in Japanese-occupied Taiwan. He went on to become a champion of Taiwanese freedom and a pioneer of Asian theology. He was an advocate of Christianity in the Global South. He was a pioneer of contextualization.

José Comblin (Born in Belgium and has lived most of his life in Brazil)—Comblin was a champion of liberation theology. He was a prominent human rights advocate.

Geevarghese Mor Coorilos (Indian)—Coorilos is the Syrian Orthodox Metropolitan of Niranam, India. Coorilos writes on integral eco-theology and ecumenical approaches to mission and unity. He writes on caring for the poor and marginalized and responding to HIV, AIDS and natural disasters.

Orlando E. Costas (Puerto Rican)—Costas was a holistic global theologian. He wrote on the mission of the church and especially mission beyond Christendom. His writings deal with issues surrounding poverty and justice and contextual evangelism. He wrote on Hispanic theology and spirituality and mission in Latin America.

Marthinus L. Daneel (Zimbabwean)—Daneel is a Zimbabwean professor of theology. He is an expert on African Independent Churches. He conducts research among African Christian and traditionalist communities.

Ruth Padilla DeBorst (Born in Colombia and grew up in Argentina)—Deborst has been involved in leadership training, church and community development, and holistic mission under the auspices of Christian Reformed World Missions. She serves as Director of Christian Formation and Leadership Development with World Vision International. She lives in Costa Rica.

Saiyuud Diwong (Thai)—Diwong runs a Thai cooking school in the Klong Toey slum, Bangkok, Thailand. She teaches students in the slums to cook and helps them find jobs. She helps slum residents get employment and education and start businesses.

Musa W. Dube (Botswanan)—Dube is a leader in postcolonial feminist theology and gender issues. She develops healing theologies and practices in societies ravaged by HIV and AIDS. She writes about people-centered and compassionate and healing mission. She is a professor at the University of Botswana.

Jean-Marc Ela (Cameroonian)—Ela developed a sub-Saharan African form of liberation theology. His focus was on social science, liberation, contextualization and community-centered forms of theology.

Samuel Escobar (Peruvian)—Escobar is involved with the Lausanne Movement. He is interested in holistic and integral mission. He is especially interested in integrating social action and justice, evangelism and mission, and holistic human flourishing.

Ajith Fernando (Sri Lankan)—Fernando is the teaching director of Youth for Christ in Sri Lanka. He writes about the mission of the church, leadership, obedience, suffering, the message of Jesus, spirituality and missional witness among non-Christian faiths.

Paulo Freire (Brazilian)—Freire was an educator, philosopher and advocate of critical pedagogy. He promoted an approach to education that leads people toward personal and social freedom. He believed that education could help people pursue the critical transformation of their situations and cultures and world.

Makoto Fujimura (Japanese American)—Fujimura is an artist, speaker, writer and theologian. He was a presidential appointee to the National Council on the Arts from 2003 to 2009. Fujimura's work is exhibited at galleries around the world.

Mitsuo Fukuda (Japanese)—Fukuda is founder of Rethinking Authentic Christianity Network. This network provides mission strategies and grassroots training systems for churches in Japan and other Asian nations. He also specializes in contextualization, cultural anthropology, Japanese culture and intercultural studies.

Segundo Galilea (Chilean)—Galilea ministered among the poor and destitute in Latin America. He wrote about liberation theology, Christian spirituality and prayer. He was interested in the relationship between contemplation and social action.

Alejandro García-Rivera (Cuban)—García-Rivera was a Jesuit theologian.

He bridged the disciplines of systematic theology and science. He also wrote about beauty and suffering.

Aruna Gnanadason (Indian)—Gnanadason is involved with the World Council of Churches. Her interests are in justice and peace, poverty and liberation, development and politics, ecology and creation care, and reproductive technologies and gender issues.

Ken R. Gnanakan (Indian)—Gnanakan ministers in slums and villages in India. His ministry helps people rise out of poverty through educational, health and environmental projects. His academic specializations include leadership, environmental issues, education and theology.

Gustavo Gutiérrez (Peruvian)—Gutiérrez is a Dominican priest. He is one of the founders of liberation theology. He serves among the poor and oppressed in Lima, Peru. Gutiérrez writes on liberation theology, literature, poverty and oppression and is interested in class, racial and gender relations. He encourages Christians to live in solidarity with the poor.

Huang Po Ho (Taiwanese)—Ho is a Taiwanese theologian and educator and ecumenical leader. He promotes forms of theological education that facilitate mission and service.

Roger Ibengi (Congolese)—Ibengi writes about the shape of missional leadership. He considers the growth and characteristics of global missiology.

Ada María Isasi-Díaz (Cuban American)—Isasi-Díaz was one of the founders of *mujerista* theology. *Mujerista* is a Hispanic womanist theology. She founded the Hispanic Institute of Theology at Drew University.

Emmanuel M. Katongole (Ugandan)—Katongole is a Catholic priest and the child of Rwandan parents—one Hutu and the other Tutsi. Many of his writings focus on peace, forgiveness and reconciliation.

Grace Ji-Sun Kim (Korean American)—Kim's writings mainly cover two areas. The first is feminist theology. She considers the experiences and theologies of Asian women in patriarchal societies. The second is postcolonial theology. Kim shows how Chinese and Korean and Japanese philosophies can enrich Christian theology. They can especially enrich our understanding of the Holy Spirit.

Kazoh Kitamori (Japanese)—Kitamori is most famous for his theology about the pain of God. Writing during and after the Second World War,

Kitamori spoke of the pain of God, which has a redemptive and healing relationship to human suffering.

Chiang Kok-Weng (Singaporean)—Kok-Weng is an Old Testament scholar. He also produces work on environmental ethics and eco-theology. He writes about the connections between Confucianism and Christianity.

Kōsuke Koyama (Japanese)—Koyama was concerned to defend a theology that was accessible to the average person in developing Asian contexts. He wrote on liberation theology, the environment and bridging the gap between Eastern and Western thought.

William Folorunso Kumuyi (Nigerian)—Kumuyi pastors one of the world's largest churches. In 2013, Foreign Policy Magazine named him one of the "500 most powerful people on the planet."[1]

Samuel Waje Kunhiyop (Nigerian)—Kunhiyop is a leading voice in the development of African contextual theology and ethics.

Simon S. M. Kwan (Hong Kong Chinese)—Kwan's research areas include Asian pastoral and practical theology. He studies cultural and sociopolitical dimensions of practical theology. He advocates a postcolonial rethinking of Asian theological methods and pastoral approaches.

Kwok Pui Lan (Hong Kong Chinese)—Kwok publishes in the areas of Asian feminist theology. She considers spiritual formation, biblical interpretation and postcolonial criticism. She cofounded the network Pacific, Asian, and North American Asia Women in Theology and Ministry.

Emmanuel Y. Lartey (Ghanaian)—Lartey develops themes around intercultural pastoral theology and mission. He is concerned about issues to do with rapid cultural change, cultural plurality and caring for the fragile and vulnerable.

Julie C. Ma (South Korean)—Ma teaches at the Oxford Centre for Mission Studies, where her husband Wonsuk is the Executive Director. She has expertise in Pentecostal church planting and evangelism, cultural anthropology and gender issues in church and mission.

Wonsuk Ma (South Korean)—Ma is a Pentecostal missiologist. He is a leader in the areas of theological education, evangelism, church planting and research on Asian Pentecostalism and mission.

---

[1]Alicia P. Q. Wittmeyer, "The FP Power Map: The 500 Most Powerful People on the Planet," April 29, 2013, *Foreign Policy*, www.foreignpolicy.com/articles/2013/04/29/the_500_most_powerful _people_in_the_world.

Laurenti Magesa (Tanzanian)—Magesa examines African spirituality. He studies moral and ethical themes in African religions and demonstrates how inculturation is transforming the church in Africa. He shows how Christianity can learn from sub-Saharan African spirituality.

Melba Padilla Maggay (Filipina)—Maggay writes about how the church can transform society. She also discusses Filipino communication patterns, proposing a culture-specific communication theory. In *A Clash of Cultures*, Maggay examines "the cross-cultural tensions that surfaced between American Protestantism and Filipino religious consciousness the first three decades of American colonial rule in the country."[2]

Nelson Mandela (South African)—Mandela shot to global fame as an antiapartheid activist, recipient of the 1993 Nobel Peace Prize and president of South Africa (1994–1999).

Vishal Mangalwadi (Indian)—Mangalwadi is an advocate for the rural and urban poor. He challenges the Indian caste system. He encourages local churches to develop and offer tuition-free, Internet-based college education. He especially wants this education delivered to the poor and disadvantaged.

John S. Mbiti (Kenyan)—Mbiti has served as a director of the World Council of Churches. He is interested in African and Asian theological themes. He writes about ecumenism and the interpretation of traditional religions.

Mmutlanyane Stanley Mogoba (South African)—Mogoba is an anti-apartheid activist. He was a Robben Island prisoner. He is well-known for his work in politics, peace, justice and racial reconciliation.

Caesar Molebatsi (South African)—Molebatsi champions social justice and empowerment in South Africa. He is a South African media personality. Molebatsi speaks internationally on issues to do with justice, reconciliation, human rights, economic development and theology.

Watchman Nee (Chinese)—Nee was a pastor and spiritual theologian and church planter. Many read and love Nee's books on Christian spirituality and discipleship.

Daniel Thambyrajah Niles (Sri Lankan)—Niles was a Sri Lankan preacher and evangelist who held various national posts. He was a president of the World Council of Churches.

---

[2]From Maggay's Micah Network profile page: Dr. Melba Maggay, Micah Network, 2015, www .micahnetwork.org/es/staff/dr-melba-maggay.

Emilio Antonio Núñez (Salvadoran)—Núñez is concerned with issues of Latin American evangelical missiology. He writes about missional effectiveness, new apostolic movements and the pastoral challenges of missional growth in Latin America.

Sarah Nuttall (South African)—Nuttall is a theologian, social commentator and critic. She examines postapartheid South African culture. She writes about African and diasporic aesthetics.

Ferdinand Nwaigbo (Nigerian)—Nwaigbo writes about a theological inculturation of Mariology. He examines African Christian perspectives on the church as communion. He also considers faith in an age of reason and science.

Mercy Amba Oduyoye (Ghanaian)—Oduyoye is the director of the Institute of African Women in Religion and Culture in Ghana. She writes on Christian theology from an African and womanist perspective. Oduyoye addresses the oppression and exploitation of women in patriarchal cultures and systems.

Izunna Okonkwo (Nigerian)—Okonkwo is a systematic theologian. He teaches ecclesiology and missiology and systematics from an African perspective. He is especially interested in inculturation and ecumenism and African thought and culture.

Oliver Alozie Onwubiko (Nigerian)—Onwubiko develops an African missionary ecclesiology and an African approach to inculturation. He shows how African thought and religion and culture converse with Christianity. Together, these can form an indigenous African Christian faith and mission and church.

Muriel Orevillo-Montenegro (Filipina)—Orevillo-Montenegro is a Filipina theologian. She focuses on ecumenical relations, Asian womanist theology, and peace and justice studies. She leads development programs alongside poor, Asian, urban women and children.

Ofelia Ortega (Cuban)—Ortega is a pioneering theological educator and ecumenical leader. She teaches theology and works with the World Council of Churches in Latin America and the Caribbean. Ortega has served as a public health volunteer in the poorer rural areas of Cuba.

Juan Carlos Ortiz (Argentinian)—Ortiz challenges Christians to pursue discipleship and spiritual formation.

C. René Padilla (Born in Ecuador, raised in Colombia and currently living in Argentina)—Padilla is involved in integral mission and the Micah Network. He specializes in theological reflection on globalization, justice and mercy issues, and integral mission.

Anne Pattel-Gray (Indigenous Australian)—Pattel-Gray explores indigenous beliefs and spiritualities. She considers gender and race relations and examines the mission of the church among indigenous cultures.

Elizabeth Petersen (South African)—Petersen is the director of The South African Faith and Family Institute (SAFFI). This institute calls clergy (across all religions) to deal with issues surrounding gender and domestic violence in Africa.

Ivan Petrella (Argentinian)—Petrella is a liberation theologian. He seeks to put the following traditions into conversation: black theology, Latin American liberation theology, womanist theology and Hispanic theology.

Peter C. Phan (Vietnamese)—Phan is a Vietnamese theologian now living in the United States. He deals with themes around culture, social thought, mission, Asian perspectives, liturgy and prayer, and church.

John S. Pobee (Ghanaian)—Pobee is an Anglican bishop in Ghana. He writes on African theology, indigenous African churches and African biblical interpretation.

Vinoth Ramachandra (Sri Lankan)—Ramachandra is involved in the Micah Network and the International Fellowship of Evangelical Students. He writes and speaks on the relationship between theology and the public issues that face our world.

Bong Rin Ro (South Korean)—Ro examines evangelical theology and biblical interpretation in Asian contexts. He is a leading thinker in the areas of Asian contextualization and mission and leadership development.

Óscar A. Romero (Salvadoran)—Romero challenged the social and political systems that perpetuated El Salvador's poverty, social injustice, assassinations and torture. He called the church to pursue social transformation. He challenged El Salvadorian society to embrace liberty and democracy and justice. He was assassinated in 1980.

Vinay Samuel (Indian)—Together with Chris Sugden, Samuel cofounded the Oxford Centre for Mission Studies. He is a pioneer in the field of holistic and integral mission. He is an expert in the field of Asian theology, microenterprise development, Christian relief and development, and faith and economics.

Lamin Sanneh (Gambian)—Sanneh studies world Christianity. He has a particular focus on the relationship between Islam and Christianity and secularity.

Fernando F. Segovia (Cuban American)—Segovia specializes in non-Western Christian theologies (especially from Latin American and the Caribbean). He considers minority Christian theologies in the West (especially from US Hispanic Americans). He writes on postcolonial and minority and diaspora studies.

Juan Luis Segundo (Uruguayan)—Segundo wrote on theology, ideology, faith, hermeneutics, social justice, oppression, suffering and liberation theology. He wrote about missional approaches to pastoring. He developed theological perspectives on the arts.

Sadhu Sundar Singh (Indian)—Singh was an Indian Christian ascetic and mystic. He devoted himself to the life of a sadhu. A sadhu is an Indian religious ascetic and holy person. He wrote on Christian meditation, contemplation, prayer and spirituality.

Jon Sobrino (Spanish born but living in El Salvador)—Sobrino has spent most of his life in El Salvador. He is a leading liberation theologian. He is well-known for his work on liberation theology and on poverty and justice. He writes about the person and work of Christ from a Latin American perspective. He considers spirituality and solidarity and hope.

Choan-Seng Song (Taiwanese)—Song attacks the Western-centric nature of Christian theology. He develops uniquely Asian theological forms and motifs and challenges all cultures to develop indigenous and contextual theology.

R. S. Sugirtharajah (Sri Lankan)—Sugirtharajah teaches biblical hermeneutics at the University of Birmingham. He is concerned for developing contextual and postcolonial mission and hermeneutics.

M. Thomas Thangaraj (Tamil)—Thangaraj writes hymns in English and Tamil. He develops Indian Christian theological responses to religious pluralism and global issues.

K. Thanzauva (Mizo)—Thanzauva studies Indian tribal cultures. He has developed a tribal theology of church and mission and community.

M. M. Thomas (Naga)—Thomas was a theologian and social activist and politician. He was a former governor of Nagaland. He wrote on Christian activism and considered the shape of Indian subcontinental mission, church and theology.

Tite Tiénou (Côte d'Ivoirian)—Tiénou was formerly the president and dean of Faculté de Théologie Evangélique de l'Alliance Chrétienne in Abidjan, Côte d'Ivoire, West Africa. He now serves as the coprovost and dean of Trinity Evangelical Divinity School. He writes on African theology, contextualization, mission and evangelicalism.

George E. Tinker (Native American—Osage)—Tinker is concerned about indigenous cultures and spiritualities. He challenges the church to care for creation. He writes about Native American theology, culture and thought. Tinker highlights the difference between Western and Native American categories of thought (especially individualism versus community).

Vimal Tirimanna (Sri Lankan)—Tirimanna is a moral theologian. He addresses ethical and moral issues in Sri Lanka and South Asia. Tirimanna writes about violence and war and peace.

Al Tizon (Filipino American)—Tizon is a missiologist. He writes about how urban-suburban partnerships can transform communities. He focuses on empowering churches to empower communities. He is interested in social action and mission. Tizon shows how churches can engage in holistic mission in their communities, especially on behalf of the poor and marginalized.

Desmond Tutu (South African)—Tutu is a prominent opponent of apartheid. He was the first black archbishop of Cape Town. Tutu promotes reconciliation and forgiveness and justice. He has sought to address global issues through his role with the United Nations. These include poverty, epidemics, unilateralism, gay rights, women's rights, climate change and church reform. His writings cover these areas. He also writes about African theology and Christian leadership and spiritual formation and prayer.

Uchimura Kanzō (Japanese)—Uchimura was the founder of the Non-Church Movement in Japan. He became influential in Asia and the West because of his theological, scientific and political views and scholarship.

Justin S. Ukpong (Nigerian)—Ukpong was a New Testament scholar who was a pioneering member of the African Biblical Hermeneutics Section of the Society of Biblical Literature. He examined biblical interpretation in the "global village" and studied approaches to biblical interpretation in Africa. He promoted an "inculturation hermeneutic." This involves people interpreting Scripture in their sociocultural setting and within their indigenous community.

John Mary Waliggo (Ugandan)—Waliggo considered the meaning and urgency of inculturation, especially in the African context. He believed that liberation meant full self-realization in ten areas of human life: spiritual, religious, moral, mental, cultural, economic, political, physical, social and personal. Waliggo also worked for the rights of women and children and the poor and silenced.

Nimi Wariboko (Nigerian)—Wariboko is a Christian ethicist. He publishes and teaches on the theology of money and on a moral philosophy of finance. He examines pneumatological ethics, economic history and corporate management. His writings also cover theology and science and social theories.

Randy S. Woodley (Native American—Cherokee)—Woodley writes about indigenous cultures, sustainability, eco-justice, microeconomics, leadership, missiology, reconciliation, societal justice and contextual theology.

Tetsunao Yamamori (Japanese)—Yamamori was the international director for the Lausanne Committee for World Evangelization. He is president emeritus for Food for the Hungry International. He analyzes global Pentecostalism, world missions and strategies for mission among unreached people groups.

Amos Yong (Malaysian American)—Yong is interested in a theology of the Holy Spirit and mission. He studies global Pentecostal theology. He constructs theologies of disability, politics, science and love. He is concerned for interreligious dialogue, comparative theology and Pentecostal scholarship.

Koo Dong Yun (Korean American)—Yun studies the "baptism of the Holy Spirit." He does this from Roman Catholic, Lutheran, dispensational, Pentecostal and Reformed perspectives. He describes three distinctive features of Pentecostal theology. These are (1) the Lukan orientation, (2) the vitality of experience and (3) the verifiability of Spirit baptism.

Hwa Yung (Malaysian)—Yung challenges the Asian church to develop an authentic Asian Christian theology. Before his retirement, he served as bishop of the Methodist Church in Malaysia. He was director of the Center for the Study of Christianity in Asia, Singapore.

RESOURCES AND GLOSSARY
AT THEGLOBALCHURCHPROJECT.COM

At TheGlobalChurchProject.com, you'll find these additional resources.

BOOK-RELATED RESOURCES

These resources include further reading lists, helpful website links, a detailed glossary and other resources.

I've even put an additional chapter up on my website. It asks, What can we learn from how Majority World Christians value and desire beauty?

OTHER RESOURCES

Bookings. Book me to speak at events, camps, seminars, conferences, churches, universities, colleges, seminaries, leadership gatherings and so on. My website lists the areas on which I speak and teach.

Links. Links to my blog, Facebook, Twitter and previous books.

Video series. Links to the GlobalChurch Project video series and my other teaching videos.

Contact. Information on how to contact me.

AUTHOR INDEX

SUBJECT INDEX

Finding the Textbook You Need

The IVP Academic Textbook Selector
is an online tool for instantly finding the IVP books
suitable for over 250 courses across 24 disciplines.

---

ivpacademic.com
